Yona Friedman
Manuel Orazi

EDITED BY NADER SERAJ

PARK BOOKS

archiZOOM

YONA

FRIEDMAN

THE DILUTION OF ARCHITECTURE

STANZAS
Photographs by Stefano Graziani, 2005.
Courtesy of Galleria Mazzoli, Modena.

Yona Friedman has lived in an apartment on the fourth floor of an ordinary and sturdy Haussmann building on Boulevard Garibaldi in Paris with his wife Denise Chavrain since 1968. Those fortunate enough to visit him see not just a series of rooms opening up before them, but a small and personal "sancta sanctorum" – or "debhir" in Hebrew.

It is a secret place filled with a large number of objects – by no means heterogeneous – that surprise visitors, capturing their attention until the pure form of the rooms almost vanishes. The souvenirs, craft pieces, models, elementary drawings and small pieces of rubbish transformed into ready-mades are, however, in line with Friedman's theoretical research.[1]

For some time now Stefano Graziani has sought to make photographs that represent anything but the *instant décisif*.[2] Graziani wants a more studied and conceptual photograph that portrays lifeless beings, soulless things suited to taxonomy – be they archive objects, vegetables or stuffed animals.[3] This is why it was completely natural for him to photograph Friedman's home, where he discovered a prominent subject in a different color in every room.

Giorgio Agamben wrote:

The 13th-century poets applied the word "stanza," i.e. "large abode and repository," to the core of their poetry because, along with all the formal elements of the song, it guarded that joi d'amor *that they saw as the only purpose of the poetry.*[4]

Similarly, Yona Friedman – not to mention Stefano Graziani – seems to use his "stanza" as the "heart" of his work.

Manuel Orazi

---

1. Friedman, Yona: *Rubbish is beautiful ou de l'utilisation des déchets*, in id., Friedman, Yona: *Utopies réalisables*, Paris, L'éclat, 2000, p. 99.
2. Cartier-Bresson, Henri: *L'instant décisif*, in id., Morgana, Fata: *L'imaginaire d'après nature*, 1996, pp. 17–32.
3. Graziani, Stefano: *Taxonomies*, Milan, A+Mbookstore, 2006.
4. Agamben, Giorgio: *Stanzas: Word and Phantasm in Western Culture*, Minneapolis/London, University of Minnesota Press, 1992, p. xvii.

PART I
Yona Friedman
THE DILUTION
OF ARCHITECTURE

PART II
Manuel Orazi
THE ERRATIC UNIVERSE
OF YONA FRIEDMAN

EDITED BY NADER SERAJ

TABLE OF CONTENTS

A SORT OF FOREWORD, Yona Friedman 25

PART I / THE DILUTION OF ARCHITECTURE / Yona Friedman

Architecture as improvisation 28
Strip cartoon: Improvisation in architecture 30
"Space-time" architecture 34
Strip cartoon: The dilution of architecture 36

ANTHOLOGY OF A PROCESS

1. MASSIVE
Mainstream architecture, "Shoe-box" 45

2. "VILLE SPATIALE"

EARLY STUDIES
Scheme of the theory, 1958 – 65 48
Level floors studies, 1958 – 62 60
Space-chain technique, 1958 – 70 64
Irregular pattern, 1959 – 90 66
The inner city, 1958 – 2000 70

EUROPEAN PROJECTS
Paris Spatial, various projects, 1959 – 2008 76
Venice of Monaco, 1959 94
Moscow, 1990 96
Milan stadium, 2004 98
Berlin, 2004 100
Vienna, 2004 102

ASIAN PROJECTS
Tokyo International Forum, 1989 104
Yokohama Triennale, 2001 106

AMERICAN PROJECTS
New York, various projects, 1958 – 99 108
Los Angeles freeway, 1964 116
San Francisco, 2006 118

AFRICAN PROJECTS
Early studies, 1958-59 120
Treichville, 1959 123
Tunis, competition, 1959 124
Dar es Salaam, Parliament House, 1967 128

BRIDGE-TOWN
Gibraltar, 1962 130
African Bridge-Town, 1963 132
Eleven Bridge-Towns to link five continents, 1963 133
Channel Bridge, 1963 134
Venice, 1969 – 2005 140
Strasbourg, Administrative Center for the EU, 1990 146
Peace Bridge, Tel Aviv, 1990 150
Centre-Bridge for London, 2004 152

3. ACCUMULATION

CONTAINERS

Trihedrical containers: A versatile technique, c. 2005	156
Container agglomeration, Semi-containers, 2002–05	158
Container Street-museum, c. 2005	160
Space-frame container, c. 2005	162
Strip cartoon: Container accumulation	164

4. TRANSPARENCY

IRREGULAR STRUCTURES

Introduction and manuals, from 1994	172
Panel chains, 1945	178
Movable boxes, 1949	180
Cylinders, 1953–58	182
Trihedral system, 1955	184
Curved panels, 1956	188
Carboard boxes, 1990–2005	190
Lamellar structures, from 1990	192
Crumpled sheets, 1992–2000	194
Macaroni, 1992	198
The Train, from 1992	200
Gribouilli, 1995–2005	202
Moebian structures, from 2000	208
Irregular & Pseudo tensegrity, 2000–05	210
Merzstrukturen, 2006	212

ICONOSTASE

Proteinic structures, 1992	216
Space-chain dome, 1970–85	218
Space-chain iconostase, various projects, 2010–13	220

5. DISSIPATED

Meuble + Plus, 2009	234

6. "NATURE MADE HABITABLE"

Street museum Como, 2004–08	238
Graffiti museum, 2006–09	240
Museum of Afghan civilisation, from 2008	242
Amorphous architecture, 2009	243
Tree museum, Rome–Paris, c. 2012	244
Shop Windows: A museum of our civilization, 2012	246
Strip cartoon: A museum is not a building	248

7. THE LABYRINTH

Nagasaki competition, 1996	256

8. BUILD LESS

Strip cartoon: Architecture without building	260

PART II / THE ERRATIC UNIVERSE OF YONA FRIEDMAN / Manuel Orazi

Prologue … 269

1. THE EARLY YEARS

Hungarian "false fascism" … 275
Science as art: Werner Heisenberg … 284
Mythology as collective psychology: Károly Kerényi … 292
Architecture in Hungary between the wars … 302
Palestine/Israel: Utopian Zionism … 314
Haifa "the Red" and the Technion Institute of Technology … 330
Konrad Wachsmann's technological utopia … 348
Europa '56 … 362

2. THEORIES. SOCIETY AND TECHNOLOGY

"L'architecture mobile" and its circulation … 385
"Groupe d'études d'Architecture mobile" GEAM … 414
Constant, Debord, Lefebvre … 426
1964: The year of the megastucture … 438
Michel Ragon's GIAP … 452
Ideology of the street … 472
Graph theory and the diagram … 484
Architecture-by-yourself: Nicholas Negroponte and the MIT … 498

3. ARCHITECTURE AND AUTOREGULATION

"Utopies réalisables" … 509
Lycée David, Angers … 526
Philosophy of participation … 536

PART III / APPENDIX

A conversation with Yona Friedman, Manuel Orazi, 2005 … 545
Seven questions for Bernard Tschumi, Guia Camerino and Manuel Orazi, 2005 … 560

EXHIBITION

Yona Friedman – Genesis of a Vision, Nader Seraj, 2012 … 562
Lecture series: Manuel Orazi, Juan Miguel Hernández Léon, Dominique Rouillard, 2012 … 566

BIBLIOGRAPHY

Books and articles by Yona Friedman … 568
Books and articles on Yona Friedman … 574

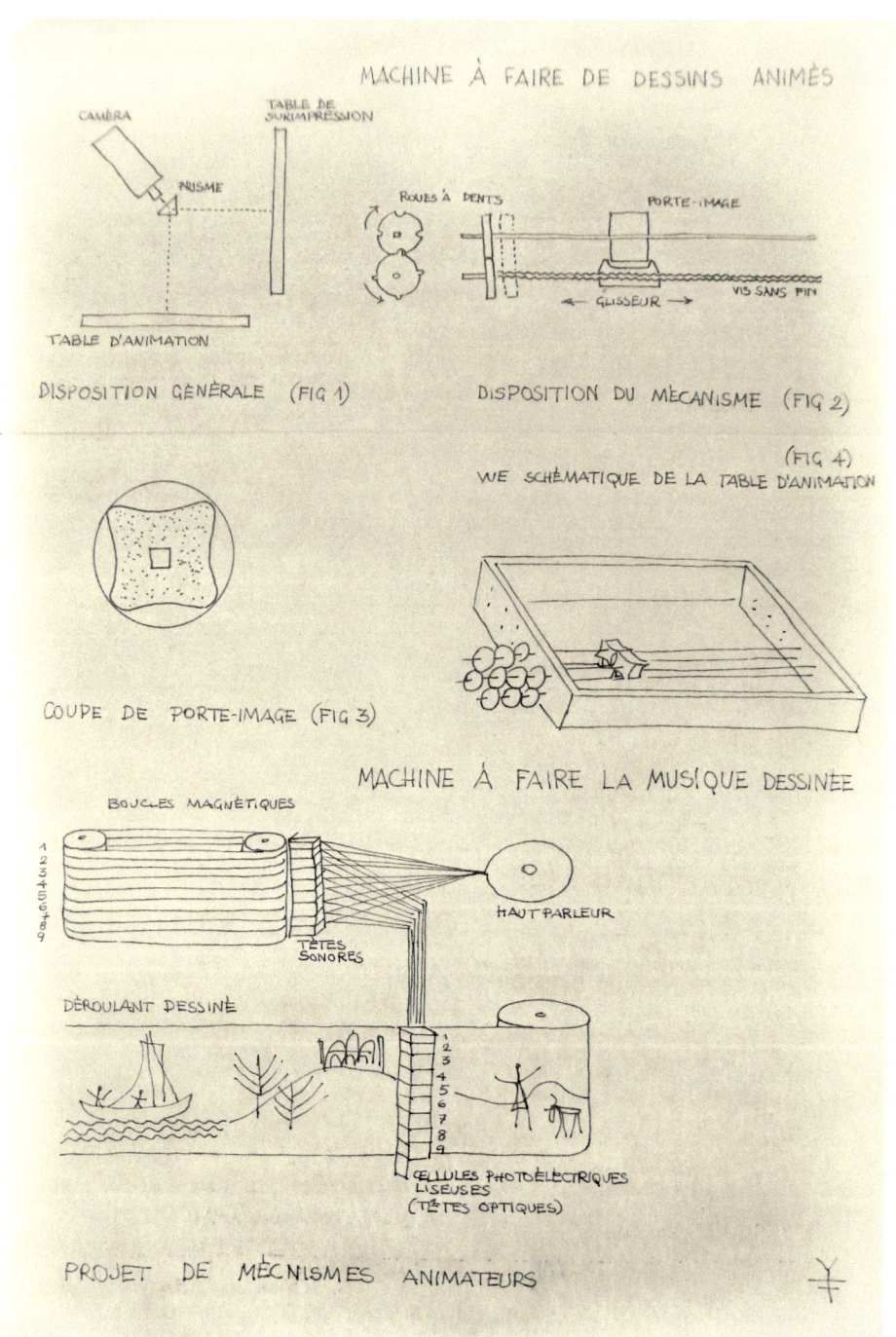

THE MACHINE TO MAKE CARTOONS, 1960–63

001 *Fig. 1. General disposition / Fig. 2. Disposition of the mechanism /*
Fig. 3. Section of the image carrier / Fig. 4. Schematic view of the animation table.

A SORT OF FOREWORD

It is always interesting to read about yourself and your work as part of history (a very small part). It gives you the impression that you "don't know this person."

This does not mean being indifferent to what people think about you and your work: my work has been much discussed for better or for worse.

I was surprised to learn from Manuel Orazi's magisterial study, that I have been living during an interesting period of architectural history without noticing it. I did not read much about architecture then and was too absorbed in my own problems to be attentive to another architect's papers or works. I see by Manuel's study that this constitutes a great loss for me.

Many of the people cited in this study I have not met or if so only superficially, like for example Alexander Klein, who refused to accept my PhD thesis that would later become *L'architecture mobile*. Other colleagues became friends without my knowing their "oeuvre."

One important influence not cited in this study was that of my wife Denise. At her instigation I started to shoot animated films (she herself was editor-in-chief). We made our first film in 1959 and received the "prime à la qualité." This was a substantial financial help for us. We then received a commission by the state TV (ORTF) for further films. One of these was shown at the Venice Film Festival in 1962 and received the Golden Lion award.

Making these movies generated my style of drawing, my explanation technique, leading to my "manuals" and slide shows.

It was Denise who corrected my manuscripts (as my French was rather poor at that time). She was also my test audience, which helped me a lot.

As for my ideas about architecture, they came from my own personal experience. Commissioned in the 1950s for some family homes, I found that there was no way to communicate with my clients. I discovered the effective non-communication and tried to forge my theory about it.

I also discovered that I am not a typical professional man but rather one interested simultaneously in many fields.

Yona Friedman, Paris, October 7, 2014

PART I
Yona Friedman
THE DILUTION
OF ARCHITECTURE

Architecture as improvisation.

Improvisation seems, at first sight, a term incompatible with architecture. Indeed, architecture, as taught in schools, implies long duration, eternity, in a way. All historically famous buildings did not disappear, at least without leaving traces.

Mobile architecture is, by definition, ephemere: its disposition, volumes, forms and elements change, according changing contexts, architecture continuously getting adapted to users' needs.

Changing continuously means being continuously improvised. But, in mainstream architecture such continuous changes also implied some prevision, some planning. I will, in this paper, try to point out another attitude: instantaneous improvisation on the site, planning to be substituted by "trial and error".

Trial and error is a fundamental method for all scientific experience. It is also determinant for all creative art.

To introduce "trial and error" and instantaneous improvisation into architecture new technical approach was necessary. Techniques, like the "tille of a tride", like "space-chairs" or "meuble + plus" make such approach effectively possible.

Improvisation for architecture is not to done on paper. Models even give only to sindication of the procedure how it can be done.

Improvisation can be done only on the site, at real scale. This requires provide will contributing parts easy to assemble, easy to handle, without special equipment and without specialist's expertise. It means parts pushed around, heaped one on the other, and similar commonplace procedures, rather inexpensive.

Outcome of improvisation in architecture is rich, collatically invigorating, personalizing. "Diluted" architecture is particularly inviting for improvisation.

Y. Friedman

ARCHITECTURE AS IMPROVISATION

Improvisation seems, at first sight, a term incompatible with architecture. Indeed, architecture, as taught in schools, implies long duration, eternity, in a way. All historically famous buildings did not disappear, at least not without leaving traces.

Mobile architecture is, by definition, ephemeral; its disposition, volumes, forms and elements change according to changing contexts, architecture continuously getting adapted to users' needs.

Continuously changing means being continuously improvised. But in mainstream architecture such continuous change also implies some prevision, some planning. I will, in this paper, try to point out another attitude: instantaneous improvisation; on site, planning should be substituted by "trial and error."

"Trial and error is a fundamental method for all scientific experience. It is also determining for all creative art."

To introduce "trial and error" and instantaneous improvisation into architecture, a new technical approach was necessary. Techniques, like the "Ville Spatiale," like "Space-chains" or "Meuble + plus" effectively make such an approach possible.

Improvisation for architecture is not done on paper. Models serve only as a visualization of the procedure of how it can be done.

Improvisation can be done only on site, at real scale. This becomes possible through constituting parts that are easy to assemble, easy to handle, without special equipment and without specialist's expertise. It means parts can be pushed around, stacked on top of each other and similar commonplace procedures, all rather inexpensive.

The outcome of improvisation in architecture is rich; aesthetically innovating, personalizing "diluted" architecture is particularly inviting for improvisation.

Yona Friedman, April 3, 2013

IMPROVISATION IN ARCHITECTURE

1 / Architecture is open for improvisation

2 / "Great" architecture was considered to be for eternity

3 / Popular architecture was often perishable

4 / Improvised on site

5 / Without preplanning

6 / And without technical drawings

7 / We have technical solutions

8 / For improvisation in architecture

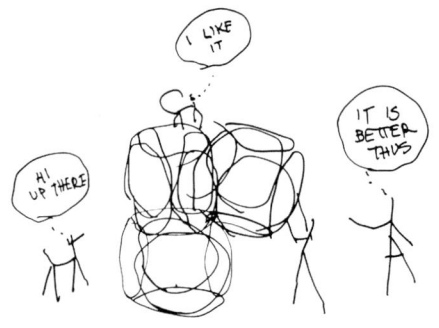

9 / Admitting "trial-and-error" procedures

10 / Techniques available to the layman

11 / Who can thus correct possible errors

12 / Or adapt and re-adapt architecture to a changing context

13 / I called this approach "mobile architecture"

14 / Which replaces "demolition" through "re-assembly" of the existing

"Space-time" architecture

Improvised architecture is "space-time" architecture: its configurations in space move in time.

Change, in "space-time" architecture is not continuous, in the mathematical sense of the term: you can not predict, knowing a given state, what will be the next one. There are no "rules", the process of change is erratic.

Improvised architecture is not "functional", in the sense as Bauhaus interpreted functionalism. It is neither estheticizing, even if it might produce esthetic effects. It is simply "living" architecture, not submitted to any theory.

"SPACE-TIME" ARCHITECTURE

Improvised architecture is "space-time" architecture: its configuration in space moves in time.

Change in "space-time" architecture is not continuous, in the mathematical sense of the term. You cannot predict, knowing a given state, what will be the next one. There are no "rules," the process of change is erratic.

Improvised architecture is not "functional" in the sense Bauhaus interpreted functionalism. Nor is it aestheticizing, even if it might produce aesthetic effects. It is simply "living" architecture, not subjected to any theory.

Yona Friedman, April 7, 2013

THE DILUTION OF ARCHITECTURE

1 / Architecture in the past always looked a compact mass

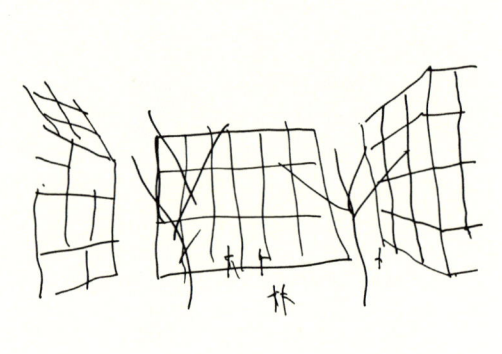

2 / In the recent past, with the use of glass this mass became transparent

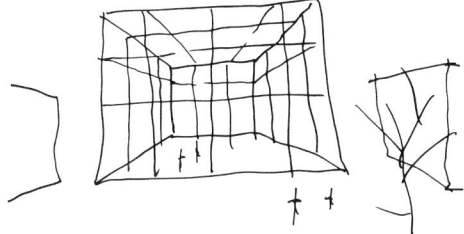

3 / Transparent but remaining compact

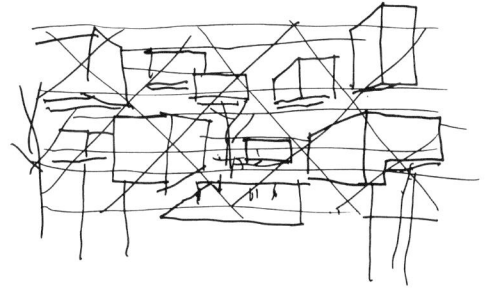

4 / The "Ville Spatiale" started diluting that mass

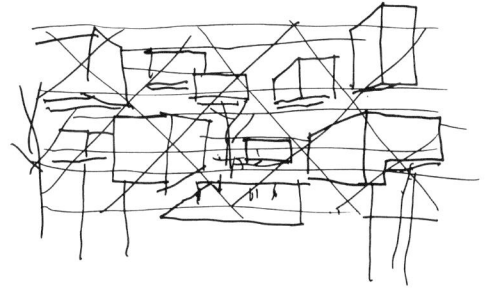

5 / Isolated volumes enter into a space-frame structure

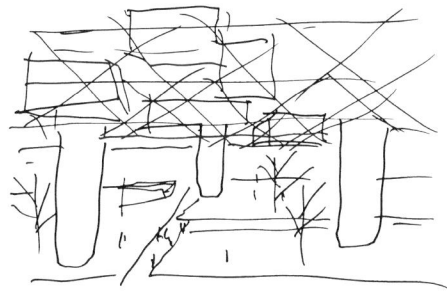

6 / Raised above ground-level on spaced staircase towers

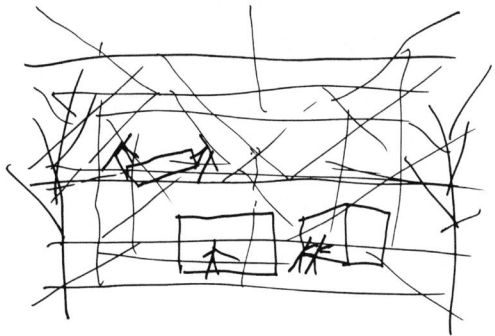

7 / Thus making mobile architecture possible

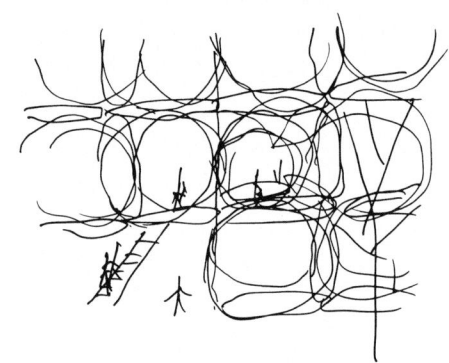

8 / In 1959, starting with a space-chain structure,

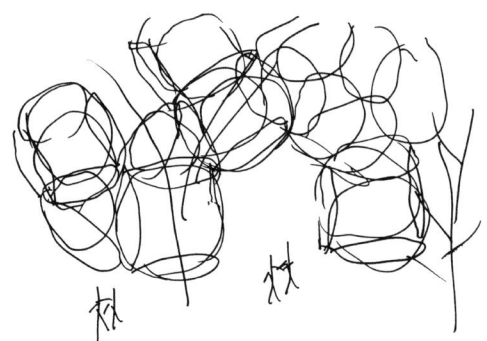

9 / The structure itself broke free of preconceived geometry

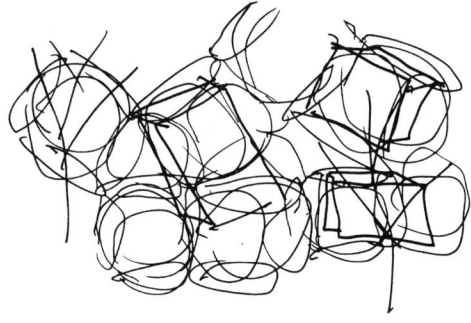

10 / Both the dispersed volumes and the structure are transformable

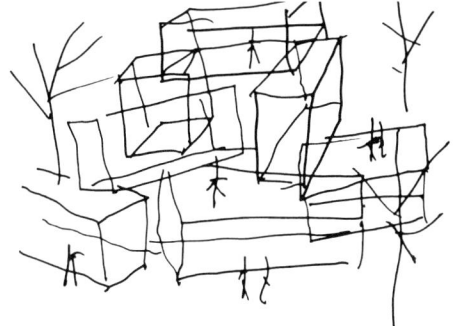

11 / Heaps of containers with no regular pattern

12 / Leaving open space between containers of the same kind

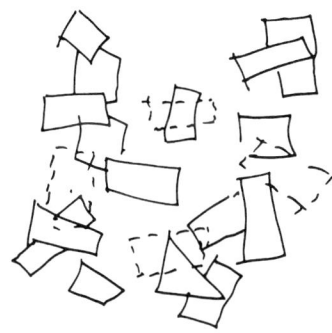

13 / Architecture became diluted

14 / Without involving preconceived plans

15 / No drawings are necessary

16 / A "building" can be improvised on site

THE DILUTION OF ARCHITECTURE
ANTHOLOGY OF A PROCESS

1. Massive

"Mainstream" architecture made of massive volumes ("shoe-box").
The building occupies the surface of the ground.

Mainstream architecture product is a "shoe-box" a simple shape with a void inside

MAINSTREAM ARCHITECTURE: "SHOE-BOX"

Originally published on the cover of *Domus*, no. 879, March 2005.

THE DILUTION OF ARCHITECTURE
ANTHOLOGY OF A PROCESS

2. "Ville Spatiale"

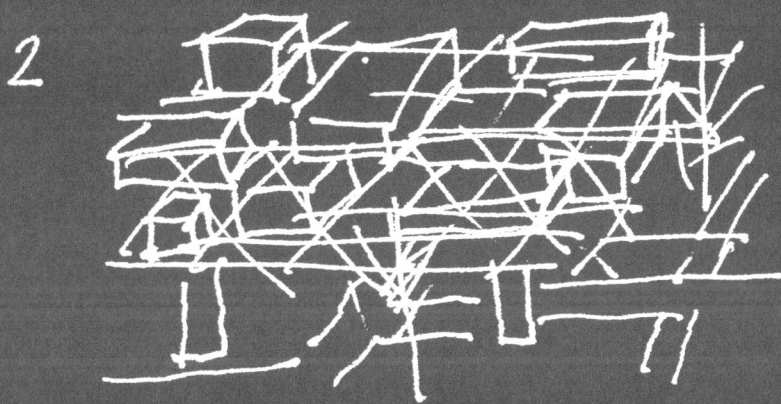

The "Spatial City." The volumes are dispersed in a structure which spans the ground space. Variable layouts without a need for demolition.

VILLE SPATIALE

Society is changing very rapidly in our time. The most important trend from the point of view of the urbanist is the need for recreation, the use of free time. The reason for the existence of towns is the struggle against boredom.

Parallel to these new changes the technical advances (communication and production) are no less revolutionary. If the trend to recreation represents a search, so the new techniques open a door for even the most eccentric solutions.

Any attempt at a static solution would be unwise. We propose a mobile urbanism which would search for techniques allowing the construction of large units within which an infinite flexibility is required; techniques allowing the provision of supplies (water, energy, sewage disposal) capable of rapid alteration and reutilization; techniques using elements, inexpensive, simple to erect, easy to transport, reusable.

The means of urban circulation should be communal; individual vehicles should stay out of town and provide for inter-urban circulation. The public centers (halls, markets) should be changeable and replaceable like the houses. These conditions assure that a town or a quarter can change its form if its inhabitants want it. Planning becomes bearable, because it is not definitive, and the possibility of correction or experimentation is still there.

FRIEDMAN, Yona and AUJAME, Roger: *Mobile Architecture*, in *Architectural Design*, no. 9, 1960.

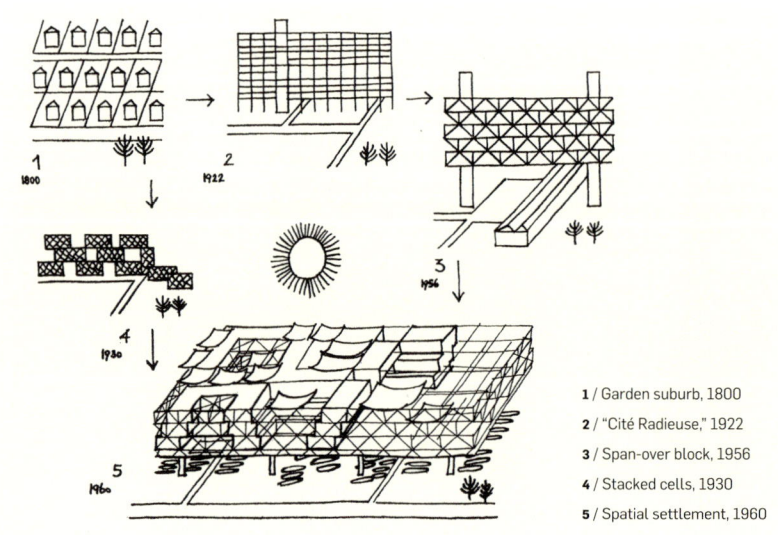

1 / Garden suburb, 1800
2 / "Cité Radieuse," 1922
3 / Span-over block, 1956
4 / Stacked cells, 1930
5 / Spatial settlement, 1960

002

EARLY STUDIES

002 Stages in the development of housing forms, from 1958.
003 Manual *The "Ville Spatiale."*

THE "VILLE SPATIALE"

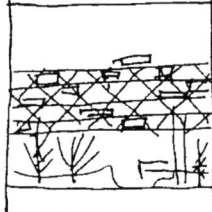
LAST, BUT NOT LEAST, I GET BACK TO MY FAVORITE IDEA: THE "VILLE SPATIALE"

IT MEANS A PARTICULAR MIXTURE OF RULES AND IRREGULARITY

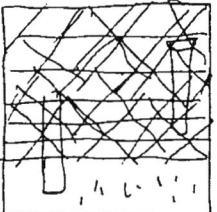
THE "VILLE SPATIALE" CONSISTS OF A MORE OR LESS REGULAR RIGID SUPPORTING GRID: THE "INFRASTRUCTURE"

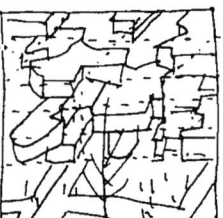
WITHIN WHICH INDIVIDUAL HOMES ARE INSERTED FORMING AN IRREGULAR PATTERN

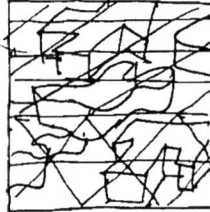
AS FOR THE SHAPE OF THOSE INDIVIDUAL HOMES ANYTHING GOES

THUS THE "VILLE SPATIAL" IS A "MERZSTRUKTUR" AT URBAN SCALE FOR A MASS-SOCIETY CONSISTING OF INDIVIDUALISTS

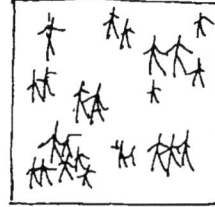
THIS IS OUR SOCIETY TODAY: A CROWD

I DO NOT KNOW HOW A "VILLE SPATIALE" WILL LOOK

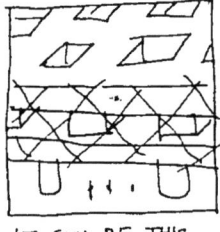
IT CAN BE THIS

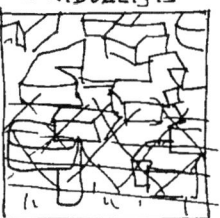
OR THIS

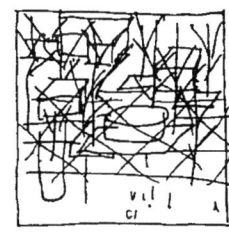
OR THIS

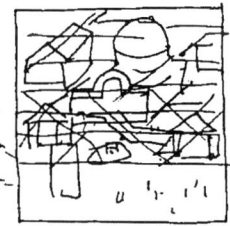
OR ANYTHING ELSE

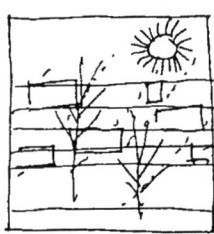
THERE IS NO GRAMAR TO THE "VILLE SPATIALE" EXCEPT RESPECT OF DAY-LIGHT

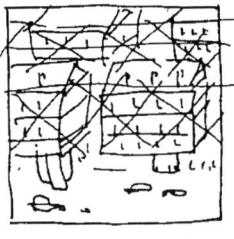
IT CAN LOOK AS WELL AS THE CITY YOU LIVE IN

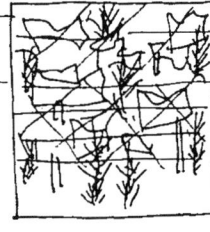
OR IT CAN BE COMPLETELY UNLIKE TO ANY CITY

IT CAN NOT BE PLANNED, IT CAN ONLY HAPPEN

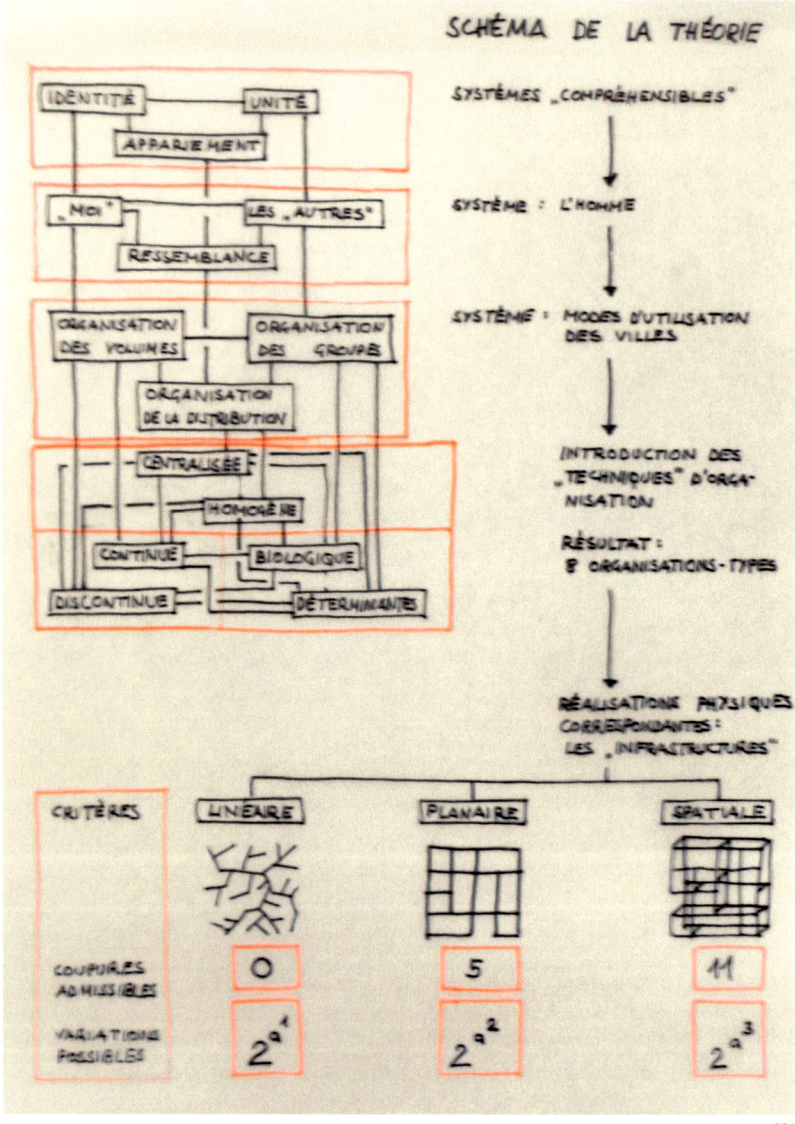

EARLY STUDIES

004 Scheme of the Theory. From *comprehensible systems* to *corresponding physical realizations; linear, planar and spatial infrastructures*, c. 1959.
005 Comparative diagrams between the *Present City* (left) and the *Ville Spatiale* (right), c. 1964.

Present City **Ville Spatiale**

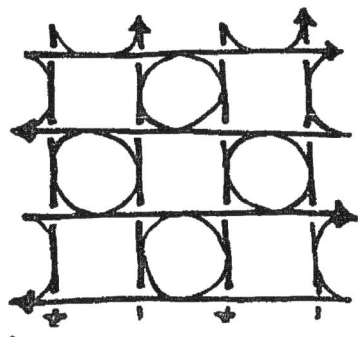

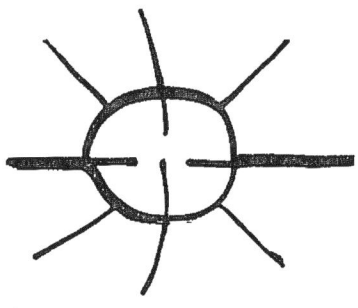

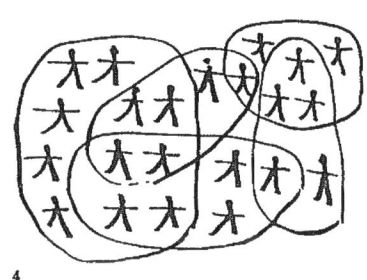

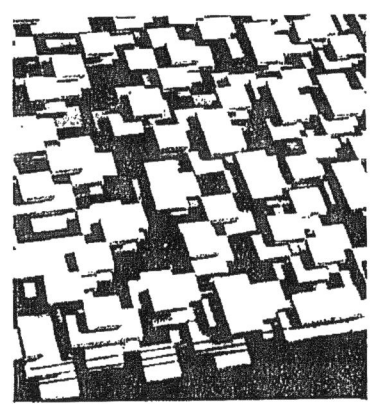

Axiome pair:
Occupation of space-mobility

1 / Centralized distribution
2 / Homogenous distribution
(network of homogenous circulation)

Axiome pair:
Communal living-communication

3 / Homogenous distribution (crowd)
4 / Centralized distribution (groups)

Axiome pair:
Rational distribution-homeostasis

5 / Centralized distribution
(network of centralized circulation)
6 / Homogenous distribution

VILLE SPATIALE / 51

L'extension de Paris, vers la hauteur:
Après le curettage des parties insalubres existantes de la ville, la densité de l'habitation sera triplée et la capacité de circulation quadruplée, tout en conservant la continuité entre les nouveaux quartiers et les anciens.

Die Erweiterung von Paris, der Höhe zu:
Nach dem Abbrechen der veralteten Slum-Konstruktionen ist doch die Wohndichte auf das Dreifache gesteigert, die Verkehrsdichte auf das Vierfache, ohne damit die Kontinuität zwischen alte und neue Stadtteile zu verlieren.

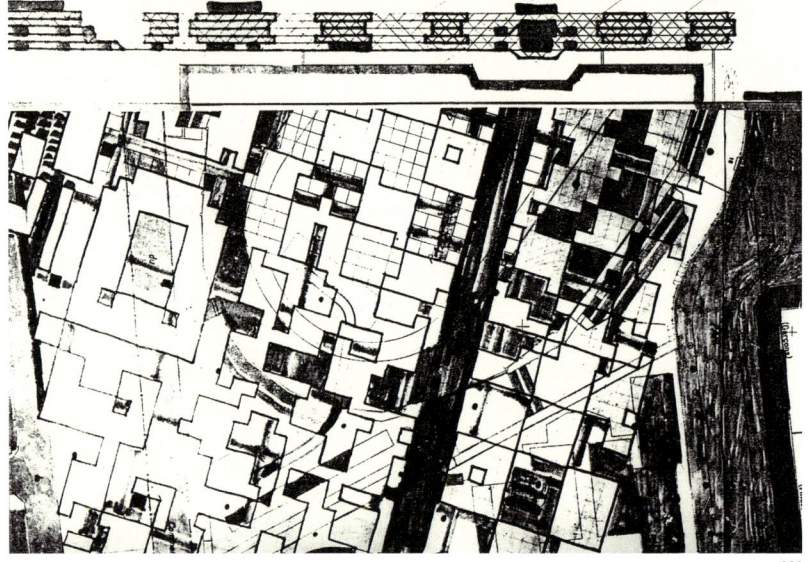

006

ELC EXHIBITION, 1959-60

006 *The extension of Paris, upwards: After the surgical removal of the existing insalubrious sections of the city, the density of habitation will be tripled and the capacity for circulation quadrupled, while maintaining continuity between the new and old districts.*
007 *The plans of different levels can be organized independently from one level to another.*

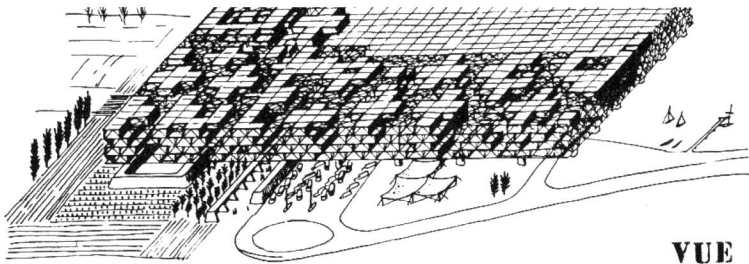

QUARTIER SPATIAL 4000 HAB

VUE AERIENNE

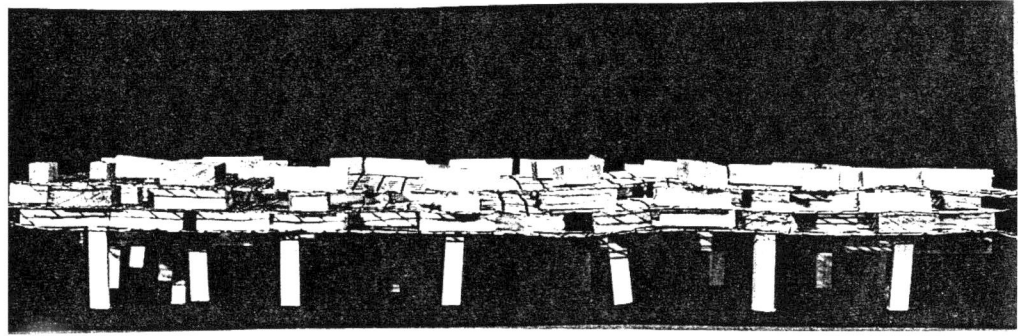

Les plans des divers niveaux peuvent être organisés différemment et indépendamment d'un niveau à l'autre.

Die Pläne der verschiedenen Ebenen können von Einander unabhängig und anders gestaltet sein von einer Ebene zur Anderen.

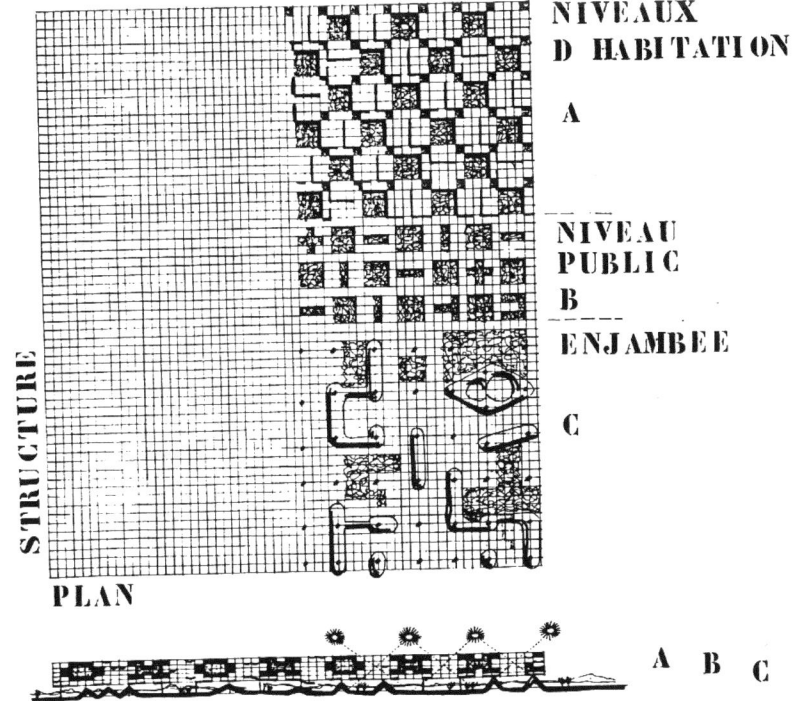

NIVEAUX D HABITATION

A

NIVEAU PUBLIC

B

ENJAMBEE

C

STRUCTURE

PLAN

A B C

VILLE SPATIALE / 53

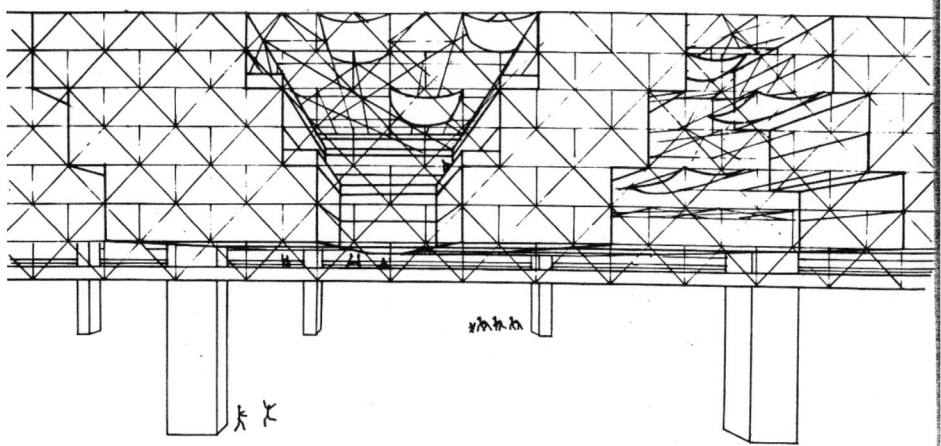

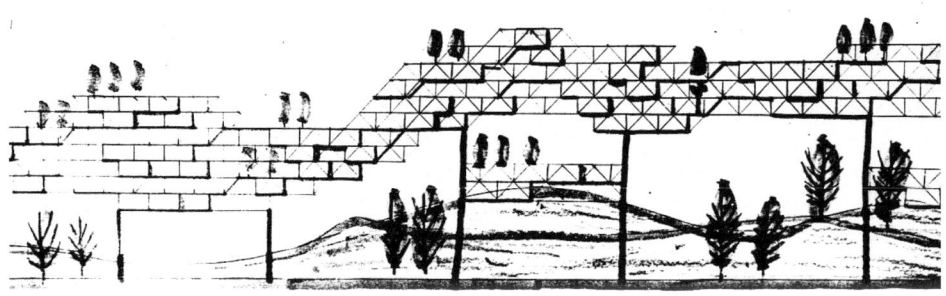

ELC EXHIBITION, 1959-60

008 *The different methods of filling the containing structures of the spatial city create a new aesthetic.*
009 Top view, *Space-frame* model of the *Ville Spatiale*.

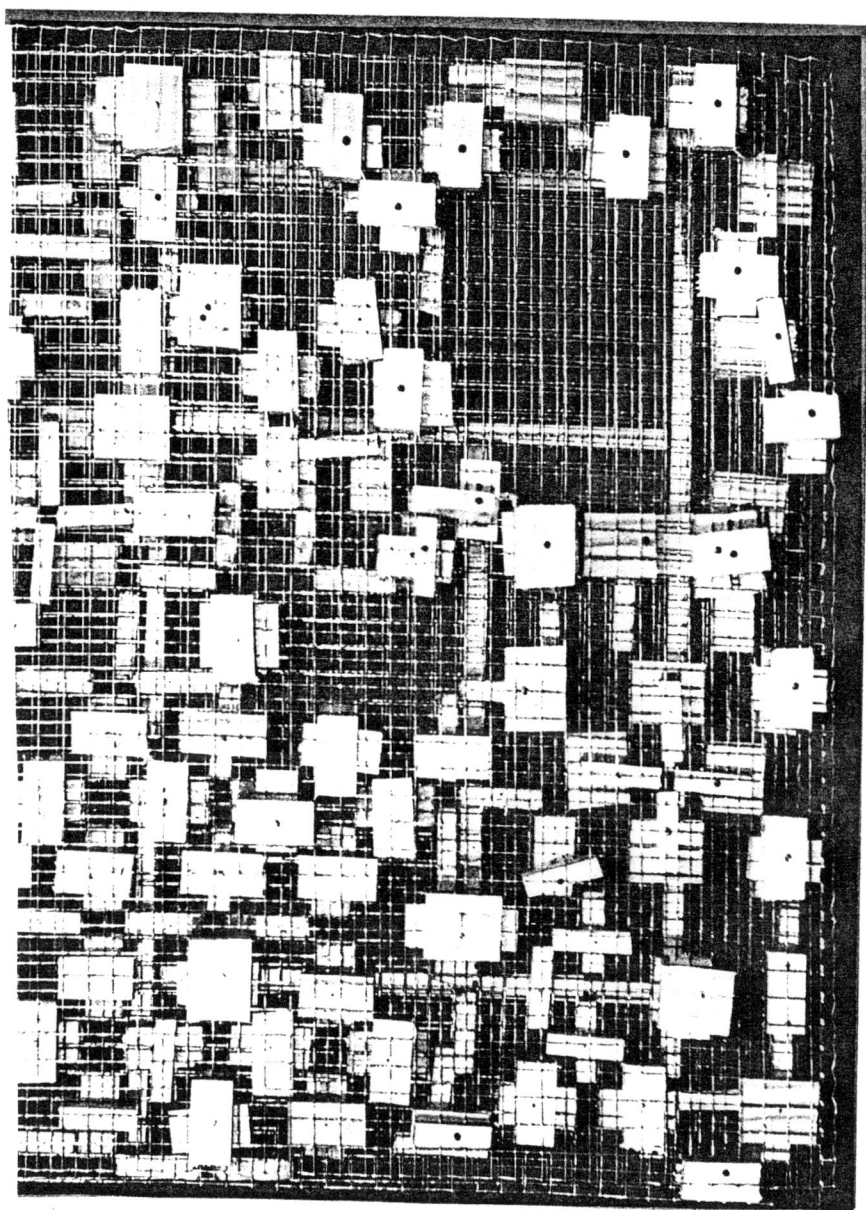

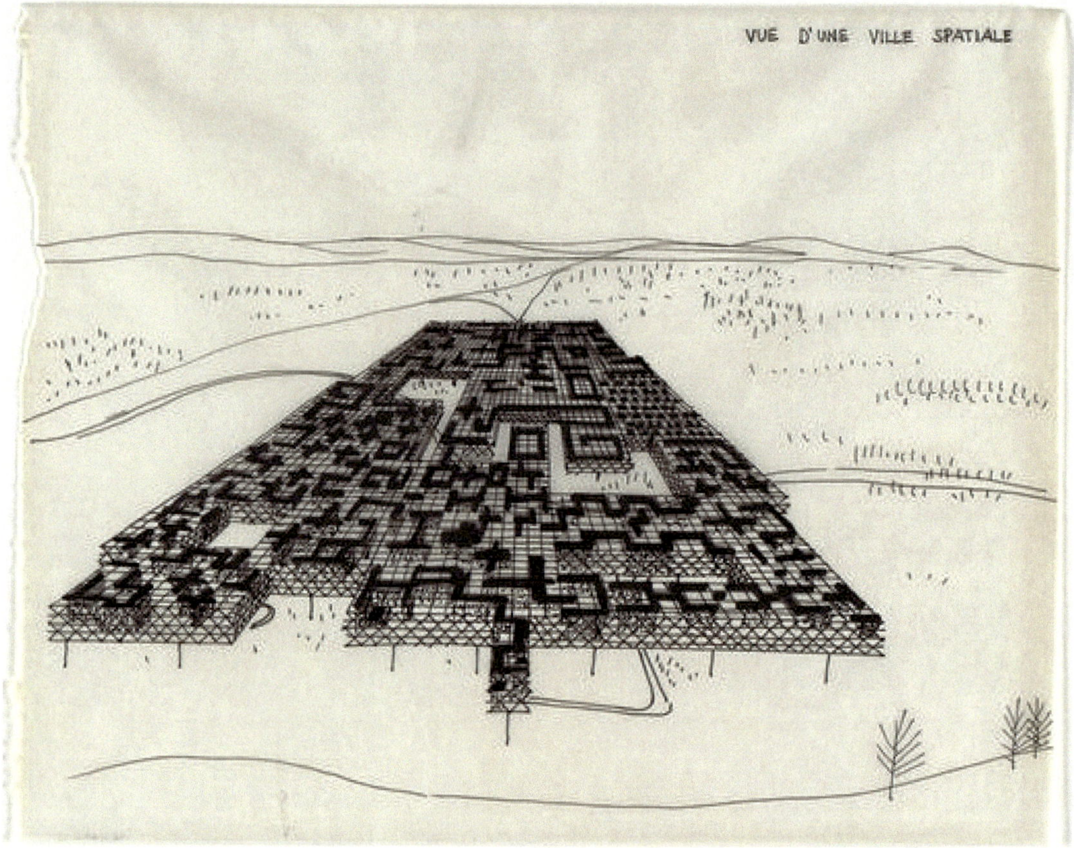

010

PERSPECTIVES

010 Aerial view of the *Ville Spatiale* for Tunis, 1958.
A spatial city makes it possible to develop the districts in height, width and length: the individual districts can either adjoin or overlap.
011 *Ville Spatiale, Perspective 3rd phase*, 1960–65.

012–014 Perspectives, *Ville Spatiale,* from 1960.

3 LEVEL FLOORS OF A STUDY

015 – 016 Cardboard models showing the floors of the *Ville Spatiale*, 1959.
017 Collage, superposition of all levels, 1958 – 62.
018 – 025 Conceptual drawings, level floor studies of the *Ville Spatiale*, 1959-60.

60 / PART I / THE DILUTION OF ARCHITECTURE / VILLE SPATIALE

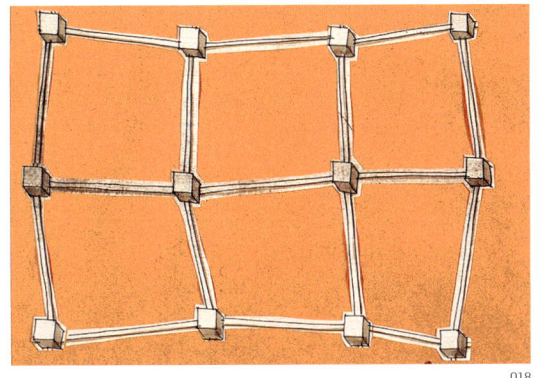
018

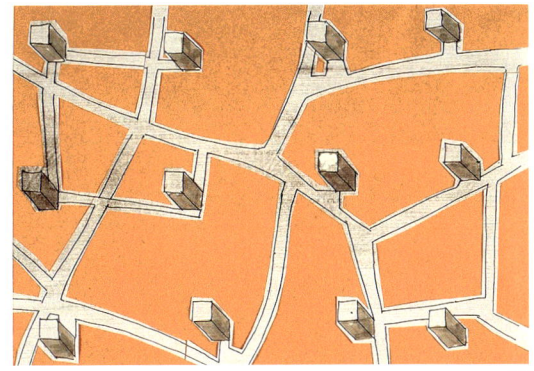
019

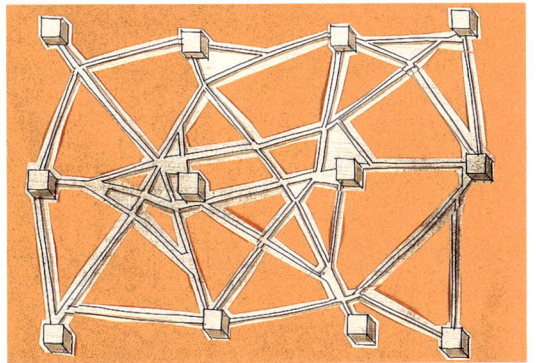
020

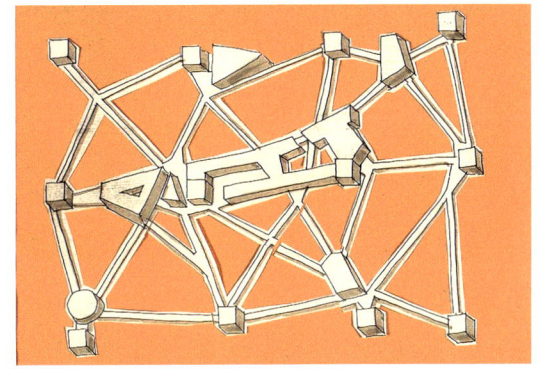
021

022

023

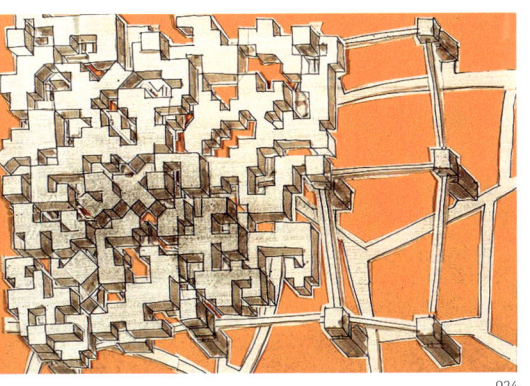
024

025

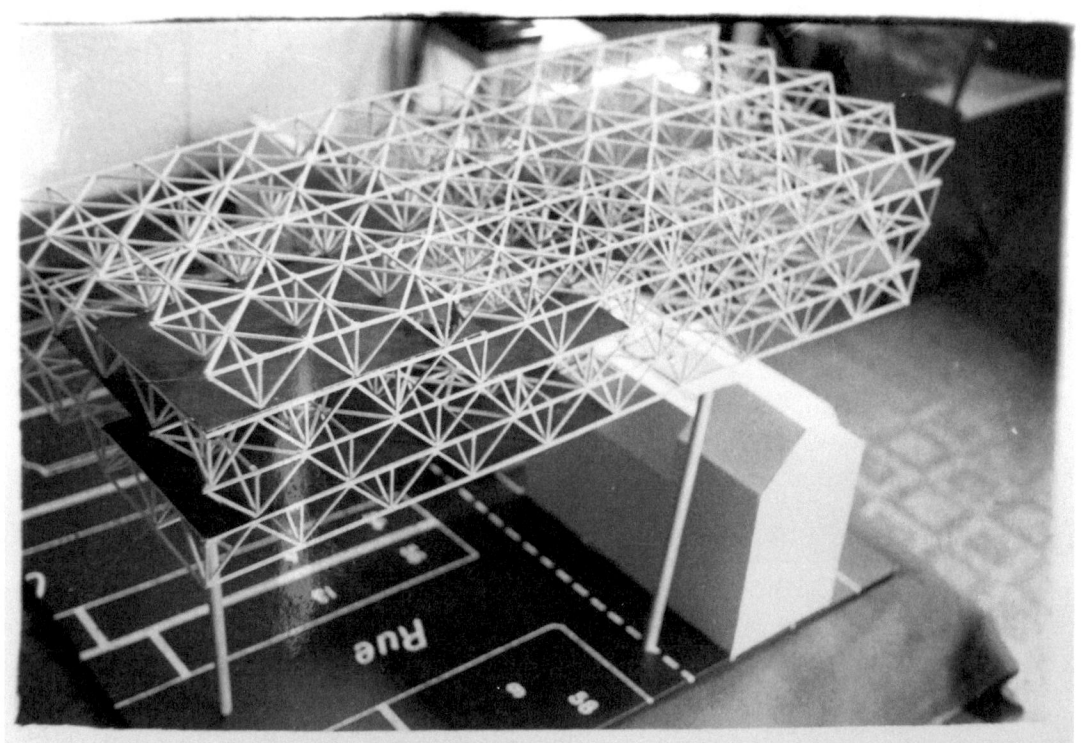

026

STUDY MODELS

026 Model of a *Space-frame* infrastructure. c. 1959.
027–028 Model views showing the complexity of the landscape, 1958–62.
029–031 Model in glass, glass paste and wood, *Ville Spatiale* studies, 1958–59.

027

028

030

031

VILLE SPATIALE / 63

032

033

034

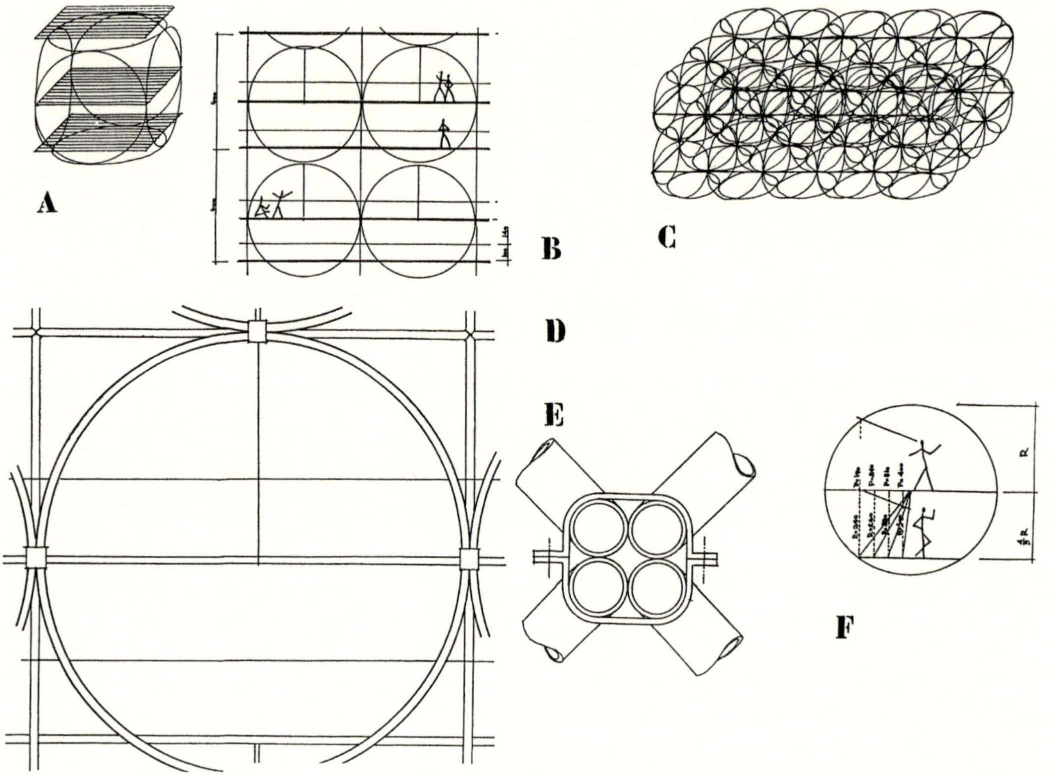

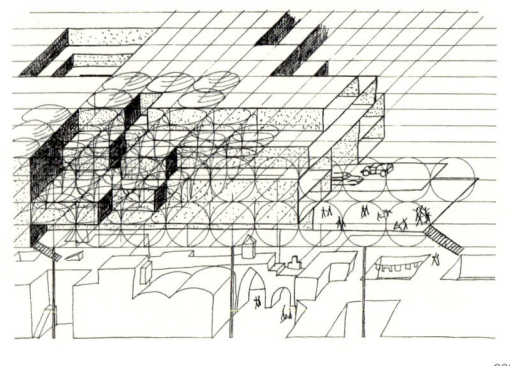

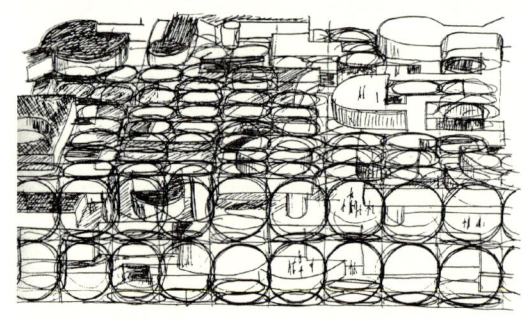

SPACE-CHAIN TECHNIQUE

032 Technical studies, *Space-frame* structure made with circles, 1959.
033 First application of the *Space-chain* technique, *Ville Spatiale* above the Medina, Tunis, 1958.
034 *Ville Spatiale* with *Space-chain* structure, from 1959.
035–**037** Top view and section of *Space-chain* infrastructure with inhabited volumes, 1970.

>> **038** IRREGULAR STRUCTURE, C. 1959

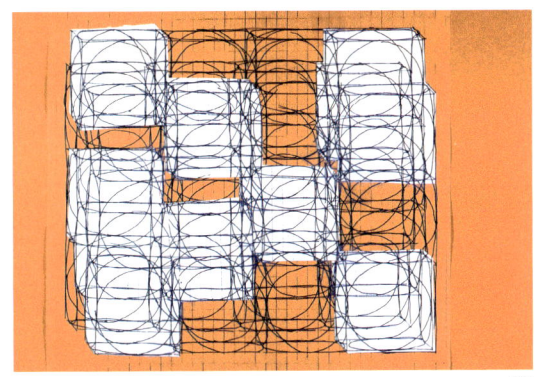

035

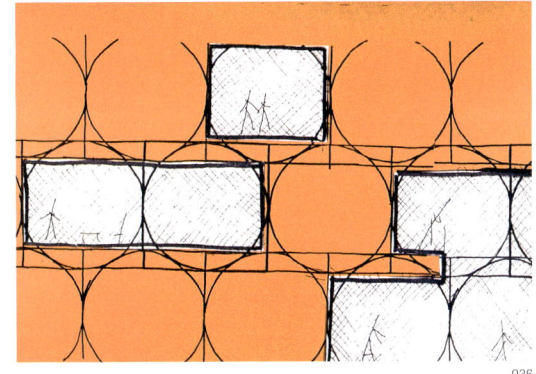

036

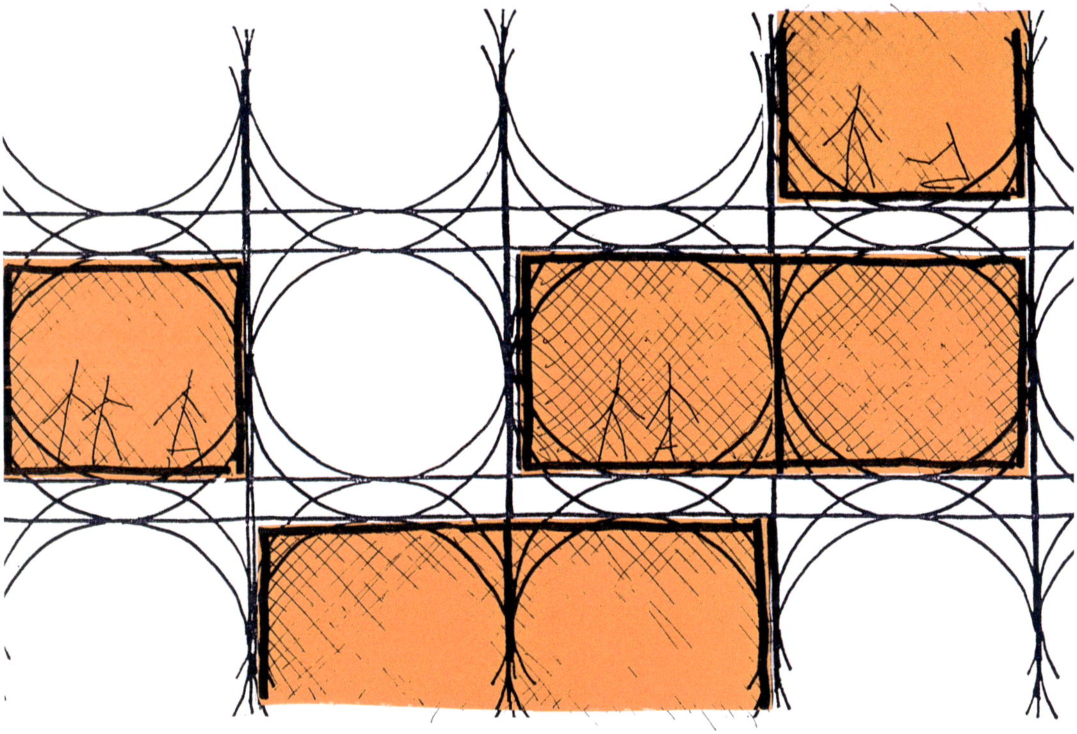

037

VILLE SPATIALE / 65

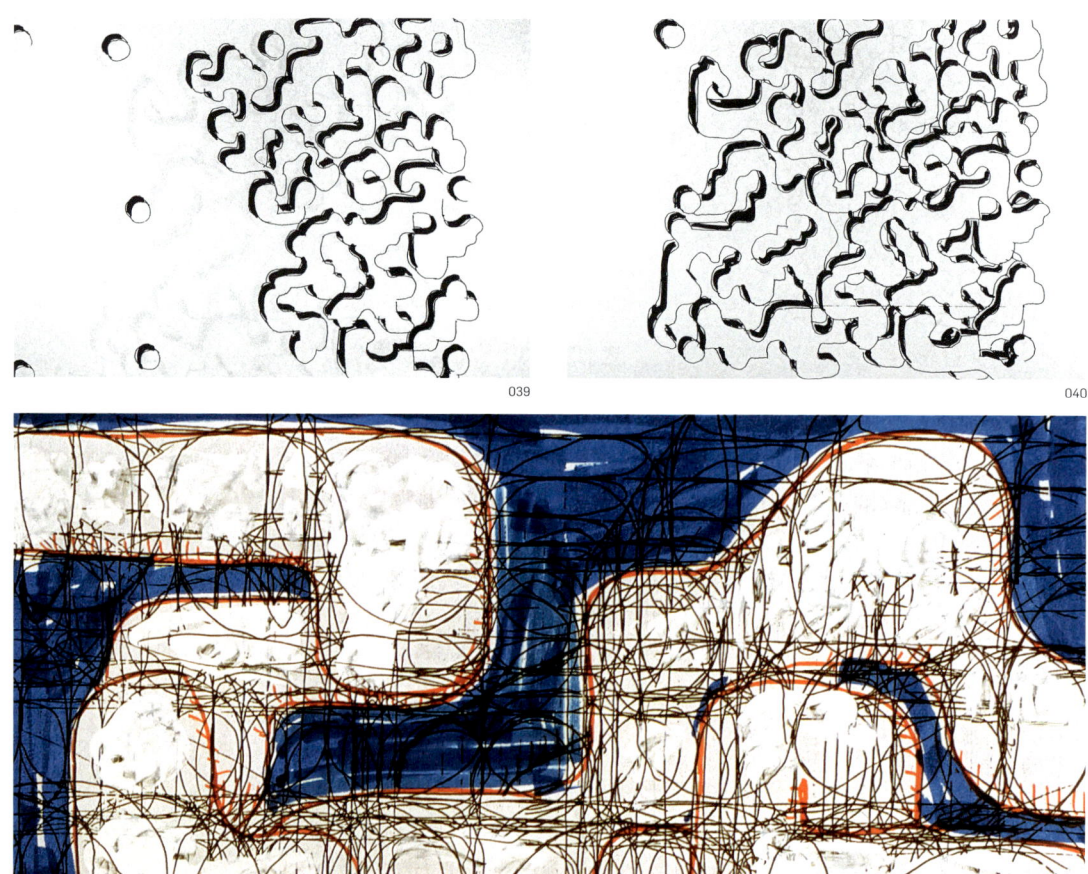

Sketches to substitute the geometrical pattern as much as technically reasonable. Architecture should not simply be "applied geometry."

FRIEDMAN, Yona: *C. 1990. Spatial town + Amorphous Architecture*, in *Yona Friedman: Drawings & Models 1945–2010*. Paris, Presses du Réel, 2010, p. 616.

IRREGULAR PATTERN

039–040 Top views, *Spatial settlement* with irregular outlines, 1970–90.
041–044 Drawing series, *Amorphous Architecture*, c. 1990.

VILLE SPATIALE

THE INNER CITY

045 Interior perspective of the *Ville Spatiale*, from 1960.
046–053 Conceptual drawings showing the *growing complexity* of the interior, 1958–62.

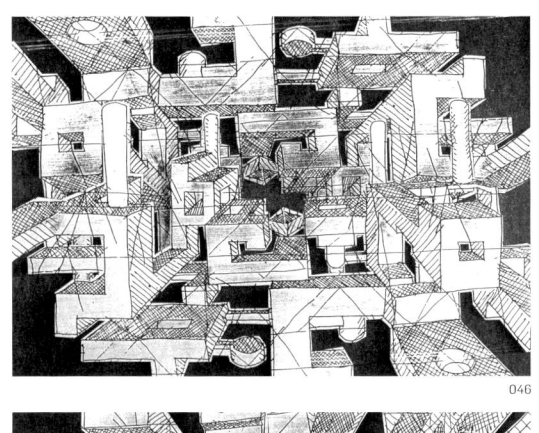
046

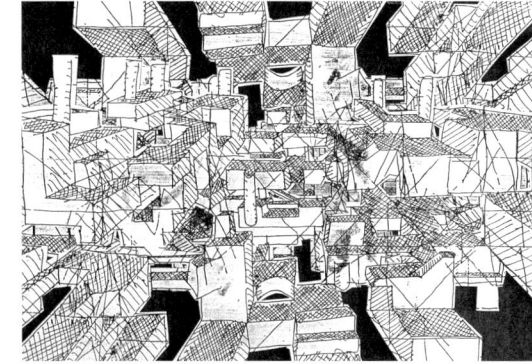
047

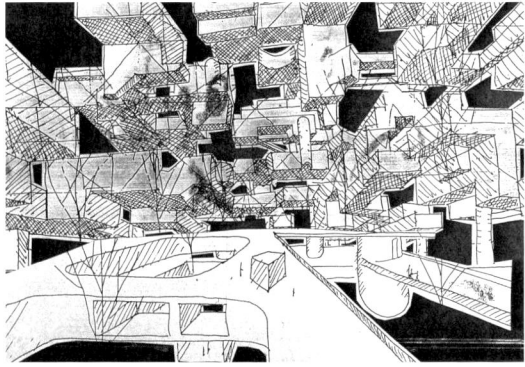
048

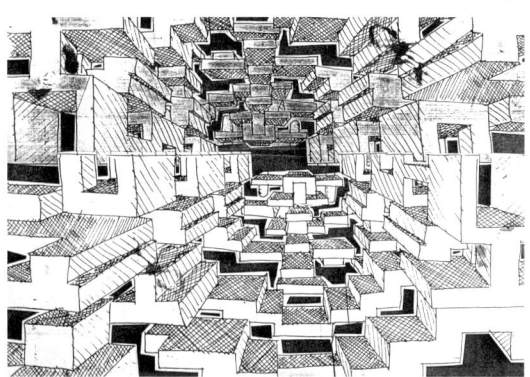
049

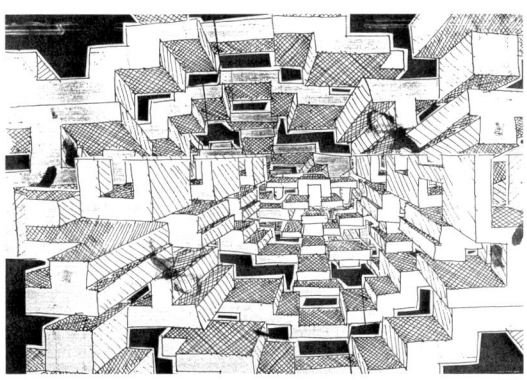
050

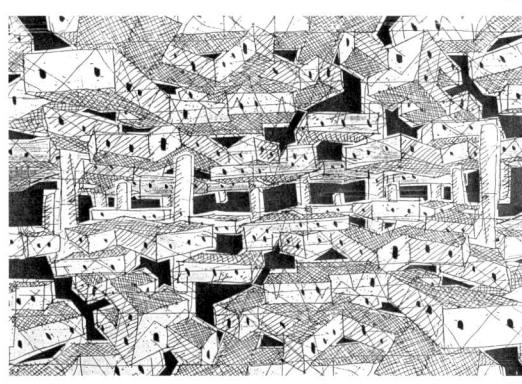
051

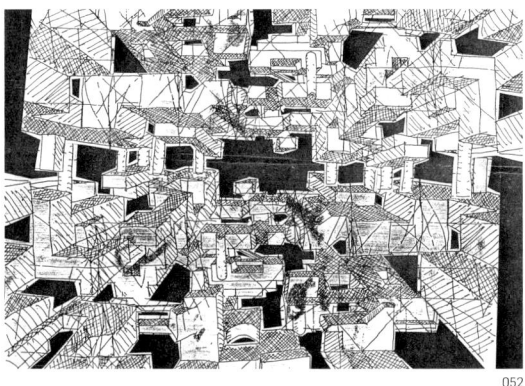
052

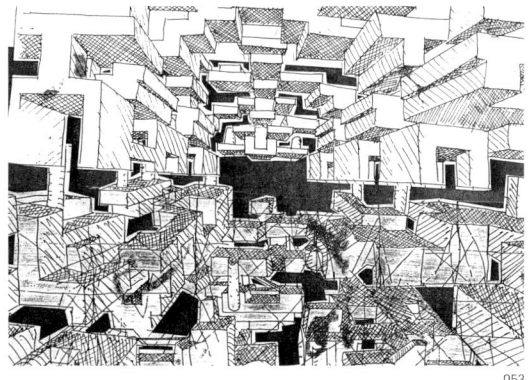
053

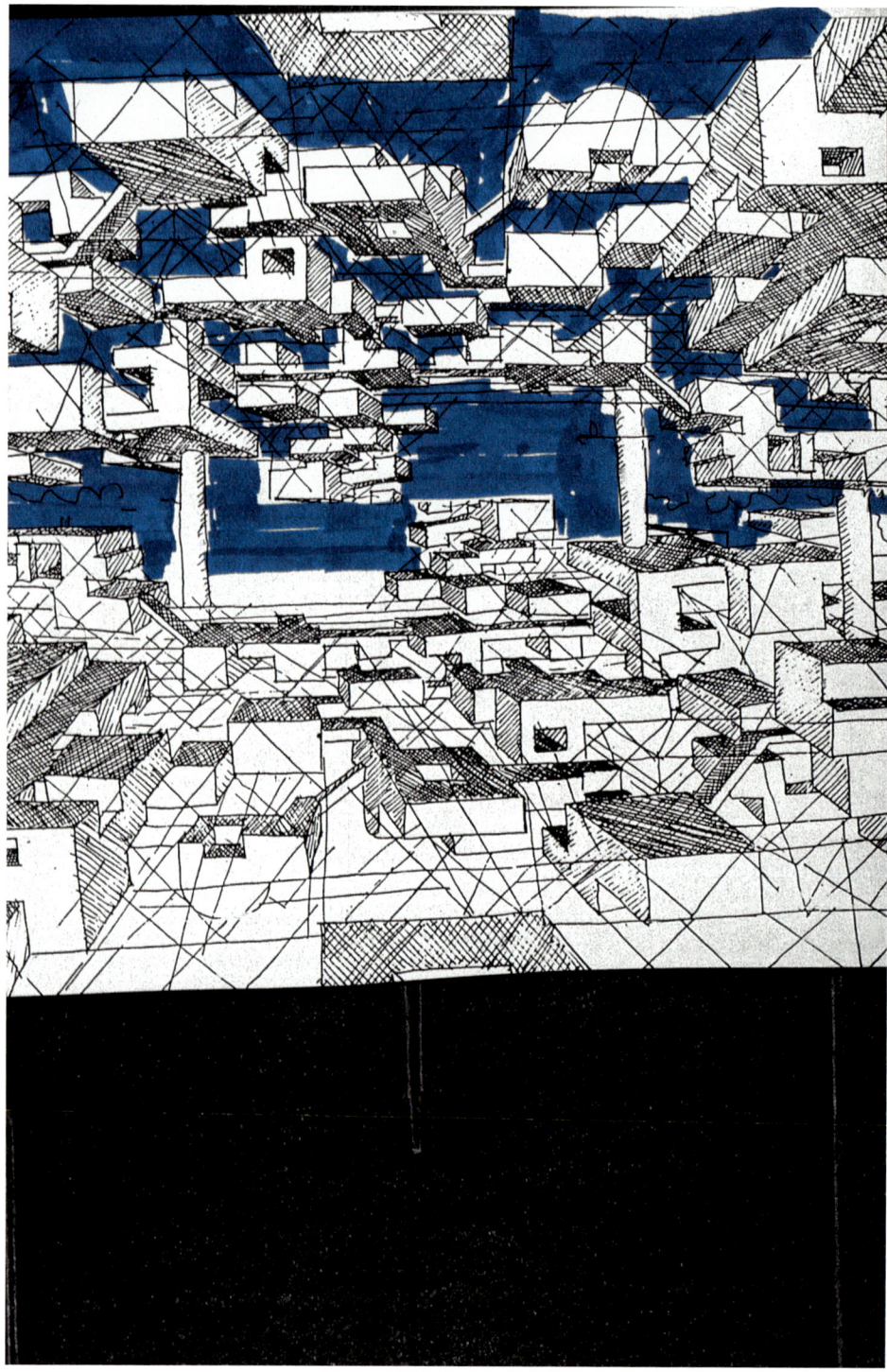

THE INNER CITY

054–055 Interior of the the *Ville Spatiale*, 1958–62.

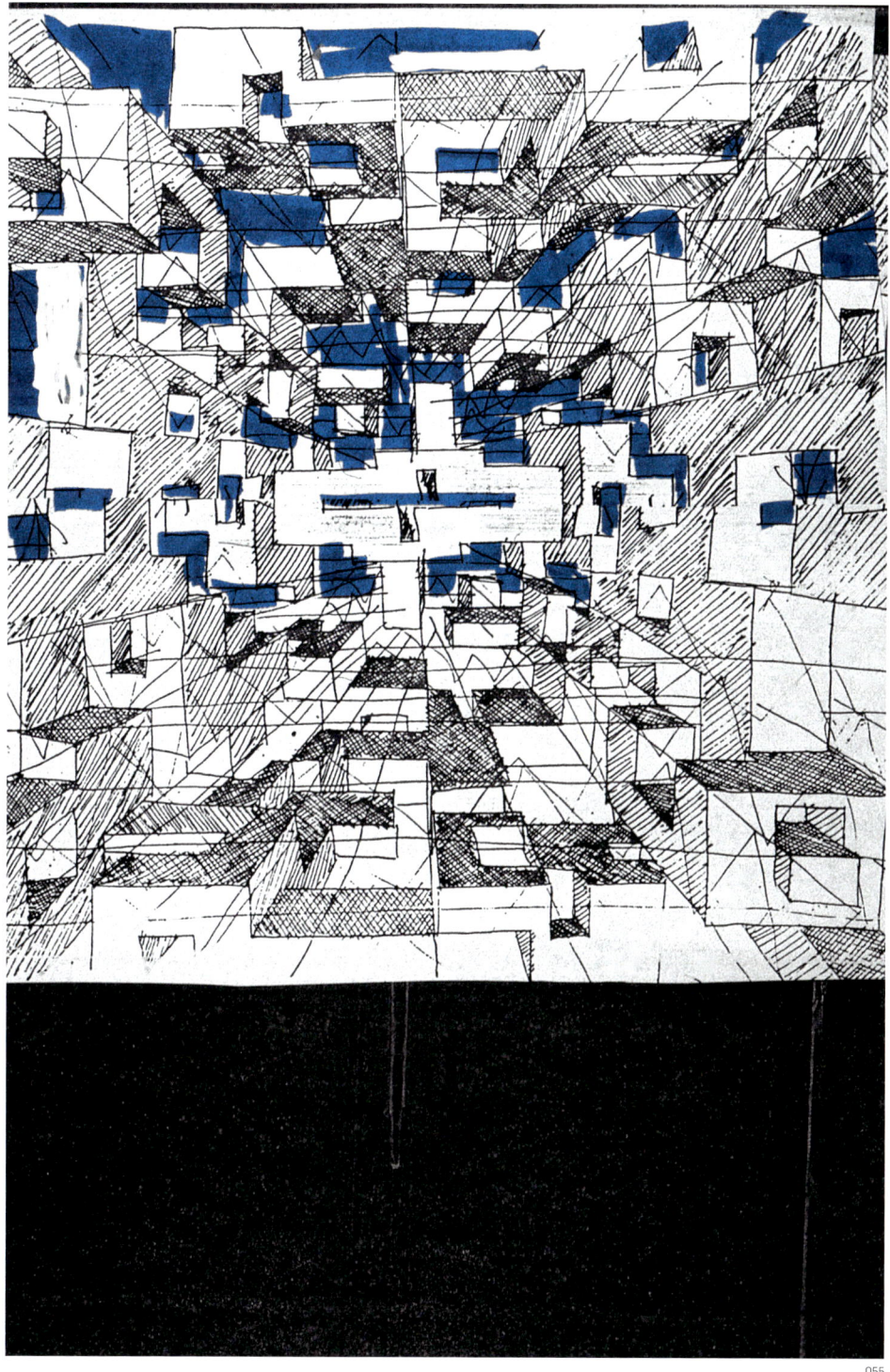

056

057

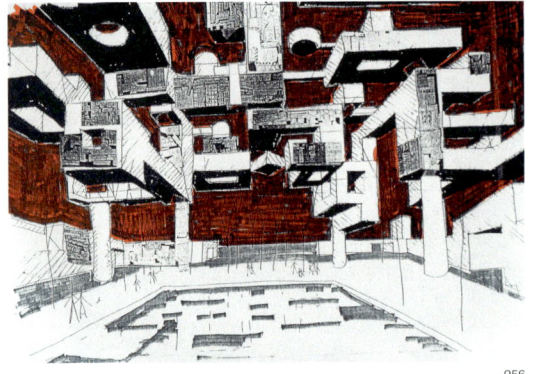

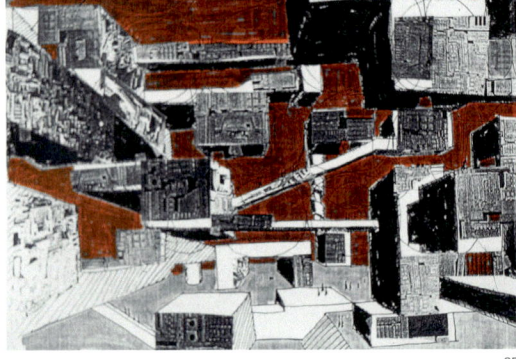

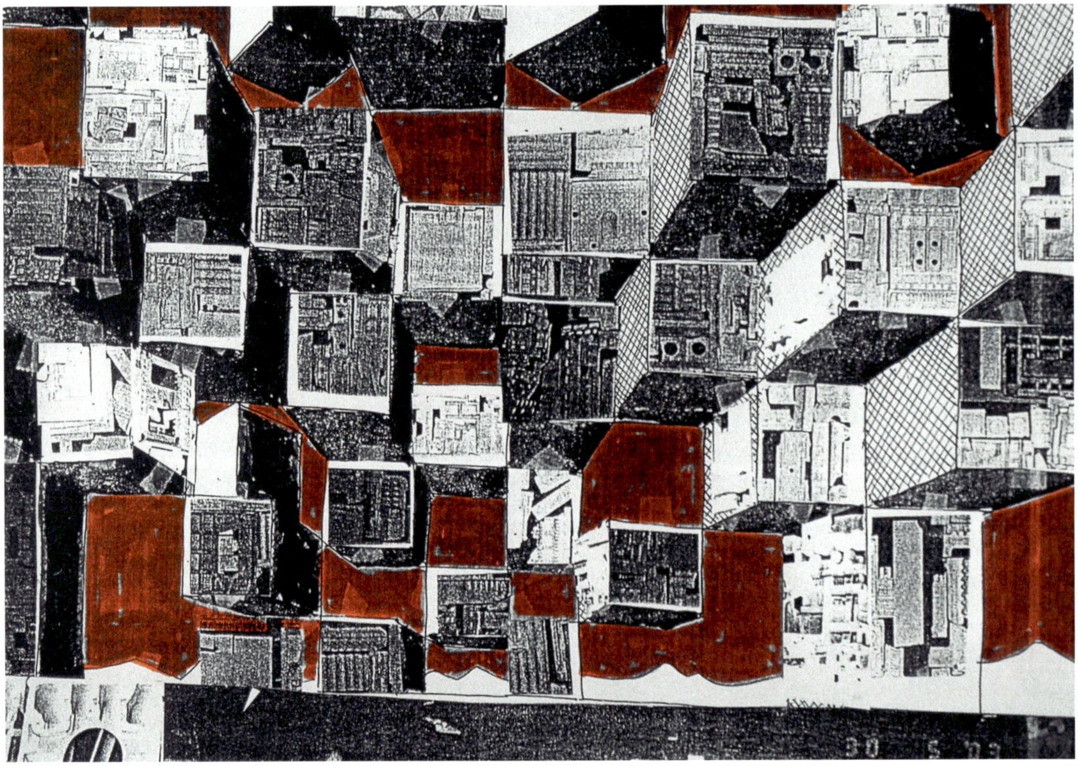

058

THE INNER CITY

056 – 061 Photomontage of a *Ville Spatiale* with polystyrene packing elements, 2000.
First real-scale application of this idea at the Venice Biennale in 2003.

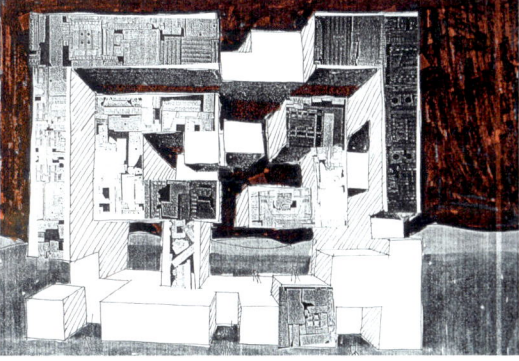

EUROPEAN PROJECTS

My project for Paris – "Paris Spatial" – proposes to triple the density of dwellings in the town itself. According to the belief that the present town will always remain the centre of attraction, it therefore appears necessary to construct the largest number of dwellings within the dimensions of the present town. The essence of the project consists in constructing new blocks above the existing town in such a way that the new constructions… does not entail important demolitions in the town itself, so that the town and its districts will keep their present character… These constructions will have to be built above the districts which are situated in the outer rings, and over certain parts of the central district (Quartier des Halles, Boulevard Sebastopol, etc.). Thus the historic town will remain intact.

FRIEDMAN, Yona: *Towards a Mobile Architecture*, translated by Veronica Bennet, in *Architectural Design*, November 1963, p. 510.

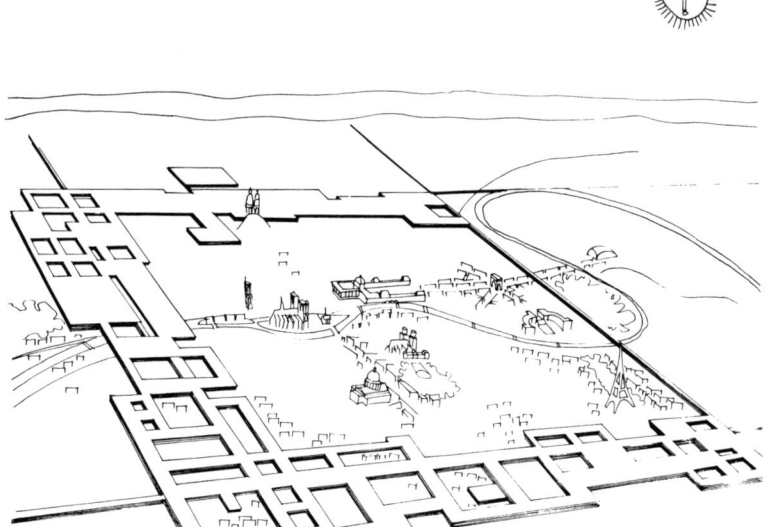

062

PARIS SPATIAL

062 Aerial view, 1960.
063 – **064** Photomontage above Place de la Concorde, 1959–70.
065 – **066** *Ville Spatiale* above Avenue des Champs Elysées, 1959.
067 – **068** Photomontage above Île de la Cité, 1959–70.
069 Photomontage above the river Seine, 1959.
070 Portrait of Friedman and Balkis, with a *Ville Spatiale* above the Hôtel des Invalides, 2000.

>> **071** *Ville Spatiale* above the river Seine, 1960.

063

064

065

066

067

068

069

070

EUROPEAN PROJECTS / 77

PARIS RAILWAY STATIONS

072 Photomontage of the *Ville Spatiale* above a Paris terminal, 1959–65.
073 The *Space-frame* above one of the roads flanking the terminal, 1964.
074 Suspended *Space-frame* in Austerlitz Station, 1964.
075–076 Proposal for Montparnasse Station, 1964.
077 Top view, development covering the railway lines, 1964.

074

075

076

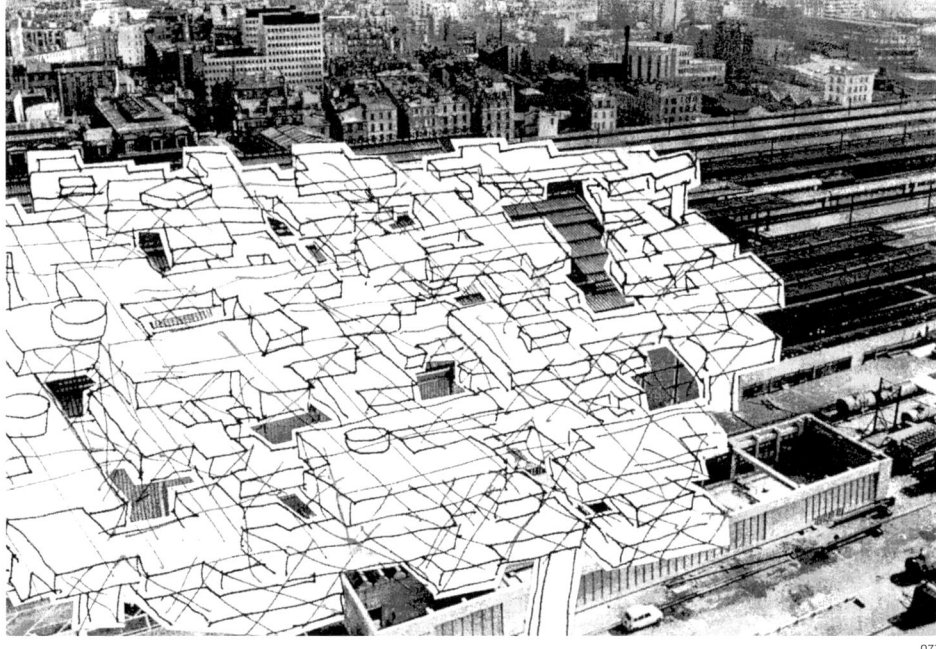
077

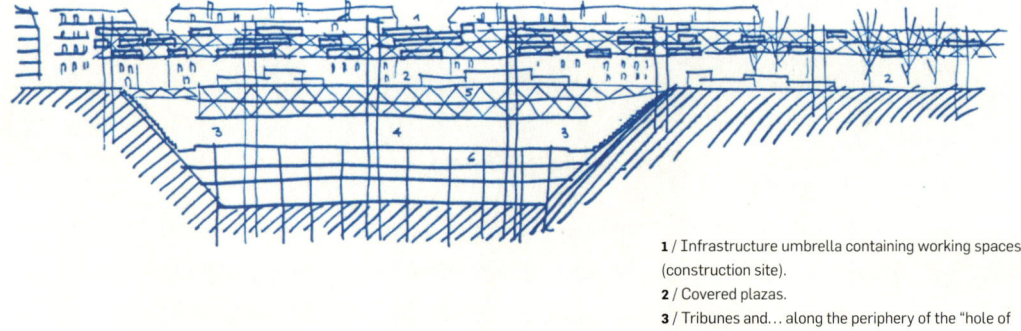

1 / Infrastructure umbrella containing working spaces (construction site).
2 / Covered plazas.
3 / Tribunes and… along the periphery of the "hole of the Halles."
4 / Covered public square bottom.
5 / Commercial center or other.
6 / Underground parking.

For the Plateau Beaubourg competition, I proposed keeping the public space intact and covering it with an umbrella roof. This roof would have contained the Center (museums, etc.) that was the subject of the competition.

For Les Halles, I would have proposed application of the same technique: covering the largest part of the surface (which had formerly been covered by Baltard's pavilions) with a roof, an airy spatial structure, standing on pilotis spaced 50 meters apart. The open spaces inside this "roof" could house – on two levels, perhaps – certain services, offices, stores, etc.

On the ground, the surface covered by the umbrella would be left open to the proposals of the Parisians: from a theater to a flea market to a Hyde Park Corner-style meeting place, everything would be allowed and possible.

And the famous hole? The hole could be filled with an underground, or semi-underground center, according to economic possibilities and other contingencies. If nothing else could be done – for lack of subsidies – it could represent an "accidental terrain," a type of reforested precipice with a "lake" at the bottom (a precedent for this being Buttes-Chaumont).

Covered public spaces whose use is left to the initiative of the public (a bit in the manner of ancient basilicas) are missing in our cities.

Yona Friedman

"UMBRELLA" FOR LES HALLES, PARIS, 1969

078 Section of the main space of the *Umbrella for Les Halles*.
079 Perspective, section and plan of the labyrinth under the umbrella.

le „parapluie" des Halles

Parapluie des Halles

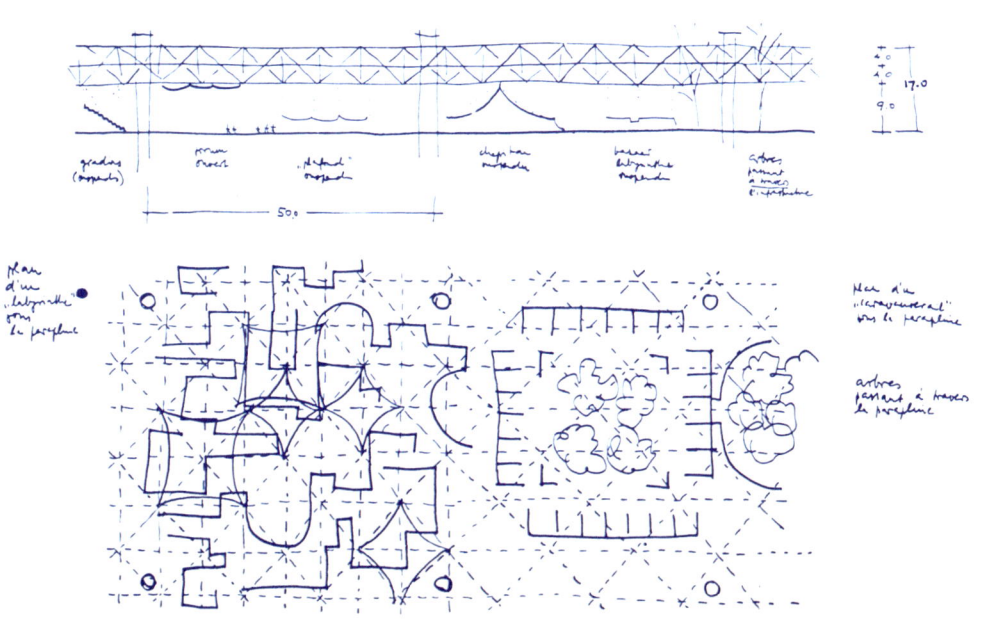

080

"UMBRELLA" FOR LES HALLES, PARIS, 1969

080 Perspective of the *Spatial-Umbrella* over Les Halles.
081–082 Photomontages, aerial views in front of the Church of Saint-Eustache, situated at the entrance of the former market of Paris Les Halles.

EUROPEAN PROJECTS / 85

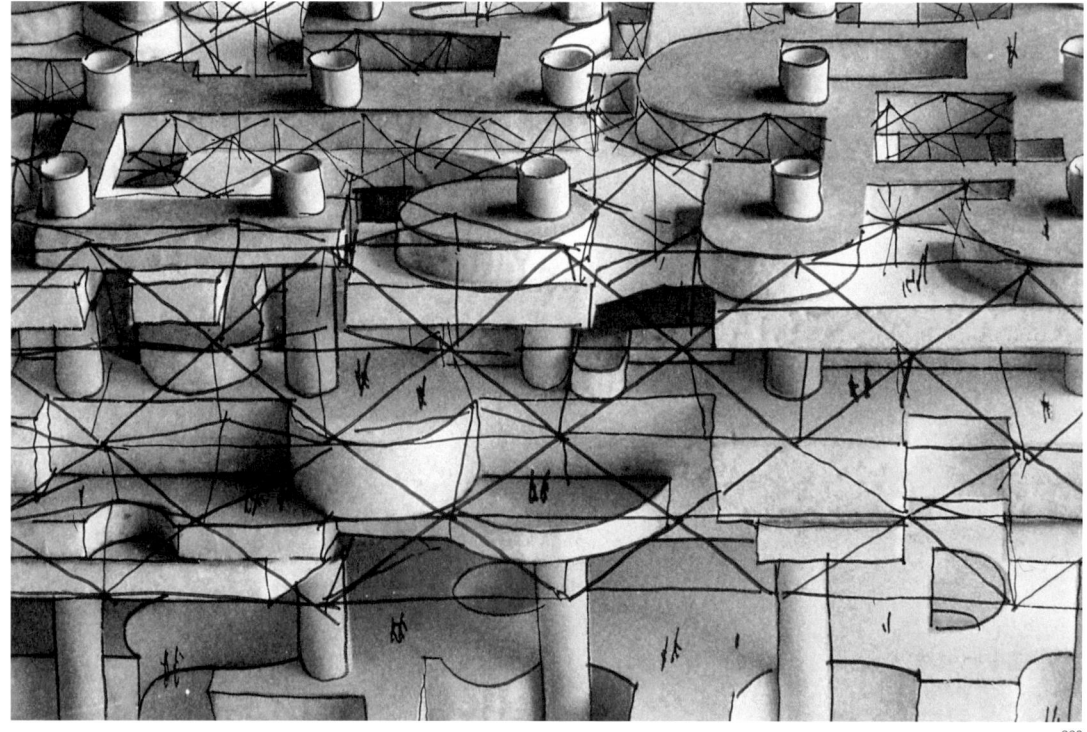

The Beaubourg project (Centre Pompidou) was a practical implementation of variable facades and building volumes within an unchanging structure. I thought that the building's exterior should change with every new exhibition.

FRIEDMAN, Yona: *1970. Centre Pompidou, Paris,* in *Yona Friedman, Drawings & Models 1945–2010,* Paris, Presses du Réel, 2010, p. 356.

POMPIDOU CENTER, PARIS, 1970

083 Model view, competition entry for the Centre Beaubourg.
084–091 Drawings of several transformations of the facade.

>> **092** Extension to the Georges Pompidou Center, Paris, 2008.

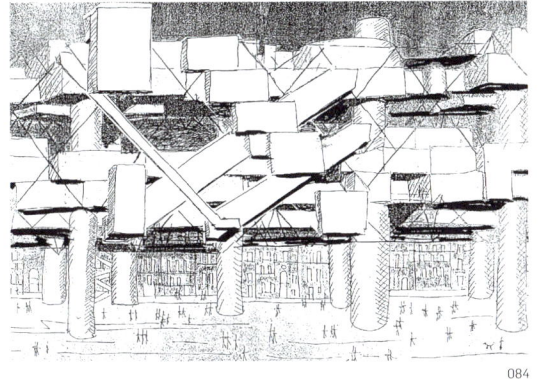

084

085

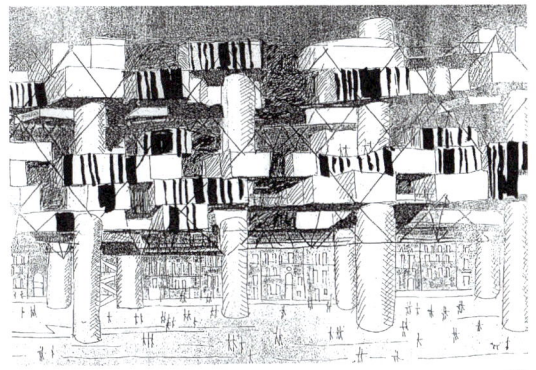

086

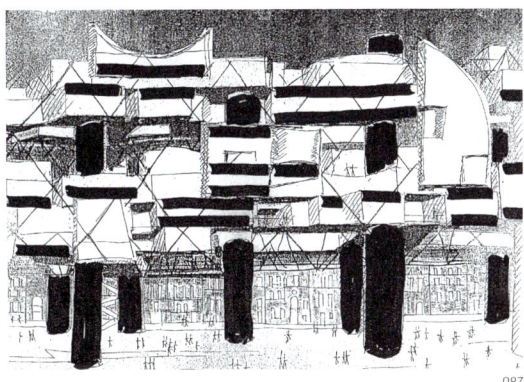

087

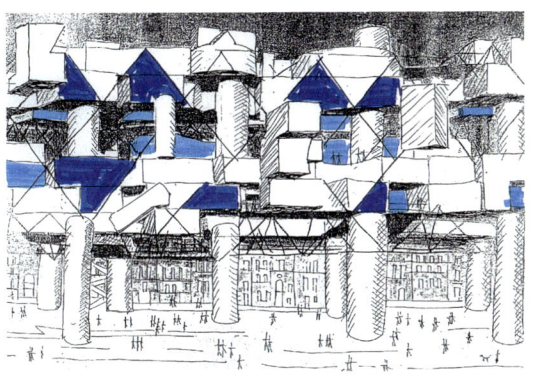

088

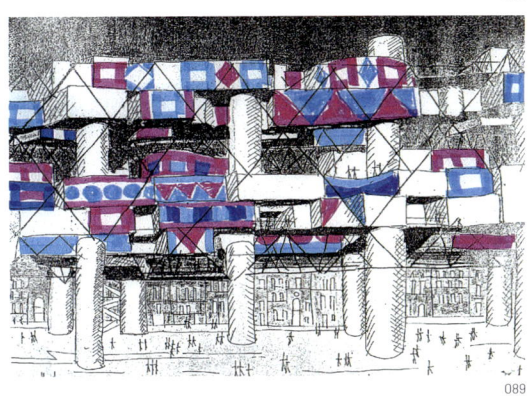

089

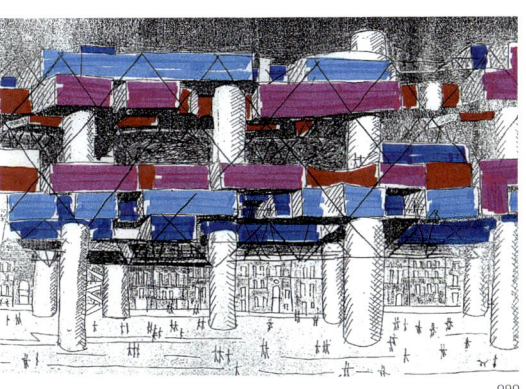

090

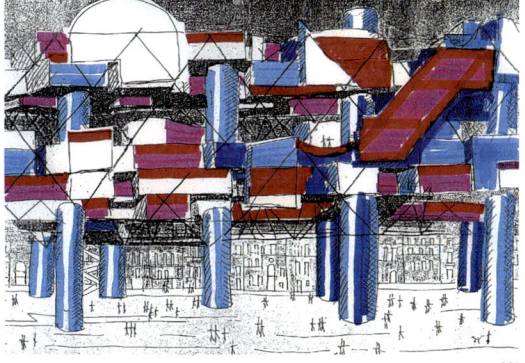

091

EUROPEAN PROJECTS / 87

Obviously – by the very definition of Museum of the 21st century – no one can predict today the appearance of this "museum-city" at the end of the century. Not even its facade, the first stage, can be determined in advance.

I have tried, in these views, to outline different possible but undefined aspects of the museum. The reality – if the project was a reality – could be even more amazing.

MUSEUM OF THE 21st CENTURY, PARIS

093–101 The *self-constructing museum*, notes and photomontages of a residential neighborhood above the river Seine in Paris, 1999.

094

095

096

097

098

099

100

101

EUROPEAN PROJECTS / 91

102

To turn certain public routes into stage sets, stadiums or promenades is natural. The Champs-Élysées lined with grandstands and terraces, with the central section pedestrianized, the Place de la Concorde surrounded by grandstands (terraces) and turned into a place for walking, is perhaps a definitive step toward making the city a public space.
At the moment, these are "asphalt wastelands."

PARIS OLYMPIC, 2004
Paris was a candidate for the 2008 Olympic Games.

102 *Paris Olympique*, view on the Arc de Triomphe and notes.
103 Schematic section and plan of the proposal for the Champs-Élysées.
104 – 106 Montage on postcards.

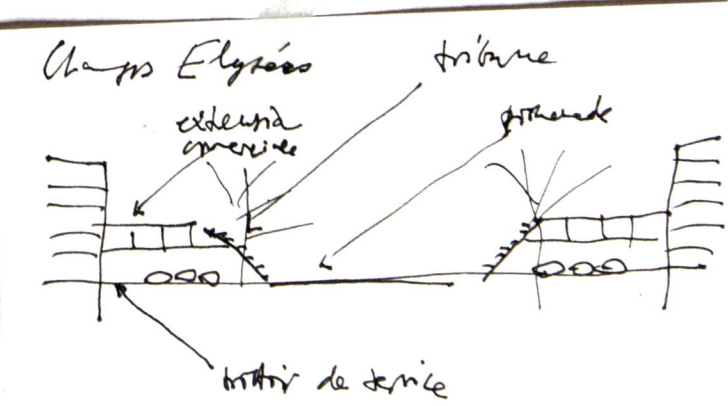

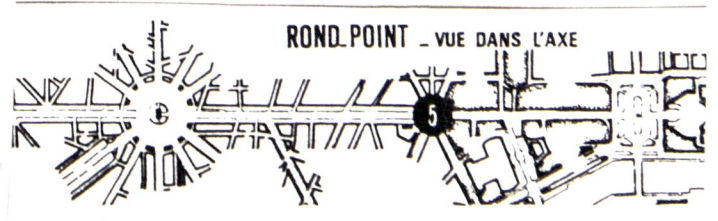

103

104

105

106

EUROPEAN PROJECTS / 93

Yona Friedman prepared a "span-over block" which, set above the pier at the edge of Monaco Harbor […] would enable him to create a sort of artificial city-bridge 400 meters long, 24 to 40 meters wide and six stories high, with the first story located 15 meters above the pier; 1,000 homes could also be constructed, as well as stores, cafes, hotels, bordering on a promenade which would be an extension of the old city, connecting the Port Neuve to the Avenue de Monte-Carlo leading to the Casino.

RAGON, Michel: *Construisons des villes sur la mer*, in *La Nation*, no. 9, 1963, p. 269.

VENICE OF MONACO, 1959

107 Photomontage on postcard, interior perspective.
108–112 Drawing and photomontages, aerial views of the *Ville Spatiale* above the harbor.

>> **113** MOSCOW, 1990

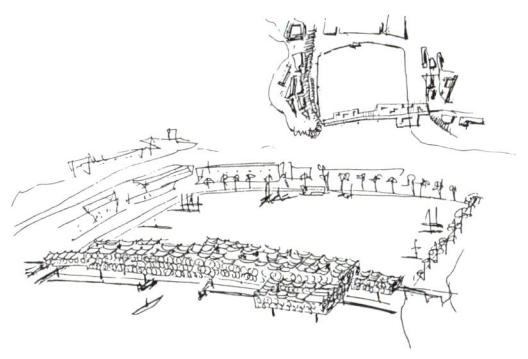

108

109

110

111

112

EUROPEAN PROJECTS

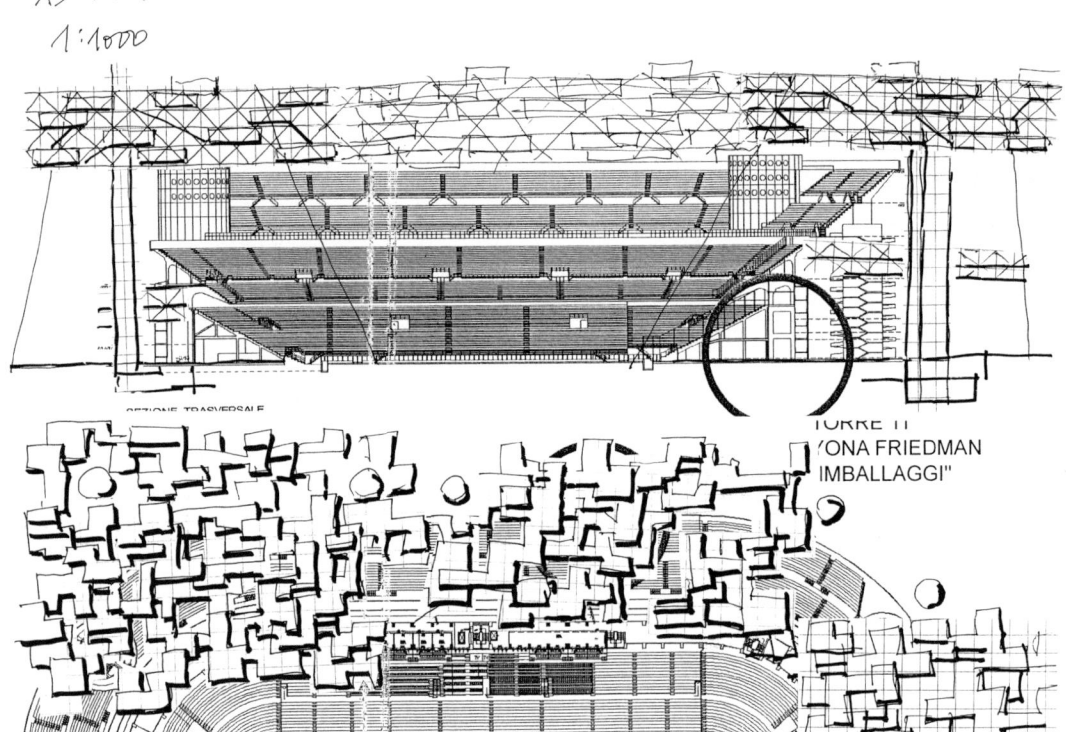

MILAN STADIUM, 2004
Project proposed by *Domus*.

114 Schematic elevation and site plan of a *Spatial settlement* covering the San Siro Stadium in Milan.
115–117 Photomontages, perspectives.

118

119

The bombed-out center of Berlin was rebuilt in a classical style, missing an occasion to build the capital with a new kind of architecture.

FRIEDMAN, Yona: *2003. Berlin*, in *Yona Friedman, Drawings & Models 1945–2010*, Paris, Presses du Réel, 2010, p. 822.

BERLIN, 2004

118–**119** Sketches, perspectives.
120–**124** Photomontages, aerial views of the *Ville Spatiale* above Berlin.

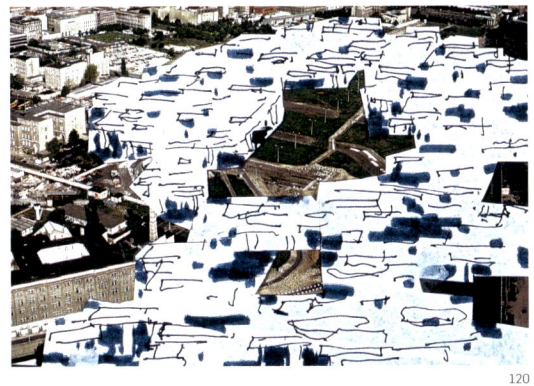

120

121

122

123

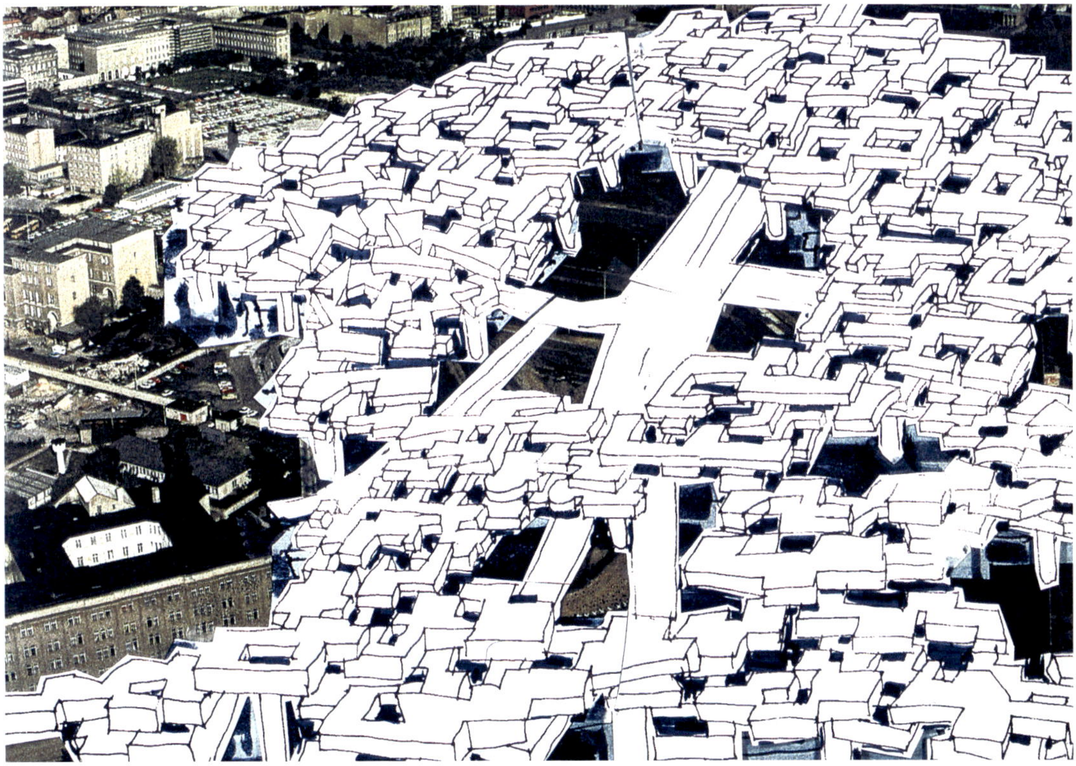

124

EUROPEAN PROJECTS / 101

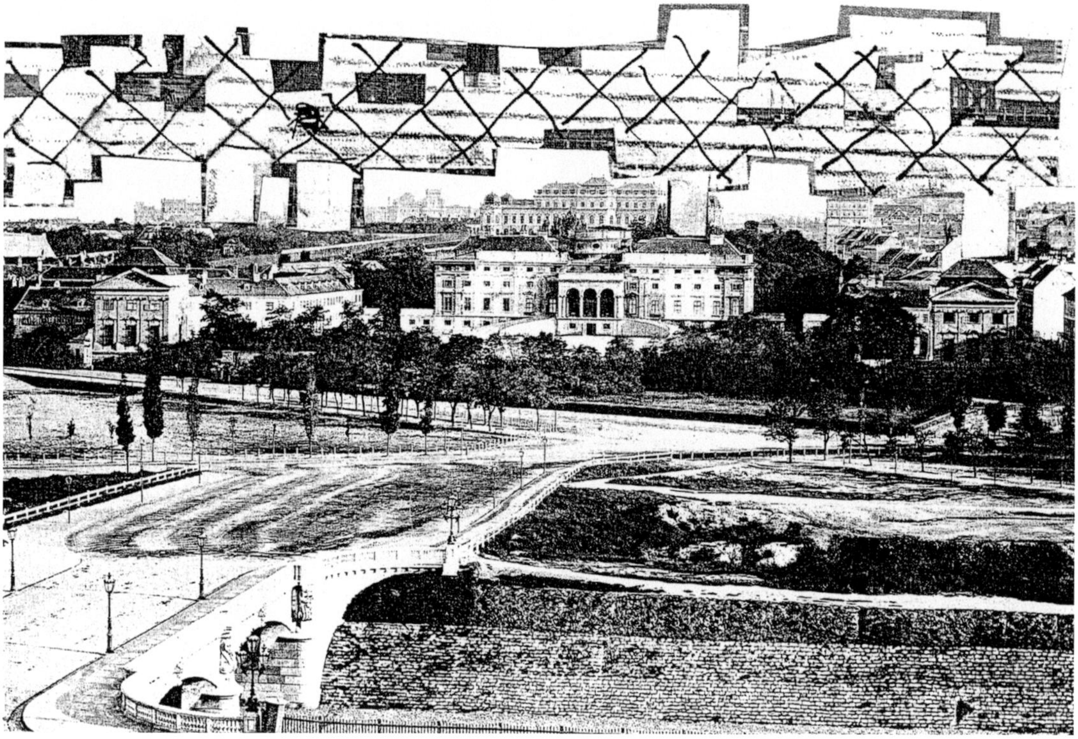

125

126

127

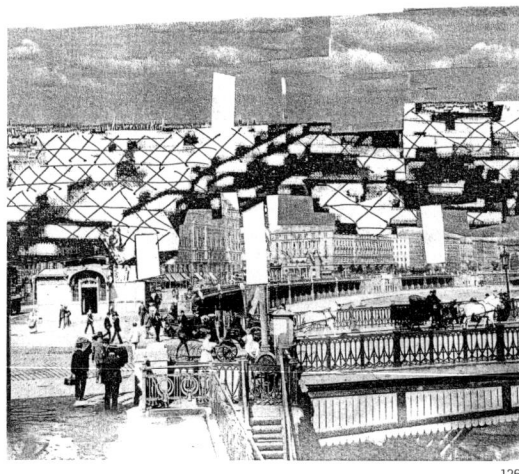

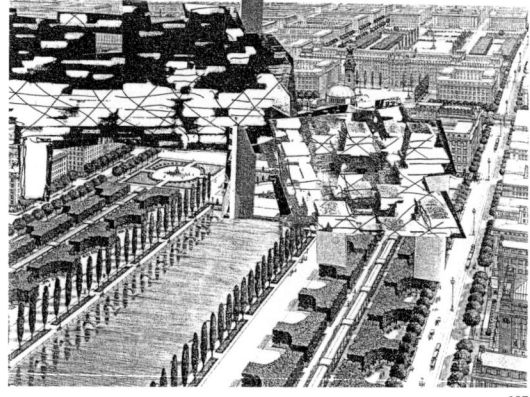

VIENNA

125–128 Photomontages on 19th-century postcards, 2004.

128

EUROPEAN PROJECTS / 103

ASIAN PROJECTS

The building we proposed essentially transformed the site into a large covered area; the program elements (hall etc.) were treated as independent pavilions, linked only underground, in a garden protected by an umbrella structure. In that umbrella were contained those functional spaces which involved only small or medium-size volumes.
To obtain the degree of conviviality desired, this project proposed the creation of a covered garden, instead of making a simple pedestrian street [...].
The pavillons in the garden (conference halls, theatres etc.) had various shapes. Their roofs were proposed to convivial use: open air tribunes, exhibition terraces, strolling places freely accessible at any hour of the day.

FRIEDMAN, Yona and SCHAUR, Eda: *Architetture per la gente / Architectures for the People*, in *Space & Society / Spazio e societa*, no. 50, April–June 1990, pp. 59–60.

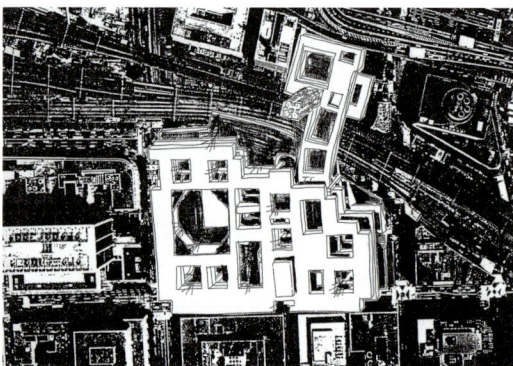

129

130

131

TOKYO INTERNATIONAL FORUM, 1989
Competition entry in collaboration with Eda Schaur.

129–130 Photomontage, aerial views.
131 Internal view on the open-air auditorium.
132 Two sections of the *Space-frame* roof and the common underground.
133–134 Front elevation, view of the facade.

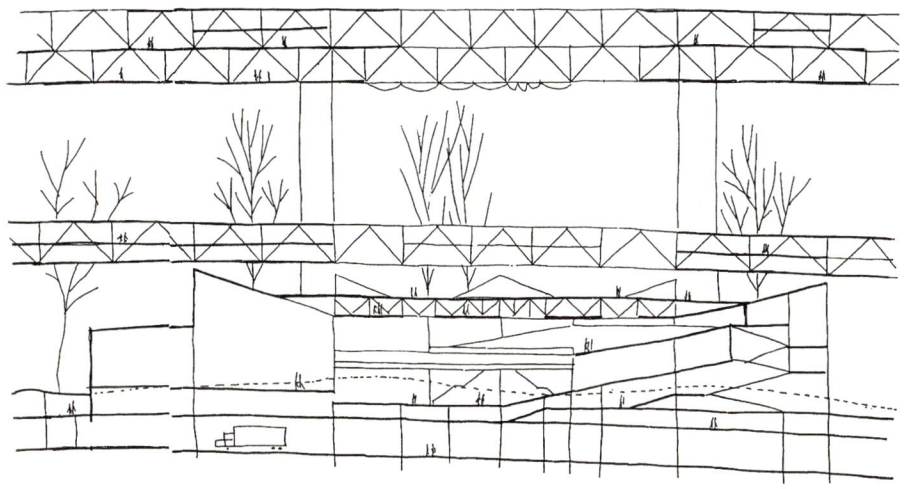

132

133

134

ASIAN PROJECTS / 105

YOKOHAMA

135–**137** Mural for the first International Triennale of Contemporary Art in Japan, 2001.

136

137

ASIAN PROJECTS / 107

AMERICAN PROJECTS

These spatial buildings could be located above the docks of the Hudson River and those of the East River. These are now poorly used areas, centrally located and under the New York Port Authority jurisdiction.
These structures which would use only the space above the docks, without disturbing their functions, could expand as bridge cities stretching over the two rivers and assuring in this way a continuous tie between the business center of Manhattan and the two sides of the port.

<small>Friedman, Yona: *Infrastructures for New York and Los Angeles*, in Arts & Architecture, no. 7, 1964, p. 26.</small>

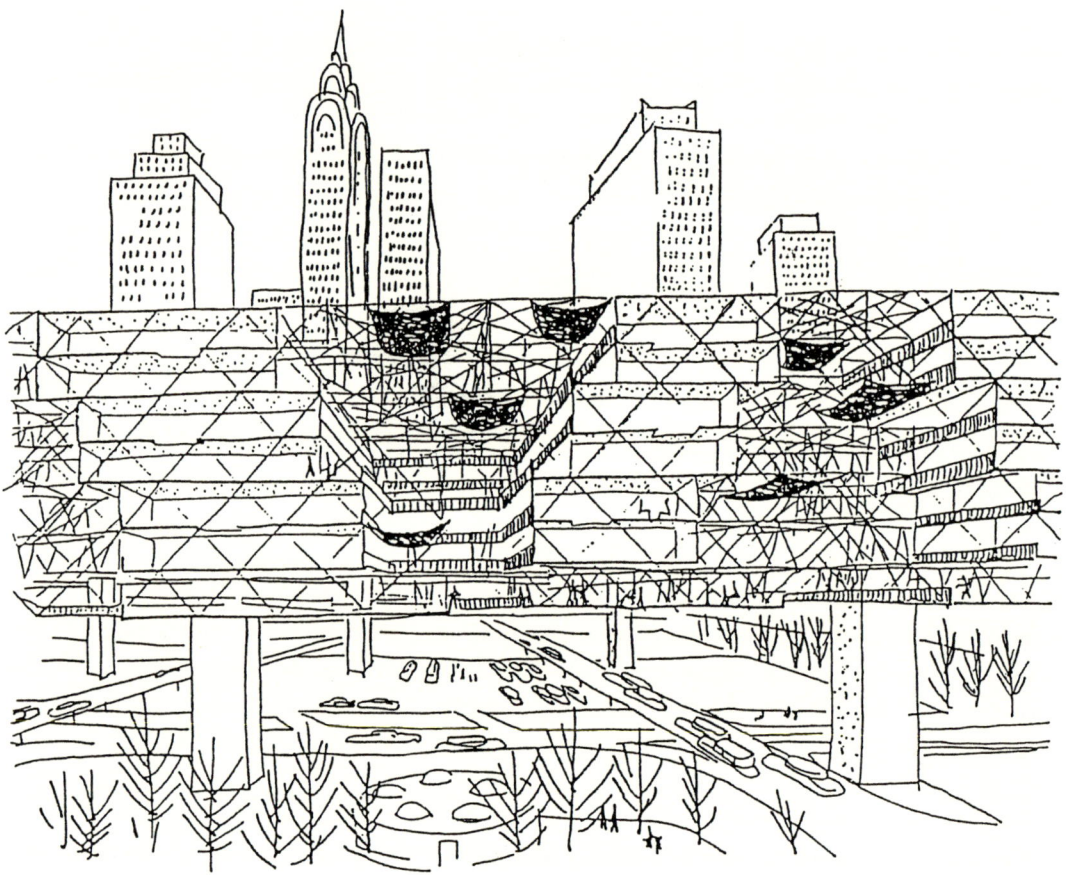

NEW YORK

138 *Span-over* development in the Central Business District, 1964.
139 *Ville Spatiale* above the Hudson River in New York, 1964.
140 Plan and section, study for Downtown New York, 1958 – 62.

139

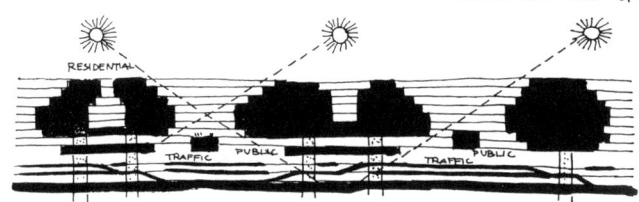

PLAN & SECTION TYPE "B"
LAND USE RATIO TOTAL 8.3

1. LEVELS FOR INDETERMINED FLOOR USE

2. LEVELS FOR CIRCULATION & PARKING

140

> The hollow-square design of Pier 40, built by the Department
> of Marine and Aviation for the Holland-America Line at
> West Houston Street on the North River, has proved a creative
> solution to some of the pier problems faced by a combined
> passenger-cargo operation. The lessons learned here may be
> useful in redeveloping the Midtown superliner piers.

New York (1964)

141

NEW YORK

141–**144** Photomontages, *Cross-block building* over the Hudson River, 1964.

>> **145** STUDIES ON NEW YORK

Vertical Cluster allowing horizontal or diagonal circulation above the ground level, 1964.

142

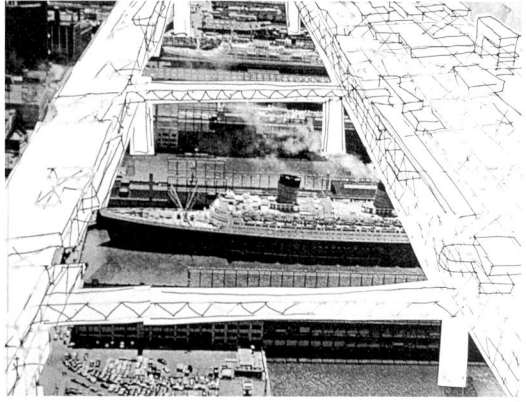

143

144

AMERICAN PROJECTS / 111

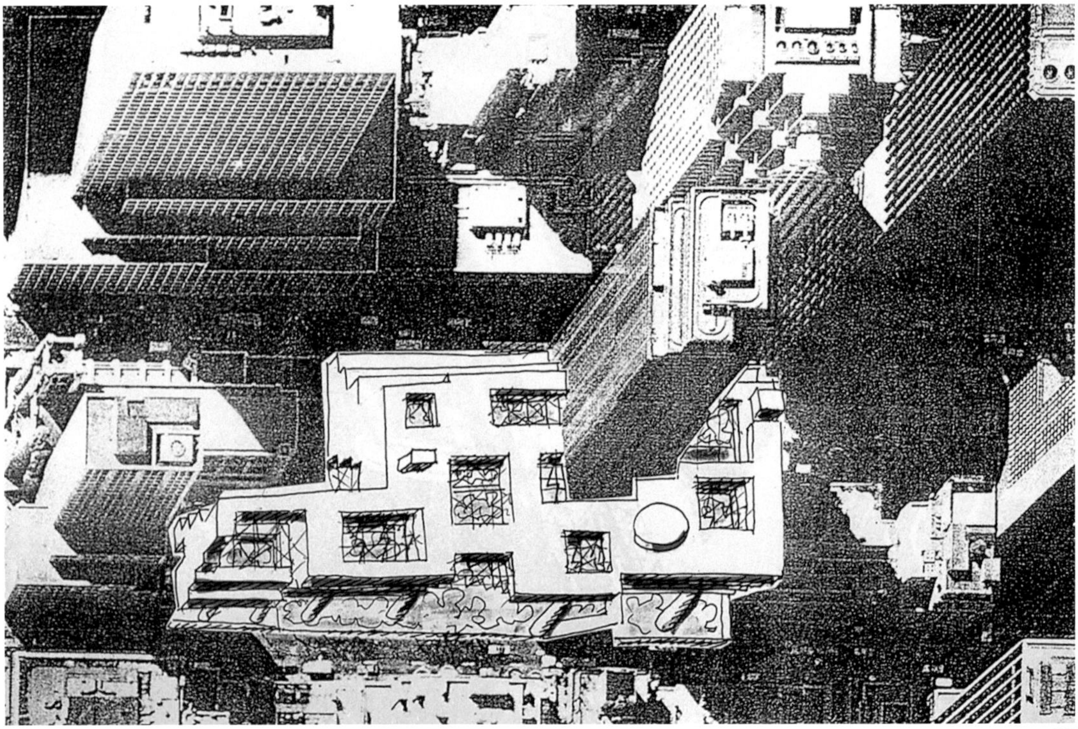

146

147

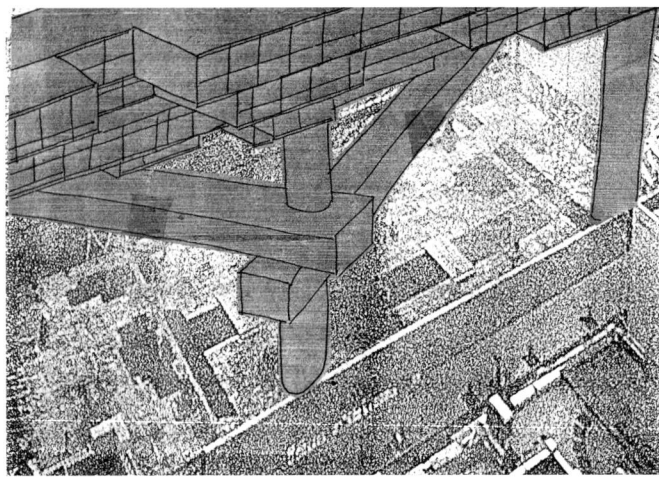

MOMA, NEW YORK, 1999

Project made after a visit to the Museum Of Modern Art in New York.

146 Photomontage, aerial view.

147 Detail of the structure.

148 Photomontage of the spatial extension covering the garden.

148

149 150

This city is actually an unorganized ensemble of suburbs supplied by a freeway network. The residential parts are situated between the meshes of this freeway network and the resident of a certain area takes the risk of loosing his way when he adventures in unknown quarter.

The succession of suburbs which compose the city has no center. Such city pattern comes from the excessive daily use of the car. The freeways that people must use to travel between large distances become the real center of the city. This situation leads to the development of "drive-in" or "drive-thru" centers over these freeways. These spatial centers could contain supermarkets, cafes, restaurants, offices and the necessary parking. On the upper platform of these centers, there could be added several miles of "tourist drives."

The "Centers" established over a certain number of miles, depending on their situation, would provide: commercial space (20,000 sq m), office space (30,000 sq m), parking space (20,000 sq m).

FRIEDMAN, Yona: *Infrastructures for New York and Los Angeles*, in *Arts & Architecture*, no. 7, 1964, p. 27.

LOS ANGELES FREEWAY, 1964

149 *Cross-block* building above crossroads in New York.
150 Aerial view of Los Angeles motorways.
151 Typical section and plan, proposed *Drive-thru Center* above freeways.

>> **152** SAN FRANCISCO, 2006

TYPICAL SECTION & PLAN

LOS ANGELES, CALIFORNIA
PROPOSED „DRIVE-THRU" CENTER
OVER FREEWAYS

LAND USE RATIO 3,0

1 SCENIC DRIVE
2 SKYVIEW PLATFORM
3 RENTAL AREA (COMMERCIAL)
4 ACCESS RAMPS
5 FREEWAY (EXISTING)

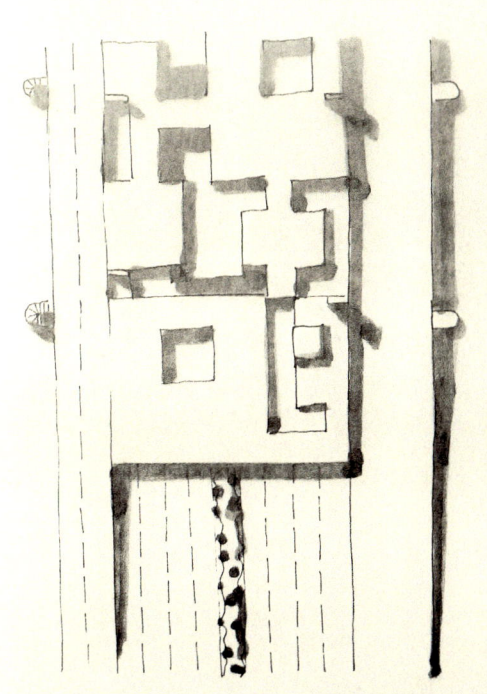

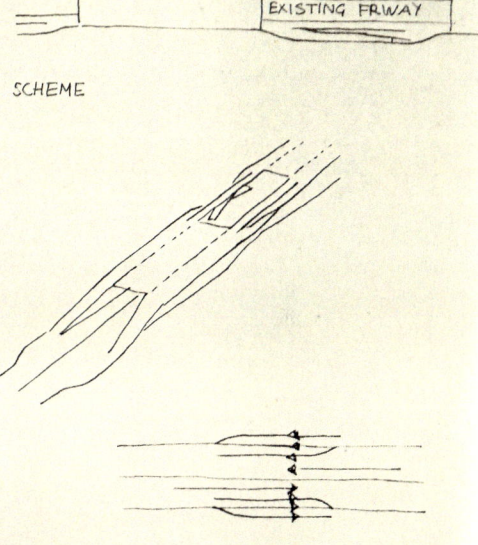

SCHEME

AFRICAN PROJECTS

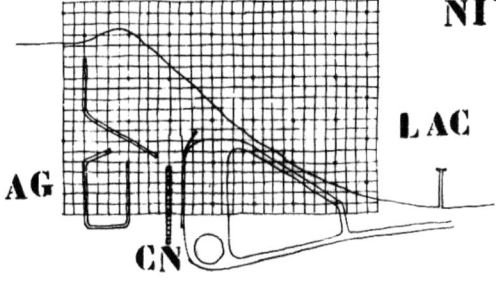

EARLY STUDIES
153 *Ville Spatiale* above a lake, adapted as a vernacular building, 1959.
154–**155** Site plan, section and perspective. Studies of *Spatial settlements for 4,000 inhabitants*, extended to the waterfront, 1958.

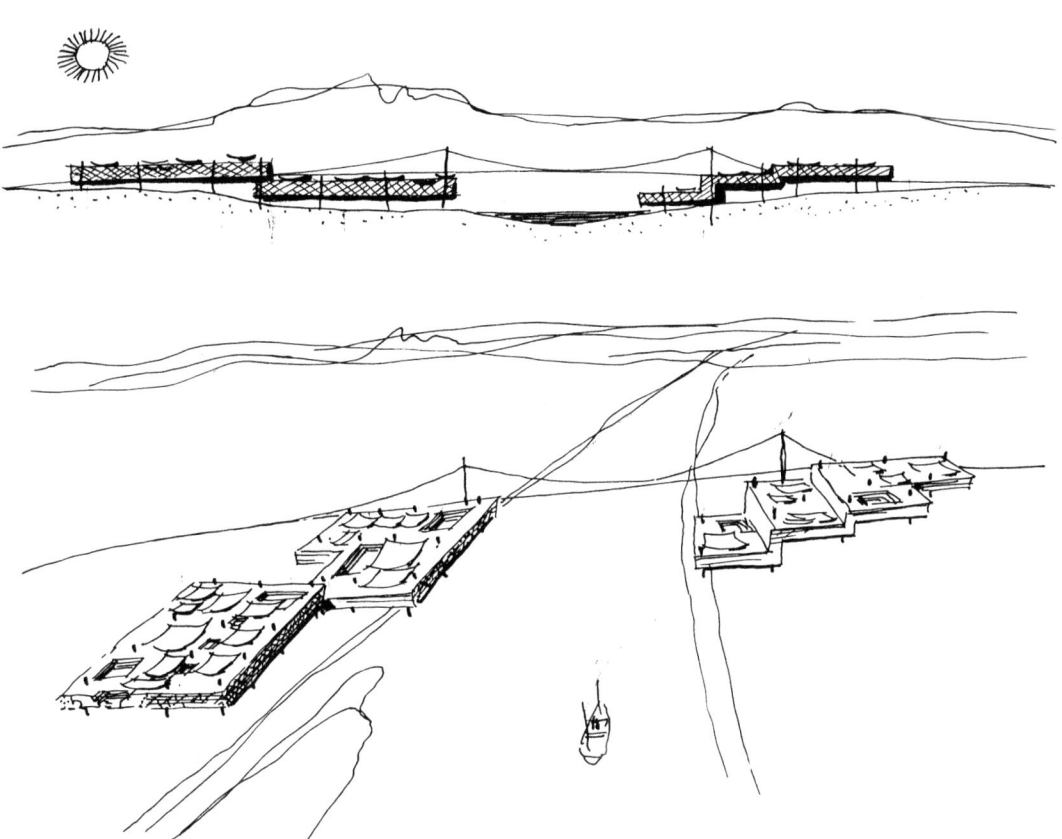

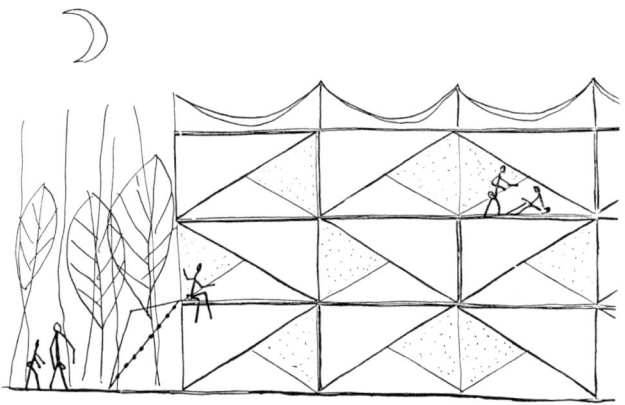

156

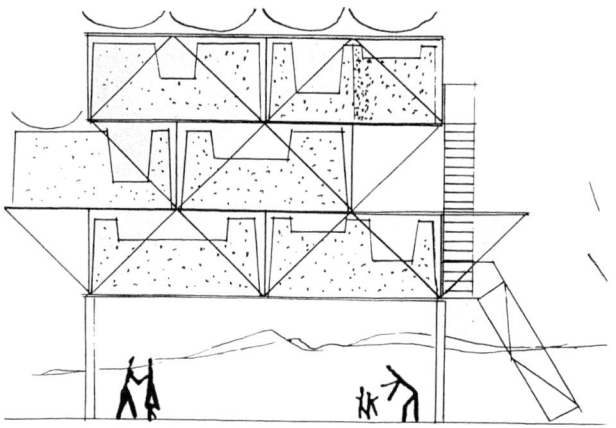

157

158

EARLY STUDIES, 1959

156–**158** *Ville Spatiale* with traditional technique. Section, elevation and plan of a unit.
159–**160** Photomontage, aerial view and plan of a hostel for Nigerian workers in Treichville, Abidjan, Ivory Coast.

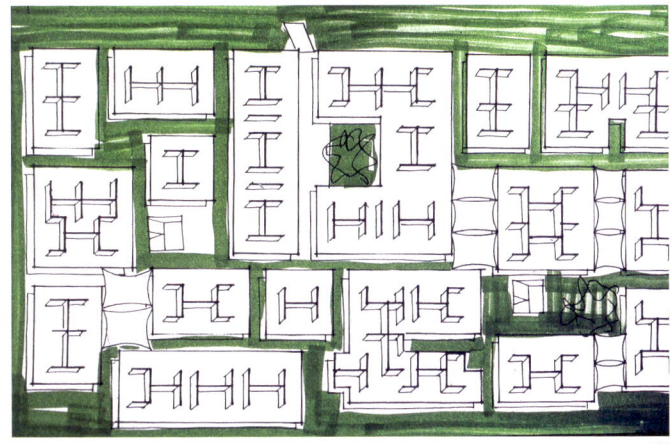

AFRICAN PROJECTS / 123

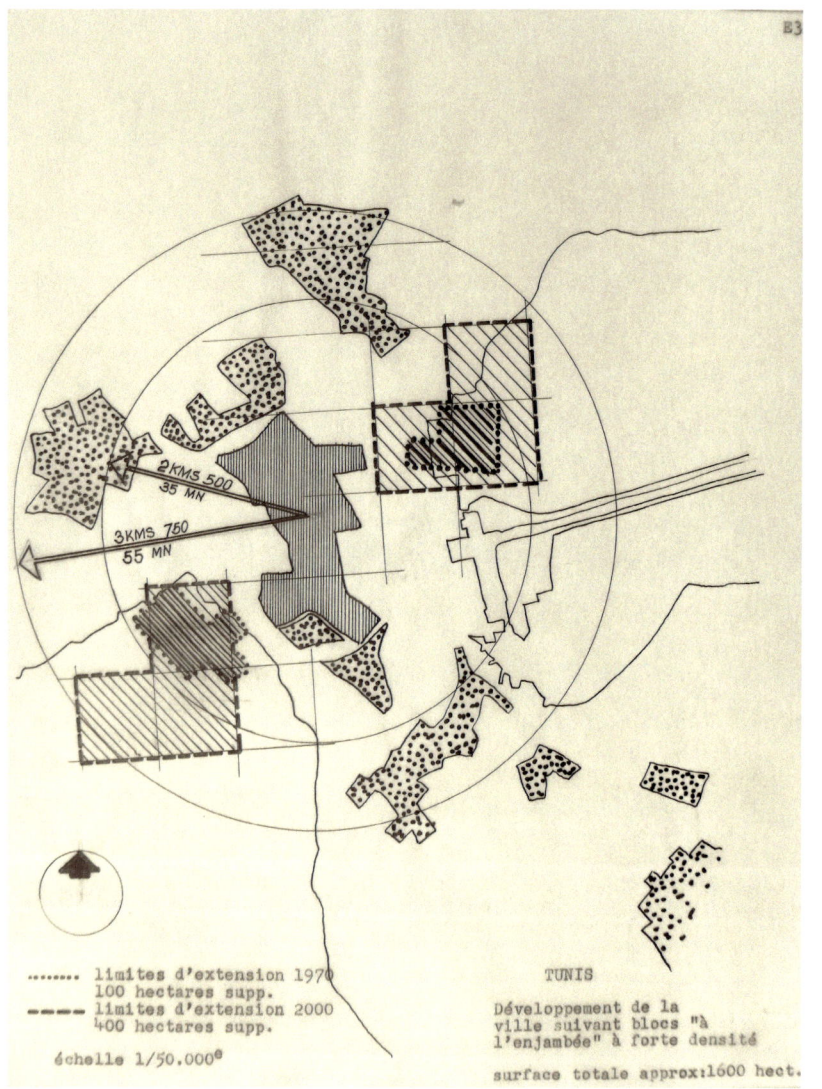

Approx. total area: 1,600 hect.

· · · · · Boundaries, 1970
Additional 100 hectares.

- - - - Boundaries, 2000
Additional 400 hectares.

Scale 1:50,000

TUNIS, 1959
Competition project in collaboration with Roger Aujame.

161 *Tunis, development of the city using "Span-over" block with high density.*
162–**165** Plans and perspectives for the *Ville Spatiale* above the Medina.
166–**167** Top view and perspective of the *Monument* with *Space-chain* roof.

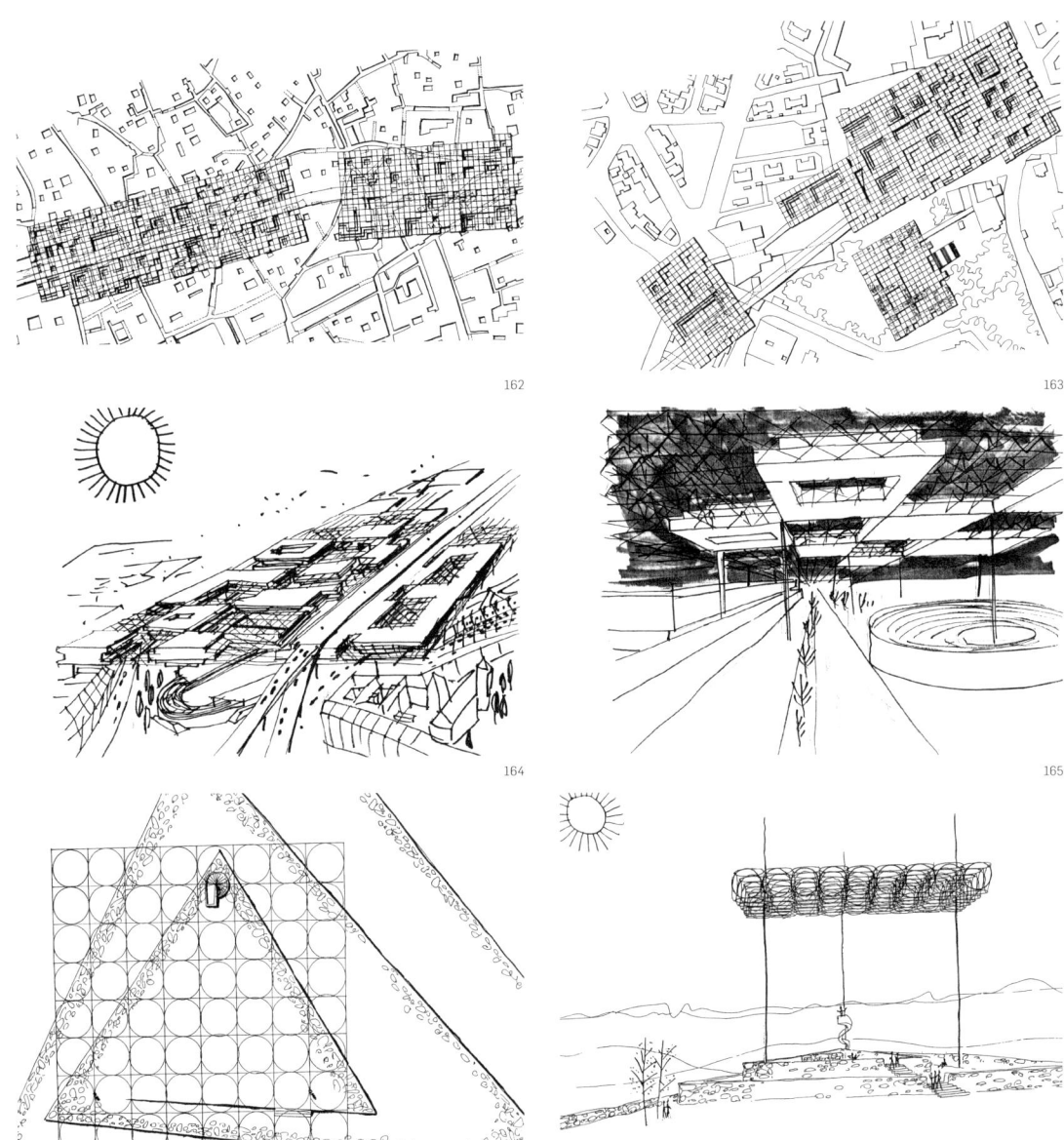

AFRICAN PROJECTS / 125

168

169

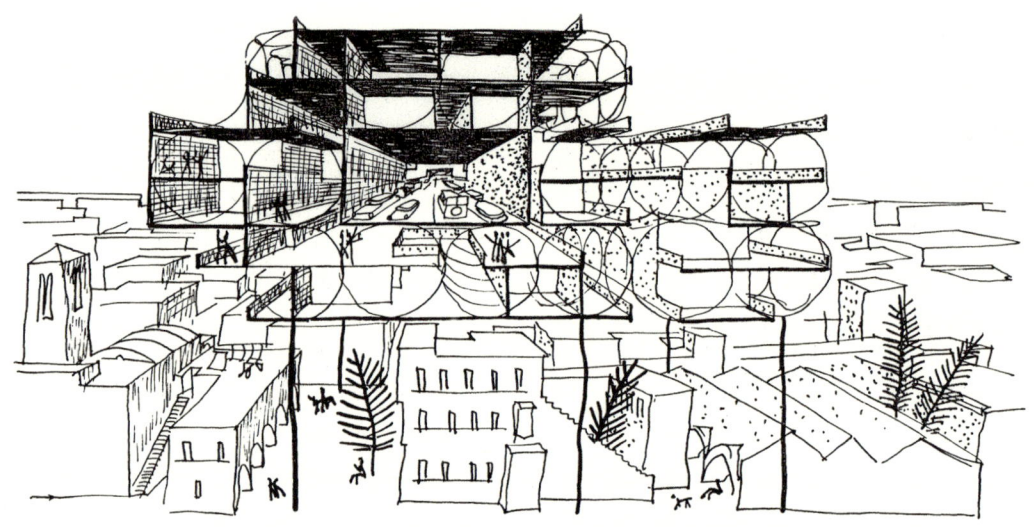

TUNIS MEDINA, 1959

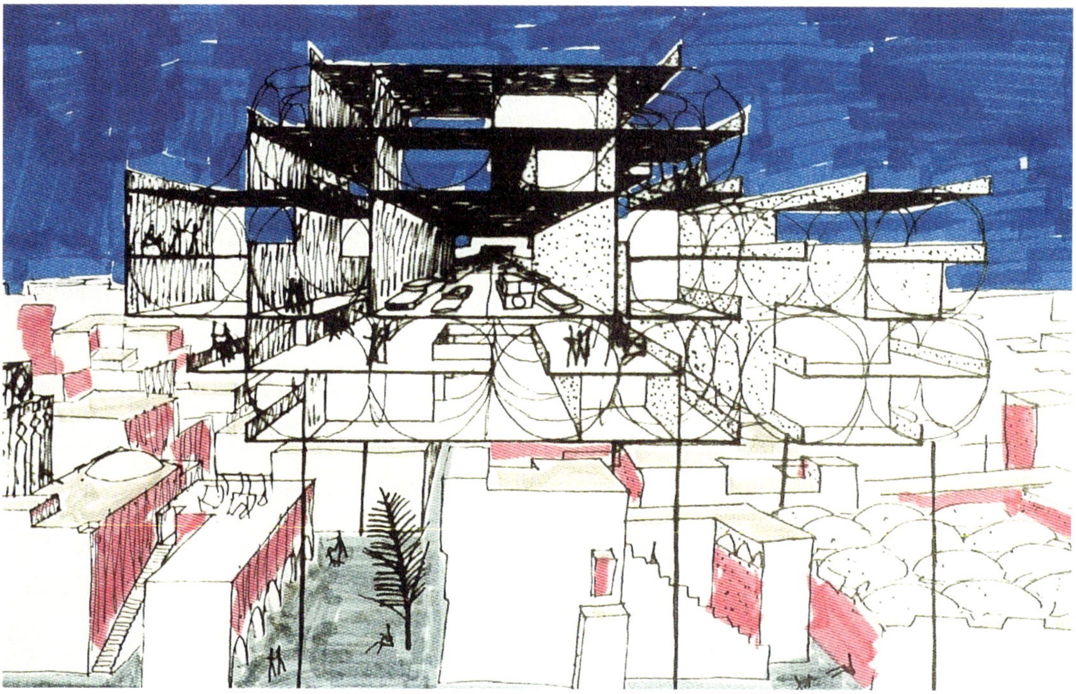

168–**169** Sectional perspectives of the *Ville Spatiale* above the Medina.

170–**173** Photomontages, performative series.

170

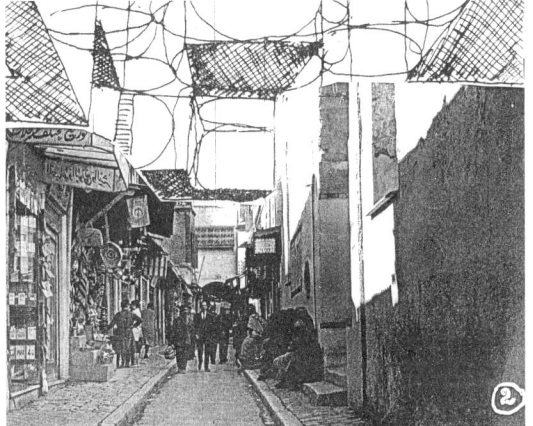

171

172

173

AFRICAN PROJECTS / 127

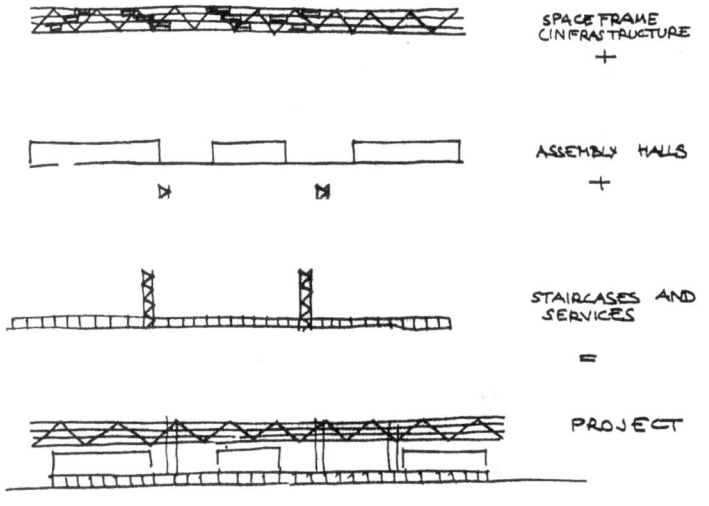

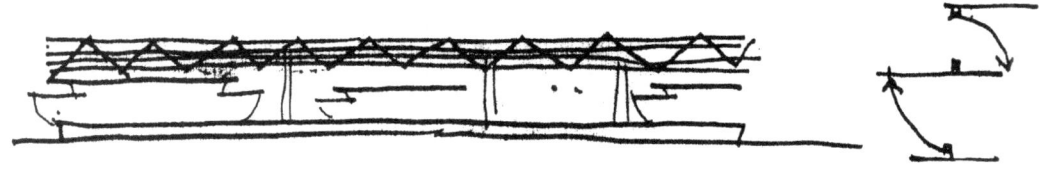

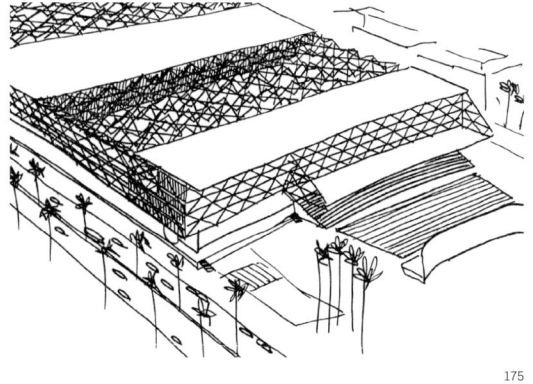

DAR ES SALAAM, TANZANIA, 1967
Competition project for the Parliament House.

174 Sketches showing stages of the project.
175–176 Aerial view and elevation of the project, showing the detail of the skeleton.
177 Perspective view from Lumumba Street and Cour d'Honneur.
178–179 North–South section, scales 1:500 and 1:200.

>> **180** BRIDGE-TOWN AT GIBRALTAR, 1962

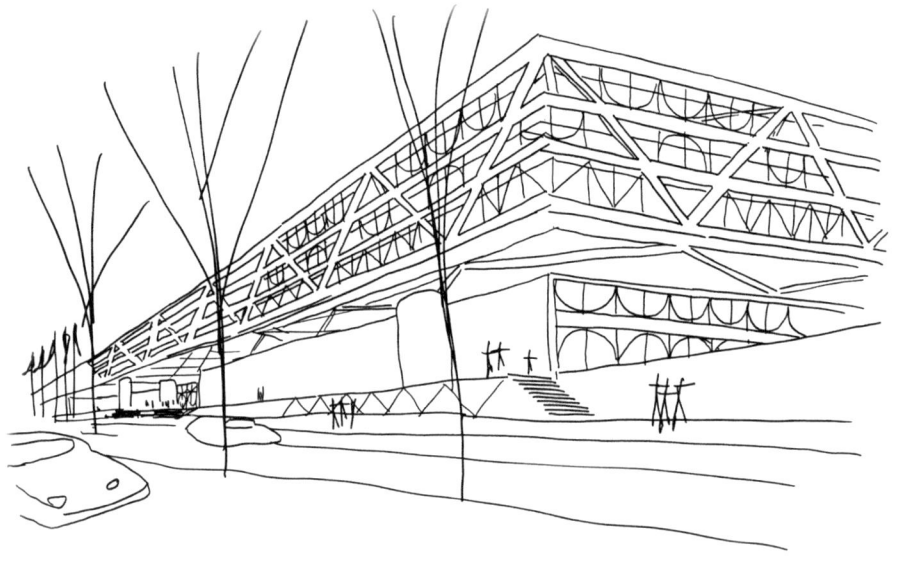

PERSPECTIVE VIEW FROM LUMUMBA STREET AND COUR D'HONNEUR

SECTION NORTH SOUTH 1:500

A 10 M HIGH REINFORCED CONCRETE SKELETON SPACE FRAME STRUCTURE (INFRASTRUCTURE) PERMITS THE FREE INSERTION OF OFFICE FLOORS, CEILINGS AND PARTITIONS, MADE OF SANDWICH PANELS WITH WOODEN LATTICE FILLING (LOCALLY PREFABRICATED).

THE SAME SKELETON SUPPORTS ALL ROOFS FOR THE LARGE HALLS. THESE ROOFS, MADE OF WOODEN PANELS, ARE SUSPENDED ON THE INFRASTRUCTURE.

LIGHTWEIGHT PLASTIFIED WOODEN UMBRELLA VAULTS KEEP RAINPROOF ALL USED PARTS IN THE INFRASTRUCTURE AND SERVE SIMULTANEOUSLY AS SUNSHADES.

THE BASEMENT LIFTED OVER GROUND LEVEL CONTAINS ALL SERVICES, ENTRANCES, CAR LANDINGS, RECEPTION LOBBIES BOTH FOR PEDESTRIANS AND CARS.

TANU OFFICES

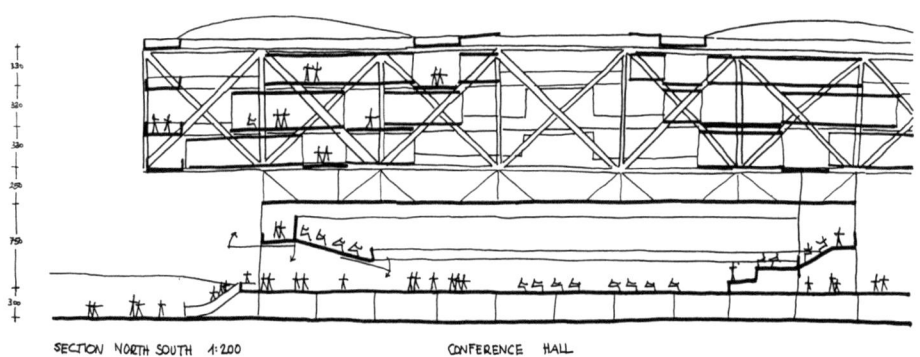

SECTION NORTH SOUTH 1:200   CONFERENCE HALL

AFRICAN PROJECTS / 129

180

BRIDGE-TOWN

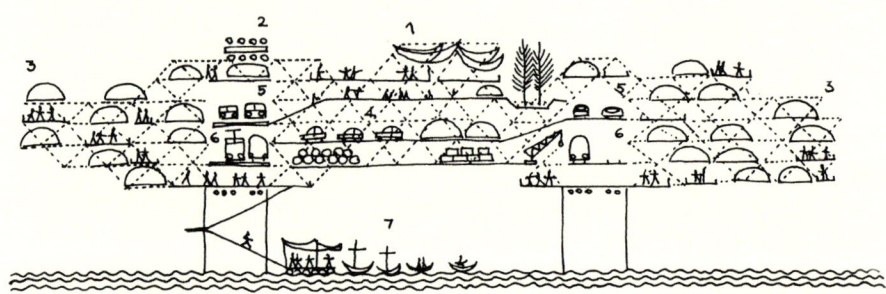

City centre
1 / Worship, recreation, public life market.
2 / Management, administration.

The Town
3 / Housings.
4 / Warehouses, industry, trade.

The Bridge
5 / The road.
6 / The railway.

The River
7 / The fishing harbor.

Advantage of the system
Important geographical position ensured.
Extension of existing bridges.
Immediate profitability for the industry.
Possibility of development of the hinterland.

Width of the bridge
150–200 m.

Number of floors
7

Available surface in slices of 100 m.
50–70 ha.

AFRICAN BRIDGE-TOWN

181 Section of an African *Bridge-Town*, 1963.

ELEVEN BRIDGE-TOWNS TO LINK FIVE CONTINENTS

182 *Links of terrestrial networks*, 1963.
1. Behring / 2. Sakhalin / 3. Hakodate / 4. Hokaido / 5. Djakarta / 6. Singapoore /
7. Aden / 8. Suez / 9. Gibraltar / 10. La Manche / 11. Panama.
Map of the world in polar projection (Azimuthal equidistant projection).

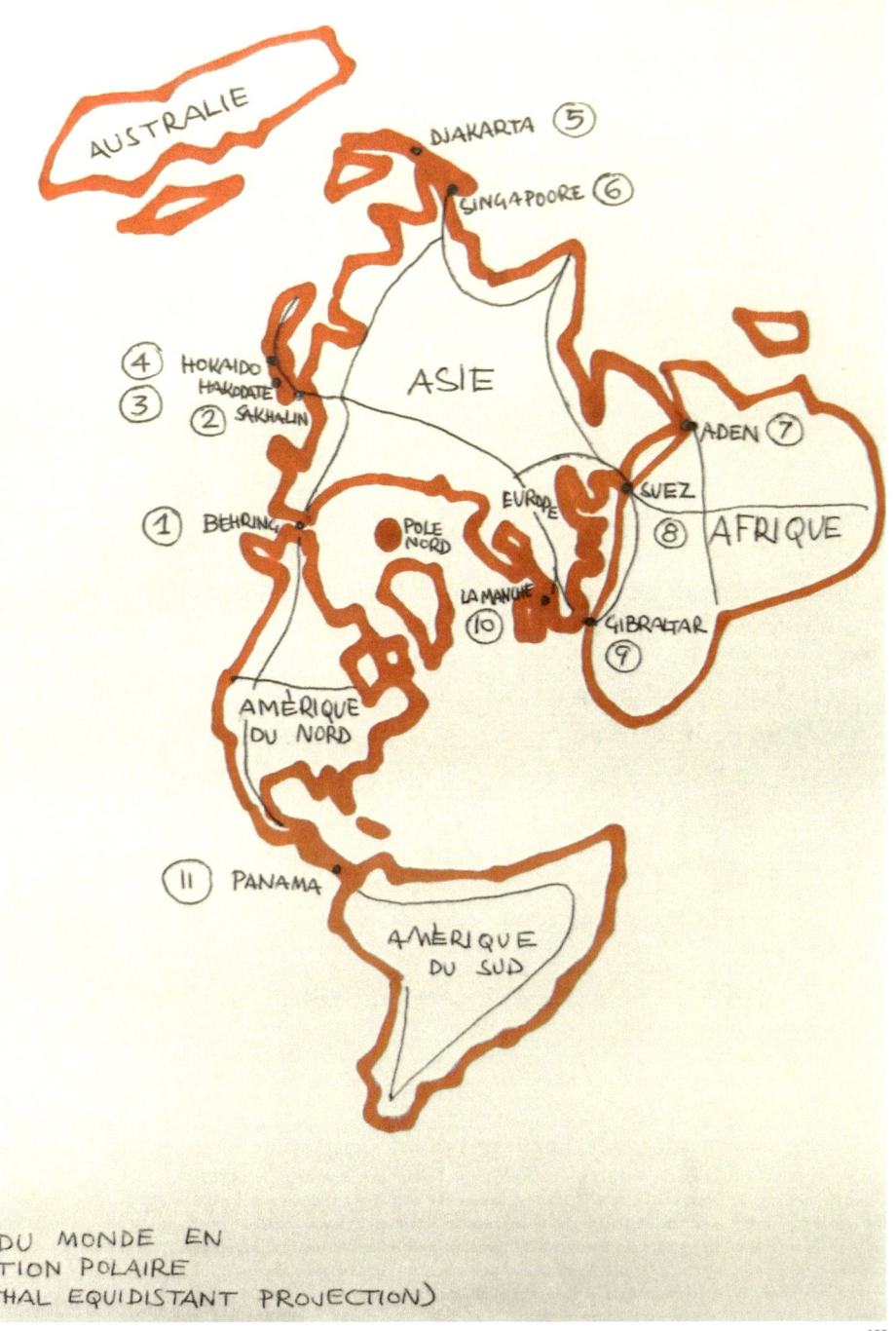

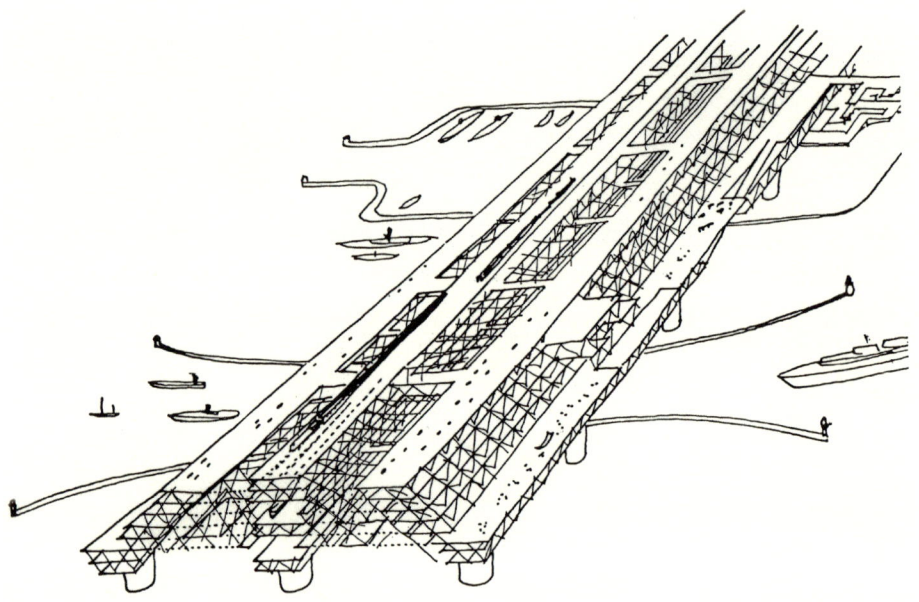

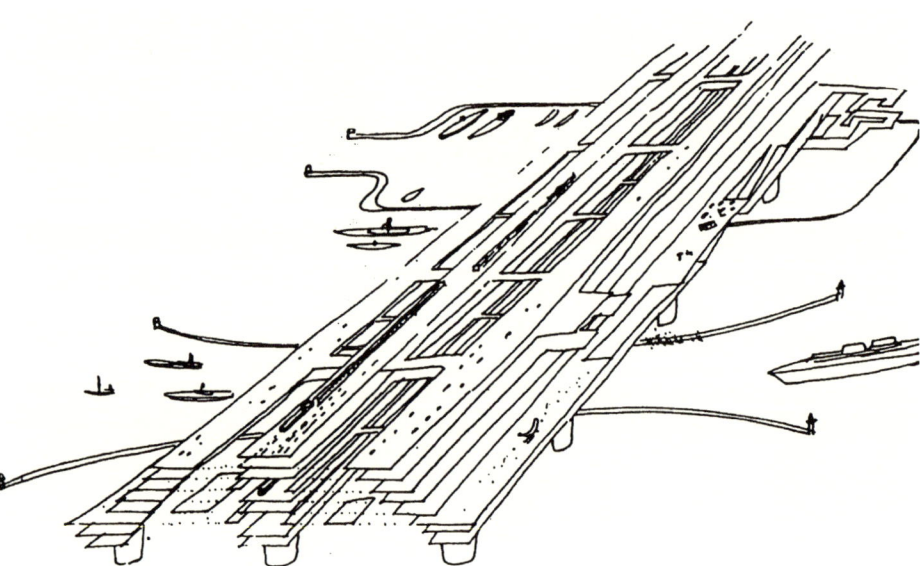

CHANNEL BRIDGE, 1963

183–**184** Diagrammatic sketches, *Space-frame* infrastructure and transport levels.
185 *Le Pont sur la Manche*, sketches and notes.

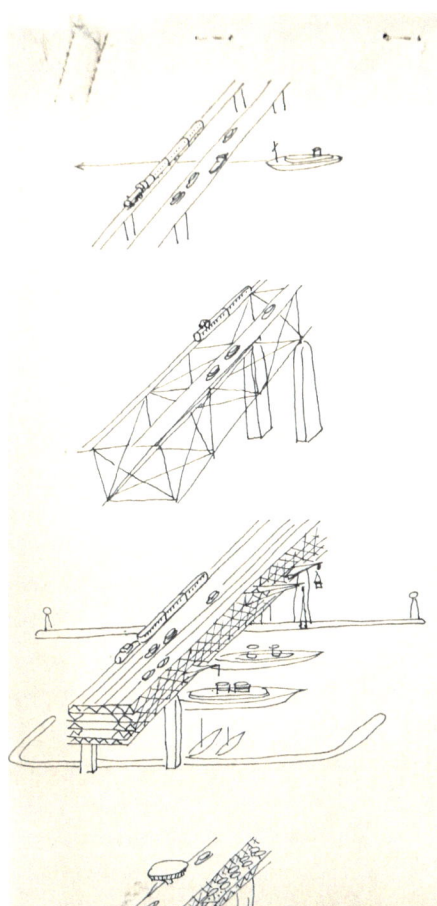

1 / The fusion of a motorway (London–Paris), a railway (London–Paris) and the shipping transport bound for London and Paris would create a need for a new port.

2 / The necessary height of the bridge entails an enormous cubic volume between the pylons.

3 / By creating a new port between the pylons of the bridge, the rent generated from stations, offices and warehouses would cover the construction costs. The vertical exchange of goods between ships, trains and lorries would make for particularly smooth management.

4 / The bridge could become a new tourist attraction. It could house restaurants, hotels, belvederes, swimming pools and artificial beaches.

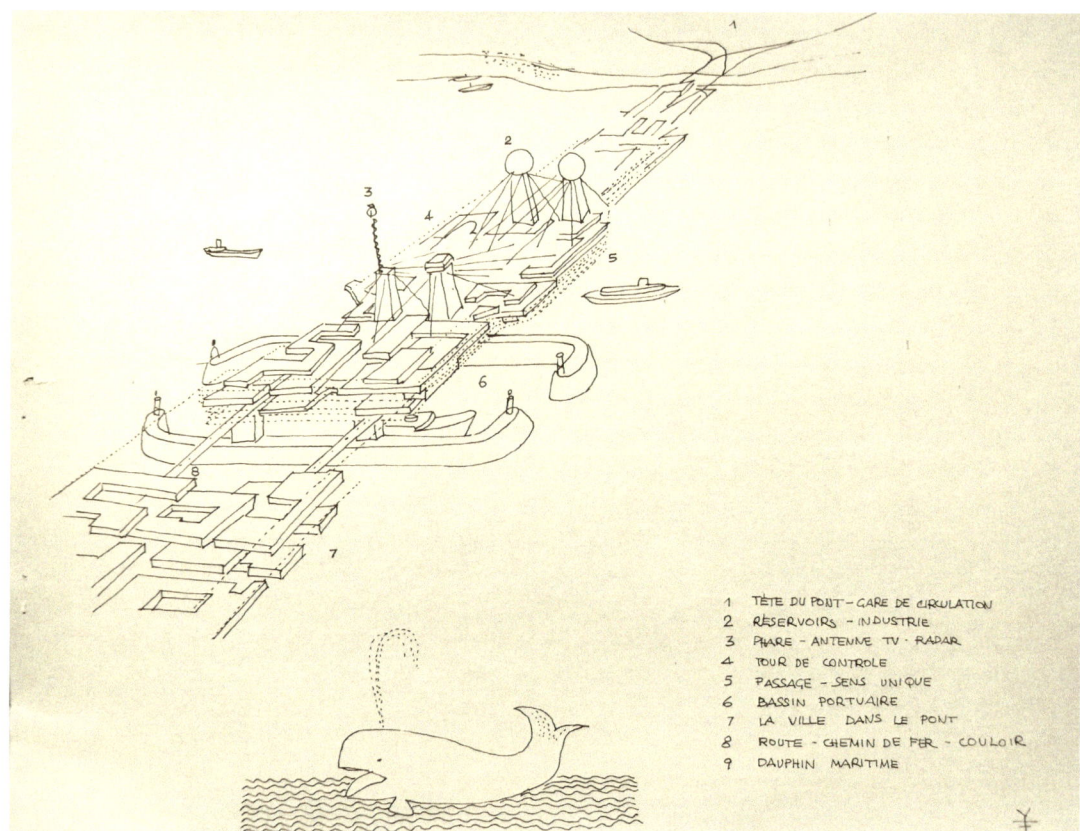

CHANNEL BRIDGE, 1963

186 Sketch of part of the project.
1. Bridge end, traffic station / 2. Water tanks, industry / 3. Lighthouse, TV-tower, radar / 4. Control tower / 5. Unidirectional waterway / 6. Port basin / 7. Town built into bridge structure / 8. Road, railway, waterway / 9. Dauphin maritime.
187 Schematic cross-section.
1. Floating dock / 2. Warehouses / 3. Tourist terrace / 4. Traffic level / 5. Offices / 6. Tourist facilities / 7. Goods station.
188 Schematic longitudinal section.
1. Control room / 2. Water tank / 3. Main cables / 4. Enclosing platform structure / 5. Pylons / 6. Access to dock / 7. Floating dock / 8. Buoy.

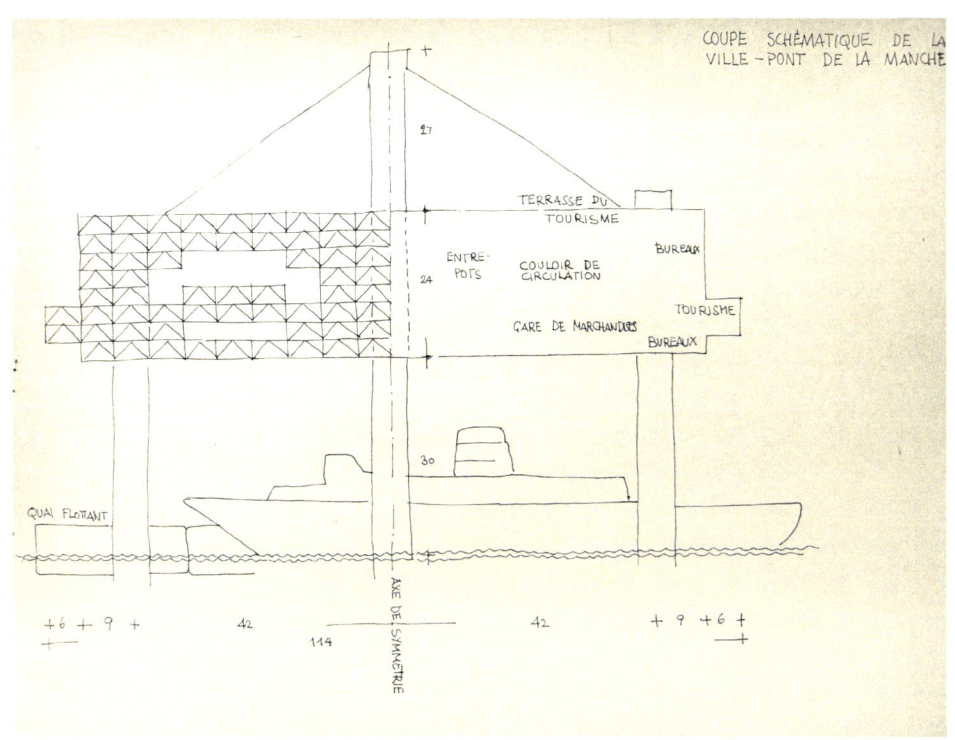

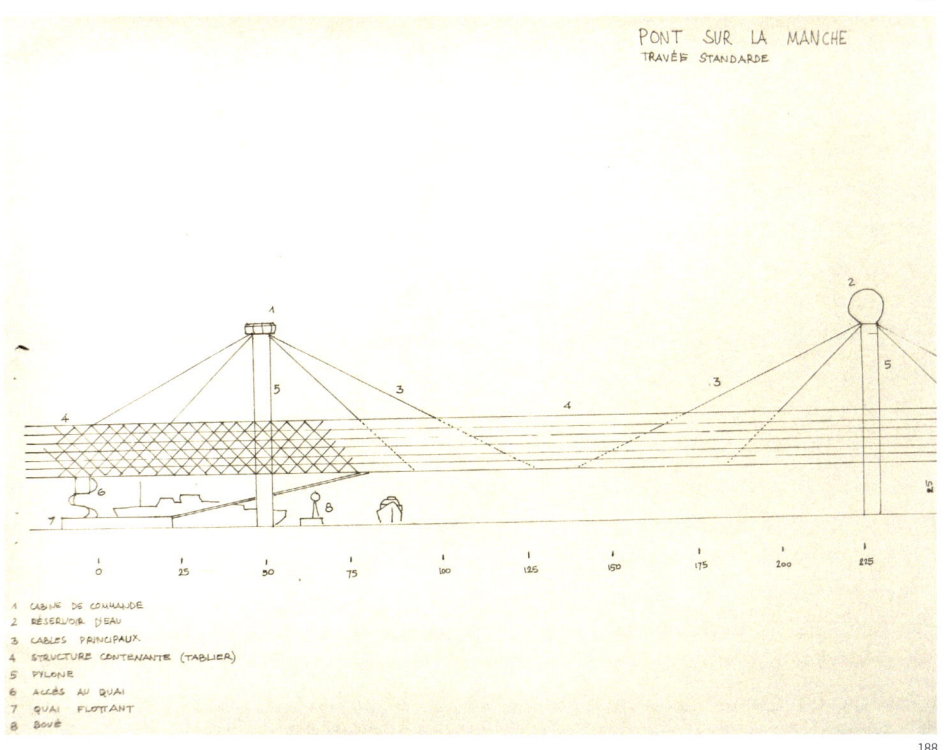

189

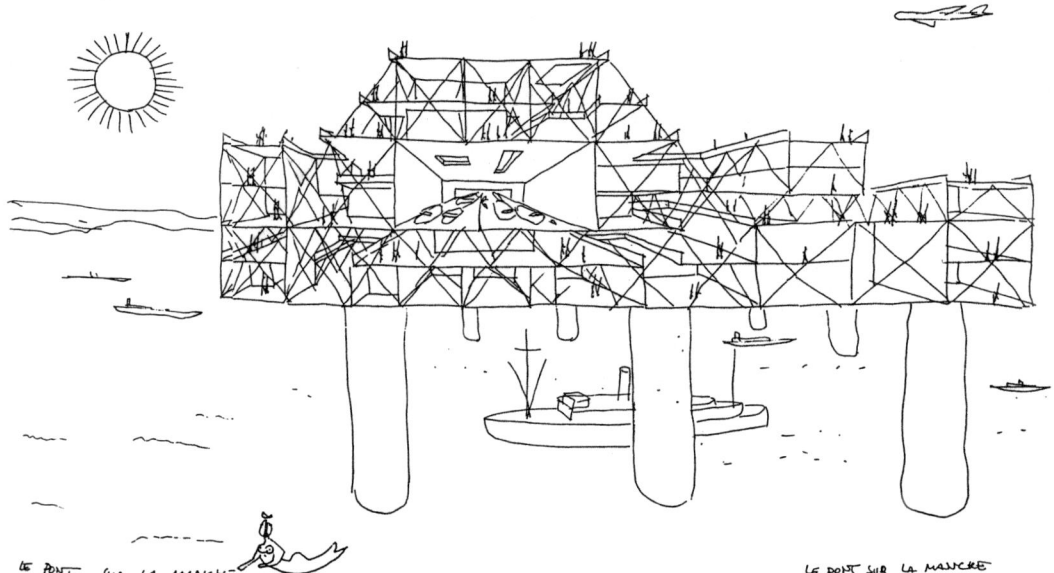

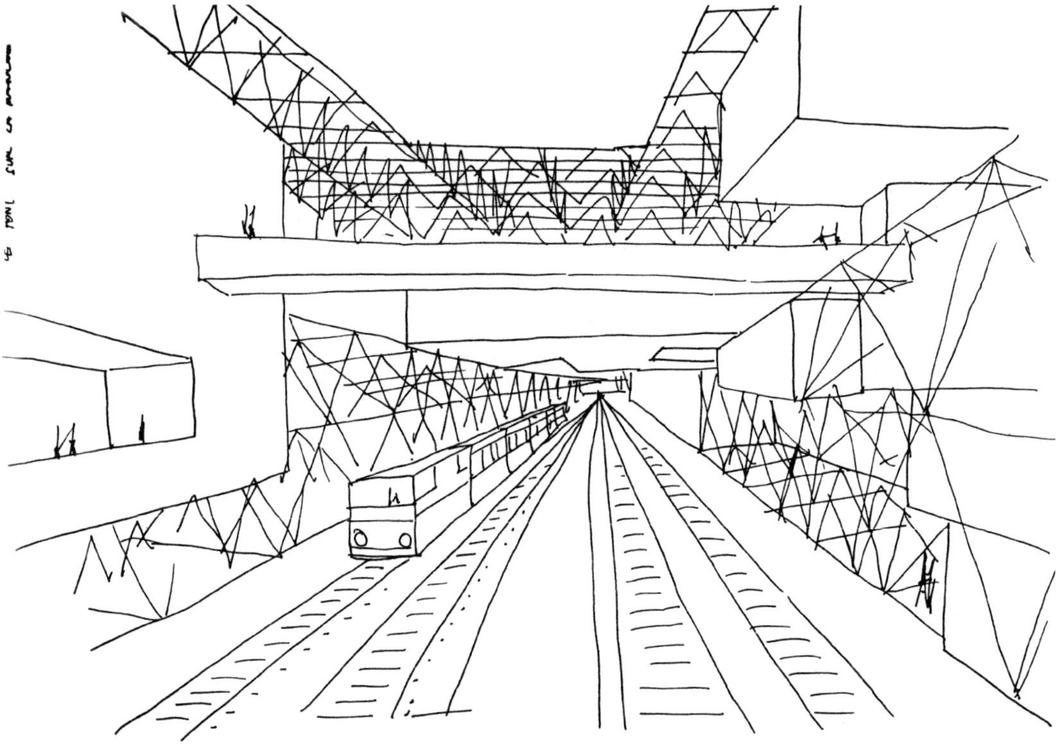

190

CHANNEL BRIDGE, 1963

189–**190** Sectional and interior perspectives of the *Pont sur la Manche.*
191–**193** Study model views of the *Bridge-Town over the English Channel.*

191

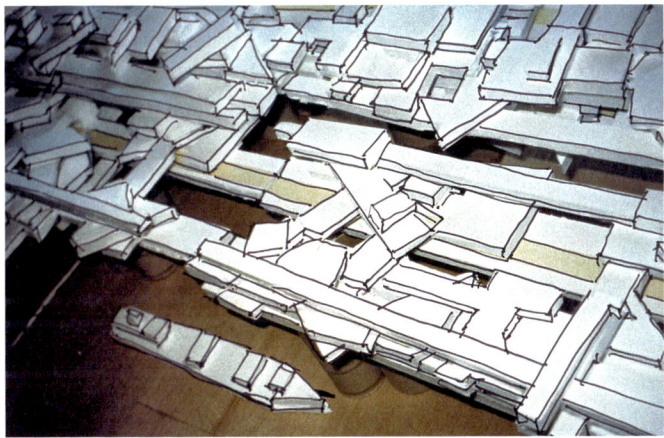

192

193

VENICE
194 *City on Stilts* is inspired by the necessity to expand the city and preserve the historical center and the fluvial traffic underneath, Venice, 1969.
195 Plan of *Street above streets* for Venice, 2005.
196–**201** Collage on paper, *Bridge-Towns* across the lagoon, *Venezia nuova*, 2005.

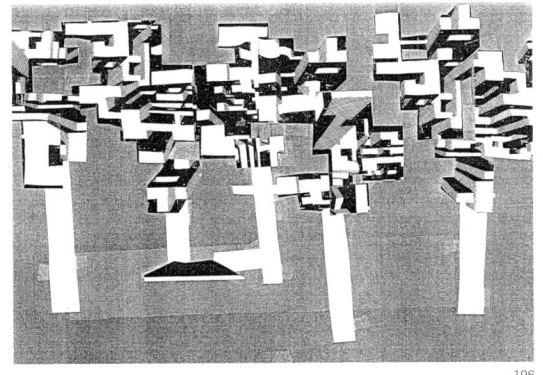
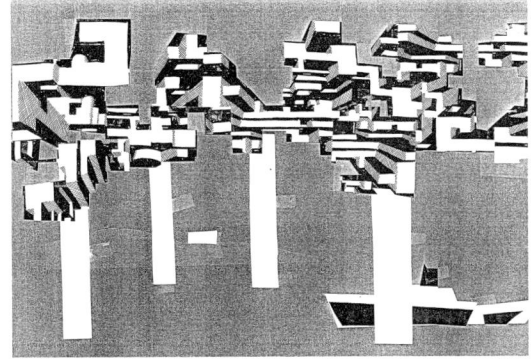

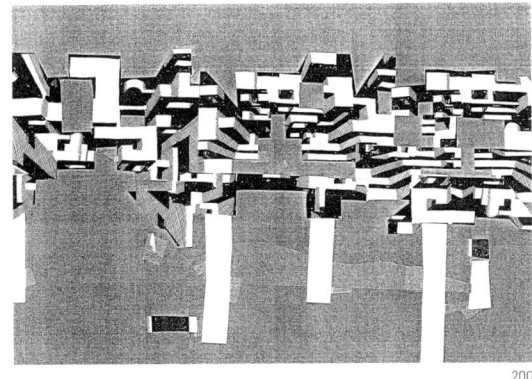
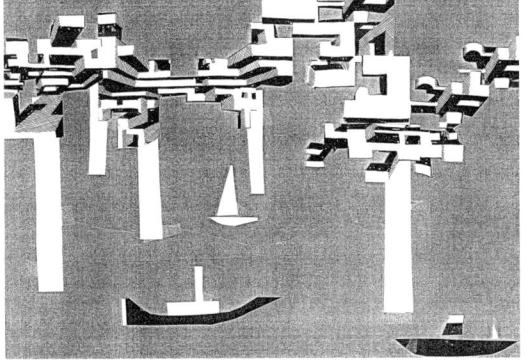

202

203

"PONTE DELLA LIBERTÀ," VENICE, FROM 2000

202–203 Photomontages, *Freedom Bridge* across the Venice lagoon.
204–211 Captions from the movie *Le Pont de la Liberté*, Balkis productions, Paris.

>> **212** VENICE SPATIAL, 2005

204

205

206

207

208

209

210

211

212

BRIDGE-TOWN / 145

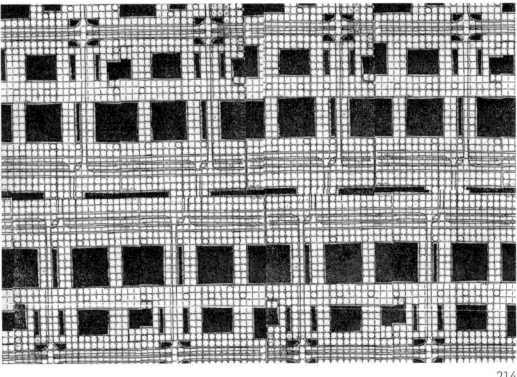

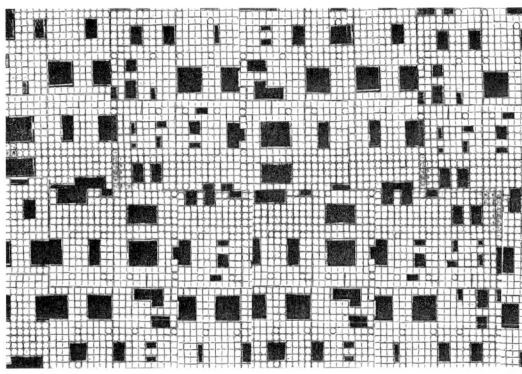

STRASBOURG, 1990
Proposition for the Administration of the European Union in Strasbourg, France.

213 Model, aerial view of the *Bridge-Town* development.
214–217 Top views and axonometric projections.
218 View of the main entrance.

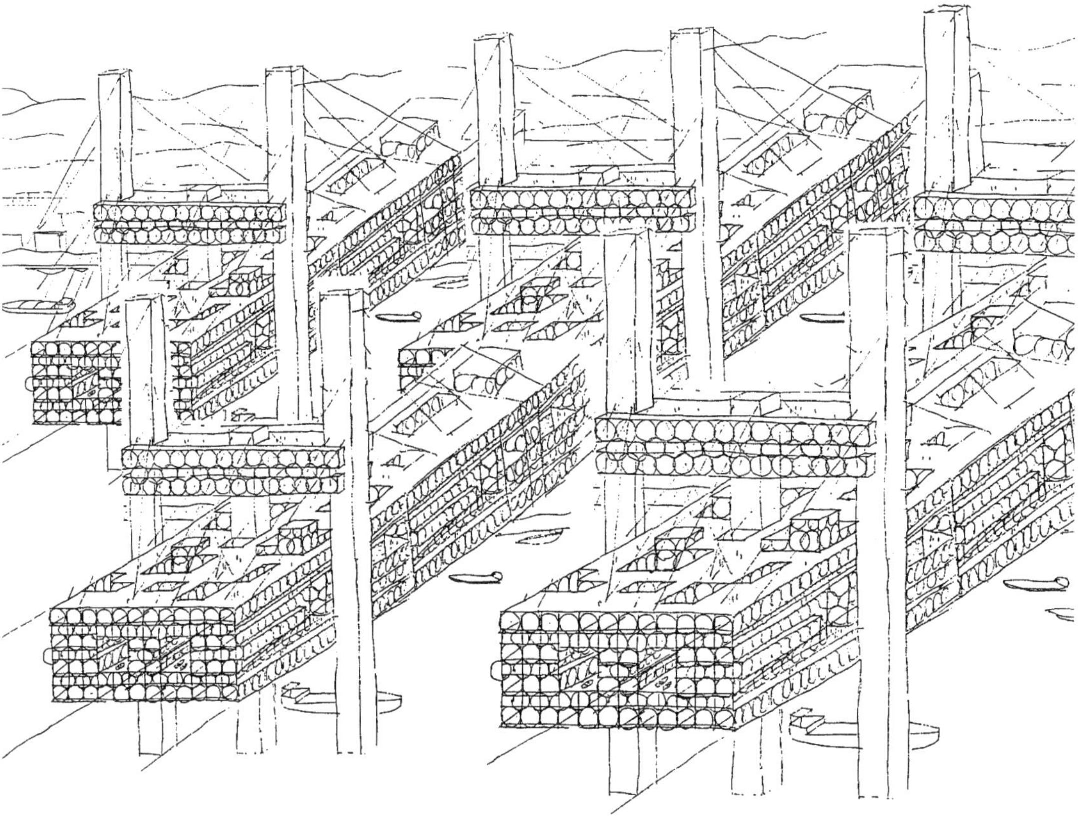

216

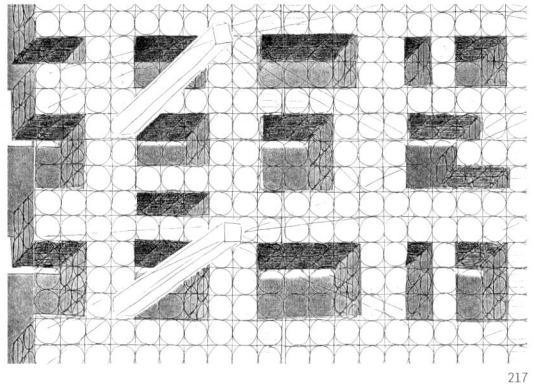

217

218

BRIDGE-TOWN / 147

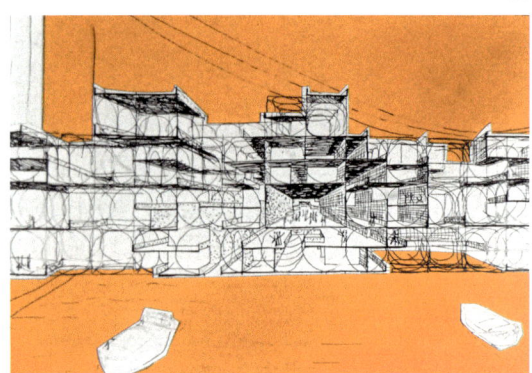

STRASBOURG, 1990

219–**220** *Bridge-Town* above the river Rhine, on the "no-man's-land" sharing borders with five European Countries.
221 Sectional perspective.
222–**225** Sections of the *Bridge-Town* with *Space-chain* structure.

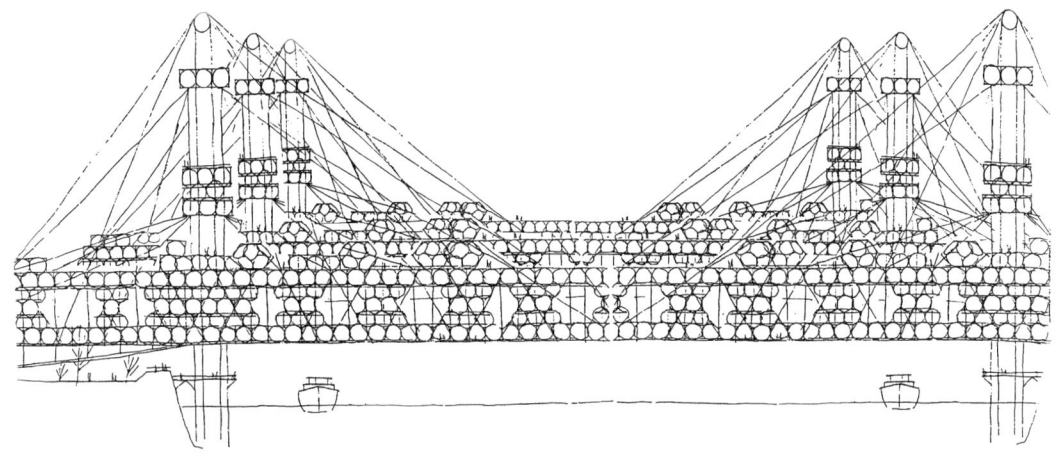

222

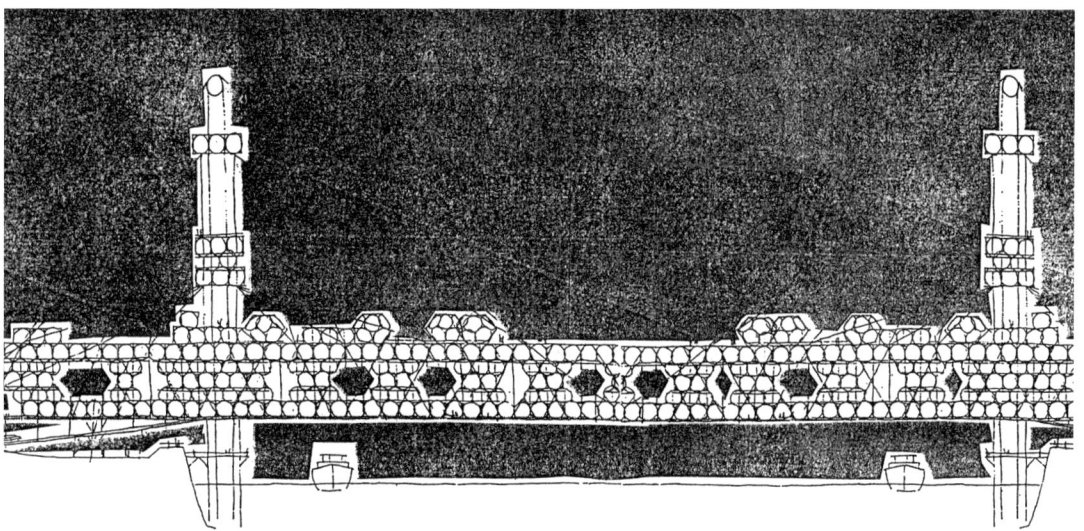

223

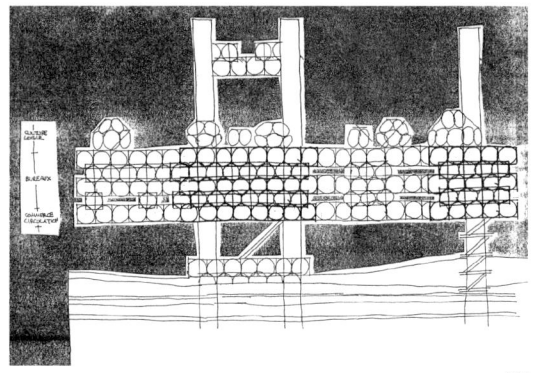

224

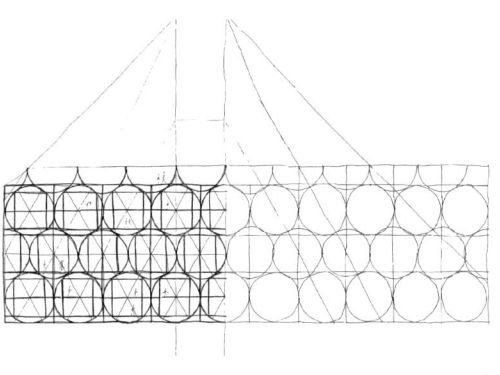

225

BRIDGE-TOWN / 149

226

The idea was to extend the territory of Israel and of the Gaza strip toward the sea, by the construction of a linear "Spatial town" along the coast.
A "parallel-country" which could settle the political problem. So I thought, naively.

FRIEDMAN, Yona: *1990. Tel Aviv Peace-bridge*, in *Yona Friedman: Drawings & Models 1945–2010*, Paris, Presses du Réel, 2010, p. 598.

PEACE BRIDGE, TEL AVIV, 1990

226 Photomontage on postcard.
227 Schematic plan and section of the linear *Bridge-Town*.

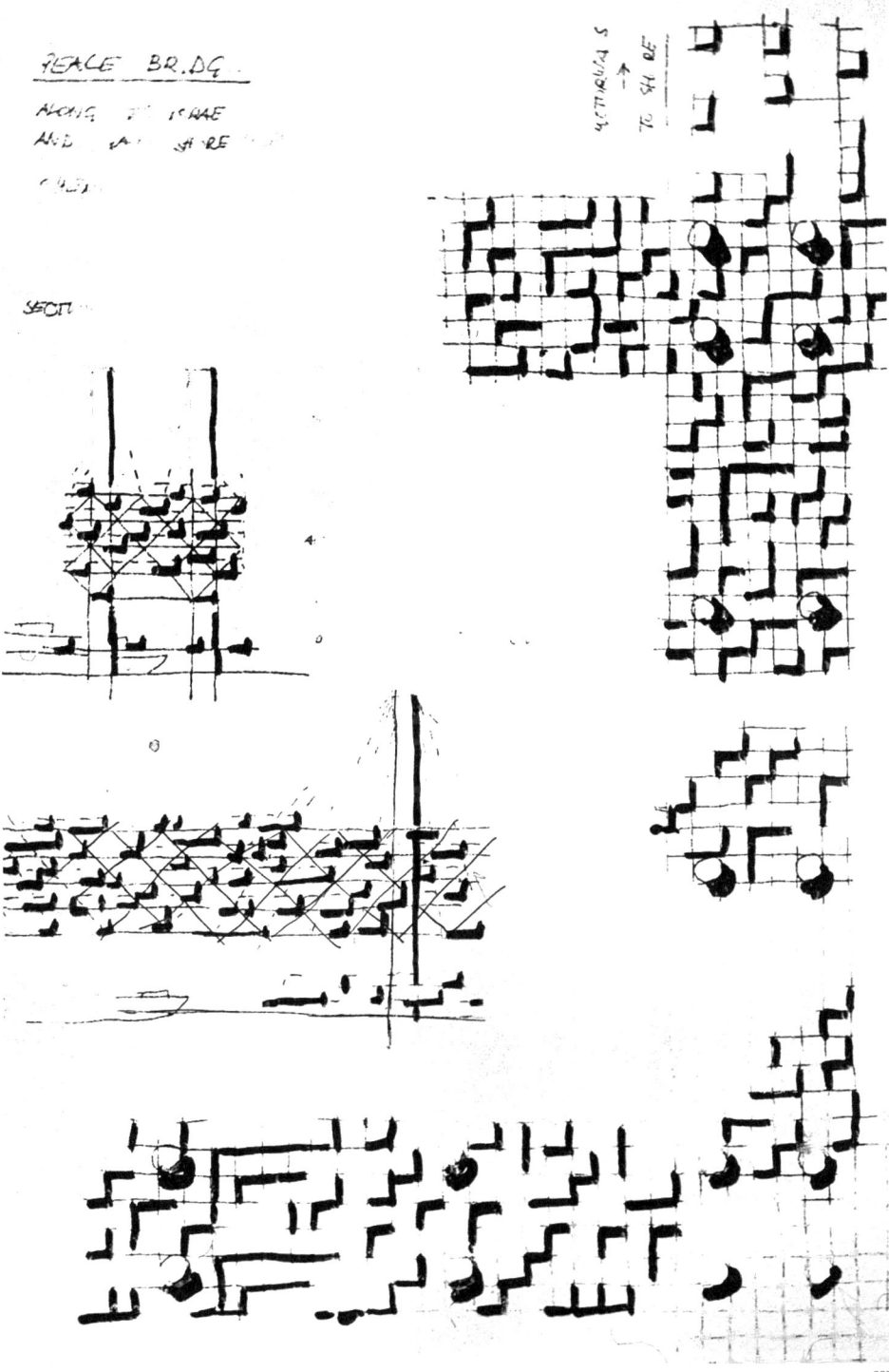

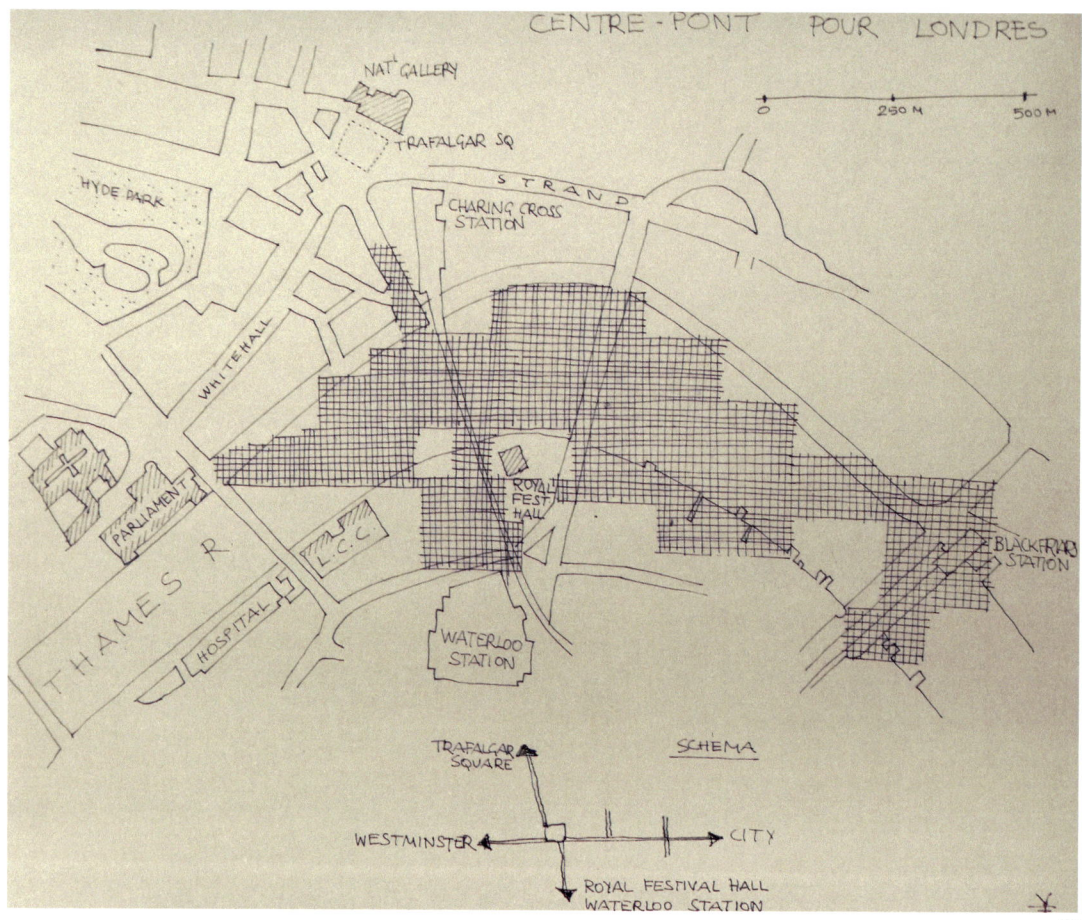

The two banks of the Thames have been developed unequally which creates many problems for the city of London. Despite the efforts of the authorities to create important centers on the South Bank, this area does not develop. Yona Friedman had the idea of creating an efficient connection between the two banks with a Center-Bridge. The Center-Bridge would extend the current commercial center across the River Thames, linking Trafalgar Square and Charing Cross Station with the Royal Festival Hall and Waterloo Station.

RAGON, Michel: *Construisons des villes sur la mer*, in *La Nation*, no. 9, 1963 p. 269.

CENTER-BRIDGE FOR LONDON, 2004
228 Site plan and scheme.
229 Photomontage on postcards, *Bridge-Towns* over the River Thames, London.

Bridge 1

Bridge 2.

Bridges 3 and 4

BRIDGE-TOWN / 153

THE DILUTION OF ARCHITECTURE
ANTHOLOGY OF A PROCESS

3. Accumulation

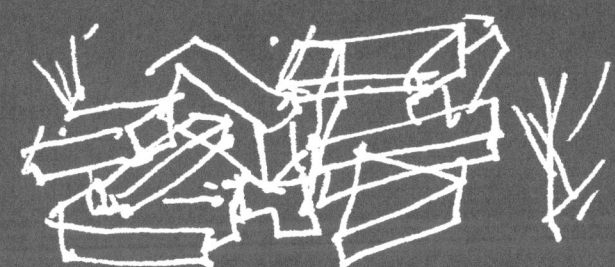

Accumulation of containers without a grid and without geometric rules. The surface of the ground is occupied, but the whole structure is transformable.

BUILDING WITH CONTAINERS, A DIFFERENT METHOD

Using containers –solid boxes stacked one on another– for living is a very old technique. I myself made a project named "Bétonbox," which proposed to stack concrete boxes with large gaps between them, using these gaps as additional inhabitable space. Mainstram container buildings have still not attained this avant-garde proposal, 1958.

My current proposition represents large improvements on my 1958 project:
1. The containers themselves are space-frame modules, supporting the transport walls and the lightweight floor slabs.
2. They (the containers) are not assembled according to some geometric grid but are "heaped" irregularly, practically improvised, into gribouillis-kind shelves (gribouillis is what I called tangled wire structures, wherein wires are fastened together in points where they cross each other).

I can simulate such container-heaps through models of space-chain modules linked at crossing points where one ring of one module crosses another ring of another module.

These models indicate both the stability of such a structure and its aesthetic quality, not to mention the social implication: they can be improvised by the inhabitant, and be fixed after a test verifying its solidity.

FRIEDMAN, Yona: *Building with Containers, a Different Method,* in RODRIGUEZ, Maria Ines (ed.): *Architecture with the People, by the People, for the People,* Coleccion Arte Arquitectura AA MUSAC, 2011, p. 51.

230

231

TRIHEDRIC CONTAINER, C. 2005

230 - 231 Study models, *Space-frame containers.*
232 Sketches and notes, *Trihedric Containers; a Versatile Technique.*

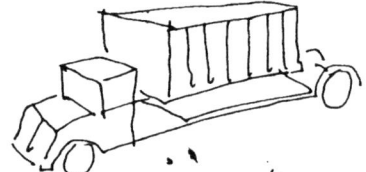

We call "container" a large tit, monolithic, used for transportation (lorries, boats etc)
1

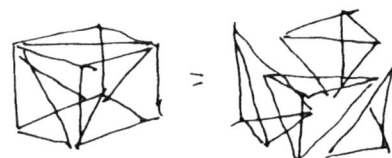

In 1956 I designed a "container"-like space-frame element which I called a "trihedron" (triedro) container composed of 4 "trihedra"
2

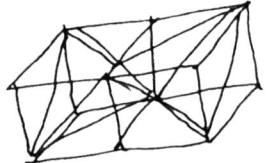

This is a trihedric container of 2 module
3

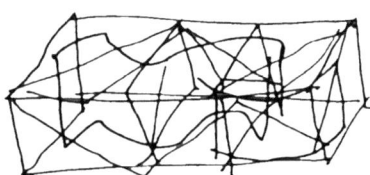

It is easy to insert in a trihedric container screens which determine the inhabited space
4

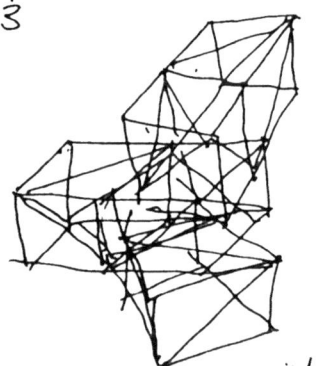

It is easy to form intricate agglomerations with such containers
5

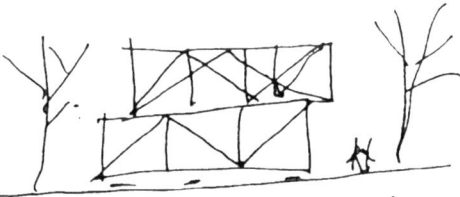

Trihedric containers (like all containers) can be disposed on the ground without the necessity of foundations
6

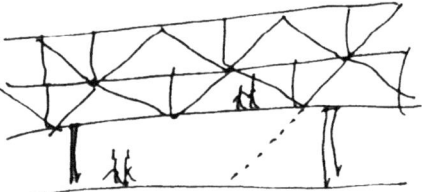

Trihedric containers can be fitted together into "span-over" structures supported by distant pillars.
7

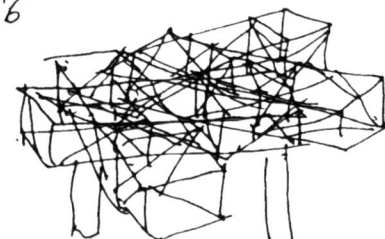

Span-over structures made with trihedra can follow intricate patterns with very little impact on the ground
8

TRIHEDRIC CONTAINER / 157

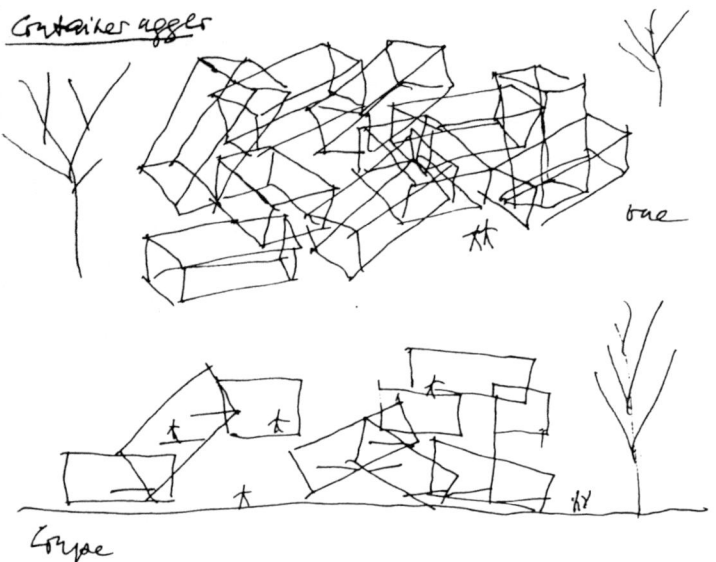

CONTAINER AGGLOMERATION

233–**233** View, section and container positions, c. 2005.

SEMI-CONTAINER, 2002

235–**236** Study model, *Blocs tridimensionnels autoportants*.
237–**238** Exercise on the *Flatwriter*.

235

236

237

238

239

CONTAINER-MUSEUM

239 *Container-museum, crumpled sheet roof merkstruktur + trees within an enclosure of about 100 m², c. 2005.*

CONTAINER STREET MUSEUM, C. 2005

240 *Container-raft Street museum.*
241 *Container-span over Street museum.*

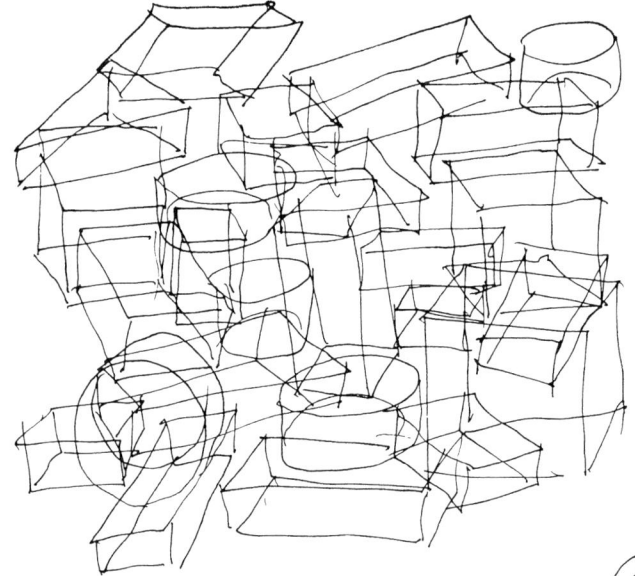

Container-raft
Street museum

240

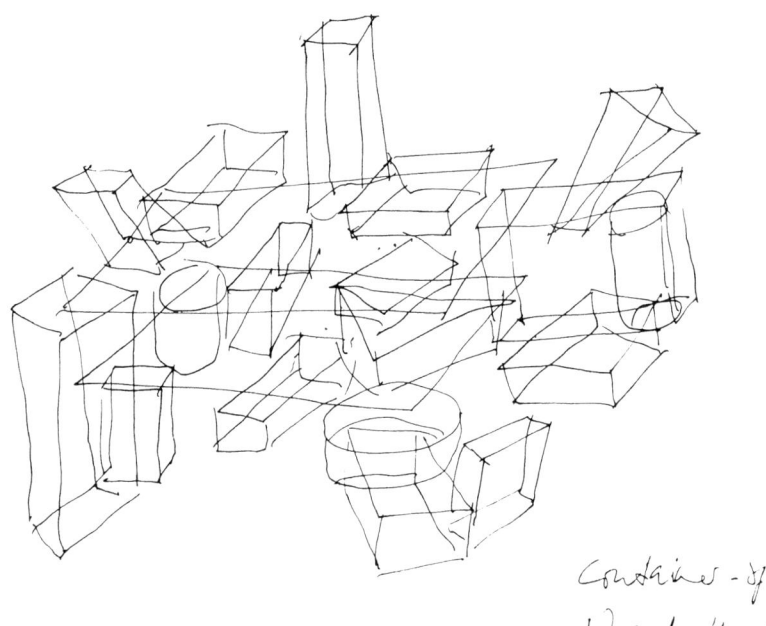

Container-shapes
Street museum

241

CONTAINER-MUSEUM / CONTAINER STREET-MUSEUM / 161

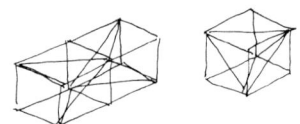
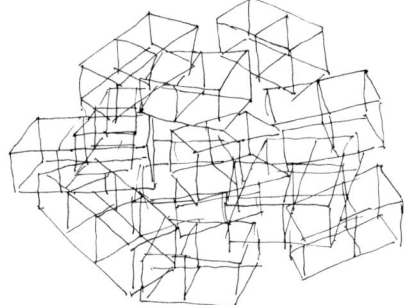
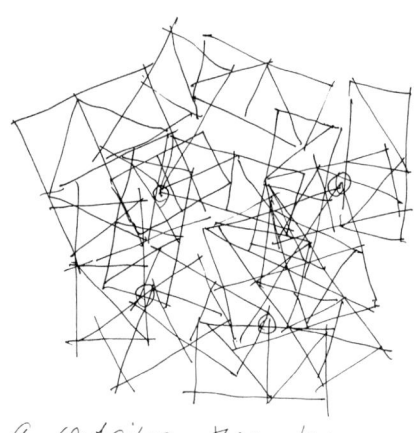
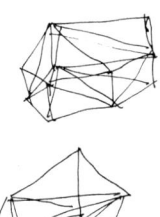
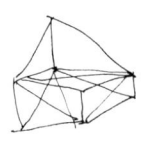

SPACE-FRAME CONTAINER, C. 2005

242 *Space-frame infrastructure made with containers* and *container agglomeration (Space-frame structure)*.
243 *A container Space-frame of 4 levels, with points of support.*
244 Models, compositions with *Trihedrical containers*.
Photographs by Jean-Baptiste Decavèle.

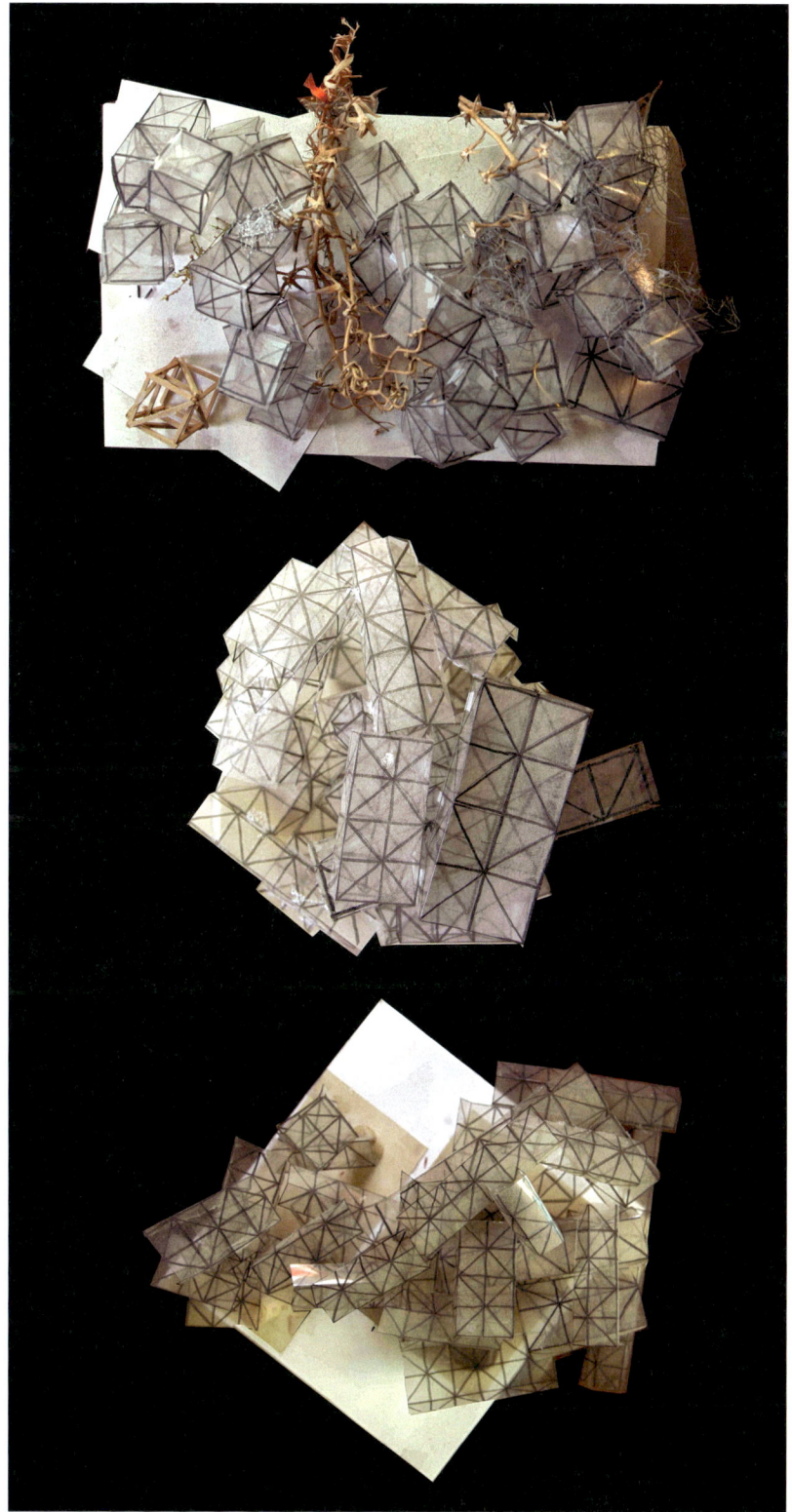

244

CONTAINERS

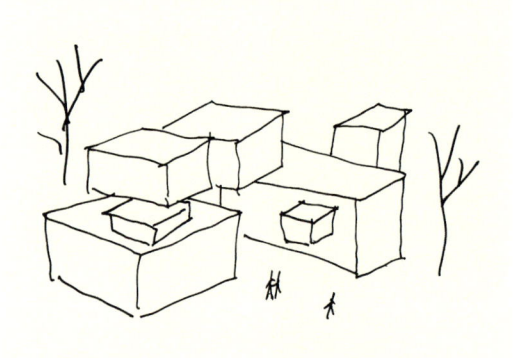

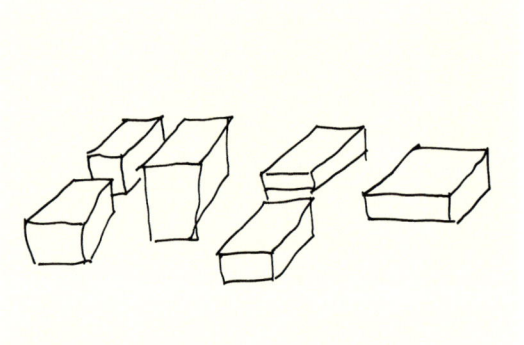

1 / One way to conceive a building is to see it as an accumulation

2 / Of container-like boxes

3 / Such boxes can be reduced to their skeleton

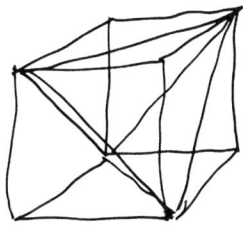

4 / Space-frame kind

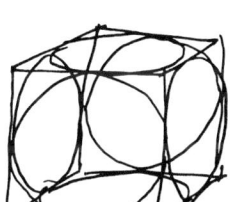

5 / Or space-chain kind

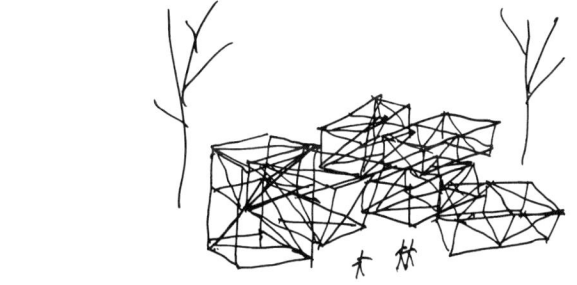

6 / The accumulation of skeleton-boxes can be irregular

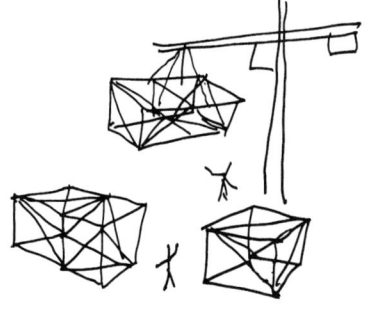

7 / Improvised

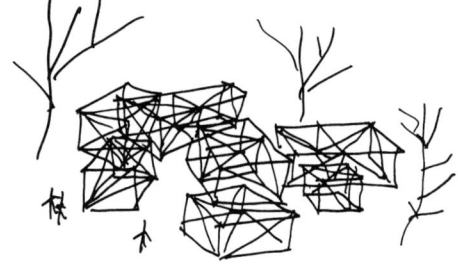

8 / And recomposed differently when desired

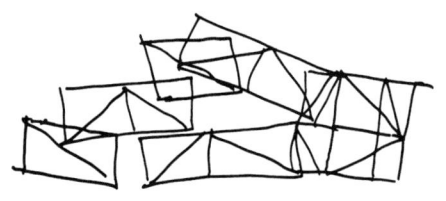

9 / Skeleton-boxes fastened together form a tridimensional structure, monolithic

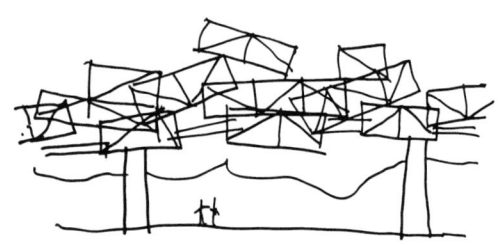

10 / That can span-over an area

11 / The skeleton structure can contain whatever the users desire

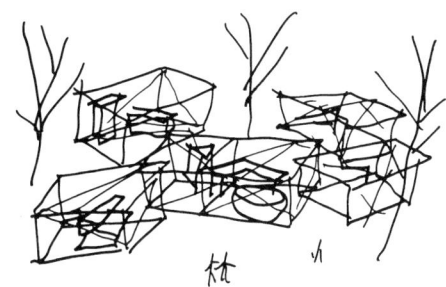

12 / Objects

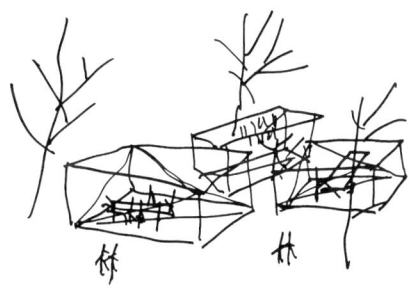

13 / Functions, etc.

14 / An accumulation of that kind is a "non-building"

15 / That can be used as a "building"

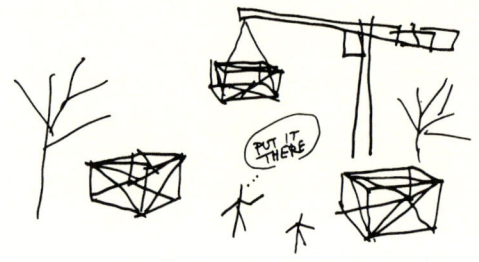

16 / It has to be assembled directly on site

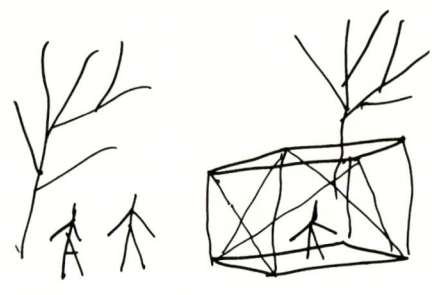

17 / At real scale

18 / That is the program of new architecture

245

CONTAINER-TOWER

245 Photomontage, Montreal, 1967.

THE DILUTION OF ARCHITECTURE
ANTHOLOGY OF A PROCESS

4. Transparency

A transformable structure without rules. It consists of objects or volumes.
Possibly constructed without impact on the ground.

IRREGULAR STRUCTURES

Irregular structures are interesting not only because of the richness of shapes they produce. Their principal advantage lies in the way they are built, which allows them an exceptional tolerance to imprecision. This makes them accessible to the layman builder, who may have mediocre skills and no sophisticated tools. Making building techniques easier can have important social consequences.

Kitchen-art is analogous to this. Cooking can be very sophisticated, but essentially it is practiced by the majority of housewives, who each use their own particular recipes. Cooking admits imprecision and improvisation.

Irregular structures admit improvisation; not only admit, but even impose it. You cannot easily draw the plans and sections etc. of an irregular structure; You have to improvise them on-site. Surely, models can help you to explore the structure's potential, and models are easy to build, and you cannot easily transfer the model into full scale.

For architecture, irregular structures might be a step towards becoming one of the "plastic-arts." Not really sculpture, not into expressing abstract (or concrete) ideals, but practical and pleasant, like kitchen-art.

On these pages, rather than theory and aesthetic considerations, I present "recipes", craftsman-like indications on how you can proceed with building irregular structures. All further initiative is left to you.

FRIEDMAN, Yona: "Introduction" and "Manuals," pp. 173–217. Originally published in *Domus*, no. 893, 2006.

IRREGULAR STRUCTURES

246 Manual *Irregular Structures.*

>> **247**–**248** Manuals, *Social Impact* and *Materials.*
>> **249**–**250** Manuals, *Ikonostases* and *Irregular Structures, What Pattern?*

IRREGULAR STRUCTURES

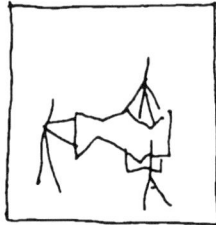
IRREGULAR STRUCTURES CAN BE BUILT EASILY

BUT IT IS DIFFICULT TO DRAW THEM ON PAPER

THEY DON'T FOLLOW RULES EASY TO FORMULATE

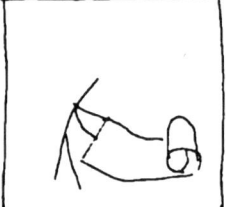
BUT THERE ARE METHODS TO BE APPLIED WHEN BUILDING

IT IS IMPORTANT THAT SUCH STRUCTURES DON'T ASK FOR PRECISION

THEY ADMIT CERTAIN NEGLIGENCE IN IMPLEMENTATION, WHAT THE PROFESSION WOULD NOT TOLERATE

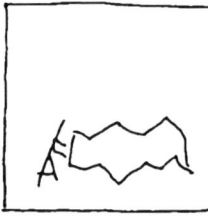
THUS LAYMEN ARE CAPABLE TO IMPLEMENT THEM

THESE STRUCTURES CAN NOT BE SHOWN COMPLETELY EVEN IN MODELS

YOU CAN TEST THEM ONLY IN FULL SCALE

ON THE SITE

IRREGULAR STRUCTURES ARE OPEN TO IMPROVISATION

TO CONTINUOUS CHANGE

THEY HAVE NO FINAL STATE

THEY ARE ONGOING PROCESSES

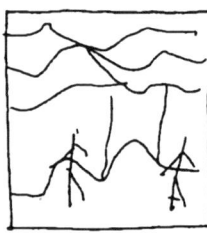
AND OPEN UP A "SOFT" ARCHITECTURE

WHICH FITS BEST A "SOFT" SOCIETY

SOCIAL IMPACT

IMPLICATIONS IN ARCHITECTURE FOR A SOFT SOCIETY

CONCERN, FIRST, WHO MAKES WHAT DECISIONS

MORALLY IT IS CLEAR: IT HAS TO BE THE INHABITANT. TECHNICALLY THIS IS MORE DIFFICULT

HIS NATURAL METHOD IS "TRIAL AND ERROR", WHAT IMPLIES ULTERIOR CORRECTIONS

CORRECTIONS DEMAND TECHNICAL FACILITY FOR THE ..LAYMAN TO PERFORM.

"TRIAL AND ERROR" IS POSSIBLE ONLY IN FULL SCALE ONLY ON THE SITE IT IS MORE THAN A GAME

CORRECTIONS ARE, IN MOST CASES, IMPROVISED

(LIKE EVERYTHING IN LIFE)

IRREGULAR STRUCTURES ARE THUS MOST APPROPRIATE

TO CONTINUOUS CORRECTIONS

EITHER SPOTWISE IN A COLLECTIVE FRAMEWORK

OR IN ISOLATED INDIVIDUAL HOMES

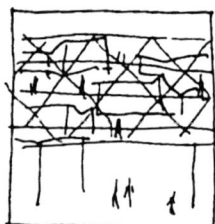

MOBILE ARCHITECTURE IMPLIES IRREGULAR RANDOM DISPOSITIONS:

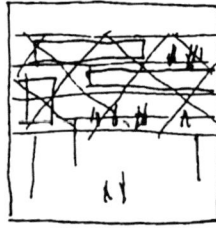

THE ARCHITECTURAL OBJECT CHANGES WITH THE INHABITANTS' LIFE PATTERN

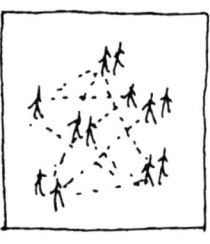

SOCIETY IS NOT A MECHANISM BUT A PROCESS

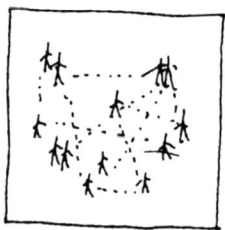

WITH NO FINAL STATE

MATERIALS

AS IRREGULAR STRUCTURES HAVE TO BE TESTED AT FULL SCALE

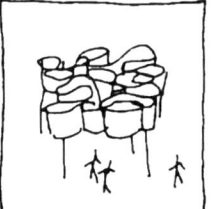
FULL SCALE MODELS CAN BE MADE WITH CARDBOARD

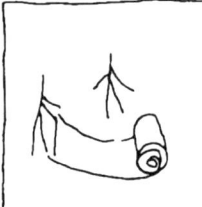
WITH ROLLS

WITH BOXES

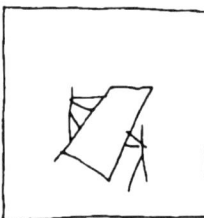
WITH PLATES

SUCH FULL SCALE DUMMIES INDICATE PHYSICAL QUALITIES OF SHAPES

ESTHETIC QUALITIES OF THE ARCHITECTURAL OBJECT TO BE BUILT

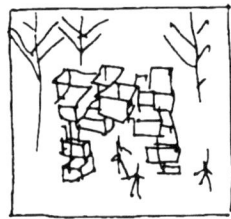
AND CAN EVEN BE USED AS EPHEMEROUS CONSTRUCTIONS

FULL SCALE CARDBOARD MODELS

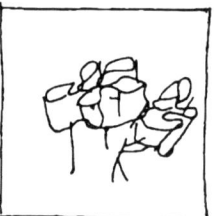
ARE THE MEANS FOR "TRIAL AND ERROR"

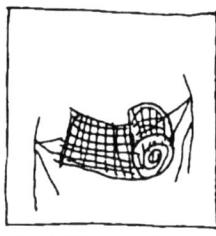
ANOTHER MATERIAL CAN BE USED: LIGHT METAL GRIDS

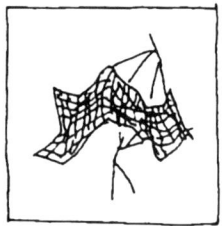
WHICH CAN BE FORMED BY BARE HANDS

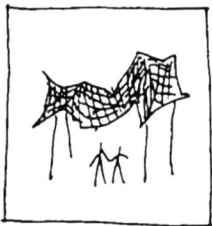
CONSTRUCTIONS MADE WITH METAL GRIDS

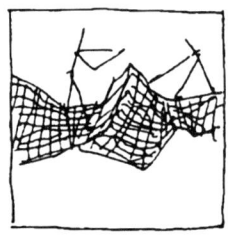
ARE LESS EPHEMEROUS: THEY KEEP LONGER

METAL GRID FOILS CAN BE COMBINED WITH SOFT PLASTICS

AND ARE ABLE TO BE USED AS OPEN SHELTERS

IKONOSTASES

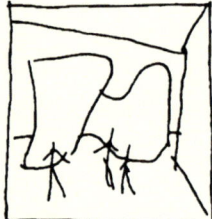
IRREGULAR STRUCTURES CAN COMPLETELY TRANSFORM SPACES WITHIN EXISTING BUILDINGS

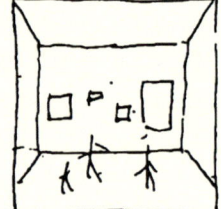
FOR EXAMPLE AN EXHIBITION ROOM

WHERE EXHIBITS ARE PRESENTED ON THE WALLS OR ON VERTICAL PANES

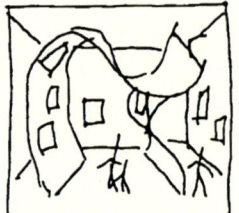
WOULD CHANGE COMPLETELY IF THE PRESENTATION SCREENS WOULD BE RESHAPED

I CALL SUCH SCREENS "IKONOSTASES" AS THEY ARE CALLED IN ORTHODOX CHURCHES

WE CAN PRODUCE EASILY IKONOSTASES OF ANY SHAPE:

CRUMPLED ONES,

LAMELLARE ONES,

MOEBIANS

OR MERZIANS.

MAINLY VERTICALS

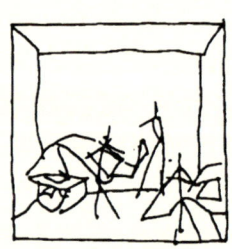
OR MAINLY HORIZONTAL.

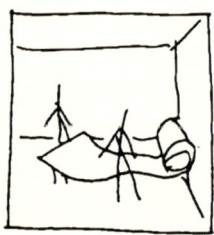
THE TECHNIQUES ARE THE SAME AS FOR ALL IRREGULAR STRUCTURES

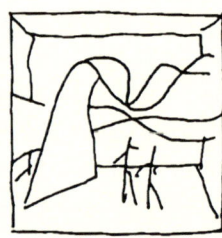
BUT THE EMOTIONAL EFFECT OF SUCH SPACES

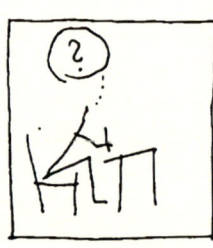
IS DIFFICULT TO DESCRIBE

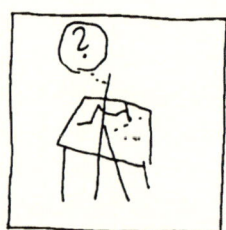
OR TO DRAW

IRREGULAR STRUCTURES WHAT PATTERN?

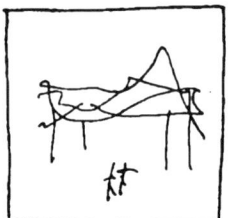

YOU CAN CONSIDER ALL IRREGULAR STRUCTURES

AS ENLARGEMENT OF MOLECULAR PATTERNS OF MATTER

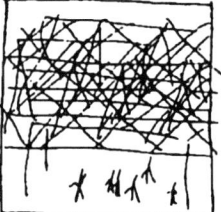

IT CAN BE CRISTALLINE LIKE THE SPACE FRAME OF THE "VILLE SPATIALE"

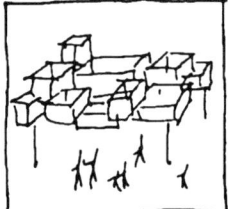

OR THE ASSEMBLY OF CARD-BOARD BOXES

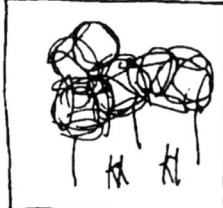

OR, EVEN, PROTEINIC SPACE-CHAINS

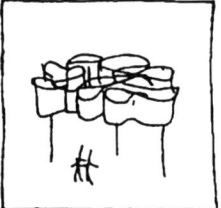

IT CAN BE FIBROUS LIKE LAMELLARY STRUCTURES

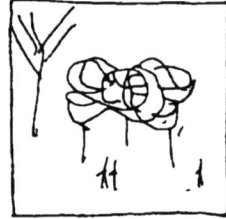

OR THE MOEBIAN ONES

SEMI-CRISTALLINE LIKE IRREGULAR TENSEGRITY

OR PSEUDO-TENSEGRITY

MERZ-STRUKTUREN ARE ALSO CRISTALLINE

AND SO ARE PANEL-CHAINS

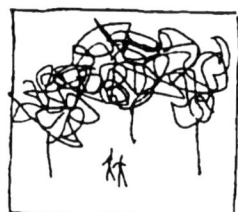

"GRIBOUILLI" IS COMPLETELY AMORPHOUS

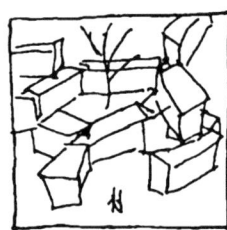

AND THE "TRAIN" IS LIKE VEGETAL FIBERS

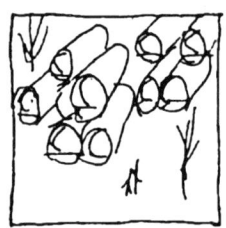

CYLINDRIC AND TUBULAR STRUCTURES ARE ALSO THE FIBER KIND

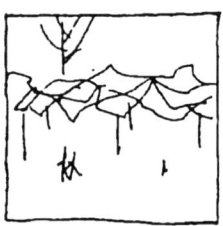

WHEREAS CRUMPLED SHEETS

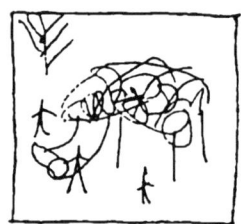

AND "PACKING" FOLLOW MODELS OF THE LIVING.

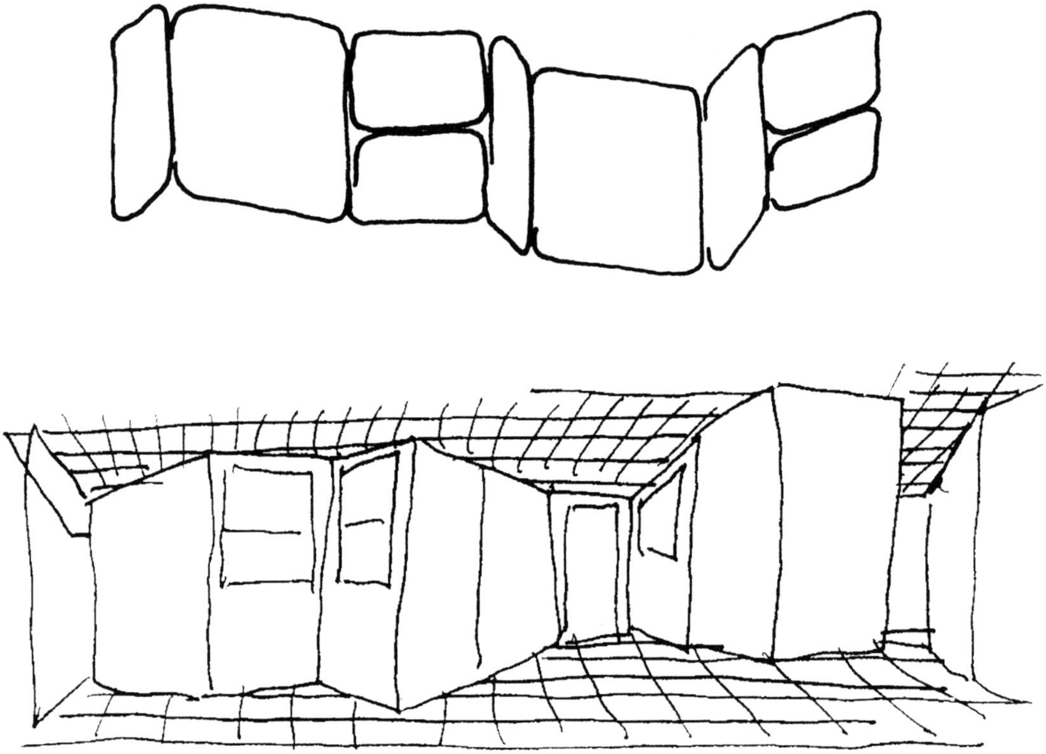

PANEL CHAINS, 1945

251 Sketch of the folding-screen system.
252 Manual *Panel Chains.*

178 / PART I / THE DILUTION OF ARCHITECTURE / TRANSPARENCY

PANEL CHAINS

THE SIMPLEST IRREGULAR STRUCTURE I CALLED "PANEL-CHAIN"

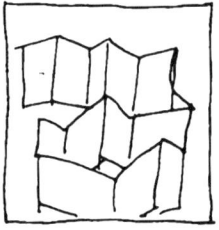
IT CONSISTS OF A RIBBON MADE WITH PANELS OF VARIOUS SIZES

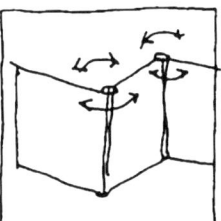
WHICH ARE LINKED TOGETHER WITH ELASTIC JOINTS

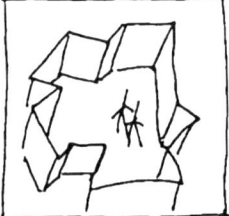
THUS THEY CAN BE DISPOSED ALONG ANY OUTLINE YOU WISH

THE PANELS OF A PANEL-CHAIN ARE NOT NECESSARILY STRONG ENOUGH TO SUPPORT A ROOF

A PANEL CHAIN SERVES TO DEFINE AN ENCLOSURE

WITHIN A LARGE SKELETON, LIKE THE "VILLE SPATIALE"

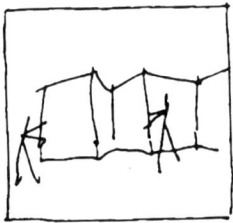
IT IS LIKE A FOLDING SCREEN

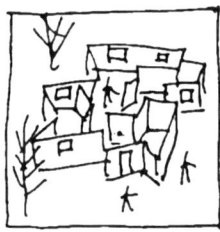
WHICH PERMITS TO INSTALL YOUR FLOOR PLAN

AND TO MODIFY IT WHENEVER DESIRED

THERE ARE NO RULES HOW TO PUT THE PANEL-CHAIN

EXCEPT THOSE OF YOUR PREFERENCE

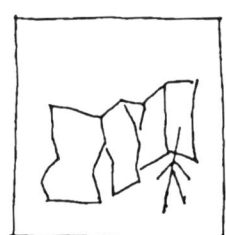
OBVIOUSLY, THE PANELS OF THE CHAIN CAN BE OF ANY KINDS

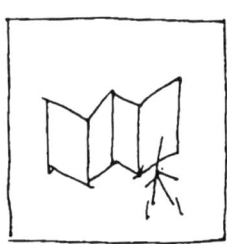
PLAN ONES,

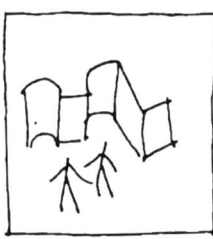
CURVED ONES

OR WHATEVER YOU WANT

IRREGULAR STRUCTURES / 179

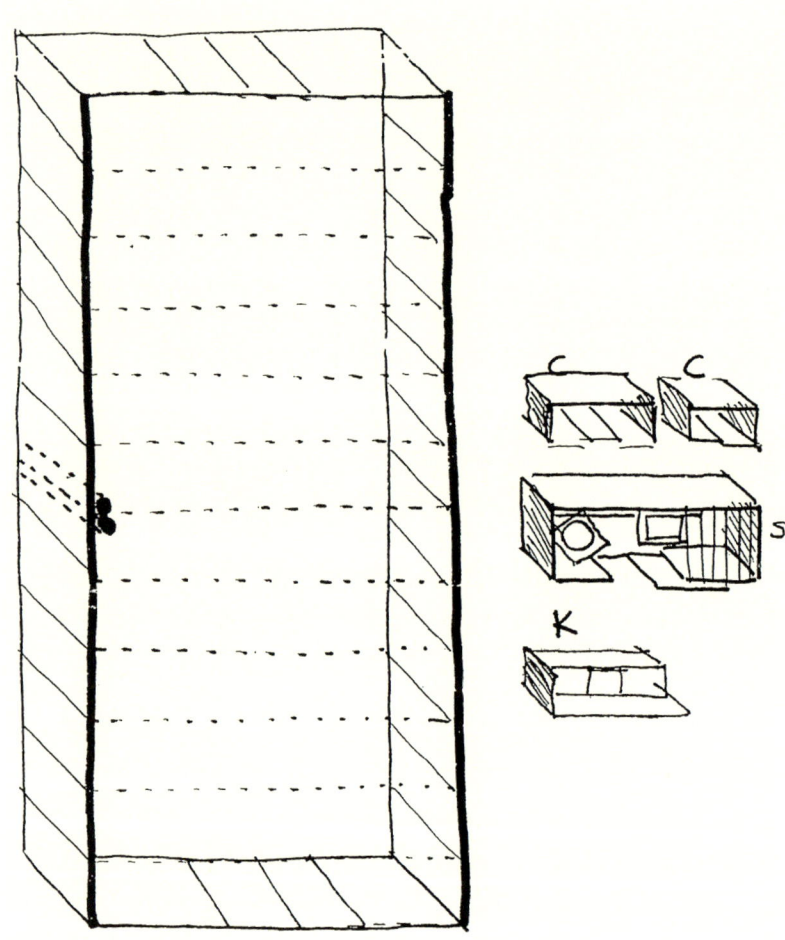

253

As a student, in Haifa, I started to work on turning premises like the bathroom, toilet, kitchen, etc. into self-contained boxes, which can be pushed, within a sort of "loft," into any position desired.
It would be easy to change the site of such boxes continuously, practically daily, if wanted. The supply and disposal of water can be assured through flexible hoses. As for electricity, the use of flexible wire is already common.

FRIEDMAN, Yona: *Movable Boxes*, in *Yona Friedman, Drawings & Models 1945–2010*, Paris, Presses du Réel, 2010, p. 10.

MOVABLE BOXES
253–254 Axonometric plan view and variations typology, 1949.

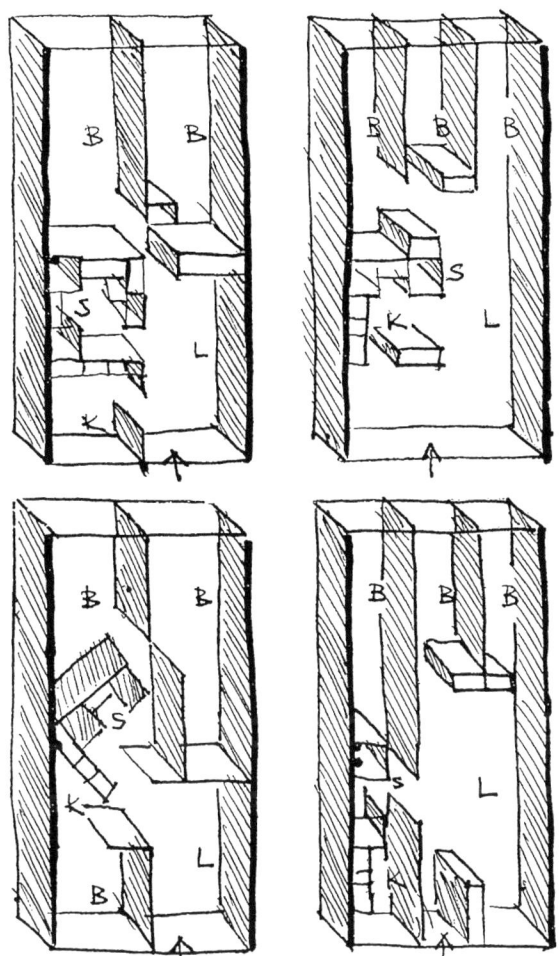

254

IRREGULAR STRUCTURES / 181

255

CYLINDERS, 1953–58

255 Photomontage, *Cylindrical Shelters*.
256 Manual *Cylinders*.

CYLINDERS

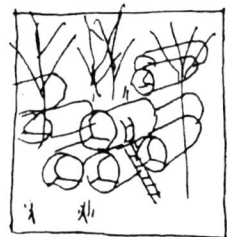
ANOTHER IRREGULAR ARRANGEMENT OF REGULAR COMPONENTS

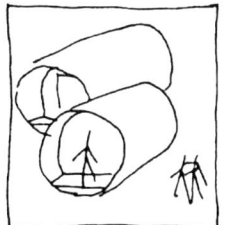
CONCERNS CYLINDRIC CONTAINERS

CYLINDERS ARE USED IN FARMING AS SILOS,

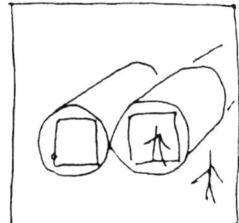
FOR STOCKAGE, FOR PASSAGES ETC

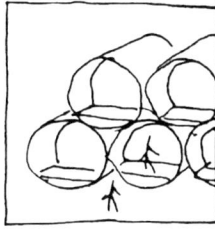
CYLINDERS CAN BE RANGED AT SEVERAL LEVELS

FORMING THUS MULTISTOREY SHELTERS

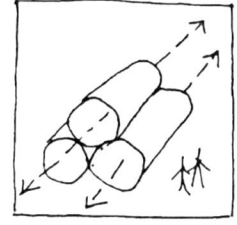
SUCH ARRANGEMENTS FOLLOW DEFINITE AXES, THIS IS A CONSTRAINT

BUT SHIFTING THE CYLINDERS ACCORDING THESE AXES STAYS FREE

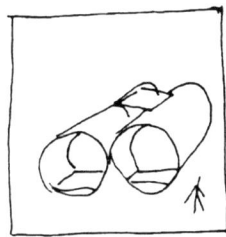
IT IS TECHNICALLY NOT TOO COMPLICATED TO LINK CONTIGUOUS CYLINDERS

SHIFTING AND LINKING CYLINDERS

PRODUCES A LARGE VARIETY OF FLOOR PLANS

WHICH CAN BE CHANGED EASILY

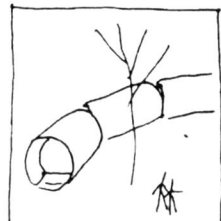
CYLINDERS ALSO CAN BE LAID OUT IN "TRAINS"

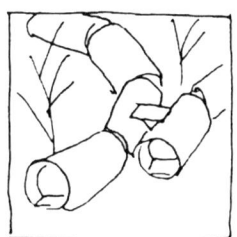
WHICH CAN BE EXTENDED THROUGH LINKING

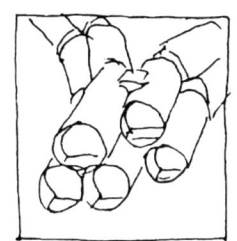
SEVERAL TRAINS HAVING ALSO MORE THAN ONE FLOOR

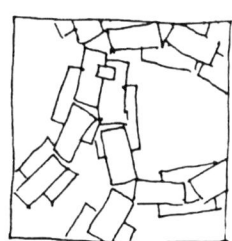
THERE ARE MANY ROADS TO NEW URBAN PATTERNS

257

258

A tetrahedron can be drawn on a cube.
Translating that fact into building elements led to the space-frame structure
used for the "ville-spatiale," and to all of my "span-over" conceptions.
I presented this idea at CIAM X, in Dubrovnik, in 1956.

<small>FRIEDMAN, Yona: *Trihedral System*, in *Yona Friedman, Drawings & Models 1945–2010*, Paris, Presses du Réel, 2010, p.18.</small>

TRIHEDRAL SYSTEM, 1955

257–258 Study models, *Trihedral system* of the *Ville Spatiale*.
259 Drawings and notes, *Trihedric element*.

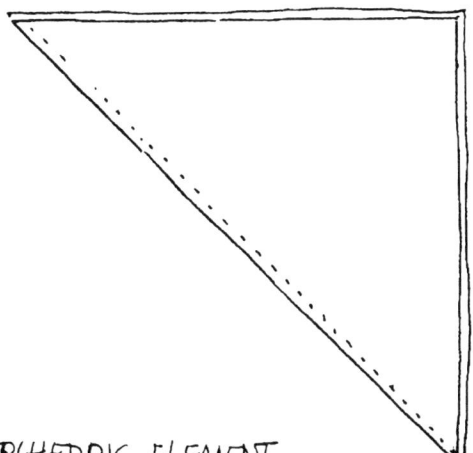

TRIHEDRIC ELEMENT

TRIHEDRA CAN BE FORMED BY 3 TRIANGULAR PANES OR BY A SPACE-FRAME OF 6 BARS

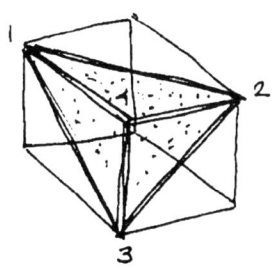

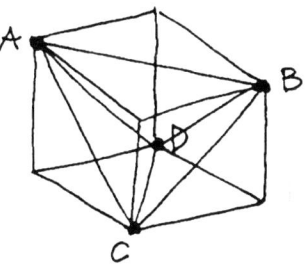

HYPOTHESIS:

4 TRIHEDRA ENVELOPE A CUBE OR A PARALLELOPIPEDE

THE 4 TRIHEDRA CAN BE FASTENED TOGETHER IN 4 POINTS (4 SUMMITS OF THE CUBE)

A SET OF TRIHEDRA FORMS A SPACE-FRAME WITH PARALLELOPIPEDIC VOIDS

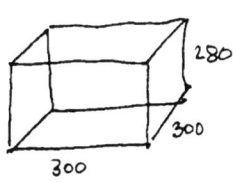

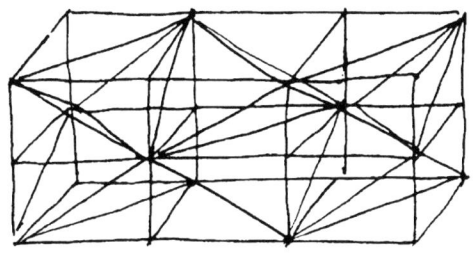

IRREGULAR STRUCTURES / 185

TRIHEDRAL SYSTEM, 1955

260 Model, *Trihedral system* of the *Bridge-Town*.
Photograph by Lucien Hervé.
261–**266** Drawing series, tetrahedrons forming a frame.
263–**264** *Space-frame* infrastructure with three levels and the same structure with freely inserted volumes.

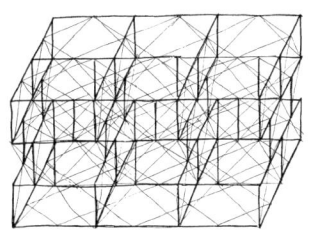 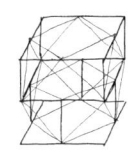

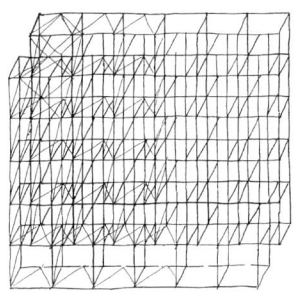 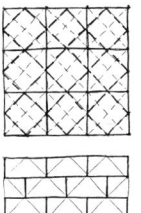

261

262

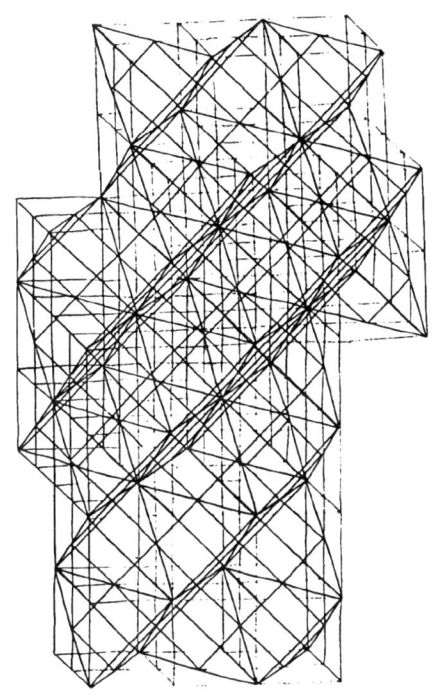

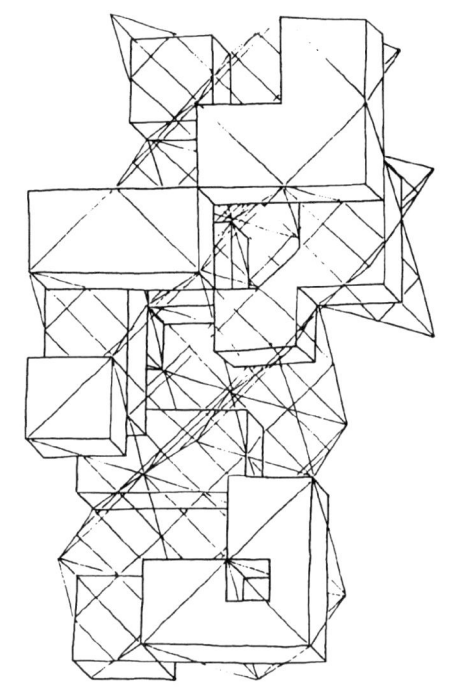

263

264

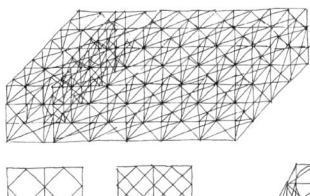

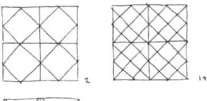
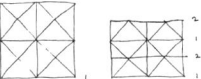
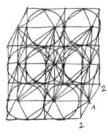
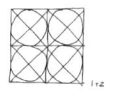
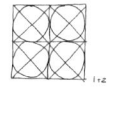

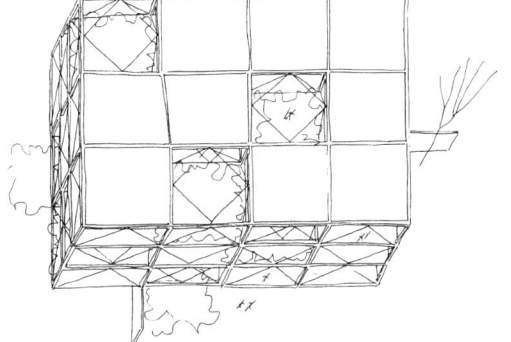

265

266

IRREGULAR STRUCTURES / 187

TEXT FOR PLATES I-VI.

PLATE I — Elements of shell-concrete for temporary housing (new immigrants). The wall-elements (W) and the roof-elements (R) are nearly identical in shape. Their surface is about 7 m2 an element; they are 3 cm thick. They are connected by screws and stress-irons. The box created by the connected elements is a monolithic structure.
The sections of the elements (W,R) are in a scale 1:25.

PLATE II — A and B are two types of movable multiuse bathing equipment. A serves in position 1 as shower-box, changed over to position 2 as a bath-tub.
B used in position 1 can be stored in this position or used for a laundry- or rinsing-sink, lifted to position 2 it becomes a washing-sink and in 3 a sitting-bath or shower.
Both units can be reproduced in plastic (perspex) or lightmetal. Their connection to the water supply tap or to the sewage disposal is secured by elastic plastic hoses.

PLATE III — 1,2 and 3 show different arrangements of bedrooms, the dotted lines indicating the different positions or placements of the washing equipment.
4 shows the living kitchen with indication of different placements of the movable kitchen-sink-desk-refrigerator.
All the flats include one living kitchen, patio, w.c. separated in the patio (indicated by circle) and bedroom-space.
The drawings are in scale 1:1oo.

PLATE IV — Different arrangements of flats and their grouping. L-shaped and I-shaped flats. Scale 1:2oo.

PLATE V — Plans for rehousing the Arab refugees arouse a problem similar to other countries to construct the walls in the traditional way by the future tenants themselves and to use for the roof prefabricated elements (R).
The way of living of the sttlers demanded less differentiation in the living-sleeping line; the main thing was to secure the upper floor (U) to the women and the lower one (D) to the men.
W and M show a possible diagram for space division; PR is another diagram for possible use of partly movable precast concrete furnishing in the public room (living). They are table (T), sink (S), bench (B) and a twopiece fireplace (F).

PLATE VI — Variations and grouping of the flat-type explained in plate V. Scale about 1:2oo.

267

CURVED PANELS

267–273 Text and drawings for Plates I to VI, 1956.

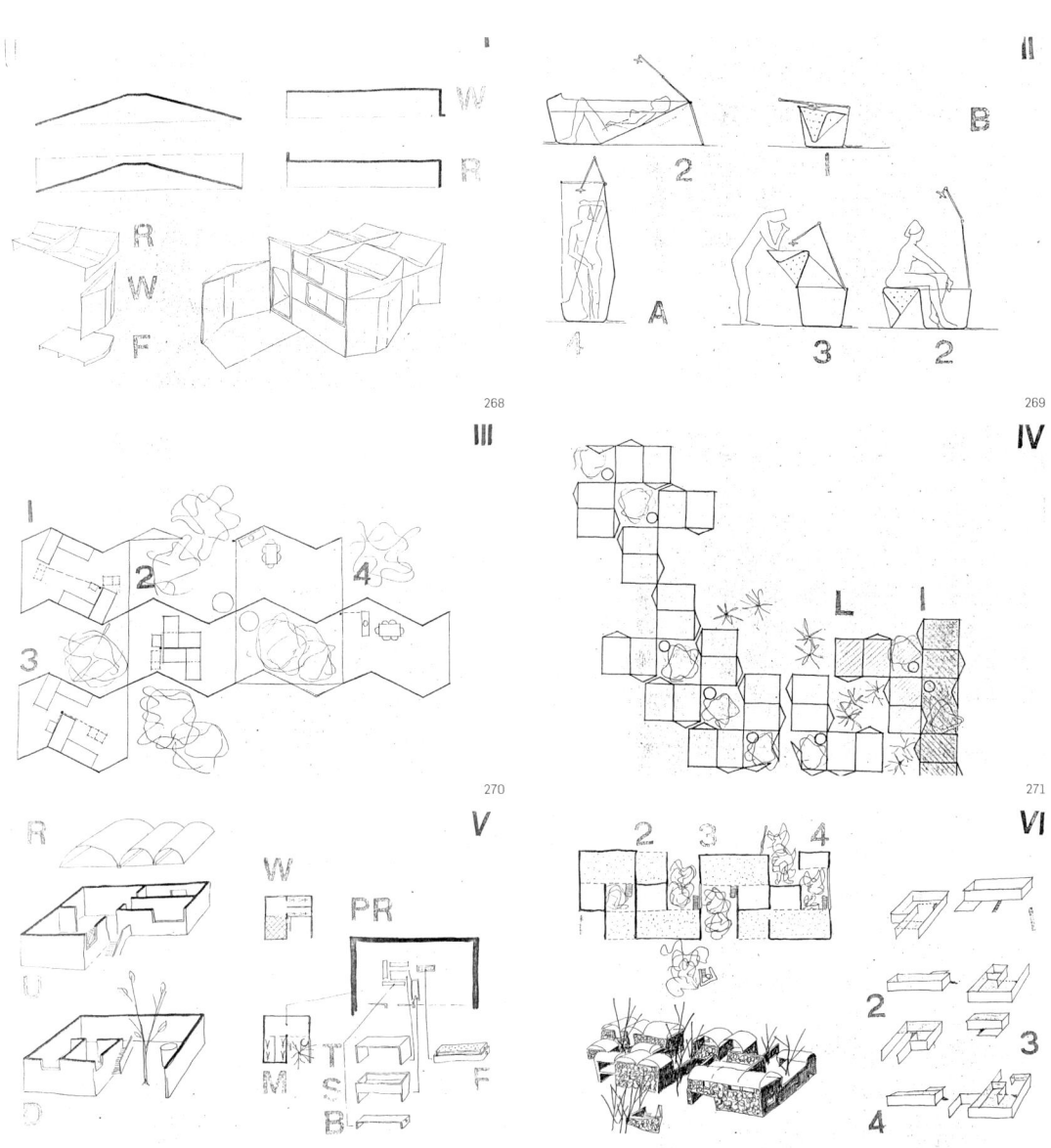

IRREGULAR STRUCTURES / 189

CARDBOARD BOXES

274 Photomontage of *Cardboard Boxes*, from 1990.
275 Composition made for testing ways of assembly, Kitakyushu, 2005.
276 Manual *Cardboard Boxes*.

CARDBOARD BOXES

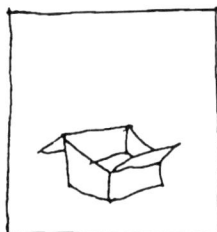

A CARDBOARD BOX ONCE USED FOR DELIVERY OF GOODS BECOMES A THROW-AWAY OBJECT

OUR INDUSTRIAL CIVILIZATION PRODUCES MANY OBJECTS OF THIS KIND

WE FORGET THAT REFUSE BECOMES A RAW MATERIAL TOO OFTEN

WE CAN BUILD EMERGENCY SHELTERS WITH CARDBOARD BOXES

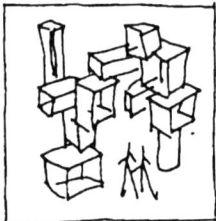

YOU CAN AS WELL ERECT MONUMENTS (EPHEMEREOUS SURELY)

IF YOU KNOW A VERY SIMPLE TECHNIQUE

ALL YOU NEED IS THE BOXES YOU CAN COLLECT ON DUMPING GROUNDS

AND GOOD SOLID GLUE

YOU LAY OUT SMALL BUNCHES OF BOXES IN ANY CONFIGURATION

AND GLUE THEM SOLIDLY TOGETHER

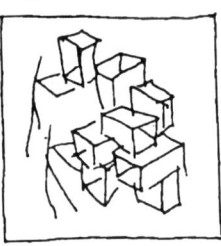

YOU USE THESE BUNCHES AS WALL ELEMENTS

OR ROOF ELEMENTS

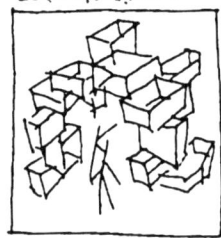

AND BUILD WITH THEM YOUR SHELTER

OR ANY ART-WORK YOU LIKE

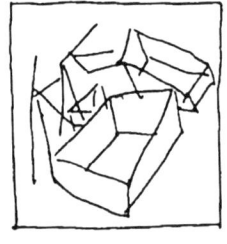

CARD-BOARD BOXES ARE THE BRICKS OF THE VERY POOR

OR OF THE SOPHISTICATED

LAMELLAR STRUCTURES, FROM 1990

277–278 Photomontages of *Lamellar Structures*.
279 Model made with undulated carboard.
280 Manual *Lamellar Structures*.

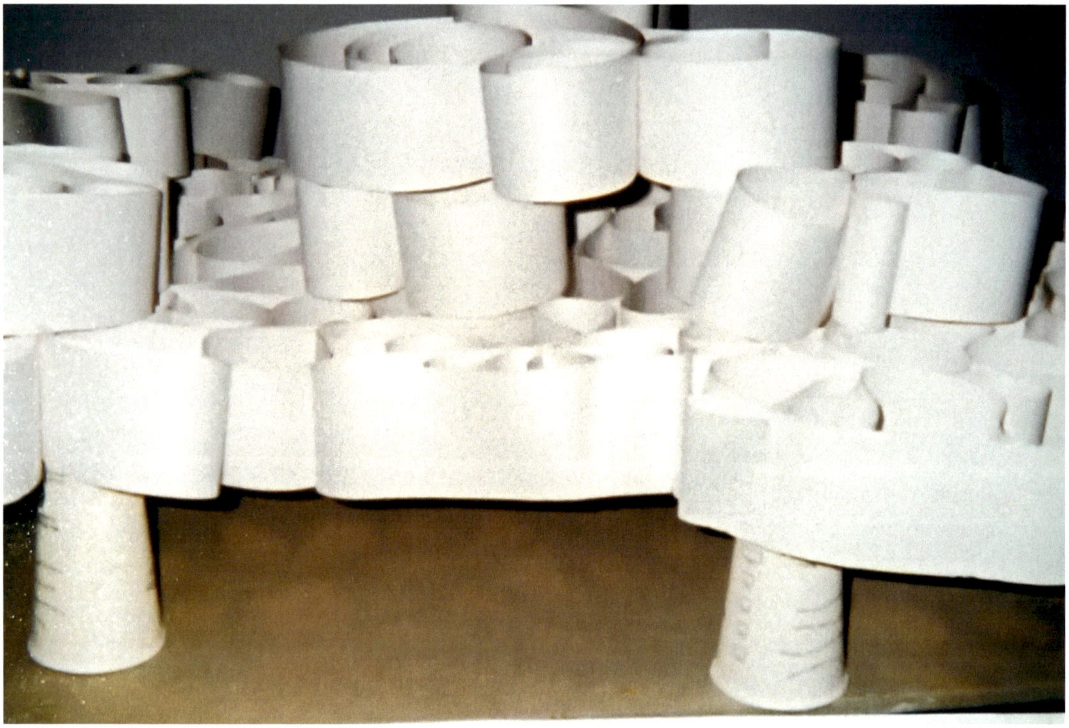

192 / PART I / THE DILUTION OF ARCHITECTURE / TRANSPARENCY

LAMELLAR STRUCTURES

USING ROLLS OF CARDBOARD OR OF METAL GRID

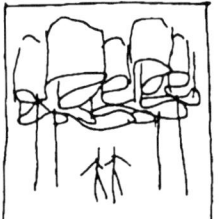
YOU CAN BUILD WHAT I CALL "LAMELLAR" STRUCTURES

FOR THIS YOU LAY OUT THE "RIBBON" INTO FREE DESIGN CONFIGURATIONS

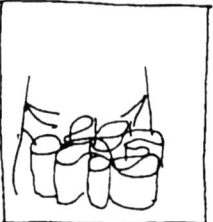
THEY SHOULD NOT BE TOO LARGE

AND NOT TOO LOSE: MAKE THE AVERAGE RADIUS NOT MORE THAN 1/2 HEIGTH

GLUE THE RIBBON LOOPS EVERYWHERE THEY TOUCH

THEN ASSEMBLE ALL CONFIGURATIONS INTO ONE LARGE SLAB

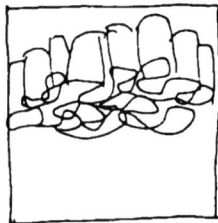
THIS SLAB FORMS A SOLID ROOF STRUCTURE

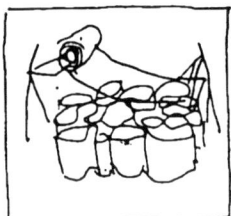
WHEN YOU GLUE ON IT BOTH UPSIDE

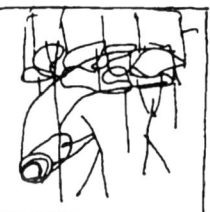
AND AT THE BOTTOM THIN PLASTIC FOILS

YOU GET THUS A TRANSPARENT ROOF WITH BUILT-IN SUNSHADE

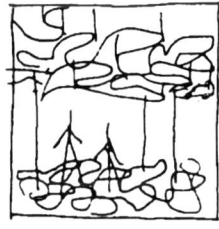
THE SHADOW OF WHICH DRAWS FUNNY PATTERNS ON THE FLOOR

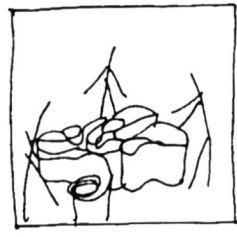
THIS KIND OF ROOF IS ENTIRELY IMPROVISED

AND EASY TO REMODEL

ANY LAYMAN CAN MAKE IT

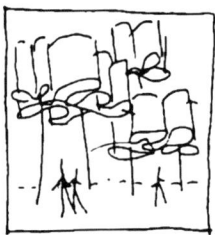
BUILDING-ART IS FOR EVERYBODY OPEN

CRUMPLED SHEETS, 1992–96

281–282 Drawing and photomontage of Temple Mount in Jerusalem, with *crumpled sheet over-roof*.
283 Manual *Crumpled Sheets*.

194 / PART I / THE DILUTION OF ARCHITECTURE / TRANSPARENCY

CRUMPLED SHEETS

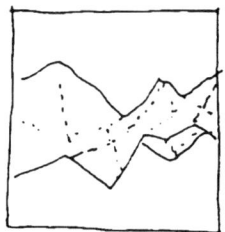

CRUMPLED SHEETS ARE A PLYWORK STRUCTURE

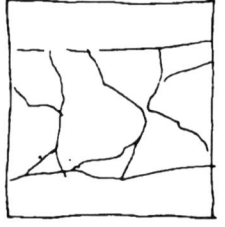

WITH NO REGULAR PATTERN

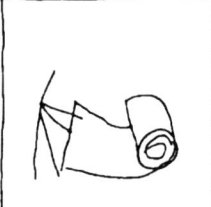

YOU TAKE SIMPLY A FOIL, OF A MATERIAL THAT KEEPS FORM

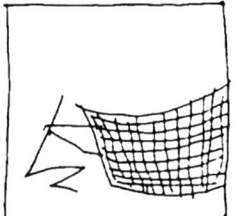

FOR EXAMPLE LIGHT METAL GRID

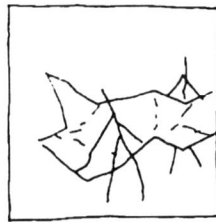

YOU BEND THIS FOIL AND CRUMPLE IT AT YOUR PLEASURE

THE CRUMPLED SHEET RESULTING IS A STRUCTURE

YOU CAN USE AS A SHADE ROOF

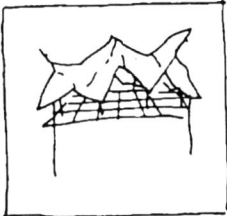

OR AS THE SUPPORT FOR THE "ROOF SKIN"; FOR EXAMPLE, HANGING ON IT

THE SOLIDITY OF THE CRUMPLED SHEET COMES OF ITS WAVE AMPLITUDE:

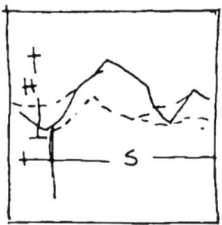

THE PATTERN SHOULD BE HIGH, FOR EXAMPLE $H \sim 1/2\, S$

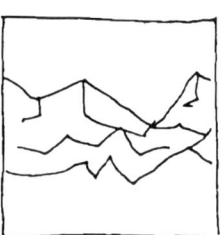

AND THE WAVES SHOULD NOT BE PARALLEL

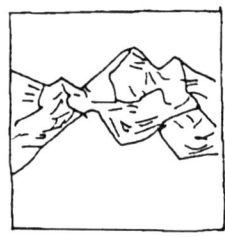

THE SMALL BENDS DISTRIBUTE THE STRESSES

A CRUMPLED SHEET ROOF CAN BE BEAUTIFUL

AND STRONG. IT CAN BE EASILY REMODELED WHEN NEEDED

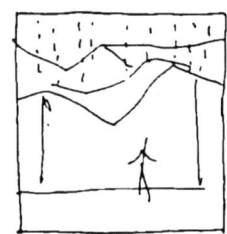

BUT IT CAN NOT SERVE AS ROOF SKIN ITSELF

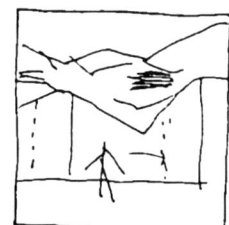

AS IN SPOTS THE RAINWATER WOULD ACCUMULATE

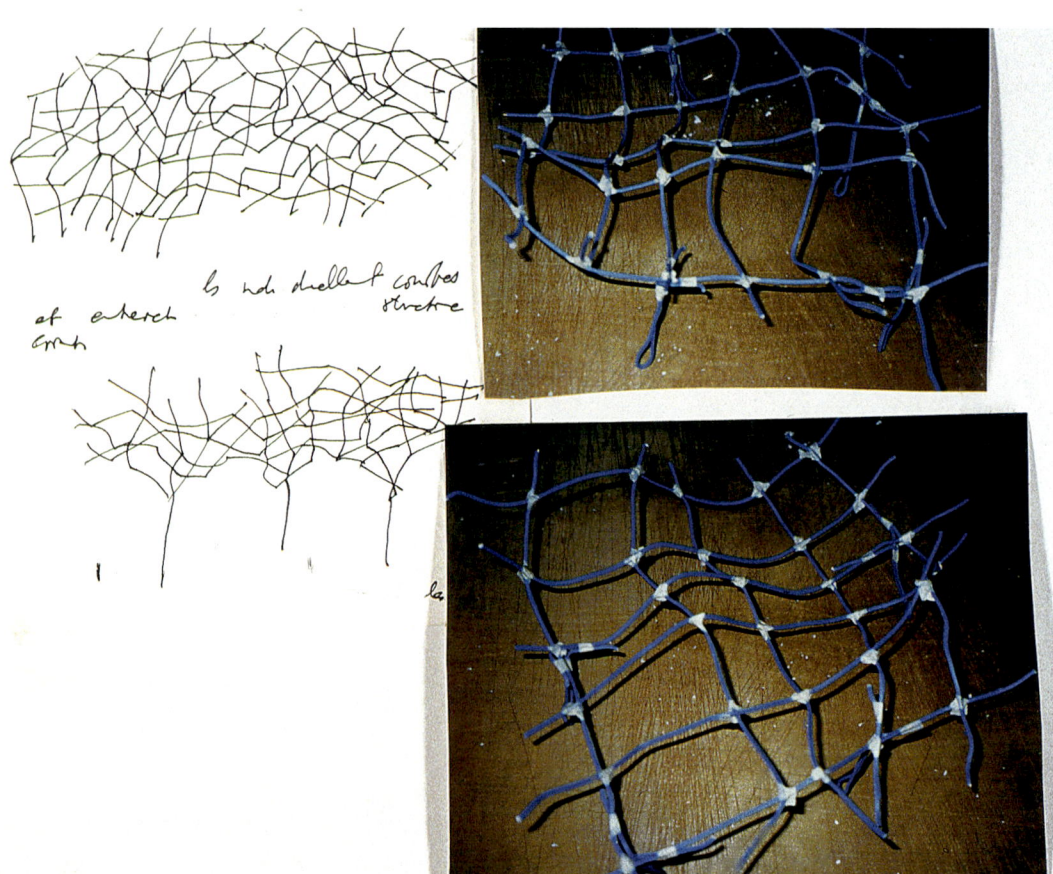

CRUMPLED SHEETS

284 Structural studies, sketches and model, from 1992.
285–**288** Study models for the real-scale materialization, from 1992.
289 Proposal for an inexpensive Museum of Modern Art in Brussels.
Cluster of plexiglass boxes, sheltered by a *Crumpled Sheet* roof umbrella, 2000.

285

286

287

288

289

IRREGULAR STRUCTURES / 197

290

"Macaroni" is the ancestor of the "train."
"Macaroni" was the orginal idea, the "train" is the translation to current technology.

FRIEDMAN, Yona: *1992. Macaroni*, in *Yona Friedman, Drawings & Models 1945–2010*, Paris, Presses du Réel, 2010. p. 634.

MACARONI, 1992

290 Perspective view of *Macaroni Ville*.
291–296 *Macaroni Ville*: *Level floor studies / The columns / Lower level / Upper level / Site plan* and model view.

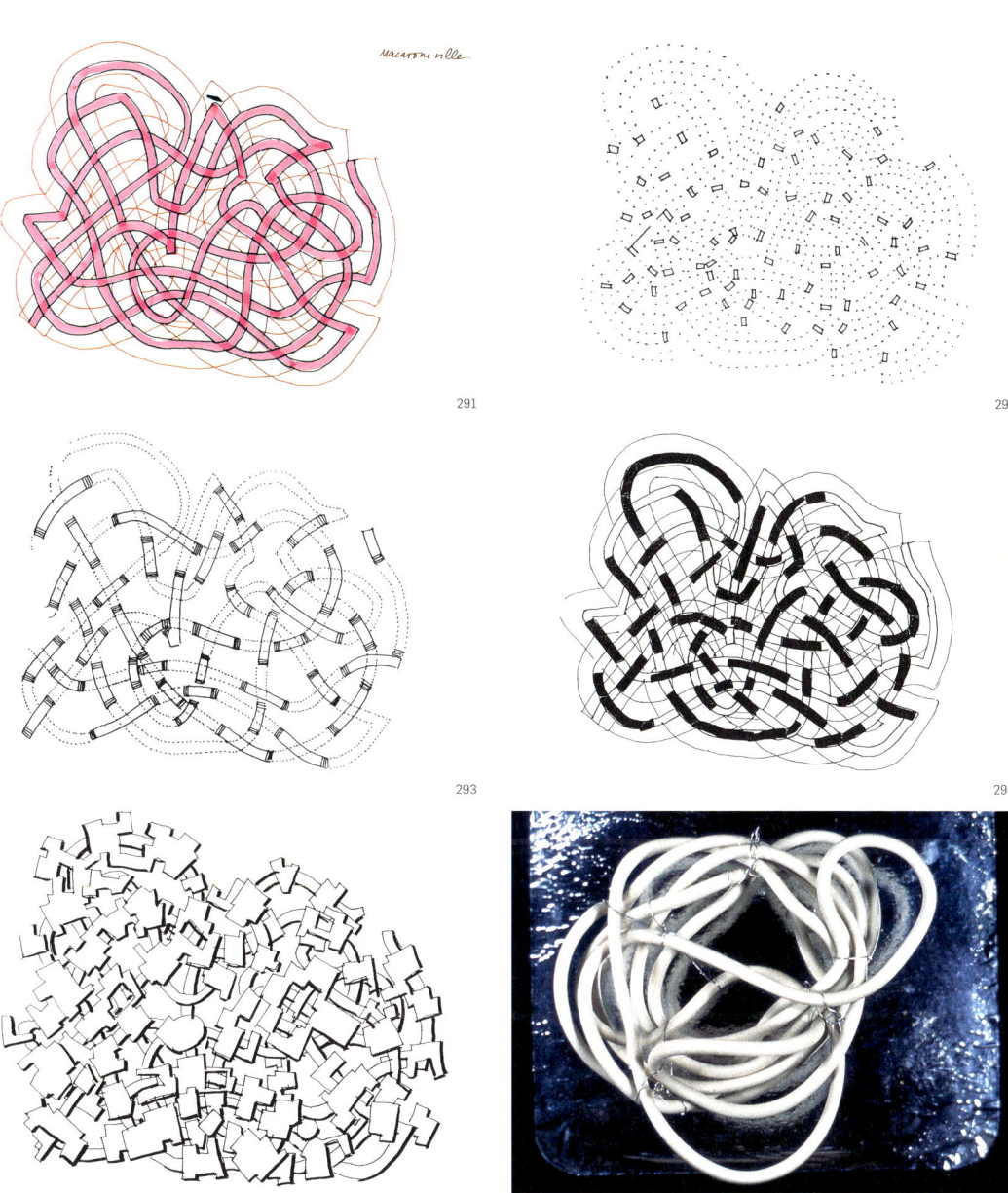

IRREGULAR STRUCTURES / 199

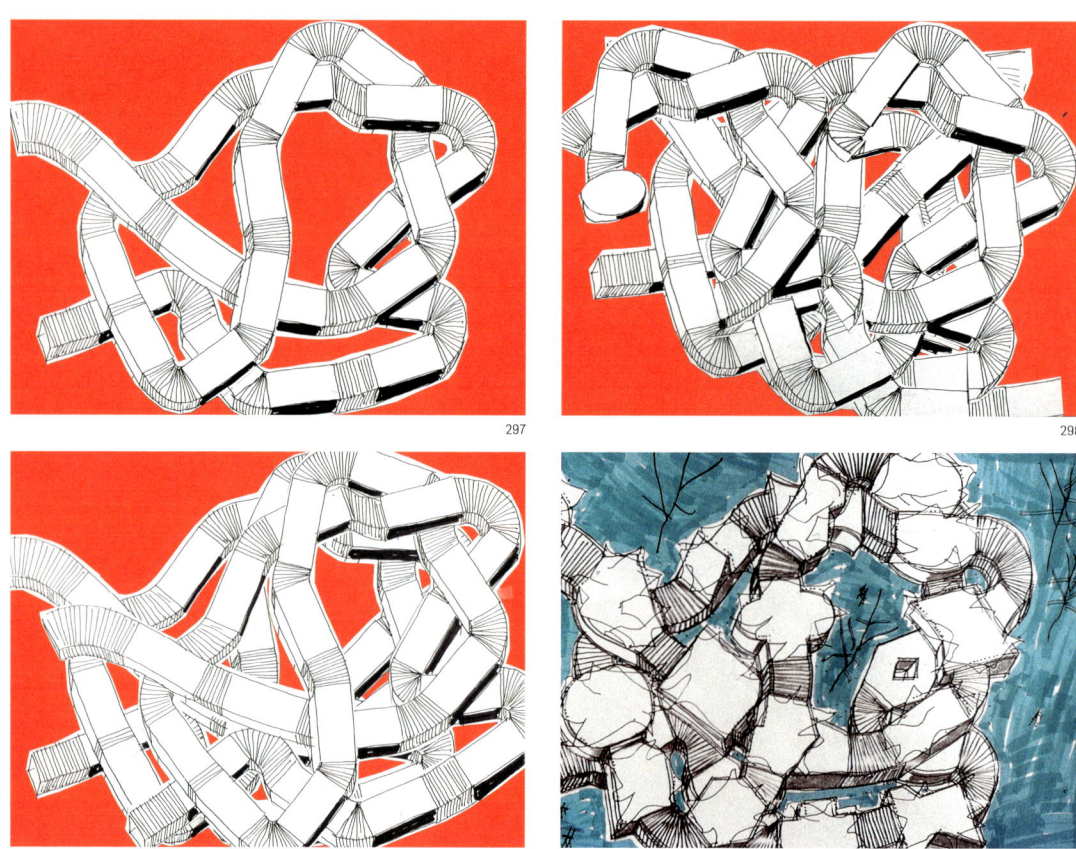

297
298
299
300

THE TRAIN, FROM 1992

297 – 300 Drawing series of another kind of *Soft Architecture*.
301 Manual *The Train*.

THE "TRAIN"

YOU CAN BUILD IRREGULAR STRUCTURES ALSO WITH REGULAR ELEMENTS

FOR EXAMPLE WITH CONTAINERS

CONTAINERS CAN BE STOCKED IN HEAPS

YOU CAN BUILD WITH THEM CONFIGURATIONS LIKE WITH CHILDREN'S BUILDING BLOCKS

ONE INTERESTING CONFIGURATION IS WHAT I CALL THE "TRAIN"

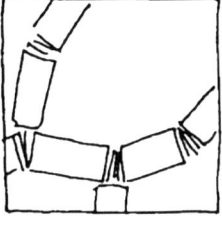
IT IS A LINEAR DISPOSITION OF CONTAINERS LINKED THROUGH SOFT CORRIDORS

LIKE THE WAGONS OF A TRAIN

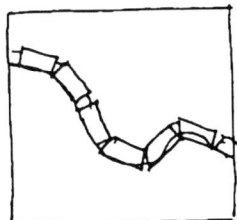
SUCH A "TRAIN" CAN FOLLOW COMPLICATED CURBS

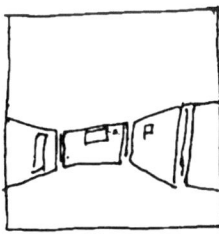
IN ONE LEVEL

OR IN LOOPS AT SEVERAL LEVELS

THERE ARE, IN ARCHITECTURE, TASKS IMPLYING LINEAR LAYOUT

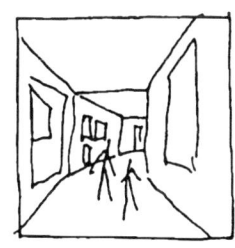
FOR EXAMPLE, EXHIBITIONS,

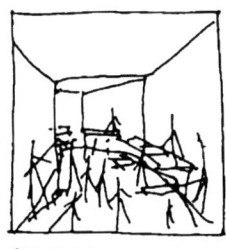
BAZARS,

EVEN TRIBUNES

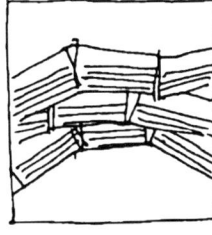
ALL WHICH HAVE NOT TO BE DISPOSED REGULARLY

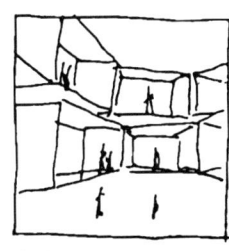
AND CAN BE DESIGNED AS TRAINS

IRREGULAR STRUCTURES / 201

GRIBOUILLI, 1995–2005

302–**303** *Scribble*, drawings on photographs.
304 Model of irregular wire structure.
305 Manual *Gribouilli*.

202 / PART I / THE DILUTION OF ARCHITECTURE / TRANSPARENCY

"GRIBOUILLÉ"

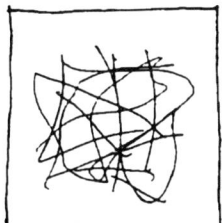
"GRIBOUILLI" MEANS IN FRENCH A "CRISSCROSSING" LINE

WHICH YOU DRAW ON A SHEET

BUT YOU CAN DO A "GRIBOUILLI" IN 3 DIMENSIONS

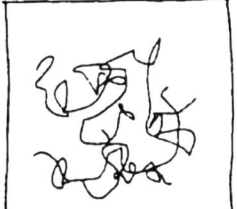
FOR EXAMPLE WITH WIRE

A 3-DIMENSIONAL GRIBOUILLI

IS, IN THE SAME TIME, A SCULPTURE

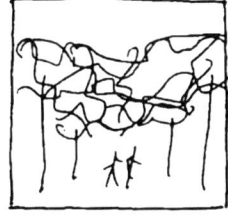
OR AN IRREGULAR SPACE-FRAME STRUCTURE

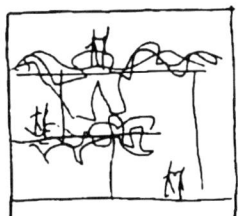
IMPLEMENTABLE IN ARCHITECTURE OR IN ENGINEERING

THERE ARE NO RULES HOW TO DO A 3-DIMENSIONAL GRIBOUILLI

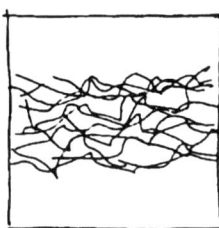
YOU CAN LOOK AT IT AS A MATERIAL MADE WITH FIBRE

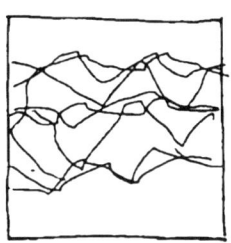
AND THE CONFIGURATIONS OF WHICH

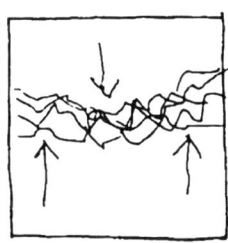
IMPLY ITS SOLIDITY

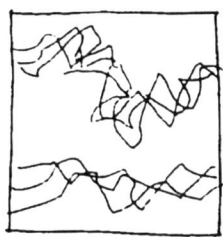
YOU CAN MAKE ANY SHAPE WITH THIS MATERIAL

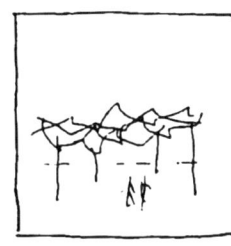
ROOFS

TOWERS

AND EVEN FIGURES

306

307

308

309

PALERMO GRIBOUILLI, C. 1990

306–309 *Tangled wire structure*, installation by students, Palermo, Italy.
310 Manual *Gribouilli 2*.

204 / **PART I** / **THE DILUTION OF ARCHITECTURE** / **TRANSPARENCY**

"GRIBOULLE" 2

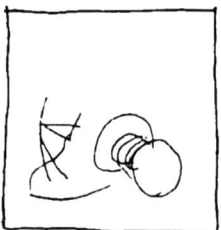 YOU SHOULD TAKE A ROLL OF THICK WIRE

 AND ENTANGLE IT

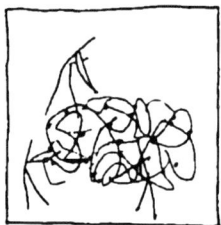 FASTEN THE CROSSINGS OF THE TANGLED WIRE

 MAKE IT AS CAPRICIOUS AS YOU CAN

 THE TANGLED WIRE FORMS THUS A SORT OF A SLAB

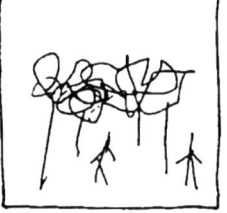 WHAT YOU CAN USE AS A FLAT ROOF SUPPORTING STRUCTURE

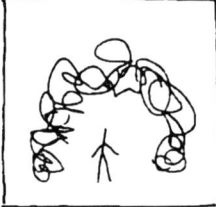 YOU CAN AS WELL BEND THE TANGLED WIRE SLAB AND HAVE A VAULT

 OR ANY OTHER SHELL STRUCTURE

 THE TANGLED WIRE STRUCTURE

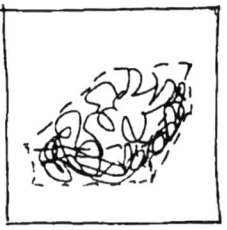 BEHAVES LIKE A THICK SHEET OF "MACRO-MATERIAL"

 YOU CAN MAKE EVEN CRUMPLED STRUCTURES OUT OF IT

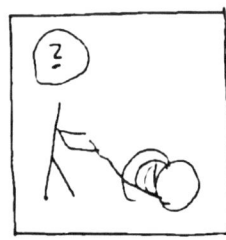 IT IS THE MOST IMPROVISED STRUCTURE WE CAN IMAGINE

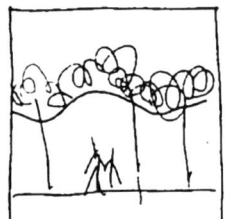 SUPPORTING SOFT PLASTIC FOIL

 IT CAN SERVE AS A ROOF,

 A SUN-SHADE,

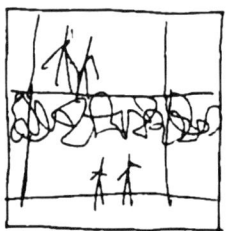 OR EVEN AS A FLOOR

Great Trafalgar Gribouilli

Piccadilly Gribouilli

LONDON GRIBOUILLI, 2004

311–**312** Drawing on London postcards, *Great Trafalgar Gribouilli* and *Piccadilly Gribouilli*.
313 Manual *Metal-Felt*.

METAL-FELT

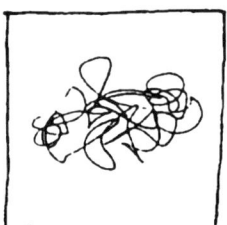 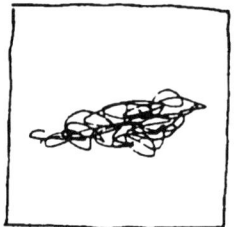 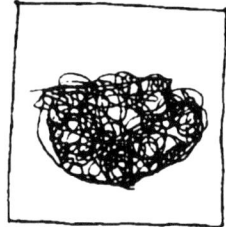 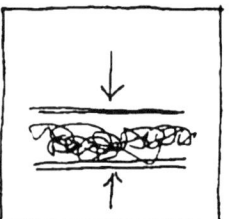

| A PARTICULAR KIND OF THE "GRIBOUILLI" | IS WHAT I CALL A "METAL-FELT" | "FELT" IS THE NAME OF A TISSUE | WHAT YOU CAN OBTAIN BY PRESSING ENTANGLED WOOL INTO A SHEET |

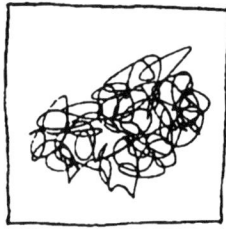 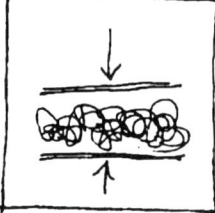 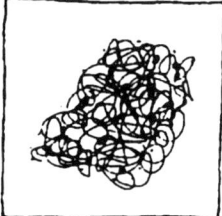 

AS THE "GRIBOUILL" IS NOTHING ELSE THAN ENTANGLED WIRE — YOU CAN PRESS THAT TANGLE INTO A SHEET — YOU SHOULD FIX THE TANGLED WIRE IN MANY SPOTS: — THE RESULT WILL BE AN IRREGULAR GRID

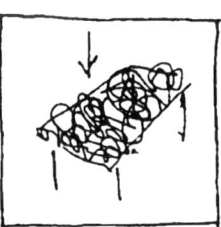 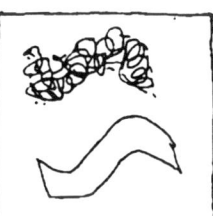 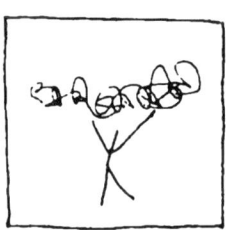 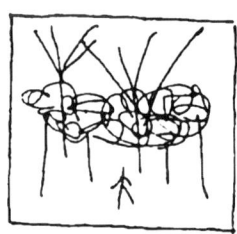

THIS "METAL-FELT" WILL BE FLAT AND VERY RESISTANT — YOU CAN USE IT AS YOU WOULD DO WITH A FULL METAL SHEET: BEND IT, STRESS IT. ETC — IT HAS THE ADVANTAGE TO BE VERY LIGHT AND SOLID — AND (OBVIOUSLY) TRANSPARENT

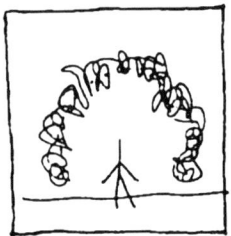 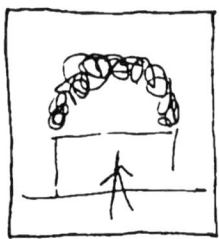  

BUILDING A SHELL OF WHATEVER SHAPE — OR A DOME — WITH "METAL-FELT" IS EASY TO DO — AND THE RESULT IS SURE TO BE BEAUTIFUL

314

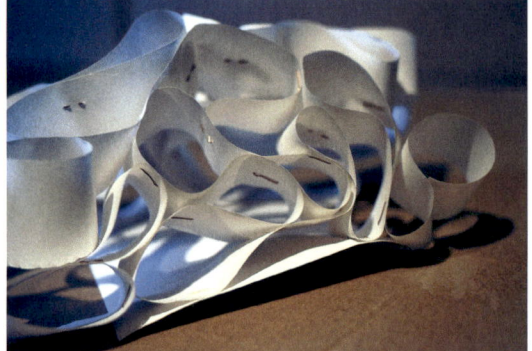
315

316

317

MOEBIAN STRUCTURES, FROM 2000

314–317 Study models made with twisted ribbons.
318 Manual *Moebian Structures*.

>> **319–320** Manuals, *Irregular Tensegrity* and *Pseudo-Tensegrity*.

208 / PART I / **THE DILUTION OF ARCHITECTURE** / **TRANSPARENCY**

MOEBIAN STRUCTURES

A PARTICULAR KIND OF LAMELLAR STRUCTURES MADE WITH RIBBONS

ARE BASED ON THE "MOEBIUS" BAND:

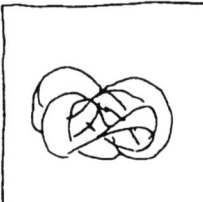
"MOEBIAN STRUCTURES"

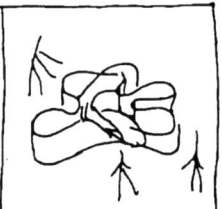
THESE STRUCTURES START WITH BAND CONFIGURATIONS, LIKE OTHER LAMELLARS

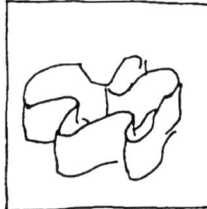
BUT HERE, BESIDE MAKING SIMPLE LOOPS

YOU HAVE TO TWIST THE RIBBON PERIODICALLY

MOEBIAN STRUCTURES ARE NOT MORE SOLID THAN OTHER LAMELLARS

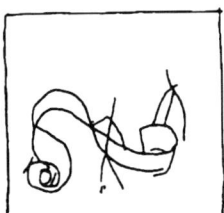
NEITHER MORE EASY TO BUILD

BUT THEIR ESTHETIC VOCABULARY IS FAR MORE RICH

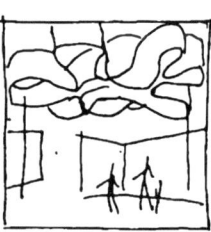
THEY SCATTER LIGHT INSIDE

AND PRODUCE SPACES UNHEARD OF

THEY ARE THE MOST BAROQUE STRUCTURES EVER MADE IN ARCHITECTURE

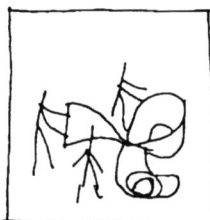
IT IS THEREFORE THAT THEY SERVE INDIVIDUALISM

BUT A VERY LARGE NUMBER OF THEM REDUCES THIS EFFECT

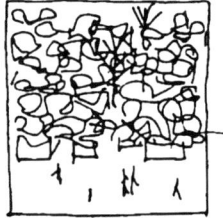
THEY PRODUCE (LIKE ALL BAROQUE) MONOTONY

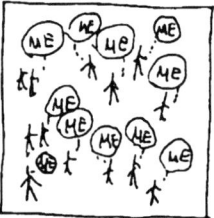
"MASS-INDIVIDUALISM" IS A BAROQUE PHENOMENON

IRREGULAR STRUCTURES / 209

IRREGULAR TENSEGRITY

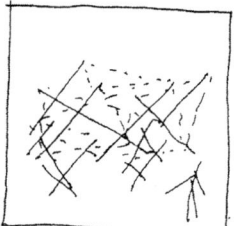
TENSEGRITY STRUCTURES WERE FIRST PUBLISHED — AS I KNOW — BY BUCKY FULLER

MANY RESEARCHERS WERE DEVELOPING FURTHER THAT IDEA

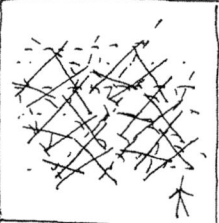
ALL THOSE STUDIES WERE BASED ON STRICT GEOMETRY

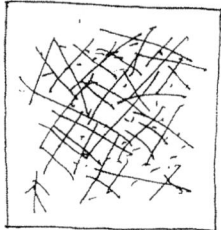
BUT IRREGULAR TENSEGRITIES CAN BE PRODUCED

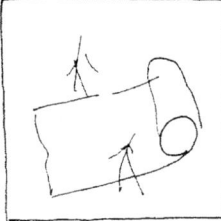
FOR IRREGULAR TENSEGRITIES MEMBRANES ARE USED INSTEAD OF ROPES

STRETCH OUT A SHEET OF SOFT PLASTIC FOIL

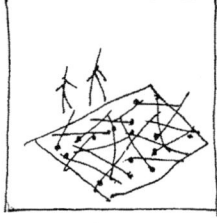
FIX THE PRESSURE RODS (I CALL THEM TENSORS) ON THAT SHEET BY ONE OF THEIR EXTREMITIES

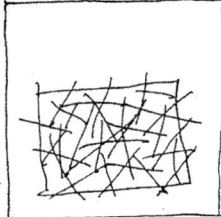
IN A CRISS-CROSS ORDER YOU LIKE

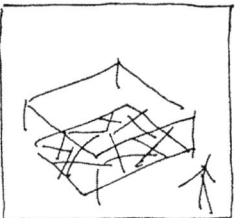
STRETCH A SECOND SHEET AT SOME HEIGHT ABOVE THE BOTTOM ONE

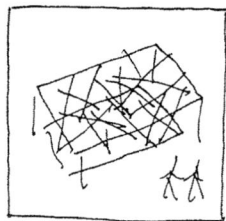
AND FIX THE FREE EXTREMITY OF THE TENSORS TO THE UPPER SHEET

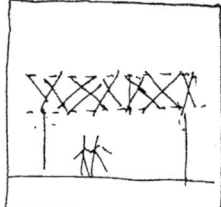
YOU GET THUS A STRUCTURE WITH THE RODS TAKING THE PRESSURE

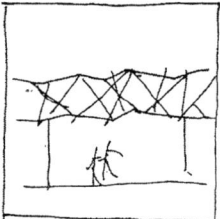
AND THE SHEETS THE TENSION SERVING IN THE SAME TIME AS ROOF-SKIN

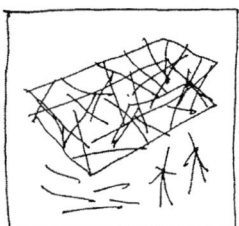
THE PATTERN OF THE RODS CAN BE ANYTHING

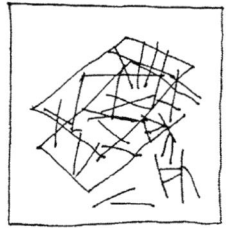
WHEN BUILDING YOU WILL SEE WHERE RODS MIGHT LACK

IT CAN BE A FANCY STRUCTURE COMPLETELY

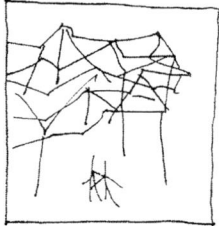
ON THE SITE HAVE FUN WITH IT

PSEUDO-TENSEGRITY

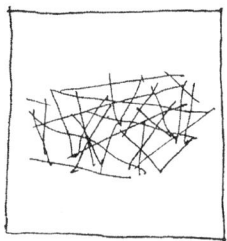
"TENSEGRITY" MEANS A STRUCTURE OF TENSION AND COMPRESSION MEMBERS

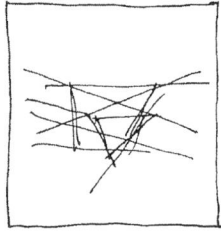
USUALLY IT IS MADE WITH ROPES AND WITH RODS

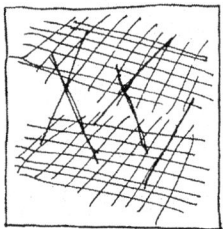
BUT IT CAN BE MADE ALSO WITH SOFT GRIDS AND STIFF COMPRESSION ELEMENTS

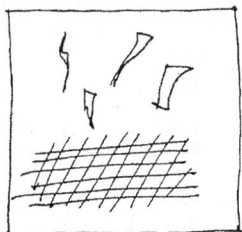
THUS GRIDS SUBSTITUTE THE ROPES AND THE RODS CAN BE OF ANY SHAPE

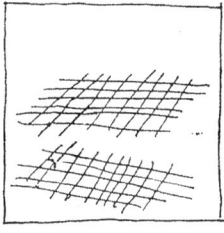
COMPOSITION OF A PSEUDO-TENSEGRITY STARTS WITH TWO LAYERS OF GRIDS

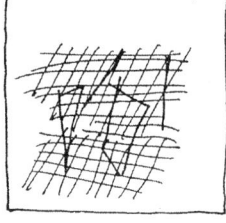
SPANNED WITH THE COMPRESSION MEMBERS

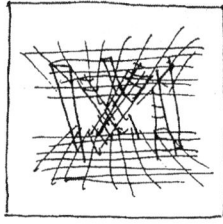
KEPT IN THEIR PLACE BY SMALLER PIECES OF GRID

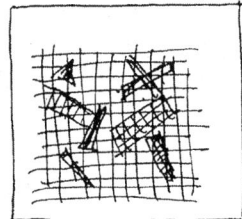
A PSEUDO-TENSEGRITY DOES NOT FOLLOW STRICT GEOMETRIC ORDER

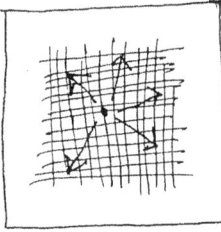
AS A GRID OPPOSITE TO A ROPE-NET DOES NOT IMPOSE PRIVILEGED AXES

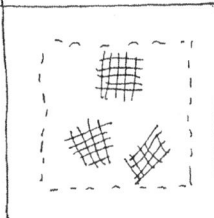
THUS... BOTH THE TENSION MEMBERS

AND THOSE FOR COMPRESSION

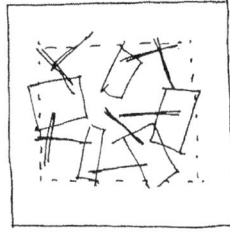
CAN BE DISTRIBUTED IRREGULARLY

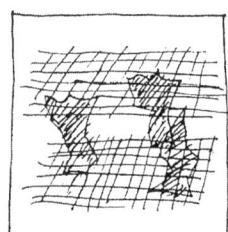
COMPRESSION MEMBERS OF ANY SHAPE

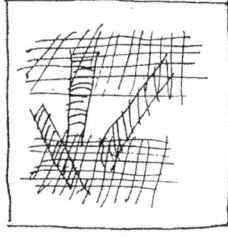
TENSION NETS ALONG ANY PATTERN

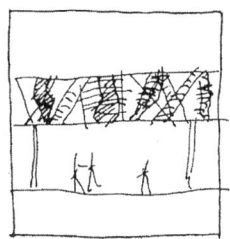
MAKE SUCH A STRUCTURE

INTO A SORT OF ARTIFICIAL JUNGLE

321

322

MERZSTRUKTUREN, 2006

321–**322** Study models for the Cabaret Voltaire in Zurich, Switzerland.
323 Manual *Merzstrukturen*.

MERZ STRUKTUREN

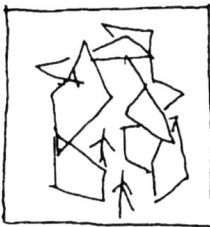
THERE ARE STRUCTURES I CALL "MERZ-STRUKTUREN" AS A HOMMAGE TO THE "MERZBAU" OF KURT SCHWITTERS

THEY ARE CONSTRUCTED FROM ODD PIECES OF ANY MATERIAL: WOOD, METAL, GLASS, CARDBOARD OR PLASTICS

WHICH ARE ASSEMBLED IN WHATEVER WAY THEY CAN FIT

PROVIDED THAT THE STRUCTURE KEEPS UP STANDING

OBVIOUSLY, SUCH STRUCTURES CHARACTERIZE, FIRST OF ALL THE SHANTYTOWNS

WHERE PEOPLE HAVE TO USE, FOR THEIR HOMES, WHATEVER THEY FIND

IN OUR INDUSTRIAL CIVILISATION THE PRODUCT PRODUCED IN THE LARGEST QUANTITY, IS REFUSE, IS INDUSTRIAL FALLOUT

IT IS THE RICHEST RAW MATERIAL OF OUR EPOCH.

WHATEVER YOU WANT TO BUILD YOU CAN FIND MATERIAL FOR IN THE DUSTBINS

IT IS THE MOST PHANTASTIC SHAPES YOU CAN BUILD WITH

SHELTERS..

MONUMENTS

OR SIMPLY EMBELLISHMENTS

YOU CANNOT PLAN, ONLY IMPROVISE

RANDOM COLLECTIONS OF THINGS ASSEMBLED FOR A SPECIFIC GOAL

IS A WAY TO DEFINE "MODERN" (OR WHATEVER) ART

324

325

MONTPARNASSE RAILWAY STATION

324–**326** Photomontages for the Nuit Blanche festival in Paris, 2006.

214 / **PART I** / **THE DILUTION OF ARCHITECTURE** / **TRANSPARENCY**

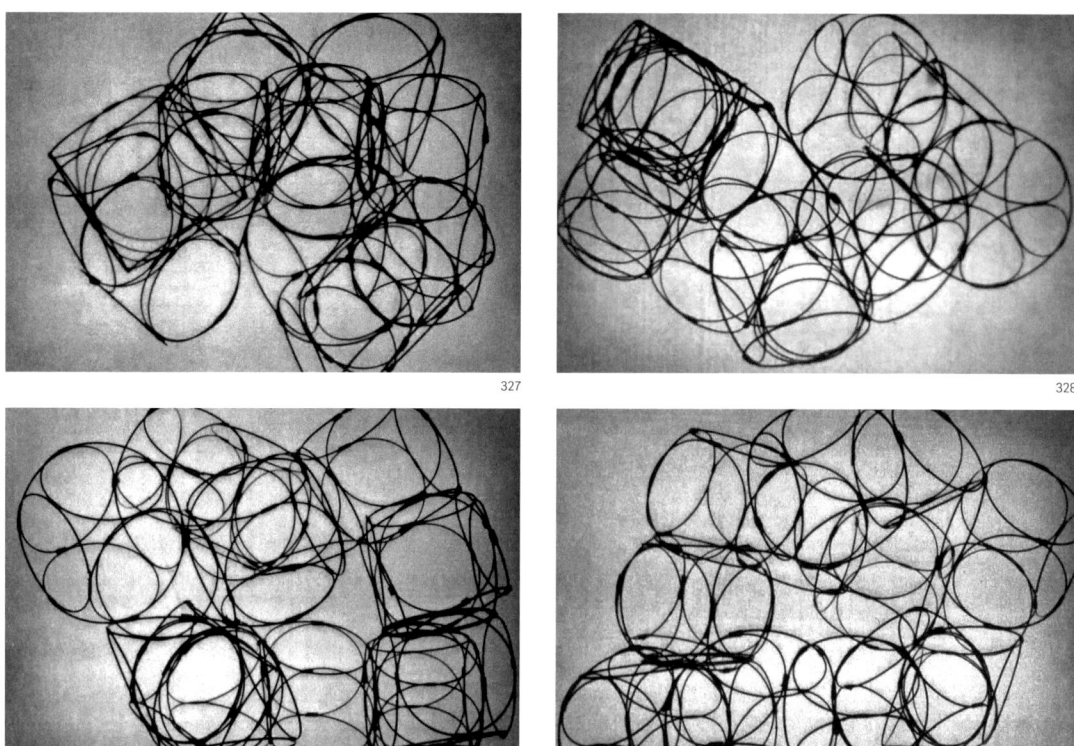

327
328
329
330

PROTEINIC STRUCTURES, 1992

327–**330** Model views, *Irregular Structures* with rings.
331 Manual *Proteinic Chains*.

PROTEINIC CHAINS

YOU CAN BUILD IRREGULAR STRUCTURES SIMPLY WITH RINGS

YOU HAVE TO START WITH REGULAR POLYHEDRA.

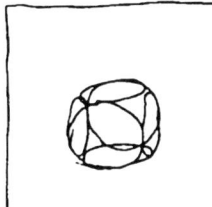

FOR EXAMPLE: A CUBE WHEREIN THE RINGS SUBSTITUTE THE SQUARES

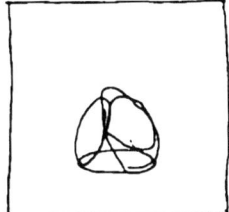

OR A TETRAHEDRON THE TRIANGLES OF WHICH ARE REPRESENTED BY CERCLES

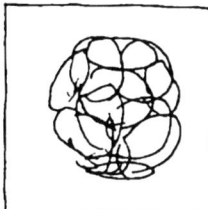

OR A DODECAHEDRON WITH CERCLES FOR ITS PENTAGONS ETC
I CALL THIS TECHNIQUE "SPACE-CHAINS"

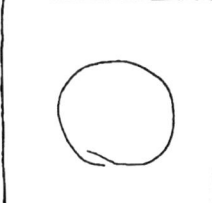

BUT A CERCLE IS AN UNDEFINED POLYGONE:

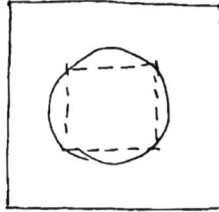

IT CAN STAND FOR A SQUARE

FOR A TRIANGLE

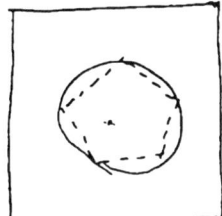

OR FOR A PENTAGONE

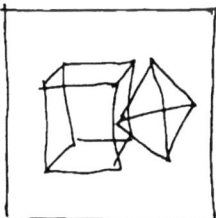

YOU CAN NOT LINK A CUBE TO A TETRAHEDRON (A SQUARE IS NOT A TRIANGLE)

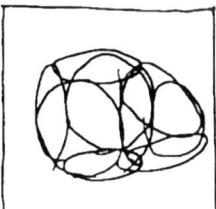

BUT, WITH THE SPACE-CHAIN TECHNIQUE YOU CAN DO IT

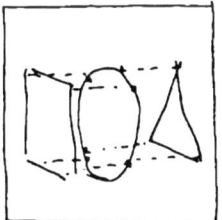

A RING IS A RING: IT CAN BE A SQUARE FROM ONE SIDE AND A TRIANGLE FROM THE OTHER

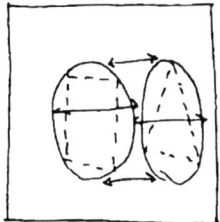

YOU CAN LINK ANY CERCLE-FACED POLYHEDRON TO ANY OTHER

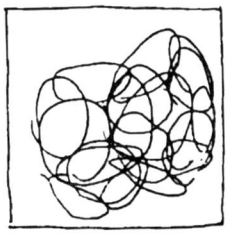

THERE IS NO MORE GEOMETRIC RULE FOR SPACE-CHAINS

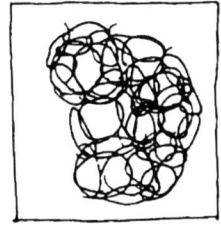

AND WILD COMBINATIONS BECOME POSSIBLE

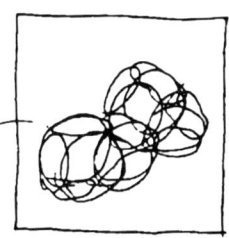

I CALL THESE WILD STRUCTURES "PROTEINIC" ONES

SPACE CHAIN

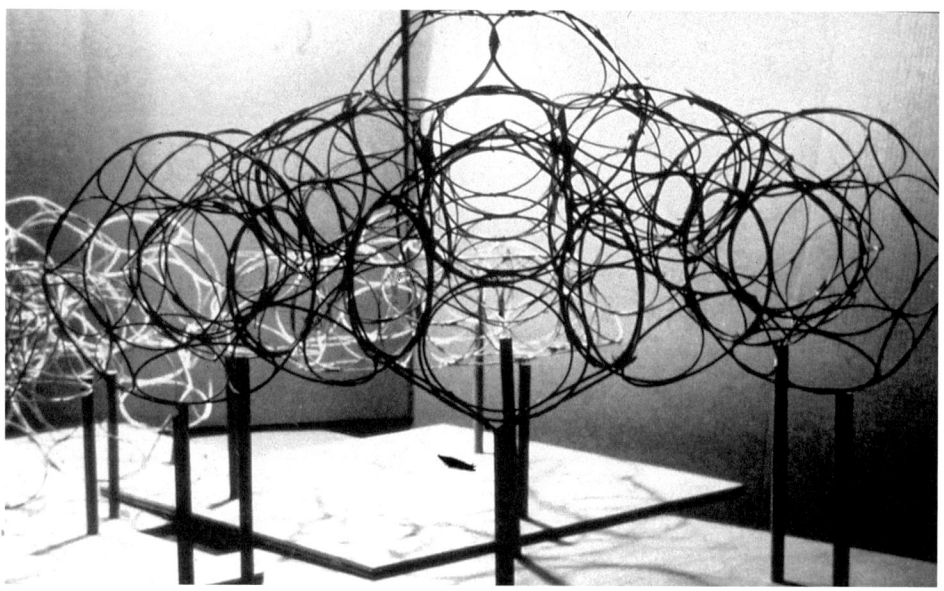

SPACE-CHAIN DOME

332 Model of a *Space-frame* structure made with circles, 1970.
333 *Space-chain Dome*, built by students in Lichtenfels, Germany, c. 1985.
334–340 *Space-chain Dome* in Terrasson, Spain, c. 1985.

334

335

336

337

338

339

340

SPACE CHAIN / 219

SPACE CHAIN - ICONOSTASE

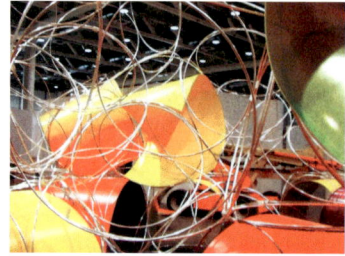

341 342 343

344

SPACE-CHAIN ICONOSTASE, BASEL

341–344 The proposed *Space-chain technique* and local improvisation was implemented for the first time at Art Basel 41 and exhibited by the Gallery Kamel Mennour, Paris, 2010.

ICONOSTASE MUSEUM, WARSAW

345–347 *Proteinic structure Space-chain* proposals for the Museum of Modern Art in Warsaw, Poland, 2011.

345

346

347

348

349

350

351

PROTEINIC MUSEUM, CHATOU

348–**351** Exhibition *Yona Friedman – Musée sans bâtiment*, with three outdoor installations, at the CNEAI, France, 2012.

SPACE-CHAIN MODEL, EPFL, LAUSANNE

352 Exhibition *Yona Friedman – Genesis of a Vision*, at the Archizoom gallery, EPFL, Switzerland, 2012.

353

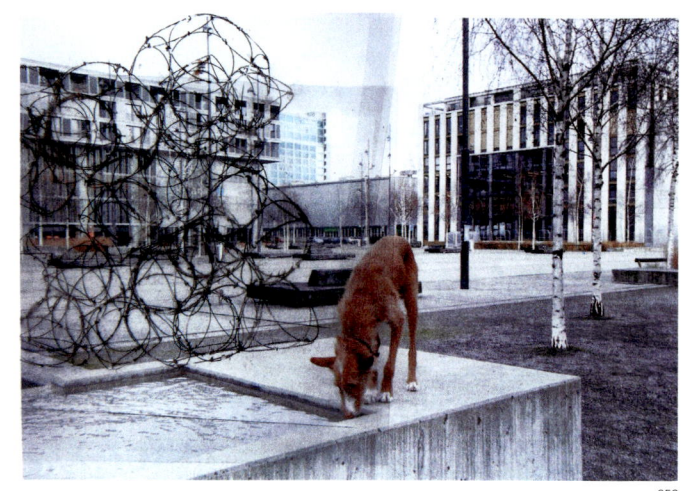

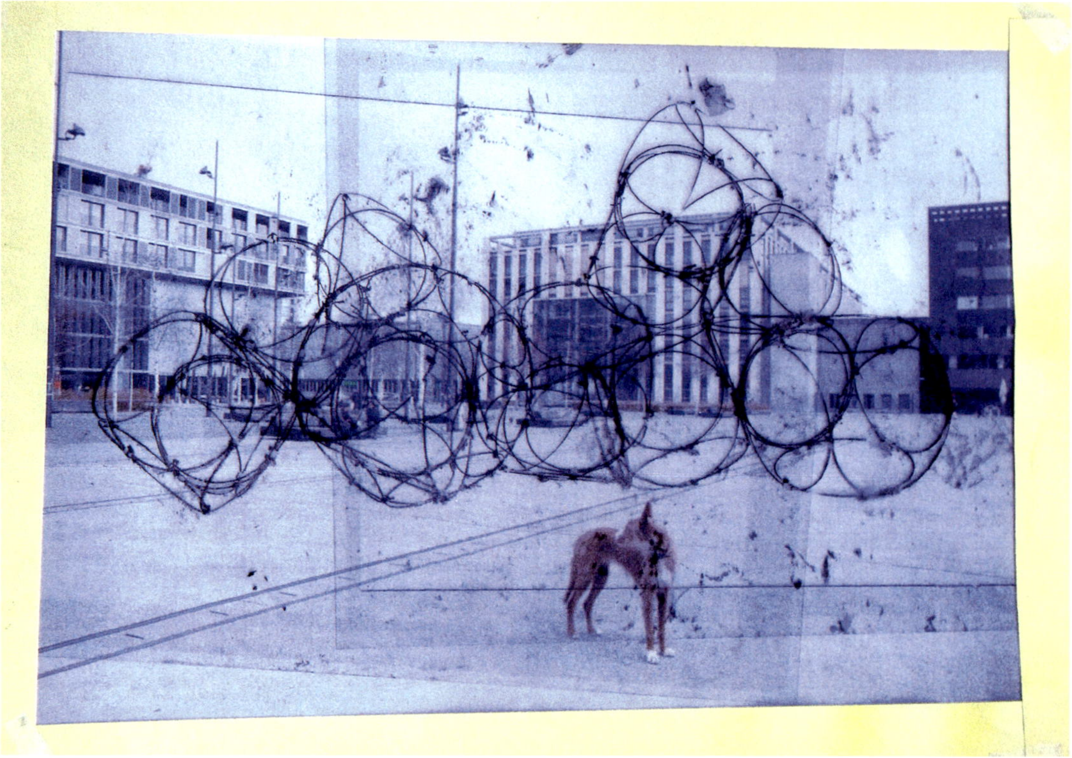

354

PROTEINIC CHAINS, ZURICH

353 – 354 Proposal in Turbinenplatz, during the exhibition *Yona Friedman – Métropole Europe*, 2012.

PROTEINIC CHAINS, BERLIN

355 – 356 Proposition for the Haus Der Zukunft Berlin, Germany, 2012.

355

356

SPACE CHAIN - ICONOSTASE / 225

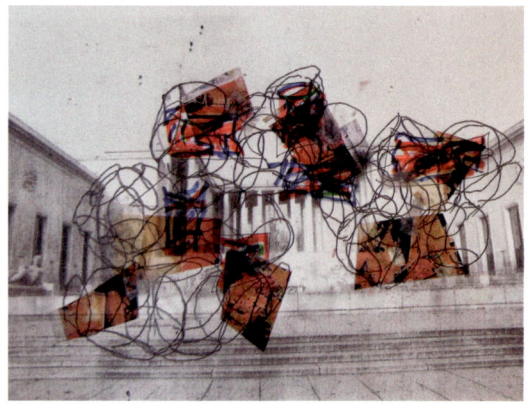

ICONOSTASE, MAM, PARIS

357–359 Proposition for the Musée d'Art Moderne de la Ville de Paris, 2012.

ICONOSTASE, MUAC, MEXICO

360–362 Exhibition *Yona Friedman – Arquitectura sin construcción*,
at the Museo Universitario Arte Contemporáneo in Mexico City, Mexico, 2013.

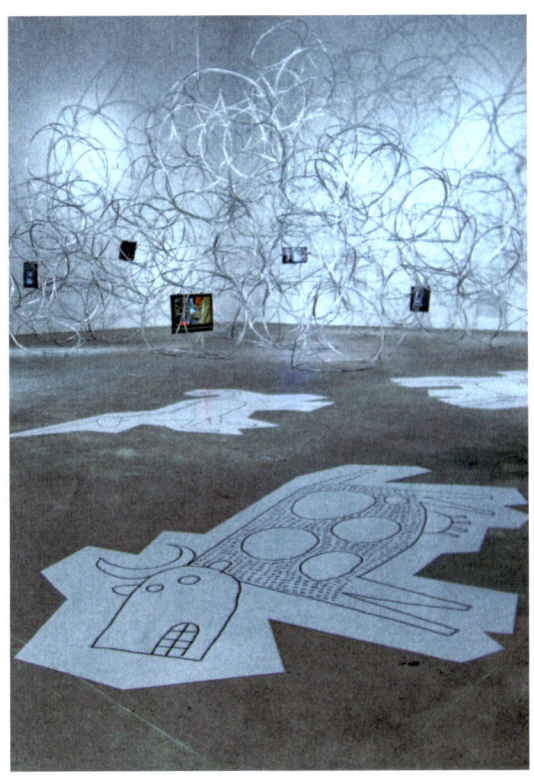

360

361

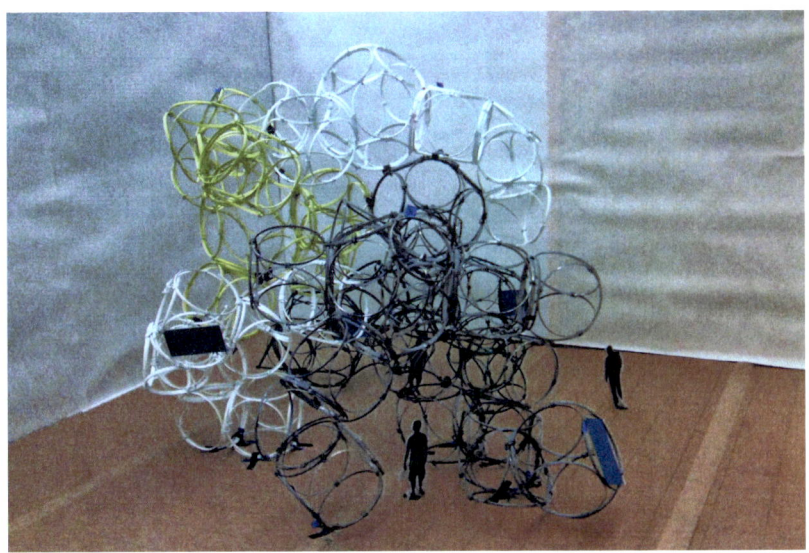

362

SPACE CHAIN - ICONOSTASE / 227

363

364

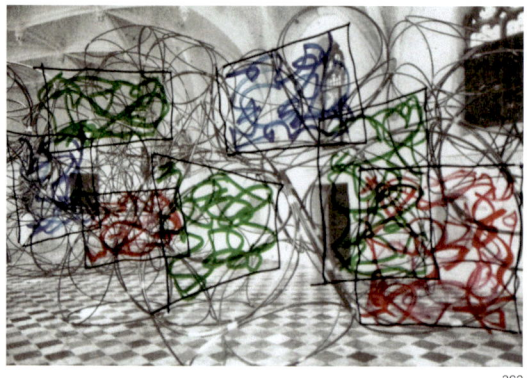

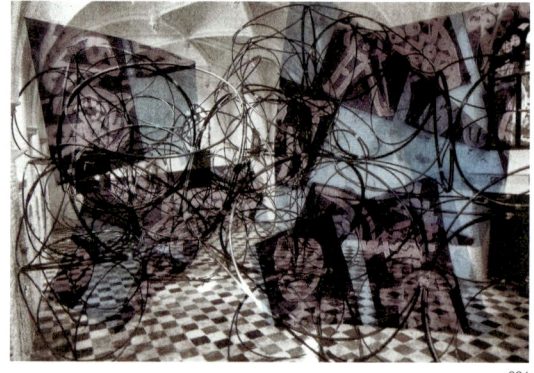

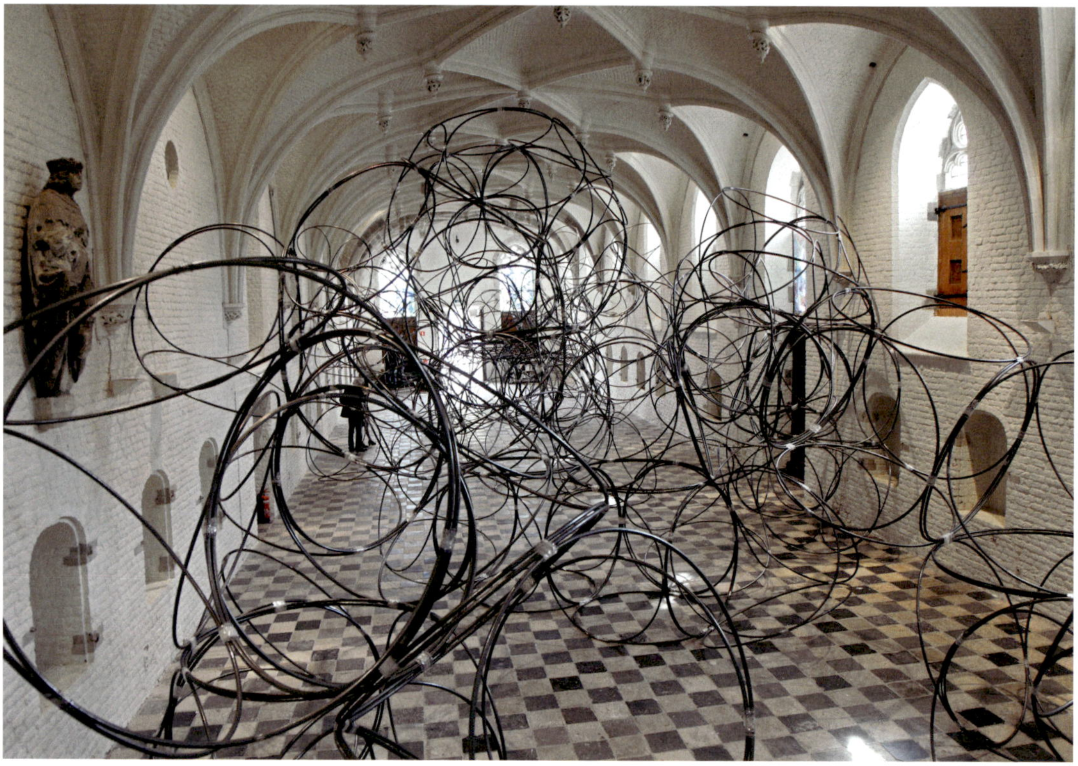

365

ICONOSTASE 150, MIDDELBURG, 2013

363 – 365 Exhibition *Yona Friedman – Architecture without Building*,
at De Vleeshal, Netherlands. Spatial adaptation Jean-Baptiste Decavèle.
366 – 368 *Iconostase 150* at the Royal Academy of Fine Arts in Antwerp, Belgium.

366

367

368

ICONOSTASE 185, ANTINORI, BARGINO

369–373 Installation at the Antinori Familiae Museum, Palazzo Antinori, Florence.
Spatial adaptation Jean-Baptiste Decavèle, 2013.

THE DILUTION OF ARCHITECTURE
ANTHOLOGY OF A PROCESS

5. Dissipated

"Furnitures + more": mini-containers at the level of contained equipment usable with or without the containing structure.

MEUBLES + PLUS

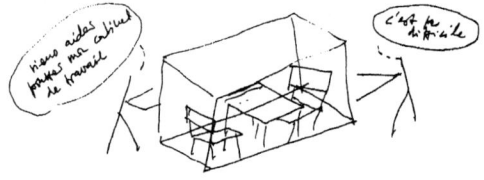

1 / The subject of this project is not really the "mobile house" but more the transformation of the home itself into furniture

2 / Let me try to explain. What we use in a "dwelling" is furniture and equipment, such as a table, a sofa, a bed, cupboards, a bath, a washbasin, a cooker and a fridge

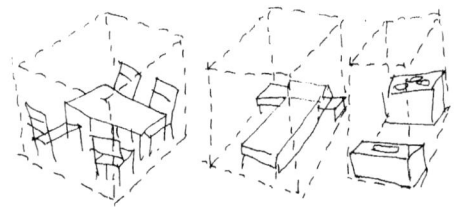

3 / Each of these pieces of furniture implies, around it, a space for use: around the table the room for the chairs, around the bed an access area, and so on for each object used

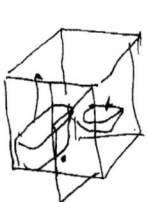 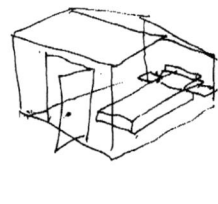

4 / What I am trying to do is contain the equipment and service space within a "quasi-cabin." (We have lots of examples from the past: for example, the four-poster bed is a kiosque, a cabin.) These "quasi-cabins" are in reality pieces of furniture plus their service-area extension. What I am proposing is that we include the furniture and its service extension within a box that is mobile and can be dismantled

FURNITURE WITH ADDED VALUE, 2009

Friedman, Yona: *The Meubles-Plus,* in Rodriguez, Maria Ines (ed.): *Architecture with the People, by the People, for the People,* Coleccion Arte Arquitectura AA MUSAC, 2011, pp. 62–65.

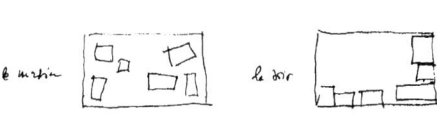 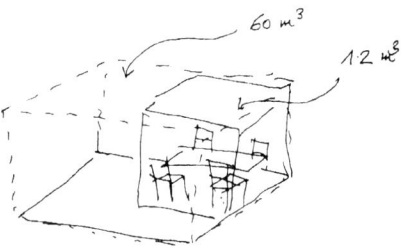

5 / This concept will allow each occupant to reorganize, if required, hour by hour, the plan of his residence, simply by pushing these "meubles-plus" where they are wanted. In the morning, he can create a home with lots of independent spaces (bedrooms) and in the evening, for example, one big room, by pushing all the "meubles-plus" into the corners, thus transforming his home into a ballroom

6 / Apart from mobility, this solution brings energy savings of up to 90 percent. This is because he would heat (or air-condition) only the spaces of the "meuble-plus" and only for the time spent in the cabin. It takes less time to heat the cabin of a piece of "meuble-plus" than to heat (or cool) a car. Likewise, a kitchen, a bathroom, a dining room, a bed, etc. will be heated/cooled only for the time we spend there

 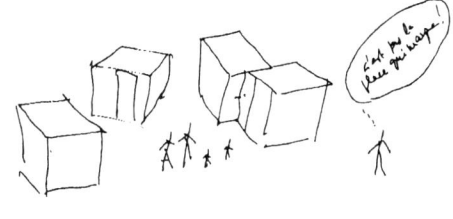

7 / Cardboard boxes give an idea of the volume of the "meubles-plus." You can play with them and compose your own imaginary apartment that will change form for each occasion and whenever you want

8 / "C'est pas la place qui manque!"

THE DILUTION OF ARCHITECTURE
ANTHOLOGY OF A PROCESS

6. "Nature made habitable"

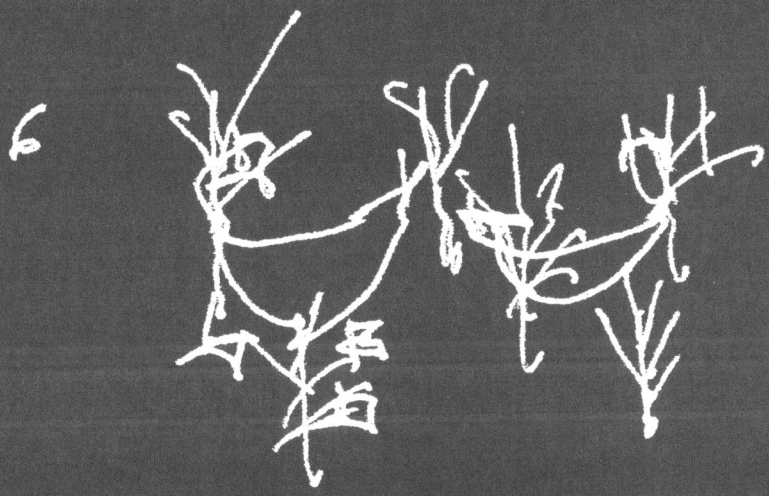

"Nature made habitable" uses trees, shrubs, etc., without making them perish.
It is the plants that replace the structure.

STREET MUSEUM

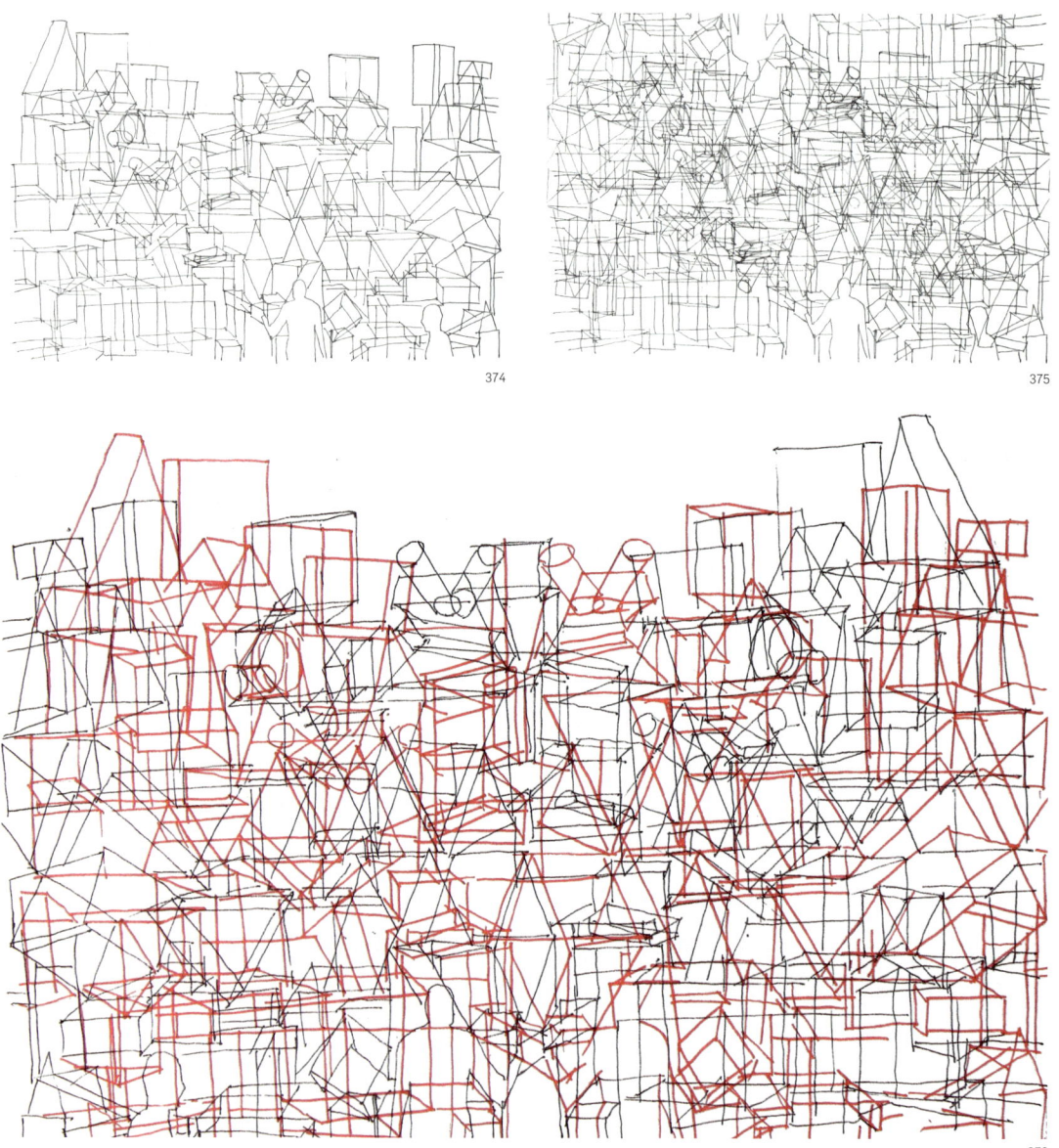

STREET MUSEUM, COMO

374–**375** Drawing series, showing an accumulation of plexiglass boxes and screen vitrines, from 2004.
376–**382** Public outdoor exhibition space during the Festival Corso Superiore di Arti Visive in Como, Italy, 2008.

377

378

379

380

381

382

GRAFFITI MUSEUM

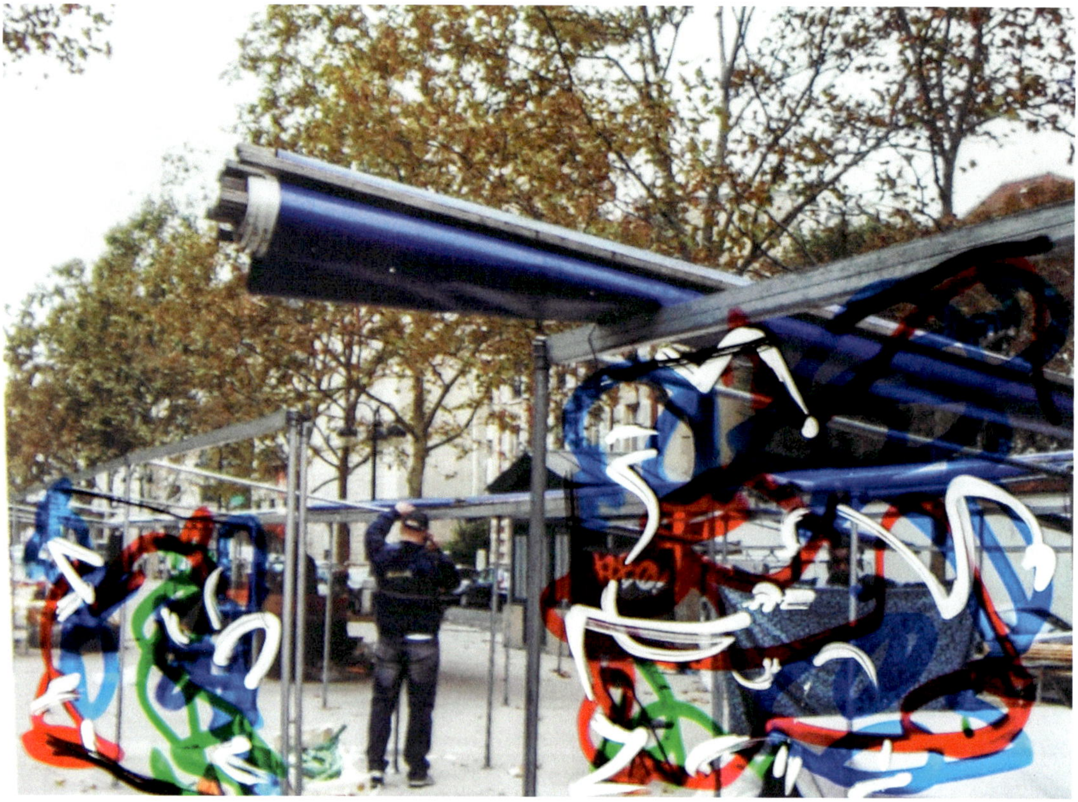

383

384

385

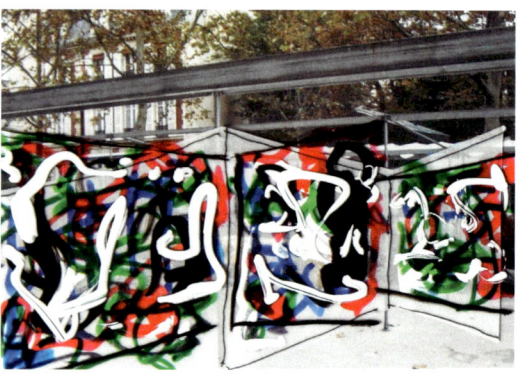

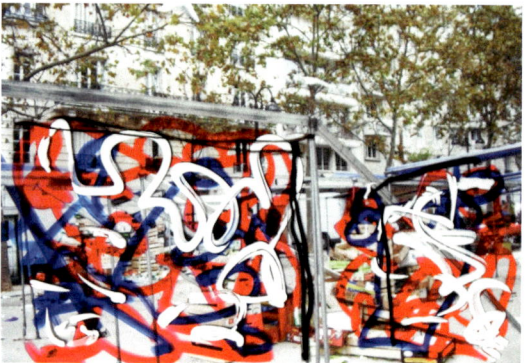

GRAFFITI MARKET, PARIS

383–**385** Drawing on photographs, *Graffiti Market*, Paris, 2006.
386 Montage, *Crumpled Sheet over-roof* system, Palmeraie, Lyon, 2009.
387–**388** *Grafitti Museum* at the Jardin Lilolila, Paris, 2009.

386

388

387

GRAFFITI MUSEUM / 241

INHABITED NATURE

389

MUSEUM OF AFGHAN CIVILIZATION

389 Proposal for a virtual museum, with *Space-chain* structure disposed around the ancient Buddhist caves of Bamiyan, Afghanistan, from 2008.

AMORPHOUS ARCHITECTURE

390 Photomontages, *Amorphous Architecture*, 2009.

Architecture Amorphe 2009

TREE MUSEUM

391

392

ROME–PARIS, C. 2012

391–**392** *Tree museum*, garden of Villa Borghese, Rome.
393–**396** Photomontages, Parc Université de Versailles, Paris.

393

394

395

396

TREE MUSEUM / 245

SHOP-WINDOWS

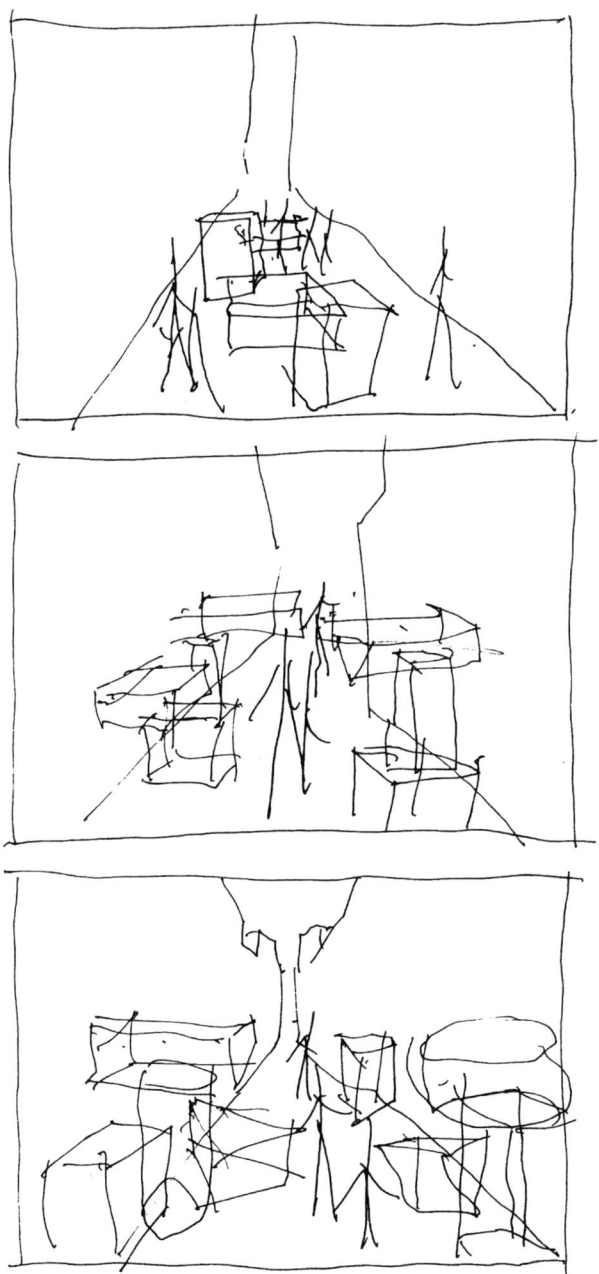

397

VENICE STREET-MUSEUM

397 Sketch, *Venice Street-Museum*, 2012.

Shop-windows, a museum of our civilization.

A museum of a civilization is not an "art-museum". It is rather a collection of everyday objects in everyday use: the civilization itself in the complex behaviors, the way how such objects are used, the social and cultural signification of such objects. An object, becoming merchandise, is different from an object randomly found.

Anthropologists and archeologists build up their images and theories about past civilizations through artifacts they find at excavation sites. A half-burnt tome at the site of a neolithic encampment triggers theories about neolithic lifestyle. Objects found in tombs are the revered treasure of large museum collections. But, as for the real value of these funds for the society which produced them, we can only guess.

Let us think about the traces of our civilization, traces that be found by generations succeeding ours. Could we ourselves "prepare" these traces, for example, have the characteristic objects accompanied by indication about their contemporary value, by instruction on how they were supposed to be used, by documents enhancing their appeal to contemporary public?

Yes, we could. All these informations are contained in shop window displays: price, technical information, advertisement. Shop-window displays are museum-ready.

There is also another advantage for the present. You don't have to pay a ticket for looking at such displays, neither to go and look at during "visiting hours". It is open for everybody, day and night, all days of the week. There is no necessity to build, for that kind of museum, a building specialized. They don't need, for the visitor, heating or weather protection: you can look at window-displays using your own umbrella to protect you.

But, there is one point I have to add to this project. Shopwindows have generally exclusively commercial motivation. Could we install also shopwindows for art, for ideas, for culture. Separately, or associated with the merchants display, for example, convening with shopowners to present, as a part of their display also works of art, cultural manifestos etc? An appropriate tax-policy could facilitate this approach.

The street as the museum of a civilization is a realist idea. I had the occasion to test it in various cities: it can be done.

The next step is with you!

A MUSEUM IS NOT A BUILDING

1 / These are the exhibits that make a museum

2 / The building itself is expensive and superfluous

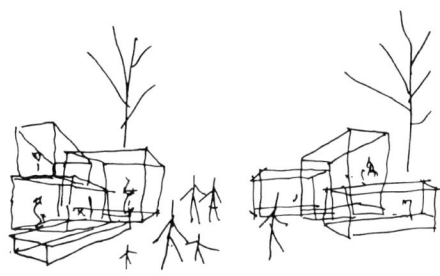

3 / You can create a museum without a building

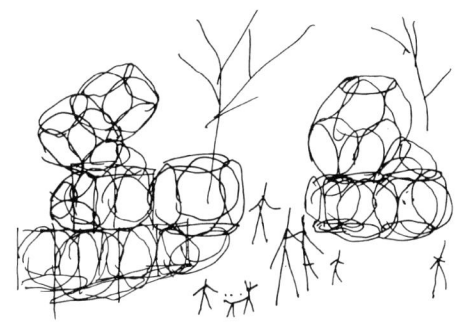

4 / A scaffolding supporting exhibits can do it

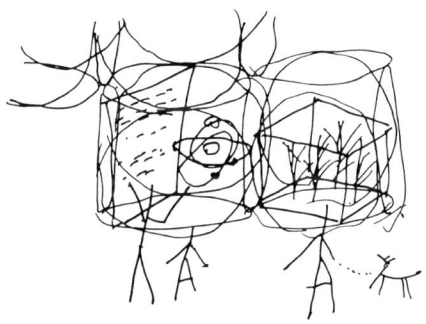

5 / Simply within a weathertight showcase or on panels protected by plexiglass

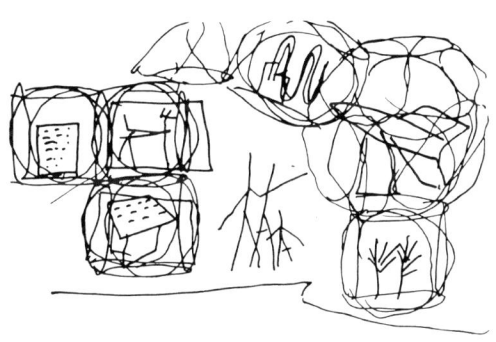

6 / You can insert the exhibits into the scaffolding

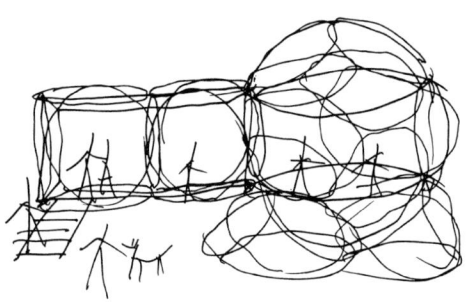

7 / You can even insert whole rooms

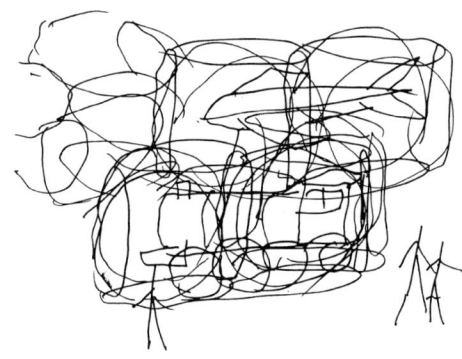

8 / Or present the exhibits directly (those which don't need weather protection)

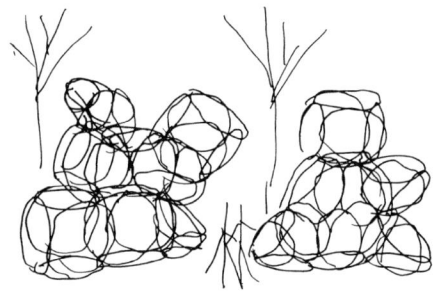

9 / A "space-chain" scaffolding permits a great variety of shapes

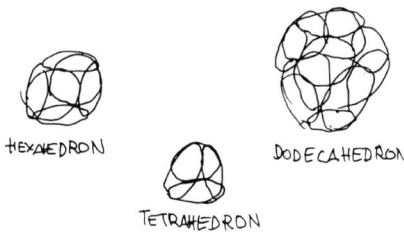

10 / A "space-chain" is built with a few basic volumes

11 / A "space-chain" scaffolding is easy to shape or reshape from one exhibition to another

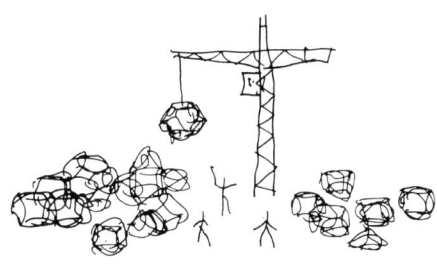

12 / A couple of fixed cranes can make handling easy, even for large scaffoldings

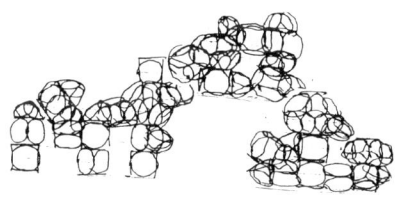

13 / "Space-chain" scaffolding can be combined into hundreds of patterns without following a particular geometry

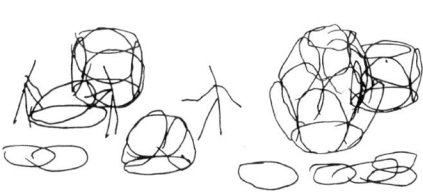

14 / Floor plans are not predetermined, you can improvise them

15 / The future is unpredictable, museum programs might change

16 / Both exhibits and exposition patterns always have to be renewed

17 / An exhibition without building can be open to the public 24 hours a day

18 / Involving less building costs, less watchmen, less costs for light, for heating. Why waste public money?

THE DILUTION OF ARCHITECTURE
ANTHOLOGY OF A PROCESS

7. The Labyrinth

The "labyrinth" is an organization of space, without introducing any change into it.

THE LABYRINTH

398

NAGASAKI COMPETITION, JAPAN, 1996

398 Top view of the *Span-over Labyrinth*.
399–400 Photomontage of the proposal designed for public use and conceived with a regular *Space-chain* structure.

399

400

THE LABYRINTH / 257

THE DILUTION OF ARCHITECTURE
ANTHOLOGY OF A PROCESS

8. Build less

*These techniques can be coordinated with one another, building less and less.
Wow! The cows...*

ARCHITECTURE WITHOUT BUILDING

1 / Architecture without building

2 / We surely build too much

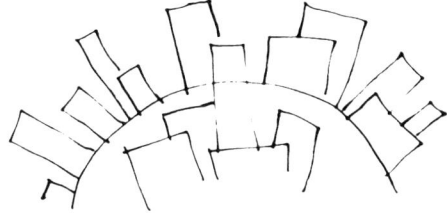

3 / Earth is overbuilt

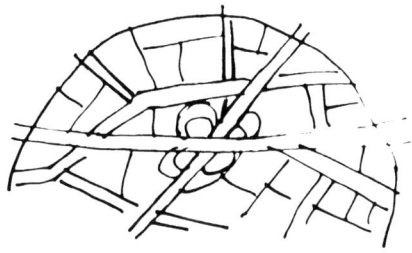

4 / Earth is overplanned

5 / Earth is overfarmed

6 / Are all these buildings really necessary?

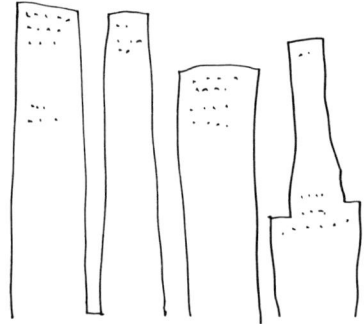

7 / We build gigantic office towers?

8 / This does not mean that we don't need architects, planners and farmers

9 / But we have to change rules

10 / There are many functions for which buildings are not indispensable

11 / Office workers, for example, need computers and not premises

12 / They can work at home

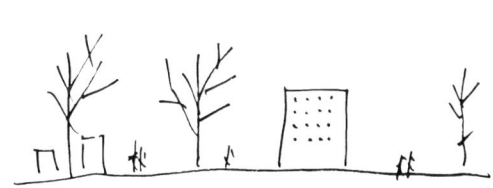

13 / We could build less offices

14 / You surely need your home but it is better if you design it yourself

15 / And put it together with container-like boxes

16 / The same with many public services

17 / Museum exhibits could be displayed in the street

18 / Assemblies can be held anywhere, they don't need large expensive halls

19 / Markets are often in the open

20 / Non-built functional supports can be designed by architects

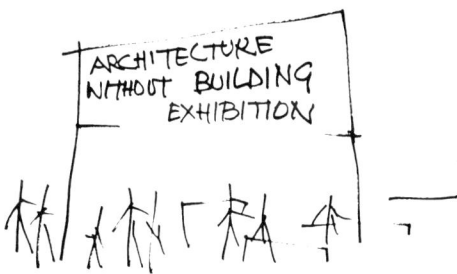

21 / The proposed exhibition presents such non-built supports

PART II
Manuel Orazi
THE ERRATIC UNIVERSE
OF YONA FRIEDMAN

TRANSLATED FROM THE ITALIAN BY HUW EVANS

PROLOGUE

The growing emphasis on specialization in architecture – from product design to landscape urbanism – has made it hard for us to understand Yona Friedman's work, inspired as it is by a constant vocation for essay writing in its purest form, free that is of apparatus like notes, citations or bibliographies. One of the most difficult to classify authors of the 20th century, Friedman's unsystematic multiplicity of interests is redeemed or masked by his plain and rational, deeply logical style of writing – for that matter "a simple language that everyone can understand is of primary importance in achieving this self-planning,"[1] i.e. the theme which more than any other has guided his theoretical production. A strictly subjective point of view, sincerity, the occasional and concretely singular nature of his approach, a sometimes ingenuous and unrealistic dilettantism and rejection of specialism that nevertheless permit a flexible adherence to the subject and to tangible experience: all these are typical of Yona Friedman. Taken as a whole, however, his work retains a sense of something precarious, equivocal and under threat, of something elegantly perplexed and ready to compromise, but always generous: his subjective and moral (or political) commitment has always driven the architect of Hungarian origin out of the territory assigned to each specific disciplinary field, just as it did his first teacher, Károly Kerényi. For this reason up until today Friedman has remained confined to a footnote in architectural historiography and his multiple intellectual connections outside the field of architecture, ranging from the physicist Werner Heisenberg to the theorists of the Situationist movement, have to a large extent been left unexplored.

This study attempts to analyze Friedman's work, following him in his progress through disciplinary and geographic areas apparently remote from one another, areas in which he has moved erratically and incessantly.

It is divided into three chapters: in the first are reconstructed the different historical contexts of his development – wholly undervalued up to now – from the Hungary of the Horthy regime to the Palestine of the British mandate, from the humiliation of the revocation of his civil rights to his joining one of the few Jewish groups of resistance to the Nazi occupation, and then from the state of refugee to his arrival in the Promised Land, in Eretz Israel, where a completely new society was ready to welcome him, but also to request his immediate engagement in another conflict. It was in these settings that a number of encounters decisive to the intellectual formation of the young Friedman took place: the lectures on physics and mythology given in Budapest by two outstanding figures in 20th century culture, his apprenticeship with an architect like Lajos Kozma, who at the time received no professional commissions, and then his technical studies in Haifa, his encounter with Zionist ideology and his debut on the international architectural scene at the CIAM in Dubrovnik.

---

1 FRIEDMAN, Yona: *Utopies réalisables*, Paris, Union générale d'éditions, 1975. Enlarged ed., Paris, Editions de l'Eclat 2000. Available online at http://www.fichier-pdf.fr/2012/07/20/utopies3/utopies3.pdf, p. 135.

The second chapter analyzes the development of Friedman's theoretical ideas and their dissemination through the identification of some key passages: a giddy series of publications, exhibitions, conferences and lectures followed his definitive move to Paris in September 1957, making him a fairly well-known figure in architecture, especially within the debate over megastructures. In this way Friedman, flanked from time to time by a series of secondary figures, established relations with a large number of architects and city planners, but it can be noted how, progressively, through a continuous series of shifts in focus, his field of intellectual action broadened, leading him to choose as interlocutors figures increasingly removed from architecture as it is traditionally understood, from Constant to Nicholas Negroponte. Friedman in fact has constantly been looking for a new role for the architect, whose crisis of identity and growing marginality in society he had sensed with clarity and disquiet ever since the fifties: this is the guiding thread that runs all the way through the second chapter.

The third section tackles instead the more mature work of the Franco-Hungarian architect, dating from the time when he put aside his interest in technology in order to concentrate on the study of society and the advantages of self-determination. His only building, a school in Angers, was realized on the principle of self-planning. It falls within the theme of participation in architecture, an elusive and problematic question but one that cannot be avoided by someone like Friedman, who has always wanted to renew his discipline root and branch. The long interview that follows has been of great value to the conduct of my research, as in it Friedman talks of themes and authors never mentioned before, especially with regard to his training, of which very few documents have survived.[2] Stefano Graziani's photographic essay on Friedman's home is intended to demonstrate the consistency between his theoretical positions and his individual practice in daily life. In addition, the appendix contains a number of documents that serve to confirm intellectual relations which have been important both to his development and to the reception of his ideas on the part of the members of a younger generation of architects like Bernard Tschumi. Finally the bibliography that closes this thesis – the first to have been compiled analytically – is arranged in chronological order in order to reveal the evolution of Friedman's research and the fluctuation in the interest shown in him by the critics over the course of the years.

When Yona Friedman took part, as an Israeli architect who had not been officially invited, in the CIAM in Dubrovnik of 1956, he was unknown. Within very few years his principle of *L'architecture mobile* and his projects of *Urbanisme spatial* would be greeted with interest and published in the principal international magazines of architecture, anticipating and influencing utopian and radical neo-avant-gardes like the British Archigram or Japanese Metabolism as well as a multitude of major and minor figures. Years later Reyner Banham would define the sixties as the age of the megastructure, in other words of the design of large,

---

[2] "History is fashioned on the basis of written documents, of course. When there are any. But it can and must be fashioned even without written documents if none is available. Then it can be made out of anything that the historian's ingenuity may lead him to employ, in order to make his honey, supposing he finds none of the usual flowers. Words, signs, landscapes…." FEBVRE, Lucien: *Vers une autre histoire*, in *Revue de Métaphysique et de Morale*, LVIII, 1949. English transl., *A New Kind Of History*, in id., *A New kind of History and Other Essays*, New York, Harper & Rowe, 1973, p. 34.

high-tech, multifunctional and extendable structures on an urban scale,[3] while Manfredo Tafuri would speak of an "academy of utopia"[4] in which Friedman could be included, too. Many still consider him a "naïve" utopian, not least Rem Koolhaas who has no hesitation in dismissing him as the emblem of the happy-go-lucky neo-Futurist avant-gardes of the early 1960s: "Yona Friedman's *urbanisme spatial* (1958) was emblematic: Bigness floats over Paris like a metallic blanket of clouds, promising unlimited but unfocused potential renewal of 'everything', but never lands, never confronts, never claims its rightful place – criticism as decoration."[5] And yet Friedman cannot really be lumped together with the other followers of "mega-fashion" owing to some significant differences that only a few, such as Alan Colquhoun, were able to grasp at the time. Up until today, Friedman provocatively claims that the *Ville Spatiale* was not a megastructure, for unlike other megastructures, it implicated the participation and auto-determination of its inhabitants. This remark echoes that of a radically different architect: Robert Venturi (who in *Learning from Las Vegas*, and together with Denise Scott Brown, wrote what may be considered as the harshest critique of the megastructure). As is well known, Venturi recently claimed, "I am not now and never have been a Postmodernist." In the same manner, Friedman, just like Venturi, "unequivocally disavows fatherhood of this architectural movement."

In any case, when the period of fascination with the megastructure came to an end, partly as a result of the publication in 1966 of two such key texts of contemporary architectural culture such as *Complexity and Contradiction in Architecture*[6] and *L'architettura della città*[7], the figure of Yona Friedman was eclipsed to the point where he almost vanished, as did so many others after the autonomy of the discipline gained the upper hand and the subsequent emergence of the "postmodern."

For he was not the only one: it suffices to cite the case of the parallel revival of Superstudio (exhibitions in London and New York in 2004 and 2005) or Archizoom, although both the Florentine Radical groups have little to do with Friedman's work. However, the Hungarian architect and theorist represents a different sort of revival, not so much because he is included in the personal genealogies of some contemporary architects as because he has been rediscovered by contemporary artistic culture. In this sphere in fact there is a growing tendency to regard the viewers as being as important as the artists and the objects they produce (pictures, sculptures, etc.); as a consequence it is the process of involvement of the public/viewer that has played a crucial role in the most recent evolution of contemporary art. In other words the spectator becomes actor (artist) and vice versa – see Friedman's participations[8] in Documenta at Kassel in 2001 and in the Venice Biennale of Visual Arts

---

3 BANHAM, Reyner: *Megastructure. Urban Future of the Recent Past*, London, Thames & Hudson, 1976.
4 TAFURI, Manfredo and DAL CO, Francesco: *Architettura contemporanea*, Milan, Electa, 1976; rpt. 1988, p. 347.
5 KOOLHAAS, Rem: *Bigness or the Problem of Large*, in id. and MAU, Bruce: *S,M,L,XL*, ed. by Jennifer Siegler, New York, The Monacelli Press, 1995, p. 504.
6 VENTURI, Robert: *Complexity and Contradiction in Architecture*, New York, Museum of Modern Art, 1966.
7 Rossi, Aldo *L'architettura della città*. Padua, Marsilio, 1966; new ed., Macerata, Quodlibet, 2011. English transl., *The Architecture of the City*, Cambridge (MA), MIT Press, 1984.
8 "I like to regard art as a communication; as a consequence I consider the receiver (the person who views, the person who receives the vision) more important than the transmitter (the artist)." FRIEDMAN, Yona: *L'architecture de survie, où s'invente aujourd'hui le monde de demain*, foreword by Michel Ragon, Paris–Tournai, Casterman, 1978. Revised and enlarged ed., *L'architecture de survie. Une philosophie de la pauvreté*, Paris, Editions de l'Eclat, 2003, p. 193.

in 2003, 2005 and 2009 at the invitation of curators like Catherine David,[9] Hans Ulrich Obrist[10] or Daniel Birnbaum. In any case, Friedman's work has never been taken into consideration as a whole and it is partly for this reason that he has made such an unexpected comeback, almost as if he were a rather elderly newcomer with a somewhat faded past in architecture. Yet Friedman never regarded himself as an artist, at least not in the sense in which this is traditionally understood.

Among the numerous theoretical texts published by Friedman – in various fields, from sociology to physics – is *Utopies réalisables* ("Feasible Utopias," written in 1974), a title that is an apparent contradiction in terms, but "believing in a utopia and being, at the same time, a realist is not a contradiction. A utopia is, *par excellence*, feasible,"[11] and becomes so if it obtains a collective consensus. Friedman is speaking of social utopias and this interest in society, in the theme of social utility, is perhaps the principal line of continuity that runs through his many-sided, Leonardesque theoretical and design activity. So his attitude is not that of a utopian of future city planning amusing himself (Dorfles[12]), of someone who "spurns the present for a desperate leaning towards anticipations of cathartic flavor" (Tafuri[13]), but a utopian realism or a *utopia of reality* (Rogers[14]) dictated by the urgency of contingent social problems, such as temporary housing for refugees. In other words Friedman, who in his life has firsthandedly witnessed at the destruction of a Central European society like that of Hungary and then played an active part in the building of a society from scratch in Israel, places the social element at the center of all his work, and this is what differentiates him from many of the purely artistic personalities with whom he has been compared, from Constant (Banham) to Schwitters (Obrist). The question of the use of architecture as a means of social and not just material reconstruction is something Friedman has in common with many architects who were trained during or after the Second World War and gravitated around Team 10, from Alison and Peter Smithson to Shadrach Woods, Giancarlo De Carlo, Georges Candilis, Denise Scott Brown and others.

Few like Friedman, however, have been able to experience in the field the construction of a completely new society like that of the state of Israel, and if "a society is a utopia put into effect" then Israel is certainly one of the most blatant examples. Zionism, especially in Martin Buber's cultural version of the movement (also known as utopian Zionism), is therefore a factor to be borne in mind when interpreting Friedman's work and the theme of mobility, so important to the architectural debate of the fifties and also at the base of his manifesto *L'architecture mobile*, is a traditionally Jewish theme.

---

9   David, Catherine and Chevrier, Jean-François (eds.): *Politics-Poetics. Documenta 10, The Book*, Ostfildern, Cantz, 1997.
10 Obrist, Hans-Ulrich: *Interviews*, vol. I, Milan, Charta, 2003. It is no coincidence that Obrist was able to invite Friedman to the Venice Biennale of 2003, directed by Francesco Bonami; see Bonami, Francesco and Frisa, Maria Luisa (eds.): *Sogni e conflitti: la dittatura dello spettatore*, Venice, Marsilio, 2003. English transl., *Dreams and Conflicts: The Viewer's Dictatorship*. New York, Rizzoli, 2003.
11 Friedman, Yona: *Utopies réalisables*, op. cit., p. 14.
12 Dorfles, Gillo: *Dal significato alle scelte*, Turin, Einaudi, 1973, p. 148.
13 Tafuri, Manfredo: *La nuova dimensione urbana e la funzione dell'utopia*, in *L'architettura. Cronache e storia*, yr. XI, no. 124, February 1966, pp. 680–83.
14 "It is a matter of putting the concept of utopia into effect: of thinking in a concrete way about a better society (certainly not a world made up solely of the honest, solely of the beautiful and good, but a world constructed with real means for real ends)."
    Nathan Rogers, Ernesto: *Utopia della realità* (1962), now in id., *Editoriali di architettura*, Turin, Einaudi, 1968, p. 269.

Finally Friedman is one of the few great producers of concepts, which for Deleuze ought to be the task of the philosopher: in a historical period like the present one, in which a theory is viewed almost as a hindrance to the practice of the profession and total realism as the only possibility of action, Friedman's substantial work stands out as a sort of humanist bulwark against professional cynicism on the one hand and against the intellectual poverty of the architectural star system on the other.

To conclude, this monographic study examines the body of Yona Friedman's work as a whole, looking at some precise theoretical and design aspects through a reconstruction of the individual contexts of reference that have made it possible for him to follow his individual course. In other words it is an attempt at a biography "reconstructed in context," according to the definition given by Jacques Revel [15], or, to put it another way, at a partial intellectual biography written *on a knife's edge*, between detachment and sympathy. On this subject, the great historian of Rennaissance Humanism, Eugenio Garin, has written:

Anyone with experience of historical research is well aware of how institutions, events and ideas sometimes appear to become more condensed than usual and take on substance "in the thoughts and feelings of men," and not be exhausted in "universal and generalized things." Trying to represent those men is certainly not easy, but well worth the attempt. [16]

---

15 REVEL, Jacques: *La biographie comme problème historiographique*, in BÖDEKER, Hans Erich (ed.): *Biographie schreiben*, Göttingen, Wallstein Verlag, 2003, pp. 327– 48.
16 GARIN, Eugenio: *Ritratti di umanisti*, Florence, Sansoni, 1967; rpt., Milan, Bompiani, 2001, p. 7.

We do not believe in the utility of derivations. Alliances are more important than derivations.

Deleuze, Gilles: *Un manifeste de moins,* in Bene, Carmelo and Deleuze, Gilles: *Superpositions,* Paris, Minuit, 1979, p. 94.

1. THE EARLY YEARS

HUNGARIAN "FALSE FASCISM"

At first sight Hungary between the two world wars presents a number of parallels with Italian history. An authoritarian government in the fascist mold led by Admiral Miklós Horthy put an end to the domestic political turbulence of the period following the First World War and within the space of two decades brought Hungary into alliance with Germany in the Second World War, introducing racial laws, until the country was occupied by the Nazis following an attempt to sign an armistice with the Allies. After liberation, the head of state, Horthy, went into exile in Portugal.

In reality, however, the differences are considerable: following the dismemberment of the Habsburg Empire, the Treaty of Trianon in 1920 recognized first of all the independence of Czechoslovakia and Serbia, rewarding countries that were allied with the victors like Romania. This was largely at the expense of Hungary, which was stripped of two thirds of its territory, losing its access to the sea (i.e. the city of Rijeka in Croatia) and large regions in the east (Transylvania) and north (Slovakia), resulting in a reduction in its population from 20.9 to 7.6 million. As a consequence almost every new neighboring state ended up with a sizeable minority of Hungarian-speaking people among its citizens, over three million of them in all. From the economic viewpoint it was a very heavy blow: 61.4% of the cultivable land, 62.2% of the railroads, 55.7% of the industrial plant and 67% of the banks of the former Kingdom of Hungary fell under the sovereignty of other nations. The army was drastically dismantled along much the same lines as the German one. This dismemberment, which has few historical precedents, was the main cause of political instability in Hungary between the wars.[17]

In any case, on November 15, 1918, a republic was proclaimed and the National Council assumed the functions of a parliament until the elections scheduled for the spring. Mihály Károlyi formed a provisional coalition government, but it was divided on every single plan of reform, from that of the electoral system to freedom of the press and expression, but above all on agrarian reform, by far the most urgent problem. The situation was exacerbated by the incessant arrival of bad news from the negotiations with neighboring countries over the new Hungarian borders, which roused the demagogy of agitators on the right and the left. The newly formed Hungarian Communist Party led by Béla Kun gained the most advantage from this situation, playing on the discontent of a working class now left without jobs, as well as on the patriotic indignation stirred by the harsh conditions of the peace treaty. In parallel, in Berlin in January 1919, the members of the Spartacus League (*Spartakusbund*), later to be renamed the German Communist Party (KPD), tried to incite a revolution, but it was harshly put down by the Social Democratic chancellor Ebert, culminating in the execution of its leaders Rosa Luxemburg and Karl Liebknecht. In Budapest on the other hand, Károlyi's provisional government, undermined by the poor outcome of the Treaty

---

17 Fejtő, François: *Requiem pour un empire défunt*, Paris, Lieu Commun, 1988.

of Versailles and by now incapable of maintaining public order, was followed by a hundred and thirty-three days of communist rule and the end of a democratic and independent Hungarian country. Kun was an adroit rabble-rouser, but did not lack pragmatism: with limited forces at his disposal he did not hesitate to merge the two workers' parties, the Communists and Social Democrats, despite Lenin's contrary view, to turn Hungary into a "Republic of Councils." Thus the Hungarian dictatorship of the proletariat had a hybrid character and partly for this reason met with very little resistance in the beginning: neither the police nor what was left of the army put up opposition. The workers, naturally, the Agrarian Party which hoped for a drastic reduction in the size of the large landed estates and even the middle class fell under the spell of the egalitarian utopia. The Hungarian variety of communism represented, especially at that moment, after defeat in the war, a reaction against the errors of the Habsburg *ancien régime*. And yet the role played by intellectuals was not unimportant: the majority of them supported the regime of the soviets, at least at the outset. The egalitarian utopia also seduced that part of the intelligentsia which had been pacifist, democratic and unhappy with the previous social inequalities, in part because their support gave them the sensation of "being on the right side of history."

In addition, the biggest names in literature and the arts, Gyula Juhász, Gyula Krudy, Zsigmond Móricz, Mihály Babits, Lajos Kassák, Frigyes Karinthy, Jenö Heltai, Béla Bartók, Zoltán Kodály, Ernö Dohnányi and Alexander Korda, gave their support following the reassurances of the people placed in charge of cultural affairs. These appointees, being influential figures like György Lukács and Zsigmond Kunfi, offered many guarantees. In 1919 Lukács was already known for two books that had stirred a great deal of discussion all over Europe, *Soul and Form* [18] and *The Theory of the Novel* [19]. Lukács, a critic and cultural historian, placed at the center of his interest the relationship between art and society, between form and life, even before embracing Marxism, which he did immediately after the October Revolution.

Among the first measures taken by Béla Kun [20], head of the united party, commander-in-chief of the army and commissar for foreign affairs, was to place the wages of manual and clerical workers on the same level. Other socialist norms were introduced in matters of health, education and labor law. The Republic of the Councils did not lead to popular violence against the bourgeoisie, landowners and the clergy. The regime itself was not responsible for repressive atrocities like in Russia. The paramilitary corps called Léninfiuk ("Sons of Lenin"), analogous to the Italian Fascist secret police force known as the Ceka, did kill people –a few hundred– but on a much smaller scale than the Hungarian White Terror that was to follow shortly afterwards. [21]

---

18 Lukács, György: *A lélek és a formák. Kísérletek*, Budapest, Franklin, 1910. German ed., *Die Seele und die Formen*, Berlin, Fleischel & Co., 1911. English transl., *Soul and Form*, New York, Columbia University Press, 2010.
19 Id., *Die Theorie des Romans. Ein geschichtsphilosophischer Versuch über die Formen der grossen Epik*, Stuttgart 1916. English transl., *The Theory of the Novel*, Cambridge (MA)/New York, MIT Press, 1974.
20 Kun, born to a Jewish family in Transylvania in 1885 and the same age as Lukács, was a journalist with social democratic leanings until, as prisoner in Russia in 1917, he became an ardent communist, in part as a result of meeting Lenin. After Horthy's counterrevolution he would flee to Moscow, becoming a leading member of the Comintern. He died in prison, a victim of Stalin's purges, in 1937.
See Borsanyi, György: *The Life of a Communist Revolutionary, Béla Kun*, Boulder (CO), Social Science Monographs, 1993.
21 Tokes, Rudolf: *Béla Kun and the Hungarian Soviet Republic: The Origins and Role of the Communist Party of Hungary in the Revolutions of 1918–1919*, New York, Praeger, 1967.

In fact the resignation of the Communist government, on August 1, 1919, cleared the way for a counterrevolution and in particular for its military strike force, the national army commanded by Horthy. He held a fairly dubious constitutional position, that of regent: in practice Horthy was supposed to exercise the functions of head of state until Parliament decided who was going to be the new king of Hungary. In point of fact, Horthy not only prevented the only legitimate pretender to the throne – Charles IV of Habsburg – from obtaining the crown, but dragged out his "regency" for twenty-four years, assuming over time an ever more central role in Hungarian political life.

The mixture of nationalism, anti-liberalism and anti-Semitism that characterized the counterrevolutionary phenomenon at the beginning has allowed historians to point to its promoters as the precursors of Fascism and Nazism. In reality Horthy's regime (1919 – 44) cannot really be described as fascist.[22] It started and ended fascist, but in between went through a very peculiar period of semi-liberal parliamentarianism, governing with authoritarian methods. Count Bethlen, one of the premiers appointed by Horthy, has defined Hungary between the wars as "a democracy based on corporative correctives."[23] In his mentality, his flexibility, his authoritarian, paternalistic attitudes and his pragmatism, the regent showed more of an affinity with Francisco Franco than with Mussolini and Hitler, of whom he was to become, however, for reason of *realpolitik*, both ally and hostage. According to the Franco-Hungarian historian François Fejtö, one of the greatest experts on the Habsburg Empire, "Horthyism" inherited the defects and flaws of the imperial system, while discarding its positive aspects and advantages.[24]

In his *Bildungsroman*, published in the mid-thirties, the great Hungarian writer Sándor Márai summed up the cultural climate of his homeland in a few adjectives: "official, inquisitorial, bedecked with flags and fanaticized."[25]

A constant element of these years was anti-Semitism, given new vigor for a variety of reasons. In periods of economic recession and high inflation like the postwar one, Jews could be used as symbols of hated financial capitalism, as well as of revolutionary agitation (so-called "Judeo-bolshevism"[26]), the corrosive influence of "déracinés intellectuels," the new means of mass communication and the economic competition – how could it not be considered "unfair?" – that bestowed on them a disproportionate share of posts in certain professions, the ones for which education and culture were required. Lastly, the Jew could be seen as the epitome of the foreigner and the outsider, given that nationalism found a

---

22   AMBRI, Mariano: *I falsi fascismi. Ungheria, Jugoslavia, Romania 1919–1945*, introductory essay by Renzo De Felice, Rome, Jouvence, 1980.
23   Quoted in HOBSBAWM, Eric J.: *The Age of Extremes. The Short Twentieth Century*, London, Pelham Books, 1994, p. 114.
24   Fejtö continues, "The real masters of Hungary between the wars were the one thousand six hundred or so large landowners, the so-called gentry, who possessed immense estates and influenced the administrative power with an upper middle class that had emerged from the minor nobility. The regime's original sin was the sabotage of the agrarian reform promised during the war from which the peasants of other countries had benefited." In FEJTÖ, François and SERRA, Maurizio: *Le Passager du siècle. Guerres, Révolutions, Europes*, Paris, Hachette, 1999. The passage has been translated from the Italian ed., *Il passeggero del secolo. Guerre, Rivoluzioni, Europa*, Palermo, Sellerio, 2001, pp. 108–9.
25   MÁRAI, Sándor: *Les confessions d'un bourgeois*, Paris, Albin Michel, 1993. The original, *Egy polgár vallomásai*, had been published in Hungary in two volumes in 1934 and 1935.
26   Several figures of Jewish revolutionaries "without a country" like Rosa Luxemburg, Karl Radek, Gregory Zinovev, Béla Kun and Leon Trotsky embodied for the Nazis the rootless universalism of Marxist culture. Indeed, it could be said that for Hitler Jews and Marxism were synonymous; see TRAVERSO, Enzo: *Giudeobolscevismo*, in id., *La violenza nazista. Una genealogia*, Bologna, Il Mulino, 2002. English transl., *The Origins of Nazi Violence*, New York, The New Press, 2003, p. 103 and p. 120.

powerful unifying force in Christianity. During the White Terror, Hungary experienced a series of pogroms that rivaled the tsarist ones in their horror: between September 1919 and May 1920 there were over fifty pogroms organized by the White Guard in rural villages in which several hundred people were killed. Eric Hobsbawm has written: "Here a straight road leads from original grassroots anti-semitism to the extermination of Jewry during the second World War. Certainly grassroots anti-semitism gave such East European Fascist movements as acquired a mass – notably the Rumanian Iron Guard and the Hungarian Arrow Cross – their foundation."[27]

So the Hungary normalized by Horthy, through the first Teleki government, stood out for the introduction of discriminative legislation into Europe in the 20th century. This was Law XXV presented to the Hungarian parliament on July 22, 1920, by the minister for Education and Religious Affairs István Haller and better known as the "Numerus Clausus." Under this law the percentage of Jews admitted to colleges and universities could not exceed 6% of the total. From the academic year 1920-21 onward only people of impeccable morality who had demonstrated their constant loyalty to Hungary would be admitted to institutions of higher education. Superficially the law seems to have been enacted to guarantee the ethnic minorities present in the country access to education. In reality it was a discriminatory law because the Hungarian Jewish community was undoubtedly the largest minority in the country. It suffices to think that the main synagogue of Budapest, designed by the Viennese architect Ludwig Förster, with its capacity of around three thousand, is still the biggest in Europe.[28] In addition, the Jews had the highest educational level in the country and were a primary component of the not very florid Hungarian middle class. In particular the number of Jews on the registers of lawyers and doctors was very high: 45% in 1910, while 50% of lawyers were Jewish in 1920.[29]

Janos Antal Friedman (he only assumed the name Yona during the resistance) was born in Budapest in 1923 to a middle-class family. His father and grandfather were indeed lawyers, and the laws passed in this period were to have a profound effect on his training as an architect. In fact, in addition to the limitations on admission to university, the profession of architect was threatened by plans of discrimination on a racial basis: the national association of engineers and architects, made up exclusively of Christians and controlling the Chamber of Engineers, set up in 1923, tried to obtain preferential treatment for its members in the award of public works, although with scanty success.

It was partly owing to this general climate of anti-Semitic hostility over the course of the twenties and thirties that many of the best Hungarian intellectuals of Jewish origin were induced to go abroad to study or seek their fortune: intellectuals like Karl Mannheim, Karl and Michael Polanyi [30], Arnold Hauser, Ferenc Molnár [31], Alexander Korda, Péter Szondi

---

27 HOBSBAWM, Eric J.: op. cit., p. 120.
28 It was in Förster's studio that Otto Wagner began his career. He would go on to design the synagogue on Via Rumbach in Budapest, built in 1868–69, in a Moorish style and with two towers on the facade as in the large synagogue on Via Dohány of 1854–59.
29 FEJTŐ, François: *Hongrois et Juifs. Histoire d'un couple singulier (1000–1997)*, Paris, Balland, 1997, p. 248.
30 In particular the economist Karl Polanyi was to become universally known for his treatise *The Great Transformation* (New York, Rinehart, 1944), in which he presented a highly original critique of the market economy.
31 Known all over the world for *The Paul Street Boys*, the writer emigrated to the United States in 1939.

and Jolande Jacobi, artists and architects like László Moholy-Nagy, Marcel Breuer and Robert Capa [32] and scientists like Dennis Gabor, Edward Teller and John von Neumann [33] are just some of the more famous names among them.

After the worldwide economic depression that began in 1929 the Bethlen government was replaced by a series of governments that were increasingly destabilized by the proliferation of rightwing movements, secretly funded by the Nazis, which pushed Hungarian politics in a pro-German direction. The most important of these movements was the *Nyilaskeresztes Párt–Hungarista Mozgalom*, the Hungarian Arrow Cross Party led by Ferenc Szálasi: in its confused ideology the dream of a restoration of a great kingdom of Hungary, ruling over the lower Danube, was mixed with extremely virulent anti-Semitism and promises of prosperity financed by the expropriation of Jewish property.[34] As a consequence the condition of the Jews grew progressively worse, falling into line with that of the other countries under German influence. We can divide this process schematically into three stages.

On April 5, 1938, the draft of a first racial law aimed at restricting Jewish influence in the press, the economy and the professions, setting a ceiling on participation at 20%, was submitted to Parliament.
After the invasion and dismemberment of Czechoslovakia, Hungary occupied Ruthenia, but to gain recognition of its rule had to obtain the consent of Germany, which demanded a quid pro quo. From the account of the German ambassador in Budapest we know that the draft of a second law against the Jews was presented to Ribbentrop on April 29, 1939.[35] A few days later Parliament passed the second Jewish law: much more restrictive than the first, it reduced the share from 20% to 6%, but above all modified the definition of "Jew" from a religious confession to a "race." This second law affected not just the "petite bourgeoisie" and middle class, but also the Jewish industrial and financial establishment.[36]
The third stage was forced labor for all those judged to be unsuitable for the armed forces, i.e. all the minorities disliked by the Hungarian regime: Gypsies, Romanians, Serbs, Ukrainians and obviously Jews. These were all grouped into gangs that were assigned to the armed units and given the job of carrying out the humblest and most dangerous tasks, like digging trenches and laying mines,[37] always with a yellow armband. In all likelihood Yona Friedman received his draft papers in 1944, at least going by the testimony of György Ligeti, a Hungarian Jew who was the same age as Friedman:

---

[32] His real name was Endre Friedmann. In 1931 he enrolled in a course of journalism in Berlin and went on to found the famous Magnum agency in Paris with Henri Cartier-Bresson and others in 1947. See WHELAN, Richard: *Robert Capa: The Definitive Collection*, London, Phaidon, 2001.
[33] Ede Teller studied with Heisenberg in Leipzig and emigrated to the US, where he became one of the fathers of the hydrogen bomb. János Neumann, who studied quantum physics and was one of the pioneers of the digital computer, emigrated to the US in the thirties.
[34] RADY, Martin: *Ferenc Szálasi, "Hungarism" and the Arrow Cross*, in HAYNES, Rebecca and RADY, Martyn (eds.): *In the Shadow of Hitler: Personalities of the Right in Central and Eastern Europe*, London/New York, IB Tauris, 2011, pp. 261–77.
[35] HILBERG, Raul: *The Destruction of the European Jews*, New York/London, Holmes & Meier, 1985, 3 vols.
[36] FEJTŐ, François: *Hongrois et Juifs...*, op. cit., pp. 279–80.
[37] HILBERG, Raul: op. cit., pp. 826–27.

People born in the same year as me, 1923, at the beginning – of 1944 – had not been drafted because Hungary continually tried to steer a middle course and did not want to back Hitler completely on the military plane. The majority of young men were drafted in March 1944.[38]

Ligeti, a central figure in the contemporary music of the second half of the 20th century, would escape the death camps only because of this forced labor: the German army moved in to occupy Hungary on March 19, 1944, and by May roundups were already being carried out all over the country apart from Budapest.[39]

Hungary was the last act of the Holocaust, carried out at a time when knowledge of the Nazi atrocities was already in the public domain, among both Jews and the Hungarian authorities. The machinery of deportation was orchestrated by Eichmann in person, who went several times to Budapest to organize the operations of transfer to Auschwitz.[40] Eichmann was so zealous that he continued to work toward the extermination of the Jews, even contravening Himmler's order to suspend their evacuation from Budapest – in November the camp at Auschwitz, for example, was supposed to have been closed and the Nazis had set about trying to destroy the evidence of the Shoah.[41]

In October 1944 the political situation rapidly deteriorated and the Germans, tired of Horthy's shillyshallying and irritated by his attempt to make a separate peace with the Soviet Union, which had routed the Hungarian army supporting the Nazis, installed by force – going so far as to abduct Horthy's son in order to make him resign – a puppet government headed by the leader of the Arrow Cross, Ferenc Szálasi. This was the beginning of the darkest period for Hungary, marked by the most ferocious and arbitrary anti-Semitic raids.

In this period Friedman was collaborating with the Zionist resistance, and in the interview published here declares that he had faked documents for this organization, as well as with the better known efforts to protect Jewry made by the Swedish embassy and in particular Raul Wallenberg, the consul that the king of Sweden had sent to Budapest with the precise assignment of saving the greatest number of Jews possible from deportation. In 1944 in fact the existence of the gas chambers was already known. However, the organization was not very efficient. Friedman himself – denounced by an anonymous informer – says that the only reason he survived was the chaos that followed the invasion by the Russians, in the early days of January 1945.[42]

---

38   LIGETI, György: *"Träumen Sie in Farbe?" György Ligeti im Gespräch mit Eckhard Roelcke,* Vienna, Zsolnay, 2003. See specifically the chapter on forced labor in the army, pp. 46–60.
39   Ibid.: "The deportation of Jews started at the beginning of May. I saw this with my own eyes at Oradea, when our company was stationed there. Every night, trains filled with Jews went past the barracks."
40   See the entire section devoted to Hungary in HILBERG, Raul: op. cit., pp. 815–74.
41   On Eichmann in Budapest also see ARENDT, Hannah: *Eichmann in Jerusalem. A Report on the Banality of Evil,* New York, Viking Press, 1963, p. 147.
42   See BENSHALOM, Rafi: *We Struggled for Life. The Hungarian Zionist Youth Resistance during the Nazi Era,* Jerusalem, Gefen, 2001. This book of memoirs of the period of the occupation of Budapest was written by a member of the Zionist resistance immediately after the country's liberation by the Russians and is one of the very few accounts of this organization, to which Friedman also belonged.

I survived only because the Russians had already started to arrive. Then total chaos broke out. That's how so many Hungarian Jews survived in Budapest: they couldn't be deported anymore, it was too late.[43]

In his posthumously published memoirs, Giorgio Perlasca, the Italian who, stuck in Hungary because of the war, posed as the Spanish consul-general in order to give thousands of Jews refuge in Spanish protected houses, is extremely critical of the action of the few legations of neutral countries that had remained open in Budapest under the occupation: in particular Perlasca accused the Swedish ambassador: "I must say that I had and have a feeling of contempt for the minister Danielsson and his assistants [...]. I believe that Danielsson's indifference gravely impaired a closer collaboration between the legations: it would have been opportune to present a united front to the government; instead this only happened on a couple of occasions and too late."[44] On Wallenberg, who disappeared in mysterious fashion following the arrival of the Red Army, Perlasca wrote: "The only decent one of the Swedes was Wallenberg, and he was not a diplomat. He did his duty to the end and met his death performing what he considered a mission; from the inquiries I've made it appears that Wallenberg was still alive when the Russians occupied the area where he lived."[45] By the time Hungary was liberated about half a million Jews had been deported to the camps and the rest were crammed into the ghetto of the capital, subjected to continual harassment down to the last day.[46] Perlasca tells us that even with Russian forces already occupying some districts of Budapest, the Arrow Cross continued its massacres:

The night of the 29–30th December 1944 a horrific massacre of Jews taken from the ghetto took place in Liszt Ferenc Tér and Eötvös Ut. [...] along the whole stretch of the riverbank facing the Hungária and the Negresco café the snow was stained red with blood and hundreds of naked corpses floated in the water, retained by the blocks of ice; they had been killed during the night and dumped in the Danube. I told the officer that I had already seen similar sights in the vicinity of the Margaret Bridge.[47]

---

43 See the interview in Lebesque, Sabine and Fentener van Vlissingen, Helene (eds.): *Yona Friedman: Structures Serving the Unpredictable*, with a note by Jean-Louis Cohen, Rotterdam, NAi Publishers, 1999, p. 116.

44 Perlasca, Giorgio: *L'impostore*, Bologna, Il Mulino, 1997, pp. 37–38. This text, written in 1946 at the request of Jënö Lévai – the first person to carry out research on the persecution of the Jews in Hungary – belongs to the genre of memoir writing and reconstructs in summary fashion a journal of the events that had been lost. Perlasca was born in Como in 1910 and died in Padua in 1992. On the story of how he saved thousands of Jews. He was awarded Israel's highest honor as one of the "Righteous Among the Nations." Also see Deaglio, Enrico: *La banalità del bene, Storia di Giorgio Perlasca*, Milan, Feltrinelli, 1991; rpt. 2002.

45 Perlasca, Giorgio: op. cit., p. 37.

46 Life in the ghetto of Budapest immediately before and during the war has been reconstructed in narrative form in an autobiographical book, Pressburger, Giorgio and Nicola: *Storie dell'Ottavo Distretto*, Casale Monferrato, Marietti, 1986. It has been translated into English as *Homage to the Eighth District: Tales from Budapest*, Columbia (LA), Readers Intl, 1990. Giorgio Pressburger, a theater director and writer who survived the German deportations by chance with his twin brother Nicola, moved with the family to Trieste in 1956, the year of the Soviet invasion of Hungary.

47 Perlasca, Giorgio: op. cit., p. 59.

401

402

403

BUDAPEST

401 Members of the Arrow Cross Party escorting Jews during deportation, Budapest, 1938–44. Photograph from the Hungarian film *Budapesti Tavasz*, directed by Máriássy Félix, 1955.
402 The liberation of Budapest by the Red Army, during the battle of 1945. Photograph by unknown Soviet journalist, published in Bauer, Eddy: *Controversial History of World War II*, vol. 7, Novara, De Agostini, 1971.
403 While retreating, the Germans destroyed the Danube bridges. Unknown photographer, Budapest, 1944.

HAIFA

404 View of Haifa from Mont Carmel, c. 1950. Published in Gitai, Amos: *Mont Carmel*, Paris, Gallimard, 2003.

404

SCIENCE AS ART: WERNER HEISENBERG

The new does not have to be visible right away, we will accept this as it is, reality will change by itself without any action on our part. [48]
Werner Heisenberg

Yona Friedman's training, although hampered by the racial laws, was not totally obstructed by the conflict: Hungary was in fact the last country to become involved in the Second World War and until the spring of 1944 research activities continued in a more or less regular way, with visits by foreign lecturers attracted by the country's substantial neutrality, on a par with that enjoyed in Switzerland or Turkey. One of the most important personalities to give lectures in Budapest during this time was Werner Heisenberg. Born in 1901, a student of Niels Bohr and Max Born, Heisenberg had won the Nobel Prize in Physics in 1932 thanks to his uncertainty principle, developed in 1927, which is at the base of the theory of quantum mechanics.[49] Among the first to recognize this authentic revolution was Max Planck, who in 1929 had written: "Now this relation of uncertainty, established by Heisenberg, is something quite unheard of in classical mechanics."[50]

The importance of Heisenberg's principle lies in its radical critique of Newtonian physics, removing the foundations of the rigid determinism on which the laws of physics had rested for almost three hundred years.
The uncertainty principle made a fundamental contribution to undermining scientific certainty, i.e. the deterministic conception of reality based on the relationship of cause and effect. In other words Heisenberg showed that there were limits beyond which our experiments are no long completely reliable. In particular, it became clear that the uncertainty of probabilistic assertions is not always the consequence of insufficient information about the objective state. From this point of view the traditional model of "objective reality" – i.e. the very notion of objectivity – was in serious trouble.

The indeterministic position in effect demonstrates that it is impossible, at least in certain areas, to make a definite scientific prediction: in the strict formulation of the law of causality – if we know the present, we can calculate the future – it is not the conclusion that is wrong but the premise.
In other words, as a matter of principle, we cannot ever exactly recognize the present. So every perception is a selection from a range of possibilities and a limitation of future possibilities.[51]
Claims like these could not leave Friedman indifferent, raised as he had been in a highly

---

48   HEISENBERG, Werner: *Ordnung der Wirklichkeit*, in id., *Gesammelte Werke*, series C, Munich, Piper Verlag, 1986. Transl. into English as *Reality and Its Order*, at http://werner-heisenberg.unh.edu/t-OdW-english.htm
49   CASSIDY, David: *Uncertainty: The Life and Science of Werner Heisenberg*, New York, Freeman, 1992.
50   PLANK, Max: *The Universe in the Light of Modern Physics*, London, George Allen & Unwin, 1931, pp. 38–39. In this book Planck cast doubt on the idea that there are fixed laws of physics, a concept that, through Heisenberg, had a profound influence on Friedman.
51   See also HEISENBERG, Werner: *Physics and Philosophy: The Revolution in Modern Science*, New York, Harper and Row, 1958.

positivistic environment and about to attend the courses of architecture at an outpost of faith in science like the Joseph University of Technology and Economics in Budapest. And yet this faith was undermined by the lectures of the German Nobel prizewinner.

Taking Heisenberg's reasoning to its logical consequences, any excessively rigid planning was doomed to fail to meet its objectives because it was no longer possible to rely on any law of nature. At the most you could take a probabilistic perspective. This conclusion in particular was to leave an indelible mark on the 18-year-old Yona Friedman, who attended both the lectures given by the German physicist in Hungary and found his conclusions so convincing that he would go on to publish a book offering an anthropomorphic vision of physics, although over fifty years later, with the unequivocal subtitle: "And if the laws of nature followed no law?"[52]

Heisenberg was in Budapest in 1941 as a guest lecturer at a seminar. I was still in secondary school, but the seminar was open to the general public. I was obviously impressed. [My] career in architecture, which was formed by my approach to science, is based on the fundamental importance of individual behaviors and actions and the unpredictability of such actions. An individual's actions are completely unpredictable even for himself.[53]

Heisenberg's theoretical production followed two lines of development: scientific papers and philosophical essays. He always felt the need to accompany his theoretical enunciations with precise and well-organized epistemological reflections, which he considered complementary to the scientific ones.

All scientific work is, of course, based consciously or subconsciously on some philosophical attitude; on a particular thought structure which serves as a solid foundation for further development. Without a definite attitude of this kind, the concepts and associations of ideas produced would be unlikely to attain the degree of clarity and lucidity essential for scientific work.[54]

A philosopher like Bachelard has also pointed out that physics has two polarities: it is a true field of thought whose specific focuses lie in mathematics and experience, and which reaches its acme in the union of these two components. In other words, physics determines, as synthesis, an *abstract-concrete* way of thinking.[55] The speculative nature of physics was in fact the subject of one of the two lectures in Budapest: experience is an adaptation of thought and is indispensable for the elaboration of thought itself, two sides of the

---

52 FRIEDMAN, YONA: *L'Univers erratique. Et si les lois de la nature ne suivaient aucune loi?*, foreword by Dominique Lecourt, Paris, Press Universitaires de France, 1994.
53 FRIEDMAN, Yona, in OBRIST, Hans-Ulrich & FRIEDMAN, Yona: *The Conversation Series*, vol. 7. Cologne, Walter König, 2007, p. 7. Also see the statement made shortly before: "I grew up in a very positivist environment, a positivist attitude towards science and faith in science. Science pretends to predict." Quoted in *Yona Friedman Relates His Beliefs and Experiences*, in LEBESQUE, Sabine and FENTENER VAN VLISSINGEN, Helene (eds.): *Yona Friedman: Structures Serving the Unpredictable*, Rotterdam, NAi Publishers, 1999, p. 115.
54 HEISENBERG, Werner: *Introduction*, in BORN, Max: *The Born–Einstein Letters*, New York, Walker and Co., 1971.
55 BACHELARD, Gaston: *Le nouvel esprit scientifique*, Paris, Alcan, 1934.

same coin for every physicist.[56] In this respect Heisenberg's lesson modeled Friedman's approach. The Hungarian architect's first projects, as we will see, were born out of firsthand experience: the forced cohabitation of several family units displaced by the war in a single room, temporary low-cost housing for new immigrants, etc.

On the outbreak of war in September 1939, Heisenberg had been called to Berlin to do his military service in the armaments department of the army. He was supposed to work on the construction of a nuclear reactor, a project known as the *Uranverein* (Uranium Club). But Heisenberg did not neglect theoretical research in his experiments. In July 1942 he was appointed director of the Kaiser-Wilhelm-Institut für Physik at Berlin-Dahlem. Heisenberg has left us a manuscript, written in 1942, that deals with philosophical matters and is entitled *Reality and its Order*.[57] It is a summary of five lectures, later included in his complete works.[58] Notwithstanding the war and his pressing responsibilities, Heisenberg was in fact still free to give lectures not only in Germany but also in neutral countries, in Zurich for example, or allied ones like Hungary. It should be said that Heisenberg, in spite of his *de facto* collaboration with the Nazi regime, was not a fervent supporter of it, at least to judge by the 1942 manuscript. Especially in the final part of *Reality and its Order,* Heisenberg speaks openly of the fact that political power "has always been founded on criminal behavior." And again: "The powerful figure who assumes the right to destroy the enemy and who throws resisters in jail is not important; it is instead the jail guard who, despite orders to the contrary, cannot refrain from slipping a piece of bread to the prisoners now and then. We need to remind ourselves again and again that it is more important to act humanely towards the other than to fulfill any professional obligations or national obligations or political obligations."[59] In short, he expressed convictions that were certainly not in line with the ethics of National Socialism. Although the situation appeared hopeless, and "even the care of others does not make it any less desolate," it was still necessary to put up a struggle: "But what is crucial now is that the few for whom the world still radiates with light stick together and recognize one another across what the others put in their way. For only to them will the meaning be unlocked that is to be given anew to the world."[60] It is not easy to tell how much of this covert political disenchantment was discernible to the people who attended Heisenberg's lectures, but is possible that to the sensitive ears of an opponent of the Germans these ideas may have transmitted at least some hope for the future, if not an invitation to resistance.

The lecture he gave in Budapest in 1941 on the theory of colors (*The Teachings of Goethe and Newton on Colour in the Light of Modern Physics*[61]) had had such a favorable reception

---

56 "In the end, all cognition rests on experience and nothing can foreshorten the journey of thought as it makes its accommodations over the centuries," in HEISENBERG, Werner: *Ordnung der Wirklichkeit,* op. cit. English transl., *Reality and Its Order,* op. cit.
57 HEISENBERG, Werner: *Ordnung der Wirklichkeit,* op. cit. English transl., *Reality and Its Order* op. cit.
58 Id., *Gesammelte Werke,* ed. by BLUM, W., DÜRR, H.-P. and RECHBERG, H.: op. cit., pp. 217–306.
59 Id., *Reality and Its Order,* op. cit.
60 Ibid., p. 197.
61 "Die Goethesche und Newtonsche Farbenlehre im Lichte der modernen Physik", *Geist der Zeit,* 19, 1941, pp. 262–75, now in id., *Wandlungen in den Grundlagen der Naturwissenschaft,* Stuttgart, Hirzel, 1959. English transl. in *Philosophic Problems of Nuclear Science,* New York, Pantheon, 1952, pp. 60–76.

that Heisenberg had been induced to reflect further on the methodological questions of the natural sciences. The outlining of a comprehensive order of reality constituted a sort of commonsense project among contemporary physicists, who all painted their own "picture of the world"[62] in a more or less articulate manner, and this aspect was fundamental for Friedman.

In 1941 Heisenberg gave a second lecture in Budapest with the title *Die Einheit des naturwissenschaftlichen Weltbildes* (*The Unity of the Scientific World View*); in it he declared that "a view of the world, at least in principle, should be able to embrace all fields, and every sphere of reality ought to find its place in it."[63] Quantum theory had in fact merged physics and chemistry into a grand unified science, a "single scientific system." Thanks to the change in the order of reality that had been made in quantum theory conceptual links were being forged between scientific fields that had hitherto been entirely separate.[64] Thus the theory of quantum mechanics was pushing its adherents toward an interdisciplinarity that was as broad as possible,[65] all the more so given that Bohr's complementarity principle, which can be considered an extension of Heisenberg's ideas on uncertainty, pointed in exactly this direction: the true lesson to be learned from Heisenberg (and from Bohr, who tried his whole life to apply his principle in other fields of cognition) consists in emphasizing the wealth of reality, which overflows any single language, any single logical structure. Each language can express only part of reality. Music, for example, has not been exhausted by any of its realizations, by any style of composition, from Bach to Schönberg.[66] No style, whether in music or in architecture, is sufficient to meet every need. Each is an expression of a different vision of the world. It follows that any personal attempt in any language has its own dignity; not just the plans of architects, but of everyone. Out of this comes the first axiom of *L'architecture mobile*. More recently Friedman has declared in this connection:

Perhaps I'm not very disciplined, but essentially I don't believe that a discipline provokes anything other than an unjustified monopoly [...] I showed that academic people attempt to interfere with language. They do it for different reasons – in some cases to maintain a monopoly or to maintain a class system.[67]

Friedman was to find this critique of the division into disciplines induced by the new theories of physics expressed in different form a few months later, in the lectures of Károly

---

62 GEMBILLO, Giuseppe: Introduction to the Italian ed. of Werner Heisenberg's two essays *Über den anschaulichen Inhalt der quantentheoretischen Kinematik und Mechanik* and *Ordnung der Wirklichkeit*, *Indeterminazione e realtà*, ed. by Giuseppe Gembillo, Naples, Guida, 1991, p. 23. Also GEMBILLO, Giuseppe: *Werner Heisenberg. La filosofia di un fisico*, Naples, Giannini, 1987.
63 *Die Einheit des naturwissenschaftlichen Weltbildes*, Leipzig, J.A. Barth Verlag, 1942. The passage has been translated from the Italian ed., HEISENBERG, Werner: *L'unità dell'immagine scientifica del mondo*, in id., *Mutamenti nelle basi della scienza*, Turin, Boringhieri, 1978, p. 121.
64 Ibid., p. 120.
65 "Perhaps we can compare the scientist who abandons the field of intuition to discover wider relations with the climber who wants to scale the highest peak of a mighty mountain range to take in the whole sweep of the land below [...]. The higher he climbs the vaster the landscape that is laid out before his eyes, and the more sparse the life that surrounds him." HEISENBERG, Werner: *Die Goethesche und Newtonsche Farbenlehre im Lichte der modernen Physik*, op. cit. The passage has been translated from the Italian ed., *La dottrina dei colori di Goethe e quella di Newton alla luce della fisica moderna*, in id., *Mutamenti...*, op. cit., p. 101.
66 PRIGOGINE, Ilya and STENGERS, Isabelle: *La nouvelle alliance. Métamorphose de la science*, Paris, Gallimard, 1979, p. 314. English ed., *Order out of Chaos: Man's New Dialogue with Nature*, New York, Bantam Books, 1984, p. 225.
67 Yona Friedman, in OBRIST, Hans-Ulrich & FRIEDMAN, Yona: *The Conversation Series*, op. cit., pp. 9–10.

Kerényi, as we will see in the next section. In his book on physics, published only in 1994, Friedman was to assert forcefully that science and art are both creative activities and that there should be no barriers between them because, founded as they are on observation and creative intuition, both communicate an *image of the world* to the greatest number of people.[68] Several years earlier the philosopher of science Paul Feyerabend had embraced this point of view, aiming at a "science as art" which, on the basis of the free construction of pure mathematics (analogous in this to artistic production) should set aside the idea of a "reality" as permanent external referent that this or that scientific model would be able to describe more or less faithfully, in favor of an epistemological pluralism:

We have not just forms of art, but also forms of thought, forms of truth, forms of rationality and, indeed, forms of reality. Wherever we turn we are never able to find an Archimedean place to stand on, but only other styles, others traditions, other ordering principles.[69]

On the other hand Heisenberg, in both the two lectures of 1941 and the essay that he derived from them, started out from the premise of the uncertainty principle. In particular in the relationship between the subject and object of reality: Heisenberg had already demonstrated in 1927, despite the misgivings of Einstein (who had also posed himself the problem of the theoretical physicist's "picture of the world"),[70] how every subject influences its own object through "regular connections."

In 1941, following along general lines a suggestion made by Goethe in his *Theory of Colors*, Heisenberg ordered reality hierarchically, subdividing it into areas that followed one another without a break and that were distinguished not by the objects to which they referred, but by the type of connections that they established at the various levels of physics, chemistry, organic life, consciousness, the level indicated as "symbol and form" and finally at the highest level, that of "the creative forces."

In this way Heisenberg intended to underline his conviction that the most important point in our theoretical activity is not what is in front of us (the "object"), but the way in which we experience it.

In 1942, in *Reality and its Order*, i.e. the reworking of the Budapest lecture, Heisenberg wrote: "Ultimately, cognition is perhaps nothing other than an ordering process, not of something that would have already been accessed by our consciousness or perception but of something that requires this ordering process in order to become the actual content of consciousness or a process we are aware of."[71]

---

68 FRIEDMAN, Yona: *L'Univers erratique*..., op. cit., p. 1.
69 FEYERABEND, Paul K. and THOMAS, Christian (eds.): *Kunst und Wissenschaft*, Zurich, Verlag der Fachvereine, 1984. The passage has been translated from the Italian ed., FEYERABEND, Paul K.: *Scienza come arte. Discussione della teoria dell'arte di Riegl e tentativo di applicarla alle scienze* (1981), in MERIGGI, Stefano: (ed.), *Dov'è la donna? Pensare l'arte e la scienza oggi*, Milan, Mimesis, 2003, p. 21.
70 "We try to make for ourselves, in the manner that best suits us, a simplified and intelligible picture of the world; we then attempt in some manner to substitute this cosmos of ours for the world of experience, and thus to surmount it. [...] The physicist's renunciation of completeness for his cosmos is therefore not a matter of fundamental principle." In EINSTEIN, Albert: *Prinzipien der Forschung: Rede zum 60. Geburtstag von Max Planck* (1918), in id., *Mein Weltbild*, Berlin, Ullstein, 1977. English transl. in *The Collected Papers of Albert Einstein*, vol. 7, it. 7 (2002).
71 HEISENBERG, Werner: *Reality and Its Order*, op. cit.

In other words, according to this new *Weltanschauung*, in any problem it is not so much the objects that count as the process by which the subject determines them.

If we apply this reasoning to architecture, the consequence is obvious: the process of ordering the city, instead of being organized around juxtaposed objects (buildings), should concentrate instead on the subjects that determine them, i.e. the inhabitants. Thus the relationship between inhabitants (subject) and buildings (object) is nothing but a system of connections regulated by a process that has to become the focus of architectural activity. And precisely this, on close examination, is the guiding thread that runs through the whole of Yona Friedman's theoretical work and design. The architectural objects in themselves, their form or even the purely professional aspect of the architecture will always seem secondary to him, if not banal.

However, there is one more kernel of Heisenberg's ideas that will have major repercussions on the subsequent development of Friedman's thought.
"Thus, something other than a sure certainty of knowledge has to exist at the beginning of an order of reality and, as history teaches, that other something results from a free decision more likely to be taken by larger human communities or by humankind as a whole than by an individual."[72] In other words it is necessary to ask what holds together a group of individuals, i.e. society, and above all why, especially in order to avoid the sort of discrimination that occurred in Hungary in the years between the wars.

---

72 Ibid., p. 88.

WERNER HEISENBERG

405 *Ascent to Herzogstand Mountain*, Germany, 1948.
From left, Martin, Werner and Wolfgang Heisenberg. Original photograph with Maria Hirsch.
406 Heisenberg, Werner: *Physik und Philosophie*, Stuttgart, Hirzel, 1959.
407 Heisenberg, Werner: *Ordnung der Wirklichkeit*, Munich, Piper Verlag, 1986.

406

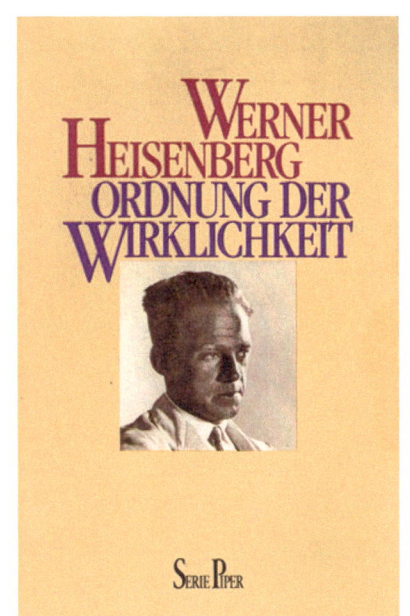

407

MYTHOLOGY AS COLLECTIVE PSYCHOLOGY: KÁROLY KERÉNYI

[The] gods have fled. The resulting void is filled by the historical and psychological investigation of myth. [73]
Martin Heidegger

The second figure to have left a deep mark on the formation of Friedman's ideas is Károly Kerényi. A multifaceted personality, he ranged in his studies from anthropology to archeology, mythology, language, psychology and philosophy, and in doing so attracted the attention of some of the principal exponents of European culture, as is testified by the close correspondence he maintained with Thomas Mann,[74] Herman Hesse,[75] and Carl Gustav Jung. Before leaving Hungary for good in 1943, Kerényi had given weekly lectures in Budapest, where he lived. The hall was fairly packed since they were open to all; for this reason, they were attended by many Jewish students like Friedman, subject to the racial laws on education, but the audience was very mixed as Kerényi's charisma attracted laypersons in large numbers.[76]

Evidence for a direct contact between Friedman and Kerényi comes from an unpublished letter of 1959 preserved in the collection of documents on Kerényi in Marbach. Many years after that association, Friedman had in fact sent his former teacher Kerényi a copy of his pamphlet on mobile architecture, confessing the extent of the intellectual debt he owed to him:

Most respected professor,
I have sent you a pamphlet (in French) on the mobility of architecture, whose basic ideas I owe to you, as a student of your course held at the University of Sciences in Budapest in 1943. I am thinking of your series of lectures on the Eleusinian mysteries, in which you presented myth as "amusement" and as "gossip" of general interest inasmuch as it is creator and center of society, referring also to Huizinga. On these bases I have tried to arrive, in architecture too, at a similar analysis, something that has taken me further forward on the technical plane, as I have tried to show in the pamphlet. (Unfortunately by now I am no longer completely sure of myself in the Hungarian language, nor in French for that matter.) I beg you to accept this pamphlet as a mark of my gratitude and, given that I have the impression of having had a fairly revolutionary effect in my profession (architecture) with that theory, I beg you also to accept the complicity connected with it.[77]

---

[73] HEIDEGGER, Martin: *Die Zeit des Weltbildes, in Holzwege.* Frankfurt am Main, Klostermann, 1950. English transl., *The Age of the World Picture* (1938), in *Off the Beaten Track*, ed. by YOUNG, Julian and HAYNES, Kenneth, Cambridge (UK), Cambridge University Press, 2002, p. 58.
[74] KERÉNYI, Károly and MANN, Thomas: *Romandichtung und Mythologie – ein Briefwechsel*, Zurich, Rhein, 1945. English transl., *Mythology and Humanism: The Correspondence of Thomas Mann and Karl Kerényi*, Ithaca (NY), Cornell University Press, 1975.
[75] KERÉNYI, Károly and HESSE, Herman: *Briefwechsel aus der Nähe,* Munich, Langen-Muller, 1972.
[76] I owe this information to Cornelia Isler Kerényi, archaeologist and daughter of the Hungarian scholar.
[77] The letter preserved in the Deutsches Literatur Archiv in Marbach is dated "Paris, 30.11.59"; it has been translated from Giorgio Pressburger's rendering of the Hungarian into Italian.

Kerényi was born in Temesvár, known today as Timisoara following its transfer to Romania, on January 19, 1897, to a family of German origin – his father had given their surname of Kintzig a Hungarian form.

The attack on positivism in general and philology in particular was a leitmotif for Kerényi in the forties and drew the boundaries of a solitude that was not just academic. As he himself put it, Kerényi very soon left the "house of erroneously triumphant scientists." Although his background was in history – he had made a thorough study of Ulrich von Wilamowitz, advocate of the ideal of classical philology as a pure science [78] – he distanced himself from his philologist and historicist teachers and colleagues. Kerényi's position on the sidelines of Hungarian academe can be explained in part by the exceptional nature of his studies, hard to classify and spanning the boundaries of traditionally separate fields. It is no coincidence that Giorgio Agamben numbers Kerényi among the pioneers of what he has defined the "nameless science": "project of a future 'anthropology of Western culture,' a study of the *Zwischenraum* in which the incessant symbolic work of social memory is carried out." This kind of science is the only one capable of breaking down the false divisions and false hierarchies that keep the human sciences separate from one another and art and literary creation separate from science; notwithstanding a century and more of anthropological studies, it is just in its early stages and in it – continues Agamben – the name of Aby Warburg can "be inscribed alongside those of Mauss, Sapir, Spitzer, Kerényi, Usener, Dumézil, Benveniste, and many – but not very many – others."[79] For Agamben in short Kerényi is one of the scholars who have done the most to build a unified knowledge, one in which the term "discipline" is more or less equivalent to that of "empty set." Another scholar who can be placed in this "nameless" category and who was as important for the development of Kerényi's thinking as he was for Friedman's is undoubtedly the Dutchman Johan Huizinga, mentioned explicitly in the letter. Huizinga regarded culture as a system in which all the elements interacted with one another: economics, politics, law, uses, customs and art. And for him history was immediately a universal history, even in the case of highly circumscribed analyses – he thought the comparative method sufficient to demonstrate this. However, the notion that to grasp the meaning of any phenomenon of modern history it was necessary to understand all the preceding cultures obliged him to work on periods of great length, and this stimulated him to develop structures on a vast scale. The most global of these is undoubtedly *Homo Ludens*, his famous essay on the social function of play: an enormous edifice of cultural anthropology founded on ethnography, historical psychology, sociology, linguistics, the study of folklore, etc.; in other words a comprehensive analysis of the role of myths and the imagination in world civilization, of play as universal principle of the generation of human culture.[80] Huizinga's name has been associated with those of Marcel Mauss, Claude Lévi-Strauss and Edward Burnett Tylor, the father of

---

78 MAGRIS, Aldo: *Carlo Kerényi e la ricerca fenomenologia della religione*, Milan, Mursia, 1975, pp. 57–58.
79 AGAMBEN, Giorgio: *Aby Warburg e la scienza senza nome*, in Aut Aut, no. 199–200, January–April 1984, p. 64. English transl., *Aby Warburg and the Nameless Science*, in Potentialities: Collected Essays on Philosophy, Stanford (CA), Stanford University Press, 1999, p. 100.
80 HUIZINGA, Johan: *Homo ludens, proeve eener bepaling van het spel-element der cultuur*, Haarlem, H.D. Tjeenk Willink, 1938. English transl., *Homo Ludens: A Study of the Play-Element in Culture*, London/Boston, Routledge & Kegan Paul, 1949. The book had already been translated into all the principal languages by the early fifties.

cultural anthropology. In any case Huizinga was far ahead of his time in developing the method of interdisciplinary research and in the study of socio-historical processes, relations and structures.[81] So this unitary conception of knowledge tallies with both Kerényi's and Friedman's. The latter, in particular, in the duplicated edition of *L'architecture mobile* that he sent to his former teacher, clearly places the theme of leisure – *loisir* – at the center of his urban studies from the very first lines. He goes further: leisure, play, is regarded as the main attraction of life in the city and would be more and more so in the future:

> *The "raison d'être" of cities is joint amusement. Dances, intrigues, and conversation, religious services, politics and theater are "amusements" (Huizinga calls them games) – it is these that have led to human agglomerations: cities, towns and villages.*[82]

This conviction, shared at least in part by future fellow travelers like Constant, had been developed by Friedman from a very young age thanks to the influence of Kerényi.
This belief in the links between play, ritual and myth was later shared by Agamben too, who has pointed out that play not only comes from the sphere of the sacred, but in a way represents its subversion:

> *The potency of the sacred act, writes Benveniste, resides precisely in the conjunction of the myth that articulates history and the ritual that reproduces it. If we make a comparison between this schema and that of play, the difference appears fundamental: in play only the ritual survives and all that is preserved is the form of the sacred drama, in which each element is re-enacted time and again. But what has been forgotten or abolished is the myth, the meaningful worded fabulation that endows the acts with their sense and their purpose.*[83]

Huizinga had already pointed out that there was an identification of play and worship in all religions, commencing with the most ancient.[84] As myth and the sphere of the sacred in ancient Greece in general were the principal subject of Kerényi's studies and lectures – and he was singled out by Huizinga as a "scientist" and his cultural ally –[85] it is worth presenting a brief profile of his intellectual achievements.
From the mid-thirties onward Károly Kerényi held the chair of classical philology at the University of Pécs, but had continued to teach classical antiquities as a private docent at Budapest University. According to various accounts, his lectures were particularly gripping,

---

81   Regarding this Umberto Eco has written: "It has to be said that Huizinga, in Italian culture, has paid a fairly high price for the fact of not being exactly either a philosopher or a historian or a sociologist or a theorist of art, and having wanted to poke his nose more or less everywhere in an interdisciplinary fashion, which is something that happens to historians of ideas." Id., *"Homo ludens" oggi*, introductory essay to Huizinga, Johan: *Homo ludens*, Turin, Einaudi, 1973, p. ix.
82   Friedman, Yona: *L'architecture mobile*, 2nd ed., Paris, 1958, p. 3.
83   Benveniste, Emile: *Le jeu et le sacré*, in *Deucalion*, no. 2, 1947, p. 165; the passage is cited, translated and amply commented on by Agamben, Giorgio: *Il paese dei balocchi*, in id., *Infanzia e storia. Distruzione dell'esperienza e origine della storia*. Turin, Einaudi, 1978. English transl., *The Game of Play*, in *Infancy and History. The Destruction of Experience*, London, Verso, 1993, pp. 69–70.
84   "Formally speaking, there is no distinction whatever between marking out a space for a sacred purpose and marking it out for purposes of sheer play." Huizinga, Johan: *Homo Ludens*, op. cit., p. 20.
85   "Kerényi's ideas about the feast as an autonomous culture concept amplify and corroborate those on which this book is built." Ibid. In drawing a parallel between play and feast, Huizinga was referring in particular to an essay that he had been able to read just before publishing *Homo Ludens*: Kerényi, Karl: *Vom Wesen des Festes*, in *Paideuma, Mitteilungen zur Kulturkunde*, I, issue 2, December 1938, pp. 59–74.

not only for their presentation of a historico-religious discourse rich in links to ethnology and literature that brought fresh blood to the rather fusty atmosphere of the Hungarian universities, but also as the expression of a vivacious and brilliant personality that was attractive in its own right. So attendance at the lectures of the course in classical antiquities and the ones given at the seminar for qualification was very high, attracting as they did students from other degree courses or graduates who wanted to take degrees in other disciplines,[86] including Yona Friedman.

The Hungarian writer Anton Szerb declared in an article of 1941:

What we will never be able to express sufficient gratitude for is the fact that Kerényi in recent years has been able to transform classical antiquity into a stimulating topic of relevance to the present day. In our university teaching, flat and lifeless beyond all bounds, in our intellectual world, which displays patent signs of aging, Kerényi represents a new tone, a lively attitude, a creative restlessness. His lectures are attended not only by students of the most diverse departments, but also by a large number of people who have no connection with the institution of the university and who are attracted exclusively by Kerényi's personality, by the cathartic and elevating power of his words. Many of his listeners perceive the spirit that he represents, the spirit that in the hours of his lectures is celebrated in a festive atmosphere.[87]

The article had been published with the intent of defending Kerényi against the rising tide of attacks on the part of officialdom. In the universities in fact the emphasis was placed on the teaching of the so-called "national sciences," at the expense of Greco-Roman classical studies among others. In the years immediately prior to the war Kerényi, who had already encountered Nazism through his contacts with the Institute for Cultural Morphology in Frankfurt, stood out as one of the most prestigious exponents of the democratic opposition in every public forum – conferences, articles, seminars. Some German scholarship holders protested and the case ended up in the newspapers and was noted by Kálmán Kollár, a Hungarian anti-Nazi publisher in exile in the Netherlands. The publishing house he ran, Pantheon Verlag, was based in Amsterdam but brought out books chiefly in German and for the most part by authors disliked by Hitler's regime.[88] So it is no accident that two of Kerényi's most important books, the one on Apollo[89] and the study of ancient religion,[90] were published by Pantheon in what was still a free country, although not for long.

In any case Kerényi was dismissed from his teaching post at the University of Pécs in 1941 and given one of lower standing at the University of Szeged, on the banks of the Tisza River, a few kilometers from the Yugoslav border.[91]

---

86 Magris, Aldo: op. cit., p. 64.
87 Cited in ibid., p. 65.
88 Edelman, Hendrik: *International Publishing in the Netherlands, 1933–1945. German Exile, Scholarly Expansion, War-Time Clandestinity*, Leiden, Brill, 2010.
89 Kerényi, Károly: *Apollon. Studien über antike Religion und Humanität*, Amsterdam, Pantheon Akademische Verlagsanstalt, 1937. English transl., *Apollo: The Wind, the Spirit, and the God. Four Studies*, Dallas, Spring Publications, 1983.
90 Id., *Die antike Religion: eine Grundlegung*, Amsterdam, Pantheon Akademische Verlagsanstalt, 1941.
91 Magris, Aldo: op. cit., pp. 114–15.

Between 1938 and 1941 Kerényi had pursued his mythological studies in Hungary "under all kinds of threat," and the first prominent result had been the publication of *Die antike Religion. Eine Grundlegung* in 1940. It is one of the fundamental texts of 20th century culture, bringing together the essays on which all his subsequent research would be based, such as *Was ist Mythologie?* or the *Vom Wesen des Festes, Paideuma* that had so impressed Huizinga and was certainly the most immediate starting point for the lectures given in Budapest. Kerényi's aversion to Nazism was public knowledge, while his positions were fairly libertarian and certainly not pro-communist. This was moreover a fairly widespread attitude in the country and in the political class, as in the case of the Kállay government.

In 1941 he had been invited by Jung to lecture in Ascona, and immediately after the war left with his family for Switzerland.[92] He would live in Ascona until his death in 1973.

Kerényi's oldest daughter, Katia, the fruit of his first marriage, joined the resistance movement while a student at university: arrested by the Gestapo following an anonymous tip-off, she was deported to Ravensbrück, where she remained until the end of the war.[93]

MYTH

[This] mythology will itself have the same effect as the most direct psychology – the effect, indeed, of an activity of the psyche, externalised in images.[94]
Károly Kerényi

In his study of Greek civilization, Kerényi, rejecting the philological specialism of traditional research, felt the need for a thorough investigation of the internal coherence of all the elements that made it up, of the "central idea," the "world vision" on whose basis these elements are structured into a unique and unrepeatable organism; in other words, of the form that underlies every partial aspect of a culture and connects it with that central vision outside which the culture itself would be obscure or incomprehensible.

The immediate consequence is that myth, far from being a metaphor for historico-social events actually experienced by a people, is a profound expression of the *image of the world* that supports – as an internal structure – an entire culture in the historical process of its becoming. However, myth is also the original form with which the spirit of a culture defines itself, it is the direct even if not unique expression of that vision of the world and existence that coherently and unmistakably characterizes a culture. Moreover, "the description of an individual event by means of historico-geographical coordinates is, if expressed in ordinary language, the story: i.e. the *mythos* [...]. For this reason every description is in the end a story, and the story a myth."[95]

---

92 MAGRIS, Aldo: op. cit., p. 115.
93 An account of her experience in the concentration camp can be found in the letter written to her father on June 25, 1945, translated into German and published in the Kerényi-Hesse correspondence, *Briefwechsel aus der Nähe*, op. cit.
94 KERÉNYI, Károly: Introduction to *Die Mythologie der Griechen*, Zurich, Rhein, 1951. English transl., *The Gods of the Greeks*, London, Thames and Hudson, 1951, reprinted 1985, p. 3.
95 MELANDRI, Enzo: *La linea e il circolo. Studio logico-filosofico sull'analogia*, Bologna, Il Mulino, 1968. Rpt. Macerata, Quodlibet, 2004, p. 513.

Yet mythology possesses a bipolarity: it is theology and anthropology at one and the same time because ancient myths would be totally incomprehensible, pure nonsense, if the human were to be eliminated from them.

"For Myth is the foundation of life; it is the timeless pattern, the religious formula to which life shapes itself, in as much as its characteristics are a reproduction of the Unconscious," [...] "any great mythology might – if one chose to ignore its artistic aspects – be styled a 'collective psychology.'"[96] The psychological nature of religion had moreover already been the subject of study by Kerényi before he devoted himself to Greek myths.[97]

The stuff of mythology is composed of something that is greater than the storyteller and than all human beings – "as they are now" said Homer – but always as something visible, perceptible or, at least, capable of being expressed in images something that can be seen, experienced or at least grasped in images [...]. Mythology must transcend the individual, and must exercise over human beings a power that seizes hold of the soul and fills it with images [...].[98]

The creation of myth is nothing but the representation of archetypes, and as such reveals an important sphere of the psyche. In other words mythology can be understood as a form of collective psychology and this is the underlying reason for the alliance between Kerényi and Carl Gustav Jung – the latter, who since the end of the First World War had devoted himself to the study of myths and religion, was interested above all in formulating a "theory of the collective unconscious."[99] For Jung, the founder of analytical psychology, the observation of individual psychological mechanisms made it possible to analyze the secrets of artistic creativity or the dynamics of historical phenomena; but to find one's way around the labyrinth of individual events it was necessary to study collective phenomena and behavior. Thus the mental dimension of humanity was no longer a sort of appendage to its biological organization, but a significant aspect of human instincts; and to understand the instincts of a society the myths on which it was founded had to be studied.

So it is possible to tackle mythology in a rational way, an intention made explicit in the title of the book Kerényi and Jung wrote together at the beginning of the forties.[100] It is a key text of contemporary psychology that was a direct consequence of the public lectures delivered in Budapest by Kerényi every Friday: in fact these were attended by Jolande Jacobi, Jung's close Hungarian associate who served as a bridge between the two scholars.

---

96 Kerényi, Károly: Introduction to *The Gods of the Greeks*, op. cit., pp. 2–3.
97 Id., *Antike Religion und Religionspsychologie*, in *Apollon. Studien über antike Religion und Humanität*, Vienna/Amsterdam/Leipzig, Leo, 1937, pp. 15–36.
98 Id., *The Gods of the Greeks*, op. cit., p. 3.
99 See Jung, Carl Gustav: *The Archetypes and The Collective Unconscious*, a collection of essays written between 1934 and 1954, Princeton (NJ), Bollingen, 1990.
100 Jung, Carl Gustav and Kerényi, Károly: *Einführung in das Wesen der Mythologie. Gottkindmythos. Eleusinische Mysterien*, Amsterdam, Pantheon, 1942; *Essays on a Science of Mythology: The Myth of the Divine Child and the Mysteries of Eleusis*, New York, Pantheon Books, 1949.

SCIENCE

In line with his criticism of German philology, Kerényi did not spare science and more in general the climate of positivism that still prevailed in Hungarian academe: "We have lost direct access to the grand realities of the spiritual world – and to these belong everything that is authentically mythological. We have lost them in part as a result of our scientific spirit, all too ready to help us out and all too abundant in subsidiary means."[101]

For Kerényi *Ergriffenheit* ("emotion") is, in the lot of the scientist, the nonscientific root of science,[102] the secret purpose that drives his efforts. It is not the scientist who chooses the subject of his research for strictly disciplinary reasons: on the contrary, the fundamental sensation of "being grasped" is that the truth chooses us, and not the other way round. But it is precisely this sensation of being chosen that induces us to assume our responsibilities at the same time.

Science and art "fused together," as in Heisenberg's lecture on Goethe's color theory, intent on grasping the "emergence of the content of the world": Kerényi's positions find affinities in those of Heisenberg and later Feyerabend. It could even be claimed, as Friedman would do many years later and on more than one occasion, that mythology always presents a complete image of the universe without internal contradictions, in relation to the culture that has generated it.[103] In his most recent essay, written at the age of around 85, *L'ordre compliqué* (2008), Friedman drives home the concept in the conclusions of the first chapter, "Constructing an Image":

Our knowledge of the world starts from the image (it cannot begin directly from the model or the prototype). All our science is based on the image: what we call a "mathematical model" is not really a model (it does not function like the thing modeled), but only an image. Sequential representation is, currently, the most precise image to which we can aspire. From it we can construct models: this is the task faced by our intellect.[104]

Friedman, in his full maturity, has finally taken the reasoning sketched out in his youth to its logical consequences, defining at last "an architecture beyond architecture."[105]
From this perspective science, like mythology, explains everything: there is no human phenomenon that lies outside these "images of the world." For this reason mythology can be considered a proto-science, and Kerényi himself suggested the possibility of a scientific study of mythology. Moreover, classical science, at least from the late Middle Ages onward, had emerged in a culture dominated by the alliance between man, seen as the hinge between divine order and natural order, and God, the rational and intelligible legislator, the supreme architect conceived in our own image. With the result that philosophers

---

[101] Kerényi, Károly: *Thomas Mann zwischen Norden und Süden*, Neue Zürcher Zeitung, July 4, 1965.
[102] See Heisenberg's contrastation of Goethe with Newton.
[103] Friedman, Yona: *L'Univers erratique...*, op. cit., p. 2, note 1.
[104] Friedman, Yona: *L'ordre compliqué et autres fragments*, Paris, Editions de l'Eclat, 2008.
[105] *Une architecture au-delà de l'architecture*, ibid. p. 11.

and theologians did science and scientists attempted to decipher and comment on the divine wisdom and power at work in creation.[106] A contemporary theoretical physicist like Ilya Prigogine – whom Friedman knew personally[107] – wrote openly of "the myth at the origin of science" and "the scientific myth" today.[108] Only later did it become clear that, as Enzo Melandri has pointed out, "in modern science there is no longer any need to recount the myth: it is implicit in our cherishing of the illusion of progress."[109]

So if science and mythology are the same thing, both must be a form of rhetoric aimed at convincing humanity:

We can describe the mythologies of "proto-sciences" as follows: they owe their consistency to what they "choose" as their references in the domain of human behavior, to what they borrow from and give back to the experience of society, for whose use they have been conceived.[110]

This means that if we regard mythologies as theories – or rather, as *anthropomorphic scientific theories* – that describe the world, they offer many advantages: they are easy to understand and communicate and capable of representing an almost unlimited complexity. Moreover Feyerabend, analyzing the surprising similarities between myth and science in the last chapter of *Against Method*, stresses that mythology (and science) leads in itself to the search for theoretical models because:

The theory places things in a causal context that is wider than the causal context provided by common sense: both science and myth cap common sense with a theoretical superstructure. [...] Theory construction consists in breaking up objects of common sense and in reuniting the elements in a different way.[111]

Friedman, however, is interested above all in a distinctive aspect of mythologies: they are the only things able to take account of completely erratic events. The main defect of mathematical models and mechanistic thinking is in fact that they are incapable, except with great difficulty, of representing phenomena linked to motion, i.e. that are erratic or unpredictable in their movement. But since our world is characterized by a dynamic, shifting nature – humanity is one of many migratory species of animal – Friedman believes that it is necessary to introduce a new model, a "neo-anthropomorphic" theory that sets

---

[106] "Science is a disguised theology: an attempt to represent the universe as the result of the application of abstract rules, rules imposed (created) by God. Modern physics (substantiated by, among others, Einstein) is based on a number of axioms of a theological nature: the laws of nature are the same at every point of the universe. The laws of nature can be reduced to a single fundamental law (these are the principles of any monotheism). Modern sciences accept the dogma that it must be possible to formulate all events examined by physics in the language of mathematics (and here we have already arrived at exegesis). In general, I feel a certain unease about mathematical models (although without questioning their utility): these models are certainly true, but insufficient, intrinsically insufficient. Other kinds of mathematics capable of overcoming these difficulties may exist, but are not yet – so I am told – very developed." FRIEDMAN, Yona: *L'ordre compliqué*..., op. cit., chapter III, fragment no. 7.
[107] "I met Ilya Prigogine back in 1977." FRIEDMAN, Yona in OBRIST, Hans-Ulrich & FRIEDMAN, Yona: *The Conversation Series*, op. cit., p. 7.
[108] PRIGOGINE, Ilya and STANGERS, Isabelle: *La nouvelle alliance*..., op. cit.
[109] MELANDRI, Enzo: *La linea e il circolo*..., op. cit., p. 516; the quotation is taken from the section with the fitting title *Science and Myth*.
[110] FRIEDMAN, Yona: *L'Univers erratique*..., op. cit., p. 7.
[111] FEYERABEND, Paul: *Against Method. Outline of an Anarchistic Theory of Knowledge*, London, New Left Books, 1975. The passage cited is available online at http://www.marxists.org/reference/subject/philosophy/works/ge/feyerabe.htm

out to deal with the continually shifting relations between people and things but is based on the individual. In fact the protagonist of any mythological account is always an individual personality and his irrational behavior implies that future events are for the most part unpredictable:

I use the term "erratic" in the sense of "not predictable on the basis of any regularity," and thus in reference to the impossibility of predicting the state of a system despite knowing the state that precedes it.[112]

After the encounter with Heisenberg and Kerényi in his formative years, no planning would be possible for Friedman any longer, except as a statistical model, and consequently architecture could only be *mobile*.

---

[112] FRIEDMAN, Yona: *L'ordre compliqué...*, op. cit., p. 56.

408

YONA FRIEDMAN
ARCHITECTE D.P.L.F.A.H.
13, RUE QUENTIN-BAUCHART
PARIS-8ᵉ   FON. 70-12

Paris, 30.11.59.

Mélyen Tisztelt Professzor Ur,

elküldtem Ünnek egy brosurát (franciául) az épitészet mobilitásával kapcsolatban, ahol az alapvető elgondolást Ünnek köszönhetem, mint egykori hallgatója a budapesti Tudományegyetemen 1943-ban. Az eleusysi misztériumokrol tartott előadássorozatát gondolom, ahol egy "szorakozást" és egy általános érdekü "pletykát" (a mythologiát) mutatta mint egy társadalom alkotóját és központját, Huysingára is hivatkozva. Ezen az alapon próbáltam az épitészetben is eljutni egy hasonló analizisre, ami természetesen a technikai nivón tovább vezetett, amit a brosurában igyekeztem kifejezni. (Sajnos a magyar nyelvben már és a franciában még nem vagyok biztos).

Fogadja, kérem, a brosurát köszönetem jeléül, és miután az a benyomásom, hogy szakmailag (épitészet) elég forradalmi hatása van a theoriának, a vele járó cinkosságot is.

Kiváló tisztelettel

Y. Friedman

409

KÁROLY KERÉNYI

408 Portrait in Rome, 1948. Photograph by Rolf Schott.
409 Letter from Yona Friedman to Professor Kerényi, Paris, November 30, 1959.

ARCHITECTURE IN HUNGARY BETWEEN THE WARS

The marked shrinking of Hungary's borders after the Treaty of Trianon (1920) and the consequent economic crisis triggered by inflation and industrial retrenchment made it difficult to contemplate architectural projects on a large scale, like some of the ones realized before the war. In general public and private works were downsized on a par with the nation itself, no longer part of the supranational Habsburg Monarchy. The binding agent of Horthy's new nationalism was the Catholic religion, a factor capable of uniting the middle class that was the social base of the counterrevolution – it is no coincidence that twenty-three new churches were built in Budapest alone in the twenties.[113]

Given that the regime professed patriotism as its guiding ideology, it might be expected that the attention of Hungarian architectural culture between the wars would have been focused on a national style. In reality, in contrast to what was declared publicly, even state architecture in this period developed in diverging directions.[114] The lines of research at the turn of the century could be assimilated for the most part to a local version of the Viennese Secession and the teachings of Otto Wagner, interpreted by authoritative figures like Ödön Lechner, Béla Lajta and József Vágó, but with the end of the war these lines died out.[115] Historicism, at times with vernacular overtones, was still preponderant of course, but on the one hand a poetics emerged that was inclined toward the general climate of "rappel à l'ordre," akin to the Italian Novecento movement, as in the work of Gyula Wälder;[116] on the other some architects did their best to introduce a profoundly renewed style of architecture into Hungary,[117] and with a "distinctly modern bias." Consequently this trend was judged as "exemplary" by as refined a critic as Edoardo Persico[118]: the Italo-Hungarian conversation on architecture was facilitated by Horthy's liking for Mussolini, especially toward the middle of the thirties.

Among the Hungarian modernists were two leading figures of the Bauhaus, Marcel Breuer and László Moholy-Nagy, with the result that in the twenties there were around a dozen Hungarian students[119] at the school founded by Walter Gropius. Among them was Farkas Mólnar (1897–1945), the only one to return from Weimar, where he had enrolled in 1921. Initially Mólnar followed the courses taught by Itten and Kandinsky[120] and then took part in the exhibition of 1923 with a paradigmatic design for a cubic detached house

---

113 FERKAI, András: *Hungarian Architecture between the Wars*, in WIEBENSON, Dora and SISA, Jozsef (eds.): *The Architecture of Historic Hungary*, Cambridge (MA)/London, MIT Press, 1998, p. 246.
114 MACSAI, John: *Competing Ideas in Hungarian Architecture*, in LESNIKOWSKI, Wojciech (ed.): *East European Modernism. Architecture in Czechoslovakia, Hungary, and Poland between the Wars, 1919–1939*, New York, Rizzoli International, 1996, pp. 113–19.
115 See respectively BIRAGHI, Marco: *Ödön Lechner: la corona dell'architettura*, in *Casabella*, no. 684–85, December–January 1999–2000, pp. 8–21; id. (ed.): *Bela Lajta: ornamento e modernità*, Milan, Electa, 1999; LAMBRICHS, Anne: *József Vágó, 1877–1947. Un architecte hongrois dans la tourmente européenne*, Brussels, AAM, 2003.
116 COHEN, Jean-Louis: *The Future of Architecture since 1889*, London, Phaidon Press, 2012, p. 260.
117 For an overview also see MERÉNYI, Ferenc: *1867–1965: Cento anni di architettura ungherese*, Rome, Accademia d'Ungheria, 1965.
118 PERSICO, Edoardo: *L'Ungheria verso l'Europa*, in *Casabella*, November 1934, now in id., *Oltre l'architettura. Scritti scelti e lettere*, ed. by MARIANI, Riccardo, Milan, Feltrinelli, 1977, pp. 130–31.
119 They included the critic Ernö Kállai, Andor Weininger, who attended the theater and dance courses, and Gyula Papp, who designed lamps and dishes. And then there was Alfréd Forbát, who was hired by Gropius between 1920 and 1924 and worked with Theo van Doesburg but had studied in Munich. See BONTA, János: *Functionalism in Hungarian Architecture*, in Wojciech Lesnikowski (ed.): *East European Modernism . . .*, op. cit., p. 128.
120 DE MICHELIS, Marco and KOHLMEYER, Agnes: (eds.): *Bauhaus 1919–1933*, Milan, Mazzotta, 1996, p. 411.

called the "Red Cube" from the previous year,[121] an idea to which he would return in later projects. He also became actively involved in scenic design in close contact with Gropius, Schlemmer and Moholy-Nagy.[122] According to Colin Rowe the "Red Cube" design suggests in particular "that approach, which has come to be considered as characteristic of modern architecture [...] an abandoning of the idea of mass and masses, a substitution of plane, an emphasis upon the prismatic quality of the cube, and at the same time an attack on the cube, which by disrupting the coherence of its internal volume, intensifies our appreciation of both its planar and its geometrical qualities. These are projects which appear as complete illustrations of that Giedionesque concept of space-time for which the Bauhaus is so justly famous.[123]

After the First World War the urban structure of Budapest was marked by a "human-environmental model of concentric circles," with a compact center and a greater dynamism of extensive development in the suburbs.[124] In 1931, on the initiative of the Hungarian association of architects and engineers, the Napraforgó experimental complex was built in a suburb of Budapest. The intent was clearly demonstrative: the aim was to prove that it was possible to construct a complete housing unit for a family on an area smaller than was prescribed by the law in force at the time, with sixteen separate residences ranging in size from 70 to 150 square meters each, as well as three duplexes, a new road and a small central square.

The Napraforgó complex was conceived for the middle class as well as for the less well-off, and in fact one of the people who worked on the plan (1930) was Lajos Kozma, previously associated with a bourgeois clientele, to whom we will return shortly. Also involved in the design of Napraforgó, however, had been the architects who had earlier belonged to the Hungarian group of the CIAM – founded in 1929 thanks to the mediation of Breuer. The leader of this group was Farkas Mólnar, who had returned to Hungary for good in 1925. Although Napraforgó cannot be compared with other "model" housing projects realized in those years – like the Weissenhof in Stuttgart (1927) and then the ones in Breslau (Wrocław), Brno, Vienna, etc. – it at least in part fits into the general climate of architectural experimentation with what was known as the *Existenzminimum*,[125] born out of the encounter between architects interested in social questions and public intervention (whether by states, municipalities or cooperatives) who found themselves in conflict with

---

121 Ibid., pp. 135–37, and FERKAI, András: op. cit., p. 254.
122 The first total theater with a stage at the center and three seating areas arranged in a U-shape was proposed by Mólnar in 1924-25 with his "U-Theater" plan, from which Gropius would later borrow some elements for the Total Theater he designed for Piscator in Berlin in 1927. See MÓLNAR, Farkas: U-Theater, in SCHLEMMER, Oskar, MOHOLY-NAGY, László and MÓLNAR, Farkas: *Die Bühne am Bauhaus*, with an introduction by Walter Gropius. Mainz/Berlin, Florian Kupferberg, 1965. English transl., *The Theater of the Bauhaus*, Middletown (CT), Wesleyan University Press, 1961. Also see HERZOGENRAT, Wulf: *Il teatro al Bauhaus*, in De MICHELIS, Marco and KOHLMEYER, Agnes (eds.): op. cit., p. 339; and WINGLER, Hans M.: *Das Bauhaus*, Bramsche, Rasch, 1962. English transl., *The Bauhaus: Weimar, Dessau, Berlin, Chicago*, Cambridge (MA), MIT Press, 1972.
123 ROWE, Colin: *Mannerism and Modern Architecture* (1950), now in *The Mathemathics of the Ideal Villa and Other Essays*, Cambridge (MA), MIT Press, 1976, p. 44.
124 On the urban development of Budapest in this period see MEGGYESI, Tamás: *La città moderna. Piani di sviluppo fra le due guerre mondiali*, in *Rassegna*, no. 78 ("Budapest 1848–1945"), pp. 47–50.
125 "The problem of the minimum dwelling is that of establishing the elementary minimum of space, air, light and heat required by man in order that he be able to fully develop his life functions without experiencing restrictions due to his dwelling, i.e., a minimum *modus vivendi* in place of a *modus non moriendi*. [...] Maximum light, sun and air for all dwellings!" GROPIUS, Walter: *Sociological Premises for the Minimum Dwelling of Urban Industrial Populations* (1929), now in *The Scope of Total Architecture*, London, Allen & Unwin, 1956, p. 112.

the building regulations in force all over Europe, as is testified by the proceedings of the 2nd and 3rd CIAM.[126] In addition, it presents a very diverse cross-section of modern Hungarian architecture at the beginning of the thirties.[127]

The CIAM group led by Mólnar and József Fischer gravitated around the monthly avant-garde magazine *Tér és Forma* ("Space and Form"), published for the first time in 1928, and through it fought politically left-leaning battles on behalf of collective and modern housing.[128] Its members were the architects most dissatisfied with the *status quo,* as is clear from Mólnar's words: "In our part of the world the new architecture for the moment appears only in the literature and already we are hearing aesthetic objections being raised, conservative attitudes opposed to everything that is new. While abroad there are already accomplished facts, here it has not been possible even to make attempts."[129] Chiefly because of their strong political connotations, the activities of the Hungarian group of the CIAM were often obstructed by the authorities of the Horthy regime: in 1932 the third exhibition held by the group was closed down by the police on the grounds of political agitation and the organizers given suspended prison sentences.[130] Finally, in 1938, the group was forced to disband.[131] For these reasons, and given the scarcity of opportunities for work, Mólnar made use of every commission to try out his ideas and in particular to investigate the possibilities of an extreme flexibility of the interiors.

"The principle of the shortest route requires the rooms themselves to become mobile, and their use convertible."[132] In his own duplex apartment, Mólnar had come up with a single sliding door which could be used, alternately, to connect two small cubicles, a studio and a dining room to the living room.[133] One of the buildings he designed at Napraforgó was a "Villa with Variable Walls." The importance of Mólnar and the Hungarian group of the CIAM, despite never succeeding in realizing the social utopia of "Constructing the City and Society," as the title of their third exhibition put it, which they had set themselves as a goal, lay in their drawing attention to the gravity of housing conditions in Hungary and to the possibilities offered by modernist architecture and urban planning. In any case their ideas continued to spread among not only architects, but also their middle-class clients.[134] In particular, their anticipation of the theme of the convertibility and mobility of buildings or some of their parts – a theme that had certainly been invigorated by the earlier experience of scenic design at the Bauhaus and which was to become a constant in Friedman's postwar work – demonstrates once again how many of the architectural theories and insights of the second half of the 20th century were in reality already present in embryo form in the early days of

---

[126] Published in Italian in AYMONINO, Carlo (ed.): *L'abitazione razionale. Atti dei congressi CIAM. 1929–1930,* Venice, Marsilio, 1971. On pp. 234 and 239 are reproduced the plans of two housing complexes located in Budapest and one of its suburbs, Rakosfalva, presented by the Hungarian group of the CIAM.
[127] Along with Mólnar, some of the other architects invited were Pál Ligeti, József Fischer, László Vágó and Gyula Wälder.
[128] In 1928 two magazines marked by their interest in modern architecture, although not from the outset, were founded in Italy too: *Domus* and *La Casa bella.*
[129] MÓLNAR, Farkas: *A lakásépités racionalizásá [Rationalization in the Construction of Apartments],* in *Tér és Forma,* no. 3, 1928, pp. 99–102.
[130] FERKÁI, Andras: *Tendenze razionalistiche nell'architettura del primo dopoguerra,* in *Rassegna,* no. 78 ("Budapest 1848–1945"), pp. 55–56.
[131] On the difficulties faced by modernism in Hungary, see BONTA, János: *Functionalism in Hungarian Architecture,* op. cit., pp. 125–72.
[132] MÓLNAR, Farkas: *A racionális építkezésro [On Rational Constructions],* in *Tér és Forma,* no. 8, 1928, pp. 198–99.
[133] Ferkái, Andras: *Tendenze . . . ,* op. cit., p. 56.
[134] BONTA, János: op. cit., p. 130.

modernism, sometimes developed by figures who have so far been regarded as secondary and are still waiting to be re-examined and placed in a historical perspective, as in the case of Mólnar. It suffices to compare some of the drawings of the Aero City project by the minor Russian constructivist Lazar Khidekel[135] with those of Friedman's *Ville-Spatiale* to make this clear, without counting the large-scale projects of El Lissitzky or Georges Vantongerloo.

Friedman's earliest projects, lost after his move to Paris in 1957, explored the principle of convertibility of furnishings invoked by Mólnar, although it is not possible to prove any direct contact between the two: his design of a "chain of panels" in 1945 and of "movable boxes" in 1949, which we will look at further on, are two different attempts to move in that direction, united by the fact that the arrangement of the interior would be determined by the occupants themselves. In the first project, conceived while Friedman was a refugee in Bucharest, the system of panels linked together only at their ends made it possible for the individual occupant to form spaces even of irregular shape at will, but also to insert housing units within larger, undivided areas;[136] the panels could be prefabricated.

But the architect who left the deepest mark on the young Friedman was without doubt Lajos Kozma: the principal representative of another spirit of modernism focused on the renewal of middle-class housing, which had to be comfortable, functional and not standardized. A versatile designer, Kozma began his career as a commercial artist before passing on to interior and furniture design and architecture.[137] Not immune to a certain formal eclecticism that was fairly widespread at the time, over the course of his professional activity in the twenties Kozma made extensive use of a variety of decorations in classical and neo-Baroque style, commencing in 1920 with the tomb of Béla Lajta,[138] whose pupil he had been, in the Jewish cemetery of Rákoskeresztúr, at the time located just outside Budapest. In the thirties, however, while remaining outside the CIAM group, Kozma chose to reduce considerably the ornamentation of his architectural designs, concentrating instead on the functional and practical requirements of his houses, with particular attention to the design of the interiors: Kozma was fairly well known for the originality and comfort of his furnishing, in general inspired by Hungarian folk art, on which he focused all his creativity. It is no accident that Giuseppe Pagano – himself the designer of some famous pieces of furniture, like the ones for the office of the editor of *Il Popolo d'Italia*[139] – devoted a highly complimentary article to him in the magazine that he edited with Persico, *Casabella*: "What are needed are constructors who are proud of having their feet firmly on the ground and who feel deeply and without arrogance their artistic, moral, economic and historical responsibility.

---

[135] KHIDEKEL, Mark: *Il suprematismo e l'architettura*, in *L'Arca*, no. 27, 1989, pp. 62–63.
[136] *Panel Chains*, in Lebesque, Sabine and FENTENER VAN VLISSINGEN, Helene (eds.): *Yona Friedman: Structures . . .*, op. cit., p. 16.
[137] FERKÁI, Andras and GADOROS, Lajos: *Lajos Kozma (1884–1947)*, in *Magyar epitomuveszet*, no. 6, 1984, pp. 43–50. Also see BEKE, László and VARGA, Zsuzsa: *Kozma Lajos*, Budapest, Akadémiai Kiadó, 1970.
[138] "A tomb [that] blends in among others, and indeed makes more of an effort than most not to stand out. It was designed by the reliable Lajos Kozma, a future protagonist of Hungarian rationalism but here still devoted to an almost neoclassical style. A sober and compact edicule surmounted by an urn, a resurrection palm in relief and the tools of his trade (triangle and compasses) crowned with laurel [...] here is buried Lajta Béla, építömüvész." BIRAGHI, Marco: *Architectura nova*, in id. (ed.), *Béla Lajta*, op. cit., pp. 73–74.
[139] BASSI, Alberto and CASTAGNO, Laura: *Giuseppe Pagano*, Bari/Rome, Laterza 1994, pp. 97–101.

One of these is the architect Ludwig Kozma."[140] Pagano was known for his advocacy of an architecture that would be at the service of the collective requirements of modern society, the satisfaction of basic needs, and thus almost anonymous, *proudly modest* like the rural architecture to which he was the first to dedicate an exhibition in 1936.[141] For this reason he was a strenuous opponent of formalist architects, be they traditionalists or rationalists, channeling his gift for design into other fields, such as graphics, furnishings or photography.[142] In this Kozma, at least in his works of the thirties, must have seemed like an ally to Pagano. On the other hand the house with a steel structure designed by Pagano for the 1933 Triennale in collaboration with Albini, Palanti and others, raised about ten meters above the ground, is a prototype made of welded prefabricated elements[143] in which the clear separation of serving and served spaces anticipates by more than twenty years Friedman's idea of mobile architecture (1956).

In similar fashion Friedman, who from the outset was more interested in the people who live in buildings than in their form, would display his greatest individual flair in the decoration of interiors – it suffices to think of his extraordinary home in Paris, the subject of Stefano Graziani's photographic essay at the beginning of this book.[144]

Among the finest examples of Kozma's architecture is the 1935-36 Atrium apartment house, with a movie theater on the ground floor, in Budapest. In the early forties the number of work opportunities diminished considerably owing to the war and Kozma concentrated instead on the writing of a book devoted entirely to the detached house and its principles of composition, illustrated in part by his own works: "The New House," for which he had been obliged to find a publisher in Switzerland.[145] The book, with spare and elegant graphics, presents in its introduction a closely argued criticism of both 19th century historicism and functionalism, judged to be too rigid and "puritan" in its excessive adherence to technique,[146] thereby marking Kozma's isolated position within Hungarian architecture, but not in Europe. Important architects like Pagano and some of his younger pupils were able to get hold of the book,[147] which in any case remains Kozma's spiritual testament.

---

140 PAGANO, Giuseppe: *Ludwig Kozma architetto*, in *Casabella*, no. 81, XII, September 1934, p. 13. Also see PICA, Agnoldomenico: *L'architettura moderna e il nuovo volto dell'Ungheria*, in *Emporium*, vol. 83, no. 496, April 1936, pp. 202–11.
141 PAGANO, Giuseppe and DANIEL, Guarniero (eds.): *Architettura rurale italiana*, Quaderni della Triennale, Milan, Hoepli, 1936. The previous year Pagano had written an article entitled *Architettura rurale in Italia*, Casabella, No. 96, December 1935. "With his *Italian Rural Architecture* Pagano carried out a piece of genuine anthropological research to find the community motivations of architecture, making his own one of the fundamental aspirations of the Modern Movement, i.e. the need to propose the model of a pre-mechanical and preindustrial society as an alternative to the tired individualism of industrial society propped up by the bourgeois economy and private capitalism." MENNA, Filiberto: *Profezia di una società estetica. Saggio sull'avanguardia artistica e sul movimento dell'architettura moderna*, Rome, Lerici, 1968, p. 111. It is worth noting that Pagano's research was contemporary with Béla Bartok's investigations of rural and folk music in Hungary.
142 See DE SETA, Cesare (ed.): *Giuseppe Pagano fotografo*, Milan, Electa, 1979.
143 Id., *Il destino dell'architettura. Persico, Giolli, Pagano*, Rome/Bari, Laterza 1985, pp. 233–34.
144 Also see RIANI, Paolo: *La casa di Yona Friedman*, in *Interni*, September 1970.
145 KOZMA, Ludwig: *Das neue Haus. Ideen und Versuche zur Gestaltung des Familienhauses mit Zeichnungen und Fotografien eigener Arbeiten*, Zurich, H. Girsberger, 1941.
146 Ibid., *Einleitung*, p. 9.
147 For example, there is a copy of Kozma's book in Albini's personal library that was put on show at the exhibition *Zero Gravity. Franco Albini, costruire la modernità*. Milan Triennale, 2006. Albini is known for his ingenuity in the design of furnishings and, along with other Milanese architects like Giancarlo Palanti and Giancarlo De Carlo, was one of the colleagues and friends closest to Pagano up until his final years of involvement in the resistance in Milan: "Not coincidentally Albini was one of the members of the new generation most closely linked to Pagano and, among these, the one that he felt nearest to in clarity of ideas, simplicity and intellectual honesty." DE SETA, Cesare: *Il destino . . .*, op. cit., p. 233. Also see BUNÇUGA, Franco: *Conversazioni con Giancarlo De Carlo*, in *Architettura e libertà*, Milan, Elèuthera, 2000, p. 44.

Yona Friedman worked for a few months in Kozma's studio in Budapest shortly after the publication of the book, in 1943. In our interview Friedman speaks of Kozma as an opponent of the Horthy regime and an unorthodox figure: it was he, continues Friedman, who introduced him to the Bauhaus, which at the time was obviously excluded from the teachings at the Palatine Joseph University of Technology and Economics in Budapest where Friedman attended the department of architecture as an auditor. As we have seen, the discriminatory legislation introduced in 1939 had reduced the quota of Jewish students admitted to the university and Friedman had been excluded at the moment of enrolment.[148] So we have to infer that the experience in Kozma's studio, which following the German occupation in 1944 must have received almost no commissions, was more one of training than of actual work. In other words Kozma, like Heisenberg and Kerényi, represented a model of an intellectual who pursued his own ideas in solitude in the face of mostly hostile public opinion.

The design of public buildings was in fact monopolized by the association of architects and the racial law limited access to this category. In addition, the worldwide depression that followed the Wall Street Crash of 1929 had arrested property development in Hungary too and the situation had certainly not improved with the outbreak of war.

Among the traditionalists there was also Iván Kotsis, undoubtedly a minor figure but one who like other Austrian and German architects attempted to steer a middle course between tradition and avant-garde, paying particular attention to the needs of the inhabitants and to the *genius loci,* as in the case of the church at Balaton Boglár (1932): the flat ceiling of the bare hall is interrupted by traditional wooden beams, as was documented in *Casabella,* in a feature on Hungarian architecture.[149] As well as with Pál Virágh, Kotsis had had direct contacts with Paul Schmittener, Paul Bonatz and their followers in Stuttgart. In particular Kotsis was the first professor at Budapest University to allow students to design according to the criteria of modern architecture.[150] This detail makes credible Friedman's claim that he was able to attend lectures with a special permit as auditor because he was regarded as deserving by Kotsis. In addition, after his emigration to Haifa in 1946, it was Kotsis again who wrote a letter of introduction for Friedman to the dean of the school of architecture of the local university, the Technion, to show that he had studied for three years (from the fall of 1941 until his arrest in the fall of 1944).[151] After the liberation of Budapest, Friedman left behind him a city that was two-thirds destroyed and filled with rubble.

---

148 György Ligeti had a similar experience: "*You took your school-leaving examination in 1941. Did you immediately apply to the university?* I took the school-leaving examination in the spring, and in the fall the university turned down my application. At the department of natural sciences in Cluj there was only one place available for a Jew. Being a "Jew" did not then indicate belonging to a religion but to a race, on the basis of the Nazi laws, although at the time these were not in force in Hungary, or at least they were not yet as severe as in Germany. Having passed the school-leaving examination with honors, I could have been given that place. But it was assigned to someone else." In Ligeti, György: op. cit., p. 43.
149 Mólnar, Jozsef and Schwarz, Dionisio: *L'architettura ungherese moderna,* in *Casabella,* no. 83, November 1934, yr. XIII, pp. 12–13.
150 Ferkai, András: op. cit., p. 273.
151 "Hungary was more or less a fascist country and there were numerous clauses for architects. I couldn't study architecture, but there was a professor who thought that I should study it. So I got a special permission to do architecture like anybody else, but I didn't get a diploma because of the law." Yona Friedman, interview in the appendix.

Friedman says that the group of resistance to the Germans which he had joined in Budapest was Zionist:

Yes, it was a Zionist group. I had some friends who took me in and we had a system. It was evident that if you were taken by an institution like the Gestapo you couldn't say that you simply didn't know anything. So, our system was very simple: you could tell them anything you knew because, if the others knew you were arrested, all the addresses would have automatically been changed. It's a guerrilla technique – they could verify that everything I said was true and realize that I could not know more. This was quite important; with these techniques the other people in the group were untouched.

Organized Zionist groups were quite rare in Europe and there is no trace of this group in the most complete study of the destruction of the Jews of Europe, divided up by nation.[152] The most striking case was certainly that of the uprising in the Warsaw ghetto led by Marek Edelman, but the situation in Poland was very different as before the war there were already Zionist political parties – as well as anti-Zionist ones, like the Bund, the Jewish workers' party – that could serve as an organizational base.[153] In Hungary, where the integration of Jews into society was very great, this did not happen: no Zionist party had been formed. The only clandestine group that could be said to have put up an active resistance to the German occupation was the one called Halutz ("Pioneer" in Hebrew), and in all likelihood this was the group which Friedman joined. However, the leaders of Halutz were not Hungarians but political refugees, a Pole (Tzvi Goldfarb) and a Slovak (Rafael Friedl),[154] from countries where the deportation of Jews had already been carried out. This group was made up of very young people, with around 500 members who often changed their names and were in conflict with the leaders of the Jewish community of Budapest, more inclined to a policy of negotiation with the Nazi command. Above all the *halutzim* had soon realized that without the support of their own community and given the very limited size of their forces, the most effective way of saving the greatest number of Jews was the forgery of papers,[155] the same method as had been adopted by Perlasca,[156] and this is the activity in which Friedman says he took part.[157] The guerrilla technique of communication of which Friedman speaks – the continual change of identity and address on the part of individual members meant that anyone arrested could confess everything without compromising the others – is certainly

---

[152] Cattaruzza, Marina, Flores, Marcello, Levis Sullam, Simon and Traverso, Enzo (eds.): *Storia della Shoah. Lo sterminio degli ebrei*, vol. 1, *La crisi dell'Europa e lo sterminio degli ebrei*, Turin, UTET, 2006.
[153] Edelman, Marek: *Getto walczy: udział Bundu w obronie getta warszawskiego*, Warsaw, Nakładem C. K. Bundu, 1945. Eng. transl., *The Ghetto Fights*, New York, American Representation of the General Jewish Workers' Union of Poland, 1946.
[154] Friedl is also known by another name, with which he signed his account of those events: Benshalom, Rafi: *We Struggled for Life. The Hungarian Zionist Youth Resistance during the Nazi Era*, op. cit.
[155] Szita, Szabolcs: *Trading in Lives? Operations of the Jewish Relief and Rescue Committee in Budapest, 1944–1945*, Budapest, Central European University Press, 2005, p. 76.
[156] "People were afraid that I was issuing too many letters of protection and passports; it is clear that I issued letters of protection and passports every time I felt I had too, and I gave out so many that by the time the Russians arrived the number of people officially protected by the legation [the Spanish one, of which Perlasca pretended to be the consul] was 5,200. Many came with their hands full of gold and valuables, or had Christian friends offer them to me, which of course I did not accept." Perlasca, Giorgio: op. cit., pp. 48–49.
[157] "Because I knew how to draw quite well I made the signatures, which was very important. These papers were not valid, but if one was stopped on the street they worked." Yona Friedman, interview in the appendix.

very similar to the one used ten years later during the Algerian war of liberation.[158] In addition, the deep-rooted community spirit and the sharing of the great danger to which they were exposed helped to create a strong sense of unity among the *halutzim* – the first model of what Friedman was to call a "critical group" – who in fact did not disband after the liberation: it was they who obtained many of the visas needed to travel abroad and even organized some flights to Palestine from neighboring Romania.

So it was not difficult for Friedman to reach Bucharest after the liberation. Although immigration was still severely curtailed and even obstructed by the British, Palestine continued to see the clandestine landings of thousands of European Jews. In reality the phenomenon of emigration to Palestine was in part due to the fact that many European countries and above all the USA, the most sought-after destination, had tightened up the laws on immigration to avoid the influx of masses of people. Nonetheless "thousands and thousands of Jews from Germany and the countries occupied by Hitler streamed into the ports of Romania, Bulgaria, Greece, Yugoslavia and Italy, seeking passage on all sorts of old, small and ramshackle ships, totally unsuited for the transport of the passengers, that were often made available by opportunists of the worst kind, promising a clandestine landing on the coasts of Palestine."[159]

To obtain a more suitable berth, Friedman was obliged to spend eleven months of inactivity in shanties built for refugees. It was not until the beginning of 1946 that he reached the Promised Land.

---

[158] See HORNE, Alistair: *A Savage War of Peace: Algeria 1954–1962*, London, Macmillan, 1977. This activity was also represented in great detail in Gillo Pontecorvo's 1966 movie, *The Battle of Algiers*.

[159] VOGHERA, Giorgio: *Gli anni decisivi per la nascita di Israele* (1973), now in id., *Quaderno d'Israele*, Milan, Mondadori, 1980, p. 179.

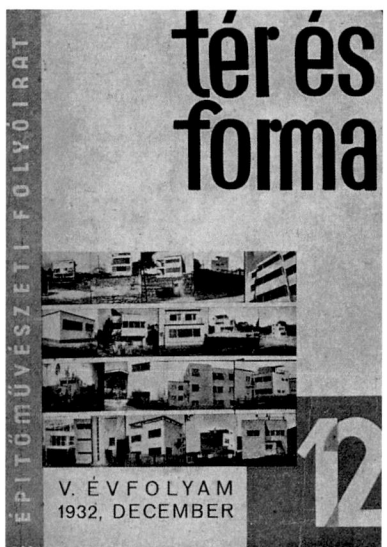

410

411

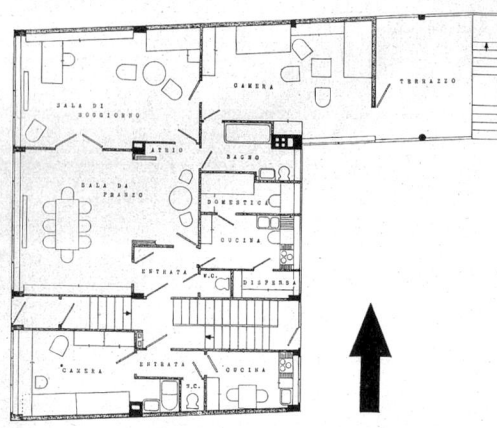

412

413

FARKAS MOLNÁR

410 Architecture magazine *tér és forma* ("space and form") for which Molnár wrote, December 1932.
411–413 Villa at Szeged, Hungary, 1934. East front view, ground-floor plan and view from the landing.

LAJOS KOZMA

414–415 Duplex house in the Rosenhügel district, Budapest, 1934. Front view and furnishings of the living room.
Photographs from *Casabella*, no. 81, 1934.

414

415

416

417

418

LAJOS KOZMA

416 *Grand fashion store*, Budapest, 1930.
417 Image from his book on detached houses, *Das neue Haus*, 1941.
418 *House for a family*, 1931. Published in Kozma, Ludwig: *Das neue Haus: Ideen und Versuche zur Gestaltung des Familienhauses mit Zeichnungen und Fotografien eigener Arbeiten*, Zurich, H. Girsberger, 1941.

IVÁN KOTSIS

419 – 422 *Church at Balaton*, Boglár, 1932. Views of the exterior, interior and detail of the pulpit. Photographs from *Casabella*, no. 81, 1934.

419

420

421

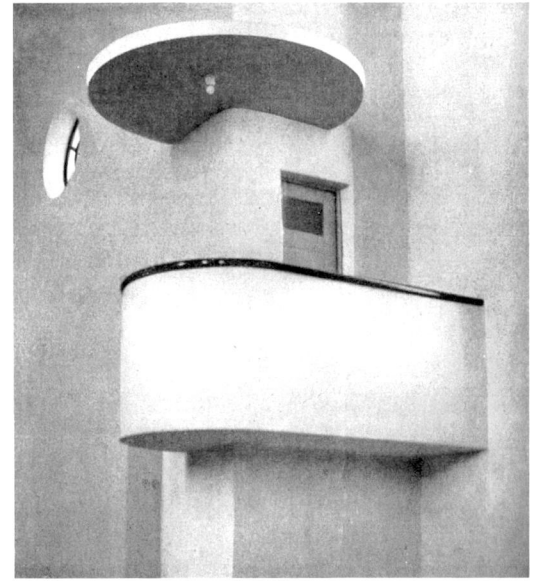

422

ARCHITECTURE IN HUNGARY BETWEEN THE WARS / 313

PALESTINE / ISRAEL: UTOPIAN ZIONISM

We shake off the old life, which has grown rancid on us, and start from the beginning. We don't want to change and we don't want to improve, we want to begin from the beginning. [160]
Aaron David Gordon, Galilean Pioneer

Hannah Arendt has explained clearly that the Zionist movement had its origin in two ideologies typical of the 19th century, socialism and nationalism. This dual root had caused a sharp division within the Zionist movement.

[The] movement was split from the beginning between the social revolutionary forces which had sprung from the Eastern European masses and the aspiration for national emancipation as formulated by Herzl and his followers in the Central European countries. […] Those who adopted the more Eastern variation of the messianic dream went to Palestine for a kind of personal salvation through work within a collective (A.D. Gordon). Spared the ignominies of capitalist exploitation, they could realize at once and by themselves the ideals they preached, and build up the new social order that was only a far-off dream in the social revolutionary teachings of the West. [161]

The state of Israel was founded and led for many decades by a workers' party that has always been a member of the Socialist International. Less well-known on the other hand is the utopian component of Zionism, which finds a direct term of comparison in utopian socialism. A current opposed and derided by communists, utopian socialism has its roots in the French Revolution and embraces some of the more heretical aspirations of Marxism: in *The Communist Manifesto*, in fact, Marx and Engels had already attacked the ideas of the principal utopian thinkers like Fourier, Saint-Simon, Cabet, Considerant and Owen,[162] arguing for the need to move on to a scientific socialism, based on revolutionary class struggle and the industrial proletariat.
The utopian socialists – linked primarily by the fact of being precursors of Marx – saw society without true classes and had varied but generally more libertarian positions.
In any case the secular and rationalist Enlightenment was the ideological base of all the components of socialism, including the Zionist one: the movement known as *Haskalah* (the Jewish Enlightenment) fought for a full integration of Jews into the society to which they belonged, for example by putting aside the Yiddish language.

---

[160] Quotation that opens the autobiographical novel of the naturalized British (but born in Budapest) writer Koestler, Arthur: *Thieves in the Night. Chronicle of an Experiment*, London, Macmillan, 1946, devoted to the construction of a Jewish farming community in Palestine in the thirties.
[161] Arendt, Hannah: *Zionism Reconsidered* (1945), now in id., *The Jewish Writings*, ed. by Kohn, Jerome and Feldman, Ron, New York, Schocken, 2007, pp. 348–49.
[162] On the urban – or anti-urban – ideologies of these thinkers, see Choay, Françoise: *Urbanisme. Utopies et réalités*, Paris, Seuil, 1965. English transl., *The Modern City: Planning in the 19th Century*, New York, Braziller, 1969, especially the first chapter "Pre-Urbanism and Urbanism: the Progressist Model."

In particular the anarchic federalism of Pierre-Joseph Proudhon constitutes one of Yona Friedman's ideological premises, concerned as he is with not imposing his choices as an architect on the users of the buildings he designs; i.e. he is always careful to preserve the rights and preferences of each individual. This is the basic principle of anarchism.[163] Marx went in exactly the opposite direction because in his view the working class was more important than the individual. Proudhon's brand of socialism on the other hand accepted the supremacy of the nation, rejecting the concept of class struggle: all the social classes had to unite in an effort to increase national wealth and ensure that their society (a sort of large, extended family) was able to compete with others. When Friedman underlined the virtues of early Israeli society it was precisely this aspect that he singled out: "When I arrived in Israel it was not really a classless society, but as near to a classless society as possible."[164]
However, Proudhon's theories could not be said to be socialist in the strict sense, based as they were on an aversion to any form of collectivism, but fitted into a libertarian and autonomist current of early 19th century French democracy (distinct from the Jacobin one which inspired Auguste Blanqui, forerunner of the communists) and were well suited to a country in which the majority of farmers were small landowners. In one of his last writings Proudhon – a great admirer of the new market of Les Halles in Paris – was prompted to outline his own aesthetics of architecture, functionalist ahead of its time:

The first thing that needs to be taken care of is housing. The most important thing is that the people are well housed; something all the more necessary in that it is sovereign and king [...] if art and the building trade are not able to provide cheap housing, then I care nothing for architecture and construction. [...] I would give the Louvre Museum, the Tuileries, Notre-Dame – and above all the Column – to live in my own home, in a little house that suits my taste, in which I would live alone, at the center of a small enclosure of a tenth of a hectare, where I would have water, shade, grass and silence.[165]

In particular he rejected a society whose sole purpose was production and consumption, and instead of the masses put the emphasis back on the person, the individual: in other words it was individuals that had to have the power to decide on political and social organization and on their own housing as well, not the state (whence his basically anarchist approach[166]). In short it is a libertarian socialism and not a "liberal" socialism [in the European sense of supporting free trade and private property, *translator's note*] like the one theorized by Carlo Rosselli in *Liberal Socialism*[167] and embraced by crucial figures in

---

163 See Ansart, Pierre: *Naissance de l'anarchisme. Equisse d'une explication sociologique du proudhonisme*, Paris, PUF, 1970. It should be noted that George Woodcock (1912–95), a Canadian writer who was one of the main contemporary ideologues of anarchism, concerned himself directly with the ideas of Kropotkin and the French thinker in *Pierre-Joseph Proudhon. A Biography*, London, Routledge & Kegan Paul, 1956.
164 See the interview in the appendix.
165 Proudhon, Pierre-Joseph: *Du principe de l'art et de sa destination sociale*, Paris, Garnier frères, 1865, pp. 351 ff.
166 The various libertarian arguments (liberal, anarchist, socialist), heirs to a long tradition that began with Locke and Jefferson, see the state as intrinsically illegitimate, since it attacks the rights of the individual, imposing norms of life on him "from the top down." See Boaz, David (ed.): *The Libertarian Reader. Classic and Contemporary Writings from Lao-tzu to Milton Friedman*, New York, The Free Press, 1998.
167 Rosselli, Carlo: *Liberal Socialism*, Princeton (NJ), Princeton University Press, 1994. Although written in the years 1928–29, it took 44 years before the book, apart from a semi-pirated edition of 1945, was published in Italy.

the Italian architecture of the 20th century like Bruno Zevi, Ernesto Nathan Rogers and others.[168] Finally there were those who found an elective affinity between neoromantic anti-capitalism and messianism, throwing into relief the libertarian roots of Jewish inspiration in many Central European intellectuals of the 20th century – Buber, Scholem and Landauer, but also in those who adhered to Marxism like Benjamin, Lukács and Bloch.[169]

The victorious camp of Zionism, i.e. the one linked to Theodor Herzl, born and raised in Budapest, got its greatest boost in all the countries of the Jewish diaspora from the idea that anti-Semitism was an "eternal" and insoluble phenomenon. It was strongly influenced by other 19th century movements of national liberation – including the Italian Risorgimento – and denied the possibility of Jews surviving in any country other than Palestine, and in any form other than that of a completely independent, sovereign Jewish state.

The other tendency, which could be traced back to Ahad Ha'am, saw Palestine as the location for a Jewish spiritual center that would influence the cultural development of all Jews in other countries, but that would have no need for ethnic uniformity and national sovereignty. Ha'am has been described as a "Cartesian Zionist" for "the lucidity and clarity of his writings, his search for the one 'objective' truth, and his critical mind and rational approach that seek in a deductive manner to explicate 'evident,' rational and general principles and apply them to the Jewish people."[170] Those who followed him, including Martin Buber, never aspired "to make Palestine as Jewish as England was English," as Chaim Weizmann put it,[171] but thought that the establishment of a center of higher culture was more important for the movement of rebirth than the foundation of a state. The most important result of the tendency linked to Herzl was the Jewish state, born – as Ahad Ha'am had feared as far back as the turn of the last century[172] – at the cost of a war between Arabs and Jews. The most important result of Ha'am's tendency was the foundation of the Hebrew University of Jerusalem, which opened on Mount Scopus in 1925 with Judah L. Magnes as its first chancellor. The buildings were designed in part by Erich Mendelsohn, linked to Magnes by their common belief in "cultural Zionism," but the university was also promoted by Buber and Weizmann.[173] In fact Mendelsohn's last work in the Holy Land was the Hadassah university hospital (1936 – 39) on Mount Scopus, about which he wrote: "No one will be disappointed who regards it in the light of the monumental austerity and serenity of the greatest spiritual

---

[168] For example Mario Fiorentino – moreover Jewish and a member of the *Giustizia e Libertà* group founded by Rosselli, as were Zevi and Rogers – who was one of the authors of the Monument to the Fallen at the Fosse Ardeatine and leader of the group responsible for the Corviale housing complex. By Zevi, an antifascist but critical of communism and for a long time president of the Italian Radical Party, see *Marxismo e ebraismo* (1976), in id., *Ebraismo e architettura*, Florence, Giuntina, 1993, pp. 33–47.

[169] See Löwy, Michael: *Rédemption et Utopie. Le judaïsme libertaire en Europe centrale. Une étude d'affinité élective*, Paris, PUF, 1988. English transl., *Redemption and Utopia. Jewish Libertarian Thought in Central Europe: A Study in Elective Affinity*, Stanford (CA), Stanford University Press, 1992.

[170] See Golomb, Jacob: *Nietzsche and Zion*, Ithaca (NY), Cornell University Press, 2004, p. 114.

[171] See Weizmann, Chaim: *Trial and Error*, New York, Harper & Bros., 1949.

[172] In 1891 he wrote: "The Arabs, especially the urban elite, see and understand what we are doing and what we wish to do on the land, but they keep quiet […]. But, if the time comes that our people's life in Eretz Yisrael will develop to a point where we are taking their place, either slightly or significantly, the natives are not going to just step aside so easily." Quoted in Kushner, Tony and Solomon, Alisa (eds.): *Wrestling with Zion: Progressive Jewish–American Responses to the Israeli-Palestinian Conflict*, New York, Grove Press, 2003, pp. 14–15.

[173] Many of the ideas typical of the Expressionist architect's cultural Zionism are set out in Mendelsohn, Erich: *Palestine and the World of Tomorrow*, London, Jerusalem Press, 1940.

creations of this part of the world – the Bible, the New Testament, the Koran."[174] In order to better reflect this cultural synthesis, the building presented three white hemispherical cupolas above a porticoed passageway that bounded the large inner courtyard and was clad with local stone.

There was a third component of the Zionist movement that sprang from the socialism of Eastern Europe and eventually led to the foundation of the collective settlements known as *kibbutzim* and *moshavim*. As a new form of agricultural economy and social and cooperative life, these became the main prop of economic life in the early Yishuv – the Jewish community in Palestine[175] – but this was not all: they were above all the location for the realization of a (socialist) utopia. Between 1954 and 1955, a barely 20-year-old Antonio Negri, at the time a member of the Italian Socialist Party, spent a year working on a kibbutz in search of a collective spirit. Later, in prison, he would recall: "in Israel, I experienced practices of communism as elementary as they were radical. It was there, this utopia, dealing with reality. It was concrete."[176] Finally, among the ideological components, there was also an ardently nationalist Zionist right wing which called for the establishment of a Greater Israel that would comprise all the lands described in the Bible. Despite being a minority, the right, led by Vladimir Jabotinsky, was able to influence the Labor Party at more than one critical juncture, partly through paramilitary organizations like the Irgun – responsible for the attack on the British administrative headquarters in the King David Hotel.

In much the same way as happened in the socialist movement, cultural Zionism has been defined as "utopian" because it diverged from the majority current of Zionism, which considered itself more realistic.[177] One of Herzl's prime concerns was to defend himself against the charge of wishful thinking right from the first page of his most important book, *The Jewish State*: "I must, in the first place, guard my scheme from being treated as Utopian [...]."[178] Thus the label of "utopian," just as in the case of socialism, was to be considered derogatory.

The most influential exponent of cultural – or utopian – Zionism after Ha'am was unquestionably Martin Buber. Born in Vienna but raised in Galicia, he lived for a long time in Berlin

---

174 Erich Mendelsohn, quoted in HEINZE-GREENBERG, Ita: *Erich Mendelsohn in Palestine, the Search for Architectural Roots*, in id. and HERBERT, Gilbert (eds.): *Erich Mendelsohn in Palestine*, Haifa, Technion, 1987. It should also be pointed out that Mendelsohn designed Weizmann's private home at Rehovot (1936–37), built out of stone and the official residence of the president of the Republic of Israel while Weizmann held the office.

175 On the role of utopian ideas in the community form of the kibbutz, see STROPPA, Claudio: *Comunità e utopia. Problemi di una sociologia del kibbuz*, Bari, Dedalo, 1970. For a closely argued critique of the model of the kibbutzim, see instead SCHOECK, Helmut: *Der Neid und die Gesellschaft*, Freiburg, Herder, 1966; enlarged ed., 1977. English transl., *Envy: A Theory of Social Behavior*, New York, Harcourt, Brace & World, 1970.

176 NEGRI, Antonio: *Pipeline. Lettere da Rebibbia*, Turin, Einaudi, 1983, p. 28. Negri continues on p. 34: "Utopia is legitimate when it reaches out for the concrete, when it is expressed in action – utopia moving toward possibility. The 1917 Revolution and Israel were pleasantly combined in my desire. Utopia is rational construction of the possible."

177 "While Herzl had to dress his utter realism in utopianism, the religious Zionists and their spiritual/cultural antipodes had to dress their utopianism in realism. It was not enough for the Zionism of the 'true' Zionists to be more real. It also had to be more real. Hence, Buber distinguished between the Zionism of realpolitik, whose politicians were 'fictitious,' and the 'Zionism of reality' (*Wirklichkeitszionismus*), whose agents acted in the domain of 'realization'; between 'actualism' and 'true' realism. 'Actualism' he called the simple 'mastering of the facts,' 'realization' 'the secret of the covenant between God and man.' Once again, the 'true' reality was not the physical reality of the land but a meta-topian, meta-historical reality transforming the people. To become real, the 'true' Zionists had to become utopian. And to become utopian, they had to become real." BIEMANN, Asher: *The Restoration of Utopia: Three Reflections on Zionism*, in *Harvard Israel Review*, no. 1, spring 2002, pp. 4–11.

178 HERZL, Theodor: *Der Judenstaat*, Vienna, M. Breitenstein's Verlags-Buchhandlung, 1896. English transl., *The Jewish State*, Rockville (MD), Wildside Press LLC, 2008, p. 51.

before emigrating to Palestine. His intense activity as an essay writer and lecturer in the years straddling the First World War had had a profound influence on the young Jews of the Central and Eastern Europe, especially in the Prague of Max Brod and Franz Kafka's Jewish-German idyll – a place where the different communities coexisted very peacefully.[179] More recent Israeli historiography, in particular that of the group of so-called "new historians" at the Department of History of Haifa University, Tom Segev, Ilan Pappe, Benny Morris (who has lately changed his mind) and Avi Shlaim, has been carrying out at least since the end of the eighties a work of revision of the history of Israel, bringing into question the Herzlian Zionist myth on which the Jewish state is founded.[180] It suffices to compare Eli Barnavi's *Une histoire moderne d'Israël*[181] with Ilan Pappe's *A History of Modern Palestine*[182] or Anita Shapira's *Israel. A History*[183] to get a measure of the great ideological rifts that have opened up within Israeli historiography, stirring fierce controversy even outside the country. What is certain is that the most recent research of the "new historians" has made it possible to identify many more lines of action that had previously been neglected, with respect to the predominant one of David Ben-Gurion and his workers' party. This is comprehensible and comparable to what has happened in other countries: according to Althusser "ideology represents the imaginary relationship of individuals to their real conditions of existence" and thus the way in which individuals think of themselves in relation to the whole of existence.[184] Ideology alludes (partly deluding itself) to reality and always aims at "totality," indeed it tries to be a faithful map of reality. When it does not succeed, because reality appears too complicated, it simply makes the map up, skipping every difficulty. So every ideology has to be able to account for everything, offering a complete understanding of things. When the attempt to refer faithfully to reality meets obstacles, it continues its course in the imaginary, adapting (and in part inventing) reality to everything that it has set out to represent, with disastrous effects on the *writing of history*.

In fact the connection between ideology and historiography is "constitutive" since the role of ideologies is decisive in understanding the dynamics of historical events. Moreover, history, like criticism, is necessarily the parasite of a larger ideology, which needs to be brought to light.[185]

The history and criticism of Israeli architecture are also undergoing this process of revision and it has been shown how contrasting tactics were present within an apparently unitary

---

[179] For an in-depth study of Buber's influence on Kafka's writing, see BAIONI, Giuliano: *Kafka. Letteratura ed ebraismo*, Turin, Einaudi, 1984, especially chapter I, "Praga el il culturismo di Martin Buber," pp. 3 ff.

[180] MORRIS, Benny: *Righteous Victims. History of the Zionist-Arab Conflict, 1881–1999*, New York: Knopf, 1999. New, enlarged ed., New York, Vintage Books, 2001. Since 2002 Morris has done an abrupt about-face, reconsidering his previous criticism of Zionism. Also see SHLAIM, Avi: *The Iron Wall: Israel and the Arab World*, London, Penguin Books, 2000; and SHAPIRA, Anita and PENSLAR, Derek J.: *Israeli Historical Revisionism: from Left to Right*, London, Frank Cass, 2003.

[181] BARNAVI, Eli: *Une histoire moderne d'Israël*, Paris, Flammarion, 1988.

[182] PAPPE, Ilan: *A History of Modern Palestine: One Land, Two Peoples*, Cambridge (UK), Cambridge University Press, 2004.

[183] SHAPIRA, Anita: *Israel. A History*, Waltham (MA), Brandeis University Press, 2012.

[184] ALTHUSSER, Louis: *Idéologie et appareils idéologiques d'Etat*, in *La pensée*, no. 151, 1970. English transl., *Ideology and Ideological State Apparatuses*, in *Lenin and Philosophy and Other Essays*, London, New Left Books, 1971.

[185] "I don't think that there is such a thing as literary criticism *in itself*; there is no critical method independent of a more general philosophy [...] criticism is necessarily the parasite of a larger ideology." BARTHES, Roland: *Le grain de la voix*, Paris, Seuil, 1981. English transl., *The Grain of the Voice: Interviews 1962–1980*, Evanston (IL), Northwestern University Press, 2009, p. 26.

ideology: Alona Nitzan-Shiftan has brilliantly pointed out the idealistic reasons that drove Erich Mendelsohn into conflict with the modernists of the "Chug" circle of Tel Aviv headed by Arieh Sharon, who were in turn opposed to the architects adhering to the garden-city movement (Richard Kauffmann et al.).[186]

The case of the Chug is very interesting from a historiographic perspective. In 1936, 166,000 people lived in Tel Aviv and its suburbs, around 41% of the entire Jewish population of Palestine. Outstanding for its activism in such a context was the "Circle of Architects" (Chug), founded in 1932, led by Arieh Sharon, Dov Karmi and Zeev Rechter. Sharon had been a student at the Bauhaus and then manager of Hannes Meyer's studio, Karmi had studied in Ghent and Rechter at the École des Ponts et Chaussées in Paris. Within a short time the group, which used to meet every evening at the Café Ginati, was joined by other young architects, mostly of Polish or Russian origin, all of them trained in Europe: Josef Neufeld, perhaps the most gifted of all, studied in Vienna and Rome and worked first for Mendelsohn in Berlin and then with Bruno Taut in Moscow; Genia Averbouch studied in Ghent and worked for a brief period in Brussels; and finally Werner Wittkower from Berlin, brother of the famous art historian Rudolf.

The group brought out a magazine that it immediately used as a way to exert pressure on the municipal authorities, trying to get them to disregard the Geddes plan for Tel Aviv and at the same time quickly edging out older professionals who were more inclined to "Deco" stylistic features like Yehuda Magidovitch or Josif Berlin. In addition, every trace of Orientalism vanished, as did any reference to a preexisting local tradition, replaced by an architecture of the *tabula rasa*, a blank, white sheet, the only kind suitable for the building of the new Zionist national society. Between 1933 and 1939 a large number of openly modern designs were approved and realized, leaving an indelible mark on the image of the city: these included Sharon's projects for housing associations (the Hod residences, the first in Tel Aviv, built for an association of stage actors), Rechter's Engel House (the first building on pilotis in Palestine), Karmi's Zlotopolsky House, Averbouch's layout of Dizengoff Square and Neufeld's Kupat Cholim Center.

Many of the protagonists of this historic space are still waiting to be investigated for the first time: reconstructing their intellectual and professional biographies through the few surviving documents would help to present a picture of the variety of cultural options – and not just in architecture – present in Palestine under the British mandate in the thirties, allowing us to gain a better understanding of why one particular political and cultural line won out over others.[187]

Some Israeli architects and historians of architecture and the city – Eyal Weizman, Sharon Rotbard, Zvi Efrat – have come up with a radical criticism of Zionist urban policy with

---

[186] Nitzan-Shiftan, Alona: *Contested Zionism – Alternative Modernism: Erich Mendelsohn and the Tel Aviv Chug in Mandate Palestine*, in Architectural History. Journal of the Society of Architectural Historians of Great Britain, vol. 39, 1996, pp. 147–80.

[187] For all the projects of the members of the Chug, see the only comprehensive study available, Metzger-Szmuk, Nitza: *Dwelling on the Dunes: Tel Aviv, Modern Movement and Bauhaus Ideals / Des maisons sur le sable: Tel Aviv, Mouvement moderne et esprit Bauhaus*, Paris/Tel Aviv, Editions de l'Eclat, 2004. Also see Freda, Gianluigi: *La collina della primavera. L'architettura moderna di Tel Aviv*, Milan, Franco Angeli, 2011.

regard to the Palestinians.[188] In contrast historians more faithful to a traditional Zionist line like Michael Levin [189] or Nitza Szmuk-Metzger nurture the myth of a "Bauhaus-style" and "white" Jewish architecture in opposition to an Oriental-style and antiquated Arab-Palestinian architecture.[190] There is nothing new about this myth of a modern "white" architecture contrasted with a vernacular "gray" one. It is an echo of the earlier wholly American dispute between "Whites" and "Grays" in the seventies, but has its ideological origins in Europe even further back.[191]

The underlying reason for these historiographical contrasts in Israel has been caught by one of that country's major contemporary writers, Abraham Yehoshua: "Zionism is not an ideology in itself but a common platform for various and even contradictory ideologies."[192] The exceptionality of the state of Israel also lies in its having succeeded in cultivating these contradictions.

From a substantial series of clues it seems legitimate to suggest Yona Friedman's adherence to the cultural Zionism of Ha'am and Buber, rather than to the official one of the Herzl/Ben-Gurion line.

When Buber in *Paths in Utopia* (1946) writes that "It is of no avail to call 'utopian' what we have not yet tested with our powers. [...] I declare in favour of a rebirth of the commune. [...] An organic commonwealth [...] will never build itself out of individuals but only out of small and ever smaller communities: a nation is a community to the degree that it is a community of communities,"[193] he comes to conclusions that are wholly in keeping with the theory of the "critical group" formulated by Friedman thirty years later, i.e. the largest size of a group of people with which the effective functioning of an organization with a defined structure can still be assured.[194] In addition, "Buber's continual call for 'realization' of the demand of the spirit in the midst of the historical realities,"[195] present in all the writings of his maturity, is totally congruent with *Utopies réalisables*.

In this book from his full maturity, fundamental to an understanding of Friedman's *Weltanschauung*, there is a paragraph that condenses, without making them explicit, some principles of cultural Zionism. His reasoning is simple: if the communities or groups are

---

[188] Weizman, Eyal and Segal, Rafi (eds.): *A Civilian Occupation – The Politics of Israeli Architecture*, Tel Aviv, Babel/London, Verso, 2003. French ed., transl., by Muriel Gilbert: *Une occupation civile – la politique de l'architecture israelienne*, Paris, Les Editions de L'imprimeur, 2004.
[189] Levin, Michael: *White City, International Style Architecture in Israel, Portrait of an Era*, Tel Aviv, Tel Aviv Museum, 1984.
[190] Szmuk-Metzger's book needs to be compared with the completely opposed thesis of Rotbard, Sharon: *White City, White Lies*, in *Territories. Builders, Warriors and other Mythologies*, supplement to the catalogue of the exhibition *Territories*, Berlin, Kunst-Werke/Köln, Walter König, 2003.
[191] The identity of modern architecture seems to be inseparable from the whiteness of its surfaces, often only presumed owing to the black-and-white photography that has bestowed an air of immaculate purity on buildings constructed before the Second World War, as in the case of Terragni's Novocomum, which was actually colored. On the whiteness of modern architecture, see Wigley, Mark: *White Walls, Designer Dresses: The Fashioning of Modern Architecture*, Cambridge (MA)/London, MIT Press, 1995.
[192] Yehoshua, Abraham B.: *La rivoluzione sionista*, in id., *Antisemitismo e sionismo. Una discussione*, Turin, Einaudi, 2004, p. 65. Part of the text has been published in English under the title *Zionism Is Not an Ideology*, in *Haaretz*, November 26, 2010.
[193] Buber, Martin: *Pfade in Utopia*, Heidelberg, Lambert Schneider, 1946. English transl., *Paths in Utopia*, Syracuse (NY), Syracuse University Press, 1950, pp. 6 and 136.
[194] Friedman, Yona, *Utopies réalisables*, Paris, Union générale d'éditions, 1975. Revised and enlarged ed., Paris, Editions de l'Eclat, 2000, p. 47.
[195] See Taubes, Jacob: *Martin Buber und die Geschichtsphilosophie*, in id., *Vom Kult zur Kultur*, Munich, Wilhelm Fink, 1996. English transl., *Martin Buber and the Philosophy of History*, in id., *From Cult to Culture: Fragments toward a Critique of Historical Reason*, Stanford (CA), Stanford University Press, 2010, p. 26.

small then their diversity increases and when the density, for various reasons, increases too, it inevitable that more than one community ends up with a very small territory.

[Territoriality] of reduced size permits the insertion of new groups or communities among the others, and the number of non-territorial groups or communities can be unlimited. [...] The closed nature of these groups increases their mutual tolerance: since the communities cannot increase the number of their members, they do not make converts (the first source of conflict between groups) without functioning as a secret society (the second usual source of conflict). The very large number of these groups does not allow the emergence of feelings of envy and rivalry except between some neighboring groups and the complexity of these relationships avoids, necessarily, any widespread or generalizable conflict.[196]

These statements are all totally in keeping with cultural Zionism. In fact it suffices to think of the different Jewish settlements (villages, kibbutzim, moshavim, etc.) that over the course of the time had grown up peacefully alongside Palestinian villages, Bedouin camps, Druse settlements, etc., at least until 1936, in British-administered Palestine.
In addition, a direct and urban model of peaceful coexistence was provided by the reality of Haifa, the city where Friedman lived for around a decade, where at the beginning of the forties the three communities of Muslims, Jews and Christians were of roughly equal size and interethnic clashes had always been relatively minor even after 1948.
So Martin Buber, an expert on Jewish mysticism and messianism, wrote his book on the search for a new social order, *Paths in Utopia*, in the Promised Land during the Second World War. Almost in parallel Adriano Olivetti, a refugee in Switzerland, presented the idea of many "communities" on a human scale with which to reshape a liberated Italy in a book "blazing with mysticism."[197] Olivetti had been the protagonist of an impossible internal reform of Fascism, partly through city planning, that found a rare but shrewd ally in Pagano, won over by Olivetti's spiritual inspirations.[198] After the war the industrialist from Ivrea would foster a genuine community movement – opposed by the Communist Party – in part through a magazine and a publishing house that would bring out the work of some of the finest intellectuals in Italy and Europe and translate Buber's book into Italian. There were architects too who took an interest in forms of community, in particular Gropius who, having fled to the US, published a little-known book on the reconstruction of communities

---

[196] FRIEDMAN, Yona: *Une multitude de communautés non communicantes*, in id., *Utopies réalisables*, op. cit., pp. 152–54.
[197] OLIVETTI, Adriano: *L'ordine politico delle comunità: dello Stato secondo le leggi dello spirito*, Rome, Edizioni di Comunità, 1946, and id., *L'idea di una comunità concreta*, Ivrea, Comitato Centrale della Comunità, 1950. The description is from ALVI, Geminello: *La memoria perduta di Adriano Olivetti* (1997), in id., *L'anima e l'economia*, Milan, Mondadori, 2005, p. 226.
[198] "Just as all his production and the organization of his workshops are decidedly oriented toward an extremely up-to-date plan of attentive and humane evaluation of the *reasons of the spirit, of art and of life*, the activities he carries out in parallel do not stray from that unity of views that characterizes all of the Olivetti company's work. [With] the aid of the liveliest forces in Italian art it aims to create that ideal world in which art and life, housing and production, material work and *the wellbeing of the spirit* will have to find the peace and the equilibrium that *the most enlightened minds* of today set as an essential condition for bringing the relations between the world of workers and that of modern industry back to a humane reconciliation and a moral justification." PAGANO, Giuseppe: *Architettura sociale della Olivetti a Ivrea*, in *Costruzioni-Casabella*, no. 172, April 1942, now in id., *Architettura e città durante il fascismo*, ed. by DE SETA, Cesare, Rome/Bari, Laterza 1976; revised ed. 1990, pp. 178 and 179. The italics are mine. It should be noted that Pagano in his last years, before joining the Resistance, taught the Mysticism of Fascism in Milan.

destroyed by the war.[199] Likewise, the foundations for the social utopias of the twenties,[200] from the communism of Lenin or Rosa Luxemburg to the social and nonviolent anarchism of Gustav Landauer in Germany,[201] had been laid during the First World War. The same thing happened during the Second and this is only natural: the breakdown or destruction of a society is the moment for reconsidering it in a new way.

The defeat of cultural Zionism in Israel was one of the reasons why Friedman would decide to return to Europe. It is no coincidence if towards the end of *Utopies réalisables* he writes from an unstated autobiographical perspective that: "Social migration represents a sort of strike in perpetuity, since an individual who leaves a group modifies its structure [...]."[202]

There were two institutions of the Yishuv rooted in permanent non-nationalistic tendencies of the Jewish tradition (universality, the predominance of culture and the passion for justice): the university and the collective settlements. From the moment of his arrival Friedman had firsthand experience of both these institutions. It is highly significant that the most consistent and eloquent of the voice raised on behalf of cooperation between the Arabs and the Jews came from the university, as Arendt has acutely observed,[203] that is to say from exactly the places frequented by Friedman.

The birth of the nation state in 1948 was not a foregone conclusion even for the Zionists: many, especially among the cultural Zionists, had hoped to live alongside the Arabs in the same state. "It was the final eclipse, at least for our generation, of the ideal of socialist Zionism, of the aspiration to cooperate with the Arabs, to struggle at one and the same time for the material and spiritual improvement of our own people and of theirs."[204] Buber's paradoxical sadness, expressed in connection with the imminent foundation of the state and the consequent war, is even more eloquent: "I cannot, however, even be joyful in anticipating victory, for I fear lest the significance of Jewish victory be the downfall of Zionism."[205] Thus Friedman's disillusionment with the form assumed by Israel is not just a personal and isolated state of mind, destined to grow more strained, but the reflection of a broader process that was underway: the reconciliation of the considerable differences within the Zionist movement left marginal splinters outside the new reality of Israel. After all even Erich Mendelsohn had decided to leave Jerusalem and move to the United States, and the crisis in construction of the early forties was certainly not the sole reason for his choice.

---

199 GROPIUS, Walter: *Rebuilding Our Communities*, with an introduction by László Moholy-Nagy, Chicago, Theobald, 1945. The basic idea of the book has been summed up well by Giedion: "Town planning and democracy have a common basis: the establishment of an equilibrium between individual freedom and collective responsibility [...] the level of a civilization depends upon how far a chaotic incoherent mass of humanity can be transformed into an integrated and creative community." GIEDION, Sigfried: *Walter Gropius. Work and Teamwork*, New York, Reinhold, 1954. Anastatic rpt., Mineola (NY), Dover, 1992, p. 84.
200 FIEDLER, Jeannine (ed.): *Social Utopias of the Twenties: Bauhaus, Kibbutz and the Dream of the New Man*, Wuppertal, Müller+Busmann, 1995.
201 See the lyrical portrait of Landauer painted in ALVI, Geminello: *Uomini del novecento*, Milan, Adelphi, 1995, pp. 122–25. "Anarchy is where there are anarchists, true anarchists, in other words those men who do not use any violence."
202 FRIEDMAN, Yona: *La migration: l'autodéfense de l'individu contre l'injustice sociale*, in id., *Utopies réalisables*, op. cit., p. 198.
203 ARENDT, Hannah: *Peace or Armistice in the Near East?*, in *Review of Politics*, January 1950, pp. 56–82, now in id., *The Jewish Writings*, op. cit., pp. 423–45.
204 VOGHERA, Giorgio: *Gli anni decisivi per la nascita di Israele*, op. cit., p. 189.
205 BUBER, Martin: *Zionism and "Zionism,"* in id., *A Land of Two Peoples: Martin Buber on Jews and Arabs*, edited with commentary and a new preface by Paul Mendes-Flohr, Chicago, University of Chicago Press, 2005, p. 223.

There was also the waning of Buber's dream of a "Semitic commonwealth" that would be a synthesis of East and West.[206] This is a fundamental but still underestimated chapter in Mendelsohn's work: while the followers of the Chug in Tel Aviv aped his Expressionism, limiting themselves to rounding corners and balconies, Mendelsohn built in local stone and with right angles, seeking a fusion between the Western and Eastern souls of Judaism. Gershom Scholem, the great German philosopher who emigrated to Jerusalem in the twenties and was a close friend of Walter Benjamin (although the writer would never follow him to Palestine), has written about those who for various reasons abandoned the Promised Land after moving there initially:

It's impossible to say how many people disappeared only to reappear unexpectedly in Paris, London, New York, Los Angeles and Toronto. The centrifugal force continued to act – as in the migration of dunes – and many did not stay.[207]

---

[206] "In opposition to Theodor Herzl, who was thinking about setting up a state of Israel on the Western European model, Mendelsohn followed the line of the so-called *Kulturzionisten*. Figures like Achad Ha'am and Martin Buber fiercely criticized the model of a 'Europe in Asia,' pushed by Herzl and his circle, while considering Zionism an extraordinary opportunity for the cultural rebirth of Judaism, through the reuniting of the people with the land from which it came, rather than as an exclusively political solution." HEINZE-GREENBERG, Ita: *Das Projekt Mittelmeerakademie und die Emigration*, in STEPHAN, Regina (ed.): *Erich Mendelsohn Architekt 1887–1953 Gebaute Welte. Arbeiten für Europa, Palästina und Amerika*, Ostfildern, Hatje Cantz, 1998, p. 222. The passage has been transl. from the Italian ed., *L'Accademia del Mediterraneo e la Palestina*, in STEPHAN, Regina (ed.): *Erich Mendelsohn 1887–1953*, Milan, Electa, 2004, pp. 204–5.

[207] Scholem continues: "But historically speaking, what was done in Eretz Israel represents the only existential creation of that generation, unlike what flowed into the diaspora." *With Gershom Scholem. An Interview*, in DANNHAUSER, W. J. (ed.), SCHOLEM, Gershom: *On Jews and Judaism in Crisis*, New York, Schocken, 1976, pp. 1–48.

423

424

425

"DER JUDENSTAAT"

423 Illustration from the first edition by Herzl, Theodor, Vienna, M. Breitenstein's Verlags-Buchhandlung, 1896.
424 Zionist propaganda picture of communal men's bathroom at a kibbutz, 1940s, from Fiedler, Jeannine (ed.): *Social Utopias of the Twenties: Bauhaus, Kibbutz and the Dream of the New Man*, Wuppertal, Müller+Busmann, 1995.

ISRAELI DECLARATION OF INDEPENDENCE

425 David Ben Gurion in the Tel Aviv Museum Hall, with a large portrait of Theodor Herzl, founder of modern Zionism, May 14, 1948.

THE NAHALAL MOSHAV

426 Project by Richard Kauffmann, 1922.
427 Aerial photograph, 1940s

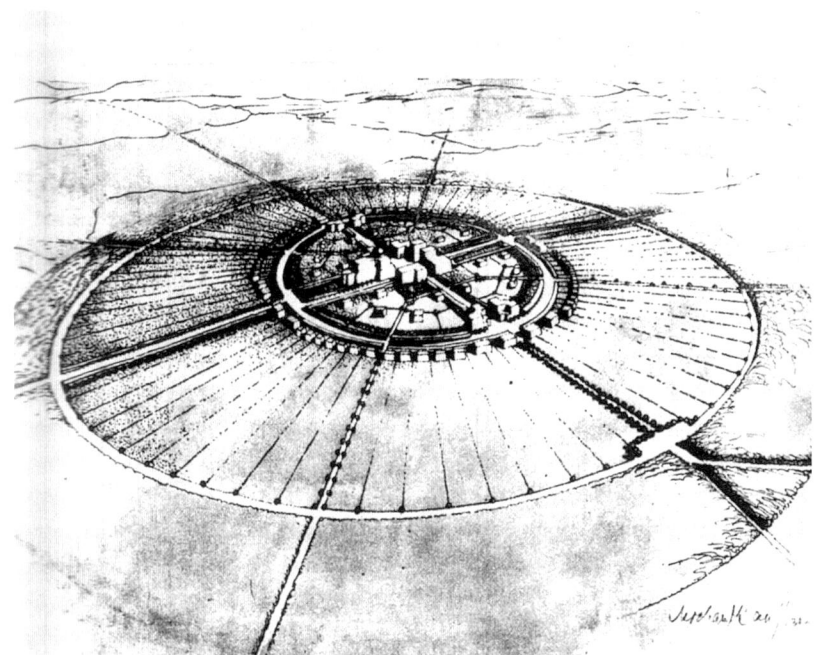
426

427

428

429

TEL AVIV

428 The city center in an aerial photograph from the 1940s.
429 Genia Averbuch: layout of *Zina Dizengoff Square*, Tel Aviv, 1935.
430 Ze'ev Rechter: *Engel House*, 1934.
431 Josef Neufeld, Israel Dicker and Carl Rubin: *Me'onot G*, 1936.
432 Josef Neufeld: *Assuta Hospital*, 1934.
Photographs from *Dwelling on the Dunes: Tel Aviv, Modern Movement and Bauhaus Ideals / Des maisons sur le sable*: METZGER-SZMUCK, Nitza: *Tel Aviv, Mouvement moderne et esprit Bauhaus*, bilingual edition English/French, Editions de l'Eclat, Paris, 2004.

430

431

432

ERICH MENDELSOHN

433–434 Hadassah University Medical Center, 1936–39, on Mount Scopus.
From: *Erich Mendelsohn 1887–1953*, Milan, Electa, 2004.
Jerusalem, a cultural Zionist synthesis of Eastern and Western, ancient and modern architecture.

HAIFA "THE RED" AND THE TECHNION INSTITUTE OF TECHNOLOGY

They call it the city of Mount Carmel
Before they used to call it Haifa the Red too
But that was still the time of the British mandate
When three mayors ran it together and fairly well
A unified city

An Englishman, an Arab and a Jew
Who did not feel the need
To divide it. [208]
Amos Gitai

Haifa was the main commercial port of the British Mandate in Palestine (1917–48) and at the end of the Second World War also became the principal landing place of Jewish refugees from Europe, who arrived on boats that were jam-packed and often in desperate conditions, as in the case of the ship *Exodus 1947* carrying 4500 ex-deportees, 905 of them children, whom the British authorities prevented from landing. Probably Yona Friedman, who was just twenty-three when he arrived in Haifa, was animated by a spirit of sacrifice and an idealism akin to those of the early militant Zionists when he got there at the beginning of 1946. But it was a concrete idealism that was never to leave him:

I knew Israel at the moment in which it was still a very interesting society, a classless society, based on immigration. But then, very rapidly, everything deteriorated. [209]

Haifa was called "the Red" for the same reasons as the epithet was applied to "Red Vienna" and other large European municipalities run by socialist administrations after the First World War. [210] Here the trade-union movement of the Histadrut, the "General Federation of Laborers in the Land of Israel" led at the time by David Ben-Gurion, was stronger than elsewhere, and there was the Workers' Council of Haifa which set up a sort of parallel state with programs of social welfare, public works, credit to workers and other supplementary services. Over the course of the thirties and forties, for example, numerous protests were staged by workers calling for low-cost housing.
Haifa is the most flourishing city in the area largely thanks to its industrial port, which in the 20th century overtook not far-off Acre – the ancient harbor used by the merchants of Venice, Genoa, Pisa and the other maritime republics – in the level of trade handled thanks to a series of infrastructure projects, some of them realized by the Ottoman Empire, like

---

[208] GITAI, Amos: *Mont Carmel*, Paris, Gallimard, 2003. The passage has been transl. from the Italian ed., *Monte Carmelo*, Milan, Bompiani, 2004, p. 18.
[209] FRIEDMAN, Yona: *Ogni utopia è realizzabile*, interview, in BRUGELLIS, Pino (ed.): *L'invisibile linea rossa*, Macerata, Quodlibet, 2009, p. 22.
[210] See TAFURI, Manfredo (ed.): *Vienna rossa. La politica residenziale nella Vienna socialista, 1919–1933*, Milan, Electa, 1980; and BLAU, Eve: "Against the Idea of Force, the Force of Ideas": Municipal Socialism and Austro-Marxism, in id., *The Architecture of Red Vienna 1919–1934*, Cambridge (MA)/London, MIT Press, 1999, pp. 20–47.

the Hejaz Railroad that connected the city with Damascus via Beirut. Under the British Mandate the port had been expanded and equipped with an oil refinery linked by a pipeline to Iraq, completed in 1938.[211]

Haifa is also the region's most ethnically and religiously diverse city. Since the thirties the vast majority of its Jewish population has been secular, and even today it is the only city in Israel where it has been possible to name a square after Heinrich Heine, the Jew who had converted to Christianity, despite the disapproval of the religious authorities.[212]

In 1920 Haifa saw the first of numerous examples of class solidarity and binational, if not downright supranational cooperation: in that year in fact Palestinians, Jews and Arabs from Syria and Egypt created the first trade union in the history of Palestine, operating on the construction sites and in the workshops of the railroads, as well as in the telegraph and mail services. Up until 1947 joint rallies were common events. On the occasion of each outbreak of violence – 1920, 1929, 1936, 1948 – studies have brought to light specific cases of cooperation between the different communities on the social or economic plane that were fiercely opposed when not stamped out by the national leaderships, in particular the Zionist one – the severity of the Histadrut was at its maximum in these cases.[213] Also present in Haifa was a strong community of German Jews, whose numbers in the country have often been overestimated. This community played a particularly active part in the foundation of the Technion university, the oldest school of engineering and architecture in Palestine: in its early years lectures were given in German and Hebrew was only adopted after an internal referendum.

Some of the best architects to have arrived from Europe were active in Haifa: Alexander Baerwald, Richard Kauffmann, the Hungarian – but who had worked in Berlin – Oskar Kaufman, Arieh Sharon,[214] Munio Gitai Weinraub, Al Mansfeld, Adolf Rading,[215] Paul Engelmann,[216] Alexander Klein, Leopold Krakauer,[217] Werner Wittkower[218] and Erich Mendelsohn all realized significant works there during the British Mandate.[219]

Above all, Haifa was the home of the Technion, the Institute of Technology at which Friedman enrolled to finish his studies while earning a living working as a laborer in the construction industry.

---

[211] INGERSOLL, Richard: *Red Haifa and Its Architectural Strategies*, in id., *Munio Gitai Weinraub. Bauhaus Architect in Eretz Israel*, photographs by Gabriele Basilico, Milan, Electa, 1994, p. 33.

[212] GITAI, Amos: *Monte Carmelo*, op. cit., p. 65.

[213] PAPPE, Ilan: *Encountering Nationalism: the Urge for Cohabitation*, in id., *A History of Modern Palestine*, op. cit., pp. 109–15.

[214] SHARON, Arieh: *Kibbutz + Bauhaus: an Architect's Way in a New Land*, with a foreword by Bruno Zevi, Stuttgart, Krämer, 1976.

[215] PFANKUCH, Peter: *Adolf Rading. Bauten, Entwürfe und Erläuterungen*, Berlin, G. Mann, 1970. Rading had worked with Erich Mendelsohn before and after his emigration from Germany to Haifa.

[216] Engelmann is a noteworthy figure; he was in order the favorite pupil of Adolf Loos, the best friend of Ludwig Wittgenstein (with whom he designed the house in Kudmangasse in Vienna) and the personal secretary of Karl Kraus. He published succint but important writings on all three. Born in Olomouc, a small city now in the Czech Republic, he settled in Tel Aviv and constructed his most important building in Haifa, Yadlin House (1937–39). See BAKACSY, J., MUNCH, A.V. and SOMMER, A.-L. (eds.): *Architecture Language Critique: Around Paul Engelmann*, Amsterdam/Atlanta, Rodopi, 2000.

[217] PERRY-LEHMANN, Meira and LEVIN, Michael (eds.): *Leopold Krakauer. Painter and Architect 1890–1954*, Jerusalem, Israel Museum, 1996.

[218] Werner Joseph Wittkower (born in Berlin in 1903) was the brother of the better-known historian of art and architecture Rudolf, who emigrated to England instead in 1934; see *Il lavoro per la comunità. Architettura di Joseph Wittkower dal 1950*, in *L'architettura. Cronache e storia*, no. 282, April 1979, pp. 218–30.

[219] HERBERT, Gilbert and SOSNOVSKY, Silvina: *Bauhaus on the Carmel and the Crossroads of the Empire: Architecture and Planning in Haifa during the British Mandate*, Jerusalem, Yad Izhak Ben-Zvi, 1993.

The dean of the department of architecture at the Technion in 1946 was Yohanan Ratner, considered a conservative and a fierce opponent of modern architecture.[220] In 1926 Ratner had designed an office building in Haifa for the Beit Hapoalim ("Workers' House") that was in net contrast to his Beaux-Arts training in Russia, as the building was totally bare and almost functionalist.[221] In general the public buildings of Haifa were extremely sober. A glaring exception to this modesty was the seat of the Technion, finished by Alexander Baerwald, who was also its president, in 1926: a cultural Zionist pastiche of Ottoman Orientalism produced by a German architect who was an adherent of the ideology of the garden city. The same year Richard Kaufmann presented to Baerwald the plan for a garden city covering sixty square kilometers to be created between Haifa and Acre, which was supposed to solve the problem of new housing. Kaufmann and Baerwald were acting on behalf of the German Zionist agency in Berlin, which in those years had espoused the ideology of the garden city, going so far as to commission from Patrick Geddes plans for the three main cities of the Palestine – the most important of which was the 1924 one for Tel Aviv.

From 1951 the president of the Technion was Alexander Klein, professor of City Planning and Architecture: Klein, born in Odessa in 1879 and educated in St. Petersburg, had left Russia for Berlin in 1920. He had taken part in the first two CIAM, presenting some important research into low-cost housing that would make a mark.[222]

After a couple of years in France following the accession of the Nazis to power in 1933, Klein had emigrated to Palestine in 1935 after publishing a study on the single-family detached home[223] that served as a direct – and avowed – model for the similar book that Kozma was preparing in Budapest.[224] His approach to urban planning and architecture was scientific: in 1943 he founded an institute of research into problems of construction and planning in Haifa and thus it is no accident that Konrad Wachsmann was a visiting professor at the Technion during Klein's presidency.

But we need to take a step back: in 1947 Klein published a noteworthy essay with the title *Man and Town:*[225] it was a proposal of urban organization that was presented as a prototype for the creation of new towns and fitted into the European current of studies on postwar reconstruction. In Italy, for example, it found a parallel in the contemporary research of Diotallevi and Marescotti[226] – begun earlier and published in Pagano's *Casabella* – which

---

[220] "As a teacher and dean in the 1950s, Ratner was considered a reactionary and one of the more ardent opposers of modernist architecture." ROTBARD, Sharon: *Wall and Tower (Homa Umigdal), the Mold of Israeli Architecture*, in WEIZMAN, Eyal and SEGAL, Rafi (eds.): *A Civilian Occupation*..., op. cit., pp. 39–58.

[221] SOSNOVSKY, Silvina (ed.): *Yohanan Ratner: The Man, the Architect and His Work*, Haifa, Architectural Heritage Research Centre, 1992, p. 16.

[222] On his life and work, see KLEIN, Alexander: *Lo studio delle piante e la progettazione degli spazi negli alloggi minimi. Scritti e progetti dal 1906 al 1957*, ed. by Matilde Baffa Rivolta and Augusto Rossari, Milan, Mazzotta, 1975.

[223] KLEIN, Alexander: *Das Einfamilienhaus, Südtyp*, Stuttgart, Hoffmann, 1934, which would have been the first volume of an "Encyclopedia of City Planning and Residential Architecture" that he never finished.

[224] "By naming here Adolf Loos, Oskar Strnad, Le Corbusier, Peter Meyer and Alexander Klein, to whose fruitful work the new architecture owes a great deal, I believe I am not so much fulfilling a duty as giving expression to the admiration I feel for these architects and writers." KOZMA, Lajos, in the introduction to *Das neue Haus*..., op. cit.

[225] KLEIN, Alexander: *Man and Town*, in *Yearbook of the American Technion Society*, New York, American Technion Society, 1947.

[226] DIOTALLEVI, Irenio and MARESCOTTI, Franco: *Il problema sociale, costruttivo ed economico dell'abitazione*, Milan, Poligono, 1948. This is a collection of drawings summarizing research carried out in the thirties and forties in close contact with Giuseppe Pagano. See CIUCCI, Giorgio: *Dalla casa dell'uomo alla casa popolare*, in CIUCCI, Giorgio and CASCIATO, Maristella: *Franco Marescotti e la casa civile 1934–1956*, Rome, Officina, 1980, pp. 7–20.

did not fail to publish some of Klein's German projects, but the essay aroused such wide interest that it was translated into many languages. In Klein's case the need for reconstruction was rendered even more urgent on the one hand by the growing immigration of Jews from Europe and on the other by the imminent foundation of the state of Israel (1948), whose sovereignty would allow a policy of construction of new settlements without the limitations imposed by the British Mandate. Work had already stated on some of these settlements, and Klein had in particular drawn up plans for a residential district in Tiberias (1938–47)[227] and another at Kiryat Yam (1938–50), on Haifa Bay,[228] in which the buildings were designed chiefly by Munio Gitai and Al Mansfeld.[229]

In *Man and Town* Klein observed that modern urban agglomerations were too big for their inhabitants to be able to form a "cooperating community" and that there was nothing that inculcated in them a feeling of love for the city, not even the garden city, because when they were conceived the problems of modern traffic could not have been foreseen. Here the criticism was directed at the illustrious founders of the Technion, such as Baerwald and his future colleague at the state planning authority, Artur Glikson.[230] In short Klein's idea was to separate pedestrian traffic completely from that of vehicles. The urban system he proposed was radial, with manufacturing activities located further out from the center and housing closer to it, as in Howard's famous diagram of the garden city, in order to create a centrifugal rather than centripetal system. However, the essay concluded with an act of faith in regional planning, fixing the area and the number of inhabitants in an inflexible way.

After graduating in 1949 Friedman embarked on a professional career and began to make his first journeys abroad (to Italy and France where he met Le Corbusier for the first time), taking an interest above all in the prefabrication of housing units for immigrants – his *Movable Boxes* project in which the occupants could decide the internal divisions for themselves, dates from the same year.

Already during the period in which I was a student I had started to come up with simple designs that allowed for a great deal of freedom: I had for example thought of creating an empty apartment in which the furniture would divide up the space; I had also treated the bathroom and kitchen as movable furniture. The basic idea was that the plan of that apartment could be modified to suit the user.[231]

This kind of research was not carried out in isolation, for obvious reasons: the prime problem faced by Israel was in fact that of taking in such a huge flow of immigrants that the population of the young state would double in the space of a few years. More in general the question of prefabrication was one that had attracted attention in Mandatory

---

227 KLEIN, Alexander: *Lo studio delle piante*, op. cit., pp. 208–9.
228 Ibid., pp. 210–11. See also Klein, Alexander: *Il progetto di una nuova città nella baia di Haifa secondo i principi dell'urbanistica organica*, in *Metron*, no. 11, 1946, pp. 64–75.
229 INGERSOLL, Richard: *Kiryat Chaim and the Workers' Suburbs of Haifa*, in id., *Munio Gitai*, op. cit., pp. 53 ff.
230 Glikson (1901–66) emigrated in 1938 and in the fifties worked for the building department of the Ministry of Public Works. See Glikson, Artur: *Regional Planning and Development. Six Lectures Delivered at the Institute of Social Studies at The Hague*, Leiden, A.W. Sijthoff, 1955.
231 FRIEDMAN, Yona: *Ogni utopia è realizzabile*, op. cit., p. 18.

Palestine and Haifa in particular for around a decade. In February 1934 the municipal Department of Civil Engineering had granted the first license for the construction of five prefabricated houses of different types.[232] These prefabricated houses, some of which are still in reasonable condition, were made in Germany and assembled on site, thanks in part to the fact that the Nazi regime was initially somewhat favorable toward Jewish emigration in Palestine, or at least did not hinder it. But the difficulty and cost of the assembly were excessive and the Jewish Agency decided to halt the activity after a few months. In all perhaps no more than twenty or twenty-five houses containing around a hundred apartments left the factories of Berlin for the Promised Land, providing a proving ground for subsequent Israeli studies of prefabrication.

From Germany, where extensive research had been carried out into the subject of prefabrication since the end of the 19th century,[233] culminating in the convergent studies of Gropius and Konrad Wachsmann, first on prototypes in wood and then in copper and other metals, this type of experimentation had moved to the United States. Gropius emigrated there in 1936, Wachsmann, a Jew, joined him shortly afterward: both would find funding for their research into emergency constructions thanks to the USA's entry into the war (1941), with the "Packaged House" of 1941–46 or the projects for the General Panel Corporation.[234] In fact modern warfare, with its devastating effects on cities and industrial zones, accelerated the study and realization of prototypes of dwellings that could be dismantled, transported and constructed almost anywhere, from the early works of Jean Prouvé in France and those of Neufert in Germany to the research conducted in the USSR and elsewhere, thereby laying the foundations for postwar reconstruction too.[235] Yet the results were wholly negative. According to Banham the failure of the General Panel Corporation was the failure of one of the most cherished dreams of Modernism as we will see in the next paragraph.[236]

In Palestine, however, prefabrication was something more than a technical hitch in the evolution of architecture: especially among the engineers and architects of the Technion, prefabrication was a philosophy and a means of dealing with an urgent problem. A design like the one for cylindrical shelters that Friedman came up with in 1953, as well as his later ones for the modular "curved panel" of 1956 and "stacked concrete boxes" of 1958 – but already sketched out three years earlier – fall within this perspective. The best-known work inspired by this kind of research is undoubtedly the Habitat complex, built for the Montreal Expo of 1967. Its designer, Moshe Safdie, was born in Haifa in 1938 but emigrated with his family to Canada in 1953 and as a student had got hold of a copy of *L'architecture mobile* – in fact he proposed a system of modular construction in three

---

[232] HERBERT, Gilbert: *The Dream of the Factory-Made House. Walter Gropius and Konrad Wachsmann*, Cambridge (MA)/London, MIT Press, 1984, p. 175 and note 34.
[233] See JUNGHANNS, Kurt: *Das Haus für alle: Zur Geschichte der Vorfertigung in Deutschland*, Berlin, Ernst & Sohn, 1994.
[234] HERBERT, Gilbert: *The General Panel Corporation*, in id., *The Dream...*, op. cit., pp. 265–98.
[235] COHEN, Jean-Louis (ed.): *Architecture in Uniform: Designing and Building for the Second World War*, in the catalogue of the exhibition at the CCA in Montreal, Paris, Hazan, 2011.
[236] BANHAM, Reyner: *I complessi della prefabbricazione*, in *Casabella*, no. 527, September 1986, p. 29.

dimensions in his graduation thesis.[237] In this seminal text that had been circulating among architects in various editions since 1958, Friedman proposed a number of much more simplified and almost elementary solutions, but all based on the use of a standardized building unit. Among these different solutions diverse were the Concrete Boxes (prefabricated concrete containers each measuring 20 square meters and weighing 12 tonnes), the cylindrical shelters (also made of concrete, and the *immeubles radiers sans fondations* ("slab buildings without foundations").[238] All, however, were conceived for warm environments, where what matters is good ventilation and protection from exposure to sunlight, and were clearly inspired by the specific conditions of the Middle Eastern climate as well as the principles of Jean Prouvé, who was Friedman's primary point of reference after his move to Paris.

In the next edition (1959) of his pamphlet, Yona Friedman reduced these solutions to just one, that of the *blocs radiers*. The *bloc radier* ("slab block") is a structure built out of prefabricated and self-supporting elements up to four of which can be stacked without foundations one on top of the other levels and staggered vertically to create a regular alternation of solid and void in a checkerboard pattern.[239]

Unfortunately the chapter of prefabricated construction and its role in the modernization of cities like Haifa, Tel Aviv and even Jerusalem has not yet been studied in depth. Gilbert Herbert's book on prefabrication came out the same year as Michael Levin's catalogue of the *White City* exhibition, the first book on the history of Israeli architecture, characterized by a wholly stylistic and often naïvely reductive interpretation.[240]

From the beginning of the fifties, Friedman worked as an assistant at the Technion while continuing his activity as an architect: in 1952 he was commissioned to design a block of public housing in Haifa. To do this he decided to get to know the occupants and discuss the criteria with them.

But it was impossible. The minister responsible for building – Golda Meir – came to the opening of the construction site and asked for a window to be positioned in a certain area and this was done. I asked myself: "But if the minister is not going to come and live in this apartment, why should this window be put where she wants and not where the people who are really going to live there want?" It was naïve to think something of the kind in the fifties, but since then I have begun to work on how to make it possible for people not only to construct or make the plan of their own apartments at the level of divisions between the various rooms, but for their views to be taken into account in giving form to the whole.[241]

---

[237] Kohn, Wendy (ed.): *Moshe Safdie*, London, Academy, 1996, p. 332. The thesis was discussed at the Department of Architecture of McGill University in Montreal, Canada, in 1961, but begun in 1958. Also see the retrospective article, Safdie, Moshe: *Post Mortem on Habitat: Anatomy of a System*, in The Royal Institute of British Architects Journal, no. 74, vol. 11, November 1967, pp. 489–94.
[238] Friedman, Yona: *L'architecture mobile*, 2nd ed., Paris, 1958, pp. 22 ff.
[239] Friedman, Yona: *L'architecture mobile*, 3rd ed., Paris, 1959, p. 18.
[240] Levin, Michael: *White City, International Style Architecture in Israel. Portrait of an Era*, Tel Aviv, Museum of Tel Aviv, 1984.
[241] Friedman, Yona: *Ogni utopia è realizzabile*, op. cit., p. 18. When the building contractor told Meir that the architect Friedman had worked for him as a laborer, the minister said: "That shows we really are a democracy!" Cited in *Yona Friedman Relates His Beliefs and Experiences*, op. cit., p. 116.

Unfortunately it has not been possible to trace the building and see what state it is in today. Not even Friedman himself succeeded in finding it on a visit to Haifa in the nineties, at the invitation of a professor at the Technion, Renzo Voghera – with whom he had shared a professional studio in the fifties.[242] It is interesting to note how Friedman had earlier paid his way through university by working as a laborer for the same construction firm that would later build this block of apartments: in this way he was able to finish his studies, graduating in 1949.[243] He had lost the previous year because of the war with the neighboring Arab countries: Friedman took part, as did the entire able-bodied population of the Yishuv, serving in a division responsible for trenches and defense works, something very similar to the Corps of Engineers.[244] It was this experience that earned him credit in the eyes of the leaders of the new state as an adviser on the fortifications of new settlements.

In an article written in 1968 Friedman recalls the importance of his experience in Israel: he relates that between 1950 and 1954 he had worked with the section of the Israeli General Staff that was responsible for the newly founded settlements – towns and villages.[245] This was an activity coordinated by offices that made meticulous statistical and sociological predictions on the future growth of the settlements. In addition to the aforementioned Klein and Glikson,[246] Arieh Sharon was involved at a higher level, having managed to earn the trust of Ben-Gurion well before 1948, thanks to a strong political and ideological affinity between the two men. In particular Sharon had been able to meld modernist architecture with the leftwing nationalism of Ben-Gurion's electorally dominant party.[247] Of course Israel was not the only country in expansion after the Second World War: in the United States the urbanistic ideas that President Roosevelt had introduced with the New Deal ever since he first stood for office in 1932 had led to the drawing up of a major program of territorial reorganization aimed at the foundation of numerous New Towns.[248] The theoretical center of this program was the Regional Planning Association of America where a small group of experts like Lewis Mumford, Henry Wright, Clarence Stein and others fought for a policy of decentralization inspired by Ebenezer Howard's garden-city movement in Britain:

For fortunately here the best policy for peace and for defense are the same: orderly, related dispersal of workers and working places in limited-size communities, surrounded by open country.[249]

---

242 The project of the cylindrical shelters, made from pipelines in the desert, was published in *L'Architecture d'aujourd'hui* in 1954 under the signature of both men prior to Friedman's move to Europe.
243 "While studying in Israel, I worked twice a week as a construction worker simply to survive. Transporting sacks of cement. That is where I got a practical knowledge of building sites." *Yona Friedman Relates His Beliefs...*, op. cit., p. 116.
244 "[...] I was in the engineering corps. I was responsible for making fortifications larger. This meant trenches. [...] MO: After the war and your graduation, did you start practicing and open a studio in Haifa? YF: I was teaching as an assistant professor at Technion. At the same time I was a counselor for the fortifications of new settlements on behalf of Yitzhak Rabin." Yona Friedman, interview in the appendix.
245 FRIEDMAN, Yona: *Une tentative pour l'avenir des villes*, in *Progrès*, no. 12, 1968.
246 GLIKSON, Artur: *The Ecological Basis of Planning*, ed. by Lewis Mumford, The Hague, Nijhoff, 1971.
247 SHARON, Arieh: *Physical Planning in Israel*, Government Printer, South Africa, 1951. Sharon was one of the very few architects living in Palestine between the wars who had attended courses at the Bauhaus.
248 STEIN, Clarence: *Toward New Towns for America*, with an introduction by Lewis Mumford, Liverpool, University Press of Liverpool/Chicago, Public Administration Service, 1951.
249 Ibid. p. 7.

As well as marking a chronological parallel, these words of Stein's, written in 1950, reveal a consonance with British policy, where in 1945 the new Labor government had set up a Ministry of Town and Country Planning and as many as fourteen new towns were founded between 1946 and 1950.[250] However, it is necessary to make a distinction: while since its beginnings in the twenties the planning policy of the World Zionist Organization – which had its headquarters in London at the time and was directed by Weizmann, who would go on to become the first president of the Israeli republic – and the Yishuv had turned on the model of the garden city, after 1948 the new and preeminent role assumed by Sharon brought a shift away from this approach.[251] According to Zvi Efrat, immediately after independence the space for improvisation, for spontaneous architecture or for speculation was minimal, to a degree almost unprecedented in the history of national states.

This country has been entirely "arranged in advance," formulated a priori by means of arithmetical, planimetrical, and demographic formulas, drafted in pencil, ink, and watercolor by planning professionals from various disciplines, who were called upon to actualize Ben-Gurion's prescript "to transform the country, the nation, our whole way of life."

According to Efrat everything was programmed on a new basis as a tabula rasa, even the geographical, environmental and agronomic roots of the place – its schemes of urbanization, socialization and work, the whole of production and services, the functioning of public life, as well as the way of mastering the land in the new state of Israel.[252]

Faced with the results – largely disregarded – of this ambitious work of total planning in the early years of the state's existence, Friedman became convinced that any attempt at prediction in urban planning was idle and illusory.
In other words the lack of success suggested two things to the Hungarian architect:
1. that it was necessary to look for a technique of construction that would leave a possible margin of adaptation for the habitat as well as for the city;
2. the urgent need to find objective and appropriate criteria to check the effectiveness of a planning process.[253]
In Friedman's view the material obstacle to change lies in the inseparable bond between the elements of the city, or the habitat, *directly utilized* by the inhabitants (apartments, public spaces, equipment, furniture, etc.) and the ones that are utilized *indirectly*: water and sewage systems, electricity grids, supporting structures: in a word, the *infrastructure*. In short, the difficulty of adaptation resides in the rigidity of infrastructure and this is the aspect in which it is necessary to intervene.

---

250 Schaffer, Frank: *The New Town Movement*, in Evansm, Hazel (ed.): *New Towns, The British Experience*, London, Knight & Co., 1972, p. 17; Hardy, Dennis: *From New Towns to Green Politics*, London, Chapman & Hall 1991, pp. 22 ff. Also see Rodwin, Lloyd: *The British New Town Policy*, Cambridge (MA), Harvard University Press, 1956; Obsborn, Frederic J. and Whittick, Arnold: *The New Towns: The Answer to Megalopolis*, London, Hill, 1963; Cullingworth, Barry (ed.): *British Planning: 50 Years of Urban and Regional Policy*, London, Athlone, 1999.
251 As mentioned earlier, Sharon was critical of the garden-city movement, to which Glikson on the other hand adhered, as is clear from the foreword written by Mumford (the best-known exponent of Howard's ideology in the US) for his book. See note 248.
252 Efrat, Zvi: *The Plan: Drafting the Israeli National Space*, in Weizman, Eyal and Segal, Rafi (eds.): *A Civilian Occupation . . .*, pp. 59–76.
253 Friedman, Yona: *Une tentative pour l'avenir. . .*, op. cit.

The reasons why Friedman decided to go back to Europe were diverse and the architect himself has avoided setting them out explicitly. Doubtless the favor with which his ideas were received at Dubrovnik, at least by some, would have been decisive. In 1956 the dean of architecture at the Technion was Alfred Neumann, a little-known figure who had studied in France under Perret and had later been the mentor of Arieh Sharon's son Elder and the young Zvi Hecker – with whom he designed the city hall of Bat Yam, crowned by large tetrahedral and polychrome forms in cement [254] – and whose orientation was diametrically opposite to that of Klein, his predecessor. Neumann was an out-and-out formalist,[255] wholly uninterested in prefabrication and in technological questions in general. Nor did he consider participation important and in fact showed no interest in the research carried out by Friedman in his department.[256]

But at bottom Friedman seems to have been induced to leave Israel for a more substantial, ideal motive: with the passing of time he saw the possibilities of a classless society crumble. For that matter any social bond, and this is something which only becomes apparent when the difficulties start, is made of precarious balances, and after about a decade these were shifting. The extreme egalitarianism of the early years, of the War of Independence, which had united people of the most diverse linguistic and social origins, now belonged to the past: more marked social differences were emerging and in general it was the less well-off who were exploited, as on the kibbutzim where working conditions were very harsh.[257] In addition, other phenomena of social disintegration were surfacing, such as discrimination toward new immigrants, especially Sephardic Jews from North Africa or the Persian Gulf. This moment of crisis was sensed by Friedman around 1953–54 and is echoed by other sources.[258]

In other words, Israel in 1956 had already become a state like many others, even if in the Middle East it was – and still is – one of the most modern thanks to its cultural openness, equipped with all the appropriate structures of a national state but at the cost of sacrificing much of its original utopianism. The politicians closest to Friedman's cultural Zionist outlook, and thus the more moderate ones like Moshe Sharett,[259] had bowed out for good

---

[254] HEKER, Zvi, NEUMANN, Alfred and SHARON, Elder: *Centre civique de Bat-Yam, Israel*, in *L'Architecture d'aujourd'hui*, no. 115, 1964, pp. 70–71. Also see *L'architettura. Cronache e storia*, no. 113, March 1965, p. 747; *Alfred Neumann and Zvi Hecker: Architectural Works*, in *Zodiac*, no. 19, 1969, pp. 99–129.

[255] NEUMANN, Alfred: *L'architecture morphologique*, in *L'Architecture d'aujourd'hui*, no. 115, 1964, pp. 72–75.

[256] In the interview in the appendix Friedman declares: "I wanted to go to the CIAM meeting in Dubrovnik, but [Alfred] Neumann, who was the dean, didn't like the idea. He was not supporting me. […] We were very far apart. He was thinking in buildings, in forms, and from the start my interest was in the inhabitants." On the subject of Neumann's opinion of the idea of participation in architecture, Friedman adds: "Neumann nicely told me: it's really not important."

[257] See, for example, Giorgio Voghera's painful account in *Quaderno d'Israele*, op. cit. A Zionist from Trieste, Voghera worked on a kibbutz near Haifa under extreme conditions and like many others left Israel to return to the city of his birth.

[258] See the account of Antonio Negri, who lived in Israel between 1954 and 1955: "There was the racism of the blond Jews against those who came from Yemen or Morocco […]. All the stigma of a class-conscious society were present internally and ready to explode on the outside. And there was the sense of guilt of the expropriator that always coarsely tinges the figure of the colonizer, in the West as in Palestine. Nor did the heroic deeds of the rediscovery of the homeland cancel out the hysterical efforts of the diaspora." In id., *Pipeline…*, op. cit., pp. 35–36.

[259] Sharett was born in a mixed Arab-Jewish village and accustomed from childhood to a peaceful coexistence. He had always distinguished himself by his policy of moderation and leniency toward the Palestinians, in contrast to Ben-Gurion. As foreign minister he would be one of the very few, along with the militant communists, to oppose the deportation of the Palestinians left within the boundaries of the state of Israel in 1948. See PAPPE, Ilan: *Storia della Palestina…*, op. cit., pp. 192–93. On the deportation of the Palestinians, also see the fundamental KHALIDI, Walid (ed.): *All That Remains. The Palestinian Villages Occupied and Depopulated by Israel in 1948*, Washington, D.C., Institute for Palestine Studies, 1992.

with the Suez War of October 1956. And yet his Israeli experience was to remain decisive: in his analysis of society in the first draft of *L'architecture mobile*, Friedman seems to speak of Israel without naming it:

The citizens of a modern state are more and more isolated, almost fragmented. There is that giant organization, the state. Here it is only anonymous interest that counts. To conclude: the more social organization grows, the more elementary grouping diminishes.[260]

---

[260] Friedman, Yona: *L'architecture mobile*, 2nd ed., 1958, p. 5.

435

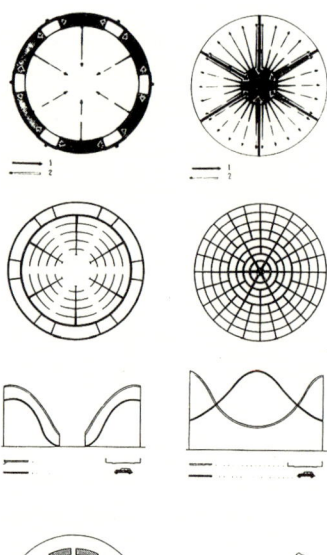

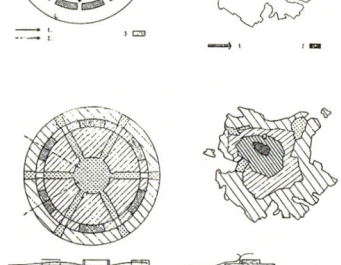

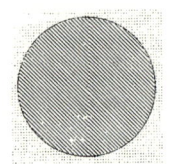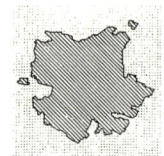

436

ALEXANDER BAERWALD

435 Original seat of the *Technion Institute of Technology*, Haifa, 1926. The German architect chose to insert Oriental decorative elements.

ALEXANDER KLEIN

436 Diagrams comparing the modern city; amorphous (left) and an ideal model (right), from *Man and City*, 1940.
437 Plan for Kiryat Yam, Haifa, from 1938, in BAFFA RIVOLTA, Matilde and ROSSARI, Augusto (eds.): *Alexander Klein. Scritti e progetti dal 1906 al 1957*, Milan, Mazzotta, 1975.

MUNIO GITAI AND AL MANSFELD

438 Housing project for immigrants, Kiryat Yam, Haifa, 1938–50. Photograph taken around 1949, shortly after Friedman's arrival, published in GITAI, Amos: *Mont Carmel*, Paris, Gallimard, 2003.
439 Kiryat Yam in an aerial photograph from 1949.

340 / PART II / **THE ERRATIC UNIVERSE OF YONA FRIEDMAN**

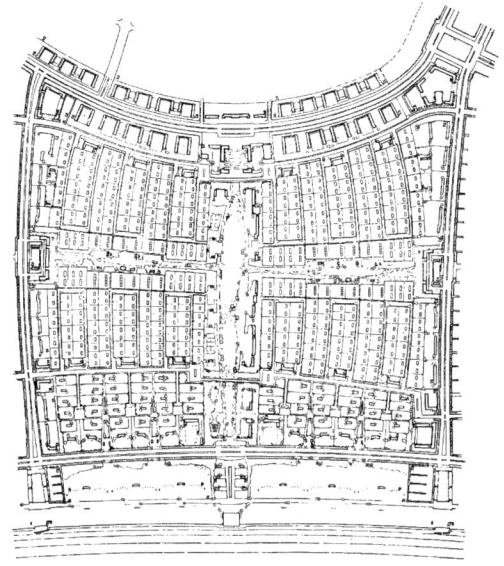

437

438

439

440

441

YONA FRIEDMAN

440 Portait from the army, 1948. Photograph with Marianne Polonsky.
441 Golda Meir, Israel's Minister of Public Works and Yona Friedman, on her left, Haifa, 1953.

"CYLINDRICAL SHELTERS" AND "CABINS FOR THE SAHARA"

442 Both were designed by Yona Friedman in Israel from 1953.
Published in the second duplicated edition of *L'architecture mobile*, 1958.

La cellule cylindrique est réalisée en tôle ondulée cintrée;
la coque est autoportante. La forme de cylindre permet une
trés bon répartiton de l'espace intérieur et des charges par
un minimum de matière. Une cellule de 15 m2 de surface utile est
de 5oo kgs environ.

Les cellules sont destinées à être groupées sur un ou deux niveaux. Les avantages sont les suivants: ventilation (réfrigeration) entre les cellules par des vides , protection contre le soleil par les cellules s'ombrageant entre elles. Les coques étant autoportantes aucune fondation n'est pas nécessaire.

Le principe des cabines sahariennes est la même. Autoportantes, juxta- or superposables sans aucune fondation, leur ossature comprend des cadres métalliques porteurs, en façade avec brise soleil, a u milieu équipés à volonté (salle d'eau, lits, etc); ces cadres sont réliés par des panneaux rigides isolés formant l'enveloppe de la cabine.

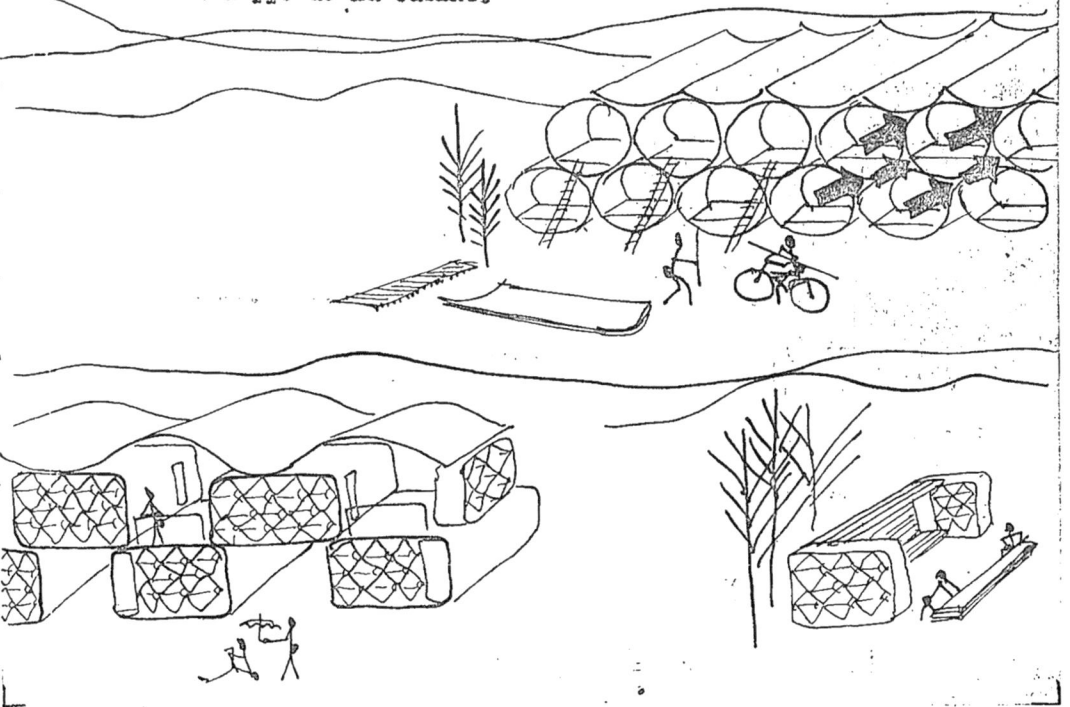

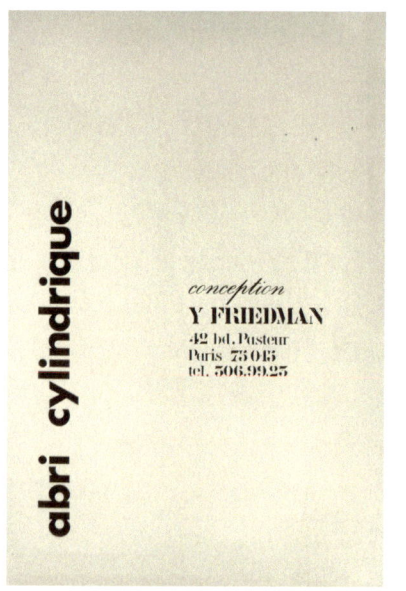
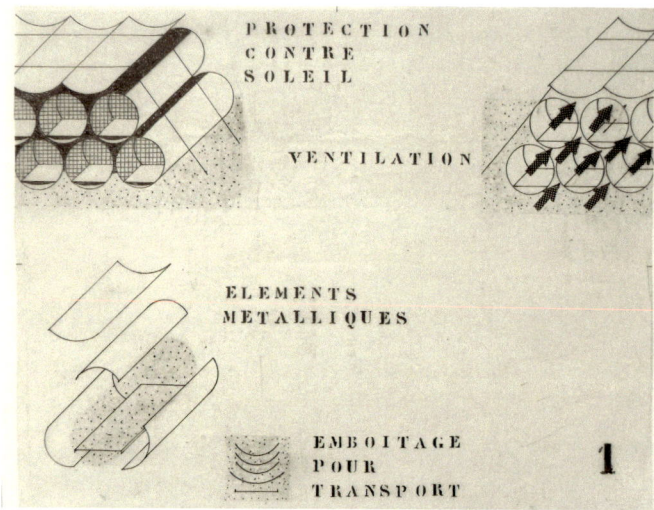
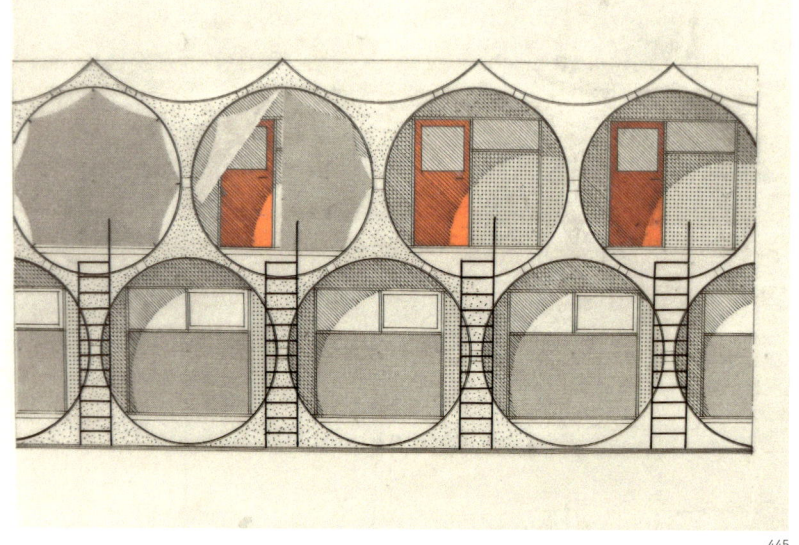

"CYLINDRICAL SHELTERS," FROM 1958

443 Friedman, Yona: *Abri Cylindrique*, cover of the first edition, 1958.
444 Yona Friedman: *Protection against the sun / ventilation / metallic elements / encasing for transportation.*
445 Yona Friedman: Front elevation, facade of groupment.
446 Yona Friedman: Plans of units type A, B, C and sections. Scale 1:50.
447 Yona Friedman: Perspective of a *Cylindrical Prefab*.

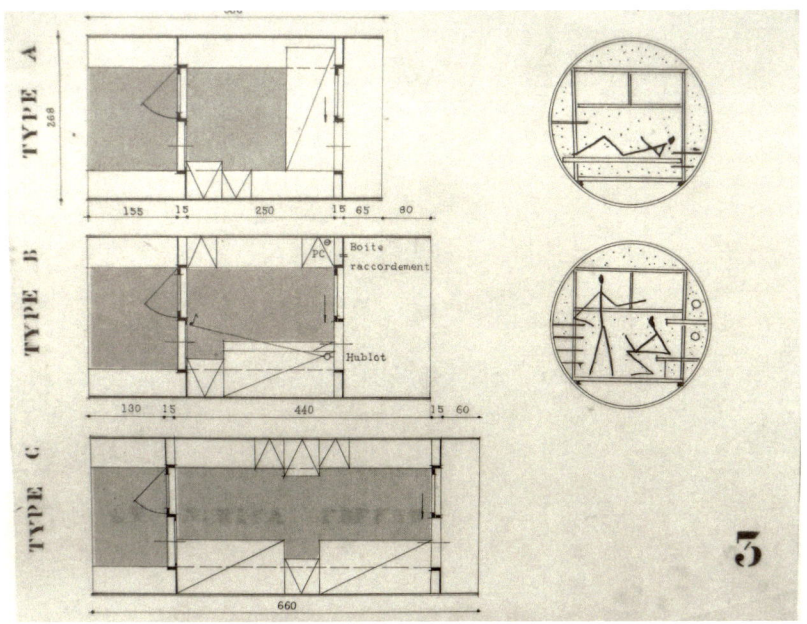

446

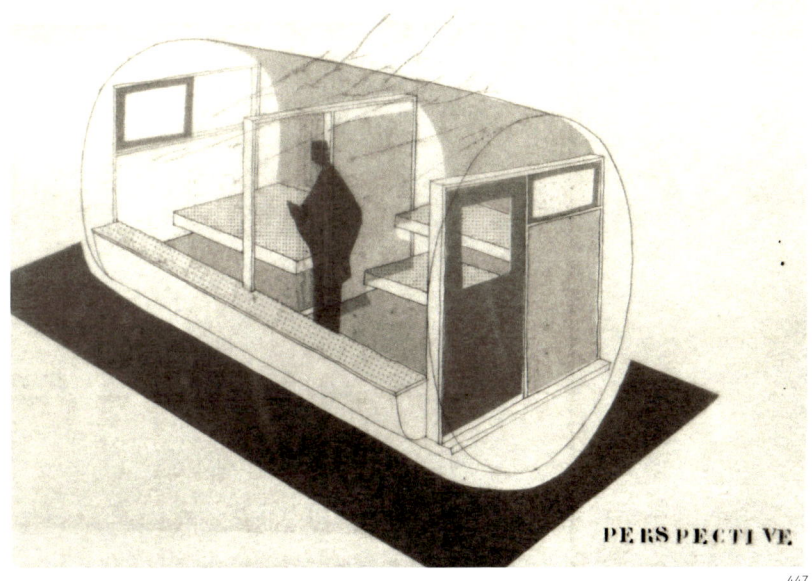

PERSPECTIVE

447

"LA MAISON DES JOURS MEILLEURS"

448 Designed by Jean Prouvé for l'Abbé Pierre, Quai Alexandre III, Paris, 1956.

STACKED CONCRETE BOXES

449 Yona Friedman: Drawing and collage, 1958.

MONTREAL EXPO 67

450 Project by Moshe Safdie in Montreal, 1967.
Construction view by unknown photographer.
Born in Haifa, Safdie read *L'architecture mobile* as a student.

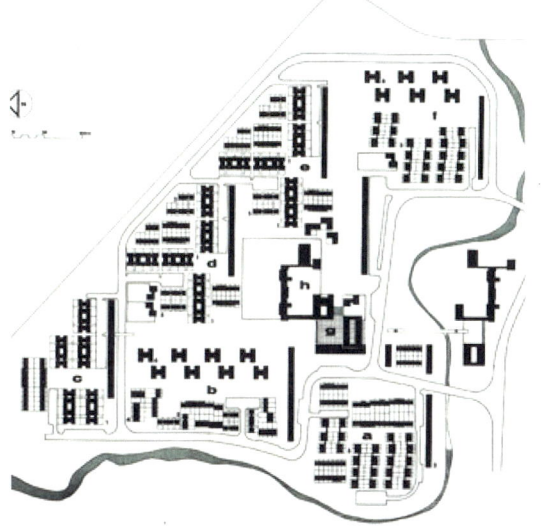

ARTUR GLIKSON

451–452 *Kiryat Gat Housing Project*, 1955–65.
Plan of civic and shopping center. Model of the *experimental neighborhood*.
Published in *Revue internationale d'architecture, Le carré bleu*, 1998.

ALFRED NEUMANN, ELDAR SHARON, ZVI HECKER

453 *Civic Center*, Bat Yam, 1964.

KONRAD WACHSMANN'S TECHNOLOGICAL UTOPIA

The machine is the tool of our age. It is the cause of those effects through which the social order manifests itself. [261]
Konrad Wachsmann

A design that is based fundamentally on showing the structure is really a superficial design. [262]
James Stirling

In the academic year 1953-54 Konrad Wachsmann was visiting professor at the Technion and so Friedman had the opportunity to get to know his theories and work firsthand. A pupil of Heinrich Tessenow and Hans Poelzig, the German pioneer of industrial prefabrication, Wachsmann was always caustically ironic in his attitude toward art. The designer of Einstein's summer house at Caputh near Potsdam in 1928, he emigrated to the United States in 1941, where he worked all through the forties with Walter Gropius. In 1950 he was appointed a professor at the Institute of Design in Chicago and as always combined practical work with theoretical research. Architecture, in Wachsmann's view, had to adopt the techniques of industrial production and make use of modular elements in theoretically infinite combinations held together by often highly sophisticated joints. Thus Wachsmann's structures, especially the hangars that he was designing in those years for the American air force, were the result of a theoretically infinite process of composition in which there was no provision for a shell, just a never-ending nodal assembly of structures supported on pillars set at a distance of up to 40 meters apart. In this process the structure tends to get confused with its own principle of unlimited extension, as has been pointed out by its clear-eyed admirer, Giulio Carlo Argan: in other words Wachsmann's works of architecture are no longer *in* space, but *of* space,[263] no longer made of skeletons but of *exoskeletons* in which to insert complete mobile units and not simple cladding. This was the theoretical principle that suggested the most new architectural possibilities on a large scale and that stirred the imagination of younger architects, from Europe to Japan where a twenty-year-old Arata Isozaki would be a student of Wachsmann's at Tokyo University in 1955.[264] Modular structures and the possibility of unlimited expansion would in fact be the two prime characteristics of the megastructure identified by Reyner Banham about twenty years later.

In the meantime Wachsmann was able to be more precise about the theoretical bases of his research. The opportunity was provided in 1956 by funding from the US Department of State for a traveling exhibition on Wachsmann's work, with a duration of seven years:

---

261 *Vom Bauen in unserer Zeit*, in *Baukunst und Werkform*, January 1957, pp. 26–31. English transl., *On Building in Our Time*, now in Ockman, Joan (ed.): *Architecture Culture 1943–1968. A Documentary Anthology*, New York, Rizzoli, 1993, p. 267.
262 Stirling, James: *Struttura di espediente o antistruttura*, in *Problemi della città*, ed. by Fernando Clemente, Padua, Marsilio, 1967, p. 149.
263 Argan, Giulio Carlo: *La sintesi spaziale di Konrad Wachsmann*, in *Casabella*, no. 244, October 1960, p. 36.
264 Rouillard, Dominique: *Superarchitecture. Le futur de l'architecture 1950–1970*, Paris, Editions de la Villette, 2004, p. 160, note 9; Koolhaas, Rem and Obrist, Hans-Ulrich (eds.): *Project Japan. Metabolism Talks...*, Cologne, Taschen, 2011, p. 120.

the preparation of the material for the exhibition was carried out at the Hochschule für Gestaltung in Ulm [265] and out of it later came a very important book, published in Germany in 1959 and in the US in 1961.[266] But in 1953–54 Wachsmann was already totally convinced of the importance of prefabrication, especially in situations of demographic emergency following wars or a major influx of immigrants.[267]

For Friedman, Wachsmann's teaching was an epiphany:

The building must evolve indirectly, obeying the conditions of industrialization, through a multiplication of cells and elements.[268]

The project of Wachsmann's that most directly inspired Friedman's theory of temporary architecture is the aforementioned 1951 design of a hangar for the US Air Force: Friedman simply thought of making it habitable, through the insertion of his "mobile boxes," elevated modular structures of large size. In particular he would make use of the structural joints to show that his designs for the *Ville-Spatiale* ("Spatial City," 1958-62) were feasible and not utopian. The principle of the spatial city is that of the multiplication of the original surface of the city by means of elevated levels, an urban intensification that Friedman would call a spatial infrastructure.[269]

However, as we have already seen, Wachsmann's ambitions of building standardization on a vast scale had already run into serious obstacles, in particular with his collaboration with Gropius at the General Panel Corporation in the forties: the "magic" joints designed by Wachsmann were ingenious and based on elegant mathematics – Argan did not hesitate to speak of "technical and scientific perfection" – but often extremely complicated and requiring extreme precision in their manufacture. For Wachsmann "the study of such joints [...] constitutes today the very essence of the secret of the building art."[270] This excessive concentration on the detail of the joints imposed a great limitation on the reproducibility of the factory-made house and was the cause of a setback, as Banham pitilessly observed:

The General Panel system might have been a minor incident in the history of prefabrication, but it was a complete disaster for modern architecture, since it marked the failure of one of the most cherished dreams of Modernism.[271]

---

265 Ockman, Joan (ed.), *Architecture Culture 1943–1968*, op. cit., p. 266.
266 Wachsmann, Konrad: *Wendepunkt im Bauen*, Wiesbaden, Krausskopf, 1959. English transl., *The Turning Point of Building: Structure and Design*, Cleveland (OH), Reinhold, 1961.
267 Herbert, Gilbert: *Gropius, Hirsch and the Saga of Copper Houses*, vol. 2, Haifa: the "Palestine Prefabs," in Architectural Documentation Unit, Faculty of Architecture and Urban Planning, Technion, Haifa, publication no. 1, 1980, pp. B1–B22.
268 Wachsmann, Konrad: *Vom Bauen in unserer Zeit*, op. cit. Cited in Braham, William W. and Hale, Jonathan A. (eds.): *Rethinking Technology: A Reader in Architectural Theory*, London, Routledge, 2006, p. 120.
269 Friedman, Yona: *Les infrastructures possibles*, in *Europäisches Bau-Forum*, no. 5, 1965, pp. 1029–30; this is the text of a lecture given at the universities of Berkeley and Strasbourg in 1964.
270 Wachsmann, Konrad: *Concetti di architettura* (lecture given at the Circolo Artistico in Rome, April 11, 1956), in *Casabella*, no. 244, October 1960, p. 41.
271 Banham, Reyner: *I complessi della prefabbricazione*, op. cit., p. 29.

Likewise, the designs for large hangars, notwithstanding all the efforts made to simplify the joints, would prove feasible only in a few specific cases, such as the ones for the American military, but were certainly not suited to being introduced on a large scale. The high cost of their production and the complexity of their assembly due to the excessive precision of the joints were the main limitations. Thus Wachsmann's technological utopia ran up against the harsh nature of reality as it could not be adapted easily to circumstances. And yet in the mid-fifties the German engineer's research seemed to open up new horizons for construction, peopled with hypothetically extendible exoskeletons that stimulated the imagination of Friedman, the Metabolists, Archigram, Schulze-Fielitz and many of the new avant-garde movements of the sixties, but the substantial failure of the designs of his German-American mentor sounded an ominous alarm bell.

In 1959 Bruno Zevi, after an exhibition of Wachsmann's work in Rome, asked polemically: "Who is Wachsmann? An architect, a critic, a technician, a utopian?" Given a career so lacking in concrete accomplishments, he found it hard to recognize him in anything but the second role.[272]

Many years later Yona Friedman would write a eulogy of imprecision, implicitly disavowing this phase of youthful technological enthusiasm in which he had become caught up, and not him alone. His mistake lay in regarding Wachsmann's designs as architectural postulates, already established from the start. Yet these postulates were merely arbitrary assumptions, founded on technological rhetoric rather than on concrete applications. For in the end even technology is first of all a form of rhetoric, and thus intended to persuade, rather than an exact science and means of salvation as Friedman and very many others after him have been naïvely inclined to believe.

---

272 Zevi, Bruno: *Konrad Wachsmann. Segmenti e giunti per un'arte insoluta*, in *L'Espresso*, October 2, 1960, now in id., *Cronache di architettura*, vol. 7. Rome/Bari, Laterza, 1971, pp. 62–64.

454

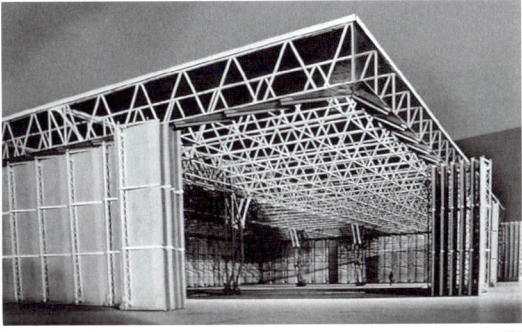

455

456

457

KONRAD WACHSMANN

454 Meeting with Walter Gropius on a prototype, at the General Panel Corporation, Lincoln, USA, 1941.
455 *Air Force Hangar*, 1940s
456 Detail of the structural joints of the hangars, published in *Wendepunkt im Bauen*, 1959.
457 Hangar design, 1951–54. The American Air Force commissioned Wachsmann to design a large-span aircraft hangar.

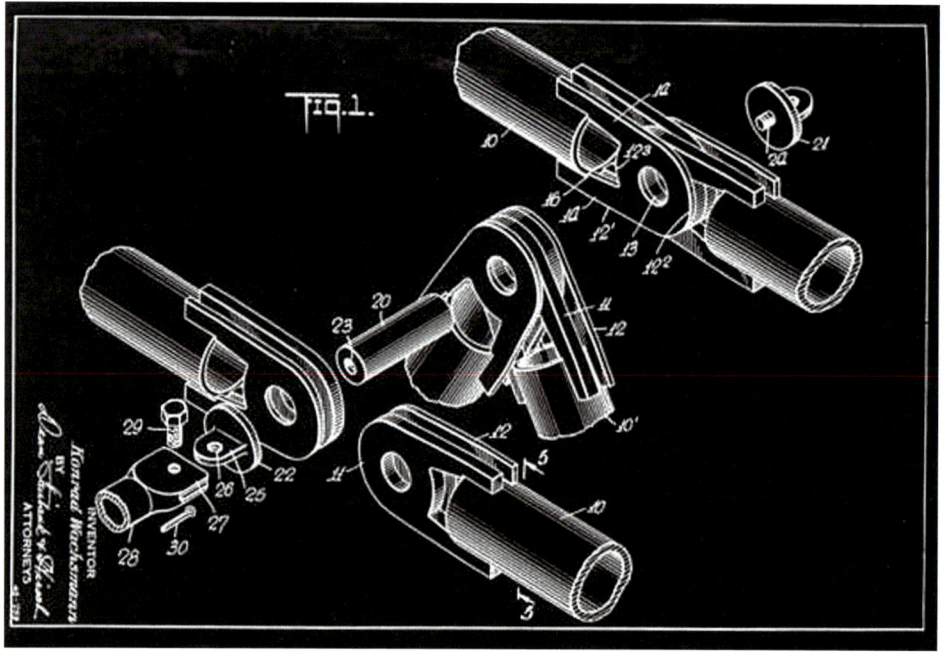

458

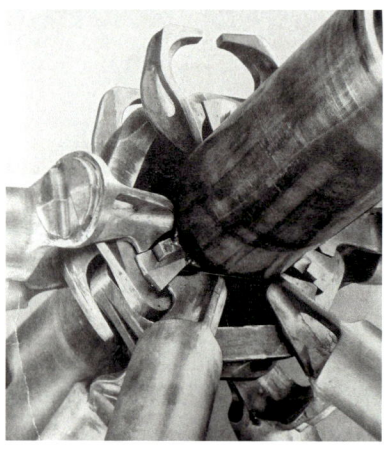

459

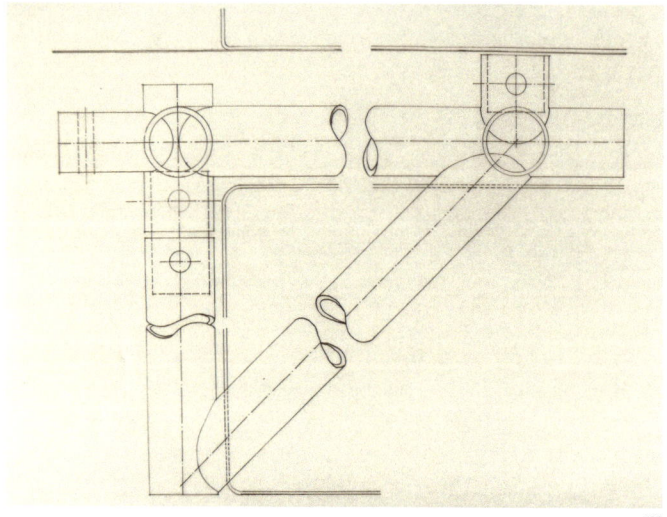

460

KONRAD WACHSMANN

458 Exploded technical drawing of a joint, 1950s, from *Wendepunkt im Bauen*, 1959.
459 View of a *Connector*, structural joint, 1950.

YONA FRIEDMAN

460 *Detail of the trihedron, standard type A–0, elevation*, 1958.
461 Joint studies, from 1958. *Node joining 4 bars. Detail of the bar / hyperboloid of rotation oblique to the axis.*
462 *Node allowing passage of 4 continuous bars for spatial constructions / superior and inferior levels of the node.*

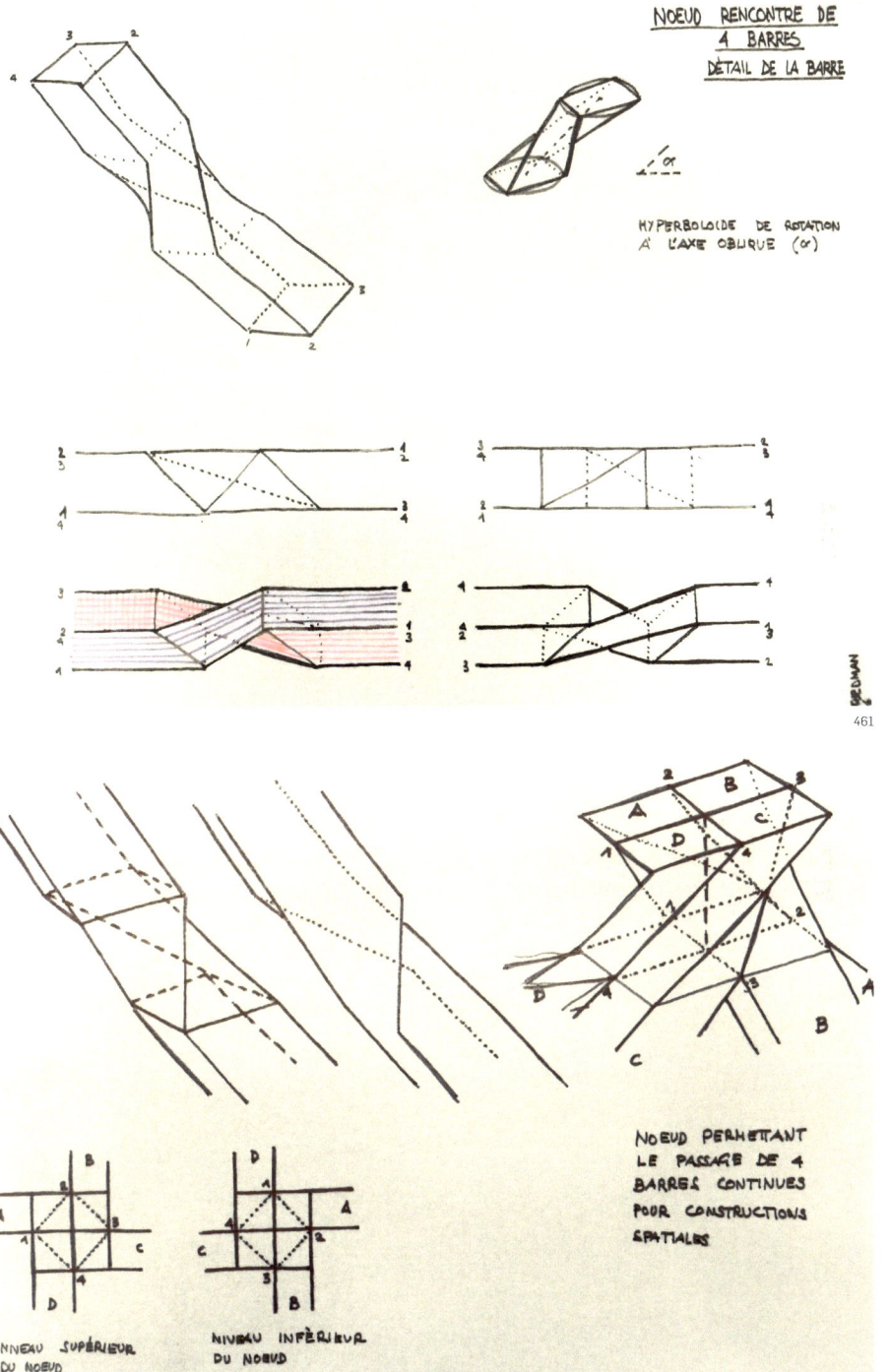

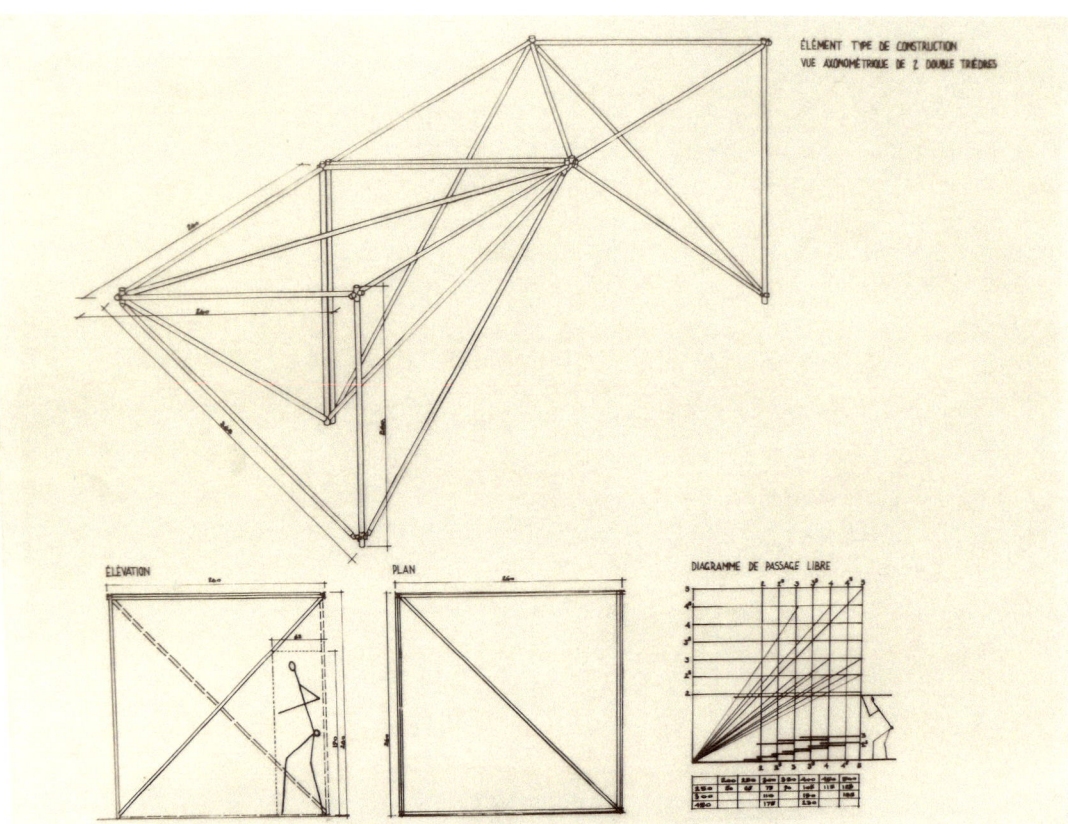

STRUCTURAL STUDIES FOR THE "SPAN-OVER BLOCK," FROM 1958

463 Yona Friedman: Element, type of construction / axonometric view of 2 double trihedrons / elevation, plan and diagram of free passage.
464 Yona Friedman: Element, type of construction / axonometric view of 2 trihedrons and diagrams.

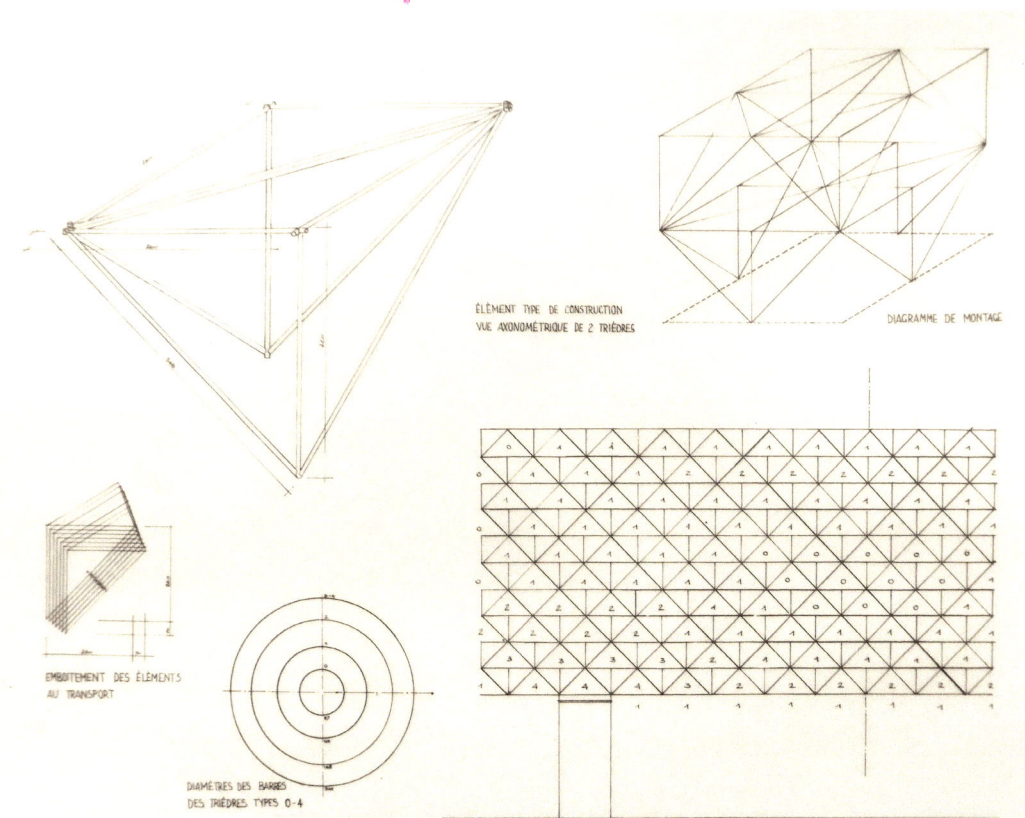

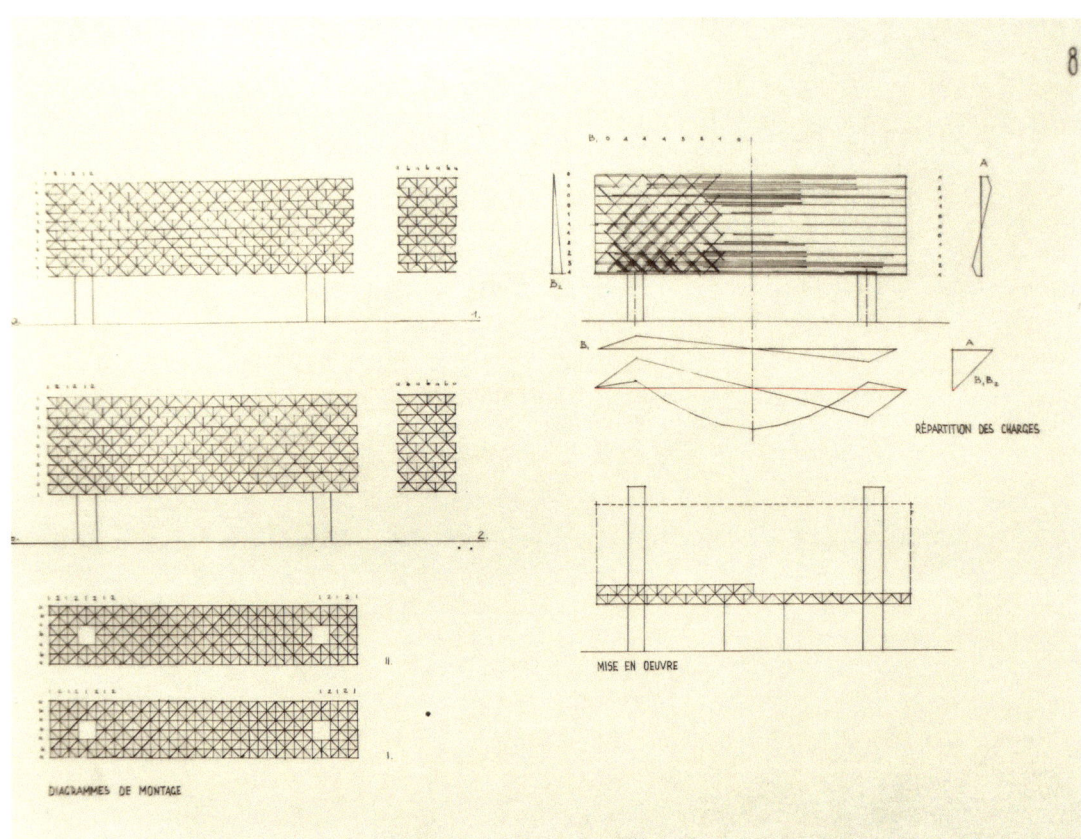

STRUCTURAL STUDIES FOR THE "SPAN-OVER BLOCK," FROM 1958

465 Yona Friedman: *Load distribution / implementation* and *assembly diagram.*
466 Yona Friedman: *Load distribution and casing of stresses.*
467 Yona Friedman: *Shear stress and bending stress / moment of inertia of the whole structure and bending by tiers.*

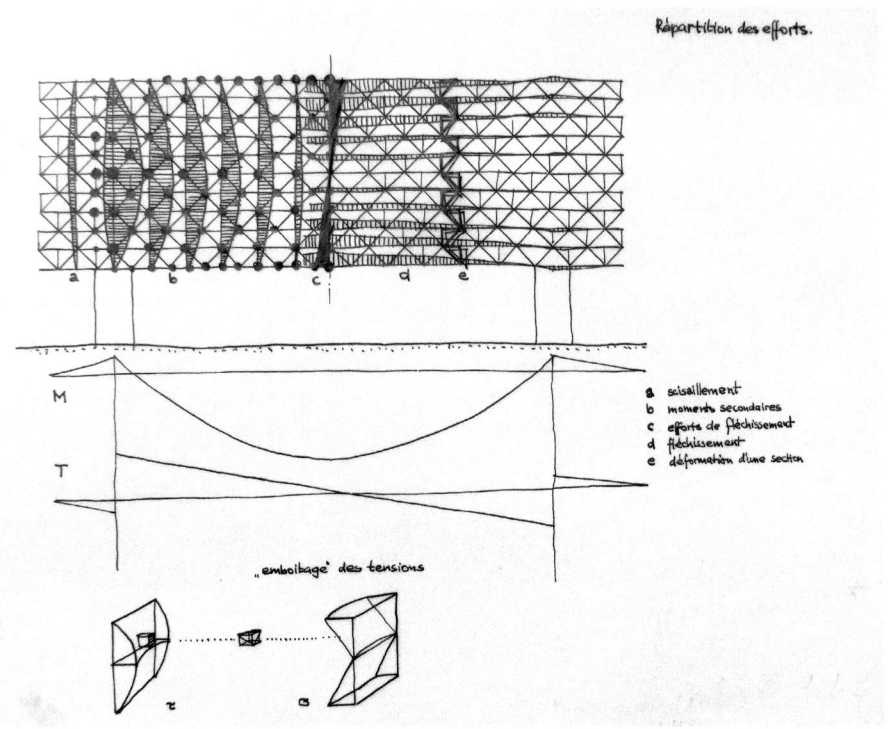

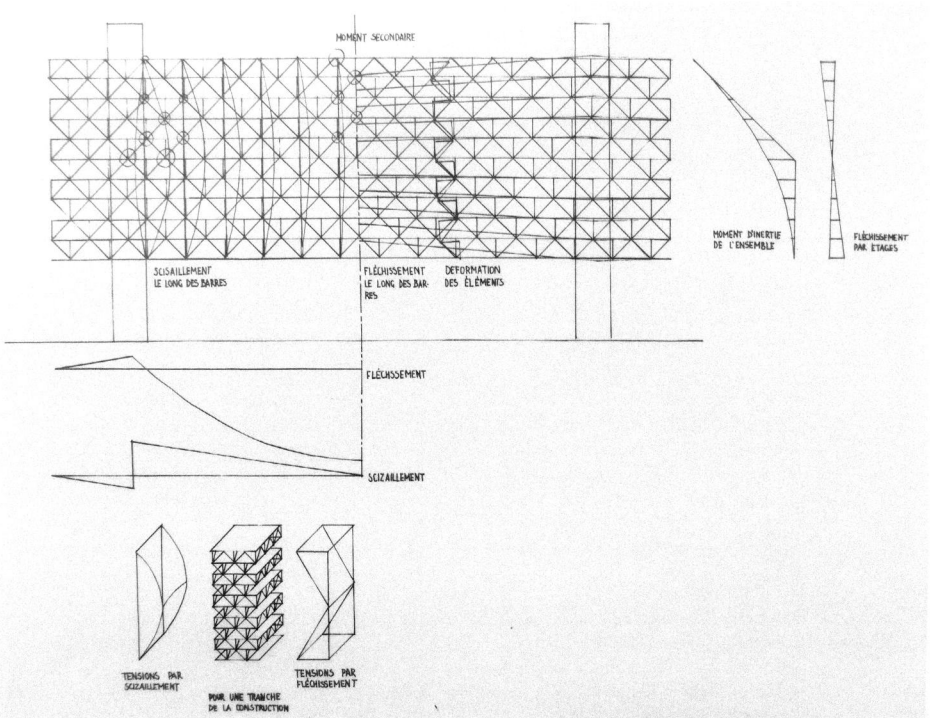

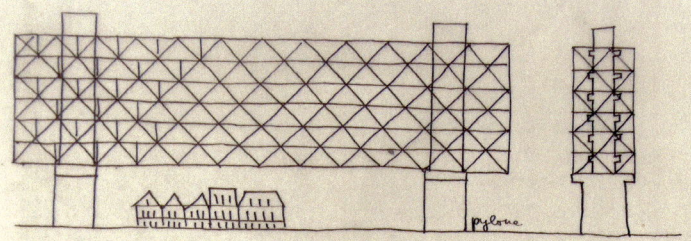

MISE EN OEUVRE.
La réalisation sera commencé par la construction des pylones en béton armé. Elle sera continué suivant deux alternatives:
a) un câble suspendu entre les deux pylones servira à construire le premier étage (qui sera la plateforme d'opération);
b) ou bien le premier étage sera soutenu par des poteaux temporaires distants de 15 à 20 mètres (suivant chaque cas particulier).

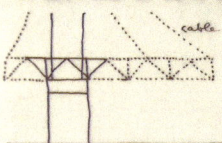 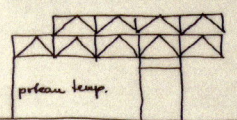

MURS ET CLOISONS.
Les cloisons sont des cloisons légers et mobiles (par exemple type Norma). Le plafond est suspendu indépendamment de l'ossature. Pratiquement les éléments forment des boites isolantes posées dans les vides de la construction, de la manière que ces boites ne participent pas aux déformations de la construction.

Le mur extèrieur, fixé sur l'ossature, est un des murs rideaux qu'on utilise habituellement.

ISOLATION.
l'isolation sonore est amélioré par l'indépendence entre les boites et l'ossature, fait qui évite la conductibilité acoustique. Les vides entre les boites (entre cloisons et cloisons, plafond et plancher) reçoivent les gaines, conduits, chauffage, ventilation etc.

Implementation
The implementation will commence with the construction of reinforced concrete pylons. They will be continued in two alternative ways:
a) a cable suspended between two pylons enabling the construction of the first floor (which will serve as the operational platform);
b) or the first floor will be supported by temporary posts placed 15 to 20 meters apart (according to each particular case).

Walls and partitions
The partitions will be light and mobile (for instance the Norma type). The ceiling is suspended independently of the framework. In practice the elements form isolating boxes inserted in the open spaces of the construction, in such a way that these boxes will not be affected by the deformations of the construction.

The outer wall fixed to the framework is a one of those commonly used curtain walls.

Insulation
Soundproofing is improved by the independence of the boxes and the framework, a fact that prevents the conduction of sound. The spaces between the boxes (between partitions and partitions, ceiling and floor) will contain ducts, pipes, heating, ventilation, etc.

"SPAN-OVER BLOCKS"
468 Yona Friedman: Stages of implementation for the *Span-over block*, 1959.
"BOX" IN THE SHELTER OF 4 TRIHEDRONS
469–470 Yona Friedman: Technical drawings, details, 1959.

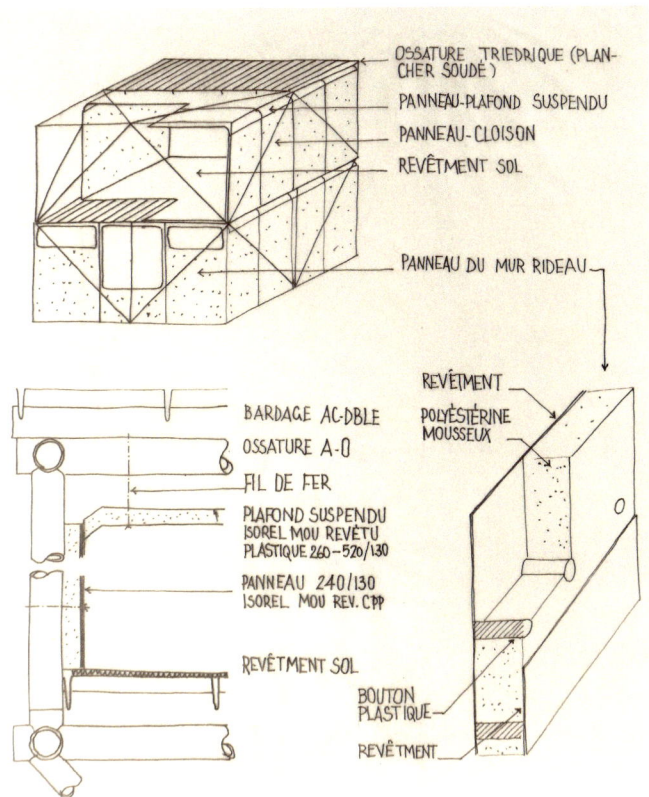

469

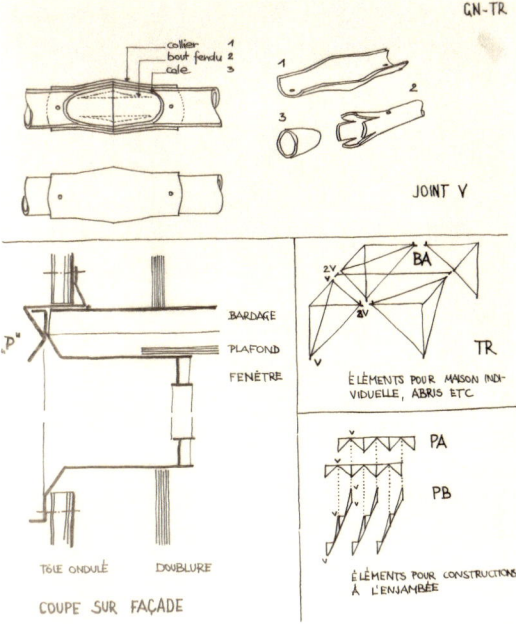

470

471

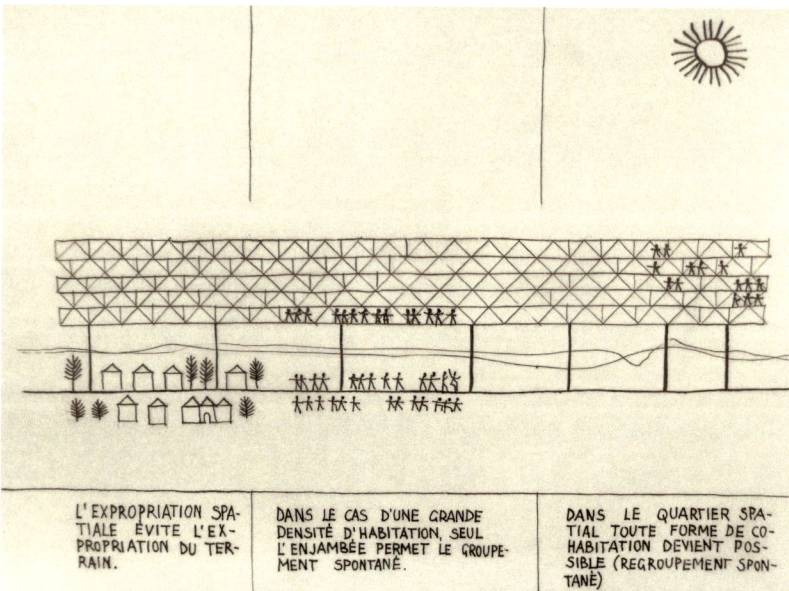

Spatial expropriation avoids expropriation of land.

In the case of high-density housing, only the span enables spontaneous grouping.

In the spatial district, all forms of cohabitation will be possible (spontaneous regrouping).

472

"SPATIAL EXPROPRIATION," 1959

471 Yona Friedman: Perspective, *Span-over* residential blocks.
472 Yona Friedman: *Spatial expropriation,* drawing and notes.
473 Yona Friedman: A *Span-over block,* urban photomontage.

UN BLOC À L'ENJAMBÉE – VUE DE MAQUETTE

EUROPE '56

What was great about the fifties is that for one brief moment – maybe, say, six weeks – nobody understood art. That's why it all happened. [273]
Morton Feldman

The year 1956 is one of the key moments in the architectural and artistic culture of the 20th century. Conferences and exhibitions of great significance were held that did not represent mere occasions of debate and the radicalization of positions, but would also have direct and immediate consequences: new groups of action were formed and individual figures who up until then had been left in the shadows came out into the open, while in parallel established work groups broke up forever. These were natural and quite ordinary historical processes, but very rarely have so many significant events been concentrated in a single year.

Between the spring and summer of 1956 followed, in rapid succession: the exhibition *This Is Tomorrow* in London, the first conference on Urban Design at the Harvard Graduate School of Design (April 9 and 10) and the tenth International Congress of Modern Architecture in Dubrovnik in August, while the Festival of Avant-Garde Art was held in Marseille and finally, on September 2, the First World Congress of Free Artists opened at Alba.

Groups that were already active, like the Independent Group (1953), or in the process of formation like Team 10 and the Situationist International, would emerge strengthened from these encounters.

This Is Tomorrow, the exhibition organized by Theo Crosby in 1956 at the Whitechapel Gallery, can be considered the final act of the Independent Group, made up of young painters, sculptors, art critics and architects, which used to meet regularly at the Institute of Contemporary Arts (ICA) in London to discuss a broad range of subjects between 1952 and 1955.[274] There can be no doubt that one of the most influential members of the group was Reyner Banham, author of the introduction to the catalogue.[275] Although he had trained as an art historian at the Courtauld Institute under Rudolf Wittkower and written a PhD thesis supervised by Nikolaus Pevsner,[276] he was a strenuous defender of modernism in architecture – which did not stop him from criticizing it, sometimes harshly, at meetings of the IG. Alison and Peter Smithson were brought into the group by Nigel Henderson and the sculptor Eduardo Paolozzi, while other members included the critics Toni del Rienzo and Lawrence Alloway, who felt that what linked the people who made up the group was a common anthropological interest in culture: any human activity was worthy of attention and

---

[273] FELDMAN, Morton: *Give My Regards to Eighth Street. Collected Writings,* ed. by B.H Friedman, New York, Exact Change, 2001.
[274] MASSEY, Anne: *The Independent Group. Modernism and Mass Culture in Britain 1945–59,* Manchester/New York, Manchester University Press, 1995.
[275] BANHAM, Reyner: *An Introduction,* in *This Is Tomorrow,* London, Whitechapel Art Gallery, 1956.
[276] The PhD thesis defended in 1957 would later be published as *Theory and Design in the First Machine Age,* London, Architectural Press, 1960. Banham broadened the scope of inquiry of the history of modern architecture, focusing in particular on his favored themes of technology and anti-rationalist currents like Italian Futurism and German Expressionism.

open to aesthetic judgment,[277] including and in particular what was generally disdained by official culture. Nigel Henderson's photographs of poor communities in the East End of London, scientific or vernacular images, simple artefacts and pictures drawn from popular magazines mixed with artistic representations all went into the exhibition *Parallel of Life and Art* in 1953, scandalizing the British middle class, which still clung to a romantic view of art.[278] This vision was moreover the butt of fierce criticism on the part of almost the whole new generation of British intellectuals to have come out of the war: the angry young men, as they came to be called following the enormous box-office success of John Osborne's play *Look Back in Anger* in the May of '56. Thus protest against the conformists of the British establishment was widespread in the arts and was not markedly ideological in character, in the sense that politico-social conservatism with a small c was opposed independently of whether it was represented by members of the Conservative or Labor parties. Writers like Kingsley Amis (who left the Communist Party following the events that took place in Hungary the same year), Colin Wilson, Philip Larkin and playwrights like the young Harold Pinter played an active part.[279]

The Independent Group was accused of producing "non-art" or anti-art, but in reality this interest in popular culture and everything that was considered ugly, ordinary and brutal can be seen as Pop Art in incubation. It is no coincidence that Denise Scott Brown, raised in South Africa, had received her training at the Architectural Association in London before moving to Philadelphia, and she never made any secret of her personal debt to the Smithsons and the IG.[280] Richard Hamilton's celebrated proto-pop picture/collage *Just what is it that makes today's homes so different, so appealing?*, anticipating by many years the better-known American Pop movement of Warhol, Lichtenstein, etc., was on show in one section of *This Is Tomorrow*.[281]

The conference called in April to define the concept of Urban Design had been organized by José Luís Sert.[282] A member of the Catalan group of the CIAM and of the GATCPAC (*Grup d'Arquitectes i Tècnics Catalans per al Progrés de l'Arquitectura Contemporània*), Sert emigrated to the US at the end of the Spanish Civil War and in 1953 was appointed dean of the Harvard Graduate School of Design,[283] where other elements of the old guard of the CIAM taught, such as Sigfried Giedion, Walter Gropius and Jaqueline Tyrwhitt. In 1956, however, Sert held another post that was not easy to handle, that of president of the CIAM at the very moment in which a fierce clash of generations was about to take place between

---

[277] WEBSTER, Helena: *Modernism without Rhetoric*, in WEBSTER, Helena (ed.): *Modernism without Rhetoric. Essays on the Work of Alison and Peter Smithson*, London, Academy Editions 1996, p. 20.
[278] SCALBERT, Irénée: *Parallel of Life and Art*, Daidalos, no. 75, May 2000, pp. 53–65.
[279] CARPENTER, Humphrey: *The Angry Young Men. A Literary Comedy of the 1950s*, London, Allen Lane, 2002.
[280] SCOTT BROWN, Denise: *A Worm's Eye View of Recent Architectural History*, in *Architectural Record*, February 1984, pp. 771–79; id., *Learning from Brutalism*, in ROBBINS, David: *The Independent Group: Postwar Britain and the Aesthetics of Plenty*, Cambridge (MA), MIT Press 1988, pp. 203–6.
[281] In a letter written to the Smithsons on January 6, 1957, Hamilton proposed organizing an exhibition on Pop Art and gave his own definition of it: "Pop Art is: popular (designed for a mass audience), transient (short-term solution), expendable (easily-forgotten), low-cost, mass-produced, young (aimed at youth), witty, sexy, gimmicky, glamorous, Big Business..." Cited in LIVINGSTONE, Marco (ed.): *Pop Art*, in the catalogue of the exhibition at the Royal Academy of Art, London, Weidenfeld & Nicolson, 1991, p. 157.
[282] KRIEGER, Alex and SAUNDERS, William S. (eds.): *Urban Design*, Minneapolis, University of Minnesota Press, 2009.
[283] The post of Dean was initially offered to Ernesto Nathan Rogers, who turned it down. See ROVIRA, Josep Maria: *José Luis Sert 1901–1983*, Milan, Electa, 2000, p. 315.

the founding members and younger recruits, still gathered generically under the label of Team 10, who were getting ready to question the meaning and the role of the CIAM from its foundations over the course of the imminent congress in Dubrovnik.

Since 1947 Sert had been the advocate of planning on a "human scale"[284] and of modern urban centers called cores in which the importance of pedestrianization was underlined. Already at Bergamo in 1949 and above all at Hoddesdon in 1951, Sert had succeeded in steering the discussion onto the themes dearest to him, so that the title of CIAM 8 was "The Heart of the City."[285] The aim was to counter the breakup of the city, which was becoming decentralized, generating suburban districts devoid of civic life, partly as a result of the spread of the new media of radio and television. Sert proposed using a "network of cores" to recentralize vast urban areas around pedestrianized civic centers where people could gather to talk about their problems instead of withdrawing into a growing individuality. In his view the four functions of the city described in the Athens Charter of twenty years earlier – housing, work, transportation and leisure – were still valid, while Team 10 considered them obsolete, as we will see. At the first conference called to establish a single and shared definition of urban design this objective was not attained, and neither would it be at the later ones (Sert himself described the debate as "a fog of amicable generalities"[286]), but the Catalan architect achieved his aim anyway as he was able to introduce his personal vision of the CIAM themes into the United States at the very moment in which he was about to be ousted as their president – and with him Giedion, secretary ever since the CIAM's foundation in 1928. At the congress the participants were invited to explore "the role of the planner, architect, and landscape architect in the design and development of the city" and the speakers included professors and professionals from all over the United States, including Richard Neutra, György Kepes and Victor Gruen; some of the participants had opposing views, like Lewis Mumford and Jane Jacobs.[287] In any case all the contributions were collected and published,[288] and since then the theme of urban design has been a constant of the American debate on the city. For Sert an urban designer had to be a coordinator, a new figure who would take on the job of facilitating the intervention of others without concerning himself with specific architectural solutions, while remaining in possession of a precise visual idea of how the city ought to be transformed. Giedion came up with a concise and almost poetic definition of his own: "Urban Design has to give visual form to the relationship between You and Me."[289]

---

[284] In reality his first definition of it had come earlier. See Sert, José Luís: *The Human Scale in City Planning*, in Zucker, Paul: *New Architecture and City Planning*, New York, Philosophical Library, 1944, pp. 392–412.

[285] The most extensive study of the history of the CIAM is the one by Mumford, Eric: *The CIAM Discourse on Urbanism, 1928–1960*, with a foreword by Kenneth Frampton, Cambridge (MA), MIT Press, 2000.

[286] Quoted in Marshall, Richard: *The Elusiveness of Urban Design. The Perpetual Problems of Definition and Role*, in Harvard Design Magazine, no. 24, spring/summer 2006, p. 28.

[287] Jane Jacobs was tenaciously opposed to the zoning adopted in policies of urban renewal as well as to the ideology of the garden city promoted in the US by Mumford. Instead, Jacobs was in favor of the participation of the inhabitants in making decisions about the use of urban areas without a single functional purpose ("mixed use") and thus opposed to pedestrianized streets as well. See Jacobs, Jane: *Death and Life of American Cities*, New York, Random House, 1961.

[288] *Urban Design: Condensed Report of a Conference on the Work of the Architect, Landscape Architect and City Planner*, held at Harvard University, in Progressive Architecture, August 1956, pp. 97–112.

[289] Marshall, Richard: op. cit., p. 31. It should be noted that it was in 1956 that Giedion published *Architektur und Gemeinshaft*, Hamburg, Rowohlt, 1956. Engl. Transl., *Architecture, You and Me*, Cambridge (MA), Harvard University Press, 1958. "The demand for the re-establishment of the relation between 'You' and 'Me' leads to radical changes in the structure of the city."

Team 10 – for some time now the focus of new attention from historians [290] – had been formed a couple of years earlier out of the unity of intentions of a number of participants in the CIAM who were in their thirties, mostly British and Dutch. In the Doorn Manifesto, illustrated by a diagram, [291] the original nucleus of Team 10 proposed the study of human association as the first principle of urban planning, subordinating to it the four functions of the Athens Charter. As a consequence they openly criticized the dogma of functionalism on the one hand and the founders of the CIAM themselves on the other, with Alison and Peter Smithson mocking the members who taught at Harvard, calling them "the professors." [292] In any case on August 3, 1956, Sert got CIAM 10 under way at Dubrovnik, in Tito's Yugoslavia, which that same year had seen the foundation of the Movement of Non-Aligned Countries, i.e. of nations that did not belong to one bloc or the other of the Cold War like Egypt and India, and thus in a perfect free zone. The title of the congress was "The Future Structure of the Human Habitat" and the great absentee was Le Corbusier, who in the letter he sent to the participants gave a nod of approval to the newcomers:

It is those who are now 40 years old, born around 1916 during wars and revolutions and those then unborn, now twenty-five years old, born around 1930 during the preparation for a new war and amidst a profound economic, social, and political crisis, who thus find themselves in the heart of the present period the only ones capable of feeling actual problems, personally, profoundly, the goals to follow, the means to reach them, the pathetic urgency of the present situation. They are in the know. Their predecessors no longer are, they are out, and they are no longer subject to the direct impact of the situation. [293]

According to Kenneth Frampton this letter was the "essential epitaph of CIAM," [294] but as we have seen, an awareness of crisis and the imminence of the end was already widespread among the older members like the "professors" at Harvard or Cornelius van Eesteren. [295] As a consequence of this feeling that a new wind was blowing attendance at Dubrovnik was very high, with 95 delegates from twenty-five countries plus an unspecified number of architects and students with accreditation who did not side with either the old guard or Team 10. Among them was Yona Friedman, coming from a country like Israel, founded just eight years earlier and not culturally up-to-date on the architectural plane, who had taken up the invitation to follow the proceedings despite the disapproval of the president of his university. [296]

---

[290] Risselada, Max and van den Heuvel, Dirk (eds.): *Team 10. 1953–81. In Search of a Utopia of the Present*, Rotterdam, NAi Publishers, 2005.
[291] Bakema, Jaap, van Eyck, Aldo, van Ginkel, Daniel, Hovens-Greve, Hans, Smithson, Peter and Voelker, John: *Doorn Manifesto-CIAM Meeting 29-30-31 January 1954, Doorn*, now in Ockman, Joan (ed.): *Architecture Culture . . .*, op. cit., pp. 183.
[292] Smithson, Alison: (ed.), *The Emergence of Team 10 out of CIAM. Documents*, London, Architectural Association, 1982.
[293] Le Corbusier: *Letter to Team 10*, in Newman, Oscar: *New Frontiers in Architecture: CIAM '59 in Otterlo*, New York, Universe Books, 1961, p. 16.
[294] Frampton, Kenneth: *Modern Architecture: A Critical History*, New York/Toronto, Oxford University Press, 1980, p. 271.
[295] "The new influence had to find its own way and the constitution of the CIAM had to regard its specific task at an end." Cited in Landau, Royston: *The End of CIAM and the Role of the British*, in *Rassegna*, no. 52, December 1992, pp. 40–47.
[296] In a letter to Alfred Neumann of May 13, 1965, Friedman makes it clear that he had only been invited to Dubrovnik thanks to Professor Roth and that they had always been in disagreement. In fact Neumann had described Friedman's research as "science fiction."

Friedman's paper presented at Dubrovnik advocated a settlement revolution:

User determination makes settlements work.
User determination is better than governmental planning.
User determination solves problems governments cannot solve.

The paper, rewritten by Friedman as soon as he moved to Paris the following year, sounds almost like a mantra and is on the one hand a proposal for reform of architecture and the role of the architect itself, and on the other an implicit criticism of the way urban planning had been handled up until then in Israel, the land of settlers.[297] Also underlined was the need to provide for urban farming and to recognize the importance of urban villages, concepts to which he was to return on many occasions.

In any case the CIAM was split into two main sections, one concerned with the past and present, which included the "professors," and the other with the problems of the future, where all the members of Team 10 were to be found. In order not to give the impression of presenting projects that were too futuristic, the latter introduced themselves with the maxim:

Team 10 is Utopian, but Utopian about the present. Thus their aim is not to theorize but to build, for only through construction can a Utopia of the present be realized.[298]

Paradoxically this coincided with the idea of a "utopia of reality" put forward by another architect of the opposing front present in Dubrovnik, Ernesto Nathan Rogers.[299] But Sert himself, at the conference in April, had expressed himself in almost identical terms:

Now we know that the new city calls for a series of new elements – that all things are not going to be what they have been [...]. In the exhibition here, Pittsburgh, Philadelphia, Chicago, and other cities show things now being realized that are the result of Utopias predicted twenty years ago. Today these Utopias are realities.[300]

This is an important detail because it is revealing: in any case Utopia – always with a capital U in Sert's text – has to be turned into a reality, and this is not just a precedent that concerns the future author of *Utopies réalisables*. Indeed this detail allows us to point out that much of the criticism made by Team 10 in general, and the Smithsons in particular, was specious: at bottom the older and the younger members championed the same ideals, and viewed from today the vision is clearer. Sert and Giedion wanted to develop a disciplinary synthesis – which they also called "orchestration" – in which architecture, landscape design and city planning would work together. Team 10 shared with them not only the starting point, which lay in holding up as a model the work of Le Corbusier and

---

[297] See the three documents relating to Dubrovnik, pp. 379–81, nos. 486–88.
[298] SMITHSON, Alison (ed.): *Team 10 Primer*, London, Studio Vista, 1968, p. 3.
[299] *Editoriali di architettura*, op. cit., p. 269.
[300] José Luís Sert cited in *"Urban Design": Extracts from the 1956 First Urban Design Conference at the GSD*, in *Harvard Design Magazine*, no. 24, spring/summer 2006, p. 9.

other architects of the twenties (considered the heroic period of the Movement Modern [301]), but also a common desire to revitalize the organization of society through architectural design.[302] Notwithstanding their rhetorical and personal conflicts, Team 10 and the directors of the last CIAM seem from a distance of fifty years to have more similarities than divergences. And Friedman, who did not belong to either camp, indirectly, confirms this overlap: "Indeed, Dubrovnik was decisive for me: not for what was said, but on the contrary for what was forgotten,"[303] referring to the theme of participation. In other words, in Friedman's view the congress devoted to the habitat did not pay enough attention to the inhabitants. So while the first drawings of *mobile architecture* found a more marked formal parallel with the "clusters" of the Smithsons, they were separated from them by an ideological gulf: on the one hand the random composition of the clusters, a picturesque disorder that was the fruit of an arbitrary decision by the English architects, on the other Friedman and his settlement revolution.

In fact the theory of mobile architecture, which in 1956 had only been sketched out, was based on impermanence and on self-determination by the users and was fairly original. Up until then the precedents for participation in architecture, like those of Ralph Erskine in Sweden, had been few and far between, and in no case had gone so far as almost to give up the traditional conception of design. This approach, which we will analyze more thoroughly in the next chapter, was bound to clash head on with that of the Smithsons and for a very simple reason: despite their much-vaunted enthusiasm for any social activity and for popular culture, the Smithsons were not populists in the way that Friedman was. The Independent Group to which they belonged – Alison would go on to claim, quite falsely, that she and Peter were the only architects in the group [304] – had clearly artistic roots. Banham, its leader, was an art historian by training, and Henderson, McHale and Paolozzi were artists, and they were not willing to completely renounce imposing a precise form on their designs. The preamble to the instructions issued to the groups of participants in the congress, contained these words:

In the presentation of their projects, groups should use whatever methods they consider necessary to arrive at a solution, for example: collaboration with engineers, anthropologists, and specialists of all kinds. But it must be emphasized that we are only interested in the outcome of this collaboration, not in diagrams of relationships or analytical studies but as architecture. We are working as architects and at this congress we are making our statement to other architects.[305]

---

301 See SMITHSON, Alison and SMITHSON, Peter: *Heroic Period of Modern Architecture*, London, Thames and Hudson, 1981. The book is partly based on an earlier study from 1965, part of which was published in December 1967 in *Architectural Design*, pp. 542–64.
302 MUMFORD, Eric: *The Emergence of Urban Design in the Breakup of CIAM*, in *Harvard Design Magazine*, no. 24, spring/summer 2006, p. 19.
303 FRIEDMAN, Yona: *Interview avec moi-même (une sorte de bilan)*, duplicated copy, Paris, 1997. It has been published in Spanish as *Entrevista conmigo mismo (a modo de balance)*, in id., *Pro Domo*, Barcelona, Actar, 2006, p. 31.
304 SMITHSON, Alison: *Anni di fermento: l'Independent Group negli anni Cinquanta / A Time of Ferment: The Independent Group in Its Setting of the Fifties*, in *Zodiac*, no. 16, 1996–97, pp. 77–81. Other architects were in fact associated with the IG: Theo Crosby, Geoffrey Holroyd, James Stirling and Cedric Price.
305 NEWMAN, Oscar: *New Frontiers in Architecture . . .*, op. cit., p. 14.

The preamble signed by Bakema, Candilis, Gutmann, Howell, van Eyck and the Smithsons is an assertion of disciplinary rights: the architect is the only coordinator of urban transformations and *must remain so*.

The clash with Friedman was inevitable: in 1956 he was still an unknown, but just a few years later, in 1960, at Bagnols-sur-Cèze – where he had been invited by Georges Candilis – Friedman was already known to everyone. And it would be then that Alison Smithson and Aldo van Eyck in particular attacked him fiercely, accusing his designs of not being architecture. In Friedman's own words:

When Team 10 started [George] Candilis invited me to Bagnols-sur-Cèze, where I had a very bad clash with the Smithsons, very very bad. Alison [Smithson] was absolutely incredible, and Aldo van Eyck also. Candilis was peacekeeping, [Jaap] Bakema too. It was really very vehement and if I had not had the backing of Prouvé, of Le Corbusier, I would have taken it very badly, but it was too late. My proposals were published; they were already published in Japan as well. It was [Masato] Otaka who asked me in '59 to publish there. It influenced the Metabolists. [...] I think Alison was very angry about the principle of mine that in this system it's not the architect who decides but the inhabitant. It was not a project with a facade and then other things. This meant it would be completed by the inhabitant and changed by the inhabitant. It might be that what Alison didn't like was that my proposal was not architecture, not art; it was not a final object. It was the start of a process, and the buildings could look completely otherwise. The use was not determined. The CIAM people were very much concerned with doing the best plan and making it definite. I was saying, "I don't know what the best plan is, and for each inhabitant the best plan is different."[306]

In short what Friedman was proposing was a radical reform of the architect's role, reducing it in favor of that of the inhabitants. This was unacceptable to Team 10 and in particular to its British leaders. The accusation of producing non-architecture that Alison Smithson leveled against Friedman was paradoxically the same that had been made against herself and her husband after *This Is Tomorrow*, i.e. just a few weeks earlier.

It is well known that Alison Smithson tended to defend the original core of Team 10 in an exceedingly blunt manner. Giancarlo De Carlo's testimony in this connection tallies with Friedman's and is sufficient to set this episode in a broader framework, that of the systematic exclusion of architects who were of indisputable capacity but did not fall into line, like Jim Stirling.[307] And yet the clash between Alison, van Eyck and Friedman had been something more than the simple exclusion of an eccentric architect: it was the conflict between

---

[306] See the interview with Friedman in the appendix.
[307] "She was always attacking everyone. At the first meeting of Team 10 she picked on some poor guy, I think his name was Lovett. He was attacked in such a way that he never recovered: his whole life was destroyed by that furious attack.... She couldn't bear encounters with architects outside the group: Jim Stirling, Kurokawa, all excellent people that however she didn't want." Giancarlo De Carlo interviewed by Boeri, Stefano, Davey, Peter and Sowa, Axel: *Il racconto dell'architettura*, in *Domus*, no. 874, October 2004, p. 70.

a moralistic conception [308] of the architect's role and another, completely unprecedented one that in order to keep pace with the new and pressing needs of reconstruction, or of a society undergoing a great expansion in its population, was ready to renounce many of its traditional prerogatives in order to allow it to get to grips with reality. To this crucial theme, which still informs the debate in contemporary architecture, we will have to return.

What needs to be pointed out here is the wholly utilitarian view that the Smithsons took of the CIAM: a promotional institution with a corporate structure and an agenda that had to be the right one.[309] Further evidence for this comes from the Smithsons' contemptuous dismissal of the last CIAM, as if it had just been a waste of time: Alison Smithson claimed that the most positive thing to have come out of the tenth congress was that the CIAM as a whole have begun to question the reasons for their continued existence.[310] A statement like this reveals the haughty attitude of the Smithsons, and Alison in particular: we know that even the older members doubted whether it was worth carrying on with the experience, but at least they had opened up the CIAM to new generations of architects and indeed they argued for its further expansion to participants from other continents, while Team 10 would always stick to a closed and elitist form, and one that was also marked by a fair amount of internal conflict,[311] and would remain within a purely European setting. The differences of opinion within Team 10 were so great that it was not even possible for them to produce a joint paper at Dubrovnik, where on the contrary mutual recriminations were already circulating.[312] Without the mediation of Jaap Bakema, who was regarded as a conservative within Team 10, the group would probably have brought its private meetings to an end long before 1981, not coincidentally the year of Bakema's death.

Organized by the French Ministry of Reconstruction and Urban Planning from July 4 to 12, contemporaneously with the CIAM, the Avant-Garde Arts Festival at the *Cité Radieuse* in Marseille was intended to serve as a showcase for what were considered the most innovative currents in every field of art, in line with the program of modernization of Mollet's Radical-Socialist government: Samuel Beckett and Eugène Ionesco for drama, the direction of Jacques Polieri (who was also the festival's coordinator), Agnes Varda and Norman McLaren for films, the Lettrists Isou and Lemaître for poetry, Pierre Boulez for music and Maurice Béjart for choreography, to mention just a few of the participants. There was also an exhibition of abstract painting with one of Yves Klein's blue monochromes alongside the young "Nouveaux réalistes" César and Tinguely.

---

[308] Also see Colquhoun's account in CHABARD, Pierre: *Entretien avec Alan Colquhoun*, in *Criticat*, no. 1, January 2008, p. 91.: "What position did you take in the generational conflict within modern architecture that led to the founding of Team 10 between 1953 and 1956? Did you have any connection with Alison and Peter Smithson? I met the Smithsons occasionally in the early fifties. I didn't go along with their mystical and apocalyptic vision. I always found them unbearably moralistic."
[309] See LANDAU, Royston: *The End of CIAM and the Role of the British*, op. cit.
[310] SMITHSON, Alison (ed.): *The Emergence of Team 10...*, op. cit., p. 71.
[311] For the clashes between the Smithsons and van Eyk and Bakema, see STRAUVEN, Francis: *The Dutch Contribution: Bakema and Van Eyck*, in *Rassegna*, no. 52, December 1992, pp. 48–57.
[312] Bakema circulated some texts in which he made public his disagreement with the Smithsons. The result was a congress in Dubrovnik where Team 10 did not develop a common point of view (as Giedion, Sert and Gropius had wished) and where the discussions were fairly uninspired. See BOSMAN, Jos: *CIAM after the War: A Balance of the Modern Movement*, in *Rassegna*, no. 52, December 1992, pp. 6–21.

No renowned architect had been invited to the festival: the presence of the recently opened Unité d'Habitation was regarded as sufficient to highlight the sense of such a variegated event as it had assumed the role of an architectural manifesto of reconstruction in France, to the point of being replicated in Nantes, Briey-en-Forêt and Firminy, as well as in Berlin. It was left to Michel Ragon and Nicolas Schöffer, Friedman's future fellow travelers, to represent the new architectural prospects at the festival, but neither was an architect: Ragon was an art historian and co-organizer of the festival,[313] while Schöffer was a sculptor. During the preparations for the festival Ragon had met and interviewed Le Corbusier and Wogenscky, sleeping and working in the Unité and becoming enthusiastic about the similarities between the struggle for a modern architecture and the one for abstract art, in which the young critic himself was involved. He quickly became convinced of the educational power of architecture in society, assigning it a primary role in his more general search for a synthesis of the arts – which was moreover the implicit theme of the festival.[314] Two years later, in the first of a long series of books on architecture, he wrote that "modern architecture helps people to understand modern art. The gap between the public and today's arts stems in part from the fact that the public still sees the works of the 20th century in the same way (or almost) as it experienced them in the Middle Ages. Thus, when we presented an exhibition of abstract art in Marseille, in the summer of 1956, on the terrace of Le Corbusier's *Unité d'Habitation,* the residents were much less shocked than the visitors by the pictures on show. They were already accustomed to living in their century."[315]

Since around 1948 Schöffer, on the other hand, had been producing sculptures with moving parts, intended to integrate the notions of space and movement in a new ideal of what he called Spatiodynamism, in part through the use of electricity and cybernetics, as in the sculpture CYSP 1, an acronym of *"Cybernétique + Spatiodynamisme."* This sculpture in black stainless steel and painted polychrome aluminum, finished in May 1956, moved under the impulses of an electronic device hidden in the base and during the summer was included in the choreography of a ballet staged by the Maurice Béjart company in Marseille.[316]

The unconditional faith in technological advances was a reflection of the equally unreserved one in the social progress promised by the system of Western civilization. In 1956 there was a strong claim for the right of the arts to place not just the instruments of modern technology at the center of their practice but also their social significance. Art, technology and society together, therefore. In that year an authoritative French art historian wrote: "The significance of art is that it permits men, who are divided over everything, to contribute to the building of a shared society."[317]

---

[313] See Thierry Paquot's interview with Ragon published in *Urbanisme,* no. 10, 1997.
[314] On the overall climate of synthesis of the arts in France in the 1960s, see BUSBEA, Larry: *From Synthesis to the Integration of the Arts,* in id., *Topologies: The Urban Utopia in France, 1960–1970,* Cambridge (MA), MIT Press, 2009, pp. 170–75.
[315] RAGON, Michel: *Le Livre de l'architecture moderne,* Paris, Laffont, 1958, p. 59.
[316] POPPER, Frank: *Origins and Development of Kinetic Art,* London, Studio Vista, 1968, p. 135.
[317] FRANCASTEL, Pierre: *Art et technique aux XIX et XX siècles,* Paris, Minuit, 1956. English transl., *Art and Technology in the Nineteenth and Twentieth Centuries,* Cambridge (MA), MIT Press, 2001.

The atmosphere of artistic koine that held sway at Marseille was spoiled by a leaflet dated July 31, and thus from just a few days before the opening. Entitled *Order for a Boycott* and signed by Asger Jorn, Guy Debord and Gil Wolman it invited artists to dissociate themselves from the festival in Marseille. What was the first joint statement to be made by the groups headed by Debord and Jorn ran:

The festival of the Cité Radieuse, which is to open on August 4 in Marseilles, will gather under the roof of Firmin Le Corbusier all the contemporary writers and artists known for having based their careers on the copying or the reactionary vulgarization of some previous novelty, itself generally lacking in reach. [...] The participants in this parade – where nothing is lacking that in twenty years will represent the imbecility of the '50s – will find themselves definitively marked by so indiscrete an adherence to the most perfect manifestation of the spirit of an era.[318]

Jorn had been a member of the CoBrA group, while Wolman and Debord had belonged to the Lettrist International. They saw Le Corbusier's Housing Unit as an ideal setting to present what they regarded as a perfect summary of the reactionary role of art in the fifties. Considered the symbol of a bright future in those years dominated by unconditional faith in progress, the Housing Unit was for them the product of a "bourgeois" architecture that needed to be knocked down, while paradoxically on the other side of the barricade Ragon also felt himself to be "anti-bourgeois." Jorn, who had worked with Le Corbusier as a decorator for the *Pavillon des Temps Nouveaux* at the International Exhibition of 1937, but after the war had dissociated himself from the architect publicly in a series of articles critical of rationalism in general. This criticism would reach its peak in the 1954 dispute with Max Bill –former student at the Bauhaus and editor of the third volume of Le Corbusier's *Œuvre complète*.[319] Jorn held the Bauhaus to be "the name of an artistic inspiration." Not only functionalism and rationalism were represented there but also alternative tendencies that Jorn defined as expressionist. In this he radically dissented from the doctrinaire and hyper-functionalist character that Bill had given to the Ulm School of Design that he directed [320] and in antithesis to this in 1955 Jorn had founded along with others the *International Movement for an Imaginist Bauhaus* (MIBI) and a review called *Eristica*.[321] The following year Bill resigned as director, leaving the post to Tomás Maldonado.

---

318 *Ordre de Boycott*, in Berréby, Gérard (ed.): *Documents relatifs à la fondation de l'Internationale situationniste. 1948 – 1957*, Paris, Editions Allia, 1985, p. 269. English transl., *Order for a Boycott*, at www.marxists.org/reference/archive/debord/1956/boycott.htm.
319 Le Corbusier and Jeanneret, Pierre: *Œuvre complète 1934 – 1938*, with an introduction by Max Bill, Zurich, Girsberger, 1939.
320 The school in Ulm echoed the designation of Gropius's Bauhaus and was conceived as an international center for "theorization, development and research in the field of the design of industrial products." See Lindinger, Herbert (ed.): *La scuola di Ulm. Una nuova cultura del progetto*, Genoa, Costa & Nolan, 1988. Bill was Director of the foundation from 1953 until 1956.
321 Sadler, Simon: *The Situationist City*, Cambridge (MA), MIT Press, 1998, pp. 8 – 9, 167 and note 24. This book is fundamental to reconstructing the intricate events dealt with in this section. For his part Jorn accused the first Bauhaus of having confined itself to the narrow domain of the handicrafts, "insignificant in comparison with that of industry and that of free art" and of not having dared to take the place of the academies of fine arts as well, "which, in contrast to the scientific departments of the universities, have remained purely *speculative* and formalist undertakings." And he pointed out the need to create an institution of artistic experiences and theories that, as he put it, "is ours but precise and direct," referring to the MIBI. See Jorn, Asger: *Contre le fonctionalisme*, now in Berréby, Gérard (ed.): *Documents . . .*, op. cit., pp. 425 – 31.

In 1956 the criticism of functionalism only superficially united Team 10 and the "free artists" assembled by Pinot Gallizio at Alba, for their political aims were different: reformist in the first case, revolutionary in the second. And yet until then Constant had also been for all practical purposes a member of the Dutch group of the CIAM – the best organized and the last to disband after Dubrovnik – taking part in the meetings of Aldo van Eyck's magazine *Forum*: "I wanted to learn," he declared retrospectively. "I was aware that there was quite a distance between us. They were thinking about present conditions, I was dreaming of the future."[322]

The First World Congress of Free Artists opened in Alba on September 2, 1956, and its theme was "The Free Arts and Industrial Activities." Present in addition to Jorn and Wolman (Debord stayed away because of his objection to its artistic connotation) was Giuseppe Pinot Gallizio, painter and a member of the town council for the independent Left, who launched the congress with his "Opening Speech"[323] – centering on an attack on the degrading use made of machinery by capitalism ("the machine is suffocating us") and on the consequent call for a revolution against the rules of the economic system and a revival of the Bauhaus experience.[324]

In Alba, just as in Dubrovnik, it did not prove possible to reach a united conclusion: Enrico Baj, for example, representative of the Movimento Nucleare, criticized Gallizio's speech on the grounds of its "very high levels of rambling rhetoric" which, in his view, doomed the discussion from the outset. Years later, Baj would write:

As had happened to me with Jorn's Surrealists I was never able to appreciate the way in which the artistic movement was politicized. In fact the encounter with Pinot Gallizio, the Lettrists and the Situationists posed the problem of our lack of understanding in that area.[325]

Thus the "rambling rhetoric" that had so irritated Baj was intended to give impetus to the activity of the heterogeneous group gathered in Alba, whose aim was to revolutionize not so much art or architecture as the entire world. This underlying intention had been present for some time and was now brought into the open, especially in Jorn's paper, but this would lead to the defection of others attending the congress as well as Baj. For example Ettore Sottsass Jr., a member of the MIBI and contributor to *Eristica*, was opposed to extremism, whether functionalist or any other kind, and consequently would leave the MIBI a few months later.[326]

---

[322] Cited in Wigley, Mark: *Constant's New Babylon. The Hyper-Architecture of Desire*, Rotterdam, 010 Publishers, 1998, p. 21.
[323] Pinot Gallizio, Giuseppe: *Discours d'ouverture* (Alba, September 1956), now in Berréby, Gérard (ed.): *Documents . . .*, op. cit., p. 595.
[324] Bandini, Mirella: *Pinot Gallizio e il Laboratorio sperimentale d'Alba del Movimento internazionale per una Bauhaus immaginista (1955–57) e dell'Internazionale situazionista (1957–60)*, Turin, Impronta, 1974.
[325] Baj, Enrico: *Mi incontrai con Jorn e gli consigliai Albisola . . .*, in *Risorse*, no. 1, Savona, March 1989, p. 28. Baj had earlier curated a small exhibition by Jorn, see id. (ed.), *Esposizione Asger Jorn*, catalogue of the exhibition at the Galleria L'Asterisco from June 20 to 30, 1954, Rome.
[326] During the congress at Alba, Sottsass declared: "all the expressive possibilities of the plastic world have to contribute to the creation of a new and finally true 'structure' that is no longer the set of pillars and beams that support the construction but the structure of an intense, modulated, open and continuous space." *Per un "Bauhaus" immaginista contro un "Bauhaus" immaginario*, in id., *Scritti 1946–2001*, ed. by Carboni, Milco and Root, Barbara, Milan, Neri Pozza, 2002. Sottsass had met Jorn at the 10th Milan Triennale in 1954 and distanced himself after reading the joint document of the MIBI published at the beginning of 1957 in preparation for the Triennale of the same year.

Criticism of functionalism in Alba was unreserved: architects, convinced that human beings all had the same needs, looked at technological resources solely from the utilitarian perspective of construction (saving of cost through prefabrication and standardization). Constant and the "free artists," faithful instead to the principle that humanity should model its existence not just on its material needs but also on its desires, wanted to use machines and material means for liberation and for the constant renewal of those desires. Just as the Lettrists revived Fourier's utopia of the liberation of humanity through the machine and Jorn wanted to make industry subject to the creativity of the artist, Constant – who on this occasion joined with the MIBI – applied the same logic to the architectural discourse. He expressed a position of technological optimism, aimed at revolutionizing the life of humanity: "Demain la poésie logera la vie."[327] In any case, just as for Ragon, architecture for Constant played the leading role in an objective horizon of a synthesis of the arts:

But today architecture has as its disposal unlimited building techniques [...]. It will be capable of incorporating into its aesthetic the manipulation of volumes and voids of sculpture, and the spatial colorism of painting, in order to create one of the most complete of all the arts, at once lyrical in its means and social in its very nature.[328]

The merger of the MIBI with the Lettrist International would lead the following year to the official birth of the Situationist International in Cosio d'Arroscia, a small town in Liguria, and in 1958 to the regular publication of a journal[329] that is fundamental to understanding the evolution of the whole of culture up until the the events of May 1968 in France.

Toward the end of 1956 an important clarification was reached in Italy too. On the editorial staff of *Casabella continuità,* Giancarlo De Carlo had been in dispute with the editor-in-chief Rogers over Le Corbusier. Both had been present, on opposite sides, in Dubrovnik. The controversy turned on the relevance of Le Corbusier's work to the present day. According to Rogers belief in that relevance was more than justified while for De Carlo it was merely taken for granted: "We are faced with problems that are limited and modest, but more subtle and profound than the ones he has dealt with up to now. We have to give architecture a measure that will allow it to play an active part in the society in which we live and for this reason it is of no use to us to continue along the road of utopia and of great adventures with plastic forms."[330] In reality it was a questioning of the historical *continuity* that Rogers had chosen to insert even in the title of the magazine and that faithfully mirrored the approach of the recent CIAM, as is demonstrated by the title of the article itself (the *misura umana* to which it refers is nothing but the "human scale" of Sert and Giedion): a position of compromise that was able to keep together the different spirits of the Modern

---

[327] This is the title of Constant's speech, given in French. Its English transl., *Tomorrow, Life Will Reside in Poetry,* is published in WIGLEY, Mark: *Constant's New Babylon...*, op. cit.
[328] CONSTANT, Nieuwenhuys: *Tomorrow, Life Will Reside in Poetry,* op. cit., p. 78.
[329] *Internationale Situationniste.* Excerpts from the journal have been transl. into English and published in KNABB, Ken (ed.): *Situationist International Anthology,* Bureau of Public Secrets, 1981; revised and expanded ed., 2006.
[330] DE CARLO, Giancarlo and NATHAN ROGERS, Ernesto: *Discussione sulla valutazione storica dell'architettura e sulla misura umana,* in *Casabella continuità,* no. 210, 1956, p. 4.

Movement, from Le Corbusier to Team 10. For De Carlo on the other hand it was necessary to radicalize the conflict and distinguish the different positions. In this he was keeping faith with the lesson of his teacher Pagano, the previous editor: "not only is there no point in reconciling the disagreements, but they need to be deepened and exacerbated, testing them on the concrete terrain of real problems."[331] In short De Carlo was accusing Rogers and some members of his editorial staff – including the young Vittorio Gregotti and Aldo Rossi – of *formalism* and essentially of being cut off from reality.

This controversy is very important because it allows us to draw a clear line of demarcation between two fundamental camps in the architecture of the last fifty years:[332] so it was not a question of form or style, but of *ideology*. On the one hand there were people like De Carlo (and Friedman) who believed that the architectural project entailed a modification of certain specific, conditions in society; consequently it ought to be society itself that makes the decision about each project on the basis of the spatial proposal made by the architect, who in turn will have to involve the users in the choices of his own work. In the admonition he made to city planners a couple of years earlier at the 10th Triennale (1954), De Carlo had expressed a hope that they would make clear "within what limits they are prepared to take on the risk of a confrontation with reality: to bring into urban planning a collaboration with all the active forces of culture that are involved and devise the means to make possible a really widespread *participation* of the community."[333]

On the other hand there were those who had complete faith in the architectural project, to the point where some (and Rossi in particular) went so far as to theorize an *autonomy* of architecture as a discipline with its own characteristics and capable by itself of transforming not just the city, but society itself.[334] To attain this end there was no need to transfer to the user any of the traditional prerogatives of the architect.

Looking closely, we can see that these were two forms of engagement, but based on radically different views of the architect's role.

Anti-disciplinarity versus disciplinary autonomy. It would take another decade before this process of divergence came to a peak: in this sense the 14th Milan Triennale[335] in 1968 would constitute the climax of an entire decade of discussions initiated by *This Is Tomorrow*. The two fronts had common origins, to which they both laid claim, and both believed that architecture was still capable of influencing human behavior, but the divergence of views on how this should happen could not have been more profound.

De Carlo's resignation[336] from the editorial staff of *Casabella continuità* serves to underline once again how in 1956 each of the figures present on the architectural scene had been obliged to take a stand.

---

[331] De Carlo, Giancarlo: *Una precisazione*, in *Casabella continuità*, no. 214, 1957, pp. i–1.
[332] See the acute analysis of Klaus Koenig, Giovanni: *Nota introduttiva*, in Brunetti, Fabrizio and Gesì, Fabrizio: *Giancarlo De Carlo*, Florence, Alinea, 1981, p. 16.
[333] De Carlo, Giancarlo: *Intenzioni e risultati della mostra di urbanistica*, in *Casabella*, no. 203, 1954, p. 24. The italics are mine.
[334] See Nathan Rogers, Ernesto: *"Casabella" per l'autonomia della cultura*, in *Casabella continuità*, no. 244, October 1960, p. 3.
[335] Nicolin, Paola: *Castelli di carte. La XIV Triennale di Milano, 1968*, Macerata, Quodlibet, 2011.
[336] "After I left, *Casabella* took another line: first it passed through neo-liberty, initiating the period of revivalisms, then it landed on the sad shores of autonomy or, in other words, academicism, which Ernesto [Rogers], an enthusiastic follower of Le Corbusier, had detested." De Carlo, Giancarlo in Bunçuga, Franco: *Conversazioni con Giancarlo De Carlo*..., op. cit., p. 92.

So Yona Friedman arrived in Europe from a situation as remote as Israel, in many ways culturally isolated from this debate, but his personal position was already fully defined: right from the foreword of *L'architecture mobile*, the text whose draft he had presented in Dubrovnik and which is analyzed in the next chapter, he had been clear that the role of architects had to be completely reassessed if they wanted to continue to have an influence in postwar society. For this reason he would find, among his colleagues in Europe, more opponents than allies. One of the latter would be Giancarlo De Carlo.[337]

---

[337] See, for example, the letter and the unpublished designs for Venice sent by Friedman on September 14, 1971, and now in De Carlo, Giancarlo: *Archives, Varie P: E-F [De Carlo – atti/003]* – Archivio Progetti IUAV, Venice.

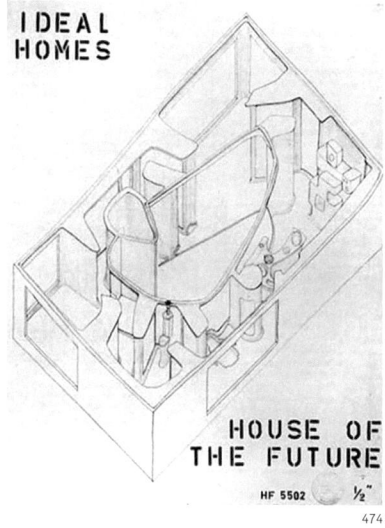

474

475

476

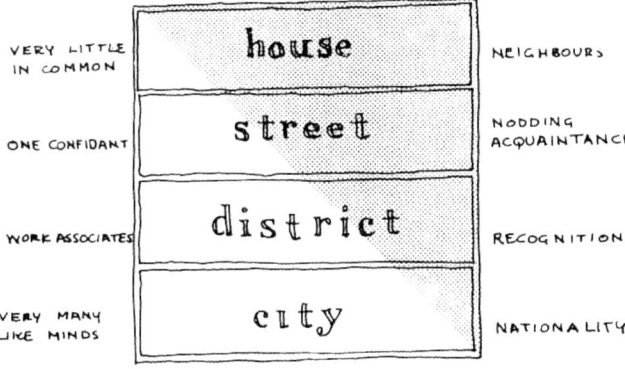

477

ALISON AND PETER SMITHSON

474 – 475 *Ideal Homes, House of the Future*, shown at the seminar art exhibition, *This Is Tomorrow*, in London, 1956.
476 *Diagram of the Scale of Human Association*, 1956. From Smithson, Alison (ed.): *Team 10 Primer*, London, Studio Vista, 1968.
477 Alison Smithson at the last CIAM and TEAM 10, Dubrovnik, 1956. Photograph from *Harvard Design Magazine*, no. 24, spring/summer 2006.

GIUSEPPE PINOT GALLIZIO

478 Portrait among gypsies, Alba, 1956.

"ART AVANT GARDE FESTIVAL"

479 See also *Cysp I* by Nicolas Schöffer, set on the roof of the *Cité Radieuse* during the Festival in Marseille, July 1956, p. 468, no. 565.

478

479

480

481

482

483

484

485

URBAN DESIGN CONFERENCE, HARVARD GSD

480–485 Some participants: Jaqueline Tyrwhitt, Lewis Mumford, Josép Lluís Sert, Jane Jacobs, György Kepes, Victor Gruen, 1956.

"THE SETTLEMENT REVOLUTION"

486 Yona Friedman: *Slogan summary of the personal statement to the meeting in Dubrovnik*, 1956.

Yona Friedman
42 Bd Pasteur
75015 Paris.

THE SETTLEMENT REVOLUTION.

User determination makes settlements work.
User determination is better than governmental planning.
User determination solves problems governments cannot solve..

The settlement revolution is a "vote by acts":
users do what the caretakers did not do for them.

Settlement problems cannot be solved than by others than by the effective users.

Information at primary school level is necessary to enable and to encourage users to rely to themselves for solving their problems.

Agriculture in cities should be promoted to assure survival in case of emergency.

Recognition of the urban village as a political entity is necessary.

Slogan summary of the personal statement to the meeting in Dubrovnik.

Yona Friedman
42 Bd Pasteur
75015 Paris.

COMPLEMENT TO PERSONAL STATEMENT AT EXPERTS MEETING IN DUBROVNIK
ON POLICIES CONCERNING HUMAN SETTLEMENT.

Actually central organisations (e.g. governments) are not in the situation to implement successfully planning for large human masses, both because such organisations are in the <u>impossibility to be sufficiently well informed about what desire the real future users</u>, and also because they are even less informed about what sacrifices real future users are ready to subscribe in order to attend their desires.

Beside this lack of information, and even if governments would be well informed about these subjects, they <u>dont possess any social apparatus which could implement the result of planning</u> within reasonable delays.

In other words, actual central organisations do <u>planning for average man, instead for the real future user</u>, and do so in the hope that the real future user will behave as the fictitious average man would do.

As governments, who are such central organisations, cannot act as planners for the masses and inspite this fact pretend to be able to plan for people, people feel themselves <u>abandoned by their governements.</u>

People want to survive and to live, and as they feel themselves abandoned by the organisations who pretend to take care of them, they are beginning to <u>act and to solve their problems themselves</u>. Squatter towns, in-town agriculture, organisation of social services by urban villages, migration etc are phenomena indicating this trend.

If problems of human settlement cannot be solved by central organisations, they can be solved by smaller communities. In such communities decision making can be done in common by the totality of the actual or future inhabitants: thus <u>decisions are made by those who could suffer or benefit from the fall-out of the decisions</u>, and who have to support the consequences of any error they might do when making decisions. This processus is entirely different from the classical planning process, wherein decisions are made by experts, who are not the same who might suffer by errors in the decision making.

Thus moral reflexions and difficulty of implementation of central planning help together to emerge the process of self-planning for human settlements self-planning effectuated by the future users themselves.

Self-planning by the users cannot be done without assuring for the user an initiation into an appropriate "interpersonal language", language which <u>facilitates direct negotiation among users</u> in case of conflict.

- 1 -

"PERSONAL STATEMENT AT EXPERTS' MEETING IN DUBROVNIK"

487–**488** Yona Friedman: *On Policies Concerning Human Settlement*, 1956.

Once planning done directly by the future users, let us see what tasks could be done by the central organisations in order to cooperate with the users:

a) central organisations (governments or supragovernmental organisations) could promote the <u>encouragement</u> of users to do self-planning, and so remove the depreciation and mistrust implanted of the user about his planning capacities, depreciation implanted in him both by school and media;

b) central organisations could prepare the means and the model of the <u>initiation</u> course (on primary school level) of the user into the interpersonal language for intracommunity negotiation;

c) selfplanning of settlement by the actual users imply the existence of an <u>infratsructure</u> (indeed, planning signifies the implementation of some particular use pattern on an existing infrastructure): the task of central organisations could be keeping the infrastructure in good working order;

d) as self planning encouragement needs examples, central organisations could finance <u>pilot projects</u>.

As the world seems to head towards a series of repeated crisis, the chances of small groups for survival might be better ones than those of larger social organisations: if alimentary or energy shortage occurs, great agglomerations might be more vulnerable than small ones. To increase the chances of survival, larger human settlements should contain agricultural land: <u>urban agriculture</u> might be necessary.

As a general goal I would propose <u>increased selfplanning and increased self reliance</u> of settlements.

=
=
=
=
=

NOTE:

Planning for other people could be considered by these others a <u>humiliation</u>: it implies that they are more stupid than you!

Y.F.

PREFACE.

Au congrès du CIAM à Dubrovnik on a beaucoup parlé de "developpement", "changements" et "mobilité" de la societé moderne.

Malheureusement ce n'était que des mots; il n-y-eut en réalité que deux projets présentés qui tenaient compte des changements sociaux et techniques actuels (M. Péré-Lahaille et moi-meme). Un délégué seulement a parlé également de l'importance de l'aviation (M. Kuehne).

J'ai pu constater après plusieurs voyages à travers l'Europe que ces changements d'existence représentent le problème principal du relogement dans presque tous les pays. La faute des architectes est de ne pas vouloir avouer l'importance de ce problème et ses conséquences, à la fois par courte vue et peut-etre par peur de perdre leur privilèges professionels.

Il est certain que la profession d'architecte a tendance à se désintègrer. Les éléments industriels des batiments seront fatalement déssinés par l'"industrial designer", leur assemblage et aménagement seront fait par l'usager, (l'habitant sur lequel les architectes ironisent si souvent) et l'ensemble des groupements d'habitation par les experts techniques de la vie communale (circulation, réseaux sanitaires, loisirs etc).

Pour suivre cette tendance une certain souplesse est nécessaire: la mobilité des constructions. Comment y arriver? A cette question un homme seul ne peut pas répondre. A seule fin de réussir à réunir des architectes qui s'intèressent à la question j'ai

proposé de créer notre groupe: le GEAM (Groupe d'Etude d'Architecture Mobile), qui s'est formé avec MM. Kuehne (Allemagne), Aujame, Emmerich, Pecquet et moi-meme (Paris), Soltan (Warszawa) et Trapman (Amsterdam), chacun apportant ses idées.
Cette brochure est le commencement d'une série de publications de chacun de nous exposant ses propositions. Mais cette série de publications n'est pas publicitaire, c'est une échange d'informations pour tous nos confréres inconnus de nous qui pensent les memes idées que nous, ou dont les idées ne différent que dans les détails.

Paris, 25.12.58.

Yona Friedman.

Mobile or immobile, everything that occupies space belongs to the domain of architecture.

Perret, Auguste: *Contribution à une théorie de l'architecture,* Paris, Cercle d'Etudes Architecturales chez A. Wahl, 1952.

It is necessary to go beyond mere appearance, and to ask these unrealized projects the reasons for their failure.

Tafuri, Manfredo: *Venice and the Renaissance,* Cambridge (MA), MIT Press, 1995, p. xi.

2. THEORIES. SOCIETY AND TECHNOLOGY

"L'ARCHITECTURE MOBILE" AND ITS CIRCULATION

It is certain that the profession of architect has a tendency to disintegrate.
Yona Friedman: L'architecture mobile

At the beginning of November 1956 the Soviet Union sent around five thousand tanks into Budapest – the same number as the Third Reich had dispatched for the invasion of the USSR during the Second World War – to put down the revolt that had broken out two weeks earlier. Taking advantage of the fact that international public opinion was focused on the Suez Crisis, with the occupation of the Sinai by Israel with the support of France and the United Kingdom, the Soviet Union was able to bring an isolated Hungary back under its control and behind the Iron Curtain, while its president, Imre Nagy, was imprisoned and later executed. The glimmer of hope that the USSR might embark on a new course after Khrushchev's shocking report to the 20th Congress of the CPSU had faded once again.

As we have seen, during the summer of the same year in Dubrovnik, in Tito's Yugoslavia, leader of the nonaligned countries, the architects present at the CIAM had been far more numerous than the officially accredited ones. Among them was Yona Friedman who, until 1956, had a studio in Haifa in partnership with Renzo Voghera, a Milanese interior architect who had moved to Palestine shortly before the foundation of the state of Israel and later became a teacher at the Technion. Friedman, thirty-three at the time, was able to present his manifesto, his charter of mobile urban planning, already sketched out while he was in Haifa. The manifesto, illustrated with a few drawings, would be rewritten and published later.[338] The architects most interested in his exposition were Günther Kühne, Roger Aujame, Jerzy Sołtan and Georges Candilis;[339] the latter would be the only one not to take part in the Groupe d'études d'Architecture mobile (GEAM) but also the only one – apart from De Carlo – who continued to invite Friedman to subsequent meetings of Team 10.

Immediately after Dubrovnik, Friedman wrote a letter to Le Corbusier asking to meet him, but would have to wait about a year before being received, on November 18, 1957.[340] On that date Friedman did not yet have a draft in French of his theory of "mobile architecture," and in fact wrote the letters in English, but just a few drawings and some projects conceived in Israel, like the cylindrical shelters. At the same time Friedman, with the assistance of André Sive (whom he got to know in Dubrovnik),[341] was able to meet Jean Prouvé, who was coming

---

[338] FRIEDMAN, Yona: *La charte d'urbanisme mobile*, in id., *L'architecture mobile*, 2nd ed., 1958, p. 20.
[339] RAGON, Michel: *Aprés Le Corbusier*, in *Les visionnaires de l'architecture*. Paris, Laffont, 1965, p. 8.
[340] See Yona Friedman's letters, T1 6309 (October 8, 1956) and T1 6310 (November 12, 1957), in which among other things he describes himself as a member of the Israeli group of the CIAM, preserved at the Fondation Le Corbusier, Paris.
[341] FRIEDMAN, Yona: *Pro Domo*, op. cit., p. 14.

to the end of his experience of running the Department of Architecture of the Compagnie Industrielle de Transport (CIMT). Both, he claims, greeted the ideas of the Israeli architect in positive fashion:

In 1957 he agreed to meet me and I talked to him about my ideas. This was quite decisive because he told me two very important things. "He said, It's not my line, I would never do this. But you have to do it." Thereby, he saw its worth. The second thing he said was, "Most of your colleagues will be against you." When somebody like Le Corbusier tells you this, and Prouvé proposes to work together with you, you don't care what other people think anymore. This was decisive for me, so I thought it was the right way – it's possible and not simply fantasy. That was very important for me.[342]

The role of Le Corbusier and Prouvé, the two most influential architects at work at the time in France, was therefore largely Socratic. Looking more closely, however, we can see that the latter was more interested in his designs for prefabricated and low-cost temporary housing: in the appendix to the first printed edition of *L'architecture mobile* can be found some proposals, eliminated from later editions, such as the "Concrete Box" system or a system of trihedral structures initially conceived for North Africa. It will not be easy to date Friedman's early projects precisely until the work of reorganizing his archives at the Getty Center is finished. The fact that Friedman himself has always been in the habit of reutilizing and re-proposing with nonchalance many of his architectural ideas, mixing up variations of a single design, as if his work had no history, certainly does not help. In any case the concrete and metal *Cabins for the Sahara*, self-supporting and stackable up to three levels, and the design for a "Cylindrical Shelter" are more or less contemporary with the *Saharan House*[343] that Prouvé designed with Charlotte Perriand for the Salon des Arts Ménagers of 1958. Prouvé, in addition to his *Colonial Houses* (1948 – 49) made of the lightweight material aluminum,[344] in 1956 had accepted the invitation of the Abbé Pierre and his company, Emmaüs, to design low-cost prefabricated shelters capable of making up for the severe lack of housing from which France still suffered: the *Maison des Jours Meilleurs*,[345] described by Le Corbusier as the "most beautiful house I know."[346]
So in his early years in Paris, Friedman worked along a dual track, and for each of them found a point of reference: on the one hand he studied the definition of prefabricated units (Prouvé), on the other an urban system that could contain them (Le Corbusier).

Friedman circulated his ideas through stapled and duplicated copies of *L'architecture mobile*, in a total of five editions all printed privately, i.e. without turning to a publisher, between 1958 and 1963.

---

342 Yona Friedman, interview in the appendix.
343 CLAYSSEN, Dominique: *Jean Prouvé, L'idée constructive*, with an introduction by Ionel Schein, Paris, Dunod 1983, pp. 34–37 and 155–57.
344 SULZER, Peter: *Jean Prouvé: Œuvre complète/Complete Works*, vol. 3 (1944–54), Basel, Birkhäuser, 2005, pp. 126–30.
345 ALLÉGRET, Laurence and VADOU, Valérie (eds.): *Jean Prouvé et Paris*, catalogue of the exhibition at the Pavillon de l'Arsenal, Paris, Picard, 2001, pp. 287–91.
346 Letter written by Le Corbusier on February 29, 1956, AD Nancy 230J, Jean Prouvé Archives.

1. The first version, unpublished and handwritten, had been prepared as a single copy for the CIAM in Dubrovnik in 1956 while Friedman was still in Haifa, and has been lost.

2. The second, mimeographed edition was prepared between 1957 and the end of 1958 (the date given in the foreword is December 25, 1958) and ten copies were printed.

3. The third edition is an enlarged reprint of the previous one and dated October 20, 1959; three hundred copies were printed.

4. The fourth edition, printed on July 1, 1962, contains additional drawings and texts that had appeared in the meantime in European and Japanese architecture magazines.

5. The fifth edition of September 15, 1963, contains an appendix of mathematical analysis and around a thousand copies were printed.

Many of the texts contained in it would be collected, along with others that had come out in the meantime, in the book *L'architecture mobile* published by Casterman in France and later translated into Italian and Spanish, but years later (from 1972 onward),[347] when the adventure of the idea of mobile architecture had almost come to a conclusion. So it is necessary to reconstruct the different phases of its development and diffusion between 1957 and 1962, the year of the breakup of the GEAM, over which time the theory was clearly delineated.

After a trip to England and holding numerous lectures, conferences and exhibitions in Germany and the Netherlands, Friedman decided to settle in Paris at the end of 1957. At the time the Parisian landscape had been radically transformed by the construction of the large housing complexes known as *grands-ensembles* in the suburbs. Even today in France there is widespread rejection of the architecture of that period owing to the rapid process of urbanization and its brutal impact on the collective imagination. It was in the same year that Henri Lefebvre pointed out that the landscape of the Île-de-France described by Gérard de Nerval in the middle of the previous century had now been lost forever.[348] In the second half of the fifties the housing crisis was at its peak, and not in Paris alone. It suffices to think of the request made of Prouvé by Abbé Pierre in 1956: a government circular of 1959 observed that five hundred thousand families were still living in degrading conditions,[349] and this explains, although only in part, what sort of situation Friedman's idea of a low-cost urban intensification was supposed to deal with. The underlying necessity that prompted the early projects described in *L'architecture mobile* has been ignored up until

---

347 FRIEDMAN, Yona: *L'architecture mobile, vers une cité conçue par ses habitants*, Paris/Tournai, Casterman, 1970. Italian transl., *L'architettura mobile: verso una città concepita dai suoi abitanti*, Alba, Edizioni Paoline, 1972. Spanish transl., *La arquitectura móvil. Hacia una ciudad concebida por sus habitantes*, Barcelona, Editorial Poseidón, 1978.
348 ABRAM, Joseph: *Rénovations, grands travaux, équipements*, in id., *L'architecture moderne en France*, vol. 2, *Du chaos à la croissance*, Paris, Picard, 1999, p. 143.
349 CLAYSSEN, Dominique: *Jean Prouvé . . .*, op. cit., p. 145.

now by architectural historians, wholly engrossed in the technological and megastructural aspect. In reality the state of emergency in housing that beset Paris was not a new problem for an architect who had just arrived from Haifa, and he was able to draw on his earlier studies in Israel.

In 1957 there were three principles of mobile architecture:
1. new constructions should touch the ground over a minimum area;
2. be capable of being dismantled and moved;
3. and be alterable as required by the individual occupant.

In the structures themselves there is a distinction between the supporting and the containing. The latter are composed of a continuous three-dimensional skeleton, in the gaps of which are located the individual living units, while in the former are concentrated the service systems.[350] The sharp differentiation between supporting and containing structures recalls the better known one between *serving spaces* and *served spaces* already partly introduced by Louis Kahn in the Yale University Art Gallery (1951–53) and in a more marked manner in the Richards Laboratories at the University of Pennsylvania (1957–65).[351]

Buildings elements of solids and voids are inherent in steel and concrete. These voids are in tune with the service needs of spaces. This characteristic combined with space needs suggests new forms. […] Storage rooms, service rooms, and cubicles must not be partitioned areas of a single-space structure, they must be given their own structure.[352]

In the laboratories Kahn had in fact concentrated all the plumbing, electric and ventilation systems in the massive brick towers with no openings, contrasting on a visual level as well with the laboratories proper, which were extensively glazed; the greater height of the towers, as well as emphasizing the verticality of the structure, gave the impression that the laboratories had been stacked one on top of the other and could therefore be detached and replaced. Although it is not possible to demonstrate any direct connection between Friedman and the American architect, what we have here is an objective theoretical correspondence. This was not the first time in fact that this had happened between Kahn and an architect moving in the orbit of Team 10. For example it has been noted that the domed spaces of Aldo van Eyck's orphanage in Amsterdam (1955–60) are fairly similar to the contemporary ones of the Trenton Jewish Community Center (1954–58).[353] In 1958, moreover, Peter Smithson stayed with Kahn in Philadelphia during his visit to the US and spoke of their "parallel aims," and the following year Kahn made an important speech at the meeting in Otterlo.[354]

---

[350] Friedman, Yona: *L'architecture mobile*, 2nd ed., op. cit., pp. 62–63.
[351] Rykwert, Joseph: *Louis Kahn*, New York, Abrams, 2001, pp. 22ff.
[352] Kahn, Louis: *Spaces, Order and Architecture*, in *The Royal Architectural Institute of Canada Journal*, vol. 34, no. 10, October 1957, pp. 375–77.
[353] McCarter, Robert: *Louis Kahn*, London, Phaidon, 2005, p. 217.
[354] Kahn, Louis: *New Frontiers in Architectures: CIAM in Otterlo, 1959*, now in Latour, Alessandra (ed.): *Louis I. Kahn. Writings, Lectures, Interviews*, New York, Rizzoli International, 1991, pp 90ff. On Kahn's contribution to Team 10, also see Smithson, Peter: *Parallel Aims*, in *Architects' Journal*, vol. 19, no. 9, March 1992, p. 54.

In any case Friedman's proposal was in line with the modernist tradition: the constructional unit is not an *object* but just the place in which the assembly of the individual cells takes on physical form. As elements that can be reproduced *ad infinitum*, these embody conceptually the prime structures of a chain of production that disregards the ancient concepts of "place" and "space." In this, Friedman's proposal does not differ substantially from Hilberseimer's urban projects for a *Großstadtarchitektur* or Alexander Klein's ideas. There is one particular difference though, the fact that the planimetric structure of the city in *L'architecture mobile* has no influence on the design of the dwelling and the room, thanks to the possibilities of elevated settlement, and shuns that "urbanistic conception of a mechanistic type that ignored the demands and needs of man" as Hilberseimer himself would note self-critically in 1963.[355] Friedman saw as central among these human needs play in the sense of recreation, which he had learned from Huizinga and Kerényi – as well as from Glikson[356] – to consider the true glue of urban life, a concept that was slowly becoming more widely accepted in the French society of those years.[357]

In addition, Friedman refused to define the elementary unit, which for him was nothing but a "shoe box,"[358] transferring the responsibility for its internal layout to the occupant, and for this reason his project is different from the Smithsons' one for the *House of the Future* and from all the later research of the Metabolists and Archigram.

While in the drawings of the founders of the CIAM the figures (the buildings) were set against a free, isotropic and homogeneous background, in the illustrations of *Urbanism spatial* the background is almost always that of a concretely present city. From the second edition (1958) onward *L'architecture mobile* contains in elevation and in plan a scheme of application of the blocks he called *"à l'enjambée"* (from the French *enjamber*, to span or straddle, which has the same root as the rhetorical figure of enjambment), which Friedman translates into English as "span-over"; that is to say a fixed width repeated a number of times in a broken line as if it had been drawn by the twirling of a pair of compasses. In other words, after deciding the length of each building block (segment) in relation to the resources and the technical solutions available at the moment, it is possible to suspend (literally "to straddle with a step") above the existing constructions a segment that can be arranged as wished so long as each of its extremities is connected with that of another segment in a large pilotis.

---

355 HILBERSEIMER, Ludwig: *Entfaltung einer Planungsidee*, Berlin, Ullstein, 1963. The passage has been transl. from the Italian ed., *Un'idea di piano*, with an introduction by Giorgio Grassi, Padua, Marsilio, 1967, p. 25. On the evolution of Hilberseimer's thinking, see DE MICHELIS, Marco: *Ritratto di un architetto come giovane artista*, in *Rassegna*, no. 27, September 1986, pp. 6–25.

356 "The more that industry and cities expand, the greater is the demand for recreation [...]. In the dynamics of city life, the demand for recreation represents a reaction against the complexity of life introduced by centralization and industrialization [...]. It [recreation] is an attempt to balance urban concentration by a temporary escape back to the places of natural and historic origin of the people: to the indigenous and rural landscape, the hamlet, the little town by-passed by modern development, in the hope of restoring, or 'recreating' health, energy and mental equilibrium." GLIKSON, Artur: *Recreational Land Use*, in THOMAS JR., William (ed.): *Man's Role in Changing the Face of the Earth*, Chicago, University of Chicago Press, 1956, pp. 897 and 912. In the volume Glikson is presented as "Head of Planning for Housing of Israel's Ministry of Labor."

357 DUMAZEDIER, Joffre: *Vers une civilisation du loisir?*, Paris, Seuil, 1962.

358 *Shoe Box* was the title of Friedman's ironic drawing on the cover of *Domus*, no. 879, March 2005; also see ibid., *Ideas at Large*, pp. 94–95.

Friedman envisaged the first application of this solution for a specific point in Paris, Les Halles de Bercy, which in 1957 were about to be demolished in order to construct new housing.[359] From the outset, the Hungarian architect had proposed his theory as an alternative to demolition. In the third edition of his manifesto, however, the example changed and so did the planimetric scheme of the "span-over" blocks: this time the part of the city in question was the freight facility in Bercy.[360] In both cases the "centres civiques" were suspended, but in the second version they became broader, elevated wharves of different shapes, while in the first case they were simple bands that ran parallel to the blocks. It is possible that Friedman had redesigned these spaces, widening them, between the second and third edition of his book after seeing the Smithsons' 1957 *Hauptstadt project* for Berlin, which saw the transition from the "street-in-the-sky" to the "street-deck," a system of suspended footbridges that in hindsight can be viewed as an inkling of the megastructure to come. Both cases were attempts to organize or make possible the communal life of a neighborhood at a different level to that of the ground, where the vehicles ran. Paradoxically, in the *urbanisme mobile* series (1959) there was no room for automobiles: the city's means of transport would be overhead, suspended like cableways running along the top of the "span-over" blocks, and have to be public; cars would have to stay out of the city as in Venice: "The city belongs to pedestrians."[361] The bridging blocks in this phase are raised 12.5 meters above the level of the ground, leaving it free, and are ten stories high, concentrating the staircases, elevators and water, lighting and gas systems in the large pillars *(piliers)*.

In the *urbanisme mobile* series, in which Friedman's simple drawings are superimposed on photographs, the sites vary and indeed are chosen to be as diverse as possible to demonstrate the universal applicability of his principle of settlement, in the best Corbusian and "machinist" tradition. Little by little, however, the "span-over blocks" became "span-over districts," further increasing the scale while remaining precise proposals of urban intensification, and there was a shift from the *Ville mobile* to the *Ville-Spatiale:* the principle of the spatial city is that of the multiplication of the original surface area of the city by means of elevated levels. The difference that sets this multiplication apart from that of the ordinary city lies in the fact that the multiplication of the surface area does not happen at points or in isolated zones (as in Manhattan, in the *Ville Radieuse,* etc.), but covers the whole area of the city, on many levels.[362]

However, there is a difference between the two and that is the introduction of more direct link between the project and its specific urban context: the photomontage. This would characterize the whole series of projects for the *Ville-Spatiale* produced between 1958 and 1963 and intended for cities like Monaco, Paris and Tunis.[363]

Reyner Banham has noted that the Smithsons were the first to insert photographs of people instead of stylized silhouettes into a plan, around the middle of the fifties. It is a common

---

[359] Ibid., p. 28.
[360] FRIEDMAN, Yona: *L'architecture mobile*, 3rd ed., 1959, p. 21.
[361] Ibid. p. 17.
[362] FRIEDMAN, Yona: *L'architecture mobile, vers une cité conçue par ses habitants*, op. cit., 1970.
[363] See LEBESQUE, Sabine and FENTENER VAN VLISSINGEN, Helene (eds.), *Yona Friedman: Structures...*, op. cit., pp. 34–38.

practice today, but at the time was clearly derived from Pop Art – it suffices to think of the photographs by Nigel Henderson that the Smithsons showed at the CIAM in 1954 – and was intended by the Smithsons to underline the importance of street life and therefore their creation of "streets in the sky." On the subject of their Golden Lane project Banham wrote, "the perspectives had photographs of people posted on to the drawings, so that the human presence almost overwhelmed the architecture."[364]

But in Friedman's case this practice was extended to the urban context for two fundamental reasons: the first was that of showing how mobile architecture could be laid on top of the existing city without upheavals and was therefore easily adaptable. Even an intransigent critic like Banham acknowledges this aptitude: "Friedman's explanatory sketches confirm and reconfirm this unitary, simplistic solution, at once convincing and universal."[365] The second reason was to set what looked like a castle in the air in existing reality and in the most direct manner. The other members of the GEAM, especially the Germans, with the exception of Frei Otto, generally presented plans that literally had their heads in the clouds – as in the case of Ruhnau and his project for an aerial work of architecture signed along with the painter Klein[366] – while Friedman by contrast, and partly out of his responsibility as leader of the group, sought to bring his own theories down to ground. Moreover, he tried to do this in a way that was connected with genuine needs: in the years spanning the fifties and sixties, many plans were drawn up for large-scale demolitions to make room for low-cost housing in certain zones of Paris, such as Bercy, and this was the basic reason for the series of projects devoted to *Paris spatiale*[367] between 1959 and 1964, among the first concrete examples of a "spatial city." Thus the alternative to costly demolitions, to the *tabula rasa*, as well as to the Herbé-Preveral Plan of 1960,[368] was intensification of the existing city, raising the density of housing by a factor of up to three times, in new districts formed by a modular grid in three dimensions straddling the great outer boulevard, but also located in a central zone, that of Les Halles.[369]

The great limitation, however, was that he stopped at a broad contextualization and went no further, to specify more precisely the functional and symbolic characteristics that were proper to each part of the city. Friedman did not go all the way, but confined himself to proposing an adaptable model and hoping that the actors on the urban scene, principally the inhabitants, would take on the task. It was the opposite attitude to that of Le Corbusier, who was always waiting for a prince to come along and make possible the realization of his ideas – whether it was Mussolini, the Americans or Nehru made little difference.

---

[364] BANHAM, Reyner: *The New Brutalism*, in *Architectural Review*, no. 118, December 1955, p. 361. See id.: *The New Brutalism. Ethic or Aesthetic?*, London, The Architectural Press, 1966.
[365] BANHAM, Reyner: *Megastructure. Urban Futures of the Recent Past*, New York, Harper and Row, 1976, p. 60.
[366] KLEIN, Yves and RUHNAU, Werner: *L'architecture de l'air*, in *Zero*, vol. 3, Düsseldorf, 1960. English transl., *Project for an Architecture of Air*, in *Overcoming the Problematics of Art: The Writings of Yves Klein*, ed. by OTTMANN, Klaus, Putnam (CT), Spring Publications, 2007, pp. 174–75.
[367] KANNENGIESSER, Jens: *Paris Spatial*, in *Bauen + Wohnen*, no. 11, 1962, pp. 36–43.
[368] Paul Herbé was the architectural adviser to the minister Eugène Claudius-Petit, who in those years was studying the possibility of constructing a major north–south four-lane expressway that would run through Paris from Aubervilliers to Place d'Italie along Boulevard Sébastopol. See ROUILLARD, Dominique: *Superarchitecture...*, op. cit., p. 151 and note 142.
[369] FRIEDMAN, Yona: *Paris Spatial: A Suggestion* (1960), in VAN SCHAIK, Martin and MÁCEL, Otar (eds.): *Exit Utopia. Architectural Provocations 1956–1976*, Munich, Prestel, 2005, pp. 19–29.

Capable instead of meeting the requirements of the client while leaving the users a certain amount of room to alter the design was the group made up of Candilis, Josic and Woods, which had always maintained excellent relations with Friedman. With respect to L'architecture mobile, the Parisian trio upped the scale of intervention in their plans for Frankfurt (1962) and Berlin (1963), tying them in every way to the surrounding parts of the city.[370]

This particular approach was to be taken to an extreme by Rem Koolhaas, who would further increase the size of the individual interventions in what he calls "red spots," i.e. the critical points at which the functions of the city are concentrated, which feed off one another.[371] In his exposition of the theory of Bigness, Koolhaas cites just one architect, Yona Friedman: he recognizes him as the precursor of the idea of the large dimension, but takes him forcefully to task for having produced a "metallic blanket of clouds, promising unlimited but unfocused potential renewal of 'everything,'"[372] and thus of never landing; in short, Friedman's was just a decorative criticism of the existing city. But as we have seen the "metallic blanket" of clouds never really existed. On the contrary Friedman utilized photomontage precisely in order to circumstantiate each proposal and "land" it, at least in his intentions.

The Dutch architect's criticism of functionalism is more radical, while for Friedman the needs of the inhabitants are fairly simple, and principally linked to subsistence and the concept of recreation. What he is criticizing is not so much functionalist architecture as city planning. Yet there is an unexpected point of contact between the two architects with regard to the nature of their profession. Koolhaas writes:

Bigness is impersonal and the architect is no longer condemned to stardom. Even as Bigness enters the stratosphere of architectural ambition it can be achieved only at the price of giving up control of transmogrification. It implies a web of umbilical cords to other disciplines whose performance is as critical as "the architect." Like mountain climbers tied together by lifesaving ropes, the makers of Bigness are a team (a word not mentioned in the last 40 years of architectural polemic). Beyond signature, Bigness means surrender to technologies, to engineers, contractors, manufacturers, politics and others. It promises architecture a kind of post realignment with neutrality.[373]

But this "after architecture" coincides with the one predicted by Friedman back in 1958 and concerns a radical refoundation of the architect's role since the war:

---

370 AVERMAETE, Tom: *Another Modern. The Post-War Architecture and Urbanism of Candilis-Josic-Woods*, with an introduction by Joan Ockman, Rotterdam, NAi Publishers, 2005.
371 According to Jean-Louis Cohen, the projects of Koolhaas's studio OMA (Office for Metropolitan Architecture, founded in 1975 in London with Madelon Viesendrop and Elia and Zoe Zenghelis) "tend to impose a new functional background on the geographical one; then, in a second operation is added a third background, on which the network of figures appears as a diffused ensemble. Far from resolving to a simple binary relationship between figure and ground, the identity of each building results from an integration of its coordinates in the network of bands and from its own functional and symbolic determination of its characteristics." *The Rational Rebel, or the Urban Agenda of OMA*, in LUCAN, Jacques: *OMA – Rem Koolhaas. Architecture 1970–1990*, New York, Princeton Architectural Press, 1996, pp. 15–16.
372 KOOLHAAS, Rem: *Bigness or the Problem of Large*, op. cit., pp. 495–516.
373 *Ibid*. pp. 20–21.

It is certain that the profession of architect has a tendency to disintegrate. The industrial elements of buildings are inevitably going to be created by the "industrial designer," their assembly and installation will be done by the user (the occupant who is so often mocked by architects) and the whole set of housing complexes arranged by technical experts on community life (traffic, sanitation networks, leisure, etc.).[374]

From Friedman's disintegration to Koolhaas's neutrality: with hindsight we can say that the role of the architect in the second half of the 20th century has been slowly sliding down a slippery slope.
On this, however, the difference between Friedman and Team 10 – especially Alison (and Peter) Smithson – could not have been more marked:

The role of architectural expression and of town planning in contemporary society is the same as that in societies of the past.[375]

The conflict between these two positions finally came to a head at the meeting in Bagnols in 1960: once again Friedman was invited by one member of the group, Candilis, and against the advice of others. The confrontation occurred between conservatives (the Smithsons, van Eyck) and reformers (including Friedman).[376] Among the latter was Shadrach Woods, who had kept a low profile within the group, and who in his project for the Freie Universität in Berlin pushed to have the design of the facades – to be made of prefabricated metal elements – entrusted to an outside specialist in the field, indeed to that past master of prefabrication Jean Prouvé. It was an unprecedented gesture in professional circles.
The first important publication on Friedman to come out in Europe had been a short article in the German magazine *Bauwelt*,[377] written by Günther Kühne, who was one of the young architects present in Dubrovnik and among the supporters (along with Jerzy Sołtan) of Friedman's theories. The article immediately caught the attention of Frei Otto, who at the time had to his credit two projects of a certain significance, the pavilions for the Federal Garden Expositions in Kassel (1955) and Cologne (1957). In addition, in 1957 the Interbau was being constructed in Berlin as part of the International Building Exhibition where Friedman says that he met Otto – in the pavilion of "The City of Tomorrow," directed by Günschel,[378] at the Interbau Café or at the Exhibition Center designed by Otto himself.[379] Otto's research into the question of suspended roofs and tensile structures had found a place of discussion and analysis in the Entwicklungsstätte für den Leichtbau, which

---

[374] FRIEDMAN, Yona: *Préface*, in *L'architecture mobile*, 2nd ed., 1958, p. 1. In this passage the influence of Prouvé is more discernible than elsewhere.
[375] SMITHSON, Alison: *Role of the Architect*, in id. (ed.), *Team 10 Primer*, op. cit., p. 24.
[376] "Candilis invited me to Bagnols-sur-Cèze, where I had a very bad clash with the Smithsons, very very bad. Alison [Smithson] was absolutely incredible, and Aldo van Eyck also. Candilis was peacekeeping, [Jaap] Bakema too. It was really very vehement and if I had not had the backing of Prouvé, of Le Corbusier, I would have taken it very badly, but it was too late. My proposals were published [...]." Yona Friedman, interview in the appendix (2005). Friedman was present at Bagnols between July 25 and 30, 1960. RISSELADA, Max and VAN DEN HEUVEL, Dirk (eds.): *Team 10. 1953–81. In Search of a Utopia of the Present*, op. cit., p. 84.
[377] KÜHNE, Günther: *Ein Architektur-Versuch*, in *Bauwelt*, no. 16, April 22, 1957, pp. 361–63.
[378] RAGON, Michel: *Histoire mondiale de l'architecture et de l'urbanisme moderne*, vol. 3, Paris/Tournai, Casterman, 1972.
[379] GLAESER, Ludwig: *The Work of Frei Otto*, New York, The Museum of Modern Art, 1972, p. 108.

also brought out a newsletter in three languages. Part of *L'architecture mobile* in its first version of 1958 was published in it, accompanied by a few illustrations, but under a different title, "Adaptable Architecture."[380] Among the architects in Frei Otto's circle in Berlin were Günschel, Werner Ruhnau and Eckhard Schulze-Fielitz,[381] all of them close in some way to the GEAM. In particular Ruhnau at the time acted as a sort of go-between, in the artistic field as well, between Germany and France, where at the end of the fifties and beginning of the sixties he was closely associated with the painter Yves Klein. They signed the *Projet d'une architecture de l'air* together. Notwithstanding the paradoxical nature of their proposal – an immaterial architecture of compressed air made up of "forms carried by the air, fire-fountains, water-fountains, swimming baths, air beds, air seats" – Ruhnau and Klein intended to underline the need for a complete air conditioning of the city which in their own eyes seemed utopian; it is no coincidence that their manifesto closes with a motto of Ben-Gurion's, "He who does not believe in miracles is not a realist."[382] At the same time Friedman was wondering about the possibilities of an air-conditioned city:

Architecture and city planning have arrived at a revolution: the air conditioning of the city. [...] The changes resulting from the air conditioning of the city will be even more important from the viewpoint of city planning: the inhabitants of an air-conditioned city will probably see their way of life totally transformed.[383]

It was an idea that Le Corbusier had foreshadowed on several occasions, but one that finally seemed within reach. So Friedman compared his proposal of a *Ville-Spatiale* with three other proposals, different in the techniques adopted but sharing the same aim: Buckminster Fuller's climate-controlled tensegrity domes, Otto's pneumatic structures – resembling gigantic tents – and Ruhnau's roof of blown air.

Friedman presented *L'architecture mobile* over the course of the joint meetings organized by the GEAM, using ten large panels propped up on each occasion against the sides of the halls in which the conferences were held.[384] These handmade drawings in bright colors were therefore very simple or rather simplistic – only two of them, numbers 3 and 5, presented axonometric projections – and had an essentially didactic character: in fact they were not conceived solely for other architects, but for as broad and undifferentiated a public as possible. The provocative title of the second for example was "The new society of cities should not be influenced by the urban planner." In other words the architecture should be determined by the inhabitants and bearing in mind the failure of the experience of total planning in

---

[380] FRIEDMAN, Yona: *Anpassungsfähig Bauen*, in *Mitteilung* [newsletter], no. 6, Berlin, Entwicklungstätte für den Leichtbau, Frei Otto, June 1959, pp. 34–42.
[381] SCHUMPP, Mechthild: *Die Raumstadt von Eckhard Schulze-Fielitz*, in id., *Stadtbau-Utopien und Gesellschaft*, Gütersloh, Bertelsmann, 1972, pp. 138–39.
[382] RUHNAU, Werner and KLEIN, Yves: *L'architecture de l'air*, op. cit., p. 149.
[383] FRIEDMAN, Yona: *La ville climatisée* (1959), in id., *L'architecture mobile*, 1970, op. cit. The passage has been transl. from the Italian ed., *La città ad aria condizionata* (1959), in id., *L'architettura mobile*..., op. cit., pp. 140–41.
[384] They are now at the Centre Pompidou in Paris.

Israel. And if as a consequence the profession of architect was falling apart, that of the city planner ought to be done away with entirely. In fact from 1959 onward Friedman would no longer use the term "city planning," be it mobile or spatial, replacing it with the word "city."

The spatial city is the result of an undetermined urban planning; in other words, it does not have to follow a plan, with exception of that of the infrastructure (of which it permits every possible transformation).[385]

A highly personal conclusion on the eve of the sixties. In other words the *Ville-Spatiale* outlined the utopia of an absolutely democratic city planning for the part of Europe that had been liberated from totalitarianism: the individual member of society was no longer solely observed, but had to be offered all the power to make decisions with regard to his environment, to his habitat, without go-betweens. "It means looking for techniques that will make it possible to pass from one solution to the other in order to adapt the city, if necessary, to the ways of life of its inhabitants, instead of adapting the inhabitants to the proposals of city planners."[386]

In any case Friedman gained more credit among architects, even if the aspect that most interested them was the technical one and not the social vision that underlay it. A comparative study of the literature by and on Yona Friedman in different national settings shows how after the CIAM in Dubrovnik of 1956 the theory of mobile architecture spread very rapidly in some key centers of architectural culture between the fifties and sixties, such as Frei Otto's Entwicklungsstätte für den Leichtbau in Germany, the Architectural Association in London and Kenzo Tange's studio in Tokyo. At the time all the architects belonging to the *Shinchintaisha* (Metabolism) group worked there: Kiyonori Kikutake, Kisho Kurokawa, Fumihiko Maki and the critics Masato Otaka and Noboru Kawazoe. The very name of the group was intended to express their view of society as a continual process of biological growth.[387] As an avant-garde movement it could be described in three ways: as a group of individuals, as a set of texts that defined a theory and as architecture.[388] There was more than one similarity between the Metabolists and Friedman's work, as is already evident in their joint publication of 1960: Kurokawa superimposed the grid of his plate-like *Horizontal Agricultural Unit* on that of the fields of the Japanese region of Aichi, devastated by a typhoon the previous year, turning on its head the idea of urban countryside proposed in *L'architecture mobile;* Kikutake, who had already designed a house raised on concrete pillars (*Sky House*, 1958), proposed in *Ocean City* mobile housing units inserted into enormous bridge structures suspended above the city center.[389]

---

[385] Friedman, Yona: *L'architecture mobile*, op. cit. The passage has been transl. from the Italian ed., *Città mobile – città spaziale* (1959), in id., *L'architettura mobile* . . . , op. cit., p. 138.

[386] Id., *L'architecture mobile*, 3rd ed., 1959, p. 11.

[387] Kikutake, Kiyonori, Kawazoe, Noboru, Otaka, Masato, Maki, Fumihiko and Kurokawa, Noriaki: *Metabolism: the Proposals for New Urbanism*, n.p., Y. Kawazoe, 1960. Kawazoe, Noboru: *Metabolism 1960*, Tokyo, Bijutsu Syuppan-sha, 1960.

[388] Wendelken, Cherie: *Putting Metabolism Back in Place. The Making of a Radically Decontextualized Architecture in Japan*, in Williams Goldhagen, Sarah and Legault, Réjean (eds.): *Anxious Modernisms. Experimentations in Postwar Architectural Culture*, Cambridge (MA)/London, MIT Press, 2000, p. 282.

[389] Kikutake, Kiyonori: *Kiyonori Kikutake. Works and Methods 1956–1970*, Tokyo, Bijutsu Syuppan-sha, 1973.

Also working in Tange's studio was the young Arata Isozaki, who had studied under Wachsmann at university and whose *Clusters in the Air* project (1960–62) consisted of enormous towers onto which could be hooked three or four cantilevered arms holding clusters of housing units held together by a new system of joints (*joint-core system*). These arms could sometimes touch one another, creating an aerial connection between the towers (they were part of a series of projects called *City in the Air*) and producing a gigantic version of the "span-over block," as in the *Shinjuku* project (1960–61) where horizontal bridge structures rested on large circular pillars.[390]

The importance of writings on architecture in spreading the ideas and projects of the Modern Movement to every continent, often with remarkable speed, is now well-established, even if there has not yet been a historical study tracing a geo-historical map of the 20th century in this sense. In any case between 1956 and 1961 articles by or on Friedman were published in *Bauwelt* (1957, 1958),[391] *L'Architecture d'aujourd'hui* (1958, 1960),[392] *Revue technique du bâtiment* (1960),[393] *Architectural Design* (1960)[394] and *The Japan Architect* (1961).[395] In 1970, at the Osaka Expo, Friedman would be one of the few Western architects invited by Tange and his pupils to visit the great roof of the Festival Plaza: Dennis Crompton of Archigram, Moshe Safdie, De Carlo, Hollein and Friedman, gathered in front of what was a unique case of a megastructure that had actually been built, even if it was temporary. As if to say: you imagined it, we have realized it.[396]

---

[390] For these projects, see the exhaustive Isozaki, Arata: *Works 30: Architectural Models, Prints, Drawings*, Tokyo, Rikuyo-sha, 1992, pp. 20–26.
[391] Id., *Ein Architektur-Versuch*, in *Bauwelt*, no. 16, 1957, pp. 361–63. Kühne, Günther: *Mobiles Planen Mobiles Bauen*, in *Bauwelt*, no. 21, 1957, pp. 491–93. Editorial, *Bauen für den Frieden*, in *Bauwelt*, no. 41/42, 1961, p. 1158.
[392] Friedman, Yona: *Plan d'une "ville mobile,"* in *L'Architecture d'aujourd'hui*, no. 80, October–November 1958; *La Ville-Spatiale*, in *L'Architecture d'aujourd'hui*, no. 87, 1960.
[393] Friedman, Yona: *Pour une architecture mobile. Les problèmes modernes de l'architecture et de l'urbanisme*, in *Revue technique du bâtiment*, no. 2, 1960, pp. 3–8. Two further parts of the article were published in later issues of the magazine: no. 3, 1960, pp. 9–19; and no. 5, 1960, pp. 8–18.
[394] Friedman, Yona and Aujame, Robert: *Mobile Architecture*, in *Architectural Design*, no. 9, 1960.
[395] *The Japan Architect*, April 1961.
[396] Koolhaas, Rem and Obrist, Hans-Ulrich (eds.): *Project Japan. Metabolism Talks* ..., op. cit., p. 516.

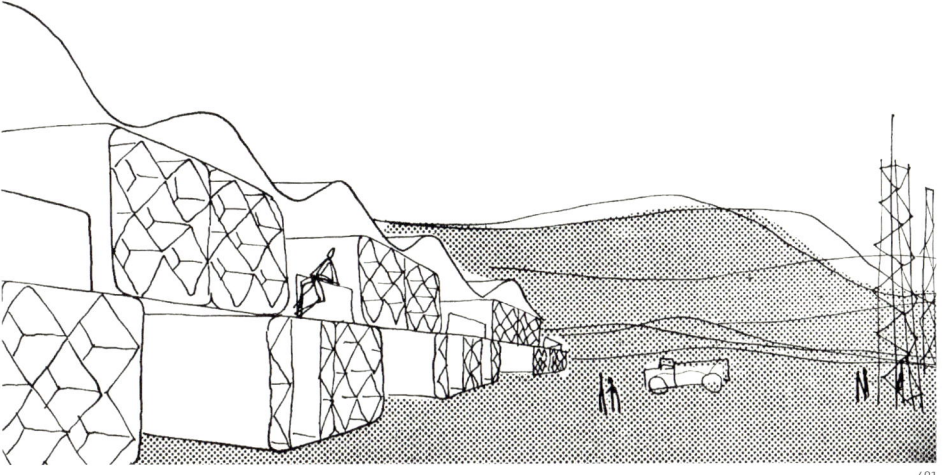

CONCRETE "CABINS FOR THE SAHARA," 1958

491 Yona Friedman: Illustration published in the second duplicated edition of *L'architecture mobile*, 1958.
492 Yona Friedman and Jean Pecquet: *Concrete Cabins for the Sahara*.

493

494

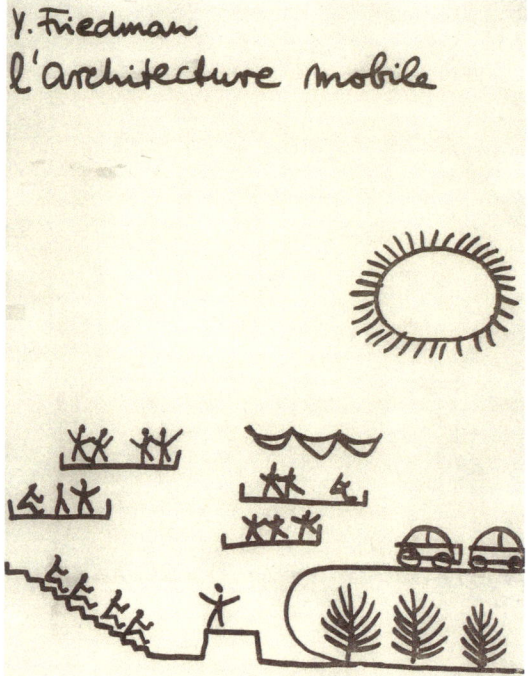

495

496

497

"L'ARCHITECTURE MOBILE"

493–494 Yona Friedman: Drawings, c. 1958.
495 Cover of Friedman, Yona: *L'architecture mobile*, 1959. This third edition consisted of 300 copies.

"VILLE-SPATIALE," MODELS, 1959

496 Yona Friedman: Structural study, model in wood and cardboard.
497 Yona Friedman: Model in metal, cardboard, wood and porcelain.

HOUSING UNITS IN THE "SPAN-OVER" BLOCKS

498 From Friedman, Yona: *L'architecture mobile*, second duplicated edition, 1958.

Dans la ville mobile les voitures n'entrent pas: elle est pour
les piétons. C'est une sorte de Venise contemporaine. Les voitures (ou tout autre moyen de circulation employé d'ici dix ans)
restent aux alentours, au parking.

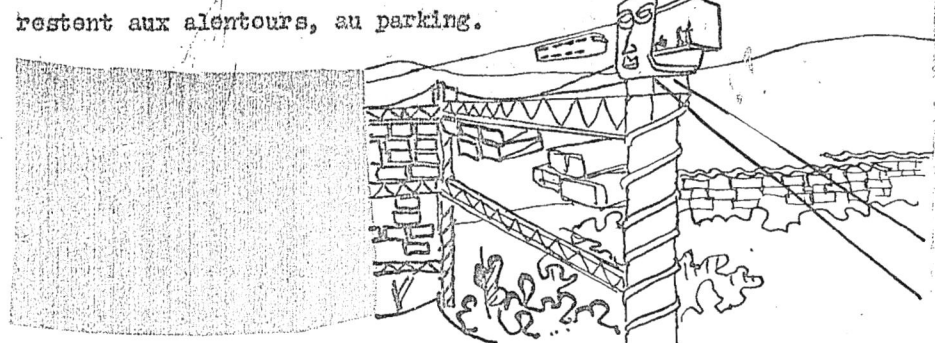

Quelqu'un arrivant en train ou en voiture prendra de ce parking
le métro aérien (ou plus exactement l'ascenseur horizontal) qui
roule sur un réseau de cables tendu entre les tours-piliers des
blocs. Arrivé à destination, il descend à l'étage voulu par l'ascenseur vertical. L'ascenseur horizontal est pratiquement un té-
léphérique qui fonctionne avec la même installation à appel au-
tomatique que les ascenseurs habituels. Ce réseau de circulation est déplaçable à volonté entre les tours qui soutiennent les
constructions à l'enjambée, puisque ces tours existent de toute
façon. Ce système d'ascenseurs horizontaux a trois avantages sur
la circulation actuelle: chaque entrée de bloc peut être désser-
vi par une ligne, - le réseau est déplaçable so déménage les
blocs, - on peut multiplier les lignes à volonté. Tous ces avantages le métro actuel là ne les a pas. Les stations se trouvent
à 120 m de distance (distance entre trois tours, variableselon
le type de construction utilisée) ce qui ne donne pas à marcher
plus de 60 m : c'est une distance moindre de celle à franchir ac-
tuellement entre la voiture et l'appartement.
Une ville de deux cent mille habitants peut être desservie complè-
tement par une boucle à grande vitesse et des lignes lentes au-

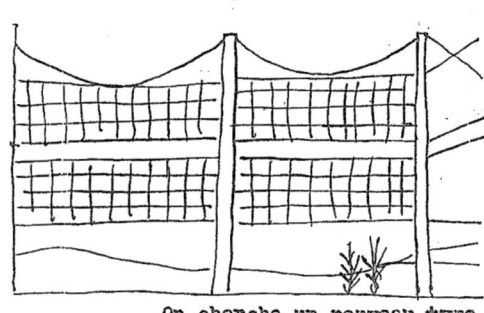

La charte d'urbanisme mobile.

Les facteurs déterminants de la société sont en flux (techniques et loisirs).

Les hypothèses habituels sont devenus fictives (valeur du terrain, groupes de cohabitation).

On cherche un nouveau type de construction qui doit:
1° toucher le sol en une surface minimum,
2° être démontable et déplaçable,
3° être transformable à volonté par l'habitant individuel.

Les moyens de circulation intérieure de la ville doivent être communaux. Les voitures ou autres moyens individuels resteront hors de la ville et ne serviront que pour la circulation interurbaine. Les points des fondations (raccords de la voirie, canalisation et alimentation d'eau et d'électricité, etc) doivent être le plus écarté possible.

La ville appartient aux piétons. Leurs passages doivent être protégés du climat (soleil, pluie).

499 Yona Friedman: *The charter of "l'urbanisme mobile,"* c. 1958.
500 Yona Friedman: *A Span-over block, facade and schematic floor plan*, scale 1:500.

Un bloc à l'enjambée

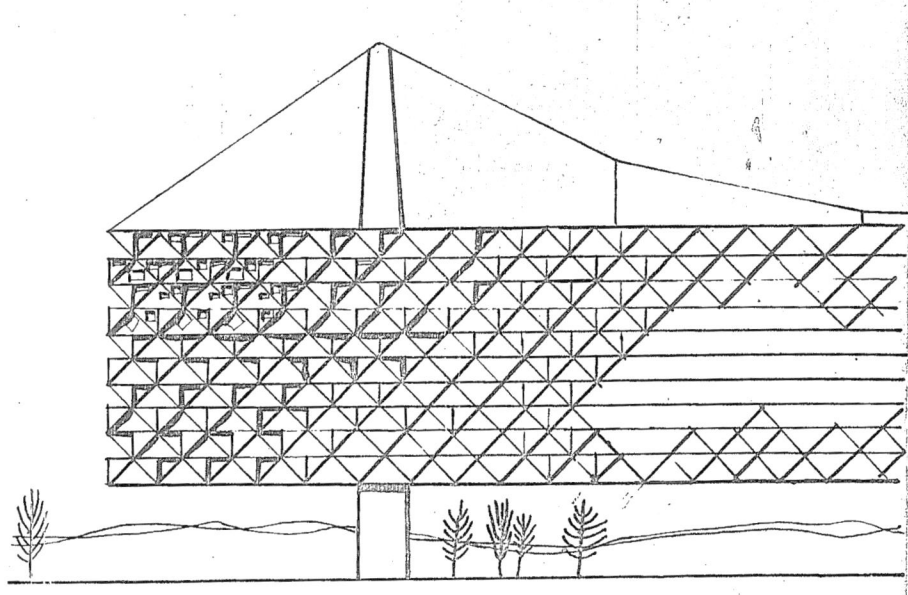

Façade 1:500

Ce bloc à l'enjambée est construit à partir de 13.200 trièdres; il contient 550 apartements en 10 étages. La portée libre entre les tours escaliers est 120 m, le porte-à-faux 25 mètres; le premier étage est situé à une hauteur de 10 m au dessus du niveau du sol.
Le principe de la construction est analogue à un pont suspendu compensé, où le rôle du bloc est similaire à celle du tablier.

Plan schématique des étages 1:500

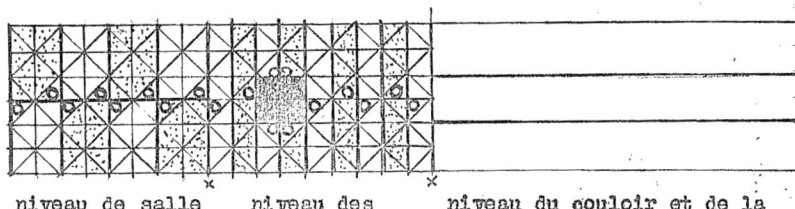

niveau de salle   niveau des   niveau du couloir et de la
de séjour   chambres   rue commerciale
(2-5-7-10)   (3-4-8-9)   (1-6)

Le plan ci-dessus sert à titre d'exemple seulement.

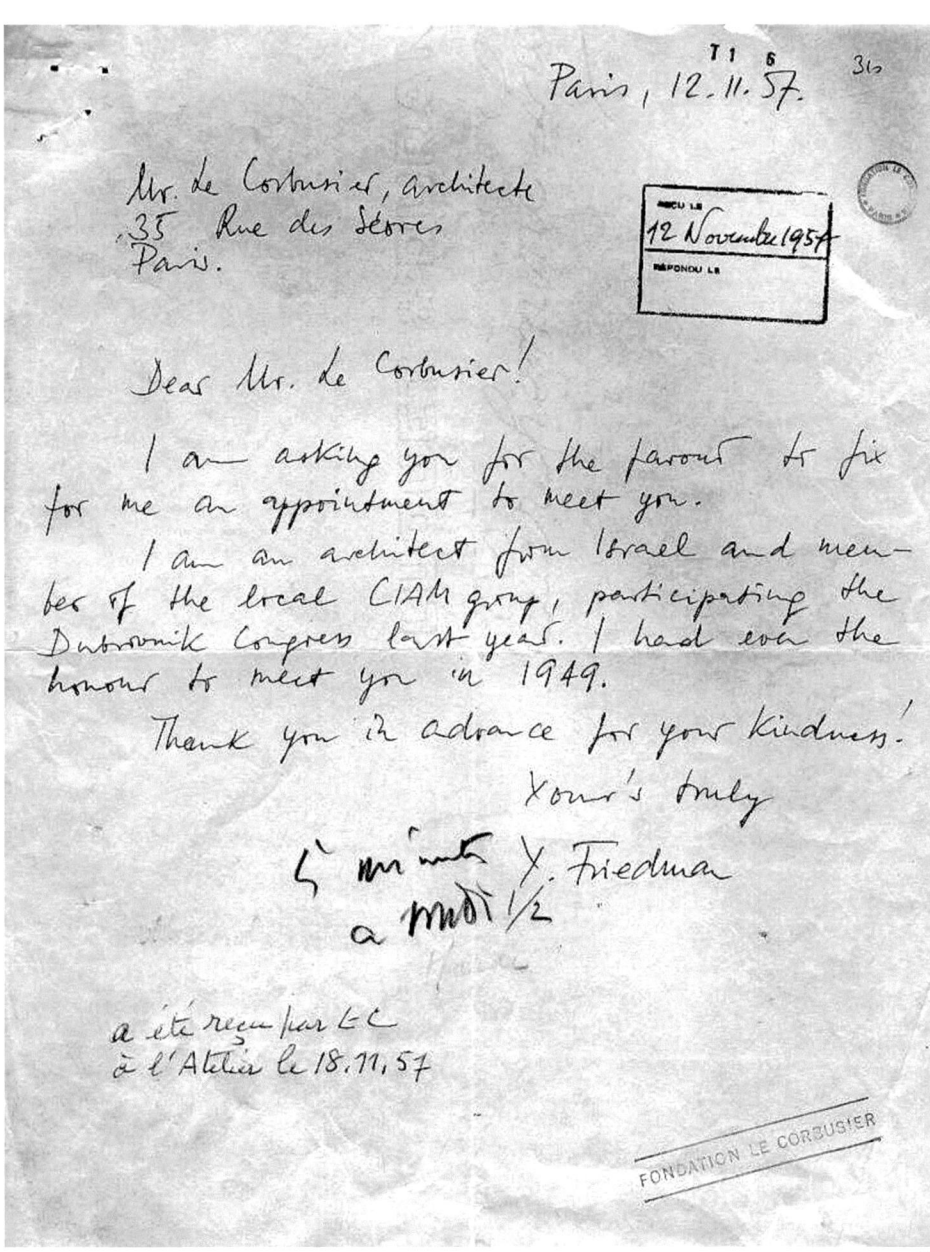

501 Letter from Yona Friedman to Le Corbusier, Paris, November 12, 1957.

SPAN-OVER BLOCKS ABOVE LES HALLES IN BERCY, PARIS

502 Yona Friedman: *Section and plan, scale 1:5,000 / residential block of ten floors / span-over civic center / existing construction*, 1958.

QUARTIER A L'ENJAMBEE AU DESSUS DE L'ENTREPOT DE BERCY.

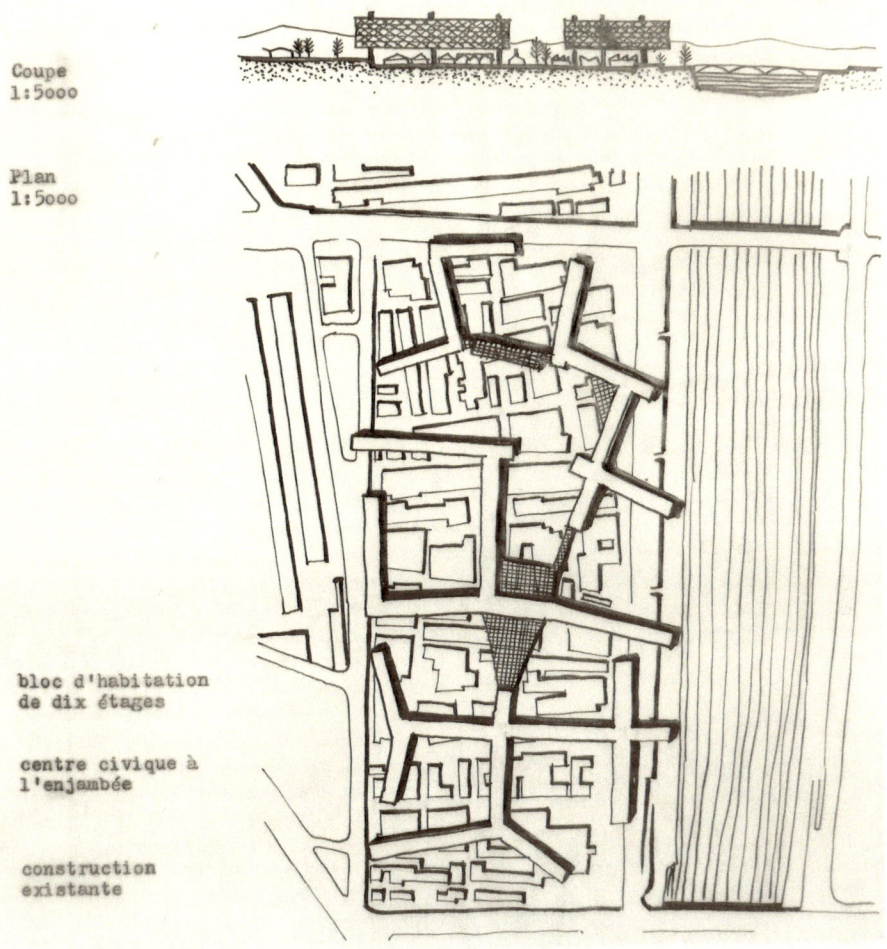

Coupe
1:5000

Plan
1:5000

bloc d'habitation
de dix étages

centre civique à
l'enjambée

construction
existante

503

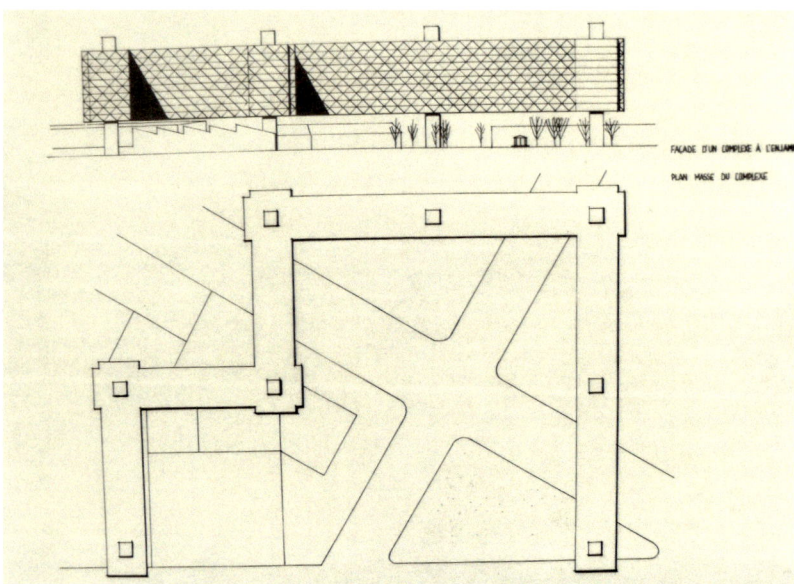

504

SPAN-OVER BLOCKS, "L'ARCHITECTURE MOBILE," 1959–60

503–504 Yona Friedman: *Span-over block* complex, perspective, front elevation and site plan.
505 Yona Friedman: *Spatial City* made of elevated blocks.
506 Yona Friedman: *Ville-Spatiale* above the existing city, sectional study and notes.

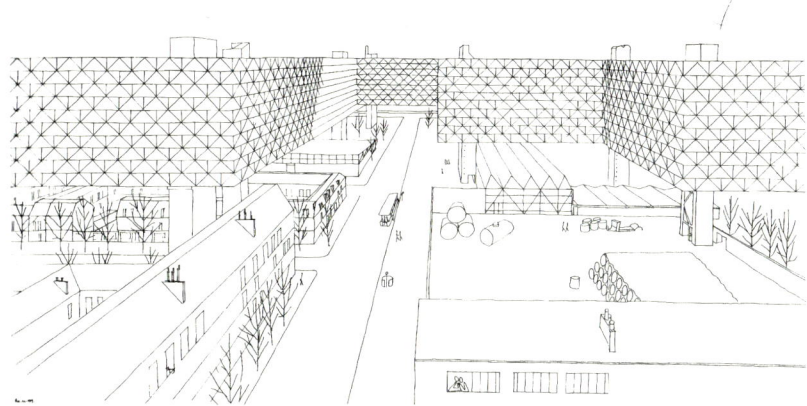

505

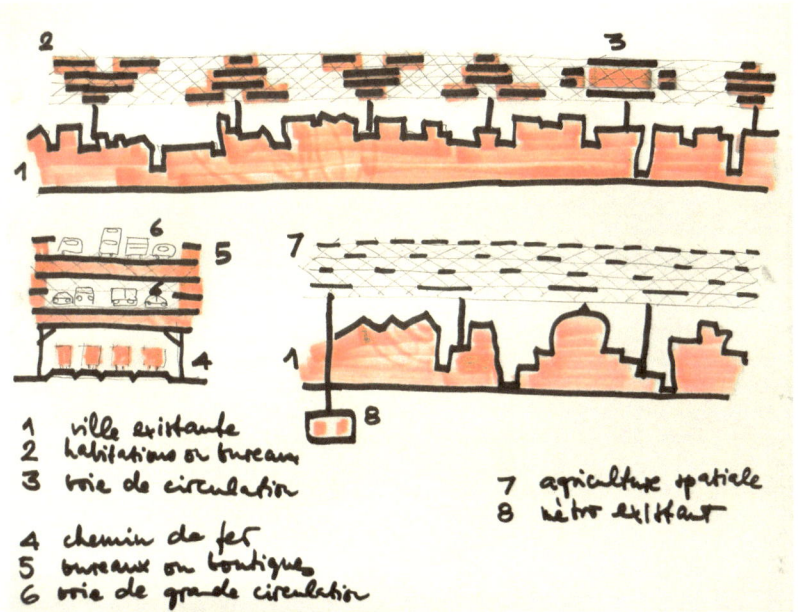

506

1 / Existing city
2 / Homes or offices
3 / Circulation route
4 / Railroad
5 / Offices or stores
6 / Highway
7 / Spatial farming
8 / Existing metro

"PARIS SPATIAL," PERSPECTIVE

507–**509** Yona Friedman: Spatial structure over the Seine with the Pont de Bercy and photomontage variations, from 1964.

508

509

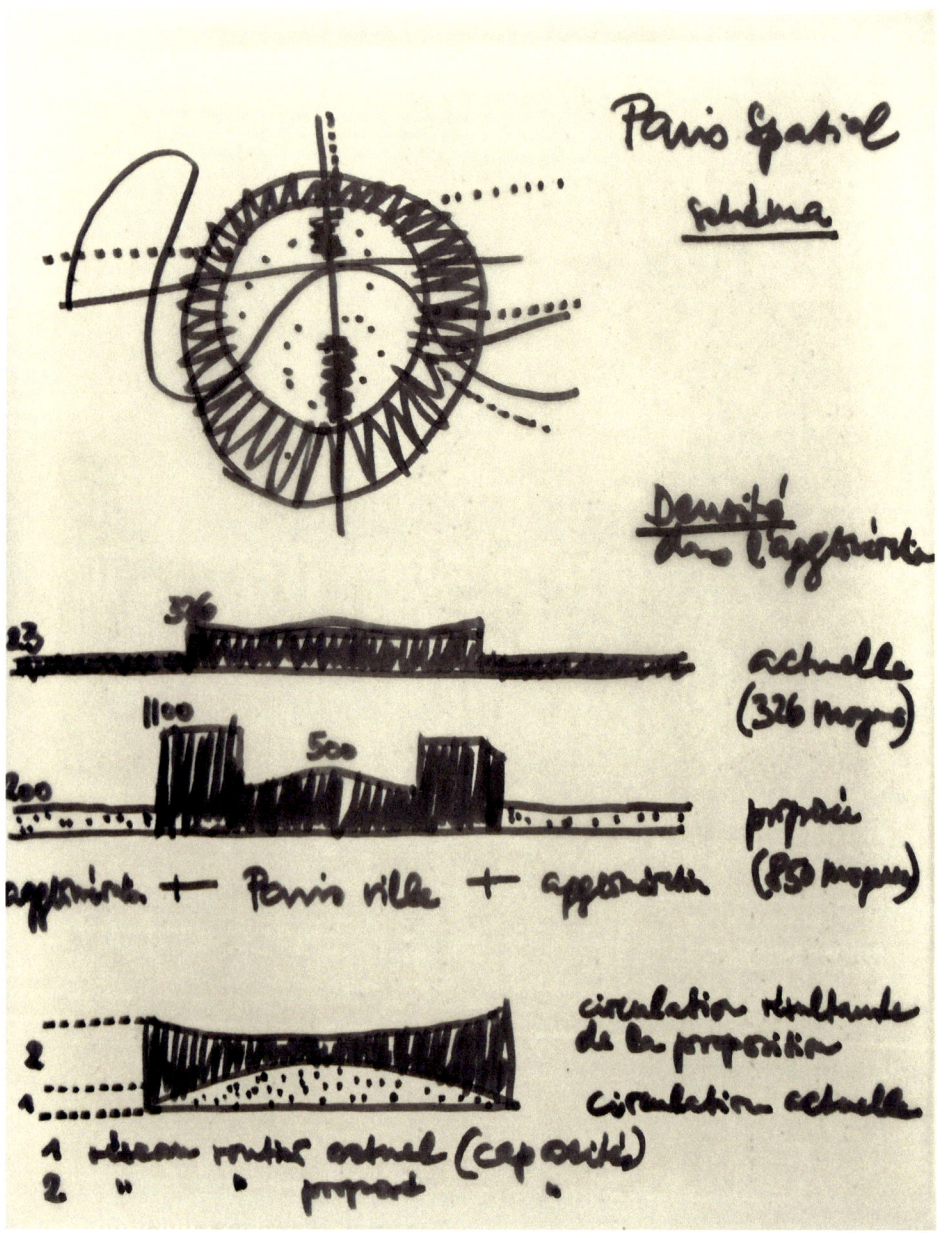

"PARIS SPATIAL," SCHEME, C. 1964

510 Yona Friedman: Density in the agglomeration: present (326 average) and proposed (850 average) / road traffic resulting from the proposition and current road traffic / existing road network and proposed road networks.
511 Yona Friedman: *Paris Radioconcentric* / *Paris – Le Corbusier* / *Paris Parallel* / *Herbé – Preveral* / *Paris Spatial*.

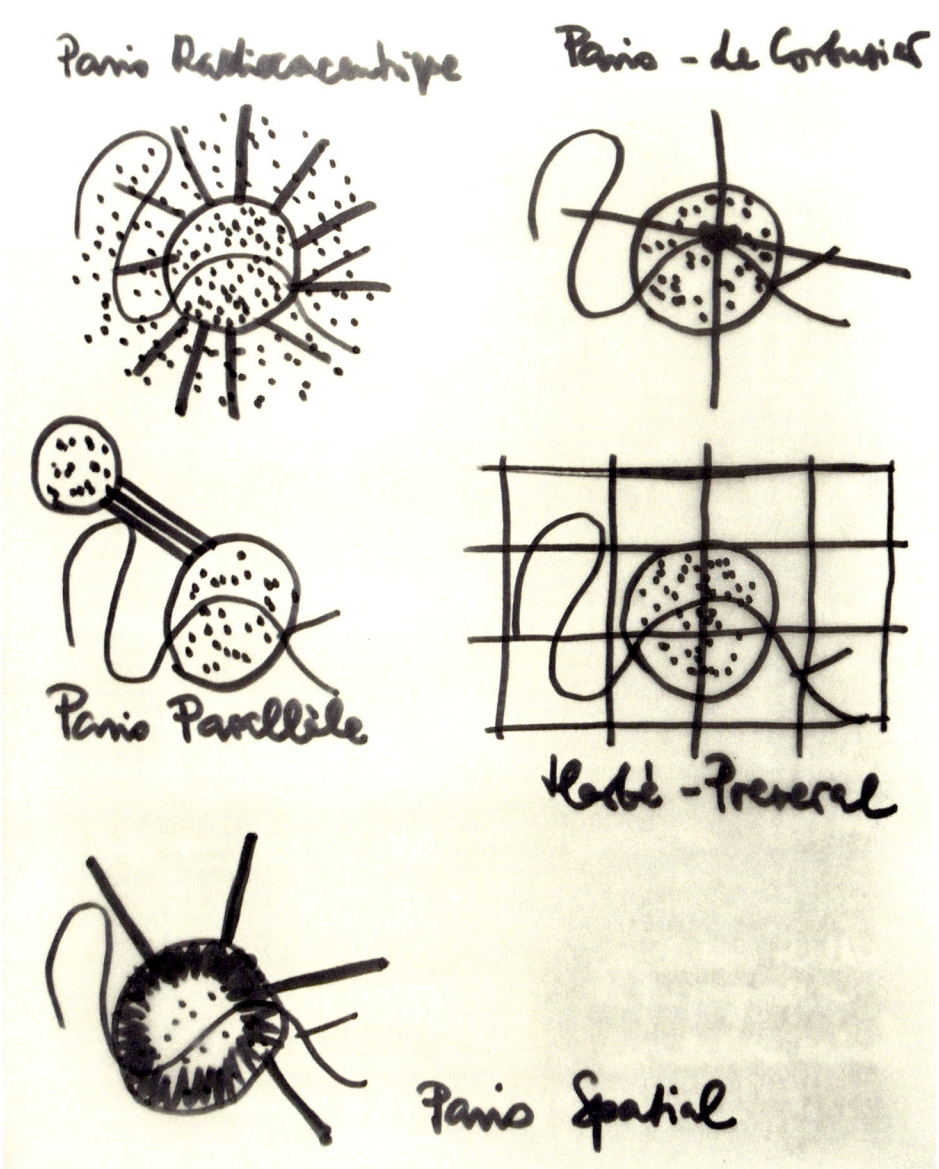

1 / The future of cities: recreation and entertainment centers, centers of public life, center of organization and decision-making.
Other functions (work, production) are increasingly automated and as a result less and less linked with major clusters. The raw material of "working" loses its importance and becomes "viewer" or "customer."

2 / The new urban society should not be influenced by the planner. Social distinctions between the different districts should be spontaneous. A housing surplus of around 10% is sufficient for residents to choose their districts according to their social preferences.

3 / Instead of industry, the major cities should be places of agriculture. The urban farmer is a social necessity.

4 / Cities must be climatized. Climatization enables the greatest freedom and efficiency in the use of cities: streets become the center of public life.

THE TEN PRINCIPLES OF SPACE TOWN PLANNING

512 Yona Friedman: *Les dix principes de l'urbanisme nouveau*, from 1959.
513 – 516 Yona Friedman: no. 1. *The future of cities; recreation centers. Other functions are increasingly automated.* / no. 2. *The new society of cities should be unaffected by the urban planner.* / no. 3. *Agriculture in the city is a social necessity.* / no. 4. *The city must be climatized.*

Drawing series, from *Les dix principes de l'urbanisme spatial*, 1961.
See principle no. 5 (p. 471 no. 573), *L'échelle technique*.

L'AVENIR DES VILLES CENTRES DE LOISIRS LES AUTRES FONCTIONS SONT DE PLUS EN PLUS AUTOMATISÉES

LA SOCIÉTÉ NOUVELLE DES VILLES DOIT ÊTRE NON INFLUENCÉ PAR L'URBANISTE

L'AGRICULTURE DANS LA VILLE EST UNE NÉCESSITÉ SOCIALE

LA VILLE DOIT ÊTRE CLIMATISÉE

KIYONORI KIKUTAKE

517 *Sky House*, 1958. Photograph by Kawasumi Architectural Photograph Office.
518 *Ocean City Project*, 1958–62. Published in Kikutake, Kiyonori: *Kiyonori Kikutake. Works and Methods 1956–1970*, Tokyo, Bijutsu Syuppan-sha, 1973.

ARATA ISOZAKI

519 *Joint core system*, elevation, Shinjuku, Tokyo, 1960.
A variation of the *Span-over block*.
520 *Clusters in the air*, model, Tokyo, 1962.
521 *The city in the sky ruins. Destruction of future city*, photomontage, 1968.

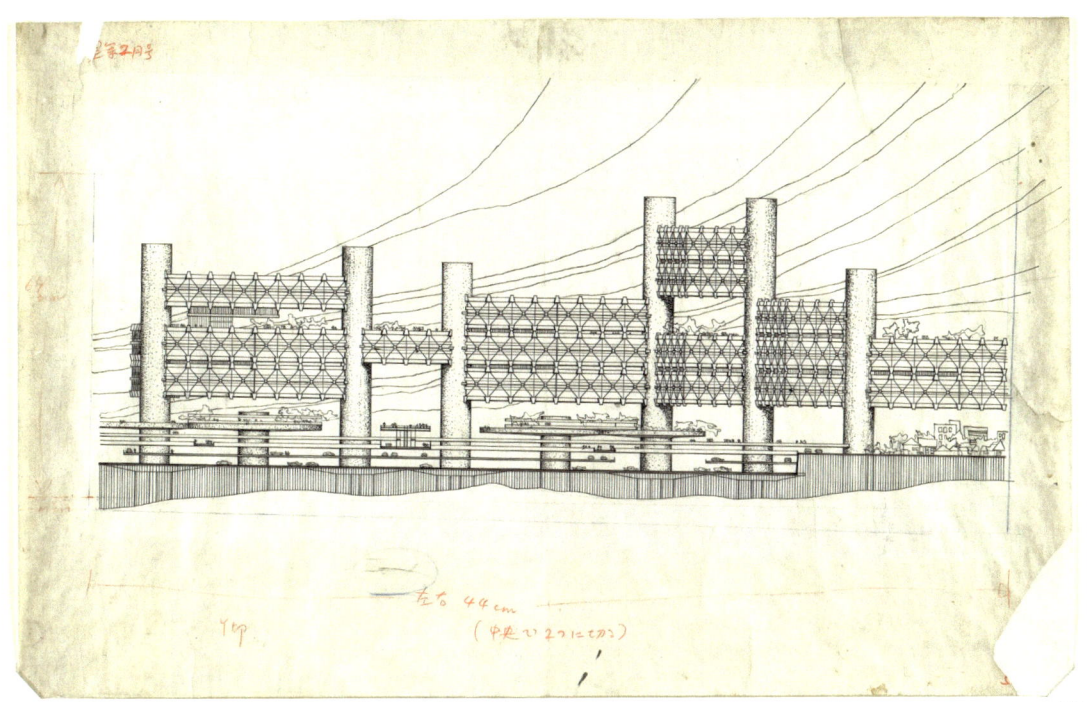

THE "GROUPE D'ÉTUDES D'ARCHITECTURE MOBILE"

In the foreword to the second edition of *L'architecture mobile*, dated 1958, Friedman announced the creation of the *Groupe d'études d'Architecture mobile* (GEAM, "Mobile Architecture Study Group"), listing its members followed by their places of origin or residence: Günther Kühne (Germany), Roger Aujame, David Georges Emmerich,[397] Jean Pecquet and Friedman himself (Paris), Jerzy Sołtan (Warsaw) and Jan Trapman (Amsterdam). Friedman's pamphlet had been conceived as a sort of open manifesto so that everyone would be able to endorse it without necessarily sharing the aesthetic inclinations of the author. *L'architecture mobile* was supposed to be the first in a series of other publications, in which each member would have made an individual proposal – Friedman's was the *Ville-Spatiale*. The minimum common denominator of these architectural proposals would be their mobile character. However, this initial intention was never fulfilled because only Friedman would go on to produce, through continual updating, systematic publications of a certain significance. These updates were facilitated by the conferences and lectures that Friedman was increasingly being invited to hold all over Europe, allowing him to discuss his ideas with a large number of experts, in architecture and other fields. For example at the conferences held at the Architectural Association in London – in 1959 and 1960 [398] – Peter Cook and the future members of Archigram, who had not yet graduated, were seated among the students.

But the group's most important meetings took place in the Netherlands, in Rotterdam or Amsterdam, primarily for reasons of convenience, owing to its geographical location halfway between Germany and France. Although Kühne was the only official German member, a lot of German architects attended the meetings, including Schulze-Fielitz, Frei Otto, Günschel and Ruhnau.

So there were many opportunities to debate Friedman's theory in the Netherlands, where in addition to Trapman there was a small community of outstanding architects: van Eyck, Bakema, Rietveld, Habraken and Constant, to mention just a few names, were therefore able to discuss things directly with Friedman. In fact the Dutch one had been the most cohesive and best organized of the former national groups of the CIAM and had continued to meet even after the disbanding of the organization at Otterlo in 1959. But the Netherlands was at the same time a decisive center for the circulation and elaboration of Situationist theories on city planning and architecture: Constant was the main point of reference and was obviously in contact with both Debord and the other exponents most involved in the development of the concept of *Unitary Urbanism*, Gilles Ivain, Raoul Vaneigem and Attila Kotányi, the latter of Hungarian origin and living in Brussels. For example Constant and Debord signed "The Amsterdam Declaration" together on November 10, 1958, in which unitary

---

[397] Hungarian by origin, he was interested chiefly in "self-supporting" structures and at the end of the sixties would carry out experiments in self-building with his students in Morocco. See Brayer, Marie-Ange (ed.): *David Georges Emmerich, architecte-ingénieur. Une utopie rationnelle*, Orléans, Editions HYX, 1997.
[398] "The AA invited me in 1959 and 1960 to give lectures." Yona Friedman, interview in the appendix.

urbanism constituted the minimal program of the Situationist International.[399] Constant was therefore, at least for a couple of years, the link between the GEAM and the Situationists and we need to take a closer look at his wholly theoretical production in the architectural field, in part because he would be the protagonist of a significant clash with Friedman.

In the meantime the first important meeting of the GEAM was held in Rotterdam in the March of 1958.

However, the founders did not sign a document together until April 5, 1960: it was a "Program for a Mobile Architecture,"[400] from which it can be inferred that the Germans Günschel[401] and Ruhnau and Camille Frieden, editor of the Luxembourg-based monthly *Europäisches Bau-Forum*, which for a while served as the group's mouthpiece,[402] had officially joined the GEAM too. Still others would be present at least occasionally, such as the Frenchman Paul Maymont, the Swede Erik Friberger, the Japanese critic Masato Otaka (who was the link between the GEAM and the Metabolists) and the Pole Oskar Hansen.[403]

In such a tangle of relations it is worth focusing on the more prominent figures in the GEAM, united by the fact that they have been relegated to footnotes in histories of architecture, in order to get a better idea of how *L'architecture mobile* lent itself to different interpretations and nuances and why it was embraced by such diverse personalities.

The most important member of the GEAM was undoubtedly Jerzy Sołtan. Born in what is now Latvia in 1913, he had trained as an architect at the Warsaw Technical Institute. Taken prisoner by the Germans, he had gone to work in Le Corbusier's studio in Paris as soon as he was released at the end of the war. Working on the *Unité d'Habitation* project with Candilis, among others. In 1949 he went back to Warsaw, staying in contact with the West through the CIAM. He was one of the first to join Team 10 and thanks to his grasp of several languages acted as a mediator between the more radical wing and the old guard of Sert and Giedion. It was partly for this reason that Sert invited him to teach at Harvard in 1958. When he met Friedman in Dubrovnik, Sołtan had just designed a "tropical pavilion" (1954) with a reticular structure, divided up internally by large folding panels[404] in a way not unlike Wachsmann's hangar design for the US Air Force. In 1957 – the year of the Interbau – another of his pavilions was built in Damascus at an international fair, with funding from the Polish state:[405] it is interesting to note how the air conditioning of these designs for

---

[399] Constant, Nieuwenhuys and Debord, Guy: *La déclaration d'Amsterdam*, in *Internationale Situationniste*, no. 2, December 1958; English transl., *The Amsterdam Declaration*, available at Situationist International online, http://www.cddc.vt.edu/sionline/si/amsterdam.html.

[400] GEAM, *Programm für ein mobiles Bauen*, in Conrads, Ulrich (ed.): *Programme und Manifeste zur Architektur des 20. Jahrhunderts*, Berlin, Ullstein, 1964. English transl., *Programme for a mobile architecture*, in *Programs and Manifestoes on 20th Century Architecture*, Cambridge (MA), MIT Press, 1970.

[401] Escher, Cornelia: *Günter Günschel, la rigueur de l'imaginaire*, in *AMC*, no. 201, 2010, pp. 99–104.

[402] *Europäisches Bau-Forum*, no. 8, 1961; the complete subtitle was: *Forum Européen d'Architecture. "Groupe d'Études d'Architecture Mobile International" (GEAM)*, Paris.

[403] Michel Ragon gets a little mixed up in the list published in his *Histoire mondiale de l'architecture . . .*, op. cit., vol. III (pp. 233 ff. in the Italian ed., *Storia dell'architettura*, op. cit., vol. III). Friedman also spoke of Hansen in the interview conducted by Obrist, Hans Ulrich: *Ever Yona, Yona, Ever 1*, in Rodriguez, María Inés (ed.): *Yona Friedman: Architecture with the People, by the People, for the People*, Barcelona, Actar Birkhäuser, 2011, p. 143.

[404] Gola, Jola (ed.), *Jerzy Sołtan. A Monograph*, Cambridge (MA), GSD Harvard University/Warsaw, Akademii Sztuk Piekuych, 1995, pp. 149–51.

[405] *Ibid.* pp. 152–53.

cities located in warm climates took the concrete form of simple sheets of cloth tied to the top of the structure. Sołtan was one of the first to invite Friedman to give lectures in the US, where Sołtan continued to teach until his death in 2005. Together with his fellow countryman Hansen, the Polish architect regularly attended meetings of both Team 10 (although he was not part of the inner circle) and the GEAM. His closeness to Sert and Giedion and the Urban Design movement from 1958 onward shows how he was able to associate with all the architectural factions of the time, not without a touch of ambiguity.

Between 1958 and 1960 the GEAM expanded, losing some of its cohesion in the process. The German group, and Ruhnau in particular, pressed for the endorsement of a unitary manifesto, the *Program for a Mobile Architecture*. Friedman's leadership was not in question, but individual contributions were limited to technological notions lacking an overall vision of society and the evolution of urban needs.
The pressure from Ruhnau and Schulze-Fielitz, both advocates of a theory of the occupation of air space,[406] is particularly evident in point C of the program signed by the whole group, in which guidelines are proposed:

Reform of property rights in building land and air space with a view to achieving easier interchange. Introduction of a system of stratified utilization of air space by the inhabitants.[407]

Here the influence of Ruhnau, fascinated like Yves Klein by an immaterial architecture consisting solely of air,[408] is clear. But perhaps the most debatable point of the program is the desire to lower the value of property on building land with the aim of encouraging the interchange of houses.
It is natural that such a proposal would encounter enormous political obstacles: ownership of one's own home is not just one of the basic forms of financial investment, but often a psychological necessity as well, as Banham had clearly understood when he wrote *A Home is not a House*.
In 1961 an interesting statement was added to the program:

Multifunctionality of the urban organism will reduce the problems of communication.[409]

But this principle would not be applied on a practical level by any member of the GEAM. Nonetheless, great hopes and expectations were roused on both sides of the Atlantic by the visions put forward by this new band of architects at a time when reconstruction had been completed and during a period of great economic growth, the years spanning the fifties and sixties: it suffices to compare Ulrich Conrads' *Phantastische Architektur* and the

---

[406] Schulze-Fielitz, Eckhard: *Une théorie pour l'occupation de l'espace*, in L'Architecture d'aujourd'hui, no. 102, June–July 1962, pp. 78–79; also see id., *Urbanisme spatial*, in L'Architecture d'aujourd'hui, no. 115, 1964, pp. 26–27.
[407] GEAM, "Programme for a Mobile Architecture" (1960), in Conrads, Ulrich (ed.), *Programs and Manifestoes . . .*, op. cit., p. 168.
[408] Noever, Peter and Perrin, François (eds.): *Yves Klein Air Architecture*, Ostfildern, Hatje Cantz, 2004.
[409] GEAM, "Programme for a Mobile Architecture," (1960), op. cit., p. 168.

exhibition *Visionary Architecture* held at the MoMA the same year.[410] A traveling exhibition of the GEAM visited many cities of Northern Europe between 1961 and 1962 and was greeted with interest everywhere – Paris, Hanover, Gelsenkirchen, Leverkusen, Berlin, Warsaw, Luxembourg City, London and Munich.[411] After the dissolution of the group, Conrads, the editor of *Bauwelt*, personally compiled an anthology of the most important architectural programs and manifestos of the 20th century and published them, in chronological order, in 1964. Among the writings that came out in 1960 he selected a total of eight (by William Katavolos, Gieselman/Ungers, the GEAM, Louis Kahn, Ruhnau/Klein, the Situationists, Eckhard Schulze-Fielitz and Constant), but the anthology concluded with a text from 1962: *The ten principles of space town planning* by Yona Friedman.[412] This explains why Friedman was so influential between 1960 and 1965, something that is also attested by Frampton, who in his capacity as a young member of the editorial staff of *Architectural Design* used to go and see him regularly in those years.[413]

In general the GEAM came up against a difficulty that went well beyond the individual case: these architects were convinced that every architectural problem could be solved if there was a sufficiently able technical advisor. In a document of the GEAM signed shortly before it disbanded they went further, expressing a hope for technological intervention in politics as well, to influence at least in part the institutional processes of decision-making:

Numerous leaders have succeeded one another since those who first made our laws and systems. They do not realize that the new applications of technology enable a reversal of their (or our) systems. If, for example, we proposed to direct the administration with the use of machines, the leaders would think that their power was thereby augmented; but in reality, machines would impose upon them their mathematical logic (which could be better than that of men) and the leaders would lose their current advantages.[414]

This is the error of naïvety into which Friedman himself fell several times, first with Wachsmann and then with Prouvé and Hansen.[415] It is not enough in fact to know that a structure can be built. What is needed is to politically persuade the client (society) to endorse such plans.

And yet even people of great experience and pragmatism like the city planner Raymond Lopez, with works in both Africa (Dakar, Cape Verde) and France (Région Parisienne) under his belt, considered the schemes of Friedman and the GEAM as feasible as those of Brasilia or Chandigarh, to the point of declaring in 1964: "Are these impossible fantasies? [The] city of tomorrow will be a real construction in space."[416]

---

410 Conrads, Ulrich and Sperlich, Hans G.: *Phantastische Architektur*, Stuttgart, Hatje, 1960. See Drexler, Arthur: *Visionary Architecture*, in catalogue of the exhibition at the MoMA (September–October 1960), New York, Museum of Modern Art, 1961.
411 Willemin, Véronique: *Maisons Mobiles*, Paris, Editions Alternatives, 2004, p. 42.
412 Friedman, Yona: *The Ten Principles of Space town Planning*, in Conrads, Ulrich (ed.): *Programs and Manifestoes*..., op. cit., pp. 183–84.
413 Frampton, Kenneth: *Yona Friedman, a Micro-Memoir*, in Rodriguez, María Inés (ed.): *Yona Friedman. Architecture with the People*..., op. cit., p. 104.
414 Friedman, Yona: *Résumé du référat à Amsterdam*, December 15, 1962.
415 See the perfunctory feasibility study published in Friedman, Yona, Hansen, Oskar and Hansen, S.: *Urbanisme mobile étude pour un bâtiment évolutif*, in *L'Architecture d'aujourd'hui*, no. 102, June–July 1962, p. 76.
416 Cited in Abram, Joseph: *L'architecture moderne en France*..., op. cit., p. 283.

Friedman's program of urban planning was reworked several times, and within the space of a few years passed from mobile city planning [417] (1957) to spatial city planning (1962). But what matters most in his revised program for spatial planning in 1962 are some almost prophetic declarations.

When he wrote that thanks to growing automation, work and production are becoming less and less connected with large urban settlements, Friedman was already seeing the emergence of the now obvious phenomenon of outsourcing manufacturing.

Where he wrote instead that "the raw material 'workers' will lose its importance and change into 'spectators' or 'customers,'" Friedman foresaw the dissolution of the social class that was shortly to become the subject of an almost mystical exaltation in Italian *operaismo*.[418] Today, in Italy at least, factory workers make up less than 10% of the labor force, in other words they are a minority of workers, but in 1962 this was certainly not a clearly perceptible trend. In this we cannot help but note Friedman's farsightedness, even if he was not of course the only one to predict this development.[419] If a utopian is someone who places his visions in the distant future so that they cannot be fulfilled, as many Marxist critics held, then Friedman cannot be called a utopian.

Friedman also declared that "the new society of towns must not be influenced by the town planner. Social distinctions between the different quarters must be spontaneous." This is not just a rejection of zoning and functionalist urban planning, but a radical criticism of the role of this discipline, which has more than one parallel with Situationist thinking, especially on the subject of participation:

Wherever bureaucratic civilization has spread, the anarchy of individual construction has been officially consecrated and taken over by the competent organs of power, in such a way that the instinct for construction [has been] extirpated like a vice and hardly survives except among children and primitives (irresponsible people, in administrative terminology).[420]

The founding theory of unitary urbanism was not intended as a doctrine of city planning but as a critique of city planning. Later Kotányi and Vaneigem would go so far as to claim that "urbanism does not exist," or rather should not exist, since it is pure spectacular ideology in contrast to architecture, which is a real production, although one "coated with ideology."[421] Previously it had been Gilles Ivain who had looked at architecture and come up with a first Situationist definition:

---

[417] FRIEDMAN, Yona: *Résumé du programme de l'urbanisme mobile*, in id., *L'architecture mobile* ..., op. cit., pp. 62–63.
[418] See TRONTI, Mario: *Operai e capitale*, Turin, Einaudi, 1966.
[419] "At a time when sociologists are joining forces to decree that the working class no longer exists, they, the urbanists, have waited for neither philosophers nor sociologists to invent the inhabitant." VANEIGEM, Raoul: *Contre l'urbanisme*, in *Internationale Situationniste*, no. 6, August 1961. English transl., *Comments against Urbanism*, available at *Situationist International online*, http://www.cddc.vt.edu/sionline/si/comments.html.
[420] Ibid.
[421] KOTÁNYI, Attila and VANEIGEM, Raoul: *Programme élémentaire du bureau d'urbanisme unitaire*, in *Internationale Situationniste*, no. 6 August 1961. English transl., *Basic Program of the Bureau of Unitary Urbanism*, now in KNABB, Ken (ed.): *Situationist International Anthology*, op. cit. Also available online at http://www.bopsecrets.org/SI/6.unitaryurb.htm.

Architectural complexes will be modifiable. Their aspect will change totally or partially in accordance with the will of their inhabitants. [...] Past collectivities offered the masses an absolute truth and incontrovertible mythical exemplars. The appearance of the notion of relativity in the modern mind allows one to surmise the EXPERIMENTAL aspect of the next civilization (although I'm not satisfied with that word; I mean that it will be more supple, more "fun"). On the bases of this mobile civilization, architecture will, at least initially, be a means of experimenting with a thousand ways of modifying life [...].[422]

It is striking how similar are the views of the leader of the GEAM and Ivain on the "mobility" of architecture and on the importance of play, or "fun," for society – a theme that runs all the way through the first issue of *Internationale Situationniste* – as is their essential contemporaneousness. Kotányi and Vaneigem's text on the other hand was published a year after the GEAM's program.

On the contrary, according to the "zoning" theories widely adhered to among city planners – and among administrators and politicians – before the First World War, urban development had fallen into line with the principle of specialization that had already been applied to systems of production; thus the city became at one and the same time means of production and merchandise; and in connection with the principle of maximization of profits, was broken up into parts with distinct functions.[423] The Athens Charter, the key text of all modernist city planning, conceived on board the *Patris II* during the 4th CIAM in 1933, was still anchored to this approach. In contrast all of Guy Debord's work, as we will see shortly, would be aimed at opposing the commodification of the city.

Finally, Friedman was decidedly opposed to newly founded cities like many of the ones in Israel. He argued that cities ought not to be created in a *tabula rasa,* in the middle of nowhere, but on the contrary should always develop gradually from a smaller and preexisting urban nucleus. For this reason every new city "must be the intensification of existing towns" (through spatial urban planning and the extensive air-conditioning of private and public areas).[424]

The GEAM disbanded in 1962, after a final conference held at Knoll International in Amsterdam where Friedman met John Habraken (born in 1929) in person for the first time.[425] He had just published his most important writing, *Supports: an Alternative to Mass Housing.*[426] Despite its generic title, the text has many points of convergence with mobile architecture.

---

[422] See IVAIN, Gilles: *Formulaire pour un urbanisme nouveau*, in *Internationale Situationniste*, no. 1, June 1958; English transl., *Formulary for a New Urbanism*, available at *Situationist International online*, http://www.cddc.vt.edu/sionline/presitu/formulary.html. Ivain (pseudonym of Ivan Chtcheglov) had first drafted this article in 1953, when he was a member of the Lettrist International, reworking it on a couple of occasions before the publication of the definitive version.
[423] See MANCUSO, Franco: *Le vicende dello zoning*, Milan, Il Saggiatore, 1978.
[424] For all the above themes, see FRIEDMAN, Yona: *The Ten Principles of Space Town Planning*, in CONRADS, Ulrich (ed.): *Programs and Manifestoes...*, op. cit., pp. 183–84.
[425] FRIEDMAN, Yona: *In the Air*, interview conducted by Martin van Schaik (October 28, 2001), in VAN SCHAIK, Martin and MÁCEL, Otar (eds.): *Exit Utopia...*, op. cit., p. 31.
[426] HABRAKEN, Nicholas John: *De dragers en de mensen*, Amsterdam, Scheltema & Holkema, 1961. English transl., *Supports: an Alternative to Mass Housing*, London, Architectural Press, 1972.

The two basic ones are:
1. The recognition of an active role for the user in decisions relating to planning.
2. The definition of support structures as "a construction which allows the provision of dwellings which can be built, altered and taken down, independently of the others."[427]
The influence of L'architecture mobile is clear: although it is never cited directly in the book and there is not sufficient evidence to prove that Habraken owned a copy, this is certainly very likely. Even the redefinition of the role of the architect within this new vision of interaction with users is consistent with the one suggested by Friedman four years earlier. In fact Habraken wrote about the architect's work:

Such a person will probably become something quite different from the current conception of the professional architect. He will in fact, be more like an industrial designer. His primary task will be to give the industrial product [...] its definitive form, in such a way that the public for which it is intended can derive the greatest advantage from it from the practical and aesthetic viewpoint.[428]

But Habraken shared some of the limitations of Friedman and the other members of the GEAM. In fact the Dutch architect never defined what might be the settings for decision-making of a collective nature or how they could be made accessible to the user, transferring them to the competence of public institutions.[429] Habraken would try to remedy this belatedly, adding a postscript giving indications about how to put the idea of supports into effect only in the reprint of 1971, i.e. at the moment when the theme of participation reached the height of its popularity, as "ideas, whether universal or not, can bear fruit only if they are cultivated in a particular social environment."[430] Friedman would write *Utopies réalisables*, with no illustrations, with the same intent.

The breakup of the GEAM occurred long before that of Team 10: however, even though the Smithsons, van Eyck, Bakema, Coderch and the others went on meeting until 1981, we can consider the phase of an effective exchange and collaboration to be almost over by 1963.[431] And it was in 1963 that two architect-engineers like De Carlo and Shadrach Woods came into the international limelight. In particular the latter – who took a degree in engineering in the US and then one in philosophy in Dublin – attracted attention with his project for Frankfurt-Römerberg, drawn up with Candilis and Josic, but developed above all with Manfred Schiedhelm. The same group would construct one of its principal works the following year after winning the competition for the new Freie Universität of Berlin with a design derived directly from the one for Frankfurt. Römerberg was the first application in design of web theory, presented the previous year in an important essay,[432] but above

---
[427] Ibid., pp. 59–60.
[428] Ibid., p. 89.
[429] Mancuso, Franco: *Nota introduttiva*, in Habraken, John N. (Italian ed.): *Strutture per una residenza alternative*, Milan, Il Saggiatore, 1974, p. 27.
[430] Ibid., p. 12.
[431] Frampton, Kenneth: *Team 10, Plus 20: The Vicissitudes of Ideology*, in id., *Labour, Work and Architecture. Selected Essays on Architecture and Town Planning*, London, Phaidon, 2002, p. 146.
[432] Woods, Shadrach: *Web*, in *Le Carré Bleu*, no. 2, March 1962.

all it was an impressive work of urban mending carried out by difference rather than by similarity: a great slab that extended from the cathedral to the River Main, leaping over the road that ran along it. Six floors, two of them below ground, made it possible to lay out, while keeping the height the same as the existing buildings, a "multi-level city"[433] organized into a complicated web of internal pedestrian streets with a certain potential capacity for both development and adaptation. In fact it was possible for users to take possession of the spaces left free in the interstices of the web.[434] The Frankfurt–Römerberg project can be seen as a piece of *urbanisme spatial*, but one that has literally landed (except in the part that arrives at the river bank, leapfrogging the road). According to Frampton it was of no importance that the concept of an arbitrarily occupied infrastructure had been anticipated by Friedman in 1956 and this in no way diminished the result of the Frankfurt project.[435] On the contrary credit was due to Woods for having revived an architectural theme that had been totally disregarded at the CIAM in Dubrovnik, rectifying the excessive abstraction of Friedman's projects. Frampton is right – although Woods probably had no direct knowledge of them until the meeting in Bagnols-sur-Cèze in 1960 – but what is not yet clear enough today is that Friedman's proposals were not and *were not intended to be* fully defined plans, but models to be applied case by case. His often naïve and vividly colored drawings, to the point where they sometimes look like those of a child, were meant to be more educational than practical because, when all is said and done, "if society has no form – how can architects build its counterform?"[436] And in the end not even the project for Frankfurt was realized and so at least in this is on the same footing as the *Ville-Spatiale*.

It was precisely this desire to communicate that constantly drove Friedman, and with him other architects of the time, to explore new means of communication in architecture such as graph theory or the diagram, in the service of a sociological approach to architecture.

---

[433] On the idea of the multi-level city, see SMITHSON, Alison and SMITHSON, Peter: *The Idea*, in id., *Ordinariness and Light. Urban Theories 1952–1960 and Their Application in a Building Project 1963–1970*, London, Faber & Faber, 1970, pp. 31–37.
[434] "Frankfurt-Römerberg comprises a megastructure that, for all the complexity and regularity of its grid, resolves the problem of the interface with the existing urban fabric in a remarkable way. [...] This megastructure is literally a city in miniature, which at its perimeter restores the contained urban space of the city in its most traditional sense." FRAMPTON, Kenneth: *The Generic Street as a Continuous Built Form*, in ANDERSON, Stanford (ed.): *On Streets*, Cambridge (MA), MIT Press, 1978, p. 331.
[435] Id., *Team 10, Plus...*, op. cit., p. 146.
[436] SMITHSON, Alison: *Team 10 Primer*, op. cit., p. 31.

YONA FRIEDMAN 42, BD PASTEUR, PARIS 15e - FON. 99-23
ANCIEN LECTEUR AUPRÈS DE LA FACULTÉ D'ARCHITECTURE DU H.T.I.

RESUME DU REFERAT A AMSTERDAM LE 15.12.62.

1)
Un gouvernement ne recherche jamais le bienêtre général. Il ne peut le vouloir: il peut s'imposer seulement quand il y a de difficultés. Le bienêtre général serait la fin de tout gouvernement, et de le chercher serait son suicide, si on se place sur le plan de l'égoisme.

2)
Tous les concepts administratifs existants (pouvoir, propriété) sont de fictions déguisant le simple fait de la malveillance de gouvernement en forme de "cadeaux moraux".
Par exemple: la propriété n'est pas un fait naturel, mais une excuse possible au meurtre de celui qui la violera (aucune loi naturelle n'est pourtant violée!)

3)
Nos idées préconçues, soigneusement conservées et conservatrices, ne nous laissent pas facilement renverser cet ordre des choses. Nous sommes trop habitués d'être commandés...

4) L
La technique nouvelle représente une percée possible dans cet état de fait. Techniquement parlant, il existe de la place, de la nourriture etc pour au moins 1000 fois plus d'individus, sans recourir au système de réservation meurtrière (comme la propriété etc).

5)
Les dirigeants se sont succédés nombre de fois depuis ceux qui ont construi nos lois et systèmes. Ils ne réalisent pas que les nouvelles applications techniques permettent renverser leurs (ou nos) systèmes.
Si, par exemple, nous proposions de diriger l'administration à l'aide de machines, les dirigeants penseraient que leur pouvoir est ainsi augmenté; mais en réalité les machines leur imposeront leur logique mathématique (qui peut être meilleure que celle des hommes) et les dirigeants perdront leurs avantages actuels.

6)
Notre tâche consiste à trouver quelle organisation technique et sociale pourra faire cette "révolution par la porte de derrière".

GEAM CONFERENCE IN AMSTERDAM, 1962

522 Yona Friedman: *Summary of Amsterdam Paper*, December 15.
523 Some participants, from left: Constant, Habraken, Hartsuyker, Trapman, Cammelbeeck. Published in van Schaik, Martin and Marcel, Otakar: *Exit Utopia: Architectural Provocations, 1956–1976*, New York/London, Prestel, 2004.

Yona Friedman, 42, bd Pasteur, Paris 15e – Fon. 99-23.
Former Member of the Faculty of Architecture of H.T.I.

1 / Government never seeks general well-being. It does not want that: It can only enforce its power when there are difficulties. General wellbeing will be the end of all government but its pursuit will be its suicide, if we place it on the level of selfishness.

2 / All the existing administrative concepts (power, property) are fictions disguising the simple fact of the government's malevolence as "moral gifts." For example: property is not a natural fact, but an excuse which makes possible the murder of those who violate it (and no natural law is violated!)

3 / Our preconceived ideas, carefully preserved, impede our ability to reverse this order of things. We are too used to taking orders.

4 / The new technology signifies a possible breakthrough in this state of affairs. Technically speaking, there is space, food, etc, for at least 1000 times more people, without recourse to the deadly system of reservation (as with property, etc.).

5 / Numerous leaders have succeeded one another since those who first made our laws and systems. They do not realize that the new applications of technology enable a reversal of their (or our) systems. If, for example, we proposed to direct the administration with the use of machines, the leaders would think that their power was thereby augmented; but in reality, machines would impose upon them their mathematical logic (which could be better than that of men) and the leaders would lose their current advantages.

6 / Our task is to find what technological and social organization could carry out this "revolution by the back door."

GEAM: list of the group's position

1 / Group for the Study of Mobile Architecture.
2 / 42 Bd. Pasteur, Paris, 15e, c/o Y. Friedman.
3 / 1957.
4 / International meeting in Rotterdam, regarding the lack of such a group.
5 / Founder: Y. Friedman, participants since the foundation: D. G. Emmerich (Paris), J. Trapman (Amsterdam), J. Soltan (Warsaw), C. Frieden (Luxembourg), R. Aujame (Kabul), G. Kühne (Berlin), G. Günschel (Hanover).
6 / Free and wide-ranging research on mobility in society; the consequences for housing.
8 / Active members: 30 architects in 10 countries participating and observing: 1,000 – 2,000 (exhibitions, lectures etc.) and publications in the country (over 100 publications and articles in 4 years).
9 / Honorary Secretary.
12 / Officially recognized by the International Union of Architects.

524

525

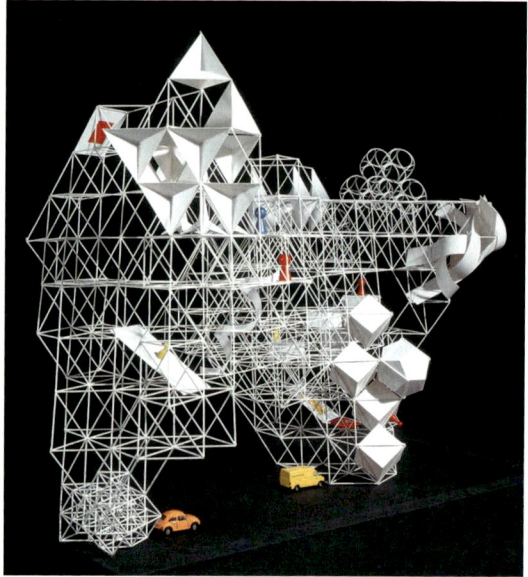

526

YVES KLEIN AND WERNER RUHNAU

524 *Gelsenkirchen Musiktheater,* 1958, from Ruhnau, Werner: *Space, Play and the Arts.* Paperback by Dorothee Lehmann-Kopp, Bazon Brock, Werner Ruhnau, Jovis, Mul (eds.), 2008.

"RAUMSTADT" MODELS, 1959

525 Eckhard Schulze-Fielitz: Portrait from *Metalanguage of Space,* by Schulze-Fielitz, Eckhard and Fiel, Wolfgand (eds.), New York/Vienna, Springer, 1961.
526 E. Schulze-Fielitz: *Raumstadt* model, in plastic, cardboard, metal, wood and paper. Photograph by Philippe Magnon.

527

528

529

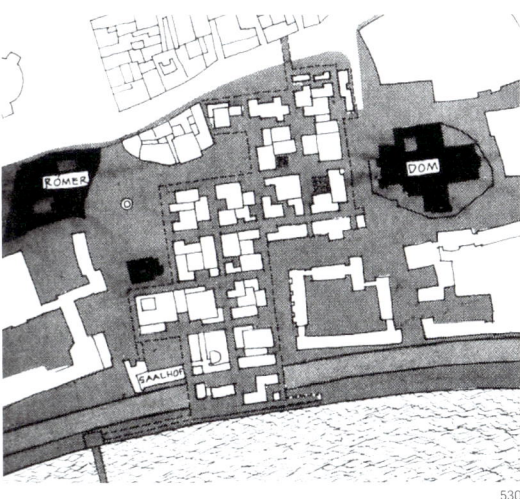

530

531

YONA FRIEDMAN AND ECKHARD SCHULZE-FIELITZ

527 At the *International Baukongress* in Grugahalle, Essen, Germany, June 1962. Photograph from *Bauwelt 26*, Berlin, 1962.

528 – 529 Yona Friedman: Interior view model of the *Bridge-Town*, 1962, and model of the *Bridge-Town across the English channel*, 1963. Both crafted by Eckhard Schulze-Fielitz.

GEORGES CANDILIS, ALEX JOSIC, SHADRACH WOODS, MANFRED SCHIEDHELM

530 – 531 *Frankfurt-Römerberg Project*, 1963. Plan and model, from Frampton, Kenneth: *The Generic Street as a Continous Built Form*, in Anderson, Stanford (ed.): *On Streets*, Cambridge (MA), MIT Press, 1978.

CONSTANT, DEBORD, LEFEBVRE

In the world of cultural decomposition we can test our strength but not employ it. The practical task of overcoming our discordance with the world, i.e., of surmounting the decomposition by some higher constructions, is not romantic. We will be "revolutionary romantics," in Lefebvre's sense, precisely to the degree of our failure.[437]
Guy Debord

Orthodox planning is much imbued with puritanical and Utopian conceptions of how people should spend their free time.[438]
Jane Jacobs

The Dutch painter Constant Nieuwenhuys was a key figure in European artistic and architectural culture in the fifties and sixties. He was in direct contact with a multitude of movements or isolated artists – CoBrA, the Lettrist International, the MIBI, the Situationist International, Team 10, the GEAM, etc.

Constant developed an interest in architecture through Aldo van Eyck, whom he met in 1947. After the disbanding of the group CoBrA to which he belonged in 1952, Constant became more and more involved with architecture[439] which, as we have just seen, also became a central theme of Situationism after 1956 thanks to the concept of Unitary Urbanism, of which it gave the following definition: "The theory of the combined use of arts and techniques as means contributing to the construction of a unified milieu in dynamic relation with experiments in behavior."[440] Constant was fairly dissatisfied with functionalism in city planning:

The total lack of alternatives involving play in the organization of social life prevents urbanism from attaining the level of creation, and the gloomy and sterile appearance of most modern neighborhoods is a shameful reminder of this.[441]

But he did believe in an evolution of the human species from *Homo sapiens* to *Homo ludens* in the sense that the Dutch sociologist Johan Huizinga, cited by Friedman too in *L'architecture mobile*, had given to this expression. In reality there was a marked difference between the condition of absolute diversion described by Constant and Friedman's conviction of a new centrality of free time ("loisir" or "amusement") in urban life. Friedman

---

[437] DEBORD, Guy: *Thèses sur la révolution culturelle*, in *Internationale Situationniste*, no. 1, June 1958. English transl., *Theses on Cultural Revolution*, available at Situationist International online, http://www.cddc.vt.edu/sionline/si/theses.html.
[438] JACOBS, Jane: *The Death and Life of Great American Cities*, op. cit., p. 83.
[439] BUCHLOH, Benjamin: *A Conversation with Constant*, in DE ZEGHER, Catherine and WIGLEY, Mark (eds.): *The Activist Drawing. Retracing Situationist Architectures from Constant's New Babylon to Beyond*, Cambridge (MA)/London, MIT Press, 2001, pp. 16–17.
[440] *Définitions*, in *Internationale Situationniste*, no. 1, June 1958. English transl., *Definitions*, available at Situationist International online, http://www.cddc.vt.edu/sionline/si/definitions.html.
[441] NIEUWENHUYS, Constant: *Le Grand Jeu à Venir*, in *Potlatch*, no. 30, July 1959, now in LAMBERT, Jean-Clarence: *New Babylon – Constant. Art et Utopie*, Paris, Cercle d'Art, 1997, p. 36. English transl., *The Great Game to Come*, in WIGLEY, Mark: *Constant's New Babylon: The Hyper-Architecture of Desire*, op. cit.

was more analytical and distinguished games into two groups: games of mimicry (theater, cinema, television and any other activity in which the spectator delegates his personality to actors according to Roger Caillois's definition,[442] cited only in passing) and creative play (do-it-yourself, Sunday painting). He went on to make it quite clear that a list of collective games had still to be compiled, but was needed in order to foresee the future of social behavior.[443] In any case at the beginning of the sixties *New Babylon* had become an icon of utopia, "a phalanstery for the love generation," and later "a totem for the architectural empowerment of the people."[444] In any case a vague shared feeling about play was spreading. Marshall McLuhan, who as we will see was in close contact with a number of eminent architects, wrote for example about the increase in free time:

We are suddenly threatened with a liberation that taxes our inner resources of self-employment and imaginative participation in society. This would seem to be a fate that calls men to the role of artist in society.[445]

On the other hand Constant focused almost exclusively on what in his eyes appeared to be a revolution, without giving adequate consideration to the fact that it was just a transformation of working conditions, thanks in part to the fierce union struggles of those years.[446] Yet there were some basic affinities between Friedman and Constant. For example the latter, quoting his friend the Marxist philosopher Henri Lefebvre, he described himself as a *utopian* and not a *utopist*: "It is necessary to distinguish utopists from utopians, that is abstract utopias from concrete utopias [...]. Utopist thinking explores the impossible, while utopian thought releases the possible."[447]

In reality, Constant was conscious from the outset of his incompatibility with the positivism of the architectural milieu of the GEAM, with which he came into direct contact between 1960 and 1961. In the Constant archives there are nine letters exchanged with Friedman, most of which date from the following year, when the GEAM met in Amsterdam shortly before its disbandment.[448]

Responding to the letter through which Friedman had made contact with him, Constant expressed his full agreement with Friedman's criticism of contemporary city planning's lag with respect to the economic and social evolution of the West (and in particular the advent of automation), but did not think that his *Mobile City* project offered innovative prospects; according to Constant, it remained a functional city:

---

442 CAILLOIS, Roger: *Les jeux et les hommes: le masque et le vertige*, Paris, Gallimard, 1958. English transl., *Man, Play and Games*, Champaign (IL), University of Illinois Press, 2001. It should be pointed out that Caillois also had a profound understanding of myth, which he saw as the place where the pressures of the individual psyche and those of communal social existence collide. See id., *Le mythe et l'homme*, Paris, Gallimard, 1938.
443 FRIEDMAN, Yona: *L'architecture mobile*, 4th ed., Paris, 1962, p. 7.
444 SADLER, Simon: *The Situationist City*, op. cit., p. 134.
445 McLUHAN, Marshall: *Understanding Media. The Extensions of Man*, New York, McGraw-Hill, 1964, p. 358.
446 The statute of workers' rights was signed, although in different forms, in the sixties.
447 Cited in LAMBERT, Jean-Clarence: *New Babylon ...*, op. cit., p. 7.
448 The letters are in the following order: April 10, 1961; April 24, 1961; March 28, 1962; August 2, 1962; August 27, 1962; November 11, 1962; November 24, 1962; August 1, 1964; plus one more and a postcard, both undated. In addition to the letters, the Constant archives at the Netherlands Institute for Art History in The Hague contain some of Friedman's writings: an article, *Réflexions sur l'architecture de l'avenir*, and two typescripts: *Une proposition: la théorie des systems compréhensibles* and *Réponses aux questions posées aux rencontres d'Amsterdam 1962*.

Your project doesn't completely deal with this social criticism. You continually accentuate private dwelling. You are evading a solution of collective life and a culture based on the game [...] a type of city completely different from today's functional city. It is not sufficient to transform the city in a technical or practical sense but above all in a social and cultural sense. The future city should not be accentuating dwelling (which is nothing but the opposition between inside and outside) nor displacement (search for needs), but a new use for social space (ecology).[449]

This criticism of Constant is fundamental because it highlights the decisive factor that would prevent him from adhering to the new architectural avant-garde of the sixties. If the Situationists, engaged in their challenge of history, had been able to dismiss Constant as a technocrat because he was too focused on the definition of the technical details of a city that could not be built, Constant could do the same with the projects of Friedman and company, seeing them as attempts to bring architecture up to date with developments in the capitalist system without questioning its foundations.

Constant would have driven these concepts home to Friedman on more than one occasion, such as the conference that the GEAM held on May 26, 1962, at the time of the exhibition in Amsterdam.[450]

Although Constant was not willing to be lumped with the megastructuralists, *New Babylon* was from that moment on regarded as one of the many projects of the architectural neo-avant-garde of those years, and the number of exhibitions on it around Europe multiplied in step with the degree of its formal complexity – what Wigley has defined as hyper-architecture.[451] Friedman's response to the criticisms of the Dutch artist was courteous, but firm: *New Babylon* was the vision of a "chef d'orchestre" who told the inhabitants of his city the way they should behave, something that in his view was unacceptable:

People could choose the direction of Constant and live together more collectively, but you cannot make this a prescription.[452]

The disagreement was ideological, not formal: perpetual play cannot be imposed on people, but only made possible by favoring mobility of dwelling and when all is said and done the voluntary adherence of the inhabitants because in general "play presupposes ritual, *collective participation* (even if temporary), awareness of the game itself."[453] On the contrary Constant, like the Situationists (especially the ex-Lettrists), designed his city for a society that was yet to come, post-revolutionary and not bourgeois but nomadic and without

---

449 Nieuwenhuys, Constant: *Letter from Constant to Yona Friedman*, April 10, 1961, quoted in Wigley, Mark: *Constant's New Babylon: The Hyper-Architecture of Desire*, op. cit. p. 40.
450 See *Réponses aux questions posées au rencontre d'Amsterdam 1962*, preserved at the NIAH in The Hague.
451 Confining our attention to exhibitions of scale models of *New Babylon* (which were accompanied by dozens of readings, catalogue texts, etc.) over the course of the sixties, we can list: in 1961, Bochum; in 1962, Amsterdam and Schiedam; in 1963, Amsterdam and Rotterdam; in 1964, Copenhagen, The Hague, Silkeborg, Krefeld; in 1965, Amsterdam, Rotterdam, Bern, Maastricht, The Hague; in 1966, Cologne, Den Bosch, Bern, Venice, Amsterdam; in 1967, Munich, Oslo; in 1968, Haarlem, Lund; in 1969, Amsterdam.
452 Yona Friedman, quoted in Wigley, Mark: *Constant's New Babylon* . . . , op. cit., p. 41.
453 Tafuri, Manfredo: *Le strutture del linguaggio nella storia dell'architettura moderna*, in *Teoria della progettazione architettonica*, with an introduction by Giuseppe Samonà, Bari, Dedalo, 1968, p. 29. The text is dated "Venice, February 18, 1966."

families; a *new city*, an alternative to the existing one and still a long way off: an authentic utopia, in the classical sense of the term (the island that is not there), or a *paternalistic utopia*, based that is only on the initiative of "someone who knows" – as Friedman would describe it in retrospect.[454]

My point of view was exactly the opposite: "I do not know." The initiatives are those of small, unknown people deciding themselves, of people who cannot express it by words: a real variety of small individual acts. In a way, Constant acts like a "maître de ballet," creating a very beautiful ballet invented exclusively by him. As for me, I do not intervene into what the real performers do. I don't even know what they do; for me, it is sufficient if they are satisfied. The difference between the ballet and the people in the street expresses our conceptual difference.[455]

Another significant point of disagreement was on the idea of city. In spite of some affinities like their being raised on great pillars, *New Babylon* and the *Ville-Spatiale* differ in one fundamental way: the former is a work of architecture set against a background cleared of other signs, as neutral as the canvas of a picture that has not been painted, while Friedman's projects are always set in the existing city, so that they can be described as an urban intensification of the city. In other words Constant, while disguising himself as an architect, remained a painter in his approach to planning. In this the Situationists were closer to Friedman than to their former Dutch associate, whom they reproached for a sort of flight from the existing city, as we will see shortly.

The foundation of Constant's theory is clearly Marxist, as is evident even from a perfunctory analysis of the terminology: "bourgeois society," "post-revolutionary culture," "slavery of the working masses," "socialization of the land and the means of production," etc.

Some of Constant's referents in the fifties and sixties were Marxists, like Lucius Burckhardt, editor of the magazine *Werk* that published *New Babylon* – as well as the *Ville-Spatiale* – in the issue devoted to "Mobile Architecture,"[456] and above all Henri Lefebvre, the Parisian philosopher close to Situationism, a movement from which he was ousted in 1962 after an intense alliance. Debord had been linked with Lefebvre since 1956, that is from the time when the Marxist philosopher had published *Vers un nouveau romantisme*.[457] Later Lefebvre was expelled from the IS for having misappropriated the fourteen Situationist points of *Sur la Commune*, in which the Paris Commune was described as "the biggest festival of the nineteenth century" (revolution as celebration would be a vital theme for the protests of 1968 in France), for a hostile magazine, *Arguments*,[458] but a certain rivalry between Lefebvre and

---

[454] "In the case of the paternalistic utopia, knowledge of the applicable technique belongs to a handful of individuals" and not the whole community. See Friedman, Yona: *Utopies réalisables*, op. cit., p. 23.
[455] Friedman, Yona: *Interview*, in Obrist, Hans-Ulrich: *Interviews*, vol. 1, op. cit., p. 239.
[456] Friedman, Yona: *Mobile Architektur*, in *Werk*, no. 2, February 1963, pp. 45–57.
[457] Lefebvre, Henri: *Vers un romantisme révolutionnaire*, in *Nouvelle Revue Française*, no. 59, October 1957; this article was later reworked and published by the author under the title *Vers un nouveau romantisme*, in *Introduction à la modernité. Preludes*, Paris, Minuit, 1962.
[458] Id., *La signification de la Commune*, in *Arguments*, no. 27–28, 2nd trimester, 1962. Later reprinted in id., *La proclamation de la Commune: 26 mars 1871*, Paris, Gallimard, 1965. The magazine *Arguments* was published between 1956 and 1962. From the outset its contributors were intellectuals who had left or were critical of the French Communist Party, including Roland Barthes, Edgar Morin, the Franco-Hungarian historian Ferenc Fejtö, Alain Touraine and Georges Perec, among many others.

Debord also carried a lot of weight.⁴⁵⁹ In fact the former mocked the Situationists, describing them as romantic advocates of an abstract utopia (the same charge that he would level against Friedman), while the latter responded that it was impossible pontificate about revolutionary practice from the height of a university chair. In any case over a period of six years Lefebvre and Debord went various times to the Netherlands – as did the GEAM – often to the Institute of Social History in Amsterdam, also frequented by Constant.⁴⁶⁰ In 1962 there was also a dispute between the entire Dutch group of former CIAM members and the Situationists over the publication, among many others, of a design for a church. Constant found himself in difficulty because he was a member of both groups, but in the end decided to resign from the Situationist International.⁴⁶¹ So Banham's claim that the Situationists had expelled Constant because he was aiming at a "bourgeois praxis" in a vision that was playful but proceeded from bricks and mortar and was closer to Habraken than to Debord is not true.⁴⁶² On the contrary not only did Debord try to persuade him to stay, but the real reason for Constant's leaving was the Situationists' total aversion to any form of aestheticism. In fact a process of purging was underway in the Situationist International, which wanted to distance itself from the world of art to make its revolutionary aims more credible. When five years later Debord finally provided the IS with a theory in his famous *La Société du spectacle*, he would write on the subject:

*As a negative movement which seeks the supersession of art in a historical society where history is not yet lived, art in the epoch of its dissolution is simultaneously an art of change and the pure expression of impossible change. The more grandiose its reach, the more its true realization is beyond it. This art is perforce avant-garde, and it is not. Its avant-garde is its disappearance. [...] The critical position later elaborated by the Situationists has shown that the suppression and the realization of art are inseparable aspects of a single supersession of art.*⁴⁶³

Logically, after Jorn and Gallizio, the turn had come of the last painter left in the group. Art hindered communication between individuals and was therefore defined as "anti-Situationist," and this meant the abandonment of the aesthetic practices that had characterized the group from its beginnings, *dérive*, psychogeography and unitary urbanism. In other words the shift in 1962 was from the "aesthetic" to the "political."
So Constant and Lefebvre started to associate more closely after 1962: both felt themselves to be "mavericks" (in 1962 Lefebvre also left the French Communist Party as he felt it to be too far to the right) and both were linked to an idea of "revolutionary romanticism" and Huizinga's *Homo ludens*.⁴⁶⁴

---
459 On the relationship between Debord and Lefebvre, see also Sadler, Simon: *The Situationist City*, op. cit., pp. 44–45.
460 Violeau, Jean-Louis: *A Critique of Architecture: the Bitter Victory of the Situationist International*, in Williams Goldhagen, Sarah and Legault, Réjean (eds.): *Anxious Modernisms* ..., op. cit., p. 255.
461 *Renseignements situationnistes*, in *Internationale Situationniste*, no. 5, 1962. The news of Constant's resignation ("Constant a choisi de quitter l'I.S.") was given at the same time as that of the expulsion of two other founders of the movement, Pinot Gallizio and Melanotte, not coincidentally also artists.
462 Banham, Reyner: *Megastructure. Urban Future of the Recent Past*, op. cit., p. 90.
463 Debord, Guy: *La société du spectacle*, Paris, Buchet/Chastel, 1967. English transl., *The Society of the Spectacle*, Detroit (MI), Black & Red, 2006. Also available online at http://www.marxists.org/reference/archive/debord/society.htm.
464 On the relations between Constant, Debord and Lefebvre, see Lefebvre, Henri: *Le temps des méprises*, Paris, Stock, 1975.

And in fact a few years later Lefebvre, whose cultural influence had increased greatly around 1968 thanks in part to the Utopie group[465] that he supported, echoed Constant's criticism of Friedman, accusing him of hedonism:

The enthusiasm for the ephemeral and nomadic, the fascination with incessant departures, will supplant the earlier sense of rootedness in the home, the traditional attachment to the place of birth. What do human beings want? Shelter. No matter where it is. Yona Friedman has built portable structures and units (boxes) that can be joined together to create one or more rooms of different sizes, ephemeral groupings. From this perspective, we could generalize and democratize the luxury life of millionaires, who move from home to home, villa to villa, or yacht to yacht. Which exposes them to the pleasures of the world. Or so it seems. Whether from above or from below this would be the end of both habiting and the urban as sites of bundled opposition, as centers.[466]

Lefebvre, following in the footsteps of Vaneigem,[467] trivialized the concept of mobility in a specious manner: obviously he had not read or was pretending not to have read *L'architecture mobile*. For Lefebvre being able to decide on the size of your house was a luxury and he mistook Friedman's structures for an enormous set of second homes, for vacations. But it was really the reflection of a top-down approach: people were not capable of making decisions for themselves, it was necessary for someone else to determine their fate (like Constant) since allowing them to satisfy their desires in housing might lead to a wrong style of life, i.e. a "luxurious" one. In particular the Utopie group formed by Lefebvre's most loyal followers – Jean Aubert, Isabelle Auricoste, Jean Baudrillard, Catherine Cot, Jean-Paul Jungmann, René Lourau, Antoine Stinco and Hubert Tonka – took it upon themselves to apply his thinking in the realm of architecture.[468] The result was an uninspired and vague reworking of the ideas of Constant, Debord or the other, minor Situationists: urban society was maimed and alienated, and a permanently playful and festive consumption of city life was required. So the constructed city was obsolete and in any case ephemeral. Hence it would have to change because it was life that in the last analysis needed to change. Urban planning was only a tool of the repression to which the city was subject and had to be rejected entirely, etc.[469]

---

[465] The group was set up in 1966 and published a magazine of the same name. See *Utopie*, no. 1, May 1967. Its members included some of Lefebvre's assistants at the university (Hubert Tonka, later a publisher, the philosopher Jean Baudrillard and René Lourau).
[466] Lefebvre, Henri: *La révolution urbaine*, Paris, Gallimard, 1970. English transl., *The Urban Revolution*, Minneapolis (MN), University of Minnesota Press, 2003, p. 95.
[467] "It appears that the working class no longer exists. Today, many ex-proletarians can have access to the comfort formerly reserved for a minority: so goes the familiar tune. But isn't it rather an increasing quantity of comfort which gives them an itch to make demands?" Vaneigem, Raoul: *Comments against Urbanism*, op. cit.
[468] See the section *Sociologie et critique radicale*, in Lucan, Jacques: *Architecture en France (1940–2000). Histoire et theories*, Paris, Le Moniteur, 2001, pp. 195–96.
[469] Baudrillard, Jean: *Le ludique et le policier et autres textes parus dans Utopie (1967–1978)*, Paris, Sens & Tonka, 2001. Compare this with Debord's statement: "Urbanism is capitalism's seizure of the natural and human environment; developing logically into absolute domination, capitalism can and must now remake the totality of space into its own setting." In id., Chapter 7, "The Organization of Territory," in *The Society of the Spectacle*, op. cit. On the application of Situationist ideas in architecture, also see Violeau, Jean-Louis: *Situations construites 1952–1968*, Paris, Sens & Tonka, 1998.

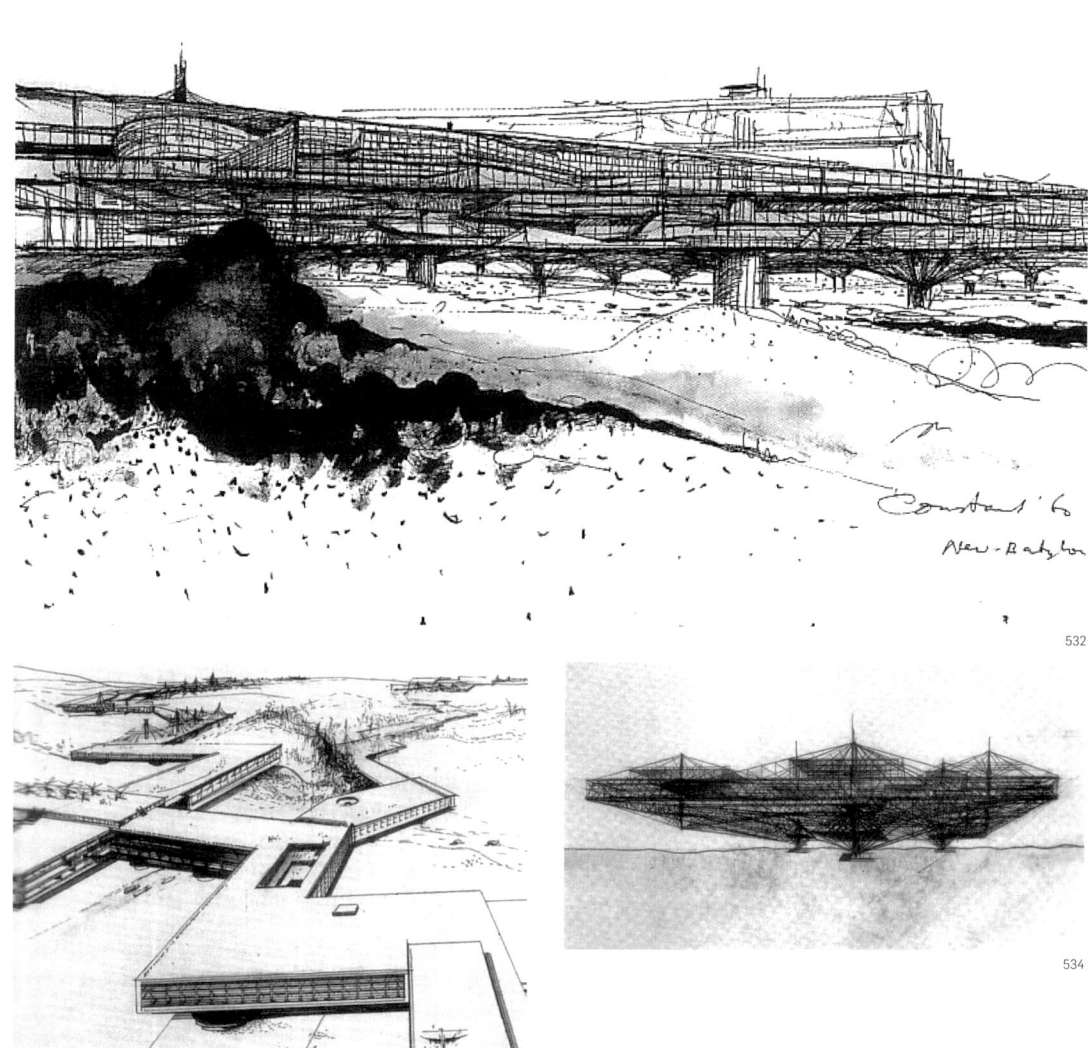

CONSTANT: NEW BABYLON

532 *View of a Sector*, drawing, 1960.
533 – 534 Two projects of *New Babylon*, from 1964. Perspective showing its expanse against a neutral landscape and view of *New Babylon* without context.
535 *The Ruhr Valley*, 1963. Drawing on map, scale 1:200,000.

Published in WIGLEY, Mark: *Constant's / New Babylon: The Hyper-Architecture of Desire*, Rotterdam, Witte de With Center for Contemporary Art/010 Publishers, 1998.

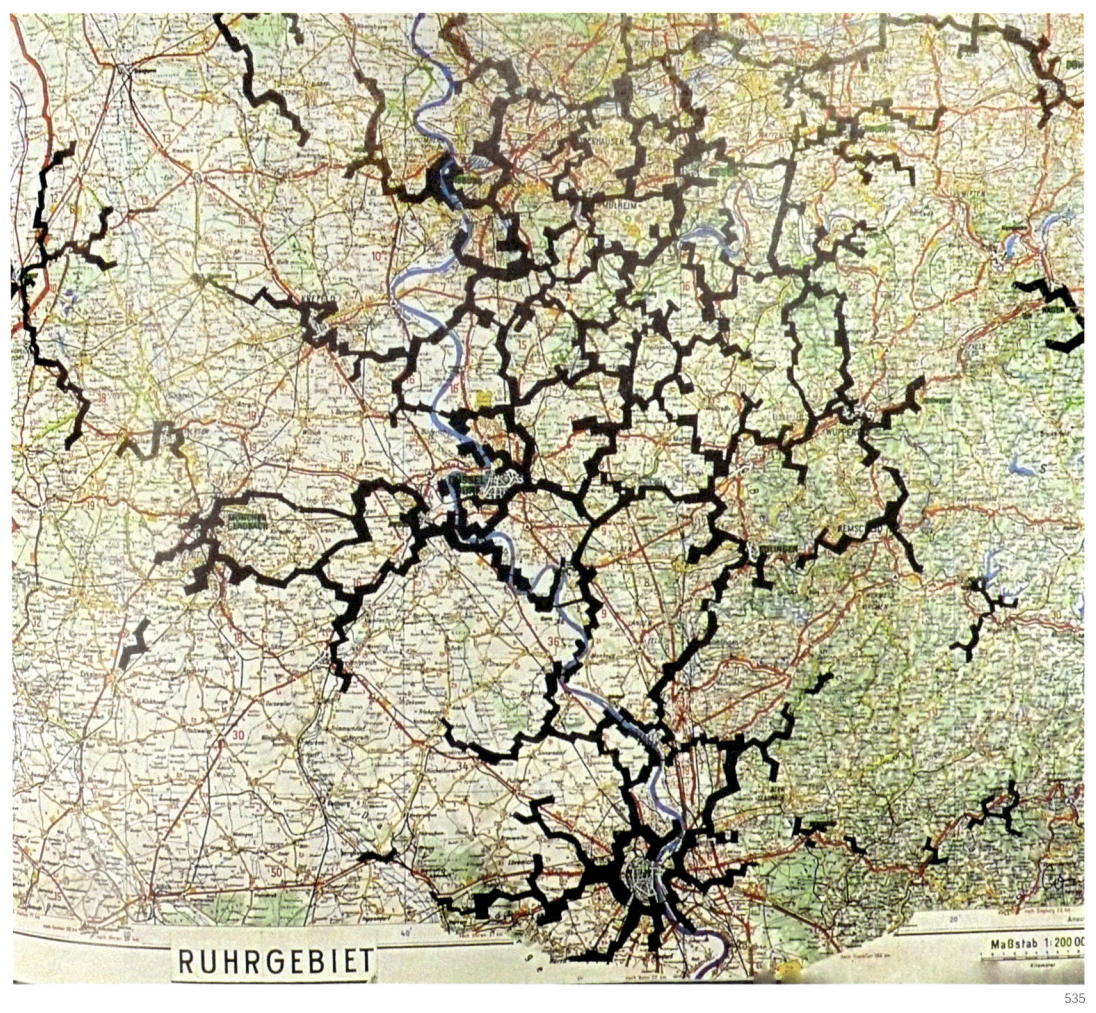

536

537

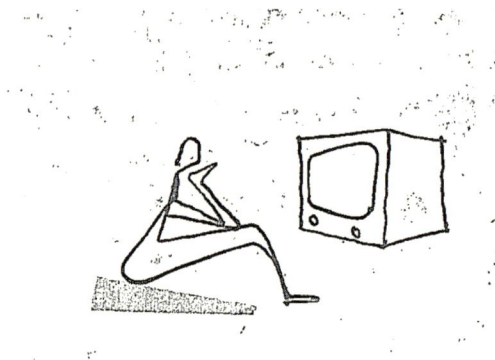

538

539

YONA FRIEDMAN AND CONSTANT NIEUWENHUYS

536 At the GEAM Conference, Amsterdam, May 1962. Published in van Schaik, Martin and Macel, Otakar: *Exit Utopia: Architectural Provocations, 1956–1976*, New York/London, Prestel, 2004.

537 Lefebvre, Henri: *La révolution urbaine*, Paris, Gallimard, 1970.

"LA SOCIÉTÉ DU SPECTACLE"

538 – 539 Yona Friedman: Sketch from the second duplicated edition of *L'architecture mobile*, 1958; and *Reckless Advertising*, from the *Situationist International Journal*, no. 8, 1963.

"AGGLOMÉRATIONS SPATIALES"

540 Yona Friedman: *Capacity ratio between spatial clusters and current clusters*, 1958.

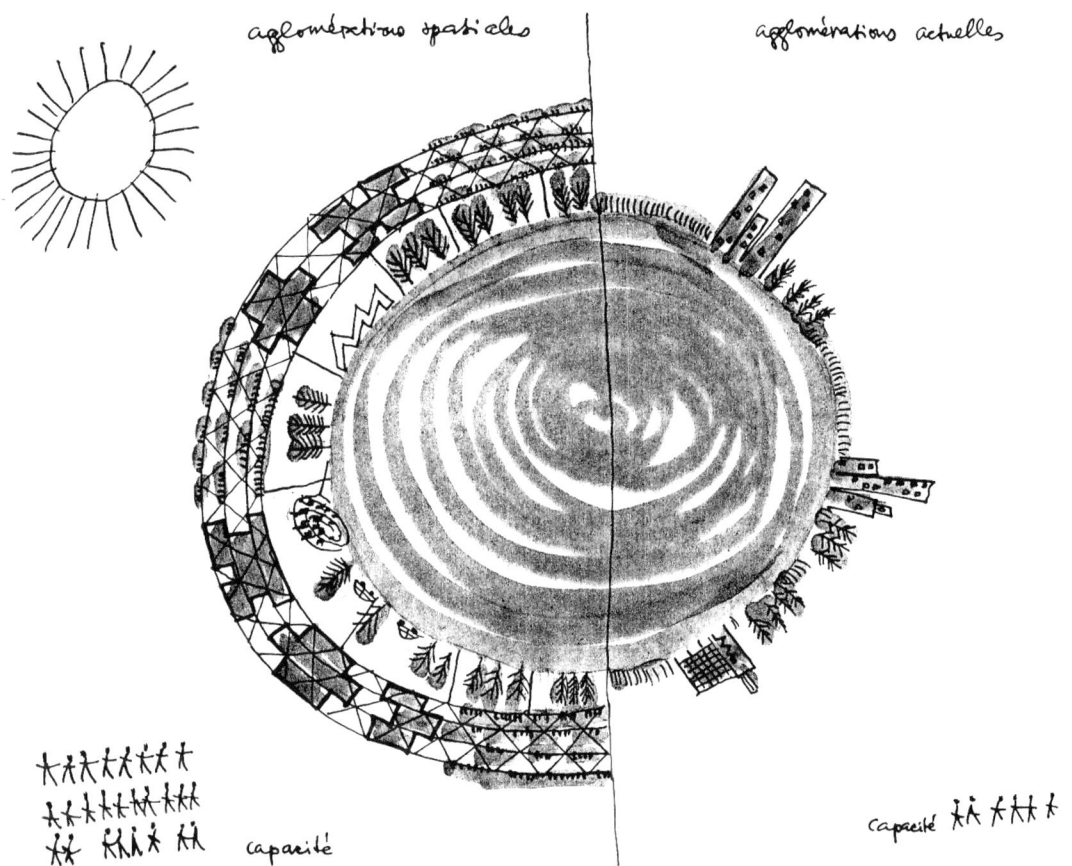

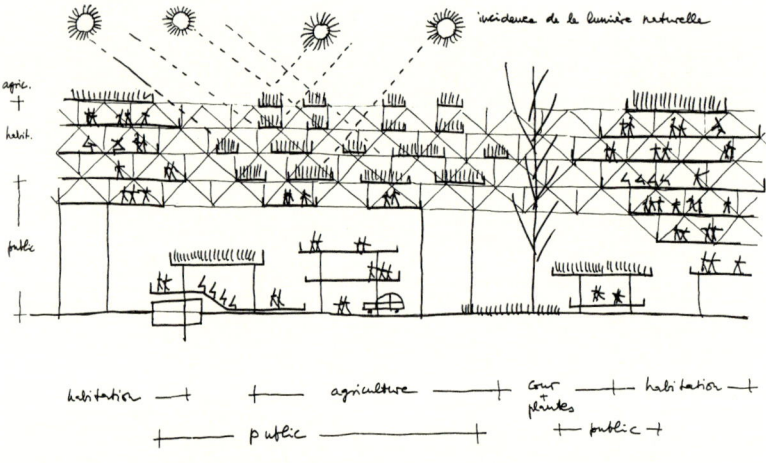

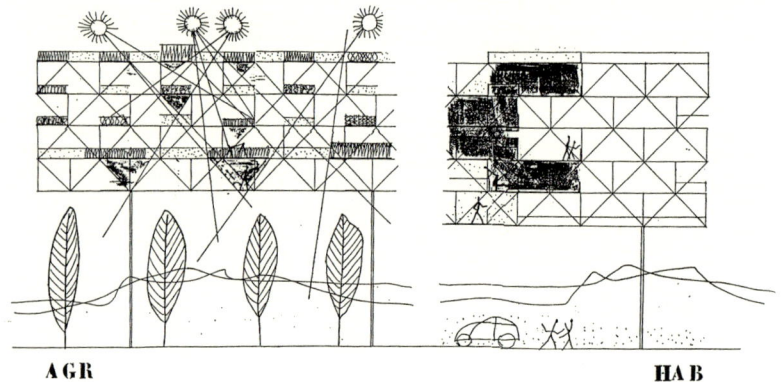

SPATIAL CLUSTERS AND URBAN FARMING

541 Yona Friedman: *L'agglomération spatiale*. Sectional studies of the incidence of natural light to favor urban farming, 1958.
542 Yona Friedman: *Spatial clusters for 10,000 inhabitants*, 1958.
543 Yona Friedman: *Spatial clusters for 7 millions inhabitants*, 1961.

Spatial clusters.
Availability for urban life and for agriculture.
A spatial cluster the size of Paris could house and feed 7 million inhabitants.

1964: THE YEAR OF THE MEGASTRUCTURE

Friedman in fact has been the Daddy of the megastructure which can move across any kind of terrain.[470]
Peter Cook

Dominique Rouillard has set the term "megastructure" in a historical perspective, identifying Peter Smithson as the first architect to have used it[471] in connection with Kenzo Tange's plan for Tokyo (1960), where a chain formed of enormous concrete rings stretched across the bay, linking the two shores.[472] Smithson's article was published in 1964, but antedated to May 15, 1962. In his book devoted to this subject Reyner Banham attributes its first use instead to Fumihiko Maki, initially a member of the Metabolists and a teacher at Harvard, but points out that the term had already been in the air for a couple of years. Tange, Maki, Metabolism: Japan was in any case a cradle of the idea of megastructure, developed in parallel – if not under the direct influence – to *Urbanisme spatial*, as we have already seen in part. The stir caused by the debate underway in Tokyo around the time of the World Design Conference (May 1960) was enormous, to the point where Banham was prompted to write about a "Japonization of world architecture."[473] Moreover, there was a grave shortage of housing in the land of the rising sun, still at grips with a difficult process of material and social reconstruction, and planners were looking for radical solutions. This shortage explained at least in part the leap in scale in the projects of young Japanese architects, which kept pace with and even went well beyond the proposals of the GEAM. For his part Tange, a highly influential figure who had attended the CIAM since 1951 (but was not present in Dubrovnik) and had been professor of urban design at the MIT in 1959-60,[474] on the one hand supported them and on the other tried to get them to take a more scientific approach, as is evident from his early disassociation from Isozaki's Metabolists.[475] Metabolism retained a basic affinity with *L'architecture mobile*, although with different origins: the conception of society as a living form in continual evolution, and thus unpredictable, was perfectly in keeping with the traditional Buddhist idea of the transmigration of souls

---

470 Cook, Peter: *Experimental Architecture*, London, Studio Vista, 1970, p. 104.
471 Rouillard, Dominique: *Superarchitecture . . .* , op. cit., p. 14.
472 Smithson, Peter: *Reflections on Kenzo Tange's Tokyo Bay Plan*, in *Architectural Design*, October 1964. See Tange, Kenzo: *A Plan for Tokyo, 1960. Toward A Structural Reorganization*, Tokyo, Shinkenchikusha, 1961. For Tange the organization comes from "the invisible *communication network* brought about by the technological revolution, and is an open organization in which it is possible to make any combination of functions with functions, of functions with people, of people with people . . . . Thanks to an organization of this kind the individual functions are grouped so as to form the overall function of a metropolis with ten million inhabitants." (The italics are mine.) Id., *Un piano per Tokyo*, in *Casabella continuità*, no. 258, 1961, p. 7, introduced by Grassi, Giorgio: *La città come prestazione vitale*, ibid., p. 5.
473 Banham, Reyner: *The Japonization of World Architecture*, in id., Suzuki, Hiroyuki and Kobayashi, Katsuhiro (eds.): *Contemporary Architecture of Japan 1958–1984*, New York, Rizzoli International, 1985, pp. 18 ff.
474 Tange, Kenzo: *Recollections*, in id., *Architecture and Urban Design 1946–1996*, ed. by Massimo Bettinotti, Milan, Electa, 1996, pp. 36–37.
475 Tange shared the GEAM's interest in the theme of mobility, as he declared in the paper he read at the World Design Conference, stating that mobility was the first problem of human settlement and involved the rapid development of technology. Id., *Technology and Humanity*, in *The Japan Architect*, October 1960. See also the personal memoirs of Isozaki, Arata: *La mia architettura*, in id., *Opere e progetti*, Milan, Electa, 1994, pp. 33–43. According to Isozaki, who quickly distanced himself from the Metabolists, there was no sense in trying to foresee future changes in design: "It is not up to the architect to talk about the future of his work." Also see id., *Japan-ness in Architecture*, ed. by David B. Stewart, Cambridge (MA)/London, MIT Press, 2006, pp. 62–65.

– the transitory nature of all things – but for Kurokawa and his companions this idea also had to condition in a consistent way architectural composition and above all city planning.[476] In other words, it was the city that had to adapt to the new requirements of individuals, and not the other way round.[477] Friedman and the Metabolists had something else in common, the disapproval of a very young Italian critic, Manfredo Tafuri. The charge that he leveled against the Japanese projects in 1964 was the same as the accusation he would later make against Friedman:

In both the formulation of their proposals and in the wording of their theoretical justifications, the young architects of the "Metabolism" group, while displaying a remarkable vitality and a sincere enthusiasm for solutions of a new kind, remain trapped in an overly generic and mannered avant-gardism, where great sociological and human problems are tackled in such an abstract and metaphorical dimension that they lose all track of possible methodological development: lacking, as a consequence, precisely that edge and incisiveness to which the utopian nature of their proposals clearly aspires.[478]

Criticisms that would soon be directed at the GEAM and the "International of Utopia" as well, but the differences between Friedman and the Metabolists are many. For example, in contrast to the majority of the protagonists of Banham's book, and contradicting the statement of Peter Cook quoted above, Friedman never fully accepted that the series of *Ville-Spatiale* projects should be included in the category of megastructures because these always envisaged a total planning of the built environment and were not always applied to specific urban contexts. It is no coincidence that Larry Busbea, author of the only in-depth study of the architectural and urbanistic milieu that turned around Friedman in the Sixties in France, chose another term as the title of his book, *Topologies*.

But let us take things in order: 1964 was the "mega-year" in which the term caught on in the US, Europe and Japan, thanks in part to the fact that several prototypes of megastructure were under construction.[479] The first English edition of Banham's book came out in 1976, but in a series of four lectures given in Naples in 1973 the British historian had already hinted at the death of the megastructure, specifying its four fundamental characteristics:

1. construction according to a modular scheme;
2. unlimited possibilities of growth;
3. structural framework in which smaller units are inserted;
4. longer duration of the main framework than the smaller units.

---

476 Guiheux, Alain: *Kisho Kurokawa architecte: le metabolisme 1960–1975*, Paris, Editions du Centre Pompidou, 1997. On the relations between the Metabolists and Team 10, see Kurokawa, Kisho: *Metabolism in Architecture*, with an introduction by Charles Jencks, London, Studio Vista, 1977, pp. 22–25.
477 "The state of confusion and paralysis in metropolitan areas is forcing us to make these proposals [...]. The huge city of Tokyo is diseased. She is even trying to conceal her illness and to justify present conditions by relying on the adaptability of her inhabitants." Kurokawa, Kisho, in Kawazoe Noboru: *Metabolism*, 1960, op. cit., pp. 6 ff.
478 Tafuri, Manfredo: *L'architettura moderna in Giappone*, Bologna, Cappelli, 1964, pp. 137–38.
479 Banham, Reyner: *Megastructure. Urban Future of the Recent Past*, op. cit., pp. 75 ff.

The lectures had been organized in more or less chronological order, but excluding the projects of Friedman and the Metabolists – and of their Italian followers.[480]

According to Rouillard, on the other hand, everything had already been said on the principles of the megastructure between 1958 and 1962 by Friedman, Constant and the Metabolists.[481] In May 1963 Banham, notwithstanding his ironic tone, still looked at the proposals of *Urbanism spatial* for Paris (associated with those of Constant and Schulze-Fielitz) with the attitude of someone who does not rule out any possibility, noting the favor and general interest they had won in the mass media.[482] According to him the Parisian authorities –thanks to the Herbé plan – took seriously the idea of erecting a gigantic "space-frame" above the French capital to solve the problems of congestion and traffic.

Reviewing Banham's book, however, Alan Colquhoun criticized it because on the one hand it had given too broad a meaning to "megastructure," failing to distinguish the first type in which the supporting structure was a neutral grid, as in the projects of Friedman and Woods, from the second in which the supporting structure was given a monumental character, as in the projects of the Metabolists or Archigram. In addition, Colquhoun rebuked Banham for having supinely accepted that the phenomenon was a passing fashion, thereby renouncing any attempt to explain the exact reasons for its disappearance.[483] Perhaps these reasons need to be sought in a wider context.

In the sixties communication science was in its infancy, just beginning to acquire the status of a discipline. It was in the "mega-year" that Marshall McLuhan published his most famous book, the one in which he stated that the "medium is the message." One passage in particular helps us to understand the general climate of hope and confidence in this type of structure:

What we are considering here, however, are the psychic and social consequences of the designs or patterns as they amplify or accelerate existing processes. For the "message" of any medium or technology is the change of scale or pace or pattern that it introduces into human affairs. The railway did not introduce movement or transportation or wheel or road into human society, but it accelerated and enlarged the scale of previous human functions, creating totally new kinds of cities and new kinds of work and leisure.[484]

So the megastructure was viewed as a means of changing society, the city and ultimately the world, which by now was just a "global village."

All the megastructuralists were intent on proposing projects that would offer decisive solutions, often disconnected from any material requirement, that can in a sense be regarded as graphic accentuations of evolutionary processes thought to be underway in society at the time, in complete accord with the above passage from McLuhan's work. In other words, the designs of megastructures were not just proposals on a larger scale conceived simply to meet

---

[480] Banham, Reyner: *La megastruttura è morta*, in *Casabella*, no. 375, March 1973, p. 2.
[481] Rouillard, Dominique: *Superarchitecture...*, op. cit., p. 15.
[482] Banham, Reyner: *Friedman's Europe*, in *Architectural Review*, no. 795, May 1963, p. 307.
[483] Colquhoun, Alan: *Frames to Frameworks. Changes in Architectural Thinking*, in *Encounter*, April 1977, pp. 41–49.
[484] McLuhan, Marshall: *Understanding Media. The Extensions of Man*, op. cit., pp. 23–24.

new needs, but attempts to modify human relations and in the end patterns of social behavior. In this connection Rouillard has rightly pointed out that, in Friedman's case too, the megastructure set out to generate the city and the organization of the territory no longer from the *human scale* so dear to the old CIAM, but from the psychological dimension of the individual.[485]

In addition, the concern for connection, the emphasis placed on bridge structures (perhaps the epitome of the connection) of which the early modernists had been so fond,[486] was in many architects an expression of the desire to intervene on a scale that went beyond the traditional urban one and in the direction of a single global city.

After the breakup of the GEAM, the dimensions of Friedman's projects became even greater: the span-over blocks expanded, turning into bridge cities, over the English Channel, over the Strait of Sicily, etc. Moreover: locating a bridge city at each of the world's principal straits (from Behring to Gibraltar, etc.) would allow rail and road networks to be joined up and the fusion of the continents into a single one, a new Pangaea. An even grander project than this would be imagined just a few years later by Superstudio in the *Continuous Monument* (1969) and the film *Interplanetary Architecture* (1970-71), but these were genuine paradoxes and not megastructures, metaphorical hyper-structures that mocked the megalomania of much of architectural culture.[487]

Of course the idea of a great inhabited bridge has its archetype in Le Corbusier's *Plan Obus* for Algiers (1931), with an expressway running along the top, and another version can be found in Bakema and van den Broek's project for Tel Aviv (1963), where the "freeway spine" ran through the city to impose order on its urban sprawl.[488] But Friedman's bridge cities were conceived in a different way: starting from the observation that since every bridge is a point of point of intersection of different flows of traffic (waterborne and land-based), it naturally generates trading places and therefore attracts other kinds of activity as well. Historical examples include the Pont Neuf in Paris, the Rialto in Venice and the Ponte Vecchio in Florence: the latter was used by Banham as one of the first illustrations of his book on megastructure. Bridges on a grand scale set in particular contexts like that of the Strait of Sicily can therefore become something more than a pure service structure, turning into entire cities: "they contain not just the transit routes, but the basic spaces of a city: public premises, industry, commerce, housing, etc."[489] In 1963 Friedman proposed a specific example of a bridge city across the English Channel, linking London and Paris, raised on pillars and with spans of around sixty meters.[490] Bridge cities were "bridges with a

---

485 ROUILLARD, Dominique: *Superarchitecture...*, op. cit., p. 100.

486 "In this emblematic figure – the bridge – 'division' and 'connection' hold a dialogue, as happens on the other hand in a 'negative' manner in the modes of metropolitan socialization." DAL CO, Francesco: *Abitare nel moderno*, Rome/Bari, Laterza, 1982, p. 49.

487 LANG, Peter and MENKING, William: *Superstudio: Life without Objects*, Milan, Skira, 2003. To the impossible, at times caricatural projects of Superstudio (1966-73) we will have to return, but it is certain that their polemic tone was also directed against some of the professors at Florence University like Leonardo Ricci's author project entitled *Megastructure for an Integrated City* (1966), later reformulated during the period he spent teaching in the US as *Macrostructure for Miami* (1970), with the advice of Riccardo Morandi. See RICCI, Leonardo: *Testi, opere, sette progetti recenti di Leonardo Ricci*, ed. by A. Nardi, Pistoia, Edizioni del Comune di Pistoia, 1990, p. 50.

488 FRAMPTON, Kenneth: *Modern Architecture: A Critical History*, op. cit., p. 274; see BAKEMA, Jaap B.: *Thoughts about Architecture*, ed. by Marianne Gray, London, Academy Editions, 1981.

489 FRIEDMAN, Yona: *Les villes-ponts*, in *Techniques et architecture*, no. 3, series 23, 1963.

490 Id., *Ports on Channel Bridge*, in *Architectural Design*, no. 4, April 1963, pp. 158-59.

containing structure" and in the final analysis the supreme application of the concept of mixed use as well as an implicit criticism of zoning, in a special case in which congestion would be guaranteed by their nature as set places of passage – an example of *Bigness* ahead of its time. In short, it was not just an innovative conception of the bridge, which historically is the natural location for urban congestion in river cities,[491] and in any case the idea of a modern inhabited bridge had already been outlined in 1958 by Paolo Soleri in a competition for Luxembourg, although on a medium to small scale.[492] The bridge city, however, was a much more ambitious project and at one and the same time an application of *urbanisme spatial* and an evolution of Friedman's project for Monaco (1959), where a continuous building was suspended on great piles – in which the plant was concentrated – arranged on the wharves of the harbor to link the two shores as a response to the problems posed by urban growth in the principality – hemmed in by an unfavorable conformation of the mountains. So Friedman proposed an expansion onto the water, a solution that among other things anticipated Kenzo Tange's plan – much more complex, but formed of a chain of rings with different functions – for Tokyo Bay by a year, as well as Maurizio Sacripanti's for the Strait of Messina (1965) and many others.[493] Two Italian architects stand out for the boldness of their proposals: throughout the sixties Soleri would design ever larger bridges, culminating in a linear bridge city called *Stonebow* (1969),[494] while Luigi Pellegrin came up with *Habitat Vectors on a Geographical Scale* (1970) raised on vertical supports, presented in a series of photomontages in which only the background changed, from the Sahara Desert to the Great Wall of China.[495]

Further increasing the scale, Friedman posed himself the problem of territorial expansion of the city in accordance with his cardinal principle of self-determination. The network of European rail links, the most extensive and oldest in the world, generated what he dubbed the *Continent-City*, blocked out in 1962 in the fourth edition of *L'architecture mobile*, where it appears as the last illustration but one. It ought to be said that the city-continent is perhaps the most realistic and at the same time idealistic proposal ever put forward by Friedman: Europe as a network of cities instead of nation states, already *de facto* in existence since the expansion of the railroad system in the middle of the 19th century

---

[491] "Fixed route, place of multiple interests, abounding in juridical, fiscal, visual and symbolic values, in the big river cities it serves in the first instance as a connection between two settlements developed on opposite banks; it identifies an intersection, sometimes a possibilty of interference, or an opportunity for contact, between pedestrian and waterborne traffic. Often in the great 'market places' it is exploited directly [...] for commercial ends; in fact activities of this kind derive an undoubted advantage from the location on a route of transit." CALABI, Donatella: *Il mercato e la città. Piazze, strade, architettura d'Europa in età moderna*, Venice, Marsilio, 1993, p. 52. The case studies examined here, including the three aforementioned bridges, are from the period between the 15th and 17th century.

[492] Soleri proposed seven types of multifunctional bridges: in the Omega bridge he placed the residences in the part above the road level, while offices and workshops were located in the lower part. See *Tomorrow's Bridge*, in *The Saturday Evening Post*, March 23, 1957; *Highway Sculptures: the Fantastic Bridges of Paolo Soleri*, in *The Architectural Forum*, no. 119, October 1963, pp. 84–87; PERSITZ, A.: *Les ponts de Paolo Soleri*, in *L'Architecture d'aujourd'hui*, October–November 1963, pp. 68–71. It should be noted that Soleri's bridges became known only after the publication of Friedman's (the first in April, see note 71).

[493] *Progetto per una città-ponte sullo Stretto, Messina*, in NERI, Maria Luisa and THERMES, Laura (ed.): *Maurizio Sacripanti. Maestro di architettura 1916–1986*, monographic issue of the magazine *Bollettino della Biblioteca della Facoltà di Architettura dell'Università degli Studi di Roma La Sapienza*, no. 58/9, 1998, p. 75. Also see PICON, Antoine and PICON-LEFEBVRE, Virginia: *Le megastrutture e i ponti abitati negli anni Cinquanta-Settanta*, in *Rassegna*, no. 48, December 1991, p. 54.

[494] LIMA, Antonietta Iolanda: *Soleri. Architettura come ecologia umana*, Milan, Jaca Book, 2000, p. 199.

[495] PELLEGRIN, Luigi: *Un percorso nel potenziare il mestiere del costruire*, Milan, Silvana, 2003, pp. 150 ff.

– Great Britain was to be connected to it by a bridge city over the Channel.[496] So this project represented an effort to move Europe in a supranational and antinationalistic direction, i.e. toward a free circulation of people and goods, in full accord with the basically anarchic vision of the architect, born a Hungarian (1923), become an Israeli (1948) and on the point of taking up his third nationality, the French one (1964).

In the *Continent-City* the existing network of rail transport, made up of a set of links (from 100 to 200 km in length) between the main cities, allowed the portions of territory excluded to remain agricultural and serve as hinterlands for the city-nodes of the network. Such a set of cities can even be considered to be a city in itself, a network in which the cities correspond to the nodes and their agricultural hinterlands to the meshes. The city-continent is a solution that permits the presence of the hinterland within the city-continent itself. Farmland, wildlife sanctuaries and natural resources are part of this new urban fabric and make the city-continent a self-sufficient entity and an alternative to the megalopolis of Africa or Asia, which on the contrary is an "agglomeration of suburbs" from which people never emerge during the day. It was not an unprecedented idea: the studies carried out at the beginning of the thirties by the geographer Walter Christaller on the cities of Southern Germany – a predominantly agricultural region – postulated the existence of a network of cities ("system of central places") and hinterlands connected with them ("complementary territories"); the mesh of this network was not fortuitous owing to a regularity in the dispersion and hierarchies of the urban centers.[497] However, this was an idea with which the majority of architects were still unfamiliar. Some of those who did know about it were fascinated, although for reasons that were not scientific, but aesthetic. For example Soleri, "desert messiah of architecture" as Banham sarcastically described him, based in the small town of Cosanti, in Arizona, was preaching that humanity should gather in a few concentrated structures and leave the surrounding land free, but his motivations were largely environmental.[498] His later project of *Arcosanti* – a city for twenty-five thousand inhabitants in a single enormous building was derived from this principle of settlement. Christian Norberg-Schulz was also inspired by a certain environmental vision – in no way in conflict with his conservative approach in architecture – and the city-continent was an extreme extension of his concept of scattered concentration, that in his view was the only possible way of preserving the integrity of nature, avoiding its breakup into isolated fragments. In this way the landscape would regain its continuity and its character as background to the works of man. So the *Continent-City* idea essentially intended to restore a structure of settlement that was normal in Europe up until the 19th century, although now on a different scale, proportionate to the needs and possibilities of our time.[499]

---

496 Friedman, Yona: *Infrastrutture possibili*, in *Casabella*, no. 297, September 1965, pp. 44–47.
497 Christaller, Walter: *Die zentralen Orte in Süddeutschland. Eine ökonomisch-geographische Untersuchung über die Gesetzmässigkeit der Verbreitung und Entwicklung der Siedlungen mit städtischer Funktion*, Jena, 1933; rpt. Darmstadt, Wissenschaftliche Buchgesellschaft, 1968. English transl., *Central Places in Southern Germany*, Upper Saddle River (NJ), Prentice Hall, 1966.
498 Banham, Reyner: *Scenes in America Deserta*, Layton (UT), Gibbs M. Smiths, 1982, p. 81.
499 Norberg-Schulz, Christian: *Existence, Space and Architecture*, New York, Praeger, 1971.

Norberg-Schulz extended this unexpected appreciation to the projects of the *Ville-Spatiale* series as well, because they did not contravene his idea of *genius loci* as they were always laid on top of part of the existing city, preserved in its entirety under the great piles. Over the years Friedman has developed his ideas about the *Continent-City* further, thanks in part to his firsthand experience of the chronic problems facing the great Asian and African cities through his work for the UN. He has more recently expressed the opinion that Europe, and more precisely the European Union, by expanding gradually to the east, is finally taking on the appearance of the first *Continent-City*: a network of cities that is expanding while preserving the agricultural areas within it. "Farmland is part of the city, filling its interstices; agriculture is becoming urban."[500] Today, however, the megastructure is absent from this prospect.

In the second half of the sixties the theme of megastructure gradually faded away, its place taken by other concerns, such as the return of values that the postwar reconstruction had put aside, such as that of collective memory. Perhaps the epitaph of the megastructure was written in 1972 by Robert Venturi, Denise Scott Brown and Steven Izenour, who in one of the most uncompromising but effective passages in *Learning from Las Vegas*, declared:

Recent Modern architecture has achieved formalism while rejecting form, promoted expressionism while ignoring ornament, and deified space while rejecting symbols. […] The megastructure has been promoted by the elaborate journalism of groups such as Archigram who reject architecture but whose urban visions and mural-scale graphics go beyond the last, megalomaniac gasps of the late Beaux-Arts delineators. Unlike urban sprawl architecture, megastructures lend themselves to total design and to extremely beautiful models, significantly impressive in the boardrooms of cultural foundations or in the pages of Time magazine but unrelated to anything achievable or desirable in the present social or technical context.[501]

At the same time, however, the architects from Philadelphia identified total design as one of the flaws that explained at least in part why no megastructure had yet been built:

Total design is the opposite of the incremental city that grows through the decisions of many: total design conceives a messianic role for the architect as corrector of the mess of urban sprawl; it promotes a city dominated by pure architecture and maintained through "design review," and supports today's architecture of urban renewal and fine arts commissions.[502]

---

[500] Friedman, Yona: *Utopies réalisables*, op. cit., p. 173. Also see id., *Die Kontinentale Stadt – eine machbare Utopie*, interview conducted by Simonetta Carbonaro, in *BDZ*, no. 10, 1995, pp. 50–53; id., *Continent City*, in *Domus*, no. 896, October 2006, p. 1.
[501] Venturi, Robert, Scott Brown, Denise and Izenour, Steven: *Learning from Las Vegas. The Forgotten Symbolism of Architectural Form*, Cambridge (MA), MIT Press, 1972; 2nd ed. 1977, p. 149.
[502] Ibid.

As we have seen, neither total design nor the messianic role of the architect nor still less the idea of a pure architecture were values to which Friedman adhered, and it is not our intention here to compare the Hungarian architect with the Venturis. It is simply a matter of pointing out that the term megastructure is still grossly misused today[503] and how much work remains to be done in order to reassess it.

---

[503] See for example the two volumes van Schaik, Martin and Mácel, Otar (eds.): Exit *Utopia*..., op. cit., and van der Ley, Sabrina and Richter, Markus: (eds.), *Megastructure Reloaded. Visionary Architecture and Urban Design of the Sixties Reflected by Contemporary Artists*, Ostfildern, Hatje Cantz, 2008. In both projects, drawings and interviews with architects who have nothing to do with one another, such as Friedman, Archizoom or Léon Krier, are mixed up, or even worse, likened to the works of contemporary artists.

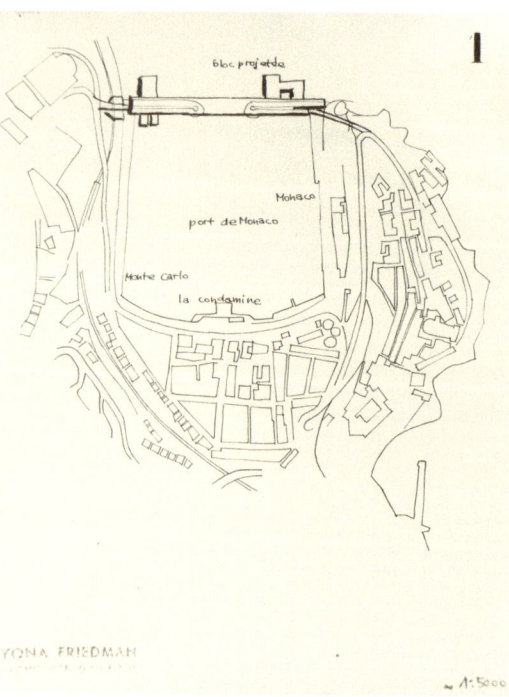

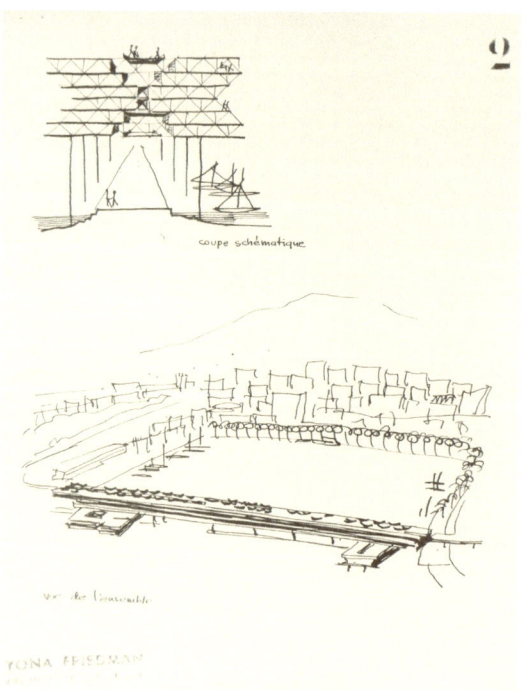

THE VENICE OF MONACO, 1959

544 Yona Friedman: Photomontage of the *Ville-Spatiale* across the harbor.
545–546 Yona Friedman: Drawings, no. 1. Site plan, scale 1:5,000; and no. 2. Schematic section and perspective view.

TOKYO BAY

547 Kenzo Tangue: Project for the extension of Tokyo into a linear city, 1960.

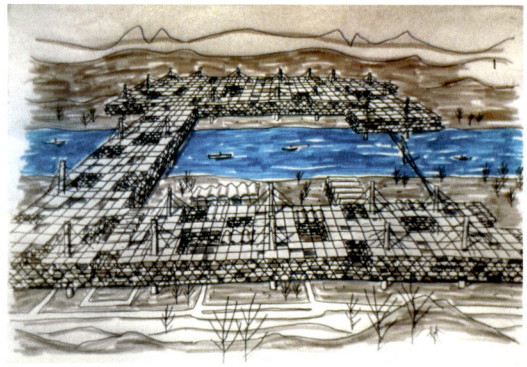
548

549

550

THE BRIDGE-TOWN

548–549 Yona Friedman: Aerial views of an independent *Spatial settlement* extended across the river, 1958–62.

MODEL OF THE BRIDGE-TOWN ACROSS THE ENGLISH CHANNEL

550 Yona Friedman in collaboration with Eckhard Schulze-Fielitz, 1963.

551

552

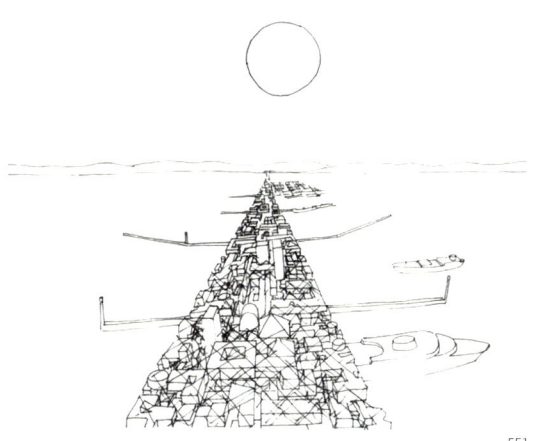

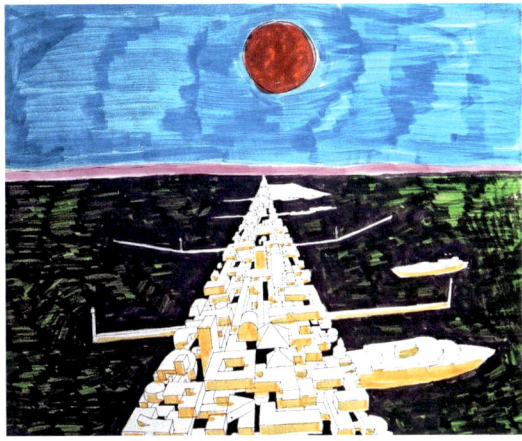

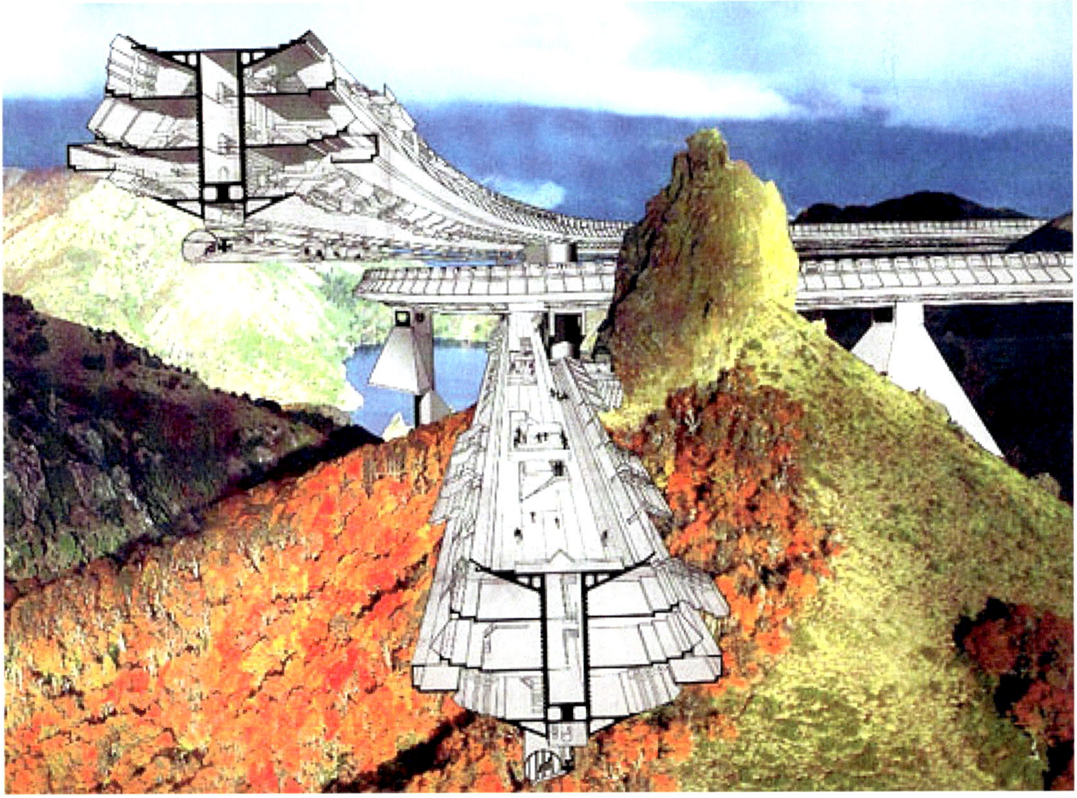

553

BRIDGE-TOWN AT GIBRALTAR

551 – 552 Yona Friedman: Perspective views of a large bridge structure, 1963.

HABITAT VECTORS ON A GEOGRAPHICAL SCALE, 1970

553 Luigi Pellegrin: Perspective from Pellegrin, Luigi: *Un percorso nel potenziare il mestiere del costruire*, Milan, Silvana, 2003.

554

555

PLUG-IN-CITY

554 Archigram: Planning study for national network, 1965.

METROPOLE EUROPE

555 Yona Friedman: *Present City-States*, c. 1961.
556–**562** Yona Friedman: *Continent-City Europe*, 1994. Map series: *network / megalopoles / nucleus / power fields (urban mechanisms model) / the real city-states / agriculture / global city.*

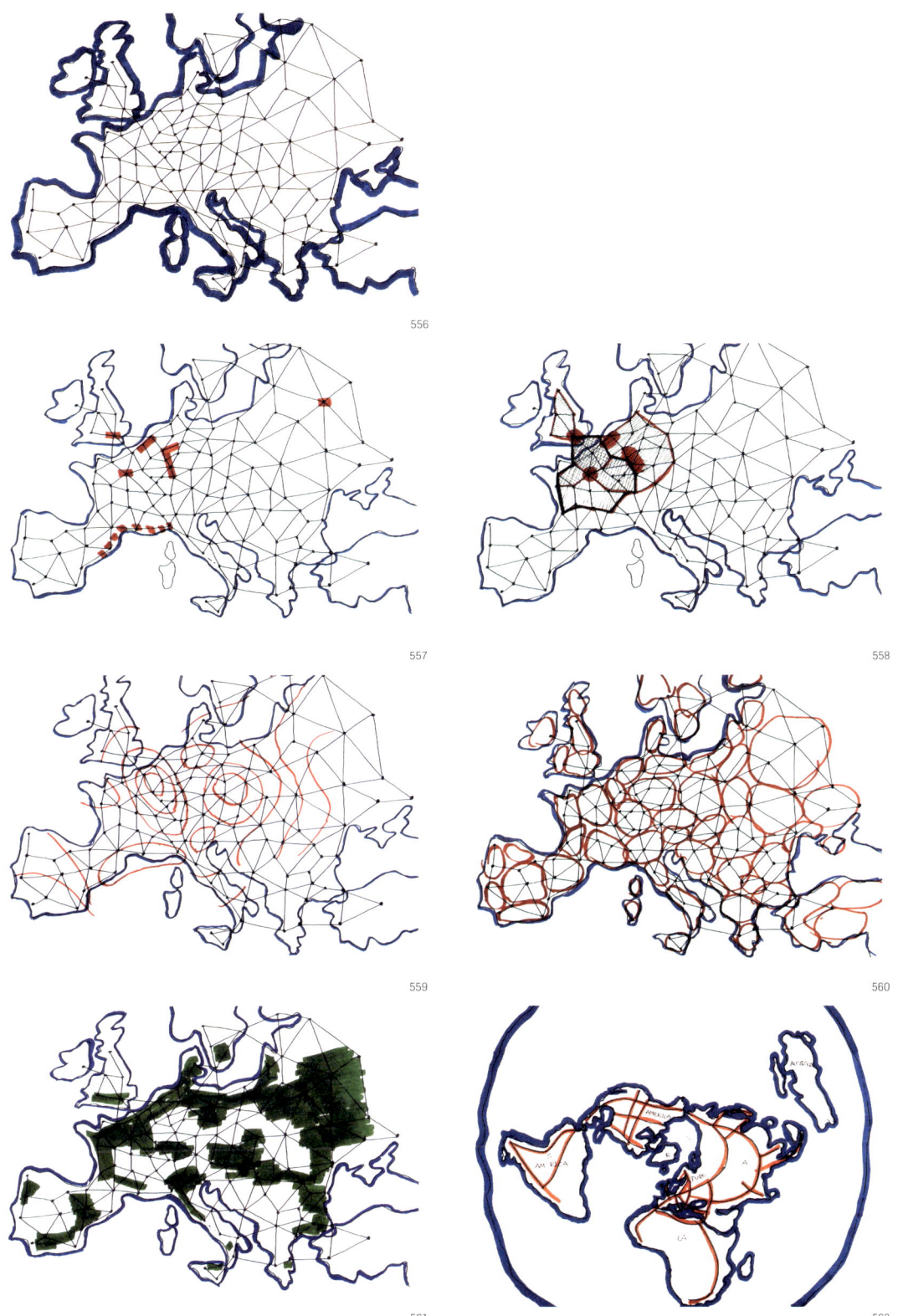

MICHEL RAGON'S GIAP

Every avant-garde (even if disdainfully called 'historical') is cynical. Because it is concerned with the possible, but never with the present as impossibility of the possible.[504]
Carmelo Bene

The role of the artist is no longer to create a work, but to create creation.[505]
Nicolas Schöffer

Yona Friedman, Paul Maymont, Georges Patrix, Michel Ragon and Nicolas Schöffer came together in March 1965 in Paris to set up the *Groupe International d'Architecture Prospective* (GIAP, "International Group of Prospective Architecture"). After a few meetings a short manifesto was written and published in May 1965, and was signed by Walter Jonas and Ionel Schein as well.

The GIAP was formed on a profoundly different basis from the GEAM: first of all the leader was not Friedman, but Ragon, and then quite deliberately there was no common platform, apart from a generic desire to come up with new ideas for improvements in the technologies available for transformation of the city: "It is becoming urgent to plan and organize the future instead of having it imposed on us."[506] The first public meetings were held at the Musée des Arts Décoratifs in Paris, while others took place informally at the studios of some of its members, including Friedman's on Boulevard Pasteur.

The purpose of the GIAP declared in the manifesto was to bring together all those "technicians, artists, sociologists and specialists of various kinds who are seeking new solutions in city planning and architecture. The GIAP aims to be a link between researchers from every country, even if their ideas are sometimes opposed. At the moment therefore the GIAP has no doctrine apart from architectural prospection." The aim was certainly a modest one when compared with that of other contemporary groups active in Paris, such as the *Situationists* or the *Utopie* group, founded the following year – both of which gravitated around a magazine: in these groups too the members were sociologists, urban planners, architects, etc., but this did not stop them from taking shared positions. As Larry Busbea has pointed out, "the architects and artists around Ragon remained diligently engaged in their respective programs of urban reform, as opposed to revolution."[507] In short the GIAP was merely a forum for debate, a legitimate offshoot of the 1956 Festival in Marseille, characterized by a chaotic lack of commitment and steeped belatedly in the general climate of *synthesis of the arts* – which had been tackled by Giedion with a great deal

---

[504] Bene, Carmelo and Dotto, Giancarlo: *Vita di Carmelo Bene*, Milan, Bompiani, 1998, p. 414.
[505] Schöffer, Nicolas: *La ville cybernétique*, Paris, Tchou, 1969, opening page.
[506] *Le Manifeste du GIAP*, May 1965, see also p. 466, no. 563.
[507] Busbea, Larry: *Topologies . . .* , op. cit., p. 7. See in general chapter 3, "The Conception and Reception of the Groupe International d'Architecture Prospective," pp. 81–104.

more rigor just a few years earlier [508] – which explains the presence of so many artists in a group intent on imagining the future of city planning, but for the most part capable only of producing curiosities.

The faith that the majority of Ragon's fellow travelers had in their demiurgic role as the vanguard of an inevitable revolution in dwelling was not just naive but anachronistic.[509] Other groups had risen from the ashes of the CIAM, bent on resuming the architectural debate in new forms, at times with ill-concealed centralizing or self-promoting intentions. From this point of view the GIAP more closely resembles the limited circle of Team 10, which continued to meet periodically after 1963, taking increasingly diverse and less and less united positions.

In any case the GIAP expanded rapidly, dividing itself into various sections including "national units"[510] and "support members,"[511] opening itself up to the contributions of many disciplines, such as photography (Lucien Hervé), set design (Jacques Polieri), sociology (Jean Fourastié, Abraham Moles), biology (Jacques Ménétrier) and criticism (Marc Gaillard, Gassiot-Talabot, Pierre Restany).

The activity of the GIAP was intense in the first two years, and then diminished gradually until it ceased altogether around 1970, in keeping with the change in the historical and cultural climate that saw the emergence of many new players on the architectural scene. At a lecture given in Venice in February 1966, Manfredo Tafuri, 31-year-old professor of the history of architecture in Rome, had already identified two directions in research that were complementary at the time, those of *jeu* and *sérieux*.[512] On the one hand there was a playful architecture in which utopias proliferated at an urban and regional level, acceptable if mindful (Archigram), but otherwise just graphic diversions that "nullify any possibility of communication, and even of design" (Metabolism and the GIAP); on the other there was an architecture of compositional rigor (Kahn, Rossi) that wanted to counter the chaos of the contemporary city with a stable formal order. And it was in this *tendency* that Tafuri placed his hopes, "if for no other reason than the value of honest testimony that its most rigorous research holds." Two years later Tafuri was to analyze the developments in this tendency in greater depth:

The situation at the end of the sixties was characterized instead by a withdrawal of architecture into itself, into an investigation of itself, of the reason for its structure, of its historical legitimacy

---

[508] A fundamental text on the cultural atmosphere that held sway in the arts and architecture in the years spanning the fifties and sixties is, in fact, GIEDION, Sigfried: *The Eternal Present. A Contribution on Constancy and Change*, London, Oxford University Press, vol. 1, *The Beginnings of Art*, 1962; vol. 2, *The Beginnings of Architecture*, 1964.

[509] See the brief and highly critical section *L'architecture visionnaire*, in LUCAN, Jacques: *Architecture en France . . .*, op. cit., p. 127.

[510] Kurokawa in Japan, Mathias Goeritz in Mexico, Jonas and Hausermann in Switzerland, Arthur Quarmby in Great Britain, Schulze-Fielitz, Ruhnau, Doernach and Frei Otto in Germany and Manfredi Nicoletti in Italy. See RAGON, Michel: *Histoire mondiale de l'architecture et de l'urbanisme moderne*, vol. 3, op. cit. Italian transl., *Storia dell'architettura e dell'urbanistica moderne*, op. cit., vol. III, p. 235.

[511] Louis Armand, Fourastié, Parinaud, Ménétrier, Le Ricolais, Buckminster Fuller, Jean Prouvé, Delouvrier, Eugène Claudius-Petit, Sauvy, Wachsmann, Makowski and Louis Pauwels.

[512] TAFURI, Manfredo: *Le strutture del linguaggio . . .*, op. cit., pp. 29–30.

[…] After denying that it was part of history it discovered, through itself, a new concept of history, one that was projected on the one hand onto the pre-18th century past, and that was inserted captiously into the process of development of the new tendencies.[513]

That the climate of interest in visionary architecture was changing can also be seen from a comparison of the writings of Tafuri himself, or for example of an art critic all too attentive to shifts in taste like Gillo Dorfles, who in 1967 asserted:

The only partly futuristic predictions of someone like Yona Friedman with his "mobile architecture" and his "nappes structurées" suspended above residential districts, the pneumatic architecture of Lundy, the regional "air-conditioning" foreseen by Frei Otto and Buckminster Fuller, the plastic structures conceived by Kowalski, etc., are solely in part impracticable fantasies and it would be a very shortsighted view not to take them into more serious consideration.[514]

But in 1973 Dorfles had already changed his tone:

It is absurd today to go on talking about building and urban planning in the terms that were dear to a Le Corbusier, or a Lucio Costa, a Gropius; and equally absurd to use those of the utopians who amuse themselves with the urban planning of the future like a Yona Friedman or a Vjenceslav Richter.[515]

Dorfles here is probably referring to Ragon's book on the city of the future and above all to *Les visionnaires de l'architecture*, in which the members of the GIAP, Schöffer, Friedman, Maymont and Jonas, were presented just before the official constitution of the group.[516] What is certain is that in the space of a few years what had seemed to be projects worthy of consideration became "fantasy architecture."[517] Friedman chose to publish three essays in the volume by the GIAP, which were them translated into various languages. Some of these were based on the papers he prepared for the numerous conferences he was invited to hold. For example on October 15, 1964, he went to Berlin at the invitation of Oswald Mathias Ungers, and then to the US, giving lectures at the Carnegie Institute in Pittsburgh, the IIT in

---

513 Id., *Teorie e storia dell'architettura*, Rome/Bari, Laterza 1968, p. 147. In particular Tafuri is referring here, and in a hardly veiled manner, to Aldo Rossi and his introduction to the new Italian edition of BOULLÉE, Etienne-Louis: *Architecture, essai sur l'art*, in the series he directed himself: *Polis, Architettura. Saggio sull'arte*, Padua, Marsilio, 1967.
514 DORFLES, Gillo: *Il divenire delle arti*, Turin, Einaudi, 1959; 1962; 3rd expanded ed., 1967, p. 160.
515 Id., *Dal significato alle scelte*, Turin, Einaudi, 1973, p. 148. See RICHTER, Vjenceslav: *Sinturbanizam [Synthetic Urban Planning]*, Zagreb, Mladost, 1964.
516 BALLADUR, Jean et al.: *Les visionnaires de l'architecture*, with an introduction by Michel Ragon, op. cit. The book came out on May 6, 1965.
517 RAGON, Michel: *Les cités de l'avenir*, Paris, Encyclopédie Planète, 1966.

Chicago, the MIT in Boston and Berkeley, as well as at the universities of Strasbourg, Zurich and others.[518] The subjects covered were spatial city planning, possible infrastructures and an architecture for billions of people.[519]

The period stretching from the end of the CIAM to the birth of *Oppositions* has still only been partly explored by historians, especially with regard to the burgeoning of discussion groups similar to the GIAP in every corner of the world. While the GIAP undoubtedly belongs to the current that Tafuri defined as *jeu*, at the same time movements were emerging that went in the opposite direction, i.e. toward the *sérieux*.
For example in the United States, between 1964 and 1969, a broad grouping of architects and critics was formed on the European model, united solely by their impatience with American professionalism and the uninspired public housing programs of the US, but on a completely new basis. Peter Eisenman, at the age of 32, returned to the States after taking a PhD at Cambridge in 1963 and settled in Princeton, where the best of the architects in their thirties and forties present on the American scene all gathered.[520] Eisenman soon emerged as the charismatic figure capable of uniting most of these architects through a research institute (the Institute for Architectural and Urban Studies, 1967), an exhibition (*Five Architects*, New York, 1972) and then a magazine (*Oppositions*, 1973)[521] – with the significant defection of Scully, Venturi and Scott Brown, the so-called "Grays," who had taken part in the first meetings.

In a period in which the masters of the Modern Movement were dying off one by one – Wright in 1959, Le Corbusier in 1965, Giedion in 1968, Mies van der Rohe and Gropius in 1969 – and after the "loss of the center," i.e. the end of the CIAM, most of the discussion between architects went on in the universities, the most important of which after 1966 were the AA in London, the IAUS in New York and the IUAV in Venice.

According to Pierre Restany, who took part in some of the GIAP meetings, the greatest merit of Ragon's group was that it made all the isolated researchers like Friedman aware of the others' existence, and of their power and responsibility. Apart from the specialists, the public who attended these conferences were awakened to the reality of a new architecture

---

[518] Id., *Aprés Le Corbusier*, in Balladur, Jean et al.: *Les visionnaires . . .* , op. cit., p. 9.
[519] Friedman, Yona: *Pourquoi l'urbanisme spatial?*, in Balladur, Jean et al.: *Les visionnaires . . .* , op. cit., pp. 34–51; *Une architecture pour des milliards d'hommes*, ibid., pp. 52–76; *Une nouvelle façon de raisonner sur l'urbanisme*, ibid., pp. 77–85. The texts are dated January 1, 1965.
[520] "At Princeton I found Michael Graves, whom I had met in Rome, and immediately we thought of setting up a group of young architects on the model of Team 10. With this aim in mind Graves and I organized a meeting in the spring of 1964 in which Colin Rowe, Vincent Scully, Bob Venturi, Richard Meier, Erik Miller, Jaquelin Robertson and others took part. We parted company straightaway and out of the disagreement with Scully and Venturi came all the later story, up to the 'Five' and the conflict between 'Whites' and 'Grays.' Expanded to take in other participants the meetings were to continue in the following years until the time when, between '67 and '69, we began to meet at the Museum of Modern Art of New York." Dal Co, Francesco and Eisenman, Peter: *Una conversazione intorno al significato e ai fini della pratica dell'architettura (e qualche ricordo)*, in *Casabella*, no. 675, February 2000, p. 32.
[521] "The institute was the product of the attraction that I felt for European culture and ideological debate that was going on there. [...] Everything that happened or 'passed through' the institute was later reflected, as you know well, in *Oppositions*, which helped to forge a special relationship between New York and Venice." Eisenman, Peter: ibid. See Hays, Michael (ed.): *Oppositions Reader. Selected Readings from a Journal for Ideas and Criticism in Architecture 1973–1984*, New York, Princeton University Press, 1998.

and its specific problems.[522] In Bruno Zevi's view, however, the group, basically French, was sustained by an unrealistic ideology. He observed that Friedman limited himself to proposing again his spatial lattices and the mobile cells to be inserted in them; in other words he had not updated his *Urbanisme spatial*.[523] Zevi did not know that Friedman had in fact joined the GIAP unwillingly, "solely out of gratitude" to Ragon, as he was at odds ideologically with its members, apart from Schöffer.[524] In general, however, Zevi saw the visionary projects of the GIAP as more prudent utopias than those of Archigram. In point of fact, none of the members, except for a few wholly epigonic figures like Édouard Utudjian – who developed the idea of an underground architecture first proposed by Maymont in 1962 with his *Paris sous la Seine*[525] – presented completely new solutions. Essentially they trotted out the ones they had developed earlier, perhaps increasing their dimensions until reached a scale as gigantic as it was improbable. The result was that the group lacked a coherent architectural approach – in contrast to the GEAM, at least in its first two years – and offered a program of mere agitation hinging on the figure of Ragon. Manfredo Tafuri was the most implacable critic of Friedman and the GIAP: he dismissed them with a brief footnote, inserting them in the category of a utopianism that was just a "rhetorical amplification of contemporary *disorder* and mythologies."[526] But while Archigram took science fiction, comic strips, technology and chaos to extremes, and in doing so renounced any semblance of experimentalism *in keeping with reality*, "[in] this sense, as purely ironic affairs, Archigram's projects are more positive than those of the Metabolism group or the GIAP." The need that Tafuri felt, unlike Zevi (perpetually dissatisfied with architectural contingency), was to separate the avant-gardes from experimentalism, distinguishing those who tried *seriously* to affect things, that is by carrying out continual reality checks (Le Corbusier, Kahn, Tange), from those who remained in the realm of ideas. Not even the Canadian experience of Moshe Safdie, who built a housing unit based on prefabricated cells that were assembled on site, under the direct influence of Friedman, was able to convince Tafuri: for the Roman historian even the case of *Habitat 67*, although actually realized, was not a genuine experiment, but only a "pedestrian technological exercise."[527]

None of the members of the GIAP succeeded in realizing any of their projects: almost all were obliged to fall back on teaching. Maymont was an assistant at the École des Beaux-Arts in Paris, Patrix[528] taught courses at the Institut Supérieur des Carrières Artistiques and Friedman had been giving lectures and carrying out research at several American universities since 1964. In particular Maymont's teaching at the academy "par excellence" is the most radical refutation of the formally anarchic intentions of the GIAP. Wavering

---

[522] RESTANY, Pierre: *Ragon, un nouveau critique pour une nouvelle architecture*, in *Domus*, no. 487, June 1970, p. 4.
[523] Zevi, Bruno: *L'architecture prospective. Troppo prudenti gli utopisti francesi* (April 30, 1967), in id., *Cronache di architettura*, vol. 12. Rome/Bari, Laterza, 1979, pp. 415–16.
[524] Unpublished letter written by Friedman's wife, Denise Charvein, December 11, 1978. Courtesy of Yona Friedman.
[525] UTUDJIAN, Edouard: *L'Architecture et l'urbanisme souterrain*, with an introduction by Michel Ragon, Paris, Laffont, 1966. See too ROUILLARD, Dominique: *Superarchitecture . . .*, op. cit., pp. 212–13.
[526] TAFURI, Manfredo: *Teorie e storia dell'architettura*, op. cit., p. 118, note 31, including the quotations below.
[527] Id., *Storia dell'architettura italiana . . .*, op. cit., p. 104.
[528] PATRIX, Georges and HUISMAN, D.: *L'Esthétique industrielle*, Paris, PUF, 1961; PATRIX, Georges: *Beauté ou laideur. Vers une esthétique industrielle*, Paris, Hachette, 1966.

between social utopia and technological utopia, the architects of the GIAP after a very short time devoted themselves to teaching within the institutions, when not to the most ordinary professional practice.

It seems, however, that there was a split into two fringes, prior to the definitive breakup of the group: on one side those more interested in morphology, in the development of forms unconstrained by social or technical factors, and therefore more artistic in their approach, and on the other the more scientifically minded. These last included Friedman, Schöffer and Moles, along with Jonas, who, although a painter by training, had tried to give his projects of urban reform a technical underpinning by turning for advice to more than one engineer. After the dissolution of the GIAP, Ragon was left with no way of reacting to this personal defeat but to write a *History of Architecture* in three volumes – a classic example of what Tafuri called "operative criticism," but when time had already run out – that would have as its climax and conclusion, it goes without saying, the GIAP.

To get a better understanding of the reasons for the formation of this short-lived group and for Friedman joining it, it is worth taking a closer look at its most representative members.

Michel Ragon had been a painter in his youth: he had been part of the French branch of CoBrA – along with Atlan, Doucet and Jaguer – becoming an indomitable promoter of abstract painting.[529] In 1949 he got to know Schöffer. He developed an interest in architecture in 1956, through his discussions with Le Corbusier and Wogenscky during the preparation of the *Festival de la Cité Radieuse* in Marseille. With his desire to make architecture a subject of popular interest and not just a discipline for specialists, Ragon was to become the principal propagandist for modernist architecture at the very moment – the sixties – in which the myth of its effectiveness was dissipating. Above all else Ragon loved imaginative architecture, designed rather than constructed, futurist or futuristic, and was incorrigibly optimistic about technology and progress. His *World History of Modern Architecture and City Planning* (1971) would be the main fruit of his conception of architecture: the result of a desire to write the history of architecture from the viewpoint of ideas more than from that of buildings.[530] After the Marseille Festival of 1956, he focused chiefly on modern and contemporary architecture. According to Restany, his *Le livre de l'architecture moderne*,[531] published in 1958, was the first book on the history of contemporary architecture in France and at the same time his personal and hagiographic tribute to Le Corbusier, who represented the hero of each historical phase – "He appeared to me as truth incarnate,"[532] he would confess many years later. Later Ragon turned to journalism: in 1959 he and Wogenscky launched the first column on French architecture in *Cimase*, a militant magazine of abstract art, and then addressed an ever broader and more general readership through regular contributions to *Arts* (1961 – 66), *L'Express* (1963 – 66) and *Planète* (from 1964). His polemical tone, the pace of his reporting and his ability to

---

[529] Many of his writings on postwar art can be found in RAGON, Michel: *Vingt-cinq ans d'art vivant: chronique vécue de l'art contemporain de l'abstraction au pop art 1944 – 1969*, Paris/Tournai, Casterman, 1969.
[530] RESTANY, Pierre: *Ragon, un nouveau critique pour une nouvelle architecture*, op. cit.
[531] RAGON, Michel: *Le livre de l'architecture moderne*, Paris, Laffont, 1958.
[532] RAGON, Michel: Interview conducted by Thierry Paquot, in *Urbanisme*, no. 10, 1997.

popularize questions of architecture opened the doors of newspapers and weeklies with a large circulation in a way that only superficially resembled the energetic and optimistic approach of Bruno Zevi and his column in *L'Espresso*,[533] but he was still able to make the theme of architecture a matter of national interest and not something just for specialists. However, the differences between the two are considerable. Zevi wrote a very harsh review of Ragon's *Histoire mondiale de l'architecture et de l'urbanisme moderne* (1972), in which he accused him of historical chauvinism and total abstraction from reality, lumping together bits of information, ideas, dates and data and integrating pages and pages of unmethodical compilation with improvised critical apparatus. Zevi went so far as to charge him with "crude futurology." On the ideological plane Ragon's mistake was to connect the utopias of yesterday with those of tomorrow, and thus undervalue all the concrete contributions of the present; on the architectural one, the distinction between architect-artist and architect-engineer resulted in the disappearance of architecture, which, "torn between 19th century 'theories' and 'visions' of the 21st century, divided between engineering and figurativeness, made dreary by the preconceived idea of French superiority, lost all importance."[534] Ragon held unorthodox political ideas that led him to differentiate himself considerably from the Situationists and gradually from the Communists as well, although he had for a while been an active supporter of the party: today he claims that he had also been associated with the *Anarchist Federation*, and it was for this that he had been shown the door by the PCF.[535] Ragon's interest in the problems of the city[536] stemmed from his enthusiasm for the utopian French socialism of the beginning of the 19th century. Many early socialist thinkers, from Saint-Simon to Fourier, had imagined ideal cities and ample space is given to these speculations – along with the anarcho-socialist ones of Proudhon and Kropotkin – at the start of the *Histoire mondiale de l'architecture et de l'urbanisme moderne*. This book represents the final act in the whole story of the exploration of architecture by the French historian and his milieu, an indisputable example of "operative historiography" that came teleologically to an end with the GIAP.[537] Attention was drawn to all the components of modern architecture considered "heretical" with the clear intention of guiding the design work of architects, in the manner characteristic of so many books on modern architecture – from Pevsner to Zevi, from Leonardo Benevolo to Charles Jencks. At the end of the seventies Ragon completely abandoned his studies of the city and architecture, going on to publish occasional essays on the history of art and a series of novels.

---

[533] The column started in 1954. See ZEVI, Bruno: *Cronache di architettura*, op. cit., vol. 1.
[534] ZEVI, Bruno: *Sciovinismo storiografico di Michel Ragon. Idee maledette del XIX frustrate dal XX*, (31 October 1971), ibid., vol. 16, note 892, p. 295.
[535] "The French Communist Party expelled me for my libertarian positions." In RAGON, Michel: Interview conducted by Thierry Paquot, op. cit. His history of architecture was published in Italian by Editori Riuniti, close to the Italian Communist Party, but the long introduction by Alfredo Lambertucci was openly critical of the author: "So we cannot agree with Ragon's argument that underestimates the importance of the contribution of the utopian socialists, as well as any later attempt based on propositions of abstract utopianism." "Introduzione," in RAGON, Michel: *Storia dell'architettura*, op. cit., vol. I, p. xx. Lambertucci contrasted with Ragon Henri Lefebvre and his *La pensée marxiste et la ville*, Paris/Tournai, Casterman, 1972.
[536] RAGON, Michel: *L'urbanisme et la cité*, Paris, Hachette, 1964.
[537] Id., *Storia dell'architettura*, op. cit., vol. III, pp. 235 ff.

In 1962 Ragon met Paul Maymont (born in Paris in 1926, he had studied under Perret and Beaudouin), who had just returned from a stay in Kyoto, where he had been teaching architecture since 1958 and had seen the birth of the projects of the Metabolists, in particular the ones for cities on water – his *Floating City* for Tokyo Bay (1960) is very similar to Kikutake's *Marine City* (1958).[538] So Ragon was the first to publish Maymont's projects[539] and it seems that he was the architect who best represented his prospective ambitions: Maymont was grappling with another floating city with an upturned conical section, proposed for Monaco (1963) and far more ambitious than Friedman's project of 1959. Maymont was interested in exploring a "floating urbanism" composed of large umbrella-shaped structures, sometimes turned upside down and always presented in idealized and not urbanized settings – one project was even conceived for a city off this planet to house a thousand inhabitants, that is to say a lunar megastructure (1962) imagined in the wake of the enthusiasm over Yuri Gagarin's first journey into space.[540] Tafuri's definition of an "academy of utopia" is particularly apt in Maymont's case, given his training at the École des Beaux-Arts. Maymont's imagination had been stirred by an article published a short time before in which the engineer René Sarger judged some of his projects to be theoretically feasible.[541] This attitude of personal exaltation betrays another, more generalized one: the use of scientific opinion as a rhetorical tool to influence society. But as David Greene of Archigram pointed out, with very English humor, "just because you can doesn't mean you should."[542] It is the same error Friedman had made with Wachsmann a few years earlier.

Maymont's flights of fancy went even further than those of Walter Jonas (born in 1910), a Neo-Expressionist painter from Zurich who like Constant had turned to architecture. But Jonas did not want to revolutionize city life. His *Intrahaus* system, made up of housing units in the form of funnels standing on their tips, could contain the ordinary activities of consumer society.[543] His main concern was the congestion and pollution caused by automobile traffic and thus he set out to free up as much ground as possible in the city, raising the residential areas in order to optimize the illumination of the apartments and improve the quality of the air breathed by their occupants. To achieve this he commissioned feasibility studies of his system from several engineers.[544] The juxtaposition of the units at their tangential points would allow circulation of air to their highest levels, as well as making the structure more solid, and in this case too "the separation of pedestrians and motorized traffic offers the greatest safety."[545] Jonas was the GIAP's representative in the German-speaking countries, Switzerland, Germany and Austria.[546]

---

[538] Id., *Construisons des villes sur la mer*, in *La Nation*, no. 9, 1963, p. 269; WILLEMIN, Véronique: *Maisons mobiles*, op. cit., pp. 168–69.
[539] For instance on the cover of Ragon's book, *Où vivrons-nous demain?* Paris, Laffont, 1963.
[540] MAYMONT, Paul: *L'urbanisme flottant à la conquête des espaces*, in BALLADUR, Jean et al.: *Les visionnaires...*, op. cit., pp. 96–109.
[541] SARGER, René: *Fantastique d'aujourd'hui, realité de demain*, in *L'Architecture d'aujourd'hui*, June 1962.
[542] Quoted in JACOB, Sam: *Topsy Turvy VSBA: Inverted Heros of an Upside Down Avant Guard [sic]*, in *Strange Harvest*, http://strangeharvest.com/topsy-turvy-vsba-inverted-heros-of-an-upside-down-avant-guard.
[543] JONAS, Walter: *Das Intrahaus*, Zurich, Origo, 1962.
[544] See the note by the engineer MATT, Peter: *Lumière, pureté de l'air, bruit*, in BALLADUR, Jean et al.: *Les visionnaires...*, op. cit., p. 120.
[545] JONAS, Walter: *La ville-cône ouverte vers la lumière et l'espace*, ibid., pp. 121 and 124.
[546] RAGON, Michel: *Walter Jonas et l'architecture*, in SCHMID, Heinrich E. (ed.): *Walter Jonas. Maler Denker Urbanist*, Zurich, Atlantis, 1980, pp. 131–37. Also see HOWALD, Stefan: *Walter Jonas: Künstler. Denker*, Zurich, Scheidegger & Spiess, 2012.

Among the participants in the meetings of the GIAP were sociologists like Abraham Moles, a professor at Strasbourg University and specialist in information theory [547] who stood out for a controversy with the Situationists.[548] Moles had worked with Schöffer and Jacques Ménétrier, studying the reactions of the individual on the visual plane.[549] Ménétrier and Moles introduced Schöffer to cybernetics in 1964, influencing the subsequent evolution of the Hungarian sculptor's art. Schöffer's first writing on the cybernetic city dates from the following year and was published in the miscellany of essays brought out by Ragon [550] to promote the GIAP, and for many years this was to remain the focus of his artistic and architectural research. Cybernetic technology did not appear to be a simple extension of the mechanical principles of industrial civilization, but marked a qualitative leap forward in the direction of closer relations between technology and aesthetics, heralded by the research into electronic music of Karlheinz Stockhausen, Pierre Boulez and Iannis Xenakis in the fifties:[551] it is no coincidence that Moles also carried out research into phonetics. In Britain too interest in cybernetics was fairly widespread among architects. In particular Cedric Price designed with Gordon Pask [552] a *Cybernetic Theater* – illustrated with a diagram [553] – for his *Fun Palace* between 1964 and 1965 and Archigram, the British group that was stepping up its production of projects and publications at the time, continued to promote cybernetics as a salvation for years to come.[554] After the disbanding of the GIAP, Moles on the other hand turned his attention back to the problems of urban space, refining his research of a scientific character together with his wife [555] in a department of the University of Strasbourg where he had been summoned to teach by Lefebvre.

Earlier Nicolas Schöffer (born in Kalocsa, in Hungary, in 1912) had been interested in *Spatiodynamism* – "the constructive and dynamic integration of space into a work of sculpture" aimed at the progressive disappearance of the object from artistic production – leading him to create metal sculptures that were articulated and animated by movement, light and noise, and perhaps indebted to some of the research of another illustrious Hungarian, László Moholy-Nagy.[556] In this it can be considered a form of kinetic art, i.e. an art of movement, usually based on mechanisms set in the body of the work so that it

---

547 MOLES, Abraham A.: *Théorie de l'information et perception esthétique*, Paris, Flammarion, 1958.
548 *Correspondances avec un cybernétique*, in *Internationale Situationniste*, no. 9, August 1964. This involved a sparring match in December 1963 between Moles and Debord, replete with personal insults on the part of the latter ("we are laughing at you!"), who would not accept debating with a university academic, and moreover a colleague and friend of Lefebvre's.
549 MÉNÉTRIER, Jacques: *Eloge de l'incertitude*, Paris, La Colombe, 1962. There is a text by Ménétrier in the volume JORAY, Marcel (ed.): *Nicolas Schöffer*, with an introduction by Jean Cassou, Neuchâtel, Editions du Griffon, 1963.
550 SCHÖFFER, Nicolas: *Nouvelles structures pour l'avenir, la ville cybernétique*, in BALLADUR, Jean et al.: *Les visionnaires...*, op. cit., pp. 14–33.
551 After the foundation of the IRCAM in Paris in 1977, directed by Boulez, Schöffer experimented with the application of his cybernetic theory in the musical field too. See LIGIER, Maude (ed.): *Nicolas Schöffer*, Dijon, Les Presses du Réel, 2004.
552 PASK, Gordon: *An Approach to Cybernetics*, London, Hutchinson, 1961.
553 LOBSINGER, Mary Louise: *Cybernetic Theory and the Architecture of Performance: Cedric Price's Fun Palace*, in WILLIAMS GOLDHAGEN, Sarah and LEGAULT, Réjean (eds.): *Anxious Modernisms...*, op. cit., pp. 130–32.
554 See GREENE, David: *Gardener's Notebook* (1972), now in COOK, Peter (ed.): *Archigram*, New York, Princeton Architectural Press, 1999, p. 110.
555 MOLES, Abraham and ROHMER, Elisabeth: *Psychologie de l'espace*, Paris/Tournai, Casterman, 1972. The publisher also brought out Friedman's *L'architecture mobile* and, above all, Ragon's books in the sixties, including his history of architecture.
556 See MOHOLY-NAGY, László: *Vision in Motion*, Chicago, Hillison & Etten, 1947.

never appears to be static in the manner of an ordinary statue.[557] In 1955 an exhibition was organized at Denise René's gallery that marked an important watershed in this sense: *Le mouvement*. On the subject Pontus Hultén wrote:

One of the great innovations of our century is the fact that the art has taken possession of and utilizes the time factor (to be precise the fourth dimension) [...]. A work of art endowed with a kinetic rhythm that never repeats itself is just one of the freest beings that can be imagined, a creation that, liberated from all systems, lives on beauty.[558]

In Paris this genre of art was explored by the *Groupe de Recherche d'Art Visuel* (GREV: Morellet, Le Parc et al.) and the *Groupe Espace* with the support of the magazine *Art d'aujourd'hui* edited by the architect and sculptor André Bloc (the same man who commissioned Candilis to follow the CIAM for *L'Architecture d'aujourd'hui*[559]), but Schöffer wanted to arrive at an integration of avant-garde art into public space, in the general climate of *synthesis of the arts*. Fundamental in this sense were his contacts with the Franco-Hungarian abstract painter Viktor Vasarely, who had produced a series of kinetic works and was developing a new plastic language applied to urban space.[560] As a consequence he would be studied by Venturi and Scott Brown in their attempt to define the order of the Las Vegas Strip:

But the order of the Strip includes; it includes at all levels, from the mixture of seemingly incongruous land uses to the mixture of seemingly incongruous advertising media [...]. It is not an order dominated by the expert and made easy for the eye. The moving eye in the moving body must work to pick out and interpret a variety of changing, juxtaposed orders, like the shifting configurations of a Victor Vasarely painting.[561]

Schöffer's project on an urban scale of a *cybernetic Tower for Liège* (1961) presents affinities both with the metal *Monument for Reconstruction* (1955) built by Constant for Bakema and with the parallel research of the *Gruppo T* in Italy – in 1963 the group constructed a temporary luminous tower in the center of Milan.[562] In fact it was by presenting them drawings and plans for a *Spatiodynamic City* that the Franco-Hungarian had made contact with Constant and the sculptor Stephen Gilbert back in the mid-fifties.[563] The three of them, together with André Bloc and Claude Parent, wrote *Neo-Vision*, a manifesto for

---

557 POPPER, Frank: *Origins and Development of Kinetic Art*, op. cit., pp. 135–37 and 170–71.
558 HULTÉN, Pontus: *Mouvement-Temps ou le quatre dimensions de la plastique cinétique*, in *Le mouvement*, brochure published on the occasion of the exhibition at the Galerie Denise René, Paris, 1955.
559 LAVALOU, Armelle: *Alison Smithson et Team Ten. Georges Candilis se souvient*, in *Architecture d'aujourd'hui*, no. 290, December 1993, pp. 28–30.
560 See VASARELY, Victor: *Plasti-cité. L'œuvre plastique dans votre vie quotidienne*, Paris/Tournai, Casterman, 1970. On the relationship between Schöffer and Vasarely, see BUSBEA, Larry: *Topologies*, op. cit., pp. 176–77.
561 VENTURI, Robert, SCOTT BROWN, Denise and IZENOUR, Steven: *Learning from Las Vegas*, op. cit., pp. 52–53.
562 The Gruppo T was born in Milan in 1959 (Giovanni Anceschi, Davide Boriani, Gianni Colombo, Gabriele De Vecchi, Grazia Varisco) and was present together with other Italian and foreigner groups at the exhibition "Arte programmata" at the space Olivetti in Milan (see A.V., *Arte programmata*, ed. by Bruno Munari and Giorgio Soavi, presentation by Umberto Eco, graphic design by Enzo Mari, photographs by Ugo Mulas, catalogue of the exhibition, Milan, Galleria V. Emanuele 1962); since 1964 the Gruppo T realized "immersivi e interattivi" ambients that created an active, mobile, provisory space stimulating all the senses. See MELONI, Lucilla: *Gli ambienti del Gruppo T*, Milan, Silvana, 2004.
563 CARERI, Francesco, *Constant. New Babylon, una città nomade*, Turin, Testo & Immagine, 2001, p. 23.

Spatiodynamism. While the characteristics of Schöffer's city are similar to Constant's *New Babylon* – a megastructure suspended at a height of sixteen meters above the ground, characterized by mobile spaces and a system of arteries that allowed it to expand gradually – it was the vision of Schöffer's world that immediately aroused the suspicion of Constant. So the dispute between the Dutch painter and Friedman was not an isolated one: in fact enthusiasm for the rapid advances in technology and for new sciences like cybernetics was combined in the sculptor French with a historical hyper-positivism so marked as to make him willing to accept society as it was and as it was developing. Thus in 1961 Gillo Dorfles questioned the very idea of an art "in movement":

The fact, then, that some of these artists – the case of Victor Vasarely (a Hungarian artist who has made Paris his home) is typical – have quickly become "fashionable" precisely for the peculiarity – more psychological than aesthetic – of their works tells us how unfortunately even in this apparently so rigorous and "scientific" sector fashion can carry more weight than an actual judgment of value. Schöffer (with his showy self-moving metal constructions) is one of the most significant examples. [564]

In 1969 Schöffer published a book, *Cybernetic City*, into which he poured all the energy he had lavished on the GIAP.[565] It is divided into three chapters, one devoted to the "social perspective," one to the "artistic perspective" and the last to the model of cybernetic organization of the human habitat. Cybernetics is defined as the theory of regulatory systems that relies in particular on analogies with machines and the animal and human nervous system. Biological analogies were very popular among architects of the period, especially the Japanese Metabolists but not them alone: it suffices to think of Shadrach Woods's theory of the stem.[566] Friedman himself has often used the example of animals to explain some phenomena of adaptation, in particular his dog Balkis – about which he has even written a book in more recent years.[567] According to Filiberto Menna, an art critic who like some of his Italian colleagues had begun to take an interest in design, with cybernetics Étienne Souriau's prophesy was going to be fulfilled:

Guided by cybernetics industry seems capable of recovering a wide margin of freedom of conception and execution with the introduction of ergonomic principles released from the need to assimilate the human gesture to the mechanical movement of the machine.[568]

One of the things that Schöffer had most in common with Friedman was his total indifference to the problem of form: the formal aspect had to be reduced to a minimum

---

[564] DORFLES, Gillo: *Ultime tendenze nell'arte d'oggi*, Milan, Feltrinelli, 1961, p. 88.
[565] SCHÖFFER, Nicolas: *La ville cybernétique*, Paris, Tchou, 1969. English transl., *Cybernetic City*, London, Architectural Association, 2009.
[566] "The process of planning from stem to cluster will tend to re-establish density and scale in the habitat." WOODS, Shadrach: *Stem*, in *Architectural Design*, no. 5, May 1960, p. 181. For a comparative analysis of the concept of stem see the section with that title in ROUILLARD, Dominique: *Superarchitecture* ..., op. cit., pp. 61–66, and the more complete AVERMAETE, Tom: *The Stem and Web Concepts by Candilis–Josic–Woods*, in *Quaderni del dottorato di ricerca in Urbanistica IUAV*, no. 3, Rome, Officina, 2006, pp. 201–19.
[567] FRIEDMAN, Yona: *Vous avez un chien. C'est lui qui vous a choisi(e)*, Paris/Tel Aviv, Editions de l'Eclat, 2004.
[568] MENNA, Filiberto: *Profezia di una società estetica* ..., op. cit., p. 146.

of signs capable of creating a language,[569] largely because "the role of the artist is no longer to create a work, but to create creation."[570] This conception of the artist's role coincided with Friedman's view of the architect's and in fact it was from him that Schöffer borrowed most of his ideas in this field, especially on the liberation of the ground, on urban intensification (although chiefly on a vertical scale) and on the importance of leisure (including sex, see the center of sexual recreation in the form of a huge pale pink breast with a vaguely Surrealist flavor), and he cites Heisenberg's view that technical equipment surrounds man like a biological extension:

Art and aesthetics also have to use the same technical arsenal to introduce works of art into the system of our technological environment, in order to create a counterweight, to counterbalance the technical elements of our technological and scientific surroundings, which run the risk of getting humanity caught up in an extremely dangerous process of conditioning.[571]

So to avoid the fate of turning into automata conditioned by machines and of enslavement to technical and scientific developments a massive use of the cybernetic art was required. It was the only thing capable of turning this threat into a benefit. Schöffer carried on with his research into the application of cybernetics to the city even after the dissolution of the GIAP, maintaining friendly and lasting relations with Friedman.[572]

At the *Salon des Arts Ménagers* in Paris (from February 1956), Ionel Schein (Bucharest 1927–Paris 2004) had exhibited a prefabricated plastic bathroom that by a very short time anticipated the Smithsons' *House of the Future*.[573] According to Ragon the "snail house" presented by Schein together with Yves Magnant and René A. Coulon was the first full-size house built out of plastic,[574] but in reality Buckminster Fuller had already designed his prefabricated *Dymaxion Bathroom* unit between 1936 and 1938.[575] Peter Cook published it in his 1967 book *Architecture: Action and Plan*, describing it as a "motel cabin in reinforced plastics," mobile and yet equipped with all the features required by its functions.[576] Schein had joined the GIAP with the intention of placing his specific research into the plastic housing unit at the disposal of the group's megastructuralists, who had exercised a great influence on him. Friedman in particular: up until the eighties,

---

569 Schöffer, Nicolas: *Non-formalisme*, in *La cité cybernétique*, op. cit., pp. 95–96.
570 Ibid., statement on opening page.
571 Ibid., p. 128.
572 Id., *La nouvelle charte de la ville. La ville cybernétique (suite)*, Paris, Denoël-Gonthier, 1974. On his friendship with Friedman, see Sers, Philippe: *Entretiens avec Nicolas Schöffer*, Paris, Belfond, 1971, pp. 68–74.
573 Webster, Helena: *Modernism without Rhetoric*..., op. cit., p. 41.
574 Ragon, Michel: *Storia dell'architettura*, op. cit., vol. III, p. 226. See Schein, Ionel: *Casa sperimentale in plastica esposta al Salon des Arts Ménagers, Parigi*, in *L'architettura. Cronache e storia*, no. 9, 1956, pp. 219–22.
575 Krausse, Joachim and Lichtenstein, Claude: *Your Private Sky: R. Buckminster Fuller: The Art of Design Science*, Zurich, Lars Müller, 1999, pp. 202–11.
576 Cook, Peter: *Architecture: Action and Plan*, London, Studio Vista, 1967, p. 24.

in fact, Schein would continue to design bridge cities and suspended dwellings along the lines laid down by the Hungarian architect.[577] In parallel he developed a rapport with Claude Parent.[578]

In France as elsewhere, research into housing built of plastic was a specific phenomenon and limited in time: it began on February 7, 1956 – date of the opening of the *Salon des Arts Ménagers* – and ended around the middle of the seventies: no significant design was ever put into production, except in the trailer and camper industry.[579]

The Italian architects who took part in the meetings of the GIAP were Enzo Venturelli from Turin and Manfredi Nicoletti (born in 1930), active in Rome. In a book whose title betrayed the influence of Friedman and Jonas, the former proposed freeing up the ground level of the city by adding to every building a story in which to transfer the inhabitants while inserting the stores on the second floor. The result was to obtain an elevated level that was completely pedestrianized and separate from the one used by vehicle traffic.[580] Zevi considered Venturelli's projects a reworking of the "ideal cities" that had appeared between the wars, an "imaginative utopia" that was only partly science fiction.[581]

At the meetings in Paris Nicoletti was able to show his 1963 project for a satellite town in the Principality of Monaco,[582] an addition that would have nothing special about it if it were not for the technique proposed. The plan envisaged an expansion onto the sea similar to Maymont's proposal, but through the sinking of reinforced-concrete boxes rather than ordinary land fill. Only subsequently would the peninsula have been filled with earth in order to build on it. Apart from this technique, the project was little more than a banal proposal of real-estate speculation, and from 1966, i.e. the time when he began to take part in the meetings of the GIAP, Nicoletti would make improvements to it: the scheme for enlargement changed and residential hills were formed in a sort of "artificial geology." These were shell-shaped mega-containers, typologically similar and made up of load-bearing diaphragms arranged in a fan to support the levels, which acted as an extension of the ground, with roads, squares and houses. Although the forms chosen by Nicoletti were fairly original, the principles of mobile architecture were adhered to: his housing complexes were completely pedestrianized, i.e. cars had no access to the "artificial hills," the vertical canalizations of the systems (including those of transport) were fixed while secondary

---

[577] SCHEIN, Ionel: *Parigi: progetto per il "vuoto" delle Halles*, in *Domus*, no. 550, September 1975, pp. 23–25. In 1989 Schein presented another design for an urbanized bridge at Tolbiac; see PICON, Antoine and PICON-LEFEBVRE, Virginia: *Le megastrutture e i ponti abitati*..., op. cit., p. 54.
[578] BERSELLI, Silvia: *Claude Parent et Ionel Schein: une collaboration symbiothique en équilibre instable*, in PARENT, Claude: *L'oeuvre construite, l'oeuvre graphique*, Orléans, HYX, 2010, pp. 48–52.
[579] SCHEIN, Ionel: *La maison plastique en France*, in MONNIER, Gérard and KLEIN, Richard (eds.): *Les années ZUP*, Paris, Picard, 2002. See DANNATT, Adrian: *Plastic house originator gets a show at last*, in *Architects' Journal*, no. 20, May 21, 1998, p. 26. Schein's scanty publications include the introduction to the French edition of Anatole Kopp's book on Soviet architecture and city planning, *Architecture et urbanisme soviétiques des années vingt. Ville et révolution*, Paris, Anthropos, 1967, pp. 3–5. English transl., *Town and Revolution: Soviet Architecture and City Planning, 1917–1935,* New York, Braziller, 1970. In which he emphasizes the way that the "utopian reality" of Soviet ideology was contained in the conceptualization of a setting built from scratch.
[580] VENTURELLI, Enzo: *Urbanistica spaziale. Integrazione dello spazio nella città*, Turin, Pozzo, 1960. The last chapter is entitled "Smog," and proposes a large-scale system for filtering the air polluted by traffic, recalling the arguments for the need for air-conditioning that Friedman had been putting forward since 1958.
[581] ZEVI, Bruno: *Urbanistica spaziale. Recise le caviglie a tutti i fabbricati*, in *L'Espresso*, April 2, 1961; now in id., *Cronache di architettura*, op. cit., vol. 7, pp. 174–77.
[582] MANFREDI, Nicoletti: *A Satellite Town for Monaco*, in *Architectural Review*, December 1963, pp. 408–10.

structures were envisaged that could be "designed entirely by the inhabitants themselves and replaced over time."[583] However, this type of structure had already disappeared in the 1969 project for the competition held by the International Atomic Energy Agency in Vienna: an "artificial sky" of offices suspended by a system of modular aggregation above a pedestrian square. In general Nicoletti was, like Jonas, one of the few megastructuralists who always had the wisdom to draw up his plans in collaboration with first-class engineers like Sergio Musmeci or Giuseppe Pizzetti – see the helicoidal skyscraper (1968–73) for the *New York Crescent Project*,[584] where he proposed the satellite town of Monaco again on the other side of the ocean.

Later Nicoletti too fell back on teaching, before moving on to a much better-established professional practice, designing buildings like the new Law Courts in Rome and the Udine University Campus[585] and more recently in some of the former Soviet countries, like the Kazakhstan Central Concert Hall.[586]

It is significant, however, that when Yona Friedman, who had been one of the main protagonists of Ragon's sketchy and teleological history of architecture, published a revised edition of his *L'architecture de survie*[587] he chose to eliminate Ragon's original introduction: a decision that can be seen as a definitive distancing from the historian.

---

[583] NICOLETTI, Manfredi: *L'aventura del progetto*, Rome/Bari, Laterza, 1991, p. 169.
[584] Ibid. pp. 53–63.
[585] Id., *Continuità, evoluzione, architettura*, Bari, Dedalo, 1978. See SHARP, Dennis (ed.): *Manfredi Nicoletti: architettura, simbolo, contesto / Architecture, Symbol, Context*, Rome, Gangemi, 1998.
[586] NICOLETTI, Luca F. and NICOLETTI, Manfredi (ed.): *Kazakhstan Central Concert Hall*, Rome, Gangemi 2011.
[587] FRIEDMAN, Yona: *L'architecture de survie, ou s'invente aujourd'hui le monde de demain*, with an introduction by Michel Ragon, Paris/Tournai, Casterman, 1978. Revised and enlarged ed., *L'architecture de survie. Une philosophie de la pauvreté*, Paris, Editions de l'Eclat, 2003.

groupe international d'architecture prospective

A.C.

DRAGO. MX001/4

MEMBRES DU GIAP, en 1965

Membres fondateurs

Yona Friedman - Walter Jonas - Paul Maymont - Georges Patrix
Michel Ragon - Ionel Schein - Nicolas Schoffer.

Membres actifs

Urbanistes - Architectes - Ingénieurs: Jacques Bardet - Jean-Claude Bernard - Biro&Fernier - Chaneac - Stephane du Chateau - Deryng - Friedman - Hausermann - Jonas - Maymont - Arthur Quarmby - Guy Rottier - Ionel Schein - Edouard Utudjian.

Plasticiens: J. Guitet - Len Lye - Carl Nesjar - Georges Patrix - Robert Risler - Nicolas Schoffer - Szekely - Vasarely.

Photographe: Lucien Hervé

Scénographe: J. Polieri

Sociologues: J. Fourastié - Abraham Moles

Critiques: Charbonnier - Marc Gaillard - Gassiot-Talabot - A. Parinaud - Michel Ragon - P. Restany.

Bureau:

Président   - Michel Ragon
Vice-Président   - Nicolas Schoffer
   "   "   - Walter Jonas
   "   "   - Yona Friedman
   "   "   - Paul Maymont
   "   "   - Ionel Schein
Secrétaire Général- Georges Patrix
Trésorier   - Robert Risler
Rapporteurs   - Biro & Fernier

99
rue de Vaugirard
Paris 6
222 17 62 - 222 13 25

"GROUPE INTERNATIONAL D'ARCHITECTURE PROSPECTIVE"

563 *Le Manifeste du GIAP*, May 1965. List of founding members.
564 The GIAP meeting in Paris. From left: Nicolas Schöffer, Yona Friedman, Georges Patrix, Paul Maymont and Michel Ragon.

564

NICOLAS SCHÖFFER

565 *Cysp I*, 1956. *Spatiodynamic sculpture* set on the roof of the *Cité Radieuse* in Marseille during the Art Avant-Garde Festival.
In the background, a performance by the Maurice Béjart ballet corps.
566 Project for a *Vertical University* of 1,200 m height, 1967.

WALTER JONAS

567 *Intrahäuser*, 1962–65, Published in Jonas, Walter: *Das Intra-Haus, Vision einer Stadt*, Zurich, Origo-Verlag, 1962.
568 Model of the *Intrapolis*, 1958–60.

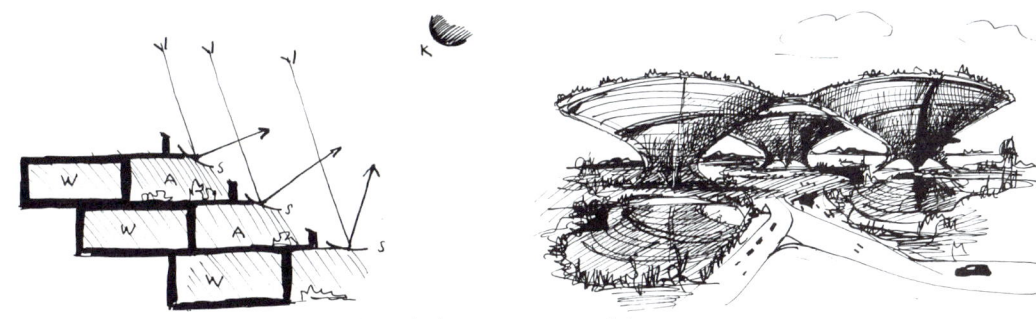

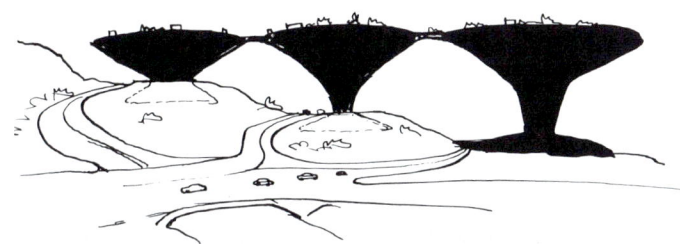

Skizzen zu Intrahäusern von Walter Jonas, TURICUM, Herbst 1961

567

568

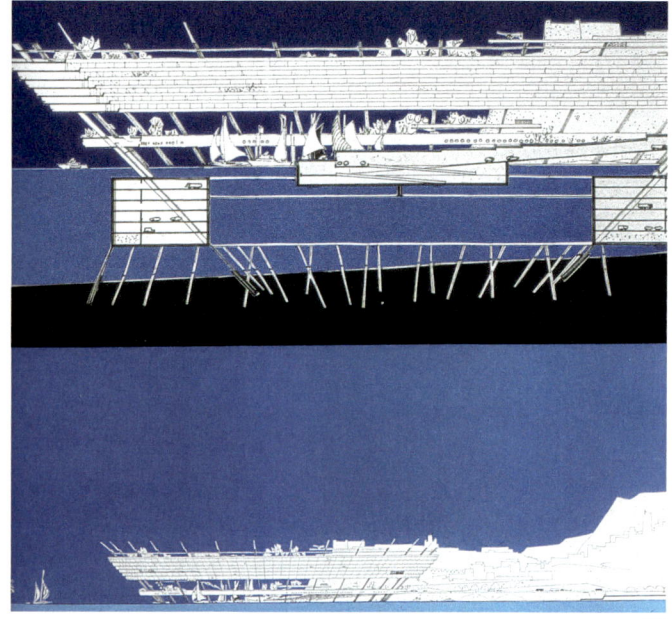

PAUL MAYMONT

569 *Floating City Thalassa*, Monaco, 1963. The system of *Floating Cities* was developed parallel to that of *City-Bridges*.
570 *Paris sous la Seine*, cross section, 1962.

"PARIS SPATIAL"

571 Yona Friedman: Aerial view of *Paris Spatial*, 1960.
572 Yona Friedman: Alterations to the plan for *L'urbanisme spatial*, at the request of Paul Herbé, 1960–64.
573 Yona Friedman: Principle no. 5. *The constructions that form the city should be on an industrial scale.* From *Ten principles of L'urbanisme nouveau*, 1961.

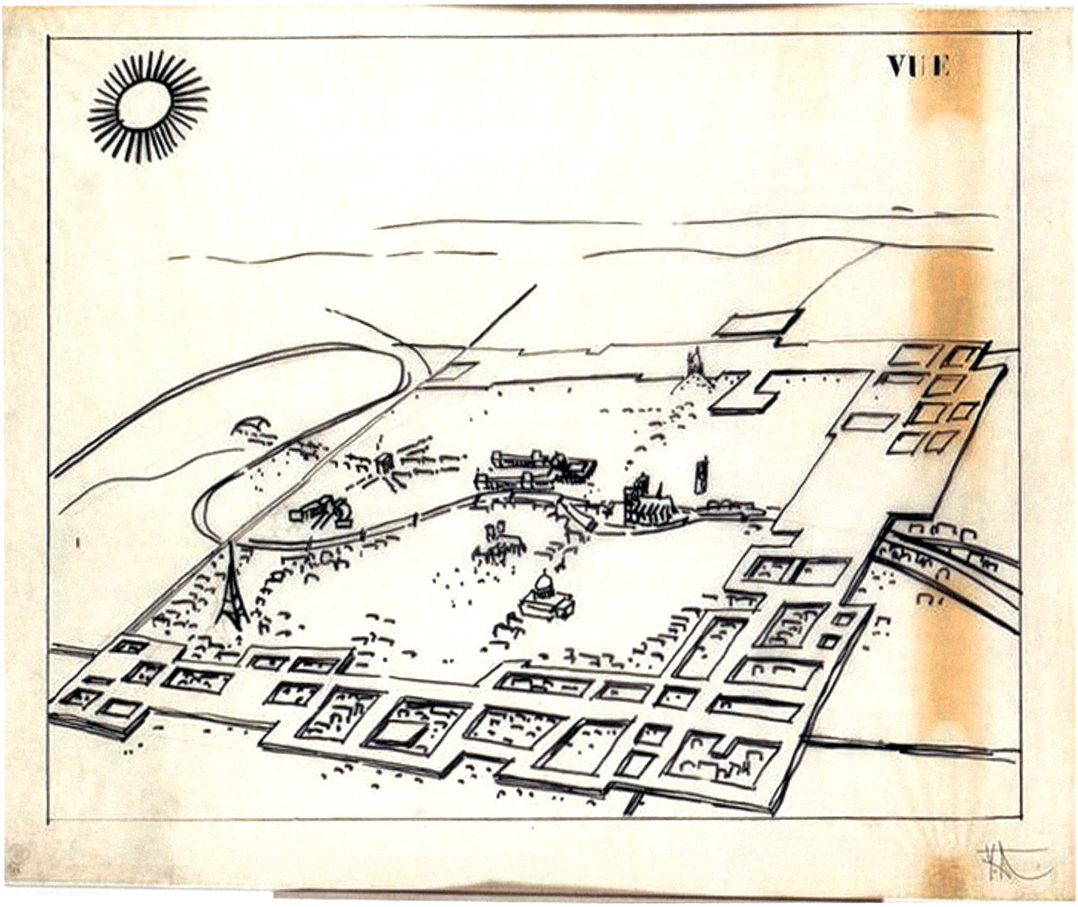

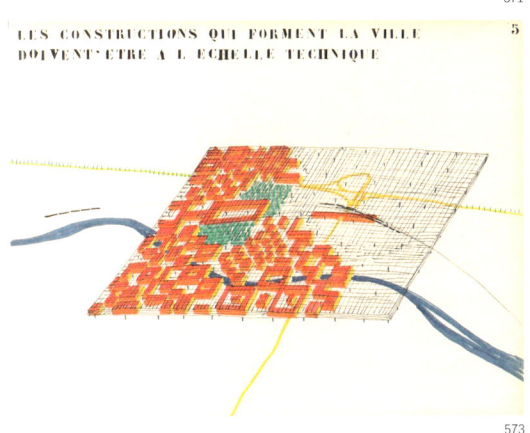

THEORIES. SOCIETY AND TECHNOLOGY / MICHEL RAGON'S GIAP

IDEOLOGY OF THE STREET

A city is measured by the character of its institutions. The street is one of its first institutions.[588]
Louis Kahn

Architects striving to renew their role in society were obliged to broaden the field of their research. The only place of social aggregation that has proved vital over the course of time, resisting all the great changes of history, is the road or street, which since the ancient Romans has been the basic element of organization of the territory and urban space. In reality, as Franco Farinelli has pointed out, the connection between house and street is so close that one has to ask whether it is possible to analyze the two terms separately,[589] even only on the level of ideas – it suffices to think of the Parisian *passages* extoled by Walter Benjamin in his *Passagenwerk* (*The Arcades Project*).

Since the rise of city planning in the 19th century, there has been no shortage of studies assigning great importance to the theme of the road. Arturo Soria y Mata has perhaps taken the most extreme position in this sense by imagining a linear city linking Cadiz with St. Petersburg via Brussels, attributing to the street urban functions that it had never had before and thereby overloading it to the point of destroying it. But the street is "human movement institutionalized"[590] and to be lived it also has to be accepted by the community that gives it its name and function. In the 20th century the first attempts at urban planning by modernist architecture had tended to rationalize streets by differentiating them, but in the process they impoverished them: too often, that is, they separated their activities, condemning them to the exclusive use of automobile traffic.

In general there have not been many studies of the street: emerging only following the criticism of zoning, they started to proliferate in the early seventies,[591] but a genealogy, however minimal, of the concept of the street in architecture from the end of the Second World War to today will help us to gain a better understanding of an element of planning that has had considerable weight in the work of both Yona Friedman and the architects most directly connected with him.

---

[588] Kahn, Louis: *The Room, the Street and Human Agreement*, in *AIA Journal*, vol. 56, September 1971, pp. 33–34.
[589] Farinelli, Franco: *Geografia. Un'introduzione ai modelli del mondo*, Turin, Einaudi, 2003, p. 124. In this connection Farinelli cites a beautiful passage by the geographer Paul Vidal de la Blache: "Ships slide through the water, the cleft waves roll together, and all trace of the passage is blotted out. But land preserves traces of the routes early travelled by mankind. The road is branded on the soil. It sows seeds of life-houses, hamlets, villages, and towns." From Id., *Principes de géographie humaine,* Paris, Collin, 1922, p. 231; rpt. Paris, UTZ, 1995. English transl., *Principles of Human Geography*, New York, H. Holt and Co., 1926, p. 370.
[590] Rykwert, Joseph: *Imparare dalla strada*, in *Lotus*, no. 11, 1976, p. 140; this essay was set to be turned into a book in its own right, devoted entirely to the street, but it was never published. I owe this information to the author. See Id., *The Street: The Use of its History*, in Anderson, Stanford (ed.): *On Streets*, op. cit., pp. 14–27.
[591] Anderson, Stanford (ed.): *On Streets*, op. cit. The book assembles a broad range of studies by architects, city planners, historians and sociologists commenced jointly in 1970 at the IAUS in New York. This cultural climate also had an influence on the contemporary historiography investigating other historical spaces. See Salerno, Luigi, Spezzaferro, Luigi and Tafuri, Manfredo: *Via Giulia, una utopia urbana del 500*, Rome, Staderini, 1973, especially Tafuri's essay, *Via Giulia: storia di una struttura urbana*, pp. 65 ff.

Our starting point has to be the *Unité d'Habitation* that Le Corbusier succeeded in building in Marseille between 1947 and 1953. As well as being the fruit of multiple earlier planning experiences – many have pointed out, above all, the debt it owes to the *Plan Obus* for Algiers [592] of 1931 – the *Unité* realized two different models of internal street. In this sort of great transatlantic liner raised on enormous pilotis we find on the one hand a dense network of "rues intérieures" and on the other the "rue commerçante," located at a height of 25 meters. All of them, however, would end up as simple expanded corridors, and not utilized at all as spaces of aggregation for the community. This first failure – the first in a long series [593] – certainly did not discourage the architects engaged in postwar reconstruction and gravitating around Team 10 or the Architectural Association in London.

Right from the first illustrations of *L'architecture mobile* (1957) Friedman showed that he hoped to separate pedestrian traffic from vehicles by means of elevated footways onto which the mobile living units faced, as well as through the use of elevators and horizontal transport systems (cableways on the roof), while Alison and Peter Smithson had observed since the fifties how in buildings of more than six stories the sense of belonging to a street disappears in any case. "Street-mesh-in-the-air," "building-as-street," "street-in-the-sky" and "street-deck" are all neologisms introduced by the couple to reconsider the space of the community in terms of the street, "the idea, not the form."

On every third floor of their project for *Robin Hood Gardens* (1966–72) in Poplar, East London,[594] the Smithsons inserted spaces of passage that were seen not as voids, but as areas where children could play and neighbors could talk, taking possession of the new space as if it were a traditional street, a bit like what went on in the street where the Smithsons lived for much of their life and where they used to meet their friends. A famous photo shows them sitting in the middle of Limerson Street in 1956 in the company of Eduardo Paolozzi and Nigel Henderson, members of the *Independent Group*. Shortly before he died, Peter Smithson declared on the subject:

That, of course, was part of the trigger that set off the idea that the invention of a new house is the invention of a new kind of street. Because the street in the late nineteenth, early twentieth century was where the children were, and where people talked and all that, despite the climate being against it. The street was the arena of life. To perceive that the invention of another sort of house was the invention of another kind of street, of another arena, or maybe not an arena, wasn't – exactly as I was saying about popular arts – a question of saying the street must be revived. It is a matter of thinking what the street did, and what is the equivalent of it if it is no longer necessary, if the street is dead.[595]

---

[592] See, for example, TAFURI, Manfredo and DAL CO, Francesco: *Architettura contemporanea*, Milan, Electa, 1976, pp. 310–13.
[593] On the subject of the formal influence exercised by the Unité on collective life in housing units, Giuseppe Samonà commented a few years later: "It would be interesting to analyze in depth the consonances and dissonances with Le Corbusier's idea, which has generally been vernacularized by shifting the internal street, which constitutes the means of access to his masterpiece in Marseille, to the outside, turning it into a balcony. The powerful unity of this work is not, in essence, reproducible." Id., *L'urbanistica e l'avvenire della città negli Stati europei*, Bari, Laterza, 1959; rpt. 1985, p. 133.
[594] SMITHSON, Alison and SMITHSON, Peter: *The Charged Void. Architecture,* New York, Monacelli, 2001, p. 296 ff.
[595] COLOMINA, Beatriz: *Friends of the Future: A Conversation with Peter Smithson*, in *October,* vol. 94, fall 2000, p. 9.

Thus the balconies of the Robin Hood Gardens were conceived as "streets-in-the sky," alternating single-story apartments with duplex ones. Unfortunately a series of structural and social drawbacks (lack of services, the high level of crime) meant that the project was a failure in this sense, despite the Smithsons having assumed a less rigid attitude than in the *Golden Lane* Estate (1951-2).[596] In 1967, commenting on some photographs of children at play taken by Henderson, they wrote:

The "life-of-the-streets" in these pictures is a survival from an earlier culture – and a subsistence culture at that. But we have not yet discovered an equivalent to the street form for the present day. All that we know is that the street has been invalidated by the motor car, rising standards of living and changing values. Any revival is historicism.[597]

Reading between the lines, we can see that this is an acknowledgment of the failure of *Golden Lane,* but not an announcement of a change in direction. In later projects like the one for the *Economist* Buildings, on the contrary, the Smithsons raised the ground floor to prevent the access of vehicles, but it was a sort of entrenchment and in the last analysis a flight from urban character.

As Peter Eisenman has pointed out, footbridges vanished from *Robin Hood Gardens,* a sign that the English couple were going through a moment of uncertainty about whether or not to contrast routes for vehicles and pedestrians – "roads" versus "streets." According to Eisenman this change in attitude was a direct consequence of Peter Smithson's study trip to the US – where the automobile was already used by the mass of the population, unlike in Europe – in 1958, during which among other things he paid a visit to Louis Kahn.[598] So 1958 marks the climax of the division between "street" and "road" in the Smithsons' work: this division reached its peak in the Berlin-Hauptstadt competition, where they came up with a system of bridge-streets raised entirely above the historic city but lacking a convincing model of interrelationship between the infrastructure for vehicles and the elevated streets.

While the theme of the "building as street" was central to all the work carried out by the Smithsons – who remained very influential until the mid-seventies[599] – there were a number of similar but more convincing attempts like Candilis, Josic and Woods's two projects for the aforementioned megastructure for Frankfurt-Römerberg and for the Freie Universität in West Berlin of 1963, where the network of corridors is conceived a priori as an internal street system but with a lower level of complexity than in the Frankfurt

---

[596] Smithson, Alison and Smithson, Peter: *The Charged Void . . .* , op. cit., pp. 86 ff.
[597] Id., *Urban Structuring: Studies of Alison & Peter Smithson*, London, Studio Vista, 1967, p. 10.
[598] Eisenman, Peter: *From Golden Lane to Robin Hood Gardens; or If You Follow the Yellow Brick Road, It May Not Lead to Golders Green*, in *Oppositions*, no. 1, September 1973, pp. 27–56; now in *Eisenman Inside Out. Selected Writings 1963–1988*, New Haven/London, Yale University Press, 2004, pp. 41–56.
[599] See the testimony of one of their detractors: "In 1975 [...] the Smithsons still exerted intellectually terror [sic] over many of their former pupils but I always found them artistically talentless and intellectually pretentious. I was disgusted by their Hunstanton school, Robin Hood Gardens, etc. They had produced nothing but instant architectural slums, based on vacuous ideas, mostly borrowed from early pre-World War II modernism." Krier, Léon: *Looking Back without Anger*, in van Schaik, Martin and Mácel, Otar (eds.): *Exit Utopia . . .* , op. cit., p. 310.

competition.[600] In both cases it was a question of giving rise to a city in miniature, permeated by a continuous movement of pedestrians. In Berlin there was one exceptional aspect: the group given the job of designing the university turned to an outside specialist for the facades, Jean Prouvé, who opted for a modular solution in COR-TEN steel.[601] This choice reflects Candilis, Josic and Woods's consistency with respect to some of Team 10's premises on group work and an authentic detachment from the formal results of the architectural project. In this sense Frampton's criticism of the "idealization of flexibility in terms of technique" made against the Berlin project are fairly trivial.[602] Unfortunately Woods did not have the opportunity to develop his conception of the street adequately. Nonetheless the fragmentary considerations that can be found in his only, and what's more posthumous book, *The Man in the Street*, bear witness to the centrality of this theme for the American architect too, as does its title.[603]

The lack of interest in form and the aversion to tall buildings (at the most they were four stories above ground) are two of the numerous points of contact between CJW and Yona Friedman's *La Ville-Spatiale*: it is obvious that the higher you go, the more you lose touch with the street and its socializing properties. The separation of pedestrian routes from the ones used by vehicles remained an objective shared by the aforementioned planners, but in Friedman's case it was renewed in different spatial configurations. Friedman has recently declared:

I met the Smithsons many times but I do not share their ideas (for example, "clusters-groups" as a work of art, conceived by the architect/artist; for me "clusters" are chance configurations and therefore not designed). I'm opposed to tall buildings and have proposed, for the "spatial city," only 4+1 stories above the ground floor. There are many reasons for this limitation:

1. In the "spatial city," to ensure natural light on every floor; if you build higher, technical restrictions will limit the possibility of conceiving the plans of the floors freely.

2. The number of the inhabitants in a highrise block of apartments is too large to facilitate social contact (think of the "critical group size" mentioned above).

3. In emergencies (blackouts, fires, evacuations, etc.) tall buildings present difficulties that are not there with less floors. If the elevator breaks down, it is inconvenient to be living on the 25th floor.

---

[600] "Frankfurt-Römerberg, on the other hand, postulates a model of disarming simplicity that not only affords urban closure and continuity, but also posits a city-in-miniature whose internal order is appropriately differentiated according to status, scale and use." FRAMPTON, Kenneth: *The Generic Street as a Continuous Built Form*, op. cit., p. 333.

[601] On the university in Berlin, see JOHNSTON, Paula (ed.): *Free University Berlin. Candilis, Josic, Woods*, London, Architectural Association, 1999. Also CAMERINO, Guia: *Candilis, Josic e Woods e il progetto per la Berlin Freie Universität: the Mat Building*, PhD thesis in the History of Architecture and of Cities; supervisor Marco De Michelis, AY, 2004-5, IUAV University of Venice.

[602] FRAMPTON, Kenneth: *Modern Architecture: A Critical History*, op. cit., p. 277.

[603] WOODS, Shadrach: *The Man in the Street: A Polemic on Urbanism*, Baltimore, Penguin, 1975. Woods died in 1974 in the US, where he had returned for good in 1968, dividing his time between the studio in New York and teaching at Harvard.

4. High-rise apartment blocks, with all the constraints they entail (repetition of the floor plans, difficulty in meeting people, etc.) are seen as "unfriendly" by their inhabitants: they are symbols of restriction and dictatorship (this is not necessarily true, but is an emotional judgment).

5. As far as the visual aspects are concerned, they are mostly oppressive: a uniformity, or an imposed order. Tall buildings with a "free" design are possible up to a certain point (I have worked on this problem myself): the best examples that I have seen, many years ago, were in Hong Kong, where the inhabitants changed the appearance of very ugly towers by adding, at their whim, balconies, loggias and trees on the front, or simply changing the design of the windows.[604]

A later idea like the *urban carpet* (1975), realized in a Parisian street during a cultural festival in the district of St.-Germain-des-Prés,[605] tried out a cheap technique, with the intention of giving an example of how it was possible to establish a direct relationship between the inhabitants and their urban environment through simple decoration, even in one of the most affluent parts of the city. Thus the street, which in those years seemed the last possible bulwark of community life, was the emblem of a periodical, and above all autonomously managed reorganization of the city.[606] If it were done today the *urban carpet* would probably be taken for an artistic operation *tout court*.
Among the Situationists the street played an essential role as it was the only possible location for a spontaneous communication, as well as the only place where the *dérive* could be practiced: "the *dérive* is, simultaneously, the street reclaimed and communication reestablished. In the end, the only authentic communication takes place in and through the street, which is the *bête noire* of the society of the spectacle."[607]

Attempts to introduce streets in order to stimulate a community life independent of that of the neighborhood and thus render buildings self-sufficient at least where fundamental necessities are concerned have been made with different layouts and in the most disparate contexts. They range from Luigi Carlo Daneri's sinuous complex in the residential district at Forte Quezzi in Genoa (from 1956 onward),[608] to the broken line of Gitai and Mansfeld's tripartite Ramat Hadar complex (1959 – 64) in Haifa[609] and the kilometer-long structure of

---

[604] FRIEDMAN, Yona: *La dimensione collettiva dell'architettura*, interview conducted by Manuel Orazi and Francesco Pezzulli, in BRUGELLIS, Pino and PEZZULLI, Francesco (eds.): *Spazi comuni. Reinventare la città*, Milan, Bevivino, 2006, pp. 60 – 61.
[605] LEBESQUE, Sabine and FENTENER VAN VLISSINGEN, Helene (eds.): *Yona Friedman: Structures . . .* , op. cit., p. 70.
[606] "You know I was going on about how everything has to be changeable, even streets. Yes, streets can be moved to another place without demolitions, without major technical instruments. The city can be reorganized periodically." FRIEDMAN, Yona: *La dimensione collettiva dell'architettura*, op. cit., p. 62.
[607] KAUFMANN, Vincent: *Angels of Purity*, in *October*, no. 79, winter 1997, p. 63.
[608] Manfredo Tafuri is more critical: "Daneri [...] responds with an image and a structure that place in tension, one against the other, the finite nature of the intervention and its frustrated aspiration to become part of the city." In id., *Storia dell'architettura italiana 1944–1985*, Turin, Einaudi, 1986 (2nd ed.), p. 62.
[609] INGERSOLL, Richard: *Munio Gitai . . .* , op. cit., pp. 112–17. This was the largest building ever constructed in Israel, a structure of concrete and prefabricated panels; bridge-streets connected the internal street halfway up with the sidewalks of the road for vehicles.

the Corviale, designed for the IACP[610] by the group headed by Mario Fiorentino (1973 – 82). In all three cases the internal streets halfway up the building were meant to accommodate the community life of the inhabitants of the floors above and below them, once again without any success – in the Genoese case the street has even been closed because of its improper use by would-be suicides. The failure to open stores and services and the unauthorized occupation of these free areas are among the principal causes of yet another negative result.

The street has long been seen as the measure of city life and some of the harshest criticisms of the architecture of the American city are based on this idea. Such criticism has come from people of European birth or training but with very different viewpoints, like Bernard Rudofsky and Denise Scott Brown. Rudofsky, a Viennese intellectual who had lived in Italy in the thirties and then moved to New York, and who has a number of affinities with Yona Friedman (with whom he was associated from the middle of the sixties), is the author of a highly original book, *Streets for People*.[611] In this book, the first on streets to be published in the US, Rudofsky harshly criticizes American society for its chronic insensitivity toward streets, all basically devoted to cars rather than pedestrians, and for this reason inaccessible to people, especially in metropolises like New York or Los Angeles. It follows that in order to make cities more livable, an improvement of the quality of their streets is a necessary step. In this connection Rudofsky wrote:

[The] street is not an area but a volume. It cannot exist in a vacuum; it is inseparable from its environment. In other words it is no better than the company of houses it keeps. The street is a matrix: urban chamber, fertile soil and breeding ground. Its viability depends as much on the right kind of architecture as on the right kind of humanity.[612]

In reality Rudofsky was adjusting his aim, because in 1961, in the exhibition *Roads* he organized at the MoMA in New York with Arthur Drexler, he seemed to be in favor of the introduction of new large highways into the city, even if he concluded that "the true utopia may yet be a road for pedestrians."[613] Immediately afterward, Jane Jacobs wrote an apologia of the city street,[614] but she was more concerned with the security of the life that went on there; for this reason, unlike in the suburbs, there had to be a clear separation between public and private spaces.

---

610 On the Corviale and the excessive "aesthetics of decay" that has accompanied its reappraisal by the world of contemporary art, see the persuasive article by Franco Purini: "The Corviale [...] cannot in any way be considered as the pretext for artistic or sociological practices, but must be thought of and treated as a *part of the city*. It is grappling with physiological problems, problems that only architecture can resolve," Id., *Un chilometro di correzioni*, in *Domus*, no. 886, 2005, p. 75.
611 RUDOFSKY, Bernard: *Streets for People. A Primer for Americans*, New York, Doubleday, 1969.
612 Ibid., p. 20.
613 "This exhibition illustrates the complexity of recently built highways and suggests that we may presently see a wholly new kind of architecture, road-inspired and road-conditioned. [...] In Europe engineers have now been joined by architects, and there is reason to hope that highways will no longer be allowed to destroy cityscapes and landscapes alike, but will be brought within the discipline of the humane arts. Indeed, the true utopia may yet be a road for pedestrians." From the brief introduction by Rusofsky and Arthur Drexler in the catalogue, rpt. in BOCCO GUARNERI, Andrea: *Bernard Rudofsky. A Human Designer*, Vienna/New York, Springer 2003, p. 300. The original title of the exhibition was *The Road as a Work of Art* and it was made up of 45 photographic panels with images from the Renaissance to modern expressways.
614 JACOBS, Jane: *The Death and Life of Great American Cities*, op. cit.

On the other hand Denise Scott Brown, who was born in what is now Zambia and grew up in South Africa, had trained in London and attended the summer seminars of the CIAM. There she came into close contact with the Smithsons, who at the beginning of the sixties advised her to carry on with her urban research in the United States, with Louis Kahn. The latter was well-known in CIAM circles, chiefly for his plan for Philadelphia, which had a decisive influence. The celebrated arrows that indicated the differentiated circulation of pedestrians and automobiles were a mark of an acute reflection on the theme of the street by someone who did not accept any kind of distinction between architecture and city planning:

The Street is a room of agreement. [...] Thru streets, since the advent of the automobile, have entirely lost their room quality. I believe city planning can start with realization of this loss by directing the drive to reinstate the street where people live, learn, shop and work as the room out of commonalty.[615]

In Kahn's entourage Scott Brown was to meet a man in his early thirties, Robert Venturi, who had been born in Philadelphia and was already teaching there, and with whom she would form a lasting sentimental and professional partnership. Publishing *Learning from Las Vegas* together, they opened the eyes of international architectural culture to the new structures that shopping streets ("strips") were bestowing on the contemporary city, and not just in America. The neglect of Scott Brown by historians up to now is somewhat ungenerous: for the most part she has been treated as Venturi's sidekick. And yet on close examination the study of the phenomenon of Las Vegas and Pop culture (which was of British rather than American origin), as well as a key aspect of the VSBA firm's work, can clearly be ascribed to her, as can the sociological aspirations of its designs: even today the corridors of her buildings, most of them for universities, are "streets within the building," designed to perform many of the common functions of a street.[616] In this the architect from Southern Africa has never repudiated the teachings she received at the AA School over fifty years ago.

Today the theme of the street is not a hot topic of architectural debate[617]: the ever wider gap that has opened up between architecture and city planning has led to its being almost totally ignored by architects. But not even city planners are able to revitalize theoretically these spaces of relationship as important as they are ancestral. The most disenchanted conclusion is, once again, that of Rem Koolhaas, who points out that the public administration is no longer in a position to respond to the innate desire for the street, often characterized by a profound nostalgia, since today streets like all collective spaces are created solely with shopping in mind:

---

[615] KAHN, Louis: *The Room, the Street and Human Agreement*, op. cit., pp. 33–34.
[616] SCOTT BROWN, Denise: *Streets as Typologies*, in VENTURI, Robert and SCOTT BROWN, Denise: *Architecture as Signs and System. For a Mannerist Time*, Cambridge (MA)/London, The Belknap Press of Harvard University Press, 2004, pp. 160–61.
[617] An exception is GIUDICI, Maria Sheherazade: *The Last Great Steet of Europe*, in *AA Files*, no. 65, 2012, pp. 124–33.

The exterior of the city is no longer a collective theater where "it" happens; there's no collective "it" left. The street has become residue, organizational device, mere segment of the continuous metropolitan plane where the remnants of the past face the equipments of the new in an uneasy standoff.[618]

His conclusion is pitiless and paradoxical:

The street is dead. That discovery has coincided with frantic attempts at its resuscitation. Public art is everywhere – as if two deaths make a life. Pedestrianization – intended to preserve – merely channels the flow of those doomed to destroy the object of their intended reverence with their feet.[619]

---

[618] Koolhaas, Rem: *Bigness or the Problem of Large*, op. cit., p. 514.
[619] Id., *The Generic City*, in S,M,L,XL, op. cit., p. 1253.

574

575

576

FOUR ARTISTS AT THE EXHIBITION "THIS IS TOMORROW"

574 From the left: Peter Smithson, Eduardo Paolozzi, Alison Smithson, Nigel Graeme Henderson, at Limerson Street, 1956. Photograph by Nigel Graeme Henderson.

THE YALE "LAS VEGAS STUDIO"

575 Robert Venturi and Denise Scott Brown in Las Vegas during their class trip, 1968.

ROBIN HOOD GARDENS, LONDON

576 Project by the Smithsons. Photographs by Sandra Lousada, 1972.

PLAN FOR MIDTOWN PHILADELPHIA

577 Louis Khan: Drawing perspective, c. 1953, from Rykwert, Joseph and Schezen, Roberto: *Louis Kahn,* New York, Harry N. Abrams, 2001.

"URBAN CARPET," PARIS

578 – 579 Yona Friedman: Drawing and photograph at Saint-Germain-des-Prés, Paris, 1975.

THEORIES, SOCIETY AND TECHNOLOGY / IDEOLOGY OF THE STREET / 481

580

SAINT-GERMAIN-DES-PRÉS, PARIS

580 Live performance by Yona Friedman, 1975.

"ART IN THE STREET," PARIS

581–584 Yona Friedman: Proposal for the intervention of ornamental facades decided by local residents, 1975.

581

582

583

584

GRAPH THEORY AND THE DIAGRAM

Information is at once a political act and the only real form of politics.[620]
Yona Friedman

In 1964, which is also the year he obtained French nationality, Friedman began to hold seminars at a number of American universities. His disappointment over the dissolution of the GEAM and the unproductive experience of the GIAP led Friedman to make a break with his previous method of research. To counter the numerous accusations of ineffectual utopianism, Friedman started to tackle theoretical speculation in a new way, concentrating on the theme of participation. He stopped illustrating his lectures with complex images, using instead just simple graphs or drawings, easy to reproduce on a blackboard. In 1970 he made a selection of his scattered writings on mobile architecture,[621] but it was as if he wished to close the accounts with that phase. In fact immediately afterward, in 1971, he collected his American lectures and reorganized them into a book that would become the most widely translated of all his writings, in four countries: *Pour une architecture scientifique*.[622] Like many other megastructuralists, Friedman was convinced that he had been misrepresented, that architects and critics had focused on his images, paying attention only to their *forms* instead of to his intense experimental research into urban reorganization. Publishing a book on architecture without images and plans is almost a contradiction in terms, but it is also the mark of a distinct inner change. According to Friedman it was a sign that the mentality of a generation of architects had changed.

Thus this research made use of instruments that were new for Friedman: from the very first pages, the book is illustrated with simplified schemes that describe the workings of the traditional relationship between the architect and the users of his architecture. He calls these schemes "diagrams." Friedman's ultimate goal is the same: to maximize the ability of inhabitants/users to determine the character of their own dwellings, but now with a further pretension of feasibility: architecture is seen as a "teachable science." In the first chapter, "Democratization," the opening section is devoted to "The Large Number," that is to say to the theme of the most recent Milan Triennale in 1968, directed by Giancarlo De Carlo. So it was not a new subject, far from it: Friedman had been invited to take part in the conference organized by the Triennale on the large number, a fairly ambiguous concept that was interpreted in an extremely varied manner, along with many other architects, artists and designers (the Smithsons, Woods, Viganò, Zanuso, Kepes, Steiner, etc.), but

---

[620] FRIEDMAN, Yona: *Pour une architecture scientifique*, with an introduction by Philippe Sers, Paris, Belfond, 1971. English transl., *Toward a Scientific Architecture*, Cambridge (MA), MIT Press, 1975. The quotation has been transl. from the Italian ed., *Per una architettura scientifica*, ed. by Rosario Giuffré, Rome, Officina, 1975, p. 37.
[621] FRIEDMAN, Yona: *L'architecture mobile, vers une cité . . .* , op. cit.
[622] FRIEDMAN, Yona: *Pour une architecture scientifique*, op. cit., Madrid, Alianza, 1973; Cambridge (MA), MIT Press, 1975; Rome, Officina, 1975; Moscow, Stroyizdat, 1982.

not in the exhibition; in any case neither the conference nor the exhibition took place.[623] This theme was not just at the base of *Toward a Scientific Architecture*, but was to remain a constant preoccupation in the reflections of the Franco-Hungarian architect, that is to say the criticism of the idea of the average man:

The "big number" is the foremost problem of our time: a "mass of individuals", possessive of their "individuality" and determined to manifest it. But this manifestation of individuality cannot occour through intermediation. Everyone must be capable of expressing it alone. "Mass individuality" is therefore opposed to the concept of the "average man", which in reality is nothing more than an illusion. An architect has to serve the individuality of a single client or – to be precise – that of a small group of clients. But it is totally impossible to serve the individuality of a thousand future inhabitants, who cannot even really express their desires. So, from this point of view, a classic building structure, where almost everything is fixed and stable, is of absolutely no use to us.[624]

In this vision the task of architecture is tantamount to the compilation of a complete list of all the possible solutions to a housing problem with the aid of a specific notation (mapping) and the development of a method that would allow directions to be associated with each number on the list. An architecture "à la carte," as in a restaurant, where the manager (the architect) does not influence the choices of his customer except through more or less disinterested advice.

Thus the future inhabitant should be put in the position of being able to choose his own dwelling in a conscious way to suit his requirements and with a clear idea of what effects his choice may have on adjacent dwellings or ones in the same building (a building that Friedman calls *infrastructure*, the hardware of architecture, while the needs of the inhabitant represent the software). The role of the architect is completely supplanted, or rather transformed: he will have to draw up these lists in a neutral way, without influencing the user and following strict rules that are valid for a range of well-defined cases as in the sciences, which can in fact be taught regardless of the teacher's personality. So if the activity of the architect and the city planner currently derive from a discipline of "apprenticeship," their new role is purely informative and stems on the contrary from a teachable science; it is that of a scientific planner. This is an extremist vision of participation in architecture where it is the architect that assists the inhabitant in the definition of his needs and not the other way round. On this Friedman admitted no distinction between architect and city planner – just like Team 10 for that matter – deliberately ignoring the deep fissure that had opened up between the two professions.[625]

---

[623] After the May 1968 events in France, as is well-known, the student protests spread throughout Europe, leading to numerous boycotts of institutionalized cultural events like the Venice Biennale and Film Festival and the Milan Triennale. On this development, which symbolically marked the end of the climate of synthesis of arts that had emerged after the war, see Zardini, Mirko: *Triennale Milano: "il grande numero,"* in Risselada, Max and van den Heuvel, Dirk (eds.): *Team 10. 1953 – 81. In Search of . . .* , op. cit., p. 158. See also Nicolin, Paola: *Castelli di carte . . .* , op. cit.

[624] Friedman, Yona: *Interview,* in *Domus,* no. 879, March 2005, p. i.

[625] For the discussion in Italy, see, for example, Samonà, Giuseppe: *L'urbanistica e l'avvenire della città negli Stati europei,* op. cit., and id., *L'unità architettura-urbanistica. Scritti e progetti 1929–1973,* ed. by Pasquale Lovero, Milan, Franco Angeli, 1975.

Thus Friedman proposed three axioms:
1. Architects and city planners mark out boundaries in the preexisting space (closed forms).
2. Each of the spaces delimited must have at least one access.
3. There will be at least two different types of spaces delimited.

"Mapping" on the other hand was a concept that heralded the use of the diagram as the preferred instrument of the new scientific planner.
To Friedman the word "mapping" signifies that there is a code that makes it possible to transcribe every operation or element of the system represented (mapped) as an operation or an element of the system that represents it (mapping), and that in each of these two systems there is only one element corresponding to another element.[626]

This is a one-to-one system of representation in which it is not just objects, enclosed spaces (rooms), that are represented, but also "operations," i.e. all the possible connections and relations between a certain number of enclosed spaces. Thus the diagram becomes indispensable, since a simple view (perspective, axonometric projection, etc.) is no longer sufficient to show the different possibilities of articulation of an architectural complex.
Translating the three axioms of the architect/city planner into rules of mapping produces the code of connected and systematic plane graphs. Thus the mapping will consist of figures formed by points connected by lines, in such a way that no point remains unconnected, i.e. isolated. Consequently the use of the mapping model allows spatial articulations that are redundant, as it were, to be discarded a priori, i.e. where some spaces are included in the plan only to make it fit with a geometric shape that has been conceived regardless of its functions. In other words it is not the functions that have to adapt to a form established in advance, but the exact opposite: the composition of the spaces should be a point of arrival and not of departure. In the following chapters, Friedman discusses the extension of a three-dimensional analysis to the city, using the model of the "urban mechanism"[627] that in turn was the fruit of his earlier studies on a theory of comprehensible systems.[628]
Friedman was looking for an "objective" way of thinking that would avoid the error shared by the majority of predictions, that of an idea which mistakes its own desires for reality. And this position, at once scientific and populist, was well received in the United States, where the themes of individualism and do-it-yourself with a marked libertarian component are fundamental elements of American culture.[629]

The diagram had been used as a tool in architecture at European and American universities since the end of the 19th century. But it is only in very recent years that architectural culture has attained a degree of awareness of the systematic nature of its employment.

---

[626] FRIEDMAN, Yona: *Toward a Scientific Architecture*, op. cit.
[627] This appeared for the first time in FRIEDMAN, Yona: *Méthode des mécanismes urbains*, in Techniques et architecture, no. 4, series 29, 1968.
[628] FRIEDMAN, Yona: *La théorie des systèmes compréhensibles et son application à l'urbanisme*, in Architecture d'aujourd'hui, no. 115, 1964, pp. 28–29. Id., *L'urbanisme comme système compréhensible*, in Techniques et architecture, no. 6, series 25, 1964, pp. 153–55.
[629] *Pour une architecture scientifique* is the only one of Friedman's books to have been translated in the US (*Toward a Scientific Architecture*, Cambridge (MA), MIT Press, 1975). In the next section we will look at the reasons for this, but paradoxically it is also the only one to have been translated in the Soviet Union, in 1982, where individualism was certainly not a traditional principle.

During his time in Israel Friedman had been able to get to know Alexander Klein, a Russian architect present at the second CIAM in Frankfurt who then emigrated to Palestine, where he was director of the Technion and worked at the Town-Planning Authority until his death in 1961.[630] A similar authority had also operated during the British Mandate for Palestine, and in the early years of the state of Israel its action played a strategically important role. In some of his analytical and rigorous studies linked to his more wide-ranging research into the *Existenzminimum*, Klein reduced the amount of information on the construction of the buildings to a minimum, while taking account of the space taken up by furniture and above all of the possible movements of the inhabitants. According to Aldo Rossi, notoriously critical of functionalism in general, in Klein "dimension becomes a way of life by determining the proportions of the acts of life."[631] while for Giorgio Grassi the value of his studies lay in the fact that "they have affirmed a scientific dimension of architecture, linked indissolubly to the form of the process of investigation itself,"[632] a dimension to which Friedman would remain faithful in his own way. In Maddalena Scimemi's view, on the other hand, Alexander Klein's technique of design constituted a phase of transition between the program and the diagram.[633]

Friedman claims to have been in direct contact with Klein. This is credible not only because Klein taught at the Technion, where Friedman had been first a student and then an assistant (1949–56), but also because he was an adviser on the fortification of new settlements owing to his having served in the Engineer Corps during the 1948 war of independence. This firsthand experience in the army and then in contact with the Planning Authority had a powerful influence on Friedman – he himself describes it as "very decisive" – orienting him toward an approach that would be as little abstract as possible; in a word: technical. It is certainly not easy to determine the best layout for a trench simply by drawing it on a map as it is not possible to take account either of the altimetry or of the movements in the field of the friendly or hostile forces – which are in turn subdivided into tactical groups that advance at different speeds, depending on the means of transport available: tanks, jeeps, etc. It is also necessary to take into consideration the nature and range of the enemy firing points. Military engineering, ballistics, geography, city planning and architecture: the diagram is able to bring together different parameters, some of which defy representation in Cartesian coordinates.

Over the course of the 20th century the diagram would find a vast field of applications, from medicine to warfare. It began to be used in the US during the Second World War and would later be introduced into university courses, thanks in part to architects: Walter Gropius at Harvard made use of the *bubble diagram* for teaching,[634] while a few years later

---

[630] WARHAFTIG, Myra: *Alexander Klein zum 110. Geburtstag*, in *Bauwelt*, vol. 80, no. 23, 1989, p. 1042.
[631] ROSSI, Aldo: *Il problema della periferia nella città moderna* (1960), now in *Scritti scelti sull'architettura e la città 1956–1972*, ed. by Rosaldo Bonicalzi, Macerata, Quodlibet, 2012, p. 126.
[632] GRASSI, Giorgio. *La costruzione logica dell'architettura*, Marsilio, Padua, 1967. New revised ed., Milan, Franco Angeli, 1998, p. 76.
[633] SCIMEMI, Maddalena: *Architettura come diagram. Il contributo inglese negli anni del II dopoguerra*, dissertation, supervisor Marco De Michelis, IUAV, ac. yr. 1997–98.
[634] HERDEG, Klaus: *The Decorated Diagram. Harvard Architecture and the Failure of the Bauhaus Legacy*, Cambridge (MA), MIT Press, 1983.

Louis Kahn would use it too in his plan for Philadelphia, as a means by which "the architect can control systems of physical communication and offer new concepts." In 1964 Christopher Alexander came up with an important definition for architectural culture:

The constructive diagram can describe the context, and it can describe the form. It offers us a way of probing the context, and a way of searching for form. [...] In all design tasks the designer has to translate sets of requirements into diagrams which capture their physical implications. In a literal sense these diagrams are no more than stages on the way to the specification of a form, like the circulation diagram of a building [...]. The form's basic organization is born precisely in the constructive diagrams which precede its design.[635]

It was in 1964 that Friedman began to give lectures at American universities and thus he had many opportunities to encounter at firsthand this kind of research, complementary to his own, on the mobility of the population.

Today the diagram is proving very popular in writing on architecture, largely due to Rem Koolhaas who in S,M,L,XL demonstrated its usefulness for large-scale projects, something in which he was promptly followed by Peter Eisenman.[636] The latter has always been acutely sensitive to variations in the architectural *zeitgeist*, but he was also a pupil of Colin Rowe who, perpetuating the method used by Wittkower to study Palladio, was in the habit of stylizing plans in his analyses to the point where they were reduced to what are called figure-ground diagrams. In his book on Terragni,[637] Eisenman gives the name diagram not just to these planimetric schemes but also to axonometric cutaways. His definition of diagram, wholly absent from the volume devoted to the architect from Como, echoes Deleuze's (made in connection with the painting of Francis Bacon): "The diagram is thus the operative set of asignifying and nonrepresentative lines and zones, line-strokes and color-patches. And the operation of the diagram, its function, says Bacon, is to be 'suggestive.' Or, more rigorously, [...] it is to introduce 'possibilities of fact.' "[638] Diagrams, in short, "mark out possibilities of fact, but do not yet constitute a fact." In reality Eisenman, paraphrasing Deleuze, limits himself to updating a passage of the dissertation he discussed with Rowe at Cambridge in 1963, where he distinguished between the surface aspects of architecture – texture, color, form – and its conceptual aspects – frontality, obliqueness, slippage – which are not perceptible through the senses.[639] No consideration is given to the internal circulation of users, or to any other requirement.

---

[635] ALEXANDER, Christopher: *Notes on the Synthesis of Form*, Cambridge (MA), Harvard University Press, 1964, p. 92.
[636] See EISENMAN, Peter: *Diagram Diaries*, New York, Universe, 1999.
[637] EISENMAN, Peter: *Giuseppe Terragni: Transformations, Decompositions, Critiques*, with essays by Giuseppe Terragni and Manfredo Tafuri, New York, Monacelli Press, 2003.
[638] DELEUZE, Gilles: *Francis Bacon: Logique de la sensation*, Paris, Editions de la Différence, 1981. English transl., *Francis Bacon: The Logic of Sensation*, London/New York, Continuum, 2003, p. 101. Deleuze had defined the diagram as an "abstract machine" a year earlier with the publication of DELEUZE, Gilles and GUATTARI, Felix: *Mille plateaux*, Paris, Editions de Minuit, 1980. English transl., *A Thousand Plateaus: Capitalism and Schizophrenia*, Minneapolis (MN), University of Minnesota Press, 1987.
[639] EISENMAN, Peter: *The Formal Basis of Modern Architecture*, facsimile, Zurich, Lars Müller, 2006.

Many contemporary architects make use of the diagram:[640] among them Bernard Tschumi, who has always been interested in the events that take place inside architecture ("there is no architecture without program, without action, without event"[641]), worked for a while as a young man in the studio of Candilis, Josic and Woods and in parallel got to know Yona Friedman, whose influence is clear in his first published article.[642] Its contemporary use, however, is distinguished by the particular emphasis given to the resolving power of the diagram, as a means of coping with the complexity of the variables and the obstacles of the profession. Toyo Ito, for example, was perhaps the first to speak of a "diagram architecture" in connection with some of Kazuyo Sejima's projects in which the architect sees the building "as essentially the equivalent of the kind of spatial diagram used to describe the daily activities for which the building is intended."[643]

Pier Vittorio Aureli and Gabriele Mastrigli have harshly criticized this kind of decorative use, which runs the risk of the diagram being reduced to an "iconographic fetish" and of the resulting designs ending up as "nothing but representations of something that is inexpressible through architecture, precisely because they are intended to represent the use of architecture, i.e. the life that goes on inside it."[644] An example might be the embossed red cover of Michael Hays's anthology *Architecture Theory since 1968*, which is covered with diagrams that have no clear function apart from decoration. The anthology ends with an essay by Robert Somol, who has had no hesitation in picking the diagram as the paradigm of the most recent generation of architects:

While the first generation of the neo-avant-garde in the early 1960s began to investigate the semiotics of form, its progeny (specifically, in the generation that came of age after the events of May 1968) have indulged a diagrammatics of function and structure.[645]

The origins of this use have for long been uncertain. The studies by members of the so-called *post-critical* camp like Somol and Sanford Kwinter[646] do not agree, but Scimemi has shown that the diagram has been utilized in architecture since the fifties, especially in British circles,[647] although by only a few architects like the Smithsons – the Doorn Manifesto is

---

[640] Toyo Ito has used the term diagram architecture in relation to SEJIMA, Kazuyo: *Diagram Architecture*, in *El Croquis*, no. 77, 1996, pp. 18–24. See also *Diagram Work: Data Mechanics for a Topological Age*, monographic issue ed. by B. van Berkel and Caroline Bos, in *ANY*, no. 23, December 1998.

[641] Tschumi continues: "These texts reiterate that architecture is never autonomous, never pure form, and, similarly, that architecture is not a matter of style and cannot be reduced to a language." In *Architecture and Disjunction*, Cambridge (MA), MIT Press, 1996, p. 3.

[642] MONTES, Fernando and TSCHUMI, Bernard: *Do-It-Yourself-City*, in *L'Architecture d'aujourd'hui*, no. 148, February–March 1970, pp. 98–105; also see the interview with Tschumi in the appendix.

[643] ITO, Toyo: *Diagram Architecture*, op. cit., pp. 18–24.

[644] AURELI, Pier Vittorio and MASTRIGLI, Gabriele: *Architecture after the Diagram: Note on the Limitations of a Concept*, in *Lotus International*, no. 127, 2006, p. 104.

[645] SOMOL, Robert E.: *Oublier Rowe*, in *ANY*, nos. 7/8, 1994, p. 8; reprinted in HAYS, Michael (ed.): *Architecture Theory since 1968*, Cambridge (MA)/London, MIT Press, 1998, pp. 780–82, where Hays dwells upon Deleuze's definition of diagram and its introduction into the American debate in the nineties.

[646] KWINTER, Sanford: *The Genealogy of Models: the Hammer and the Song*, in *ANY*, no. 23, December 1998, pp. 57–60. See SOMOL, Robert: *The Diagrams of Matter*, ibid. See also SOMOL, Robert and WHITING, Sarah: *Notes around the Doppler Effect and other Moods of Modernism*, in *Perspecta*, no. 33 ("Mining Autonomy"), 2002.

[647] SCIMEMI, Maddalena: *The Unwritten History of the Other Modernism. Architecture in Britain in the Fifties and Sixties*, in *Daidalos*, no. 74, October 2000, pp. 15–21.

a diagram, the text of the *Team 10 Primer* (1968) is illustrated with many diagrams and Cedric Price, whose reputation has not coincidentally risen greatly in recent years but who was not very well-known at the time,[648] was prompted to make use of the diagram by the spread of cybernetic theory in the mid-sixties, shifting the attention of the architects from the standardization of building to the new needs not amenable to standardization induced by the society of spectacle and information: without taking these factors into consideration a project like the *Fun Palace* and its gradual evolution "from participatory architecture to a cybernetic machine" would be incomprehensible, like much of so-called diagram architecture.[649]

Yona Friedman would only have an opportunity to apply his graph theory and utilize a diagram in 1978, in the Lycée Bergson at Angers which we will look at in the next chapter. From a simple scheme made up of points and lines determined by the inhabitant, the architect would make a *bubble diagram* – a specific type that had been introduced into teaching at Harvard by Gropius in the forties: this was "a method of design that made it possible to process functional interactions in topological terms prior to their geometrical and distributive determination."[650] In other words it allows the drawing up of a rough scheme of the most necessary spaces on the basis of the planned use and is one of the simplest forms of communication that can be used to discuss architecture with the uninitiated.

So the diagram is a special form of *representation for the purposes of communication*, but not for that alone as it can easily be adapted to other uses. It lends itself equally well to communication with users in medicine and in journalism. Another advocate of participation in architecture like Christopher Alexander soon became aware of its powerful impact: "I found that the diagrams themselves had immense power, and that, in fact, most of the power of what I had written lay in the power of these diagrams."[651]

Friedman started work on the project for Angers in 1978, and so as an application of the diagram it is fairly belated, just as it is the only building he constructed, for that matter. But it is significant nonetheless because the French megastructuralists of the GEAM, GIAP, etc., unlike the British neo-avant-gardes for instance, had never accompanied their projects with diagrams. It is partly for this reason that the designs of Maymont, Schöffer and the others seem to us today to be so naïve and obsolete, in contrast to the playful utopias of Price[652] or the best projects of Candilis, Josic and Woods.

---

[648] On his reappraisal, see in particular PRICE, Cedric: *Re: CP*, ed. by Hans Ulrich Obrist, Basel, Birkhäuser, 2003. The book contains an incoherent collection of materials, an introduction by Rem Koolhaas and essays by Arata Isozaki and Patrick Keiller.
[649] See LOBSINGER, Mary Louise: *Cybernetic Theory and the Architecture of Performance* . . . , op. cit., pp. 130–33.
[650] CORBELLINI, Giovanni: *Diagrams. Instructions for Use*, in *Lotus International*, No. 127, 2006, p. 88–95.
[651] ALEXANDER, Christopher: *Preface to the Paperback Edition*, in *Notes on the Synthesis of Form*, op. cit.
[652] "Cedric Price was a friend and an ally in thinking about architecture. I met Cedric in the early 60s and we hit it off immediately. He saw in architecture not simply a technical gadget or a propaganda item (as many of the avant-garde of the time did). Indeed, architecture is not simply an applied technology and a decor for theatre performance. It also has a strong social and emotional overtone (it is difficult to separate the two). We were in agreement on these precepts." FRIEDMAN, Yona: *Cedric Price: Friend and Ally*, in *Domus*, no. 870, May 2004, p. 56.

Friedman, although only belatedly and following long periods of teaching in American universities, realized the power of the diagram and put it at the service of his philosophy of participation after writing *Utopies réalisables* (1975), his treatise on society and communication. For this reason, among others, Peter Cook was right when he wrote that Friedman "has little real spiritual similarity with the French tradition."[653]

---

[653] Cook, Peter: *Experimental Architecture*, London, Studio Vista, 1970, p. 86.

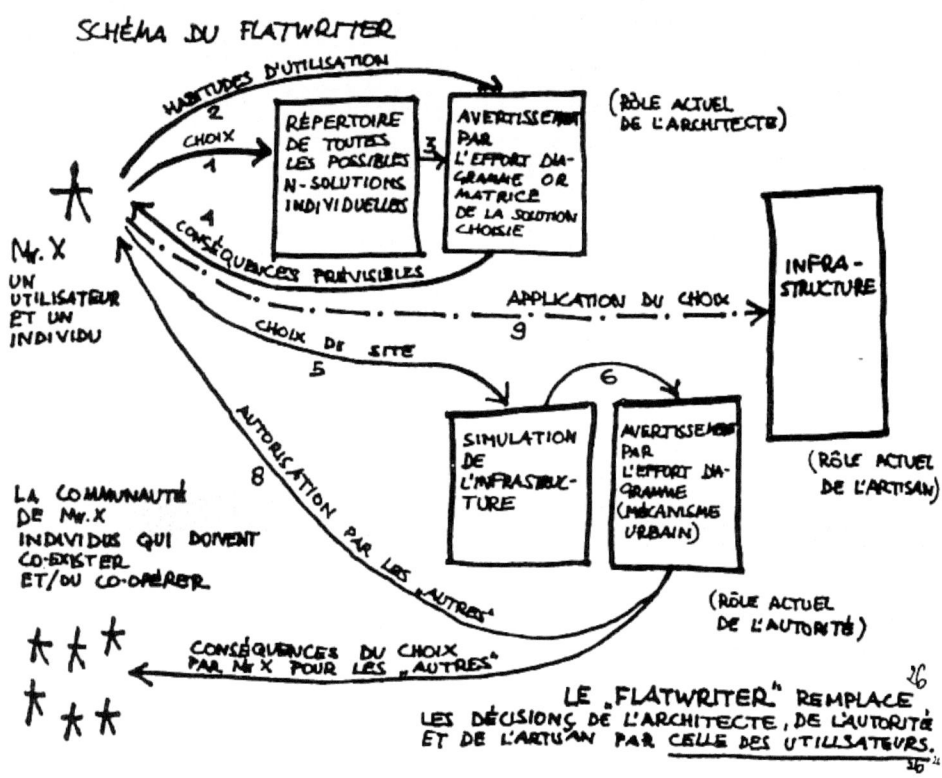

SCHEME OF THE FLATWRITER, 1967

585 From Friedman, Yona: *Pour une architecture scientifique,* with an introduction by Philippe Sers, Paris, Belfond, 1971.

"URBAN MECHANISM"

586–589 Yona Friedman: Abstract effort diagram series, 1966–72.

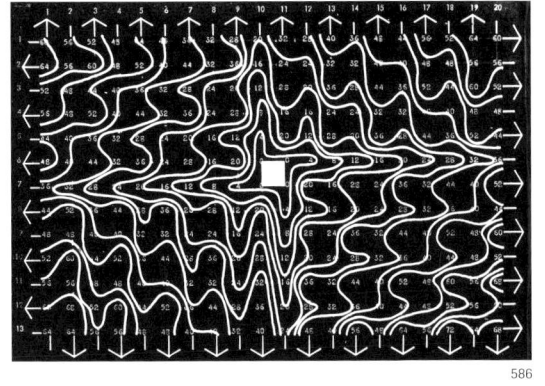
586

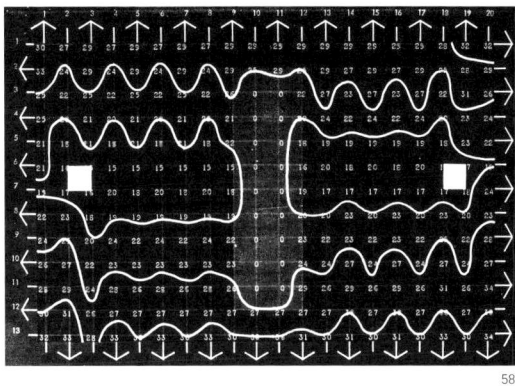
587

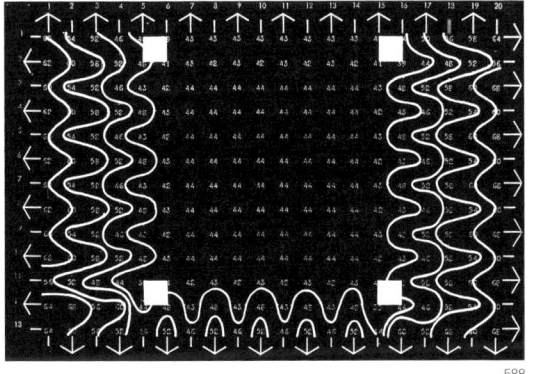
588

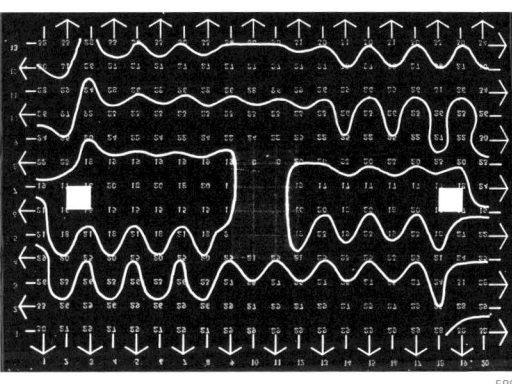
589

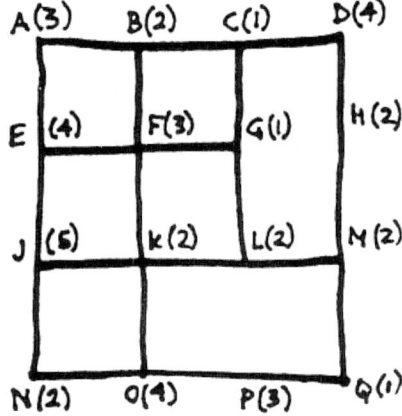
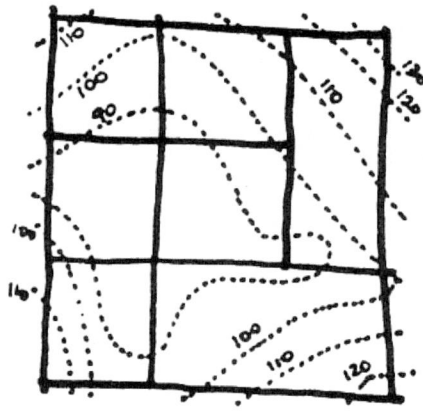

The knowable data of a city

1 / The network of roads (infrastructure).

2 / The number of people who travel past a given point in the city during a specific interval.

This data can be summed up in the matrix of local efforts following the formula.

This matrix can be replaced by the effort diagram of the city. This diagram is easier to read.

"STRESS DIAGRAM" OF A CITY, 1971

590 Yona Friedman: Diagrams and notes.

ALEXANDER KLEIN

591 *Studies of circulation and the use of space inside buildings*, 1928. Published in Baffa Rivolta, Matilde and Rossari, Augusto: *Alexander Klein. Scritti e progetti dal 1906 al 1957*, Milan, Mazzotta, 1975.

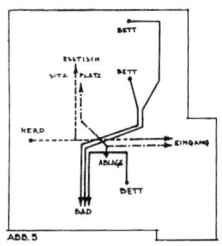
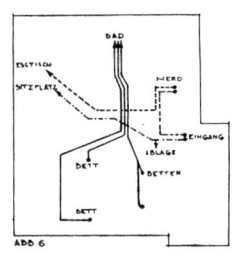
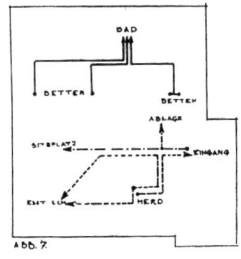
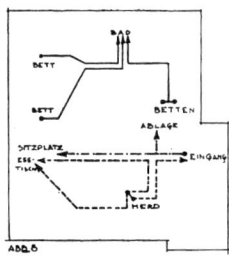

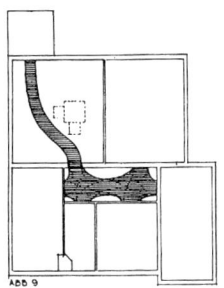
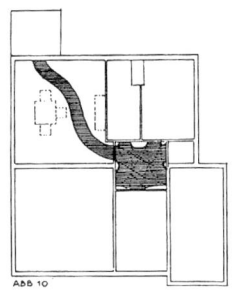
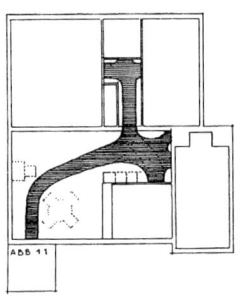
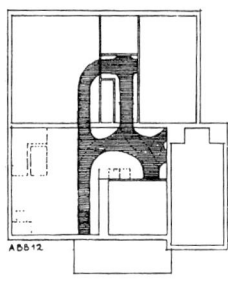

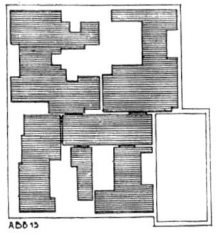
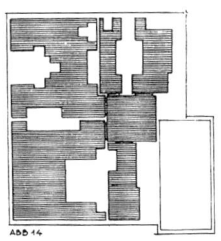
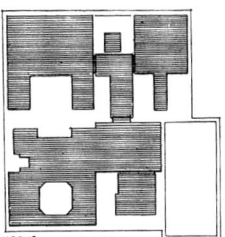
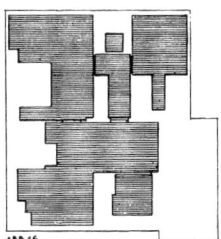

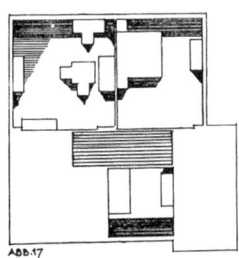
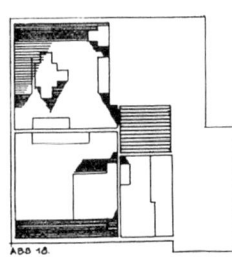
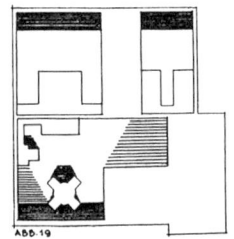
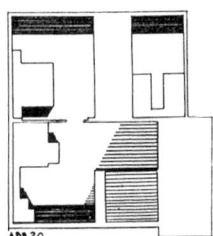

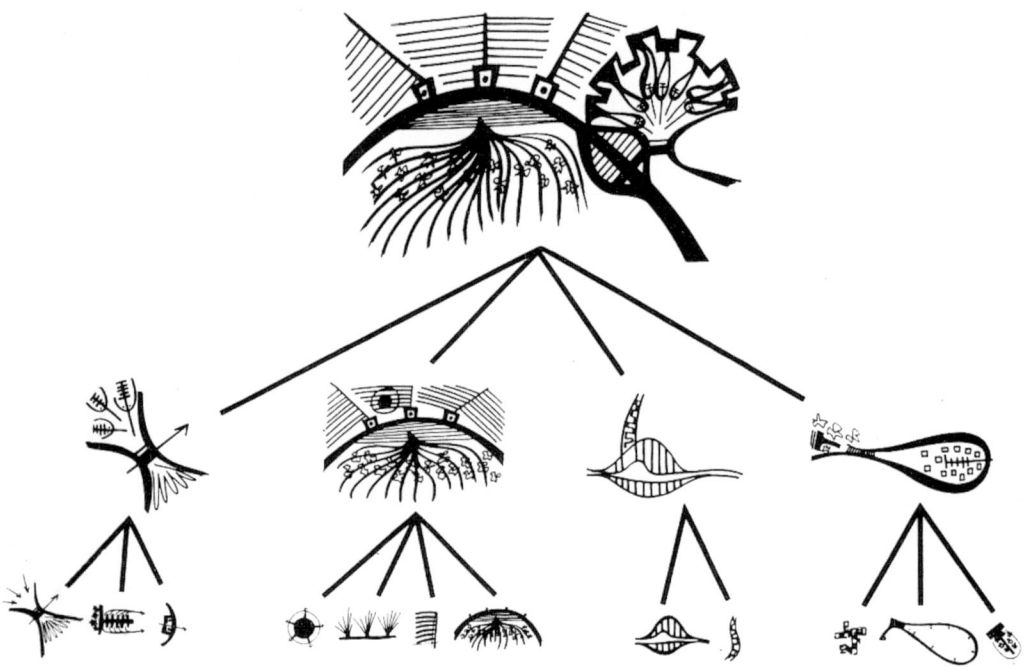

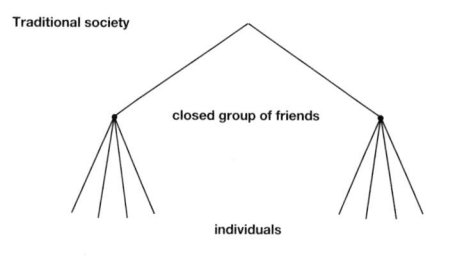

CHRISTOPHER ALEXANDER

592 Diagram from Alexander, Christopher: *Notes on the Synthesis of Form*, Cambridge (MA), Harvard University Press, 1964.
593 – 594 Diagrams from Alexander, Christopher: *A City Is Not a Tree*, 1965.

YONA FRIEDMAN AND BERNARD TSCHUMI

595 Friedman's *Bubble* diagram for the *Lycée David*, Angers, 1978.
596 Scheme of play in American football, 1981, from Tschumi, Bernard: *Architecture and Disjunction*, Cambridge (MA), MIT Press, 1996.

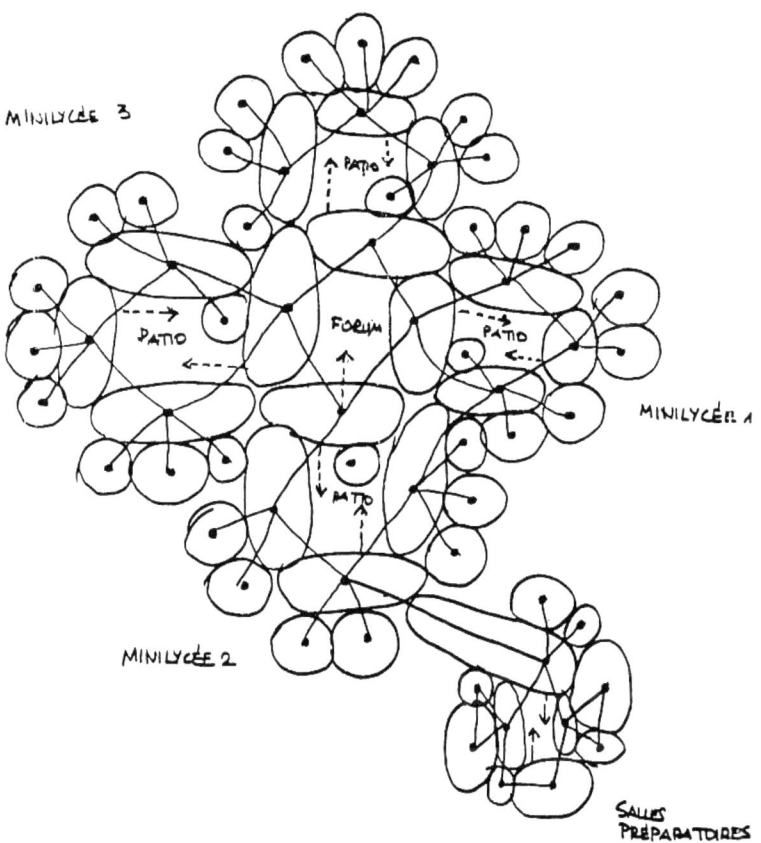

ARCHITECTURE-BY-YOURSELF: NICHOLAS NEGROPONTE AND THE MIT

My aim is to understand and explain things in a way that works for everyone. Staying within the system in order to answer for it is a weaker position.[654]
Iannis Xenakis

As the problem of reconstruction eased with the passing of the years and at the same time popular discontent with the new housing complexes grew, the architects who felt the distance of their profession from society most keenly adopted a more scientific attitude toward design. In short *Pour une architecture scientifique* was no exception: more and more architects, especially in the English-speaking countries, became fascinated by the computer, mathematical analyses, diagrams and the idea of basing design on new and less arbitrary logical approaches, a sentiment that seems to be rising again today with the supporters of parametric architecture. At the time however, in England, at Cambridge, this fascination found expression in lines of research that were heterogeneous and sometimes contradictory, but had a powerful influence on the development of some key figures in contemporary architectural culture, like Christopher Alexander and Peter Eisenman.[655]

Iannis Xenakis, designing the Philips Pavilion on behalf of Le Corbusier at the Brussels World's Fair in 1958, completely changed the Swiss architect's initial idea, using mathematical procedures to determine the form of the enclosing structure.[656] Xenakis – an engineer by training – said that he arrived at the characteristic final form of the structure through mathematical calculation, but at that point the logic came to a standstill and he had to rely on intuition to finish the work.[657]

According to the British architect and critic Alan Colquhoun, who attended a lecture he gave at the Architectural Association in 1966, Yona Friedman also utilized these methods to arrive at an organizational hierarchy in the program of design:

Friedman, in describing methods of computing the relative positions of functions within a three-dimensional city grid, has acknowledged that the designer [is] always faced, after computation, with a choice of alternatives, all of which are equally good from an operational point of view.[658]

Colquhoun set out to demonstrate that the approach he called "biotechnical determinism" was one of the two traditional conceptions adopted by the Modern Movement, in permanent

---

[654] Xenakis, Iannis: *Conversations*, in *L'Arc*, no. 51, 1972, now in id., *Musique. Architecture*, Paris/Tournai, Casterman, 1976.
[655] Keller, Sean: *Fenland Tech: Architectural Science in Postwar Cambridge*, in *Grey Room*, no. 23, spring 2006, pp. 40–65. Also see his dissertation discussed at Harvard, *Systems Aesthetics: Architectural Theory at the University of Cambridge, 1960–1975 (Peter Eisenman, Lionel March, Leslie Martin, Christopher Alexander)*, supervisor Michael Hays. Ann Arbor (MI), ProQuest-UMI, 2006.
[656] Cohen, Jean-Louis: *Le Corbusier 1887–1965: The Lyricism of Architecture in the Machine Age*, Cologne, Taschen, 2005, p. 85. According to Cohen: "The surfaces bore a pattern of hyperbolic paraboloids, which recalled his score for *Metastasis*, composed in 1954." Ibid. In fact Xenakis was also a composer of music, an activity to which he devoted himself exclusively after 1958.
[657] Xenakis, Iannis: *Le Pavillon Philips à l'aube d'une architecture*, in id., *Musique. Architecture*, op. cit., pp. 123–42.
[658] Colquhoun, Alan: *Typology and Design Method*, in *Arena*, vol. 83, no. 913, June 1967, pp. 11–14; now in id., *Essays in Architectural Criticism: Modern Architecture and Historical Change*, Cambridge (MA), MIT Press, 1981, pp. 43–50.

tension with the other, the free expression that is the result of an *intention*. In other words the British critic wanted to refute the idea of architecture as the fruit of a deterministic process, which paradoxically was also Friedman's aim, but from a completely different perspective: Colquhoun demanded more freedom of choice for the architect, Friedman for the inhabitant. Colquhoun was one of a large number of British architects and historians – Colin Rowe, Reyner Banham, Robert Maxwell, Kenneth Frampton, Anthony Vidler – who moved from England to the United States. A contributor to *Oppositions*, Colquhoun tended to assign value to the disciplinary autonomy of architecture, basing his ideas in particular on his personal interpretation of Le Corbusier, partly in opposition to some of the technological tendencies that, especially in America, architects like Alexander had espoused.[659] Moreover, Colquhoun was not new to criticism of the technological approach. His stern reviews of Banham's books remain points of reference today.[660] However, the technological research carried out by architects in the USA that we want to look at here is not the fanciful and delivering kind invoked by Archigram in Europe or the Metabolists in Japan. Rather it is a technology controlled "from the bottom up," determined by the user instead of the requirements of industrial mass production.

In particular, between 1970 and 1975, the Massachusetts Institute of Technology became the main center of this scientific-technological tendency, whose results were so disappointing that they have subsequently been wholly ignored by historians of the discipline. And yet it is a tradition that has proved capable of renewing itself periodically, always giving rise to new messianic expectations about the application of the latest generation of technology to the running of the city. In any case Nicholas Negroponte had graduated in architecture at Boston in 1966 with a thesis on "computer-aided design." The following year *The Architecture Machine Group*, a workshop of ideas for the development of human-computer interfaces headed by the young architect of Greek origin was set up at the MIT. In 1985 the Media Laboratory, also known as the MediaLab, would grow out of the work of this group. Negroponte and his collaborator Groisser published a short article in *Ekistics*, the magazine edited by Constantinos Doxiadis, on a computerized system – URBAN5 – that illustrated some parallels between graphical and natural language.[661] Negroponte and Groisser were just at the beginning of their numerous attempts to develop a friendly interface between architect and machine. They defined the interface as the point of contact and interaction between a machine and its "information environment." Two years later, thanks in part to subsequent private funding (from Ford and IBM among others) and the collaboration of the MIT and Harvard University, Negroponte was able to announce the launch of an ambitious research program, the result of his experiments with systems of computer-aided design.

---

659 "*Notes on the Synthesis of Form* came out just when the movement of rational methodologies of design was getting under way." BANHAM, Reyner: *L'eterno modo di cambiare rotta*, in *Casabella*, no. 522, March 1986, p. 34.
660 Id., *The Modern Movement in Architecture*, in British Journal of Aesthetics, January 1962, pp. 59–65; now in id., *Essays in Architectural…*, op. cit. The book reviewed is *Theory and Design in the First Machine Age*, op. cit.
661 NEGROPONTE, Nicholas and GROISSER, Leon: *URBAN5*, in *Ekistics*, no. 142, September 1967, pp. 289–91.

This rescarch was motivated by a fundamental faith in the evolution of machines and a lack of confidence in architects:

The general concern of machine-assisted architecture is twofold. First, architects cannot handle large scale problems, for they are too complex; second, architects ignore small scale problems, for they are too particular and individual (and, to them, trivial).[662]

This belief in the inadequacy of architecture was justified quantitatively through the statistic that "less than 5 percent of the housing built in the United States and less than 1 percent of the urban environment is exposed to the skills of the design professions."[663] For this reason the researchers in Boston wanted to develop information systems, computer graphics and computing services to make the architect in the traditional sense practically useless – theorizing a network of computers capable of communicating with one another over the telephone.[664]

The book he brought out the following year, *The Architecture Machine*,[665] goes into the question more deeply, disclosing two general principles: the first is the "do-it-yourself" approach proposed by Marshall McLuhan a few years earlier in *Understanding Media. The Extensions of Man* (1964), declaring that mass consumption becomes interactive in the automation circuit. This is the best known book by the Canadian philosopher of communication theory, which opens with the chapter "The Medium Is the Message." Negroponte was immediately aware of McLuhan's text because, in addition to having several positions in common, both had been contributors to *Ekistics*.[666] McLuhan wrote:

Automation or cybernation deals with all the units and components of the industrial and marketing process exactly as radio or TV combine the individuals in the audience into new interprocess. [...] Automation affects not just production, but every phase of consumption and marketing; for the consumer becomes producer in the automation circuit, quite as much as the reader of the mosaic telegraph press makes his own news, or just is his own news.[667]

So the inhabitant can and should become a designer. In short Negroponte wanted to automate architecture in an integration between architect (intermediary between the physical form and human needs) and machine (processor of alternatives and incompatibilities), with the character of a public service. In other words he aspired to turning architecture into

---

[662] NEGROPONTE, Nicholas: *Toward a Theory of Architecture Machines*, in *Journal of Architectural Education*, vol. 23, no. 2, March 1969, p. 9.
[663] For these figures Negroponte cites an article by EBERHARD, John: *A Humanist Case for the Systems Approach*, in *AIA Journal*, no. 1, July 1968, pp. 34–38.
[664] "Away from the designer would be a parent machine to which all architecture machines could talk via telephone lines." NEGROPONTE, Nicholas: *Toward a Theory ...*, op. cit., p. 11.
[665] Id., *The Architecture Machine. Toward a More Human Environment*, Cambridge (MA)/London, MIT Press, 1970.
[666] A possible intermediary between the two may have been Harvard professor Jaqueline Tyrwhitt (1905–1983), editor-in-chief of *Ekistics* and secretary of the CIAM, who had worked with McLuhan on a UN program in 1955 and then met up with him again on visits to Greece in the summer as guests of Doxiadis. During one of these stays, in 1963, Giedion and Bucky Fuller were present as well as McLuhan and would be co-authors of the Delos Declaration in which the idea of the world as a global village was first presented. See WIGLEY, Mark: *Network Fever*, in *Grey Room*, no. 4, summer 2001, pp. 83–122.
[667] McLUHAN, Marshall: *Understanding Media. The Extensions of Man*, op. cit., pp. 348–49.

what McLuhan called a "cold" medium, i.e. a medium with a high degree of participation or completion on the part of the public.[668] For this reason it was necessary to bring a machine for architecture into every home, like the television or the telephone (both cool media):

The computer at home is not a fanciful concept. As the cost of computation lowers, the computer utility will become a consumer item, and every child should have one.[669]

The architecture machine would prove a flop. The book itself was born out of the failure of the URBAN5 prototype, whose defects of development, dialogue and flexibility are prudently laid bare only in the last chapter.[670] The scientific, and thus empirical according to the classical scheme of "trial and error," method admits self-criticism: Alexander himself had given a demonstration of this in his celebrated *A City is not a Tree* after the setback undergone with the *San Francisco Bay Area Rapid Transit District (1964).*[671]

Yet Negroponte still considers the architecture machine a feasible (technological) utopia, clinging as he does to the concept of a technology determined or at least modified from the bottom up, on the basis of the requirements and tastes of the users, but in a wholly nonpolitical sense:

In other words what Negroponte was proposing to do, instead, *was* not advocacy planning with the aid of the computer, but helping the inhabitants of the city to play a part in the design of their environment, by increasing the availability of planning services rather than mobilizing political power.[672]

First of all it should be noted that Negroponte is an architect dissatisfied with the traditional role of his profession and that, like Friedman, he is striving to give it back the effectiveness it has lost in reality through research in new fields of knowledge. Both men are the expression of a crisis in the discipline, a crisis to which people have reacted in two ways: withdrawing into the self-referentiality of their own imagination or trying to reform the profession on totally new bases. Negroponte was able to found his research on some studies that had been carried out not long before or were almost contemporary, those of Serge Chermayeff and Christopher Alexander into districts of low-rise, high-density housing as the best possible form of urban expansion, in which the use of technology in architecture and city planning was praised in no uncertain terms:

---

668 *Media Hot and Cold*, ibid., pp. 31 ff.
669 NEGROPONTE, Nicholas: *The Architecture Machine . . .*, op. cit., caption to fig. 2, p. 6. This educational (and redeeming) idea of the computer is a constant of Negroponte's thought: in 2006 a very low-cost laptop for children, developed by the MediaLab at MIT under his supervision, was launched on the market. See the feature ed. by MASCHERONI, Loredana: *A Computer Will Save You –Weighing up and Analysing a Visionary and Ambitious Project: the New 2B1 for One Laptop per Child by MIT in Boston*, in *Domus,* no. 896, October 2006, pp. 100–9.
670 *Urban5: A Postmortem,* ibid. pp. 95–96.
671 ALEXANDER, Christopher: *A City Is Not a Tree*, in *Architectural Forum,* vol. 122, no. 1, April and May 1965, pp. 58–61.
672 NEGROPONTE, Nicholas: *The Architecture Machine . . .* , op. cit.

Designers need to come face to face with the facts of science and technology: their real hope for the restoration of humanism lies in their ability to exploit technique to its limits. The biggest obstacle to the improvement of design standards is the obsolescence of designers themselves.[673]

It should be noted that Chermayeff and Alexander could count on funding from the MIT and Harvard, that is to say the same institutions that were later to support Negroponte. In particular Alexander, thanks to the use of the IBM 704 supplied by the Computation Center at the MIT[674] (in the sixties computers were rare, being extremely bulky and expensive), was able to write a seminal essay, *The Question of Computers in Design*.[675] However, Negroponte's training as an architect also drew on sources from within the disciplines, such as Stanford Anderson's essay on the nature of design – "I suggested that architecture is concerned with structuring man's environment to facilitate the achievement of human purposes (intellectual, psychological and utilitarian)"[676] – and Sigfried Giedion and Lewis Mumford's studies on mechanization.[677]

Other basic affinities with Friedman are evident too: the centrality of the user/inhabitant (for this reason De Carlo published an Italian translation of the book in his "Structure and Urban Form" series for Il Saggiatore), a faith in technology, but a stronger one, messianic and almost animistic, to the point of regarding machines as capable of intelligence in their own right. In fact according to Negroponte computer-aided design implies at least three elements:

1. Mutual interruptability for man and machine,
2. Local and dedicated computing power within the terminal, and
3. A machine intelligence.[678]

And again:

Machines that poll information from many designers and inhabitants, directly view the real world, and have a congenial dialogue with one specific designer are architecture machines. They hint at being intelligent machines.[679]

---

[673] CHERMAYEFF, Serge and ALEXANDER, Christopher: *Community and Privacy*, New York, Doubleday, 1963, p. 111. It is worth pointing out that Chermayeff (1900–96) had been a partner of Mendelsohn in London before the war (1933–36); moving to the US on the outbreak of war, he shared a studio with Wachsmann from 1947, while from 1953 to 1962 he taught at the MIT and then Harvard and Yale. Also see id. and TZONIS, Alexander: *Shape of Community: Realization of Human Potential*, London, Penguin, 1971; PLUNTZ, Richard (ed.): *Design and the Public Good. Selected Writings 1930–1980 by Serge Chermayeff*, London/Cambridge (MA), MIT Press, 1982.
[674] CHERMAYEFF, Serge and ALEXANDER, Christopher: *Community and Privacy*, op. cit., p. 7.
[675] ALEXANDER, Christopher: *The Question of Computers in Design*, in *Landscape*, no. 3, spring 1965, pp. 6–8.
[676] ANDERSON, Stanford: *Problem-Solving and Problem-Worrying*, in *American Institute of Architects Teachers Seminar*, Bloomfield, Cranbrook Academy, June 1966.
[677] GIEDION, Sigfried: *Mechanization Takes Command: A Contribution to Anonymous Design*. New York, Oxford University Press, 1948. MUMFORD, Lewis: *The Myth of the Machine*, New York, Harcourt, Brace & World, 1967. Also see id., *Technics and Civilization*, New York, Harcourt, Brace & World, 1934.
[678] NEGROPONTE, Nicholas: *The Architecture Machine . . .*, op. cit., p. 23.
[679] Ibid., p. 29.

Negroponte foresaw not only a terminal in every home, linked to one another over telephone lines, but also virtual reality, i.e. the simulated experience of theoretical spaces, videophones with keyboards and interactive cable television. The guiding thread running through all these mechanisms is the fulfilment of particular needs, do-it-yourself in other words.
The relations between man and machine are represented through diagrams, and the processual aspect of architecture is clearly underlined: a process is a progressive course, a series of procedures. A procedure [...] is replicable in an algorithm; its parts have a chronological cause-and-effect relationship that can be anticipated. Thus a procedure is deterministic and can be computerized, but a process is not. It can only be aided by the computer, and is not predictable.

In 1967, the year in which a newly graduated Negroponte published his first article on his idea of the machine, Yona Friedman announced his "Flatwriter" in a series of lectures given at Michigan University:

Thanks to a machine that I call the Flatwriter, each inhabitant of a city can imprint his personal preferences with respect to his apartment (flat) to be, using symbols which put in visual form the different elements of his decision so that the builder as well as his neighbors can understand what his choice is.[680]

In 1971 the Flatwriter was published first in a magazine [681] and then in *Pour une architecture scientifique*. The similarity of these lines of research is clear, but there is one fundamental difference: the Flatwriter has no need of electricity to work (the first version was an adaptation of a simple typewriter), and so is not a cybernetic project like those of Negroponte, Schöffer, Price or Archigram.

A meeting between Negroponte and Friedman was inevitable. Even outside observers noted the parallels,[682] but for Negroponte it was an elective affinity:

The happy correspondence between (1) our interests in graphic communications and nonpaternalistic guidance, (2) the conclusions derived from our case study, and (3) the capabilities of the graph theory approach led quite naturally to the implementation of this approach on the Architecture Machine Group's mini-computers.[683]

First of all Friedman signed one of the four forewords to *Soft Architecture Machines*, Negroponte's second book which he finished in the summer of 1972, brining the second phase of the work of the *Architecture Machine Group* (1968 – 72) to a close.[684] It was fol-

---

[680] http://yonafriedman.blogspot.it/2006/11/during-this-first-meeting-we-intervied.html.
[681] FRIEDMAN, Yona: *The Flatwriter: Choice by Computer*, in *Progressive Architecture*, no. 3, March 1971, pp. 98–101.
[682] FRIEDMAN, Yona, TANGE, Kenzo, NEGROPONTE, Nicholas and BUCKMINSTER FULLER, Richard: *La ville totale*, in *2000*, no. 24, 1971, pp. 5–7.
[683] NEGROPONTE, Nicholas and WEINZAPFEL, Guy: *Architecture-by-Yourself. An Experiment With Computer Graphics for House Design*, in *Computer Graphics*, vol. 10, no. 2, summer 1976, p. 75.
[684] Id., *Soft Architecture Machines*, Cambridge (MA)/London, MIT Press, 1975. For the date, see the author's preface and p. 1.

lowed by a new and more elaborate project, that of *Architecture-by-Yourself*, an attempt to combine graph theory with design on the computer. The solution that the group at MIT came up with was "The YONA System," through which the user could discard impossible linkages between the requested spaces. Bubbles appeared in the pre-shape spaces, to represent the appropriate areas around the nodes in the network of connections inside the future building. In other words, it was a "bubble diagram." However, the result was not satisfactory – as we have seen it is an intuitive process that was already in use in the forties – for the "paternalistic" predominance of the computer over the results obtained could be noted, but Negroponte proposed to improve its capabilities the following year. In the meantime other studies were published, along with the English translation of Friedman's book on scientific architecture.[685]

Notwithstanding the proliferation of theoretical studies and the experimentation with new computers, the hoped-for effects were not obtained in this period, and no experiment would be carried out on a large scale.

The year after "The YONA System" the cultural climate changed yet again, and together with the last publication of the group in Cambridge, the dense book by Bill Mitchell,[686] *The Language of Post-Modern Architecture*[687] also came out, two years before Lyotard's celebrated essay marking the decline of the machine age.[688] With the end of the "grandes narratives" (the Enlightenment, idealism, Marxism) the utopias they implied disappeared as well, and architectural culture could find nothing better to do than take refuge in the regressive dream of the past or in an uncritical pragmatism.

---

[685] NEGROPONTE, Nicholas (ed.): *Reflections on Computer Aids to Design and Architecture*, New York, Petrocelli–Charter, 1975. See FRIEDMAN, Yona: *Toward a Scientific Architecture*, op. cit.

[686] MITCHELL, William J.: *Computer-Aided Architectural Design*, New York, Petrocelli–Charter, 1977. The book had been anticipated by the article, id., The Theoretical Foundation of Computer-Aided Architectural Design, in *Environment and Planning B*, vol. 2, no. 2, December 1975, pp. 127–50.

[687] JENCKS, Charles A.: *The Language of Post-Modern Architecture*, London, Academy, 1977.

[688] The reference is to the famous book by LYOTARD, Jean-François: *La condition postmoderne. Rapport sur le savoir*, Paris, Minuit, 1979. English transl., *The Postmodern Condition*. Minneapolis (MN), University of Minnesota Press, 1984.

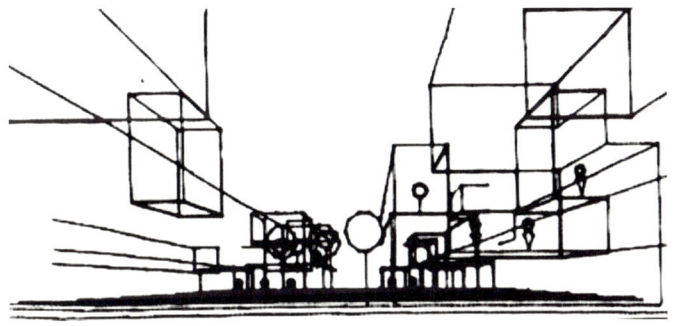

597 Negroponte, Nicholas: *The Architecture Machine; Toward a More Human Environment*, January 1973.
598 First image produced on a computer by Negroponte's Architecture Machine Group, c. 1973.

   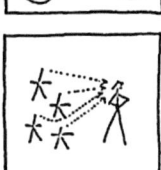  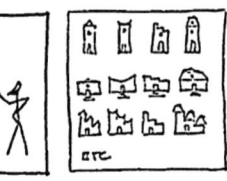   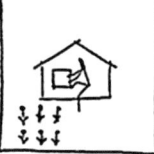    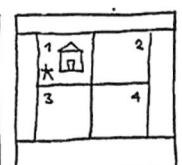     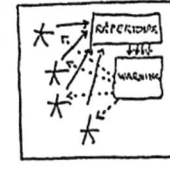 

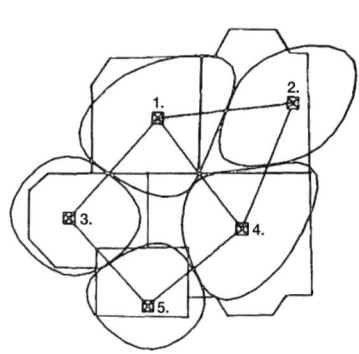

1 / Bath
2 / Bedroom
3 / Kitchen
4 / Living room
5 / Entry

THE ARCHITECTURE MACHINE GROUP

599 Yona Friedman: Pictograms from Negroponte's *Computer Aided Participatory Design*, in Negroponte, Nicholas: *Soft Architecture Machines*, Cambridge (MA), MIT Press, 1975.
600 *The Yona System*, 1976, by *The Architecture Machine Group*. Possible shape diagram drawn over bubbles. It combines graph theory with diagrams.
601 Gordon Pask: Diagram for *The Architecture Machine Group*, 1976. Pask worked with Cedric Price on the Fun Palace in London in the early sixties.

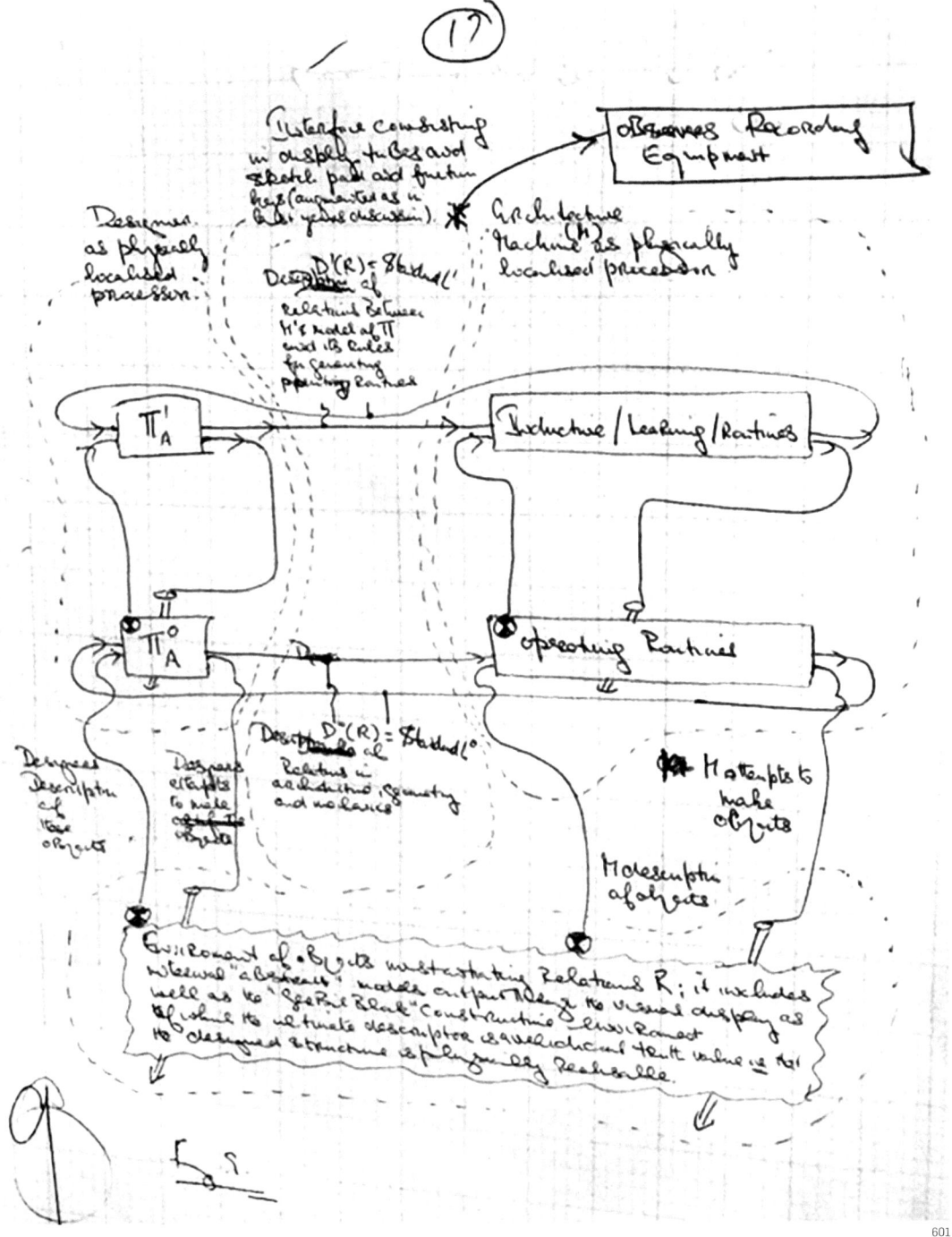

Utopias are much the same as possibilities [...]. The present is nothing but a hypothesis that one has not yet gotten beyond.

MUSIL, Robert: *Der Mann ohne Eigenschaften,* Berlin, Rowohlt, 1930. English transl., *The Man without Qualities,* New York, Knopf, 1995, pp. 265 and 269.

3. ARCHITECTURE AND AUTOREGULATION

UTOPIES RÉALISABLES

Utopian thinking, as I came to regard it, then, was the opposite of one-sidedness, partisanship, partiality, provinciality, specialism. He who practiced the utopian method must view life synoptically and see it as an interrelated whole: not as a random mixture, but as an organic and increasingly organizable union of parts [. . .].[689]
Lewis Mumford

The theme of utopia has resurfaced regularly in modern architectural culture since its early days, before and after the catastrophe of the Second World War. The idea of utopia is born in fact when people have suffered a great deal and are imagining a possible way out – it is no accident that the proponents of megastructural utopia, Friedman and the Metabolists above all, experienced the two greatest calamities produced by the conflict: the Nazi death camps and the atomic bomb. After the neorealist period, utopia would return forcefully to the limelight in the sixties, partly in the wake of widespread frustration with the results of reconstruction, especially among the younger generation, with an escalation in the production of philosophical and architectural writings on the subject. Around 1968 this climate intensified further, as the historian of Italian literature Alberto Asor Rosa has evoked at a distance of many years, and in words laden with disillusionment, in a long essay written in memory of Manfredo Tafuri:

Literature, culture, history, philosophy and architecture, the history of architecture and of art turned around this center: namely the utopia of a harmonious universal understanding, linked in turn to an equally global and equally utopian (the word is not chosen at random) plan for the transformation of the world. But don't expect me to tell you now which part and how much of this plan has turned out to be mistaken or short-lived: you only have to look around to find a bleak answer to this question. What interests me instead is to try to get across to the reader of today, by reassessing it, the unique fragrance of that attempt, which, rightly or wrongly, had a fascination that from then until today we have not felt for anything else: the idea (to put it very schematically) that anything would have been possible, if only we had wanted it.[690]

Without an awareness of this generalized *will to power*, of this faith that led to the breaking down of every disciplinary barrier, it is not possible to understand fully either Friedman's most mature books (Utopies réalisables, L'architecture de survie) or the substantial literary

---

[689] MUMFORD, Lewis: *The Story of Utopias*, New York, Boni and Liveright, 1922. Rpt. with a new introduction, New York, Viking, 1962, pp. 5–6.
[690] ASOR ROSA, Alberto: *Manfredo, Tafuri: Progetto e utopia. Architettura e sviluppo capitalistico*, in *Bollettino di italianistica*, special issue, year II, no. 1, 2005, p. 180. English transl., *Manfredo Tafuri, or Humanism Revisited*, in *Log*, no. 9, 2007, pp. 29–30.

production of historians like Tafuri or architects of wholly divergent orientations like Andrea Branzi or Hans Hollein.

Philosophers had tackled utopia directly from discordant positions. Their books were translated or reprinted in those years – Martin Buber was published by Olivetti's Edizioni di Comunità, as was Lewis Mumford,[691] to mention just two examples. The Marxist current of writing was undoubtedly the most prolific of the sixties, with the Hungarian Karl Mannheim,[692] Ernst Bloch and Herbert Marcuse in particular.

Ernst Bloch's *The Spirit of Utopia*, published in the mid-sixties, was an obligatory point of reference in the debate of the time.[693] The initial premise from which Bloch moves is that given reality never fully satisfies people and so from this perspective is not "true": the truth to which people aspire, imagining and desiring what they lack, is not given, but is utopia, which transcends the present in its focus on the future. So Bloch rejects any kind of contemplative thought, seen as a merely passive reflection of what has already been, frozen in an eternal present. The German philosopher spoke out against the myth of the impartiality of a presumed objective knowledge: in reality, thought is always biased and contemplation amounts, essentially, to the acceptance of existing reality. Utopian thinking, on the other hand, can find clues to the future in the past and always goes beyond the facts of the present to aim at the future, which rises to a position of precedence. It differs, however, from pure and simple daydreaming in so far as it takes account of what it intends to supersede, i.e. actual tendencies operating in the present: from this perspective, it is *concrete utopia*, real possibility. Also at the center of utopian thought, therefore, is the notion of dialectics, indispensable to dealing in an effective way with the contradictions inherent in reality and connecting up with the real movement of history in order to realize utopian truth. In the same year as Bloch published his book, Marcuse brought out *One-Dimensional Man: Studies in the Ideology of Advanced Industrial Society*, which was to become required reading during the years of student protest in the United States and Europe.[694] In 1967, in front of an audience of students in Berlin, Marcuse announced the end of utopia, not in the sense of its failure, but on the contrary in that of its imminent fulfilment. What was finished, in fact, was precisely its utopian character. The conditions of contemporary society allowed people to think of it no longer as a dream but as something possible and feasible. The eternal aspiration of humanity to freedom, justice and happiness was within reach.[695]

---

[691] MUMFORD, Lewis: *The Story of Utopias*, op. cit., 1962. Italian transl., *Storia dell'utopia*, with an introduction by Pierluigi Giordani, Bologna, Calderini, 1969. The same year Giordani, editor of Calderini's series on architecture, published *Il futuro dell'utopia* (Bologna, Calderini, 1969), in which Yona Friedman is cited. Also see MUMFORD, Lewis: *Utopia, the City and the Machine*, in *Daedalus*, spring 1965, no. 2, pp. 271–92.

[692] MANNHEIM, Karl: *Ideologie und Utopie*, Bonn, Cohen, 1929. English transl., *Ideology and Utopia: An Introduction to the Sociology of Knowledge*, New York, Harcourt, Brace & Co., 1954. Mannheim was born in Budapest in 1893, emigrated to Germany in the twenties and then in 1933 to London, where he died in 1947.

[693] BLOCH, Ernst: *Geist der Utopie*, Frankfurt am M., Suhrkamp, 1964. English transl., *The Spirit of Utopia*, Palo Alto (CA), Stanford University Press, 2000.

[694] MARCUSE, Herbert: *One-Dimensional Man: Studies in the Ideology of Advanced Industrial Society*, Boston, Beacon, 1964.

[695] Id., *Das Ende der Utopie: Vorträge und Diskussionen in Berlin 1967*, Berlin, Maikowski, 1967. English transl., *The End of Utopia*, in *Five Lectures: Psychoanalysis, Politics, and Utopia*, Boston, Beacon, 1970, pp. 62–81.

Today, however, not only have we established the impracticability of those aspirations, but we have also begun to question the very idea of a different form of social organization, the very idea of alternative social and economic relations to the existing ones. The ideal and the real have been put back together again. In front of us there is only one possible world, the one that actually exists. Utopia seems to be dead, and in a sense that is the complete opposite to the one meant by Marcuse. It has become almost unthinkable, inconceivable, unimaginable.

For his part Michel Foucault in 1967, after bringing out the books in which he presented his "archeology of the present," seeking to demythologize and reconstruct the origins of modern thought and its institutions (*The Birth of the Clinic*, *The Archaeology of Knowledge*, *The Order of Things*, etc.), gave a lecture at *Centre d'études et de recherches architecturales* in Paris in which he tackled for the first time the theme of space, or rather the "spatialization of knowledge."[696] In contrast to utopias he identified *heterotopias*:

First of all, the utopias. These are arrangements which have no real space. [...] There also exist, and this is probably true for all cultures and all civilizations, real and effective spaces which are outlined in the very institution of society, but which constitute a sort of counter arrangement, of effectively realized utopia, in which all the real arrangements, all the other real arrangements that can be found within society, are at one and the same time represented, challenged, and overturned: a sort of place that lies outside all places and yet is actually localizable. In contrast to the utopias, these places which are absolutely other with respect to all the arrangements that they reflect and of which they speak might be described as heterotopias.[697]

Heterotopias can assume many forms, but according to Foucault one can clearly be identified in the post 19th century cemetery, which is located outside the city and no longer attached to a church. As an example of a heterotopia that played a crucial role in territorial organization, Foucault singles out the English Puritan colonies founded in America in the 17th century, which in his view were "absolutely perfect places" in this sense.[698] It is no coincidence that these settlements in particular would be the subject of urban studies carried out by European and American architects in the years immediately afterward, as we will see shortly.

---

696 OCKMAN, Joan: *Architecture Culture* ..., op. cit., p. 419.
697 FOUCAULT, Michel: *Of Other Spaces: Utopias and Heterotopias*, in LEACH, Neil (ed.), *Rethinking Architecture: A Reader in Cultural Theory*, New York, Routledge, 1997, pp. 330–36.
698 On the reception of Foucault and his analytical method in architecture, see CACCIARI, Massimo, TAFURI, Manfredo and TEYSSOT, Georges: *Il dispositivo Foucault*, with an introduction by Franco Rella, Venice, Cluva, 1977.

ARCHITECTURE AND UTOPIA

Publications devoted to utopian forms of community flourished in architectural literature as well. In the United States the brothers Paul and Percival Goodman, a philosopher and an architect respectively, brought out a new edition of their book *Communitas* in 1960, which was then translated into Italian.[699] Percival Goodman, for many years a professor at the Columbia University School of Architecture, took on the young Peter Eisenman in his studio in 1960 and would be one of the first to invite Friedman to the US for a conference.[700] Paul Goodman is considered the theorist of the student protest movement in America, but both brothers were convinced of the need for a decentralization of power and of the population and studied various forms of utopian community.[701] Still in the US, Martin Meyerson published *Utopian Traditions and the Planning of Cities* in the special issue of *Daedalus* devoted to "The Future Metropolis" and edited by Rodwin in close collaboration with Kevin Lynch.[702] Immediately afterward Reiner wrote *The Place of the Ideal Community in Urban Planning*.[703]

In Milan Rogers, along with his assistants (Piergiacomo Castiglioni, Vittorio Gregotti, Guido Canella, Francesco Tentori, et al.), external contributors (including Bernardo Secchi and Gillo Dorfles) and students (among them Pierluigi Cerri and Pierluigi Nicolin), published in 1965 a miscellany entitled *L'utopia della realtà*[704] which developed a theme dear to him: "It is a question of putting the concept of utopia into effect: of thinking in a concrete way about a better society (certainly not a world made up solely of the honest, solely of the beautiful and good, but a world constructed with real means for real ends)."[705] This concept was favorably received, as a stimulating harbinger of the future, in the fateful year of 1966 by Manfredo Tafuri, who wrote an essay entitled *La nuova dimensione urbana e la funzione dell'utopia* (The New Urban Dimension and the Function of Utopia) for the magazine edited by Zevi in which he denounced the megastructures presented in magazines as "absurdities of a nihilistic flavor,"[706] opposing the optimistic approach to city planning widely adopted at the time in Rome, from Pellegrin to Maurizio Sacripanti.[707]

---

[699] GOODMAN, Paul and GOODMAN, Percival: *Communitas. Means of Livelihood and Ways of Life*, New York, Vintage Books, 1947; revised ed., 1960. Italian transl., *Communitas. Mezzi di sostentamento e modi di vivere*, Bologna, Il Mulino, 1970.

[700] FISHMAN, Robert: *Utopian Freedom: Percival Goodman's Social Thought*, in ELMAN, Kimberly and GIRAL, Angela (eds.): *Percival Goodman. Architect, Planner, Teacher, Painter*, catalogue of the exhibition at the Miriam and Ira D. Wallach Art Gallery, Columbia University, New York, New York, Wallach Gallery, 2001, pp. 111–25. Also see EISENMAN, Peter: *Percival Goodman*, ibid. pp. 141–42.

[701] Alexander included the *Communitas* project in the category of the tree city in his *A City Is Not a Tree*, op. cit., no. 2, pp. 58–62.

[702] MEYERSON, Martin: *Utopian Traditions and the Planning of Cities*, in *The Future Metropolis*, special issue of *Daedalus*, ed. by Lloyd Rodwin, vol. 90, no. 1, 1961. Rpt. as *The Future Metropolis*, New York, Braziller, 1961. Other contributions to the issue included LYNCH, Kevin: *The Pattern of the Metropolis*, pp. 103 ff., and the essay from KEPES, György: *Notes on Expression and Communication in the Cityscape*, pp. 151 ff. In the introduction to the Italian ed., *La metropoli del futuro* (Venice, Marsilio, 1964), De Carlo calls it "the most penetrating and stimulating of all collections" (p. xv).

[703] REINER, Thomas A.: *The Place of the Ideal Community in Urban Planning*, Philadelphia, University of Pennsylvania Press, 1963.

[704] NATHAN ROGERS, Ernesto et al.: *L'utopia della realtà. Un esperimento didattico sulla tipologia della Scuola Primaria*, Bari, Leonardo da Vinci Editrice, 1965. The volume was the third in the series "Problemi della nuova dimensione" directed by Carlo Aymonino.

[705] NATHAN ROGERS, Ernesto: *Utopia della realtà (1962)*, op. cit., p. 269.

[706] TAFURI, Manfredo: *La nuova dimensione urbana e la funzione dell'utopia*, in *L'architettura. Cronache e storia*, year XI, no. 124, February 1966, pp. 680–83. Also see the earlier id., *Razionalismo critico e nuovo utopianismo*, in *Casabella-continuità*, no. 293, November 1964, pp. 20–42.

[707] "If the planning of large cities has always been utopian with respect to its time, never as much as today – to bring the future into the present – has the utopia been necessary as a redemption of reality, as a liberation from the embrace between city and countryside." SACRIPANTI, Maurizio: *Un geroglifico spazio-temporale*, in *Lineastruttura*, no. 1, 1966, p. 43.

In 1967 Ludovico Quaroni published *La torre di Babele*, in which he devoted two chapters to utopia,[708] and even Aldo Rossi defended the utopian designs of the French "revolutionary architects,"[709] while in Germany Mechthild Schumpp published *Stadtbau-Utopien und Gesellschaft*, looking at the utopias of the Expressionists, the Bauhaus, Friedman and the German group of the GEAM and finally Archigram. The following year Filiberto Menna analyzed the artistic and architectural avant-gardes jointly, investigating their roots in Romanticism and entitling the last chapter "Return of the Utopia."[710] Finally Soleri, who in 1956 had founded the community at Cosanti in the Arizona desert following his apprenticeship in his youth with Frank Lloyd Wright at Taliesin West, published a first assessment of his experience, "Architettura e/o utopia."[711] The case of the Turinese architect is emblematic for Italy: Soleri was in fact a child of the cult of Wright's work as a dependable model of democratic architecture, officiated after the Second World War by the Association for Organic Architecture (APAO) and its high priest, Bruno Zevi.[712]

In addition to Ragon's numerous writings,[713] France in 1965 saw the publication of Françoise Choay's important anthology, *Urbanisme. Utopies et réalités*, in which ample space was given to the urban and anti-urban ideas of the 19th century utopian socialists – during what Benevolo defined as "the age of great hopes"[714] – along with the principal architects and philosophers of the 20th century, with a clear indication of their intellectual lineage. Constantinos Doxiadis (1913 – 75), an architect, engineer and city planner born in Bulgaria but of Greek origin who was active in the United States, wrote a short book in which he fingered the problem faced by his contemporaries with irrefutable accuracy:

This is the problem of humanity today: it builds cities which are bad, the dystopias; *it dreams of cities for which there is no-place, the utopias; while it needs good cities for which there will be a place, the* entopias.[715]

After serving in an espionage unit of the resistance against the invasion of Greece by the Nazis and Fascists, Doxiadis became directly involved in postwar reconstruction, managing the aid of the Marshall Plan in his capacity as head of the development program. From 1948

---

[708] QUARONI, Ludovico: *La torre di Babele*, Padua, Marsilio, 1967. The chapters in question are "L'armonia della città antica e l'architetto artigiano" and "Il mito della città ideale e l'architetto artista."
[709] "To speak of a supposed utopia in artists like B[oullée] has little significance as the meaning of the word utopia is contentious in architecture, in so far as those works of architecture whose realization encounters notable difficulties of an economic or sociological character are regarded as utopian. Hence they are 'difficult' works rather than utopian works. Especially in architecture where the difficulties are so great and so many that the realization even of more modest works is always rendered problematic." Rossi, Aldo: *Introduzione*, in BOULLÉE, Etienne-Louis: *Architettura. Saggio sull'arte*, op. cit., p. 15.
[710] MENNA, Filiberto: *Profezia di una società estetica . . .*, op. cit., pp. 131–51.
[711] SOLERI, Paolo: *Architettura e/o utopia*, in *Marcatre*, nos. 50/55, 1969, a monographic issue on architecture in which Friedman also features.
[712] For a comparative analysis of Wright and Soleri, see BANHAM, Reyner: *Scenes in America Deserta*, op. cit., especially chapter 4, "Frank Lloyd Wright Country," pp. 69 ff.
[713] As well as the aforementioned publications devoted to the GIAP, see RAGON, Michel: *La cité de l'an 2000*, Paris/Tournai, Casterman, 1968. Also see CHRIST, Yvan, *Paris des utopies*, Paris, Balland, 1970.
[714] BENEVOLO, Leonardo: *Le origini dell'urbanistica moderna*, Bari, Laterza, 1964. English transl., *The Origins of Modern Town Planning*, London, Routledge & Kegan Paul, 1967. See in particular the chapter "Nineteenth century Utopias," pp. 39–84, where he analyzes the urbanistic ideas of Owen, Saint-Simon, Fourier, Godin and Cabet, previously excluded from his *Storia dell'architettura moderna*, Bari, Laterza, 1961. English transl., *History of Modern Architecture*, Cambridge (MA), MIT Press, 1977.
[715] DOXIADIS, Constantinos: *Between Dystopia and Utopia*, London, Faber and Faber, 1966, p. xx.

he worked in the Coordination Office of the Greek government, supervising the planning of three thousand new settlements and the construction of two hundred thousand new housing units. The professional firm he founded in 1951 received commissions in various parts of the world, and especially in the USA thanks in part to his role as chairman of the UN's study group on housing policies.

Doxiadis included linear cities among the dystopias, i.e. negative versions of the utopia, because in his view they were not feasible except on a very small scale.[716] His criticism was directed against Arturo Soria y Mata,[717] who had earlier theorized about its structure (1922), and turned on four points: a linear city can exist only in small areas, it can be static, it has the same dimensions at every point of its axis and it can grow in only two directions.[718] To the linear city Doxiadis contrasted his proposal of a *Dynapolis* ("dynamic polis"), an evolving city with a complex form that can grow in all directions except one – i.e. the line tangent to the generating center.[719] However Doxiadis's critique corresponds to Friedman's bridge city – which moreover was published immediately afterward in the same anthology – because, in fact, the linear form is conserved "if all the forces with the same direction are much greater than the forces that point in all the other directions."[720]

Doxiadis had also criticized Archigram, without naming them, as representatives of those thoughtless architects and city planners who pretend to believe that we should be living in larger and more inhuman buildings where the container is more important than the contents, the construction more important than the space, the shell more important than the people, lines of transport more important than human values. These enormous cities were like steel tanks that moved mechanically and probably crushed nature and everyone outside them.[721]

The problem came to the fore in the middle of the decade: the communitarian utopia offered an alternative to the technological utopia, regarded as inhuman, and Doxiadis's title was symptomatic, *Technological Dystopias*. His criticism of technology was not isolated, indeed he found an ally in James Stirling, who was the same age as Friedman and who in 1969 urged architects not to overvalue the structural aspect of design even though buildings were growing ever larger and more complex, and to stick to the fundamental logic that underpins the drawing up of a project in the realm of humanistic considerations.[722] However, Stirling was inconsistent in his disapproval of British high-tech architecture since just a few years earlier he had adopted just such a solution in the *Dorman Long Steel Headquarters* (1965), although under pressure from the client.

---

716 A brief comparative analysis of theories of linear cities can be found in the section entitled "La ville linéaire: plans et chantiers" in COHEN, Jean-Louis: *Le commissaire prend le crayon*," introduction to MILIOUTINE, Nikolaï, *Sotsgorod. Le problème de la construction des villes socialistes* (1930), Besançon, Editions de l'Imprimeur, 2002, pp. 17–20.
717 SORIA Y MATA, Arturo: *La cité linéaire: conception nouvelle pour l'aménagement des villes (1926)*, Paris, Centre d'études et de recherches architecturales, 1979.
718 DOXIADIS, Constantinos: *On Linear Cities*, in LEWIS, David (ed.): *Urban Structures*, London, Elek Books, 1968, pp. 49–51. The article had already been published a year earlier in *The Town Planning Review*, vol. XXXVIII, no. 1, April 1967, pp. 35–52, and in *Ekistics*, June 1967.
719 On Dynapolis, see id., *Architecture in Transition*, London, Hutchinson, 1963, pp. 102–6.
720 DOXIADIS, Constantinos: *On Linear Cities*, op. cit., p. 51.
721 Id., *Between Dystopia and Utopia*, op. cit., p. 20.
722 "Stirling Stuff," James Stirling in conversation with Sunand Prasad and Satish Grover, *Architecture and Design* (New Delhi), no. 5, July–August 1987.

In his most important book on architecture, *Progetto e destino*, Giulio Carlo Argan wrote:

The utopianism of our time, which begins in the model factory and ends in science-fiction, is technological. Since technological progress is the salient fact of the age in which we live, the modern utopia follows the general rule: imagine a world in which there is nothing but technological progress.[723]

A response to Argan's book came with *Progetto e utopia*,[724] the text that Tafuri derived from an expansion of his long essay "Per una critica dell'ideologia architettonica"[725] published in 1969 in *Contropiano*, the magazine of "Marxist materials" edited by Alberto Asor Rosa and Massimo Cacciari that came out between 1968 and 1971. This magazine, born from the ashes of *Quaderni rossi*, stood at the intersection between the revival of critical Marxism carried out earlier by philosophers like Della Volpe and Colletti[726] on the one hand, and Mario Tronti's *operaismo*[727] on the other. Antonio Negri contributed to the first two issues, before resigning contentiously. Even in a workshop of political ideas of such a high level architects played a leading role, something literally inconceivable today: in addition to Tafuri, the historians Giorgio Ciucci, Francesco Dal Co and Marco De Michelis, among others, wrote for *Contropiano*. Cacciari's analyses, particularly the essay "Utopia e socialismo,"[728] judged to be "fundamental" by Tafuri, were at the root of a partial revision of the text between its essay form and the final one of the book. Tafuri echoes Marx's criticism of the romanticism of the utopian socialists and accuses the utopia of condemning itself to concrete failure in practice, "revealing as well the secret desire for ruin implicit in the very birth of the utopian notion." [...]

"The end of utopianism and the birth of realism are not automatic moments in the formative development of the ideology of the modern movement. On the contrary, around the 1830s realist utopianism and utopian realism begin to overlap and complement each other. The decline of social utopianism confirmed ideology's surrender to the politics of things created by the laws of profit. Architectural ideology, in both its artistic and urban forms,

---

[723] Argan, Giulio Carlo: *Progetto e destino*, Milan, Il Saggiatore, 1965, p. 13.
[724] Tafuri, Manfredo: *Progetto e utopia. Architettura e sviluppo capitalistico*, Bari/Rome, Laterza, 1973. English transl., *Architecture and Utopia: Design and Capitalist Development*, Cambridge (MA), MIT Press, 1976. The book has been translated into several other languages, including French, German and Spanish.
[725] Tafuri, Manfredo: *Per una critica dell'ideologia architettonica*, in *Contropiano*, no. 1, January–April 1969, pp. 31–79. English transl., *Toward a Critique of Architectural Ideology*, in Hays, Michael (ed.): *Architecture Theory since 1968*, op. cit., pp. 6–35. The essay is the first in the anthology because according to Hays: "Contemporary architecture's situation was never more radically theorized than by Manfredo Tafuri" (p. 2).
[726] See Della Volpe, Galvano: *Critica dell'ideologia. Saggi di teoria dialettica*, Rome, Editori Riuniti, 1967; Colletti, Lucio: *Ideologia e società*, Bari, Laterza, 1969. In France a critique of ideology was presented in the same years by the neo-Marxist Althusser, Louis: *Idéologie et appareils idéologiques d'Etat*, in *La pensée*, no. 151, 1970; English transl., *Ideology and Ideological State Apparatuses*, in *Lenin and Philosophy and Other Essays*, New York, Monthly Review Press, 1971. It should be noted that, apart from Della Volpe's, these convergent texts were brought out in Italy by the same house that published *Teorie e storia* (1968) and *Progetto e utopia* (1973) in its series on architecture.
[727] Tronti, Mario: *Operai e capitale*, op. cit.
[728] Cacciari, Massimo: *Utopia e socialismo*, in *Contropiano*, no. 3, September–December 1970, pp. 563–86. The essay is a review of *La tradizione socialista in Inghilterra. Antologia di testi politici 1820–1852*, ed. by Gino Bianco and Edoardo Grendi, Turin, Einaudi, 1970, but the prose is so convoluted and stuffed with quotations that it is practically illegible; in it he extols Marx's value theory and essentially denies any continuity between the different forms of socialism.

was left with the utopia of form as a project for recuperating the human totality in the ideal synthesis, as a way of mastering Disorder through Order."[729]

Tafuri was writing about the first half of the 19th century, but in reality he was talking about something extremely pertinent to the architecture of that moment: what else could the "utopia of form" be but the autonomy of form put forward by Aldo Rossi just three years earlier in *L'architettura della città*?[730] Colin Rowe on the other hand, returning in 1973 to an earlier writing – *The Architecture of Utopia* – added that despite the enormous obstacles encountered by the now traditional programs/fantasies of modern architecture, "some affirmation of a limited Utopia remains a psychological obligation," but to preserve the myth of utopia and the reality of freedom without producing authoritarian monstrosities, the utopia "should persist as possible social metaphor rather than probable social prescription."[731] This is precisely the metaphor that Yona Friedman was pursuing in those same years.

Utopies réalisables,[732] the book that Friedman decided to publish when the notion of utopia had completely vanished from the architectural debate, can be considered the retrospective manifesto of *L'architecture mobile*. The immediate antecedent was an exhibition held at the Musée d'Art Moderne de la Ville de Paris,[733] but some of the themes that would be treated more systematically in the book can be traced in a number of writings published earlier.[734] Friedman's primary motivation for writing it was that "the theories lack rules that would allow their application."[735] The basic argument of the book is simple: every utopia is feasible if the necessary consensus is achieved. In this the concept of *feasible utopia* is not so distant from the one of *entopia* put forward by Doxiadis: the place that "satisfies the dreamer and is accepted by the scientist, where the projections of the artist and the builder meet."[736] The city, for example, is utopia materialized "par excellence": "The city is the 'material framework' of a society" and it is certainly no coincidence that the early utopians, from Plato to Thomas Moore, Rabelais or Fourier, imagined their utopias in the form of cities. The city in itself, as a synthesis of human organization and territory, can be regarded as a utopia materialized, "perhaps even the first human utopia to have been realized."[737]

In this essay teeming with ideas we once again find a vision that does without either plans or images and that formulates its reasoning chiefly on the need to place a physiological

---

[729] TAFURI, Manfredo: *Toward a Critique of Architectural Ideology*, op. cit., p. 15.
[730] On the importance of the magazine *Contropiano* in Tafuri's work and in relation to Rossi's book see AURELI, Pier Vittorio: *The Project of Autonomy. Politics and Architecture within and against Capitalism*, New York, Princeton Architectural Press, 2008.
[731] Rowe, Colin: *The Architecture of Utopia* (1959), now in id., *The Mathematics of the Ideal Villa and Other Essays*, op. cit., p. 216.
[732] FRIEDMAN, Yona: *Utopies réalisables*, op. cit.
[733] FRIEDMAN, Yona: *Une utopie réalisée*, with an introduction by Pierre Restany, Paris, Musée d'Art Moderne de la Ville de Paris, 1975. The volume is a compendium of 19 years of work (1956–75).
[734] FRIEDMAN, Yona: *About the Possibility of Social Utopias*, in *Proceedings of the Inst. of Electrical and Electronic Engineers*, Mexico City, 1971, with essays by A. Concheiro, C. Ruiz and R. Viqueira, Mexico City, Inst. of Engineering, National University of Mexico, 1971. Id., *On Models of Utopias and Social Ecology*, in *Leonardo*, vol. 5, 1972, pp. 37–41.
[735] FRIEDMAN, Yona: *Utopies réalisables*, op. cit., p. 161.
[736] DOXIADIS, Constantinos: *Between Dystopia and Utopia*, op. cit., pp. 51.
[737] FRIEDMAN, Yona: *Utopies réalisables*, op. cit., pp. 125–26.

limit on the functioning of the community, and thus constructing a *social ecology*.[738] For this reason Friedman abandons the simple suggestions of neutral and abstract settings that had characterized the earlier period and concentrates its constitutive logic, the theory of the *critical group*, on definition of the idea of limit and dimension.

We will call a critical group *the largest set of elements (people, objects and connections) with which the efficient operation of an organization with a defined structure can still be guaranteed.*[739]

Undoubtedly, we can see in this concept, which the author describes as a parapolitical phenomenon, the influence of Friedman's experiences as an architect and structural engineer in Israel during the construction of the first settlements – the relational economy of the *critical group* can be traced back to the principles of the kibbutz – and the spread in the United States and Europe, between the sixties and seventies, of communes in which small groups managed their existence "autonomously" on ideological, religious or secular bases.[740] One of the most interesting cases, of religious origin, was the Waldensian Monte degli Ulivi community space designed and coordinated by Leonardo Ricci at Riesi, in Sicily, which referred explicitly to the kibbutzim of the Zionists.[741] In general, as we have already seen, there was great interest in those years among architects, artists and city planners in the idea of community as a clearly defined space in which to instantly bridge the gap between desire and fulfillment without having to wait the lengthy time required for political reform of the whole urban territory. In the historic 1972 issue of *Casabella* (the one whose cover has a gorilla beating its breast, inscribed with the words "Radical Design"), sandwiched between Superstudio's "Life, education, ceremony, love, death: five tales" and an essay by Germano Celant on Sol LeWitt was the leaflet of an agricultural commune founded – and evicted – the previous year in Monferrato. In it we read:

More or less everyone looked forward to the prospect of a life in common in a new world. Traditional culture with its lack of opportunities was killing us. We were firmly convinced that the commune was the only meaningful way of life. There were those who tried to discourage us, accusing us of being inveterate utopians or runaways; but after all why shouldn't we run away from these disgusting crappy metropolises, where now even human relationships have to be subject to the laws of supply and demand?[742]

Yet the anti-urban ideology evident in this text is wholly absent from Friedman's writings. It suffices to think of his idea of Europe as a network of cities (*Continent City*): the differences between Friedman and the advocates of communes are profound and irreducible,

---

[738] Aureli, Pier Vittorio: *Il fascino discreto dell'utopia*, in Brugellis, Pino (ed.): *L'invisibile linea rossa*, Macerata, Quodlibet, 2009, pp. 11–13.
[739] Friedman, Yona: *Utopies réalisables*, op. cit., p. 47.
[740] "The term 'commune' today embraces a wide variety of experimental communities that range from housing cooperatives, usually set up with a very precise purpose, to communes in the city and self-governing communes in the countryside." Ungers, Liselotte and Ungers, Oswald Mathias: *Kommunen in der Neuen Welt 1740–1971*, Cologne, Kiepenheuer & Witsch, 1972. The passage has been transl. from the Italian ed., *Le comuni del Nuovo Mondo. Alle fonti dell'utopia urbanistica*, Faenza, Faenza Editrice, 1975, p. 93.
[741] Costanzo, Michele: *Leonardo Ricci e l'idea di spazio comunitario*, Macerata, Quodlibet, 2009, pp. 34–39.
[742] *Comune agricola*, in *Casabella*, no. 367, July 1972, p. 27.

not so much for generational reasons as for ideological ones. The metropolis for Friedman is not "disgusting," but can be improved through correctives like urban farming or other means of fostering self-sufficiency.[743] In any case it was the United States, the land where traditionally "not a reading man but has a draft of a new community in his waistcoat pocket"[744] (Emerson), that became in the early seventies a privileged case study on both sides of the Atlantic. While in the US John Reps offered a first systematic study on the urban planning of utopian communities,[745] in parallel Francesco Dal Co commented from Venice that "it can be said that America as 'utopia materialized,' or the 'land of utopia,' is a persistent myth in Europe"[746] in the collective volume devoted to the American city by the Venetian study group led by Tafuri – immediately after carrying out parallel studies on the socialist city in the USSR.[747] Again between 1972 and 1973 Dolores Hayden embarked on a detailed study of a selection of American communities, four of them religious and three nondenominational, for a research project funded by an influential department of architecture, the one at Berkeley, and the American Institute of Architects, leading to the publication of a book, *Seven American Utopias*.[748]

This proliferation of studies had been inaugurated by a book that appeared without much fanfare in 1972, in which the idea of community was developed through a complete urban program and in which were collected the studies that Oswald Mathias Ungers and his wife Liselotte had carried out on American communes in the 19th and 20th centuries at the time when Ungers was president of Cornell University (1968–74), *Kommunen in der Neuen Welt*.[749] In their book the German couple shows, at the end of a comparative analysis of communities with an ideological basis in religion (Amana, Hutterites, Shakers[750], Rappites, Moravians), socialism (Owenites, Fourierists, Icarians) or a hybrid of the two (the religious-communalist Oneida Community), that the idea of utopian communitarian life had survived in the USA for over 300 years alongside and as an alternative to urban individualistic society, oriented instead toward profit and competition, what Friedman called "competitive society."

It may seem paradoxical that an architect like Ungers, passionately fond of historical studies and a collector of Renaissance treatises on architecture, should have written a book of

---

743 Something written by Friedman many years later seems to be a direct description of these Proudhonian ideas: "Une économie ni socialiste, ni capitaliste," in Friedman, Yona: *Alternatives énergétiques ou la civilisation paysanne modernisée. Pour une réelle économie des resources: comment désindustrialiser l'énergie*. Saint-Jean-de-Braye, Dangles, 1982, pp. 65–66. See id., *Votre ville est à vous. Sachez comment la conserver*, Strasbourg, Conseil de l'Europe, 1975.

744 Rush, Ralph L. (ed.): *The Letters of Ralph Waldo Emerson*, 6 vols., New York, Columbia University Press, 1939, vol. 2, p. 353. This passage was cited first by the Ungers at the beginning of their introduction (p. 19) and later by Hayden, too.

745 Reps, John: *Town Planning in Frontier America*, New York, Princeton University Press, 1971, in particular the chapter "Cities of Zion: The Quest for Utopia."

746 Dal Co, Francesco: *Dai parchi alla regione. L'ideologia progressista e la riforma della città americana*, in Tafuri, Manfredo et al.: *La città americana, dalla guerra civile al New Deal*, Rome/Bari, Laterza 1973, p. 160. See in particular the section "La comunità utopica," pp. 157–64. In those years Eugenio Battisti was also studying the utopian communities of America; see the essay he published many years later: *Breve storia illustrata delle comunità artificiali e alternative*, in *Oz*, no. 3, 1995, pp. 19–33. Also see Saccaro Del Baffa, Giuseppe: *Eugenio Battisti e la storia delle utopie realizzate*, ibid., pp. 15–17.

747 Tafuri, Manfredo et al.: *Socialismo, città, architettura URSS 1917–1937. Il contributo degli architetti europei*, Rome, Officina, 1971.

748 Hayden, Dolores: *Seven American Utopias. The Architecture of Communitarism 1790–1975*, Cambridge (MA)/London, MIT Press 1976. An Italian translation was published in a "Library of Architecture" series directed at the time by Dal Co.

749 Ungers, Liselotte and Ungers, Oswald Mathias: *Kommunen in der Neuen Welt 1740–1972*, op. cit.

750 See Lassiter, William Lawrence: *Shaker Architecture*, New York, Bonanza, 1966; Schiffer, Herbert: *Shaker Architecture*, Exton Schiffer Publishing, 1979.

sociology to describe the different forms of community and utopia in America; the same man who in his 1960 manifesto had declared polemically: "It is not possible to deduce any plan from sociology."[751] There can be no doubt that the contribution of his wife, who went on to write a book on the German Siedlungen, was substantial. The interest shown by Friedman, philosopher of self-determination and poles apart from Ungers on the architectural plane, is much more logical. And yet Ungers's book dates from 1972, while Friedman's article on the theory of the *critical group*[752] was published at the beginning of 1973. This shows just how central was the notion of utopia in the sixties, and especially after 1968, bringing into dialogue figures who in abstract we might consider very distant from one another. In 1963 Ungers was called to teach at the Technical University (TU) in Berlin and took it upon himself to reinvigorate discussion of architectural theory, wholly neglected at the time. At the end of the sixties students, and not just in Germany, were not so much interested in architecture from a formal viewpoint as from that of the social, political and economic relations from which it sprang and in which it developed. They were interested in criticizing the conditions under which housing was constructed, in demonstrating the impossibility of "solving the housing question" (Engels) in a capitalist system and, above all, in condemning the latter; the student revolt had entered a political phase in which architecture, city planning and history were regarded as completely useless. In this atmosphere of political and social strife,[753] teaching as Ungers conceived it had become impossible and as a consequence he accepted the chair of the Department of Architecture at Cornell University in New York in 1968.

In the brief but intense period in which he taught at the TU, however, Ungers invited Ernst Bloch and Yona Friedman to hold seminars (both in 1964) and organized the Berlin meeting of Team 10 (1965) and then an international congress on theory in architecture in which, among others, Colin Rowe, Reyner Banham, Giedion and Kenneth Frampton took part (1967).[754]

In addition, Ungers was the first to take an interest in German Expressionist architecture, i.e. in the group of architects and artists who were authors of the chain letter initiated by Bruno Taut and called the *Utopian Correspondence*, in which his brother Max, Gropius, Mendelsohn, Scharoun and others were involved. In particular the socialist anarchism of Bruno Taut and his model of dissolution of the city constituted the closest theoretical antecedent to the book on American communes.[755]

---

[751] "The subject-object relationship has been done away with." See Ungers and Gieselman's manifesto (1960) now in CONRADS, Ulrich (ed.): *Programs and Manifestoes* . . . , op. cit., pp. 165–66.

[752] FRIEDMAN, Yona: *The Critical Group Size*, in Architectural Design, no. 1, 1973, pp. 44–45.

[753] For a close examination of the events in France in May 1968 written on the spur of the moment, see CACCIARI, Massimo: *La comune di maggio*, in Contropiano, no. 2, 1968, pp. 455–63.

[754] On this phase and Ungers' career in general, see STIMMAN, Hans: *Oswald Mathias Ungers. Il reticolo delle idee*, in Area, no. 70, September–October 2003, pp. 154–68. See DE MICHELIS, Marco: "Architectura artificialis," in UNGERS, Oswald Mathias: *Opera completa 1991–1998*, Milan, Electa, 1998, pp. 9–18.

[755] Up until then Ungers had organized a small exhibition in Berlin in 1963–64, without publishing much on the subject. See KULTERMANN, Udo and UNGERS, Oswald Mathias: *Die gläserne Kette. Visionäre Architekturen aus dem Kreis um Bruno Taut 1919–1920*, in the catalogue of the exhibition in Leverkusen and Berlin, Leverkusen, Stadtverwaltung, 1963. The text of the lecture he gave in Florence, at the invitation of Giovanni Klaus Koenig, is in UNGERS, Oswald Mathias: *Die Erscheinungsformen des Expressionismus in der Architektur*, Cologne, Studioverlag für Architektur, 1964.

As Pier Vittorio Aureli has pointed out,[756] Ungers and his wife understood the idea of community as an archipelago of micro-cities capable of rapidly colonizing the New World a long way from any true urban setting. This idea had been inspired by the concerts at Woodstock and Altamont during which rural and isolated locations were instantaneously urbanized by groups of people who identified with well-defined and socially selective ideals, thereby recreating the situation of the political and religious communities of the previous century. Ungers also had in mind the peculiar circumstances of West Berlin after the construction of the wall, a city completely cut off from the rest of the territory and made up in turn of scattered boroughs, independent of one another, and inhabited by people resigned to living in an enclave. Over the course of the seventies this insight would be developed in positive terms, culminating in the 12 *Theses on the City* in which Ungers and his assistants, including Koolhaas and Hans Kollhoff, imagined Berlin as a *Green Archipelago*:[757] a federation of small urban communities highly characterized on both the social and the formal level, immersed in an unattended forest that had to absorb everything that was transitory and generic. This idea of city has exercised a decisive influence on two urban conceptions that represent two of the most recent manifestos on the contemporary city, Koolhaas's *Bigness* and Léon Krier's *Ville dans la Ville*[758] – his brother Rob had been Ungers's assistant in Cologne, before Koolhaas went to work with him at Cornell.[759] Both these theories propose the shrinkage of the city into autonomous parts to counter the illusion that the city can be organized as a continuum.

In *Utopies réalisables*, Friedman totally abandons the "universalist utopia"[760] (i.e. the utopia whose realization depends on a universal, impossible consensus) of the global village of the sixties, assuming a position clearly opposed to the more or less naïve enthusiasm for the myth of generalized global communication that had characterized much of architectural culture: Friedman tries to show that the impossibility of generalized communication is not the result of its technical impracticability but of our structural inability (in the biological sense of the term) to coordinate a surplus of inevitably ambiguous information. In other words "mass communication stifles new ideas."[761] The most direct and persuasive of all forms of communication, the face-to-face one, is therefore only possible within a critical group, and so utopias, including architectural ones, can only be realized in a critical group: "the key to utopias could be, on the contrary, *coexistence in diversity*. Each group would look for its own utopia, which it would then realize, and each of these utopias would

---

[756] See AURELI, Pier Vittorio: *The City within the City. Oswald Mathias Ungers, OMA and the Project of the City as Archipelago*, in id., *The Possibility of an Absolute Architecture*, Cambridge (MA), MIT Press, 2011, pp. 177–227.
[757] UNGERS, Oswald Mathias: *Cities within the City: Berlin as a Green Archipelago*, in *Lotus International*, no. 19, 1978, pp. 82–97.
[758] KRIER, Léon: *A City within a City. The New Quartier de la Villette*, in *Architectural Design*, no. 3, vol. 47, March 1977, pp. 200–13.
[759] On the relations between Ungers and Koolhaas, see the latter's (autobiographical) essay, in AMO/Rem Koolhaas (eds.), *Post-Occupancy*, special issue of *Domus*, 2006. It should be noted that the issue centers on the modifications that some of OMA's recent buildings have undergone on the basis of their use by occupants, a theme very dear to Friedman.
[760] FRIEDMAN, Yona: *Utopies réalisables*, op. cit., p. 43.
[761] Ibid., p. 72.

be peculiar to a precise group."[762] The change in direction with respect to his proposals of the GEAM years is evident, as for example no critical group would ever be able to create a bridge city, just buildings or entirely self-planned parts of the city.

The ideas on participation that Friedman expressed in his little treatise were not isolated: the early seventies saw a moderate dissemination of movements of thought such as bottom-up urbanism or advocacy planning aimed at boosting the degree of participation of inhabitants in the decision-making processes of city planning, "hard to define appropriately and even more difficult to achieve."[763]

Friedman, in contrast to this tradition, which as is well known has almost never succeeded in really achieving its goals, developed his "anti-utopian" *Utopies réalisables* not simply as a protest against or counterproposal to the institutional processes of public decision-making, but as a theory that formulated a clear hypothesis of non federal self-government. In fact he declares that the federative formula is the cause of wars while the simultaneous presence of different and non-communicating critical groups in the same territory guarantees peaceful coexistence because "the *closed* nature of these groups increases their mutual tolerance: given that the number of their members cannot grow, they do not try to make converts (the first source of conflict between groups) or behave like secret societies (the second habitual source of conflict)."[764]

Friedman was unwittingly fulfilling the hope expressed by the urban designer Martin Meyerson when he wrote about a decade earlier:

Planning, like utopia, depicts a desirable future state of affairs, but unlike utopia, specifies the means of achieving it. [...] If production and technology do wane, utopian formulations can more readily shift from the authoritarian to the permissive view of the human personality, from a kind of statistical concept of central tendency to one of dispersion, satisfying many minority aspirations.[765]

This is exactly where the change of tack in this book devoid of images lies, in the way it presents in a simple and accessible manner the proposal of a management of the territory based on the physiological principle of necessity, setting aside all the megastructural technological utopias and the meticulous mathematical calculations of *Pour une architecture scientifique* and avoiding the smug rigidity and long-windedness of the social utopias of the past.

From this time on Friedman would only show an interest in *modest, ordinary techniques*, or rather the simple technologies to which he would devote a museum around the middle of the eighties.

---

[762] Ibid., p. 53.
[763] FRAMPTON, Kenneth: *Modern Architecture: A Critical History*, op. cit., p. 288.
[764] FRIEDMAN, Yona: *Utopies réalisables*, op. cit., pp. 153–54. See the section on utopian Zionism in this book.
[765] MEYERSON, Martin: *Utopian Traditions...*, op. cit., pp. 247–49.

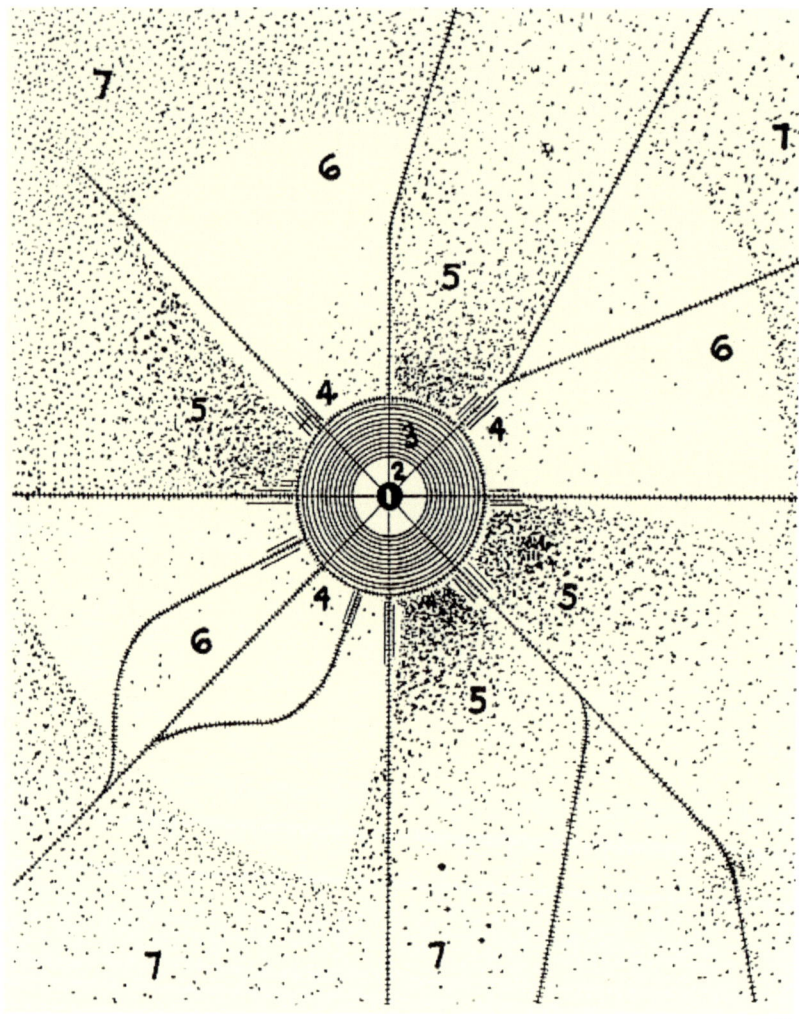

602

PAUL AND PERCIVAL GOODMAN

602 *Communitas*, 1974. Scheme of an ideal community, divided into four concentric major zones, conceived at an urban as well as social level. Published in Alexander, Christopher: *A City Is Not a Tree*, 1965.

CONSTANTINOS A. DOXIADIS, 1966

603 Doxiadis, Constantinos: *Between Dystopia and Utopia*, London, Faber and Faber, 1966.
604 Conceptual scheme: *Connections of elements, internal cohesion of conceptions*.
605 *The ideal Dynapolis* is a city with unidirectional growth, which prevents any of its parts from suffering from pressures by foreseeing and planning for growth in time.

BETWEEN DYSTOPIA AND UTOPIA

by Constantinos A. Doxiadis

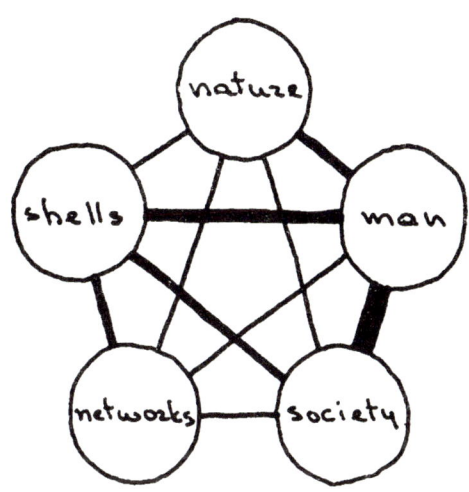

fig. 3   the growing city

we need:

wide streets

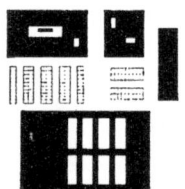
big parking plots

large regular plots

freedom for new designs

freedom for expropriation

but we have:

narrow streets

small parking plots

small irregular plots

no room to move

the largest investment.

606

THE PROBLEMS OF URBAN GROWTH

606 Published in Doxiadis, Constantinos: *Between Dystopia and Utopia*, London, Faber and Faber, 1966.

THE "WATERVLIET SHAKER SETTLEMENT," NEW YORK, 19TH CENTURY

607 Scheme from Ungers, Liselotte and Ungers, Oswald Mathias: *Kommunen in der Neuen Welt, 1740–1971*, Cologne, Kiepenheuer & Witsch, 1972.

"THE CRITICAL GROUP," C. 1975

608 Illustration from Friedman, Yona: *Utopies réalisables*, Paris, Union Générale d'Editions, 1975.

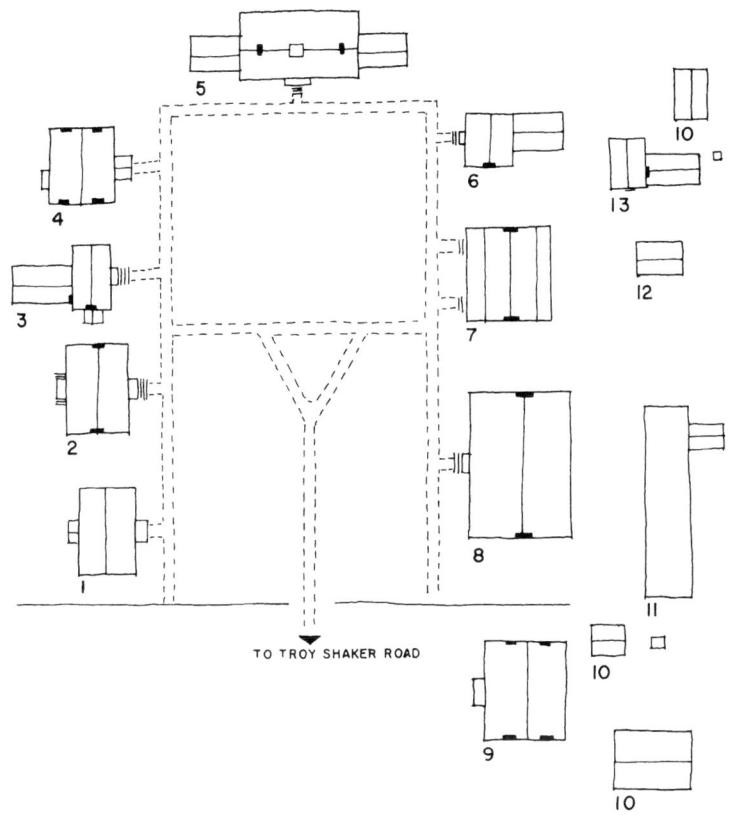

1. HERB HOUSE
2. BRETHREN'S SHOP
3. DWELLING HOUSE
4. SISTERS' WORKSHOP
5. MAIN DWELLING HOUSE
6. MINISTRY'S HOUSE
7. MEETING HOUSE, 1791
8. MEETING HOUSE, 1846
9. OFFICE
10. BARN
11. WOOD SHED
12. MODERN GARAGE
13. SEED HOUSE

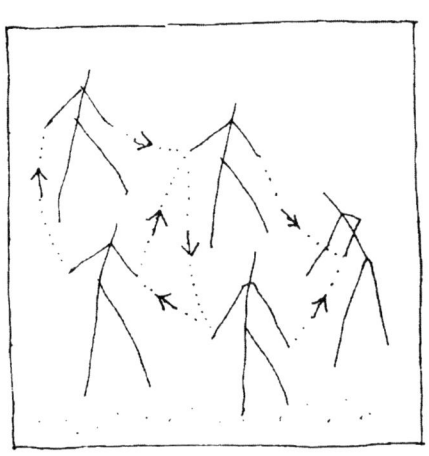

LYCÉE DAVID, ANGERS

Can an idea without an archetype be anything but a chimera?
Paul Thiry d'Holbach, 1772

Friedman takes the concept of participation to an extreme because the ultimate aim of his projects is to delegate the maximum power of choice to the inhabitants, moving in the direction of an absolute self-planning and self-determination. In his theoretical essay that comes closest to sociology, *Utopies réalisables*, Friedman postulates the equivalence of the terms *society* and *environment*. The implication for architecture is all too clear: to remodel an urban environment it is necessary to remodel first of all the society that will live there. Friedman goes so far as to propose an idea of society in addition to concrete proposals for its reorganization, as we have just seen.

The same year as he wrote the book, Friedman received his first major commission, the design of the new administrative headquarters of the CDC Dubonnet liquor manufacturer in Ivry.[766] A large disused factory was available and the first concrete step to take according to Friedman was to turn it into an *infrastructure*: eliminating the side walls and internal partitions, the bare skeleton that remained would be able to provide the maximum of freedom. The second step to take, on the other hand, was to inform the *critical group* of the company's employees, the futures users of the building, about their new possibilities of choice in the layout of their own offices. The internal partitions would be based on the principle of the "panel-chain," the simple system of prefabricated screens linked in a chain that Friedman had devised immediately after the war. The project was already at a fairly advanced stage when Dubonnet was taken over by its direct competitor, Ricard, and consequently all that survives are a scale model and some plans. But four years later, in 1979, another opportunity presented itself.

With the exception of a small and now completely transformed building in Israel, the only work of Yona Friedman to have been realized stands in Angers, a city in the Anjou region that currently has around 60,000 inhabitants, halfway between Paris and Nantes.
The Lycée David, located in a late 18th century building in the historic center, had become totally incapable of coping with the number of schoolchildren in the small city, whose population had been growing rapidly since the war. Under pressure from the mayor and some members of parliament, the National Ministry of Education announced its approval of the allocation of the funds needed to build a new high school outside the city walls, in a newly developed district near the Maine River, in 1971.[767]
At the beginning of the seventies the constant emergence of "biological spikes" in education, i.e. of sudden increases in school attendance, led many administrations in Europe to

---

[766] Lebesque, Sabine and Fentener van Vlissingen, Helene (eds.): *Yona Friedman: Structures...*, op. cit., pp. 68–69.
[767] Letter from the Secretary of State Pierre Billecocq to René La Combe, member of the National Assembly for Maine-et-Loire, June 23, 1971, Archive Lycée Bergson, Angers (henceforth ALB).

set up *mobile schools*, housed in improvised trailers (the municipality of Milan for instance bought fifty of them in 1972). Since the "biological spike" typical of newly urbanized outlying areas, as at Angers, was a transitory phenomenon, it became necessary to construct buildings that could vary over time, accompanying the demographic surge from elementary school to high school, and remaining available at the end for a more generic use. For this reason they had to be convertible as well as cheap, and allow for the possibility of being dismantled. These kinds of school first emerged in the sixties as single-story wooden pavilions with two classrooms, and then were transformed in 1969 into two-story pavilions that could be taken down, to be added to existing complexes, but with structural characteristics similar to those of a normal school. In the seventies instead a series of multistory buildings with a steel framework were constructed to house schools of every level and type with requisites like those of permanent structures; as these lent themselves more to being dismantled than to being converted, they opened up the new possibility of transfer to other districts or cities where the need was greater. In Frankfurt am Main both solutions were adopted, but the cost of production was 40% higher than similar constructions in Italy, and the level of technical skill required still fairly high; for example the bolts of the steel framework had to be inserted on site.[768]

It was partly to meet these requirements of convertibility of school buildings that the ministry singled out Friedman as the most suitable architect, since he was an expert on adaptable habitats and self-planning.[769]
In the meantime in Angers, after a series of bureaucratic delays, the necessary funds were set aside – with the municipality contributing around two hundred million francs – but what is more interesting is the letter sent by the principal to the representative of the students' parents in 1977 in which he declared:

I have the honor to inform you that the future Lycée David in Angers will be built using the method of self-planning.[770]

In 1977 Friedman officially received the commission and immediately sent out a manual of self-planning compiled on the basis of his experience with the Dubonnet offices and similar to others he had published in the meantime.[771] Choosing Friedman to coordinate this particular project seems to have been the ideal solution as he had always fought for an architecture shaped by its occupants. Thus the project for the Dubonnet headquarters constituted the closest precedent and can be considered the model for the subsequent one at Angers. The majority of the parents and students was opposed to the site chosen by the ministry because it was on the outskirts of the city, and it was partly to placate such protests that the ministry agreed to let the new building be designed using the self-planning method.

---

768 On this, see issue no. 10 of *Acciaio*, 1972, and Bolocan, Andrea G. and Mendini, Francesco: *Scuole: smontabili e rimovibili*, in *Casabella*, no. 376, 1973, pp. 4–5.
769 Ragon, Michel: *Yona Friedman: de l'habitat évolutif à l'autoplanification*, in *Urbanisme*, vol. 43, no. 143, 1974, pp. 75–77.
770 Letter from R. Chausseray, "Proviseur du Lycée d'Etat David d'Angers," October 27, 1977, ALB.
771 Friedman, Yona: *Votre ville est à vous. Sachez comment la conserver*, op. cit.; id., *Comment habiter la terre*, Paris, 1976.

Friedman fixed November 9, 1977, as the date of the first meeting, which was attended by thirty teachers, fifteen students, four school attendants, four parents and some representatives of the administrative staff. He took care not to invite officials of the ministry or the municipality to ensure that they did not influence the future users, and excluded himself as from the meetings as well. He handed out a manual with the title *Collective Planning and the School*.

The plan of the work was defined through this manual, which Friedman then adapted to the building standards and regulations. The consultations were completed by March 1978 and a preliminary plan was drawn up, and approved the following year.[772]

To do this Friedman left the decisions on the number of rooms needed and their arrangement to the participants in the meetings and then drew a graph that had the distinctive feature of being able to change shape without radically altering its structure.[773] After this, Friedman moved on to a *bubble diagram*: in other words he allowed the users to determine the routes of circulation, focusing solely on ensuring that the size of the rooms met the rigid requirements laid down by the ministry.

After this the rooms were strung out along the lines of circulation like simple *bubbles* along a thread. So it is evident that from this point of view the internal circulation played a preponderant role: it bound all the parts of the building together but also made sure that each classroom communicated with the outside. As a result the corridors are very long, like small streets, but this was a precise request on the part of the users: walking some distance between one lesson and the next, when the classroom changed, allowed them to stretch their legs and meet their friends or colleagues as if on a walk in the city. In addition, from discussion with the teachers it emerged that long corridors, with corners kept to a minimum, made it easier to keep peace among the younger students: it seems in fact that the children were in the habit of withdrawing into the corners of the buildings and forming cliques, out of sight of the schoolteachers.

Thus the rooms are lined up along the internal streets, which converge on a central open space, the large courtyard around which the whole life of the high school turns.

The panels between the classes, on the other hand, are interchangeable and can be removed fairly easily, permitting continual adaptations of use and later alterations, but in reality they have never been modified.

The building is organized for what originally were intended to be four separate schools (including scientific, technical and commercial colleges) but were then combined in a single institution – along with a small section with a lecture hall to be used for preparatory courses for young teachers.

When it was opened, the teachers had a very communitary intention. They wanted to accommodate four independent mini-schools in the same building [...] I had to guarantee that it could be transformed into an ordinary lycée if they wanted.[774]

---

[772] Dossier des Ouvrages Executives, October 30, 1979, ALB.
[773] The graph and the bubble diagram are reproduced in FRIEDMAN, Yona: *Théorie et images*, Paris, Editions Institut Français d'Architecture, 2000, pp. 76–77.
[774] OBRIST, Hans-Ulrich and FRIEDMAN, Yona: *The Conversation Series*, op. cit., p. 28.

One of Friedman's responsibilities was to ensure that the construction met a number of technical standards without exceeding the allotted budget; however, the French Ministry of Education had chosen only four possible processes of prefabrication in advance. Friedman decided to accept these limited possibilities, in the case of the windows for example, in order to preserve the freedom in the overall plan of the work.[775] This meant renouncing leaving any formal mark on the construction. In any case there were numerous compromises. For instance the ministry would have preferred the internal courtyards to be roofed with plexiglass, but in the end only the central one was covered. The teachers and Friedman agreed on a request for a tree to be planted in all the others.

The plan of the building was fully in keeping with the fire regulations as it was possible to go directly outside from each classroom without having to use the long internal corridors. Moreover, the teachers did not like the idea of a multistory building as had been envisaged in an earlier alternative design promoted by the local architect Thellier, with whom Friedman quickly came into conflict.[776] It is partly for this reason that the plan of the high school is so sprawling and complex: the large number of classrooms required and the desire to have each of them open onto the outside or one of the internal courtyards explains the size of the area covered by the building.

Friedman tried to keep the whole building on a single level raised two meters above the ground and with basements underneath. However, yet another compromise was reached and the result was a base of just 60 centimeters and two stories above ground. In particular one teacher asked for the installation of a small astronomical observatory on the second floor, but the proposal was considered too costly and rejected. Finally decorative murals were planned for the outer facades but were not executed, even though Friedman had prepared designs for the purpose, visible in a photomontage.[777] It was a fairly simple decoration made up of a few geometric elements vaguely akin to Vasarely's work in those years.[778] Even before this, in the early seventies, Friedman had produced models of urban decoration of both the road surface (*Urban Carpet,* 1973) and the blind facades that are so common in Paris (*Art in the Street,* 1975).[779] In this last case the decoration was to have been composed of just three geometric shapes – triangle, circle and square – arranged in a pattern chosen by the inhabitants of the condominium. In a similar manner Friedman wanted to leave the decoration of the high school to its students, but then prepared some designs for the outside walls, clearly visible in the photomontage. The Lycée David soon changed its name to Lycée Bergson, by which it has been known since the end of its construction in 1981 and up until the present day.

---

[775] "Actually I wasn't free in conceiving the structure itself, because this was specified by the ministry. Nevertheless, it was a skeleton-type structure, which allowed for a certain degree of change," ibid., p. 29.

[776] They would end up in court – in a case won by Friedman – partly because Thellier had tried to keep the entire fee for himself. See the interview with Friedman in the appendix.

[777] Lebesque, Sabine and Fentener van Vlissingen, Helene (eds.): *Yona Friedman: Structures . . .* , op. cit., p. 73.

[778] Vasarely, Victor: *Plasti-cité,* in *L'œuvre plastique dans votre vie quotidienne,* op. cit.

[779] Lebesque, Sabine and Fentener van Vlissingen, Helene (eds.): *Yona Friedman: Structures . . .* , op. cit., pp. 70 – 71.

In any case Yona Friedman still regards the Lycée David as a demonstration of his hypothesis that ordinary people can shape a design and that the role of the architect is to let the community make the choices, adhering to the decisions they take. In other words, Friedman is trying to shift architecture onto a different plane from that of art, getting it to take a step back in order to place itself at the service of society.

While no one doubts that an owner can determine the design of a detached house like a little Louis XIV in Versailles, the majority of ordinary people and architects do not believe that it is possible for three hundred and fifty people to do the same, influencing the project to suit its future collective use; in general they dismiss self-determination as utopian or unrealistic. Friedman on the contrary claims to have shown that it is possible and to have put into practice the theory first formulated in his manifesto *L'architecture mobile* way back in 1956 and set out clearly on many occasions over the following years:

Architects and city planners today are no longer artists or "the people who take decisions," but just public servants; the inhabitants (or users of the products of the architect and the city planner) should not be regarded as consumers, but as highly specialized professionals and experts on the subject of habitats, each of whom has had a long enough experience of the way of life that suits him to know what he wants.[780]

From this point of view the building in Angers is a demonstration prototype: it is not very interesting in itself, as an object. Indeed its aesthetics are wholly secondary because it is the process of involvement in decision-making that really counts.

In conclusion, if society and environment are one and the same thing then the quality of urban life depends on the relations that are established between people, ideas and constructions. So the architect has to give up what has traditionally been his oldest and most cherished prerogative, the power to leave a personal and lasting mark on a building, and go beyond his customary role, equipping himself with new tools. But few architects are willing to pay such a price, sometimes not even the ones who give their ideological support to the need for participation.

---

[780] FRIEDMAN, Yona: *L'architettura mobile*, op. cit., p. 5.

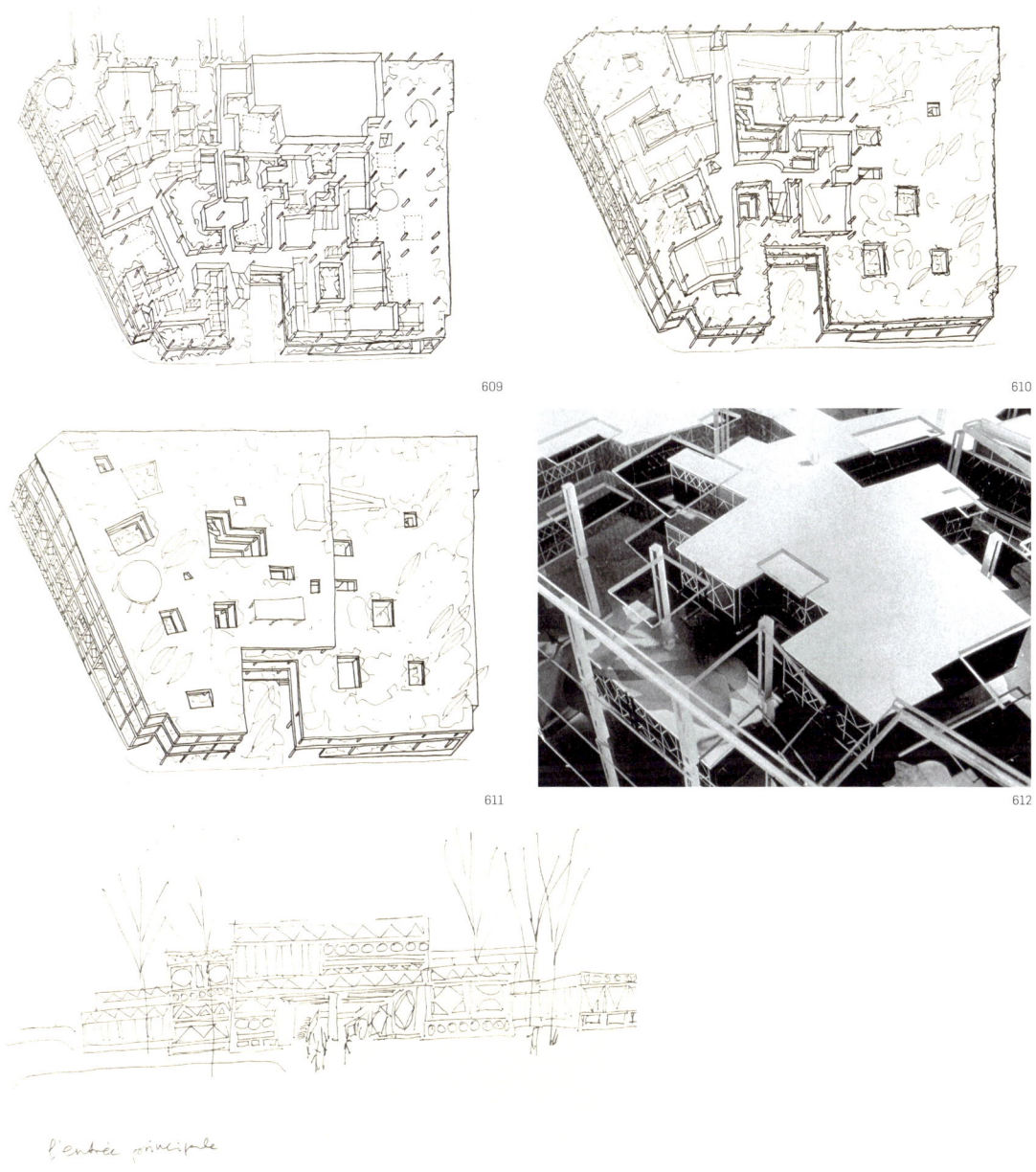

ADMINISTRATIVE CENTER OF THE DUBONNET COMPANY, IVRY, 1974

609 – 611 Yona Friedman: Axonometrics, level 2 and 3, scale 1:400.
612 – 613 Yona Friedman: Model view and elevation of the main entrance.
Photograph of the model by Robert Doisneau.

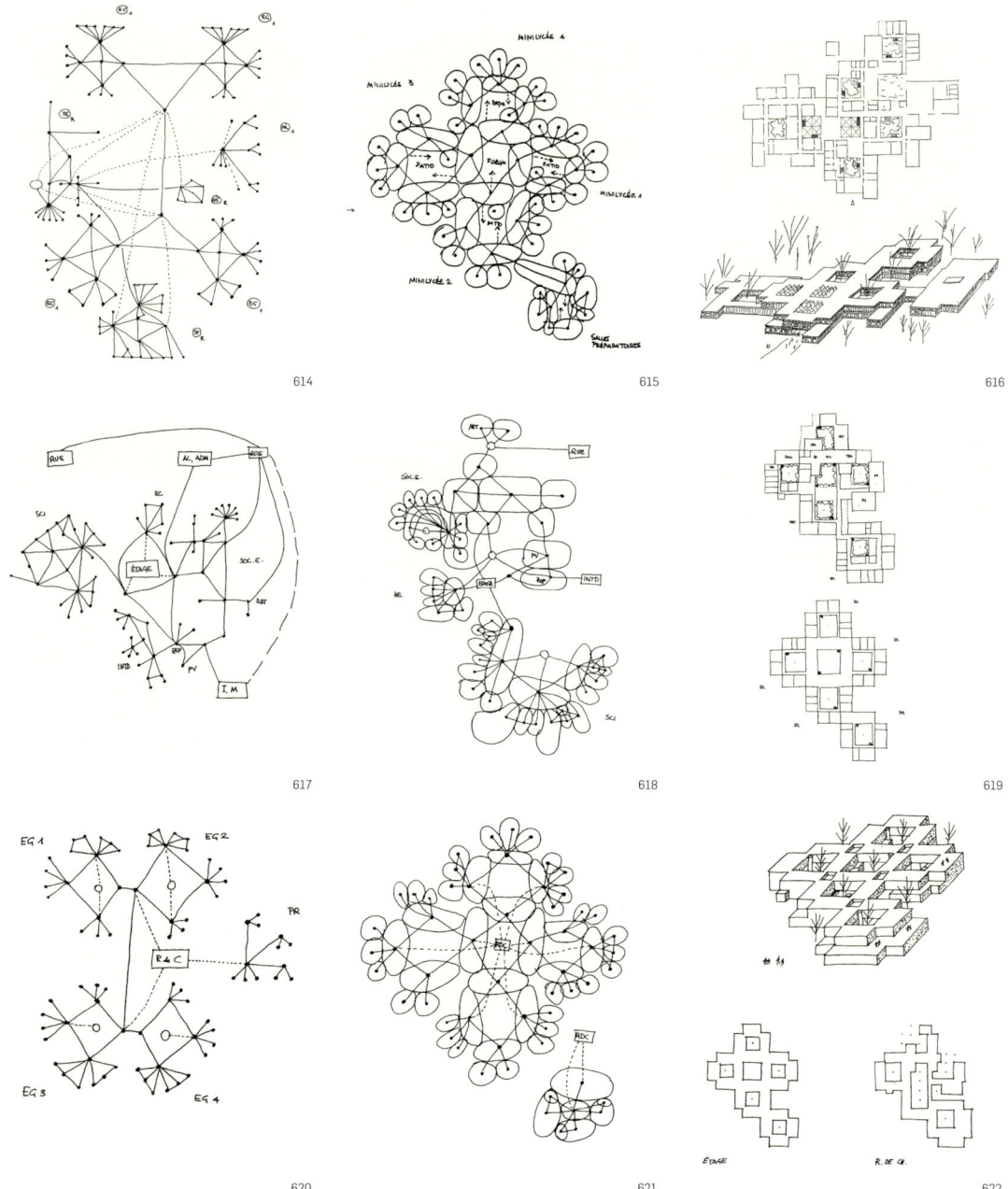

"LYCÉE DAVID D'ANGERS," FRANCE, 1978

614 – 622 Yona Friedman: *Bubble diagrams: preparatory room / general scheme / plan and axonometry / ground floors / ground floor and first floor / first floors / axonometry.*
623 – 625 Yona Friedman: Photomontage, aerial view, internal perspective of the patio and ornamentation for the external facade.

Patio

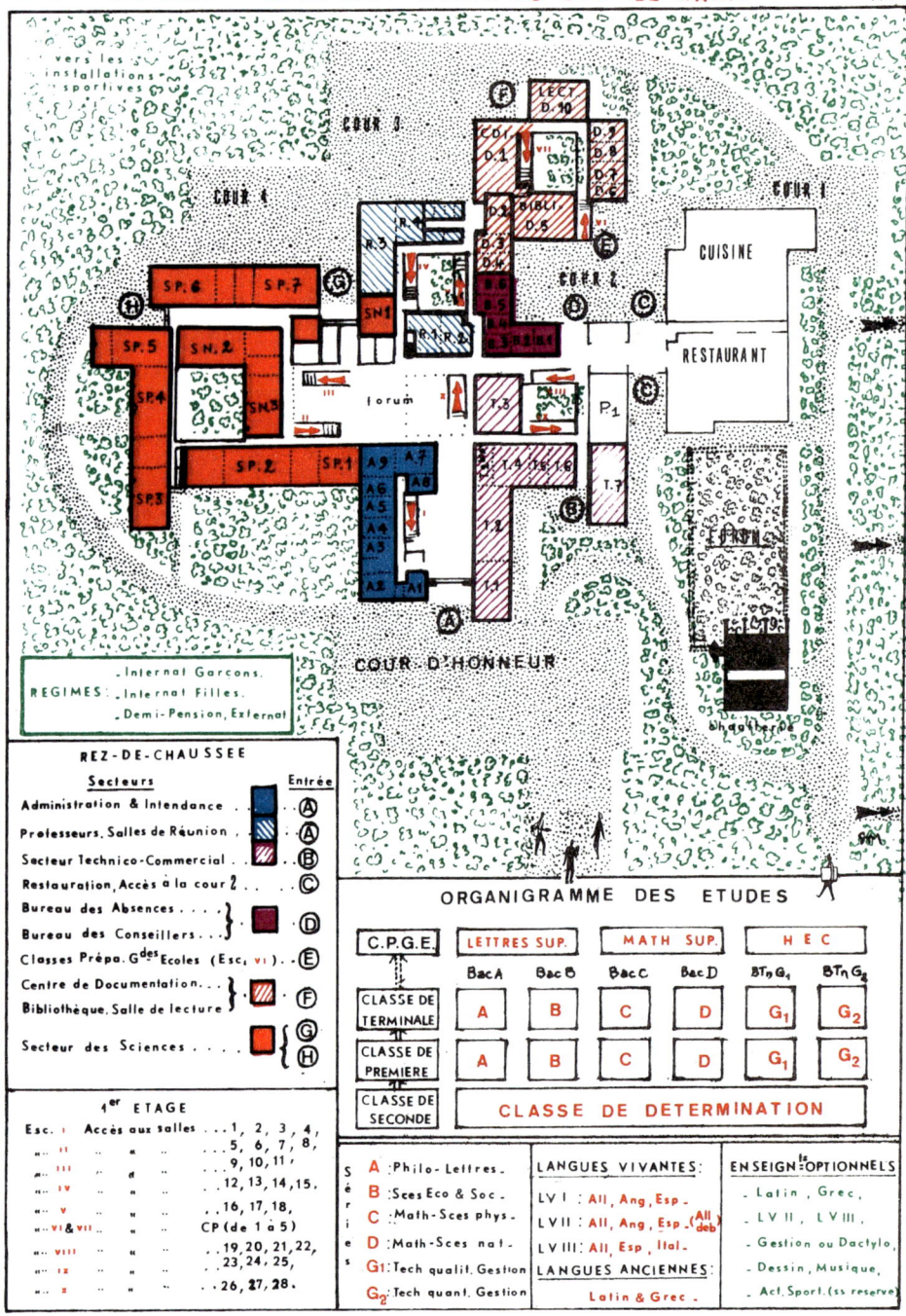

"LYCÉE DAVID D'ANGERS"

626 Organization chart: uses of the rooms, just after its opening, 1981.
627–633 Internal and external views of the high school, 2005.
Photographs by Manuel Orazi.

PHILOSOPHY OF PARTICIPATION

Is politics a theoretical or practical science? Both of them. In truth it comprises all the other sciences.[781]
Friedrich Schlegel

The seventies were years of retrenchment for Friedman. After the great success of *L'architecture mobile* in the sixties, Friedman gave up producing formal images to concentrate on new forms of representation to be used for communication, such as graph theory and the diagram, but he also produced many manuals of self-planning. These contain mostly elementary drawings, almost stylized cartoons, that provide the basic information for self-determination on various planes, from the building of a roof to how to behave in nature; handbooks that were therefore accessible even to uneducated people. The themes of these manuals are: designing your own house, living with others in big cities,[782] modifying your own urban environment to measure and how to design your own natural setting.[783]
In the second half of the seventies he began to work steadily with the UN and above all with UNESCO – which has its headquarters in Paris, a very short distance from Friedman's home. So the Hungarian architect undertook a series of journeys to developing countries (Africa, the Middle East, India) and took part in international meetings like the Conference on Human Settlements in Vancouver in 1976.[784] The Yom Kippur War (1973) and the energy crisis that ensued from the interruption in the supply of oil from Arab countries had paralyzed Europe, undermining the climate of optimism that had characterized the previous decade. Once again Friedman reacted to an alarming situation with lucid rationality, presenting technical solutions, even if they were now extremely simplified.
An early result of this research was *L'architecture de survie*,[785] a book that reflects on many of the experiences of those years and is perhaps the author's own favorite,[786] and one in which the ultimate goal of this new commitment emerges clearly: restoring to the people of the West the versatility they had lost with the advent of industrial society, that is to say the way that in agricultural societies the farmer was also an architect and builder and completely self-sufficient – capable of carrying out any everyday activity, sewing, cooking, smithery, etc. Obviously, the greater a man's versatility the greater his chance of survival, and Friedman took care to indicate in his manuals – of which he wrote dozens – basic

---

[781] SCHLEGEL, Friedrich: *Teoria del bello nella poesia*, in id., *Frammenti di estetica*, ed. by Michele Cometa, Palermo, Aesthetica, 1989, p. 53.
[782] FRIEDMAN, Yona: *Comment vivre entre les autres sans être enclave et sans être chef*, Paris, Pauvert, 1974; "Friedman, in one chapter of his booklet, supposes a future world of poverty (partly in the light of the recent economic and energy crises), due to unavoidable circumstances to which humanity will be forced to adapt in order to survive; and, indeed, to live better than it does today, torn between capitalist selfishness and totalitarian restrictions." DORFLES, Gillo: *Il divenire della critica*, Turin, Einaudi, 1976, p. 36.
[783] FRIEDMAN, Yona: *Je veux projeter ma maison*, Paris, Ministère de la Culture, 1973; id., *Votre ville est à vous. Sachez comment la conserver*, Strasbourg, Conseil de l'Europe, 1975; id., *Comment habiter la terre*, Paris, Ministère de l'Environnement, 1976; id., *Où commence la ville?* Paris, UNESCO, 1978.
[784] LEBESQUE, Sabine and FENTENER VAN VLISSINGEN, Helene (eds.): *Yona Friedman: Structures . . .*, op. cit., p. 128.
[785] FRIEDMAN, Yona: *L'architecture de survie, où s'invente aujourd'hui le monde de demain*, with an introduction by Michel Ragon, Paris/Tournai, Casterman, 1978. Revised and enlarged ed., *L'architecture de survie. Une philosophie de la pauvreté*, Paris, Editions de l'Eclat, 2003.
[786] "When I wrote it, it was not simply theoretical speculation. I had proof that it could actually be done." In OBRIST, Hans-Ulrich and FRIEDMAN, Yona: *The Conversation Series*, op. cit., p. 115. In the following pages Friedman speaks of his collaboration with UNESCO.

techniques of survival for Europeans as well as Africans. In particular Friedman wanted to dovetail the figure of the inhabitant with that of the architect, or rather of the builder: the builder should not take precedence over the inhabitant because the latter is "the spouse of the architectural object." The architect instead should be like a language teacher, in other words he should limit himself to teaching a grammar that can be used by inhabitants in his absence – in the same way as the professor does not interfere with the literary decisions of his former students.

So the architect 'teaching grammar' is equivalent to a language teacher, while the architect who applies the participation of the inhabitant is nothing more than an interpreter.[787]

The Museum of Simple Technologies in Madras (now Chennai) that he designed with Eda Schaur in 1986–87, a series of pavilions constructed out of bamboo and aluminum foil with the aid of local craftsmen, on the initiative of UNESCO, held a special value for Friedman: it was a prototype for the application of the techniques of self-building expounded in the manuals.[788]

In the seventies participation was no longer Friedman's privileged and exclusive theme. Other architects had set off down the same road with decision: Habraken and his SAR[789] in the Netherlands, Ralph Erskine[790] in Sweden and Britain, Christopher Alexander[791] in the United States and above all Giancarlo De Carlo in Italy – who had published Alexander[792] and Habraken,[793] but not Friedman, in his series for Il Saggiatore – who had provided a highly controversial concrete example in the *Matteotti housing project* for workers at the Terni steel mills.[794] De Carlo had declared clearly that participation would be a central theme of the seventies right at the beginning of the decade, in what remains his most important theoretical text, *An Architecture of Participation*,[795] published first in English and then in Italian, and anticipated in *Parametro*:

Participation turns architectural design from the peremptory act that it has been up to now into a process. A process that starts with the revelation of the users' needs [...].[796]

---

787 FRIEDMAN, Yona: *L'architecture de survie ...*, op. cit., p. 58; see in general the whole of chapter II, "Les rôles nouveaux: celui de l'habitant et celui de l'architecte," pp. 55–71.
788 STEVENS, Albert: *Tecnologie semplici a Madras*, in *L'Arca*, no. 35, 1988, p. 44.
789 BOSMA, Koos, VAN HOOGSTRATEN, Dorine and Vos, Martijn: *Housing for the Millions: John Habraken and the SAR (1960–2000)*, Rotterdam, NAi Publishers, 2000.
790 "In 1948 Erskine started designing the enlargement of a small village, Gästrike–Hammarby some 100 miles north of Stockholm. Participation was entered into for the first time, and has become fundamental to Erskine's design methods since." COLLYMORE, Peter: *The Architecture of Ralph Erskine*, London/New York, Granada Publishing, 1982, p. 13. Also see RAY, Stefano: *Ralph Erskine, architettura di bricolage e di partecipazione*, Bari, Dedalo, 1978.
791 GEROSA, Pier Giorgio: *Christopher Alexander. Le ipotesi metodologiche dell'ultimo razionalista funzionale*, in DI BIAGI, Paola (ed.): *I classici moderni dell'urbanistica*, Rome, Donzelli, 2002, pp. 269–87.
792 ALEXANDER, Christopher: *Note sulla sintesi della forma*, Milan, Il Saggiatore, 1967.
793 HABRAKEN, John: *Strutture per una residenza alternativa*, Milan, Il Saggiatore, 1974.
794 MIONI, Angela and OCCHIALINI, Etra Connie (ed.): *Giancarlo De Carlo. Immagini e frammenti*, Milan, Electa, 1995, pp. 64–67.
795 In RICHARDS, J.M., BLAKE, Peter and DE CARLO, Giancarlo: *A Critic's View: Architecture in the 'Seventies*, Melbourne, Melbourne, The Chapter, 1969–72. Id., *L'architettura degli anni Settanta*, Milan, Il Saggiatore, 1973, pp. 87–142. Now in DE CARLO, Giancarlo: *L'architettura della partecipazione*, ed. by Sara Marini, Macerata, Quodlibet, 2013.
796 DE CARLO, Giancarlo: *Il pubblico dell'architettura*, in *Parametro*, no. 5, 1970.

In all his experiments with participation, and especially now, De Carlo worked, taught and wrote with particular attention not to theory but to the dynamic relations between society and the organization of space.[797] However, Sara Marini has noted how "De Carlo does not undermine but on the contrary magnifies the figure of the architect, associating his function with a broader process of design, and at the same time he denounces the problem of the exclusiveness of architecture and the entrenchment of its language that follows from it, something he stressed even in his last writings,"[798] pointing in this way to a substantial difference from Friedman.

Even Ungers tried to find a remedy for the divorce between architect and society:

A design concept with an orientation toward an adaptable systems of order, however, searches for a minimal design in which the organization of the elements in space will be minimized to allow or even to provoke a maximum participation of those who are using the space. [...] In reality, adaptability in architectural design means a transformation from an authoritarian act into an act of participation?[799]

In a brilliant essay, Jean-Louis Cohen has outlined two types of populism in architecture since the Second World War: the first, linked to vernacular forms of housing in both their traditional (Rudofsky,[800] Fathy) and their modern sense (Venturi and Scott Brown), pursues an autonomy of form while pretending not to. The second type, on the other hand, uninterested in form, wants to allow the inhabitants to make real choices, but harbors the ambition common to "democratic populism governed by the hegemonic discourse of politics and technocratic populism, governed by the methods of mathematics or those of engineering."[801] Yona Friedman can undoubtedly be placed within this second current of populism, which for Cohen has remained a constant temptation in the architecture of the 20th century. This trend toward participation, harshly criticized by Franco Purini, who spoke of "selling out design,"[802] extended in the seventies to other areas, such as product design, thanks to the migration of many young architects like Riccardo Dalisi into this specific sector – which was also explored, although to a much lesser degree, by Friedman: see his ring chairs.[803] Dalisi wrote:

If "participation" means "relationship," the architecture of participation is born at the moment it turns into an opportunity and instrument of social relations. For this purpose in addition to use everything can become a means of participation: construction, design, preparatory analyses and decisions on the contents and objectives of architecture.[804]

---

[797] Lyndon, Donlyn: *Giancarlo De Carlo negli Stati Uniti*, in Samassa, Francesco (ed.): *Giancarlo De Carlo. Percorsi*, Padua, Il Poligrafo, 2004, p. 58.
[798] Marini, Sara: "Scegliere la parte," introduction to De Carlo, Giancarlo: *L'architettura della partecipazione*, op. cit., p. 12.
[799] Ungers, Oswald Mathias: *Criteri di progettazione*, in *Lotus International*, no. 11, 1976, p. 13.
[800] See the fundamental Rudofsky, Bernard: *Architecture without Architects. A Short Introduction to Non-Pedigreed Architecture*, New York, Doubleday, 1964.
[801] "Yona Friedman's approach is representative of a technocratic component [...] it proposes utopian technical solutions, but with all the features of rationality with regard to the question of appropriation by the people and change." Cohen, Jean-Louis: *Promesses et impasses du populisme*, in *Cahiers de la recherche architecturale et urbaine*, January 2004, pp. 167–84.
[802] Purini, Franco: *Nove tesi* (1979), in id., *L'architettura didattica*. Rome: Gangemi, 1980, p. 17.
[803] Lebesque, Sabine and Fentener van Vlissingen, Helene (eds.): *Yona Friedman: Structures...*, op. cit., p. 94.
[804] Dalisi, Riccardo: *La partecipazione creativa è possibile*, in *Casabella*, nos. 368/369, August–September 1972, p. 93.

Shortly afterward Ugo La Pietra published his own definition of participation in the *Casabella* of the "Radicals":

Our operations will more and more tend to urge the individual to give serious thought to the need:
1. to broaden his range of choices;
2. to take a direct part in the shaping of his environment;
3. to enrich his processes of perception and understanding;
4. to increase his freedom of behavioral and thought.[805]

La Pietra hoped that the active participation of individuals would be able to introduce structural modifications in the organization of urban society "breaking down the process of uniformity and formal planning typical of our cities."[806]

Manfredo Tafuri criticized designers who countenanced participation because in his view it was not possible to break the cycle of production–distribution–consumption. All the anti-consumer utopias that "seek to redress the ethical 'distortions' of the technological world by modifying the system of production or the channels of distribution only reveal the complete inadequacy of their theories, in the face of the actual structure of the capitalist economic cycle."[807] In fact the early series of Enzo Mari's or Dalisi's anti-designs have a very high market value today, selling for large sums. But not everyone was trying to get away from the capitalist system, or rather this was not their priority.

For Tafuri social participation in architecture was a myth, and moreover an extremely ambiguous one.[808] Indeed Tafuri saw it as a "form of social control" since it was a current that came from the United States. According to Eisenman, Tafuri was deeply distrustful of the US in those years.[809] But one point is clear: he was openly opposed to flying this flag and even considered it dangerous as the state-controlled institutions – already in crisis, especially in Italy – would be weighed down by an expansion of those at the base. It was a consistent aversion on the part of the Roman historian: in *Contropiano* he had espoused Tronti's idea of the competitive spirit of a federation of allied but distinct forces independent of the political parties (unions, students and workers' committees, etc.) that would struggle *within* the capitalist system, without ever harboring much faith in the people. So populism was an enemy that always had to be treated with suspicion.

---

[805] La Pietra, Ugo: *Modelli attivi di comportamento*, in *Casabella*, no. 376, April 1973, p. 35.
[806] La Pietra, Ugo: *Il sistema disequilibrante*, with an introduction by Gillo Dorfles, Genoa, Masnata, 1971, p. 39.
[807] Tafuri, Manfredo: *Design and Technological Utopia*, in Ambasz, Emilio (ed.): *Italy: The New Domestic Landscape: Achievements and Problems of Italian Design*, in the catalogue of the exhibition at the MoMA, May 26 – September 11, 1972, New York/Florence, The Museum of Modern Art/Centro Di, 1972, p. 397.
[808] Manfredo Tafuri interviewed by Andrea Branzi and Benedetto Gravagnuolo in *Data*, nos. 28/29, October – December 1977; now in Branzi, Andrea: *Moderno Postmoderno Millenario, Scritti teorici 1972 – 80*, Turin/Milan, Studio Forma Alchymia, 1980, p. 83.
[809] "Manfredo was profoundly anti-American and this was a problem for me […]. America, in spite of its questionable political conditions, guarantees you a certain freedom and independence of thought." Aureli, Pier Vittorio: *Ding an sich. Autonomia rivisitata. Una conversazione con Peter Eisenman*, in *Parametro*, nos. 252 – 53, July – October 2004, p. 36.

Thus opposition to any form of architectural populism was logical for Tafuri and his fellow travelers: very different experiences and reflections like those of Rudofsky (not even mentioned in passing in the history of contemporary architecture he wrote with Francesco Dal Co), Venturi and Scott Brown and Friedman were openly resisted.

This partly explains the dearth of studies and research devoted to Friedman by architectural culture in the over forty years that has passed since he established his reputation –since the seventies, more or less. If in the first decade of the new century Friedman has experienced a substantial revival in his popularity,[810] if he has begun to publish almost a book a year and these are now being translated and reprinted in many countries, it is because he has been rediscovered, not by the world of architecture or its historiography, but by contemporary art. The relational art of many of today's artists, supported by the critical activity of curators like Nicolas Bourriaud or Hans Ulrich Obrist, explores the possibilities inherent in interaction with the public, often locating itself in critical zones of the contemporary city such as some of the most degraded peripheral urban areas in Europe, as if in an inadvertent attempt to make up for the shortcomings of the architects who designed them.

It is partly for this reason that relational art [811] is today almost naturally rediscovering many figures like Friedman who are atypical but relevant to this trend, and it is against this background that we need to set Friedman's ambiguous collaborations with many young and not so young artists, from Camille Henrot to Rä di Martino. The danger, however, is that this will diminish Friedman's rational proposals by aestheticizing them, stopping at the surface of a generic involvement of the public, whereas his ideas are always addressed to the whole of society and to the developing world in particular. So it is undoubtedly a paradox that a prototype of a cardboard shelter for the homeless – constructed by Friedman with the help of some students – is now in the collection of a museum of contemporary art like the MART, but at the same time it is the sign of yet another failure: what ought to have been an extremely useful solution to an everyday problem has instead been mummified and put on display in a museum like a chloroformed butterfly – placing art in a museum always results in its neutralization in any case. Friedman's message has, once again, been dramatically misunderstood, elevated to the status of a work of art while exorcizing all its *political* significance.

---

810 ORAZI, Manuel: *Utopia's Revival*, in *Log*, nos. 13/14, fall 2008, pp. 37–40.
811 BOURRIAUD, Nicolas: *Relational Aesthetics*, Dijon, Presses du Réel, 2002.

634

GIANCARLO DE CARLO

634 First example of participatory architecture in Italy, with workers and local residents from the Matteotti Village in Terni, 1973. Photograph by Studio Giancarlo De Carlo.

PART III
APPENDIX

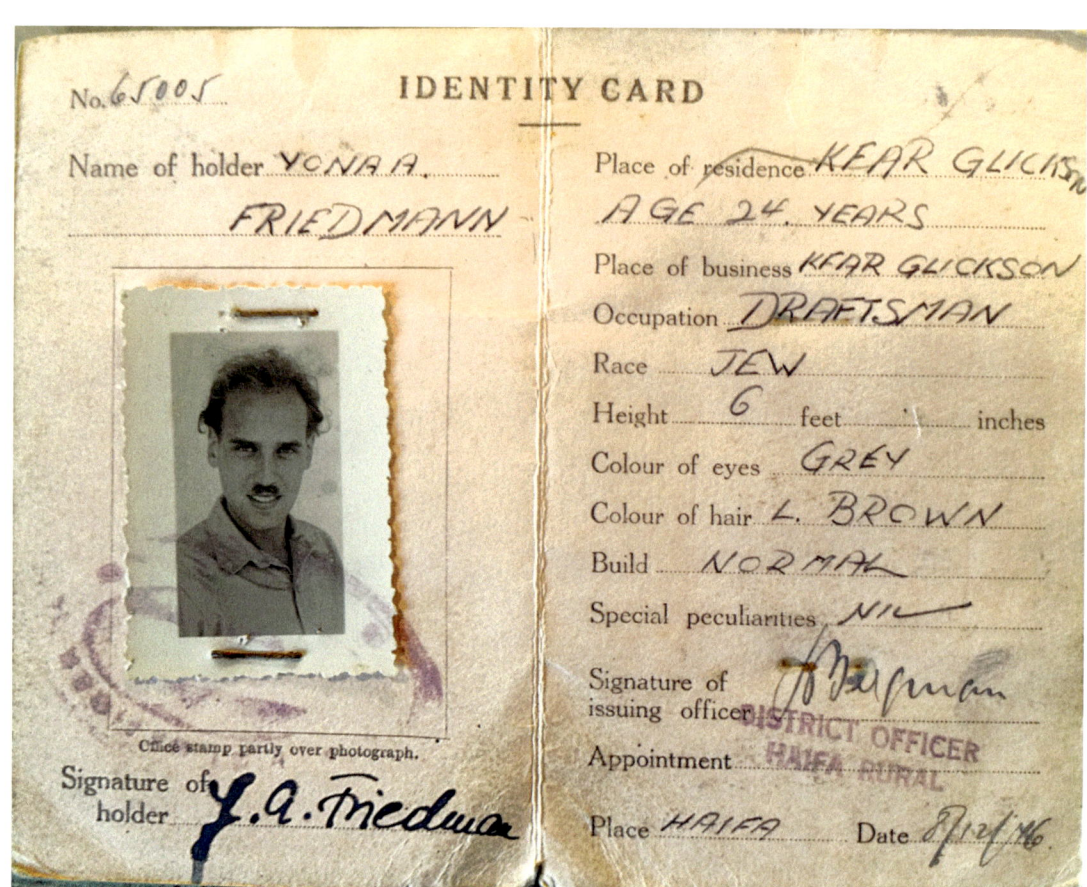

GOVERNMENT OF PALESTINE

635 Yona Friedman: Identity card, Haifa, 1946. Original document with Marianne Polonsky.

A CONVERSATION WITH YONA FRIEDMAN
CONDUCTED BY MANUEL ORAZI, PARIS. 2005
Originally published in *Log* No. 26, fall 2012.

<u>Manuel Orazi:</u> To begin I would like to ask you about your education in Budapest, which was not strictly disciplinary, before and during the Second World War.

<u>Yona Friedman:</u> Well, it's quite complicated. I was interested in many things in high school, and it was possible to listen to public lectures at the university. I was mainly interested in two topics, physics and mythology. I had the chance to listen to the physicist Werner Heisenberg, who impressed me very much, and to Károly Kerényi, a quite significant professor of mythology. Both matters were really important for me, especially at that age. I kept following Kerényi when I studied architecture and later we became quite friendly – we even corresponded when I came to Paris.

<u>MO:</u> Kerényi was living in Ascona, Switzerland, at that time.

<u>YF:</u> Yes, he left Hungary during the war.

<u>MO:</u> In what sense was Kerényi formative for you?

<u>YF:</u> He very much insisted on one point: that mythology is not just a collection of stories but a system. Much later I got more and more into the idea that mythology is essentially a protoscience, because it gives a complete description of the world. This was Kerényi's influence, although he was presenting it as an image of the Greek world. At the same time I realized that official science is somewhat questionable. Heisenberg was talking about Goethe's Farbenlehre [Theory of Colors]: it's not scientific and it doesn't fit with science, but at he same time it fits. For me it was quite important to realize that you can build up a system. I am calling it the image of the world.

<u>MO:</u> In this sense can we say that you learned how to create a personal mythology?

<u>YF:</u> I learned not to look that way [he holds his hands up like blinders]. This is important at the age of 17 or 18, and not the way that universities are generally compartmentalized – it was an opening. That's why you can look at my *Utopies réalisables* or my work on physics in another way, and not care about the specialists. At the same time this helped me to be daring in architecture, to not look at the specialists. Hungary was more or less a fascist country and there were numerous clauses for architects. I couldn't study architecture, but there was a professor who thought that I should study it. So I got a special permission to do architecture like anybody else, but I didn't get a diploma because of the law.

<u>MO:</u> You are talking about the law against the Jews, aren't you?

<u>YF:</u> Yes, and when the law was overturned I immediately got the degree.

MO: *In Hungary?*

YF: In Hungary. And when I went to Israel, to Technion, I entered in the sixth semester because the dean said, Okay, you should manage to pass this semester and everything will be okay. Otherwise I couldn't work as an architect there without the necessary papers. So my situation became normalized.

MO: *Who was the professor that let you study in Budapest?*

YF: Iván Kotsis, who was a very important person at the time.

MO: *In Budapest you also worked for a short period in the studio of quite a famous architect, Lajos Kozma, didn't you?*

YF: Yes, although he was considered bad because he was evidently an enemy of the regime. Kozma was in a way very interesting because he was doing architecture differently from the mainstream. In the technical university you got a mainstream, practically 19th century training. But through Kozma I discovered that the Bauhaus existed! So, about my education in Hungary, I think that I was actually lucky: as I couldn't go down the main road, by necessity I got into a situation in which I was more informed than the main road allowed. I also learned quite a lot during the occupation in Budapest. I learned what it means to survive. We had a small resistance organization – maybe you heard about Wallenberg – that made falsified papers for people in order to escape the usual controls. It saved people.

MO: *Did you collaborate with this group?*

YF: Yes. Because I knew how to draw quite well I made the signatures, which was very important. These papers were not valid, but if one was stopped on the street they worked. In October of 1944 somebody from the Technical University denounced me.

MO: *Do you know who it was?*

YF: No, I don't, but I was taken with two bunches of the forged papers.

MO: *Who exactly took you?*

YF: The fascist party handed me over to the Gestapo. They said I was a political prisoner, which is why I was not liquidated as a Jew. Then, during the time I was in the Gestapo's prison, the Russians arrived in the city. The Gestapo handed me over to the Hungarian police and after that I was released. It was a peculiar situation, but I was practically saved by the Red Army. They arrived very suddenly, even though everybody knew that the Germans couldn't keep the city for long.

MO: *Was the resistance group you joined a Zionist association?*

YF: Yes, it was a Zionist group. I had some friends who took me in and we had a system. It was evident that if you were taken by an institution like the Gestapo you couldn't say that you simply didn't know anything. So, our system was very simple: you could tell them anything you knew because, if the others knew you were arrested, all the addresses would have automatically been changed. It's a guerrilla technique – they could verify that everything I said was true and realize that I could not know more. This was quite important; with these techniques the other people in the group were untouched.

MO: What was the name of your group?

YF: There was no name; or perhaps it had a name I didn't know.

MO: Were there leaders of this group?

YF: Yes, but I knew only some of them. Because of the resistance technique I was talking about, you could not know them.

MO: But you must have known some of their names.

YF: Yes: Szigfrid Roth and a friend of mine, Gesa Samosci. I tell you this because for me it was a kind of preparation. You simply could not do the mainstream, it was too disturbed. I had a very funny coincidence: exactly 20 years after the day I was arrested, I was invited to give a talk at the TU in Berlin, which I began by saying, "I'm very glad to be here, only 20 years ago I was arrested by the Gestapo!" The young people at that time had obviously been Nazis, you know. For me it was satisfying. I mean that everybody who survived had defeated the most powerful army in the world, simply by surviving. Okay, all this doesn't matter to architecture.

MO: I disagree, your background is very important. For example, because you work very much with ideas, your experience with guerrilla techniques was significant and anticipates your later studies on communication. I also think it is important with regard to your idea of system.

YF: Surely in many of my systems I was very influenced by this period.

MO: You once told me that your work is the product of the Second World War. Do you mean that the war was the most important formative experience for any of the disciplines you deal with?

YF: After the Russians came in I knew what survival meant: you need water! You know I wrote a book about survival architecture [L'architecture de survie: une philosophie de la pauvreté]. I was in a big city and there was no water and no food. There were no windows, and you had to eat. The situation was worse than in the shantytowns. This gave me major doubts about the very positivist attitude at that time; I saw what it can produce and that it doesn't work.

MO: Do you mean that immediately after the war you looked at positivism critically?

YF: Yes. The approach that says "everything is good, everything is well organized."

MO: *Then you decided to leave Hungary and go to what was then called Palestine.*

YF: Yes, I didn't want to stay in Hungary. People in the Zionist organization were mostly going to Bucharest because Romania permitted illegal ships to Israel – I mean Palestine. Waiting in Bucharest for practically one year was interesting as well. It was a city with an attitude very different from Budapest. Bucharest was French influenced, whereas Budapest was somewhat German–Austrian influenced. It was important for me, because at that age everything had an impact.

MO: *How were the months spent in Bucharest?*

YF: It was a waiting period. They gave you a small amount of money, monthly, for survival.

MO: *Can we say that you have been a Zionist?*

YF: Well, my grandfather was a Zionist, so it was not a foreign idea. I even spoke some Hebrew. But when I got to Israel it was a very double-edged experience. From one side it was very important, because in Israel I was not a second-rate citizen. I was a citizen like anybody else. At the same time, in certain places the exploitation was very bad. At first I was in a kibbutz, and this was perfect.

MO: *What was its name?*

YF: I left the kibbutz when I was accepted at Technion. Its name is now Kfar Glikson. It is near Pardes Hanna and Benyamina.

MO: *You are talking about 1946, aren't you?*

YF: Yes, 1946 . . . a long time ago!

MO: *How about Technion in Haifa?*

YF: I survived by working as a construction worker two days a week. I spent the other three days at Technion. My knowledge of Hebrew was not enough to start practicing in an office, but I had to work – there was no other solution. Hebrew learned abroad had nothing to do with the Hebrew you found on the spot. Working on a building was important for me. Most architecture students don't know how the work is done on the site. I was an unskilled worker, but I could see how it all worked. Later, when I was teaching at Technion, students were trying to make prefabricated systems. I was always asking them, "Where is the worker putting his hands?" You have to think about a technical proposition not only so that it fits on paper – you have to do it! Another example was the staircase. How are they building staircases? Students were drawing stairs, but what do they mean? All these technical things were quite important for me. I realized that the solution is not simply on paper or in the model.

MO: When did you graduate from Technion?

YF: In 1949.

MO: After the independence of Israel, then?

YF: Yes. Along with the entire school, I lost one year because of the war. We were in the army.

MO: Did you actively take part in the war? Which detachment were you in?

YF: Sure, I was in the engineering corps. I was responsible for making fortifications larger. This meant trenches. This was not Second World War technology, but old techniques. This was an important experience because I learned, again, that you cannot do it on paper! You can only do it on the spot. This was a very decisive thing at that age.

MO: You must have been about 25 years old.

YF: Yes, I was 23 when I arrived in Israel, so I was 24 when I went into the war.

MO: After the war and your graduation, did you start practicing and open a studio in Haifa?

YF: I was teaching as an assistant professor at Technion. At the same time I was a counselor for the fortifications of new settlements on behalf of Ytzhak Rabin.

MO: So you knew Rabin personally.

YF: Yes, I knew him, I knew Eshkol, I knew Golda . . . you know, it was a small country. I was a newcomer before the foundation of the State and the large immigration that followed, but I was thought of as someone who had been there for a long time since I was part of the war, and at Technion . . . I was part of the establishment. They saw that I had a sort of competence in fortification so I continued working there after the war.

MO: Can I ask how the fortifications were made?

YF: They were trenches, built so that people in the street were not sniped. Experience was needed and I suggested things like "this street would be better if you do it that way," for defensive reasons. Everything was at a primitive level; it was not a modern army. The Arabs were also not a modern army.

MO: You also started working as an architect after the war.

YF: Yes, at the time I was making a few private homes for people I knew and who more or less trusted me. Together with several friends we tried to make a little cooperative, but it didn't work too well and we stopped it. I had some ideas for very simple but improved apartment plans. When they made the first Shikun Amami, popular social housing, in Haifa, I got the commission to do it.

MO: *Did you build it?*

YF: Yes. For that period it was a large project, but now something like 150 flats would be considered ridiculous.

MO: *Do you have photographs of it?*

YF: I don't have any of that one, but after that they approved the type and repeated it in Jerusalem and again in another place in Haifa, and from those two I have photos.

MO: *Was there a town planning administration in Israel?*

YF: Yes, of course there was. It continued from the British Mandate.

MO: *Was it well organized? I know that some cases were like Michel Ecochard's work in Africa.*

YF: The people determining it were Alexander Klein and Artur Glikson. I find them very close to the garden city idea. I speak about those years because things changed. Israel changes very fast.

MO: *That's because many immigrants arrived. Early Israel was a completely new society. I know you appreciated that condition. Can you tell me in what sense?*

YF: Yes, I was trying to tell you I had an ambiguous feeling. When I arrived in Israel it was not really a classless society, but as near to a classless society as possible. In the society I knew before the war, it was absolutely unimaginable that you would be studying architecture and working as a construction worker at the same time. It was normal in Israel. You were surviving as you could and it didn't define your class. But this didn't keep up for a long time.

MO: *When and how did this situation change in your opinion?*

YF: Well, by 1953 or '54 this had already changed. During the war it was not really important if I knew you, even if you were an officer – we were speaking to very important people using only their first names. Then it slowly became like any other society, but superficially. I will give you an example: the first building I designed in Haifa was made by the company where I was working as an unskilled worker. Golda Meir came for the opening because it was the first operation in Haifa. The director of the construction company told her that the architect had worked as an unskilled worker, and she responded: "This is democracy!" It's true, it's true. All this disappeared somehow.

MO: *Is that one of the reasons you left Israel?*

YF: I wanted to go my own way in architecture and I saw it was impossible, that's all.

<u>MO</u>: Do you mean at Technion?

<u>YF</u>: It was impossible for many reasons. Now I am accepted by many people, but at that time it was really very difficult. Technion was very old-fashioned in spirit and I had to find somewhere I could go my way. I wanted to go to the CIAM meeting in Dubrovnik, but Alfred Neumann, who was the dean, didn't like the idea. He was not supporting me.

<u>MO</u>: I have the impression that your attitude in architecture was the opposite of Neumann's. For you, form is a secondary problem.

<u>YF</u>: We were very far apart. He was thinking in buildings, in forms, and from the start my interest was in the inhabitants. In 1945, when I was still in Romania, I was trying to imagine a system, what Sabine Lebesque calls the "panel chain." It means that the shape of the walls, prefabricated walls, can be changed by the inhabitants, just like paravent. I was trying to propose this system for the British and for the Russians, but the only ones who were interested were the Yugoslavians. But among the Russians I met the deputy minister of housing. We both spoke French, and we had a long conversation about the metro in Moscow, but I got no reaction, no interest in the project. Now that I am digging it up again there's another thing: at Technion I made a raw house in which the bathroom, the kitchen, and so on were simply furniture. You could move it where you wanted.

<u>MO</u>: Was this a project you did at the university or was it produced?

<u>YF</u>: It was not a project; it had nothing to do with the university. It was a housing proposal. When I asked whether I could do this . . . flatout "no." I understood them. At that same time I was commissioned for a larger object. "Keep it as classical as possible," they said. There were people like Yohanan Ratner who were very positive toward this proposal.

<u>MO</u>: So do you think that supposedly classical people like Ratner were paradoxically more modern than the openly modernist Neumann?

<u>YF</u>: Yes, in a way Ratner was more modern. He was old-fashioned and Neumann was modern on the surface. It is a difference, not a criticism. Subsequently, when I went to Dubrovnik I suddenly realized that I was coming to something new. Israel was isolated. Neumann nicely told me, "It's really not important," but I got a positive reaction from people in Dubrovnik. Jerzy Soltan and Roger Aujame were positive, but most importantly, Bauwelt agreed to publish my proposal.

<u>MO</u>: That was the first of many articles in magazines and publications in different countries.

<u>YF</u>: Yes, and I realized, "Okay, they take me seriously." After the article in Bauwelt, I got a letter from somebody completely unknown in that period, Frei Otto, and

we met in Berlin in 1957, when I went to see the Interbau. I was trying, first in Berlin and then in Holland, to look for young architects who accepted this trend. This is how the group was made in 1958.

MO: You are talking about the Groupe d'études de l'Architecture mobile?

YF: Yes, GEAM. I was staying in Paris because of the Cylindrical Shelters project. Jean Prouvé told me we should make it together. You can imagine that for me this absolutely justified my research. Prouvé was somebody. We couldn't do it after his factory broke down in December, but I completed it with somebody else. So this was very positive. Personal reasons also have a certain weight. I never thought I would move to Paris, but I met my wife here. I was thinking of eventually going to London, but I didn't meet too much sympathy there. Personal sympathies, but not too much understanding.

MO: The first time you were in London, was it at the Architectural Association?

YF: No, I went there later. The AA invited me in 1959 and 1960 to give lectures.

MO: What happened before?

YF: I met with people from Dubrovnik and with Goldfinger. They were very friendly, but afterward, when I went to Paris, I phoned Prouvé in order to show him my projects and he said, "Okay, come and see me." I met Le Corbusier the first time I was visiting Paris, in 1949. I was then freshly graduated and Le Corbusier received us very superficially. In 1957 he agreed to meet me and I talked to him about my ideas. This was quite decisive because he told me two very important things. He said, "It's not my line, I would never do this. But you have to do it." Thereby, he saw its worth. The second thing he said was, "Most of your colleagues will be against you." When somebody like Le Corbusier tells you this, and Prouvé proposes to work together with you, you don't care what other people think anymore. This was decisive for me, so I thought it was the right way – it's possible and not simply fantasy. That was very important for me.

MO: Did you have other opportunities to work with Prouvé after your failed collaboration?

YF: After 1957 Prouvé was employed by a company that fabricated wagons and he was not doing prefabricated housing anymore. I met him once or twice after that, but it was simply a sort of friendly nicety.

MO: Let's talk more about your CIAM experience. Did you only take part in the meeting at Dubrovnik?

YF: Yes, only that one. When Team 10 started [George] Candilis invited me to Bagnols-sur-Cèze, where I had a very bad clash with the Smithsons, very very bad. Alison [Smithson] was absolutely incredible, and Aldo van Eyck also. Candilis was peacekeeping, [Jaap] Bakema too. It was really very vehement and if I had not had the backing of Prouvé, of Le Corbusier, I would have taken it very badly, but it was too late.

My proposals were published; they were already published in Japan as well. It was [Masato] Otaka who asked me in '59 to publish there. It influenced the Metabolists.

MO: Why was the clash with the Smithsons so hard?

YF: *I have absolutely no idea. I met the Smithsons again something like 30 years later and Alison turned her back to me. I really don't know why.*

MO: But what was their specific accusation against you, exactly?

YF: *It was after I presented La Ville-Spatiale. Soltan liked it very very much, Soltan and [Oskar] Hansen. I really had backing . . .*

MO: Maybe it was because of the role of technology.

YF: *I really don't know. The thing was realistic, since in 1959 the engineering part was already worked out.*

MO: Was it a technical critique?

YF: *I think Alison was very angry about the principle of mine that in this system it's not the architect who decides but the inhabitant. It was not a project with a facade and then other things. This meant it would be completed by the inhabitant and changed by the inhabitant. It might be that what Alison didn't like was that my proposal was not architecture, not art; it was not a final object. It was the start of a process, and the buildings could look completely otherwise. The use was not determined. The CIAM people were very much concerned with doing the best plan and making it definite. I was saying, "I don't know what the best plan is, and for each inhabitant the best plan is different." I was looking for a technical possibility to make that realizable.*

MO: To make the start of a process realizable.

YF: *Yes, I was calling it the triggering of the process.*

MO: Can you speak about the role of technology and the relationship you had with engineers?

YF: *In 1953 I met Konrad Wachsmann at Technion. He was making propaganda all over the world about space-frame structures. He was convincing, and when I was looking for Ville-Spatiale's structure I eventually tried to make it hang, but it was the space frame that fit best. Personally I would have preferred hanging, because it could be completely soft. But the space frame was best adapted to the technology at the moment. I thought it should be realizable, not a utopian best; something one really knows how it works.*

MO: *Did you ever try to modify the engineering solutions? Or did you simply accept the existing ones?*

YF: Yes, I did try. In 1959 I started with rings, what I was calling "space chains," because of the disadvantage of the space-frame structure's nodes. The space chain, the circle, has no nodes. The points where elements meet are parallel. There were several engineers who were interested in Serge Kétoff, who recalculated it.

MO: *You used the space chain several times, didn't you? I think that even the chair you are sitting on now was made with this technology.*

YF: Yes. I think you can make even a hypohydra with circles. At the point where the elements touch there is this parallel. It's like this chair. The other point I am insistent upon is that it permits high inexactitude. Because I was a construction worker I know what exactitude in a building is. It's very difficult and never perfect – so let us plan it that way. It's a very simple idea, which I used for my proposal for Tunis in 1960. It was completely understood.

MO: *With the Tunis project, it's impossible for me not to think of Le Corbusier's Plan Obus project for Algiers, since yours is also a kind of bridge. Am I wrong?*

YF: No, you're right. They wanted a sort of Champs-Elysées, so I proposed a main Champs-Elysées over the Medina without destroying it.

MO: *Yes, but my point is that your big bridge is inhabited, just like the Plan Obus.*

YF: In the detailed plans there were courtyards on the ground floor, which would stay completely free. That way they gave us the plan of the Medina with the exact indication of the courtyards. In this kind of Arabic city the courtyards are relatively small so it was very easy to coordinate.

MO: *I'd like to ask you more about your work in Paris during the '60s. You founded GEAM in 1958 and through that you were in contact with many architects, artists, and critics until the foundation of Groupe International d'Architecture Prospective (GIAP) in 1965.*

YF: First of all I'd like to say that GEAM and GIAP are not the same thing. I did not at all agree with GIAP. The difference was that for GEAM, people had to have an idea. GIAP was very banal. I was friends with Michel Ragon and he asked me to join, so it was simply because of friendship. In GEAM there was a program, L'architecture mobile. It was a clear program and all the people who entered made their own interpretation; this was not necessarily La Ville-Spatiale. Later on the Germans wanted to make a new program for GEAM, but this was a compromise.

MO: *So GIAP was a very divided group without a common position. Did you meet Nicolas Schöffer only then? He was Hungarian and wrote some books parallel to yours.*

YF: Well, GIAP wasn't really a group. I met Schöffer earlier, in '59 or '60, and Ragon too.

<u>MO</u>: Later on Schöffer wrote La ville cybernétique. Do you find there were points of contact with your idea of the city?

<u>YF</u>: Yes, because he was intelligent. My idea is not that certain persons have to control the decisions of other people. He could take over my ideas or not, but he had to have something, a solid way of thinking. We were very good friends; we met every two weeks. We had a sort of traditional lunch in a restaurant on Boulevard Pasteur. Our ideas were not fundamentally contradictory. He had the artist's point of view and I had the sociologist's, not the architect's, point of view. They're not contradictory, fairly less contradictory than Constant's view, since Nicolas accepted the idea that the city is not a final solution as well. His title, La ville cybernétique, means that he accepted the same idea of process.

<u>MO</u>: But this idea was shared also by Candilis and Shadrach Woods, especially about town planning as a process.

<u>YF</u>: Yes, surely, but not in 1960. At Bagnols-sur-Cèze they didn't say anything about that. Later, Woods presented an idea he was calling the web. But in 1960 I didn't hear anything about that. I didn't know him really, but I think he was a very valuable person.

<u>MO</u>: Did you have any contact with Candilis?

<u>YF</u>: Once or twice, somewhere, we had a small talk, and I had a relation with Team 10 at Bagnols-sur-Cèze, where I presented La Ville-Spatiale. I knew about the idea of the web, but they were actually realizing it in the Free University, Berlin.

<u>MO</u>: I ask you because I think that the Free University has many points in common with your work.

<u>YF</u>: Yes, there is much similarity to what I was doing, but in a different period.

<u>MO</u>: The Free University project was in 1963.

<u>YF</u>: Yes, four years later! You know La Ville-Spatiale had an impact on several people who were involved in these problems. [Eckhard] Schulze-Fielitz was writing to me in '60 because of my publication, and Moshe Safdie, and Soltan knew it in '58 or '59, in Holland. So at Bagnols I was presenting the proposal in its mature form.

<u>MO</u>: May I ask you something about the diagram? Have you ever used it as an instrument of design?

<u>YF</u>: I realized around '63 that there is something called graph theory – it has a mathematical background. Then, in '64 I was giving guest lectures in the United States and talked about it there.

MO: But what did the diagram represent to you in the '60s? Can you give me a definition?

YF: Areas or volumes have a connection scheme. You can see how they are connected. Graph theory indicates the limits: certain connections are absolutely mathematically impossible. I had this exercise: make four rooms, each connected, completely interconnected, and each with a door to the outside. Students worked on it, but it's not possible. Graph theory is a very valuable thing. I don't remember who made the first demonstration . . . I think it was Euler, so it's old. Strangely enough, I was surprised that architects use all kinds of connection schemes in the design process without knowing where the impossibilities are. Therefore, I was really working out a method. The Flatwriter project was based on it, for example.

MO: This whole study is in your book Toward a Scientific Architecture, isn't it?

YF: Yes. This book was the result of my teaching in the States, so it was really elaborated, with notes, etc. – and I worked it out.

MO: How were you invited to teach in the US? From what I know, you went to many different universities.

YF: Soltan invited me to Harvard, then, at the same time, I was invited to Columbia by Percival Goodman, to Berkeley by . . . what was the name . . . I don't remember anymore. They offered me 10 years. I was going with Denise, and we decided that we didn't like the way of life in the States. I continued to give a guest seminar twice a year because I needed the money.

MO: Where exactly?

YF: At Carnegie, Michigan, and UCLA. At that time it was important for me, since certain tools, computers, were not very accessible except in big American universities. Then I was invited to MIT for a particular project.

MO: Which one?

YF: "Architecture-by-Yourself," this was really complete.

MO: When?

YF: I think it was roughly '70 or '71 . . . . Yes, surely, because it was after the Flatwriter, which I planned for the Osaka exhibition in the late '60s. This experience at MIT made me see that the computer is not the best tool because it's too fast, and not transparent. People have to decide slowly, they need time. Plus, it has to be transparent.

MO: What do you mean by transparent?

YF: When you use a computer you put in a symbol, but you don't know what the machine does. Transparency is knowing the steps. Computers work that way because you have to do many steps.

MO: *Do you mean that we need to see the process clearly? If so, then process comes back as a central theme of your work again.*

YF: *Yes, and that's why at MIT I developed a counter-computer for small operations, but with instant reading. It's easier and this is evident for people, it is tangible.*

MO: *I want to ask you about the only project you were able to realize, apart from the housing in Haifa —the Lycée David in Angers.*

YF: *I realized the whole plan, but I had no control over the object itself.*

MO: *Was this done in the seventies?*

YF: *No, it was in '80, or 1979-80. The Dubonnet project was in 1974-75.*

MO: *The Dubonnet experience was important, as you used the diagram. In this sense, I believe Lycée David is a son of the Dubonnet project.*

YF: *Exactly, exactly. The Dubonnet project was really the laboratory project. When I did Angers I already knew the technical as well as the human technique.*

MO: *Both projects are based on consultation with the users of the buildings.*

YF: *The users have to do the project really.*

MO: *Do they have to define the number of volumes and rooms?*

YF: *And where and what size. Everything depends on them. My responsibility was to control the budget and make it fit the technical structure. There were more constraints with the Angers project because the sizes of the rooms were devised by the Ministry of Education, but not the situation. It had to be that size. What the users accepted was the customer model. In the Dubonnet project everything was free, with the panel chain technique. The directors asked, "If we really realize it, can it be changed two years later, five years later?" I had to guarantee that it could be changed.*

MO: *Were all the internal divisions in the Dubonnet project made using the panel chain?*

YF: *Yes, and also the outside. You could get everything back to an anti-skeleton.*

MO: *What were the main problems with the Lycée in Angers?*

YF: *Very simply, I was imposed on by a local architect who was leading the operation, and that's usual. But the local architect was trying to push me out of the project. He had a relationship with the city hall and he succeeded. The mayor told me they would not do the project. And what happened? The users protested and went to the minister.*

MO: Was your project done directly for the Ministry of Education? Who called you exactly?

YF: The ministry was financing the project. I was called by the rector of the department, the chief of the district. The story is essentially simple: they had an old school and they wanted to do a new school outside of the city center. All the people were protesting.

MO: Why?

YF: Because they didn't want to go outside the center. Then the ministry told them: Okay, you will get a new building, but you will do it. This was accepted and then they called me because of the Dubonnet experience. They knew I was the only person who had the experience to do this. And then I had this problem with the municipality people, you know, the local interests.

MO: But the school was realized.

YF: Yes, it was realized because these people were going to the ministry. The counsellors asked if it cost more, or if it caused any problems. Since it didn't, they said that it should be done as the people want it to be. It's logical.

MO: How did you organize the work? Did you hold meetings with the teachers?

YF: No, no, I was never present at the meetings, in either Dubonnet or Angers. They had to decide without me. The high level of bureaucracy had no right to be present; if the director general is there, people will not speak freely.

MO: What did they produce when they were alone?

YF: Graphs.

MO: Can we call them diagrams?

YF: Yes, and from these graphs bubble diagrams were made that gave the locations without defining the exact shape. In Dubonnet the users did define the exact shape. I had to see if technically it was possible.

MO: So who decided the final shape in Angers?

YF: The final shape and the organization of the building were decided by the people. Only the sizes of the rooms were decided by the ministry's standards.

MO: So in the end your project was focused on the process and the budget. You merely had a coordination role.

YF: Yes, for me the important thing was to show it could be done. You know, I was told – I still am now – that it was impossible, that people cannot conceive a plan. So I had an argument, since in two cases it was done. It is possible.

MO: Can we say that this is your definition of the role of the architect: a coordinator?

YF: I had one part of the role of the architect, a very little part, because I wanted to do a decoration on the exterior walls, and obviously the municipality stopped it. They wanted control. It turned out to be a very grotesque thing. The ministry was doing the project as planned, but then the people asked if the electric switches could be in other places, and the answer was no. They said it was completely idiotic that the ministry leaves them to plan a building of several million francs and doesn't allow them to decide where to put the blackboard. But the same department of the ministry was not responsible for the internal furniture, electricity, so . . . .

MO: Were you satisfied with the result?

YF: I couldn't do anything more. The building was done. What I had to guarantee was fire security, access for the handicapped . . . all the rules were respected. The colleague who was trying to push me out persuaded the mayor, telling him that the corridors were too long. The people who made the plan said that was exactly what they wanted because they didn't want to go from one classroom into another across the corridor – they wanted to have a little walk. It's for relaxation. They also wanted a number of internal courtyards and for the school not to be one school but four small schools that had certain services together. The ministry agreed but said it should be possible to transform it into a classic school later, which happened a number of years after. This really was my work: to see that it could be transformed.

MO: Did the ministry repeat this operation for other schools?

YF: No, this was a particular political moment.

MO: It remains a sole example or experiment then.

YF: Yes, it is the only example. I was so disgusted by my experience with the local architect that I really thought about not continuing with architecture. It was so nasty. Then there was a process and the court rehabilitated me because the fee was retained by the local architect. It was such a nasty thing . . . you know the business side of architecture is so essentially unfair. Anyway, in the end my project was made tangible. For me it is important that people can conceive very complex buildings. So I used it to justify my basis for the best projects: it depends on the people. The architect has to organize the project, but it must be possible to transform it, it must not be frozen. Believe me, in the '60s this was not taken very well. Now it is . . . not completely accepted, but it seems possible.

7 QUESTIONS FOR BERNARD TSCHUMI
CONDUCTED BY GUIA CAMERINO AND MANUEL ORAZI, NEW YORK, 2005

Guia Camerino, Manuel Orazi: When and where did you get first come into contact with the ideas and projects of Yona Friedman? Do you think Friedman had an exceptionally solitary role in postwar French architectural culture?

Bernard Tschumi: I probably saw the projects of Yona Friedman published around 1965 or 1966 when I was a student. I met him in 1967 in Paris. Yes, I believe he was a solitary figure, slightly detached from the rather conventional French scene of the time, yet quite provocative and charismatic.

GC, MO: Yona Friedman says that you are the only contemporary architect who generally mentions the debts you owe to his ideas. Some of these debts are quite evident (unpredictability of society, importance of process in design, unimportance of form), but what is the main point of disagreement with Friedman's proposals – if there is one?

BT: He dealt with ideas first. Forms were just means to express ideas. I liked that.

GC, MO: Who are the international architects that you consider most in tune with him, if there are any in particular? Must we really consider him a utopian dreamer?

BT: He's not a dreamer, but often a poet who says very simple and clear things while everybody else tries to make them very complicated and obscure.

GC, MO: In the Le Fresnoy Art Center project you decided to keep the existing buildings and design on top of them, working on an in-between space. I think you did something similar in the Factory project on an ex-industrial area for a competition in Beijing last year. Is it possible to see those projects as interpretations of Friedman's proposal for La Ville-Spatiale?

BT: Le Fresnoy somehow has different implications as it is mostly concerned with envelopes and in-between spaces, but of course there is a connection between Factory 798 and La Ville-Spatiale. In the process, I discovered that Friedman's La Ville-Spatiale has less density than the existing city it covered. In our Factory 798, the opposite is true: there is much more density in the new elevated part that in the existing ground level neighborhood.

GC, MO: With the project for the Freie Universität Berlin, in 1963, Candilis Josic and Woods transferred into a real architectural context the abstract notion of "web" that Woods had come up with the year before for that competition. Do you think that their attempt to turn a theoretical model into an architectural form was successful?

BT: Yes, the FU Berlin was an extremely powerful concept, and therefore successful as such. Nevertheless, this concept challenges notions of private vs. public, object vs. field, infrastructure vs. superstructure, etc., and these challenges are what has made the project controversial, and led to its being attacked sometimes.

GC, MO: What role did technology have in this passage from theoretical model to project? What is your opinion of this, in view too of your experience in their studio at the end of the sixties (with the "trames directionelles," etc.)?

BT: At the time, it seemed to be capable of adding an increased level of efficiency. We know today that this is not the most important thing, as there are dozens of equally efficient ways to use appropriate technology.

GC, MO: Both Candilis, Josic and Woods and Yona Friedman have looked at the problem of architectural feasibility from the perspective of technology. But with the wire mesh of La Ville-Spatiale Yona Friedman definitely gave up any attempt to convey the form of the project. In our view Candilis, Josic and Woods took a different attitude in the FU Berlin project, though it is apparently equally radical in its renunciation of any formal approach. If "anarchitecture" means architecture that gives up form in order to deal with other problems (unpredictability, communication, ideology), then we believe that Yona Friedman is closer to this definition than Candilis, Josic and Woods.
Do you agree?

BT: Yona Friedman and Candilis, Josic and Woods were addressing two very different problems, one conceptual and "futuristic," the other conceptual and "realistic." Whence the resulting difference is formal, which stems from the problem, and should not be discussed in terms of the result. An alternative way to formulate your question would be to look at these two projects in relation to the current tendency to produce "iconic" designs without reference to programs, social patterns and growth, in contrast to the agenda followed by Friedman and by Candilis, Josic, and Woods.

YONA FRIEDMAN – GENESIS OF A VISION
EXHIBITION AT THE ARCHIZOOM GALLERY – EPFL, 2012

▸ http://archizoom.epfl.ch/Yona-Friedman

. . . I do not feel like a utopian, nor an architect, nor a writer, but rather all these things together as they complete each other and it is impossible to separate them.
Yona Friedman

Genesis of a Vision presents the development of Yona Friedman's creative pursuits, the Hungarian architect, artist, and author of *Utopies Réalisables* (Feasible Utopias). His avant-garde ideas explored new conceptions of the city and ways of life existing on the fringes of "mainstream" architecture, from the second half of the 20th century to nowadays.

The exhibition is based on a programme created for Archizoom by Yona Friedman, entitled *The dilution of architecture*. It covers its emblematic themes: mobile architecture, the spatial city, urban agriculture, network cities, autoplanification, and the role of the architect. At the centre of the space, a video installation showcases an interview with Yona Friedman on the genesis of his vision conducted in the very particular and gainful atmosphere of his Parisian apartment. In parallel, various architecture thinkers analyse his creative and philosophical approach within its historical context, as well as within present-day developments.

Through his prioritisation of the process over the object, Friedman lays out an architectural design that accentuates communication prior to the creation of the shape itself. For users to entirely take in his ideas, he puts forth architectural programmes that are reduced to what is essential, comparable to guidelines for a plural society. These are presented within the exhibition through a documenting of his drawings, writings and concepts that are at each and everyone's scale. More than just a collection of projects, the exhibition attempts to comprehend and communicate the seed of such revolutionary thought, which feels all the more relevant today.

Curator:
Nader Seraj
With the participation of:
Jean-Baptiste Decavèle, Luis Antonio Gutiérrez Cabrero, Juan Miguel Hernández León, Marianne Homiridis, Marc Vincent Kalinka, Emmanuele Lo Giudice
and José Miguel de Prada Poole.

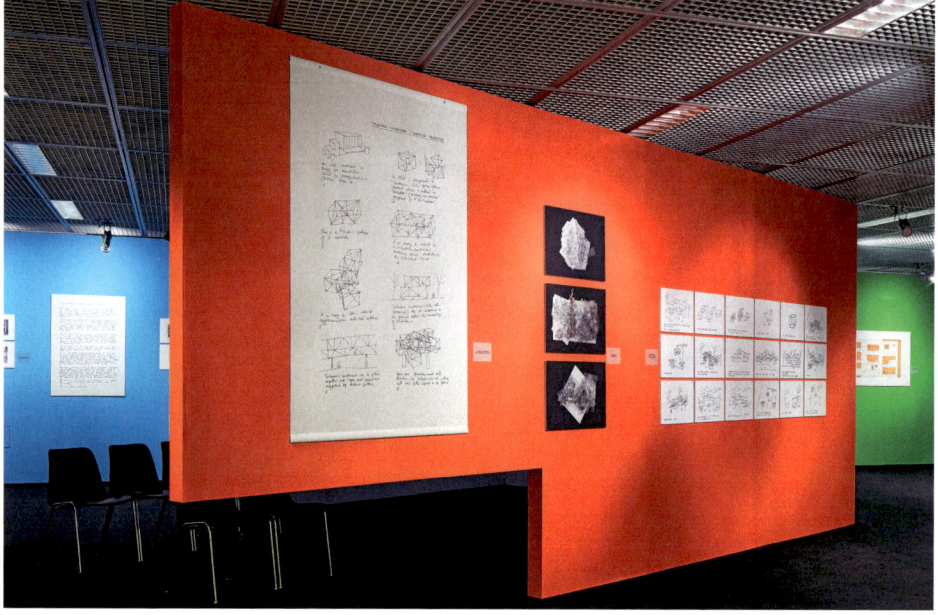

ARCHIZOOM EXHIBITION

Photographs by David Quattrocchi

YONA FRIEDMAN – GENESIS OF A VISION
LECTURE SERIES

MANUEL ORAZI

Yona Friedman – Genesis of a Vision
▸ http://archizoom.epfl.ch/Manuel-Orazi

The French-Hungarian architect Yona Friedman is well known among architects for his theory of a Mobile Architecture. He was also one of the protagonists of the "Age of Megastructure" during the 50's and 60's. After having been classified as an utopian architect he disappeared from the disciplinary publications for almost thirty years. Recently Friedman's work is having a revival of general interest but forgetting much part of it. Since his education as an architect at first in Hungary and then in Palestine–Israel, Friedman progressively has investigated problems beyond architecture. His theoretical production, developed after moving to France in 1957, is extremely heterogeneous and rich. In fact Friedman's publications matter with city planning, sociology, anthropology and physics. For these reasons is now urgent to give a unique critical view of his multiple activity rebuilding some of the contexts in which he operated. For too much Friedman has been judged separately from the environments where he was part of.

EPFL / September 19, 2012 / Duration: 1h30mn / English.

JUAN MIGUEL HENANDEZ LÉON

Yona Friedman and the Ghost of Utopia
▸ http://archizoom.epfl.ch/Hernandez-Leon

The creative and theoretic process of Yona Friedman could be understand as a derivation of the coincident aim within the lucky expression of Reinhold Martin: "Not in order to build utopies but to live with their ghosts." Although his thought and activity has been keeping in step to the glide of the modern system in its transition to the condition of post-modernity.
A parallel thought, that came from the same, and contradictory sources, to the technological utopia of Archigram, global topology of Fuller, or the critic theory of the Situationists. That proposes a constellation of key-words, (such as *process*, *Ville-spatiale*, *Continent City*; but also, *mapping*, *random* or *translator*), shaping a line of thinking that leaves no testimony of our contemporaneousness.

EPFL / October 10, 2012 / Duration: 1h10mn / French.

DOMINIQUE ROUILLARD

Just what is it that makes megastructure so appealing? Hier et aujourd'hui
▸ http://archizoom.epfl.ch/Dominique-Rouillard

The rediscovery of the work of Yona Friedman is in itself a question: Is it the utopian tale that narrates the city projected space developed at the turn of the 50s and 60s, which is fascinating us once again? Or do we assist in the creation of the megastructure, dormant in a state of drawings and collages in the design culture that we see exhibited in art galleries and fashion?

This unexpected media coverage of the work of Friedman could make us forget what, nevertheless remains his essential contribution to the history and theory of architecture. We will present five of his concepts, which will show the pertinence of his subject matter: five theoretic cities, to see and think of the city of today.

EPFL / October 17, 2012 / Duration: 1h53mn / French.

BIBLIOGRAPHY
BOOKS BY YONA FRIEDMAN

L'architecture mobile, vers une cité conçue par ses habitants, Paris/Tournai, Casterman, 1970 / Italian transl., *L'Architettura mobile: verso una città concepita dai suoi abitanti*, Alba, Edizioni Paoline, 1972 / Spanish transl., *La arquitectura móvil. Hacia una ciudad concebida por sus habitantes*, Barcelona, Editorial Poseidón, 1978.

Pour une architecture scientifique, with an introduction by Philippe Sers, Paris, Belfond 1971 / Spanish transl., *Hacia una arquitectura científica*, Madrid, Alianza, 1973 / English transl., *Toward a Scientific Architecture*, Cambridge (MA), MIT Press, 1975 / Italian transl., *Per una architectura scientifica*, ed. by Rosario Giuffré, Rome, Officina, 1975.

19ᵉ siècle bis. Scenario d'un film de science-fiction (politique fiction), 1972, printed by A. Chaize and A. Froment, 2003.

Comment vivre entre les autres sans être esclave et sans être chef, Paris, Pauvert, 1974 / Spanish transl., *Como vivir entre los demás sin ser jefe ni esclavo*, Mexico City, Trillas, 1980.

Meine Fibel, Düsseldorf, Bertelsmann, 1974.

Une utopie réalisée, Paris, Musée d'Art Moderne de la Ville de Paris, 1975.

Utopies réalisables, Paris, Union Generale d'Editions, 1975 / Enlarged ed., Paris, Editions de l'Eclat, 2000 / German transl., *Machbare Utopien. Absage an geläufige Zukunftsmodelle*, with an introduction by Robert Jungk, Frankfurt a. M., S. Fischer, 1977 / Spanish transl., *Utopías realizables*, Barcelona, Gustavo Gili, 1977 / Italian transl., *Utopie realizzabili*, Macerata, Quodlibet, 2003.

Les Pictogrammes de la Genèse, Paris, Belfond, 1975.

Votre ville est à vous. Sachez comment la conserver, Strasbourg, Conseil de l'Europe, 1975 / English transl., *Your Town Belongs to You*. Strasbourg, Council of Europe, 1975.

Comment habiter la terre, Paris, Ministère de la Qualité de la Vie, 1976.

Où commence la ville?, Paris, UNESCO, 1978.

L'architecture de survie, où s'invente aujourd'hui le monde de demain, with an introduction by Michel Ragon, Paris/Tournai, Casterman, 1978 / Revised and enlarged ed., *L'architecture de survie. Une philosophie de la pauvreté*, Paris, Editions de l'Eclat, 2003 / Italian transl., *L'architecture di sopravvivenza. Una filosofia della povertà*, Turin, Bollati Boringhieri, 2009.

Des villes pour vivre, Strasbourg, Conseil de l'Europe, 1980 / Italian transl., *Città per vivere*, Strasbourg, Consiglio d'Europa, 1982.

Alternatives énergétiques ou la civilisation paysanne modernisée. Pour une réelle économie des ressources: comment désindustrialiser l'énergie, St.-Jean-de-Braye, Dangles, 1982 / New ed., *Alternatives énergétiques. Plaidoyer pour une autosuffisance locale*, Escalquens, Dangles, 2011 / Italian transl., *Alternative energetiche. Breviario dell'autosufficienza locale*, Turin, Bollati Boringhieri, 2012.

Roofs 1 and Roofs 2, Paris, UNESCO, 1992.

L'Univers erratique. Et si les lois de la nature ne suivaient aucune loi?, with an introduction by Dominique Lecourt, Paris, Press Universitaires de France, 1994.

Interview avec moi-même (une sorte de bilan), duplicated, Paris, 1997.

Théorie et images, Paris, Editions Institut Français d'Architecture, 2000.

The "trompe l'œil" Universe, Kitakyushu, Center for Contemporary Art (CCA), 2002.

Vous avez un chien. C'est lui qui vous a choisi(e), Paris/Tel Aviv, Editions de l'Eclat, 2004 / Italian transl., *Hai un cane? È lui che ti ha scelto(a),* Macerata, Quodlibet, 2011.

Cities, Kitakyushu, Center for Contemporary Art (CCA), 2005.

Pro Domo, Barcelona, Actar, 2006.

Manuels, vol. 1 – 3, Paris, CNEAI 2008.

Etc. Balkis Island, with DECAVÈLE, Jean-Baptiste, Milan, Silvana Editoriale, 2009.

L'ordre compliqué et autres fragments, Paris, Editions de l'Eclat, 2008 / Italian transl., *L'ordine complicato. Come costruire un'immagine,* with a note by Manuel Orazi, Macerata, Quodlibet, 2011.

Drawings & Models / Dessins & Maquettes 1945 – 2010, Paris, Presses du Réel, 2010.

Architecture without Building, CNEAI, 2012.

ARTICLES BY YONA FRIEDMAN

Ein Architektur-Versuch, in *Bauwelt,* no. 16, 1957, pp. 361–63.

Plan d'une "ville mobile," in *L'Architecture d'aujourd'hui,* No. 80, October–November 1958.

Anpassungsfähig Bauen/Adaptable Architecture/L'architecture adaptable, in Mitteilung [newsletter] no. 6, Berlin, Entwicklungstätte für den Leichtbau – Frei Otto, June 1959, pp. 34–42.

De la mobilité en urbanisme et en architecture, with PECQUET, Jean, in *Techniques et architecture,* July 1959.

Mobile Architecture, with AUJAME, Roger, in *Architectural Design,* no. 9, 1960.

Pour une architecture mobile. Les problèmes modernes de l'architecture et de l'urbanisme, in *Revue technique du bâtiment,* no. 2, 1960, pp. 3–8.

Pour une architecture mobile. Les problèmes modernes de l'architecture et de l'urbanisme (II), in *Revue technique du bâtiment,* no. 3, 1960, pp. 9–19.

Pour une architecture mobile. Les problémes modernes de l'architecture et de l'urbanisme (III), in *Revue technique du bâtiment,* no. 5, 1960, pp. 8–18.

Les constructions "ruches", in *Europäisches Bau-Forum,* no. 6, 1960, pp. 65–67.

Rome Technic, in *Bâtiment,* no. 79, 1960, pp. 17–22.

La Ville-Spatiale, in *L'Architecture d'aujourd'hui,* no. 87, 1960.

Architecture mobile, in *La journée du bâtiment,* December 30, 1960, pp. 7–8.

Urbanisme mobile étude pour un bâtiment évolutif, with HANSEN, Oskar and HANSEN, Zofia, in *L'Architecture d'aujourd'hui,* no. 102, June-July 1962, p. 76.

Vers un urbanisme tridimensionelle, *L'Architecture d'aujourd'hui,* no. 102, June – July 1962.

Mobiler Städtebau, in *Bauwelt,* no. 1, 1963, pp. 14–15.

Les villes-ponts, in *Techniques et architecture,* no. 3, series 23, 1963.

Mobile Architektur, in *Werk,* no. 2, February 1963, pp. 45–57.

Ports on Channel Bridge, in *Architectural Design,* no. 4, April 1963, pp. 158–59.

Towards a Mobile Architecture, in *Architectural Design,* November 1963, pp. 509–10.

Development over a Paris Terminal, in *Architectural Design,* no. 1, 1963.

L'industrialisation et la ville, in *Techniques et architecture,* no. 4, series 25, 1964, pp. 176–77.

La théorie des systèmes compréhensibles et son application à l'urbanisme, in *L'Architecture d'aujourd'hui,* no. 115, 1964, pp. 28–29.

L'urbanisme comme système compréhensible, in *Techniques et architecture,* no. 6, series 25, 1964, pp. 153–55.

Résumé de la théorie des systèmes compréhensibles et son application à l'urbanisme, in *Europäisches Bau-Forum,* no. 5, 1964, p. 815.

Infrastructures for New York and Los Angeles, in *Arts & Architecture,* no. 7, 1964.

Gestaltungsprobleme der Gegenwart, in *Werk,* no. 3, 1964, pp. 112–13.

Problems of Town Planning, in *Arts & Architecture,* no. 6, 1965, pp. 26–27.

L'industrialisation et la ville, in *Techniques et architecture,* no. 4, series 1965.

L'urbanisme spatial, in *Architecture, Formes, Fonctions,* no. 12, 1965.

Les infrastructures possibles, in *Europäisches Bau-Forum,* no. 5, 1965, pp. 1029–30; lecture given at Berkeley and Strasbourg in 1964.

Infrastrutture possibili, in *Casabella,* no. 297, September 1965, pp. 44–47.

Une architecture pour des miliards d'hommes, in Problèmes, no. 96, 1965, pp. 31–48.

Une nouvelle façon de rançonner sur l'urbanisme, ibid., pp. 56–59.

Réflexions sur l'architecture de l'avenir, in Réalisations du bâtiment et des travaux publics, no. 2, 1st quart., 1966.

Kriterien der Stadtplanung, in Werk, no. 2, 1966, pp. 23–24.

Riflessioni sull'architettura dell'avvenire, in Lineastruttura, 1966/1.

Réflexions sur l'Architecture de l'Avenir in Europäisches Bau-Forum, no. 11, 1966, p. 7.

Teoria generale della mobilità, in Casabella, no. 306, June 1966, pp. 10–13.

La théorie des systèmes compréhensibles et son application à l'Urbanisme, in Chiesa e quartiere. Quaderni trimestrali, yr. 10, no. 39, September 1966, pp. 10–11.

Infrastructure Joint, in Architectural Design, no. 11, 1966, p. 7 / Code 6.

A Research Programme for a Scientific Method of Planning, in Architectural Design, August 1967, pp. 379–81.

Recherches de solutions aux problèmes urbains, in Techniques et architecture, no. 2, series 27, 1967.

Cahiers du Centre d'études architecturales, in L'architecture mobile, Liège, 1967.

L'art et la ville, in Leonardo, vol. 1, no. 1, 1967, pp. 51–61.

Recherche d'une méthode, in Techniques et Architecture, no. 2, series 29, 1968, pp. 76–82.

Méthode des mécanismes urbains, in Techniques et Architecture, no. 4, series 29, 1968.

Grands immeubles, in Techniques et Architecture, no. 6, series 29, 1968.

The Revolt of the Young. A Statement Made in April before the Recent Events in France, in Action, no. 3, May 21, 1968 (reprinted in Log, no. 13/14, 2008, pp. 3–35).

Die Wohndichte: Ein falsches Problem? in Bauen + Wohnen, no. 2, 1968, pp. 40–41.

Seminar on Methods for Architects/Planners, in Arch +, no. 2, 1968, p. 48.

Toward a Coherent System of Planning, in Urban Structures, Architects' Year Book 5, ed. by David Lewis, London, Elek Books, 1968, pp. 52–64.

Cahiers du Centre d'études architecturales: Les mécanismes urbains, Liège, 1968.

Une tentative pour l'avenir des villes, in Progrès, no. 12, 1968.

Gegen den Demokratismus der Planung: Wer die Wahl zu treffen hat und wie die Durchführung gestaltet werden soll. Eine "Nicht-Utopie" von Yona Friedman, in Europa baut, December 27, 1968, pp. 13 and 18.

Cahiers du Centre d'études architecturales: La planification urbaine, Liège, 1969.

Vers une démocratisation de la planification, à qui revient le choix et comment le faire, in Techniques et architecture, no. 1, series 30, 1969.

Vers une démocratisation de la planification, in Neuf, no. 19, 1969, pp. 6–8.

Nice Future, with ROTTIER, Guy, in Neuf, no. 19, 1969, p. 20–21.

Vers la démocratisation de l'environnement, in Techniques et architecture, no. 3, series 32, 1970.

Umfrage zur Architektenhausbildung, in Werk, no. 10, 1970, p. 682.

The Flatwriter: Choice by Computer, in Progressive Architecture, no. 3, 1971, pp. 98–101.

The Total City, with TANGE, Kenzo, NEGROPONTE, Nicholas and BUCKMINSTER FULLER, Richard in Japan Architect, no. 178, September 1971.

La ville totale, with Tange, Kenzo, Negroponte, Nicholas and Buckminster Fuller, Richard, in *2000*, 1971, no. 24, pp. 5–7.

L'expression individuelle, son rôle et ses possibilités dans l'architecture de l'avenir, in *Architecture, Formes + Fonction,* vol. 16, 1971, pp. 77–80.

About the Possibility of Social Utopias, in *Proceedings of the Inst. of Electrical and Electronic Engineers,* ed. by A. Concheiro, C. Ruiz and R. Viqueira, Mexico City, Inst. of Engineering, National University of Mexico, 1971.

On Models of Utopias and Social Ecology, in *Leonardo,* vol. 5, 1972, pp. 37–41.

Société & environnement, in *Vers une stratégie de l'environnement,* "Les Cahiers de l'environnement" series, Brussels, Mignot, 1972.

Où va l'architecture? in *Cadre de vie,* Institut de l'Environnement, 1973.

L'organisation des "autres," in *Techniques et architecture,* no. 6, series 34, 1972.

The Critical Group Size, in *Architectural Design,* no. 1, 1973, pp. 44–45.

Planning Proposal for Paris Tested by the Urban Mechanisms Group, in *Architectural Design,* no. 12, 1973, pp. 790–91.

Groups and Networks, in *Associations Internationales,* 1974, pp. 274–85.

Une pauvreté nécessaire, in *Gulliver,* no. 11, summer 1974, pp. 52–65.

Arguments for a Poor World, in *Futures,* August 1974, pp. 334–39.

Euroharbour, in *Architectural Design,* no. 8, 1974, p. 177.

User Design, in *Architectural Design,* no. 11, 1974, pp. 699–700.

Yona Friedmans Fibel, in *Bauwelt,* no. 28, 1974.

The Babel Syndrome. Global Communication Being Impossible, the World Is Headed toward a State of Poverty Compatible with Civilization, in *Ceres,* September–October 1975, pp. 48–52.

Food and Shelter: How to Achieve It? in *Royal Institute of British Architects Journal,* September 1976, editorial, *World Future Studies Federation newsletter,* Rome, November 1977.

Art and the Future, in Alisjahbana, Margret (ed.): *Art and the Future,* contributions to the First International Conference on Art and the Future, Indonesia, July 8–15, 1978, Toya Bungkah (Bali), The International Association for Art and the Future, 1978, pp. 131–34.

About Routine, in editorial, *World Future Studies Federation Newsletter,* Rome, September 1979.

Environment is Everything, in *Intermedia,* vol. 8, no. 3, May 1980, pp. 35–36.

The Quaternary Sector, in *Human Systems Management,* no. 2, 1981, pp. 44–52.

The Visual Arts and the Future, in *Leonardo,* vol. 14, no. 4, 1981, p. 310.

Communication Centre of Scientific Knowledge for Self-Reliance, in *Leonardo,* vol. 19, no. 4, 1986, pp. 333–36.

Lezioni di tecnologie semplici, in *Spazio e società. Rivista internazionale di architettura e Urbanistica,* no. 37, 1987, pp. 42–47.

Uno strumento di crescita – Museum of Simple Technology: a Tool for Development, with Schaur, Eda, in *Spazio e società. Rivista internazionale di architettura e Urbanistica,* no. 40, 1987, pp. 86–93.

Una nota sui disegni, in *L'Arca,* no. 35, 1987, p. 48.

Appropriate Technology for Self-Reliance, in *Open House International,* vol. 13, no. 2, 1988, pp. 10–13.

Un savoir pour survivre, in *Alliage,* no. 3, spring 1990, pp. 47–56.

Space Frames and Span-Over Buildings, in *International Journal of Space Structures,* vol. 6, no. 4, 1991, pp. 257 – 65.

Aid for Development through Knowledge, with Schaur, Eda, in *Trialog,* no. 34, 1992, pp. 35 ff.

Homeless Become Shelved in Radical French Squat, in *The Big Issue,* November 1992, p. 13.

Program of Mobile Urbanism, in Ockman, Joan (ed.): *Architecture Culture 1943 – 1968. A Documentary Anthology,* New York, Rizzoli International, 1993, pp. 274 – 75.

Scientific Theory as One of the Fine Arts, in *Leonardo,* vol. 26, no. 4, 1993, pp. 359 – 63.

Die kontinentale Stadt – eine machbare Utopie, interview conducted by Simonetta Carbonaro, in *BDZ,* no. 10, 1995, pp. 50 – 53.

Structures without Rules and Their Implementation in Architecture, in *International Journal of Space Structures,* vol. 11, nos. 1/2, 1996, pp. 85 – 91.

Strutture in "fogli accartocciati," in *Zodiac,* no. 16, 1996/97, pp. 124 – 25.

Tall Building Aesthetics: a New Style for Skyscrapers, in Viswanath, H.R. (ed.): *Multi-Purpose High-Rise Towers and Tall Buildings,* London/New York, E & FN Spon, 1997, pp. 29 – 37.

Function Follows Form, in Hughes, Jonathan and Sadler, Simon (eds.): *Non-Plan. Essays on Freedom, Participation and Change in Modern Architecture and Urbanism,* Oxford, Architectural Press, 2000, pp. 104 – 15.

Paris 30/12/2000. The Best Possible Universe Where Anything Can Happen, in *032c,* Berlin, no. 4, winter 2002/03, pp. 96 ff.

Interview, in Obrist, Hans-Ulrich: *Interviews,* vol. I, Milan, Charta, 2003, pp. 233 ff.

Everyone's an Architect, Hans Ulrich Obrist and Molly Nesbit in discussion with Yona Friedman, in *Janus,* no. 14, June 2003, pp. 43 – 46.

Point d'ironie, no. 35, October 2004.

Cedric Price: Friend and Ally, in *Domus,* no. 870, May 2004, p. 56.

In the Air, interview conducted by Martin van Schaik (28 October 2001), in van Schaik, Martin and Mácel, Otar (eds.): *Exit Utopia. Architectural Provocations 1956 – 1976,* Munich, Prestel, 2005, pp. 30 – 35.

Interview, in *Domus,* no. 879, March 2005, p. 1.

Ideas at Large, in *Domus,* no. 879, March 2005, pp. 94 – 95.

Austrian Pavilion, in *Domus,* no. 883, July – August 2005, p. 25.

Conversazione su Scattered City, with Gabriele Basilico, Stefano Boeri and Hans Ulrich Obrist, in Basilico, Gabriele: *Scattered City,* Milan, Baldini Castoldi Dalai, 2005, pp. 6 – 10.

La dimensione collettiva dell'architettura, an interview conducted by Manuel Orazi and Francesco Pezzulli, in Brugellis, Pino and Pezzulli, Francesco (eds.): *Spazi comuni. Reinventare la città,* Milan, Bevivino, 2006, pp. 53 – 61.

Continent City, in *Domus,* no. 896, October 2006.

Yona Friedman in Conversation with Hans Ulrich Obrist, in Obrist, Hans Ulrich and Notz, Adrian (eds.): *Merz World, Processing the Complicated Order,* Zurich, Jrp Ringier Kunstverlag, 2007, p. 100 – 18.

Afterword, in Obrist, Hans Ulrich: *Everything You Always Wanted to Know about Curating But Were Afraid to Ask*,* London, Sternberg Press, 2011.

A Conversation with Yona Friedman, with Orazi, Manuel, in *Log,* no. 26, fall 2012, pp. 61 – 75.

BIBLIOGRAPHY ON YONA FRIEDMAN

Kühne, Günther: *Mobiles Planen Mobiles Bauen,* in *Bauwelt,* no. 21, 1958, pp. 491–93.

Temporäre zylinderförmige Wohnungen, in *Luxemburger Bau-Forum. Kultur und Technik,* no. 8, August 1959.

Japan Architect, Aestheticism and Vitalism – CIAM, October 1959, pp. 8–10.

Un art économique: le cinéma d'animation, in *Afrique,* no. 9, 1960, pp. 55–61.

La journée du bâtiment, December 30, 1960, pp. 7–8.

T.S.V.P.: *Le cinéma d'animation français en 1961,* in *Telerama,* July 9, 1961, pp. 4–5.

Japan. New Plan for Tokyo, in *Architectural Design,* no. 4, 1961.

Bauen für den Frieden, in *Bauwelt,* no. 41/42, 1961, p. 1158.

Kannengiesser, Jens: *Paris Spatial,* in *Bauen + Wohnen,* no. 11, 1962, pp. 36–43.

Die Stadt als Basis des Gesellschaftslebens, in *Journal,* Luxembourg, August 10, 1962.

Forum européen d'architecture, in *La Meuse,* Liège, January 1962.

Forum européen d'architecture, in *Républicain Louvain,* January 22, 1962.

Image et son, no. 150, 1962, p. 28.

Rouch, Jane: *Le festival des peuples,* in *Jeune Afrique,* December 24–30, 1962.

Yona Friedman: urbanisme mobile, in *L'Architecture d'aujourd'hui,* no. 102, June–July 1962, p. 76.

Joachim: *Ohne Bart vor jungen Bärten,* in *Bauwelt,* no. 26, 1962, p. 730.

No title, in *Werk,* no. 2, 1963.

Ragon, Michel: *Construisons des villes sur la mer,* in *La Nation,* no. 9, 1963, p. 269.

Paris Spatial, in *Bauen + Wohnen,* no. 5, 1963.

No title, in *Der Spiegel,* no. 10, 1963, p. 89.

Stachelhaus, Heiner: *Raumstadt über dem Revier. Pariser Stadtplaner Friedman entwickelt revolutionäres Schema,* in *Unterhaltung,* June 21, 1963.

Kühne, Günther: *Die Brückenstadt über dem Ärmelkanal,* in *Bauwelt,* no. 14/15, 1963, p. 386.

Forum, in *Le carré bleu,* no. 1, 1963.

Rowntree, Diana: *A Community to Span the Channel. Bridge that Would Pay,* in *The Guardian,* April 3, 1963, p. 3.

Banham, Reyner: *Friedman's Europe,* in *Architectural Review,* no. 795, May 1963, p. 307.

Ragon, Michel: *La arquitectura movil,* in *El Imparcial,* May 18, 1964.

No title, in *Civis,* no. 11, 1964, pp. 19–20.

van der Mühll, H.R.: *L'architecture mobile de Yona Friedman,* in *Architecture, Formes, Fonctions,* no. 11, 1964.

Conrads, Ulrich (ed.): *Programme und Manifeste zur Architektur des 20. Jahrhunderts,* Berlin, Ullstein, 1964 / English transl., *Programs and Manifestoes on 20th-Century Architecture,* Cambridge (MA), MIT Press, 1970.

Ragon, Michel: *L'urbanisme et la cité,* Paris, Hachette, 1964.

Construire la ville de l'avenir, in *Suède d'aujourd'hui,* no. 7, 1965, pp. 46–48 and 71.

Balladur, Jean et al.: *Les visionnaires de l'architecture. Textes de Balladur, Friedman, Jonas, Maymont, Ragon, Schöffer,* Paris, Laffont, 1965.

Ragon, Michel: *Les visionnaires de l'architecture,* in xxe siècle, no. 25, 1965.

Les visionnaires du bon sens, in *L'Express*, July 12 – 18, 1965, p. 38.

No title, in *Rheinischer Merkur*, January 22, 1965.

L.B.: **Wozu Utopien?** in *Werk*, no. 6, 1965, p. 121.

KULTERMANN, Udo: **Elementare Architektur. Visionen des Bauens mit Erde, Wasser, Feuer und Luft,** in *Europäisches Bau-Forum*, no. 1, 1965, p. 946.

TAFURI, Manfredo: **La nuova dimensione urbana e la funzione dell'utopia,** in *L'architettura. Cronache e storia*, year XI, no. 124, February 1966, pp. 680 – 83.

No title, *Studio International*, no. 4, 1966, p. 146.

RAGON, Michel: **Les cités de l'avenir,** Paris, Encyclopédie Planète, 1966.

ANDRIELLO, Domenico: **Il pensiero utopistico e la città dell'uomo,** Naples, Minerva, 1966.

BODNAR, Ron F.: **Architect Friedman Ups Ford Plans. Europe on Beam in Sky,** in *Michigan Daily*, January 15, 1967, p. 2.

GEIGER, Martin: **Ein Beispiel für die Beschreibung städtischer Mechanismen,** in *Werk*, no. 6, 1967, pp. 366 – 68.

Die Raumstadt, in *Baumeister*, no. 6, 1967, p. 38.

COLQUHOUN, Alan: **Typology and Design Method,** in *Arena*, vol. 83, no. 913, June 1967, pp. 11 – 14, now in id., *Essays in Architectural Criticism: Modern Architecture and Historical Change*, Cambridge (MA), MIT Press, 1981, pp. 43 – 50.

COOK, Peter: **Architecture: Action and Plan,** London, Studio View, 1967.

Die individuelle Freiheit ist eingeplant. Architekt Yona Friedman erläuterte seine Grundlagenforschung, in *Tages Anzeiger*, April 9, 1968.

HOLZ, Hans Heinz: **Mathematisierte Stadtplanung. Yona Friedman im Zürcher Centre Le Corbusier,** in *National Zeitung*, no. 169, April 10, 1968, p. 15.

Bauen als Wissenschaft. Yona Friedman im "Centre Le Corbusier," in *Neue Zürcher Nachrichten*, April 11, 1968, p. 33.

Progressive Architecture, July 1968, p. 101.

Yona Friedman expose à Loches ses théories sur l'architecture et l'urbanisme de demain, in *La Nouvelle République*, August 9, 1968.

Rf. L.: **La ville de l'an 2000.** "Nous la construisons mal, parce que c'est finalement l'argent qui transforme nos cités" déclare Claudius Petit, in *Le Figaro*, December 30, 1968.

La ville utopique, Eurêka. Une émission de Michel Treguer, in *Téléfilms*, September 23, 1969, p. 59 [a broadcast with Ungers, Archigram, Soleri, Friedman and Virilio].

Unsigned article, in *L'architettura. Cronache e storia*, year XV, no. 167, September 1969, pp. 310 – 11.

Architekt präsentiert Speisekarte, in *Tagesgeschehen. Kleine Zeitung*, June 21, 1969, p. 20.

GIORDANI, Pier Luigi: **Il futuro dell'utopia,** Bologna, Calderini, 1969.

RUDOFSKY, Bernard: **Streets for People. A Primer for Americans,** New York, Doubleday, 1969.

Architekt Friedman erhielt Lehrauftrag an der SHfbK, in *Braunschweiger Presse*, February 12, 1970, p. 48.

COGNIAT, Raymond: **La part de l'imagination,** in *Le Figaro*, July 2, 1970, p. 16.

Objective Methods, in *Werk*, no. 8, 1970, pp. 537 – 38.

RIANI, Paolo: **La casa di Yona Friedman,** in *Interni*, September 1970.

COOK, Peter: **Experimental Architecture,** London, Studio View, 1970.

LEFEBVRE, Henri: *La révolution urbaine,* Paris, Gallimard, 1970 / English transl., *The Urban Revolution*, Minneapolis (MN), University of Minnesota Press, 2003.

SIMONCINI, Giorgio: *Il futuro e la città. Urbanistica e problemi di previsione urbana,* Bologna, Il Mulino, 1970.

ZEVI, Bruno: *Storia dell'architecture moderna,* Turin, Einaudi, 1950; 5th ed. 1970.

ZEVI, Bruno: *Spazi dell'architecture moderna,* Turin, Einaudi, 1970.

DACRE, Paul: *Pennine City – You Could Live Here in 20 Years' Time,* in *Daily Express*, March 12, 1971.

NORBERG-SCHULZ, Christian: *Existence, Space and Architecture,* New York, Praeger, 1971.

SERS, Philippe, *Entretiens avec Nicolas Schöffer,* Paris, Belfond, 1971.

Berliner Kunstpreis 1972, in *Bauwelt*, no. 14, 1972.

RAGON, Michel: *Histoire mondiale de l'architecture et de l'urbanisme moderne,* Paris/Tournai, Casterman, 1972 / Italian transl., *Storia dell'architettura e dell'urbanistica moderne,* with an introduction by Alfredo Lambertucci, vol. III, Rome, Editori Riuniti, 1974.

SCHUMPP, Mechthild: *Stadtbau-Utopien und Gesellschaft. Der Bedeutungswandel utopischer Stadtmodelle unter sozialem Aspekt,* Gütersloh, Bertelsmann, 1972.

Expert's Views on City Expansion, in *The Sunday Standard*, March 4, 1973, p. 3.

Yona Teaches the Kids, in *Architectural Design*, no. 7, 1973, p. 420.

No title, in *Architectural Design*, no. 12, 1973, p. 767.

DORFLES, Gillo: *Dal significato alle scelte,* Turin, Einaudi, 1973.

PORTOGHESI, Paolo: *Urbanistica e utopia,* in *Civiltà delle Macchine*, May – August 1973.

GRANET, Danièle: *Les deux manuels de Yona Friedman. Un architecte sociologue propose une méthode pour changer la société, et d'abord l'éducation des enfants,* in *L'Express*, February 4 – 10, 1974, pp. 46 – 47.

Urban Carpet, in *Architectural Design*, no. 10, 1974, p. 669.

DE FUSCO, Renato: *Storia dell'architecture contemporanea,* Rome/Bari, Laterza, 1974.

NAVONE, Paola and ORLANDONI, Bruno: *Architettura "radicale",* in *Documenti di Casabella*, Segrate, Milani, 1974.

RAGON, Michel: *Yona Friedman: de l'habitat évolutif à l'autoplanification,* in *Urbanisme*, vol. 43, no. 143, 1974, pp. 75 – 77.

GROBBEN, Renate: *Do-it Yourself? Yona Friedmans "Fibel" für Stadtbewohner,* in *Panorama*, no. 2, February 15, 1975, p. 57.

DORFLES, Gillo: *L'utopia della fabbrica autoprogettata,* in *Il Corriere della Sera*, May 29, 1975.

NEGROPONTE, Nicholas: *Soft Architecture Machines,* Cambridge (MA)/London, MIT Press, 1975.

HILL, Anthony: *Yona Friedman, an Appreciation,* in *The Royal Institute of British Architects Journal*, March 1976, p. 105.

NEGROPONTE, Nicholas and WEINZAPFEL, Guy: *Architecture-by-yourself: an Experiment with Computer Graphics for House Design,* in *Computer Graphics*, vol. 10, no. 2, summer 1976, pp. 74 – 78.

STEADMAN, Philip: *Science of Architecture?,* in *Architectural Review*, August 1976, pp. 101 – 2 [review of *Toward a Scientific Architecture*].

RABENECK, Andrew: *Non-Paternalist Systems,* in *Architectural Design*, no. 12, 1976, p. 712 [review of *Toward a Scientific Architecture*].

BANHAM, Reyner: *Megastructure. Urban Future of the Recent Past,* London, Thames & Hudson, 1976.

TAFURI, Manfredo and DAL CO, Francesco: *Architettura contemporanea,* Milan, Electa, 1976, rpt. 1988.

Mayr, Max: *Die moderne Stadt – das sehr zerbrechliche Wesen,* in *Tagesgeschehen. Kleine Zeitung,* October 23, 1977, p. 11.

Emanuel, Muriel: *Yona Friedman,* in Richards, J.M. (ed.): *Who is Who? Architecture from 1400 to the present day,* London, Weidenfeld and Nicolson, 1977, p. 264.

Bauwelt, no. 33, 1978, p. 119.

Frampton, Kenneth: *Modern Architecture: a Critical History,* London, Thames & Hudson, 1980.

Guratzsch, Dankwart: *Eine große Stadt ist doch kein Autoreifen,* in *Die Welt,* February 10, 1981.

Curtis, William Jr.: *Modern Architecture since 1900,* London, Phaidon, 1982; enlarged ed., 1996.

Elia, Gian Franco: *L'arcipelago urbano. Sociologia della pianificazione territoriale,* Milan, Franco Angeli, 1983.

No title, in *Omni,* no. 7, 1984, p. 43.

Alimentaçao è mais importante que moradia, in *Folha de S. Paulo,* August 30, 1985, p. 23.

Congreso sobre ciudades del futuro, a realizarse en San Pablo, in *Tiempo Argentino,* July 17, 1985, p. 16.

La ciudad como diseño total: Peter Cook y Yona Friedman en Buenos Aires, in *Tiempo Argentino,* August 21, 1985, p. 16.

Viratelle, Gérard: *Learning Skills for Survival,* in *Development Forum,* September 1986, pp. 8–9.

Bild der Wissenschaft, no. 9, 1986, p. 49.

Inexpensive Building Techniques for the Poor, in *The Hindu,* March 27, 1987.

Kahn, Badiuddin: *Communication for Self-Reliance,* in *Science Age,* May 1987, p. 54.

Noblet, Dorothée: *Yona Friedman: La santé et l'agriculture en bd,* in *Nations Solidaires,* March 1987, pp. 11–12.

Renaudie, Serge: *Yona Friedman: l'architecture degré zéro,* in *M,* December–January 1987/88, p. 63.

Stevens, Albert: *Tecnologie semplici a Madras,* *L'Arca,* no. 35, 1988, p. 44.

Dorfles, Gillo: *L'architettura moderna,* Milan Garzanti, 1989 (3rd ed.).

Picon, Antoine and Picon-Lefebvre, Virginie: *Le megastrutture e i ponti abitati negli anni Cinquanta-Settanta,* Rassegna, no. 48, December 1991, p. 54.

Der große Preis von Osaka, in *DBZ,* November 1991, p. 1568.

Bonomo, Fabrizio: *E per tetto la semplicità,* in *Costruire. Produzione, economia, cultura,* no. 108, 1992, pp. 142–43.

Geipel, Kaye: *Yona Friedman und die weltweite Stadtentwicklung,* in *DB,* no. 8, 1993, pp. 41–45.

Ockman, Joan (ed.): *Architecture Culture 1943–1968. A Documentary Anthology,* New York, Rizzoli International, 1993.

Koolhaas, Rem: *Bigness or the Problem of Large,* in id. and Mau, Bruce: *S,M,L,XL,* ed. by Jennifer Siegler, New York, The Monacelli Press, 1995, pp. 495–516.

Guiheux, Alain (ed.): *Collection d'architecture du Centre Georges Pompidou,* Paris: Editions du Centre Georges Pompidou, 1998.

Sadler, Simon: *The Situationist City,* Cambridge (MA), MIT Press, 1998.

Violeau, Jean-Louis: *Situations construites,* Paris, Sens & Tonka, 1998; enlarged ed., 2006.

Wigley, Mark: *Constant's New Babylon. The Hyper-Architecture of Desire,* Rotterdam, 010 Publishers, 1998.

Lebesque, Sabine and Fentener van Vlissingen, Helene (eds.): *Yona Friedman: Structures Serving the Unpredictable,* with a note by Jean-Louis Cohen, Rotterdam, NAi Publishers, 1999.

ABRAM, Joseph: *L'architecture moderne en France. Du chaos à la croissance 1940–1966,* Paris, Picard, 1999, vol. 2.

LOYER, François *Histoire de l'architecture française, vol. 2. De la Révolution à nos jours,* Paris, Mengès, 1999.

DE ZEGER, Catherine and WIGLEY, Mark (eds.): *The Activist Drawing. Retracing Situationist Architectures from Constant's New Babylon to Beyond,* Cambridge (MA)/London, MIT Press, 2001.

LUCAN, Jacques: *Architecture en France (1940–2000). Histoire et théories,* Paris, Le Moniteur, 2001.

FRAMPTON, Kenneth: *Labour, Work and Architecture. Selected Essays on Architecture and Town Planning,* London, Phaidon, 2002.

AURELI, Pier Vittorio: *Oltre il fascino discreto dell'utopia,* in Arch'it, no. 8, October 2003, www.architettura.it [review of Utopies réalisables].

PURINI, Franco: *L'utopista didascalico della misura urbana,* in Alias, supplement to Il Manifesto, November 22, 2003, p. 23 [review of Utopies réalisables].

SANTUCCIO, Salvatore: *L'utopia nell'architettura del '900,* Florence, Alinea, 2003.

COHEN, Jean-Louis: *Promesses et impasses du populisme,* in Cahiers de la recherche architecturale et urbaine, January 2004, pp. 167–84.

CAMURRI, Edoardo: *L'uomo insegue l'utopia, il cane ci si siede sopra,* in Il Riformista, March 16, 2004, p. 4 [review of Utopies réalisables].

MICHELI, Silvia: *Ma l'utopia è realizzabile,* in Il Giornale dell'Architettura, no. 16, March 2004, p. 34 [review of Utopies réalisables].

LEGRENZI, Susanna: *Il profeta Yona,* in Io Donna, supplement to Il Corriere della sera, June 19, 2004, p. 57.

BANDINELLI, Angiolo: *La polis senza politica, l'utopia chic di Friedman,* in Il Foglio, June 25, 2004, p. III [review of Utopies réalisables].

GAGLIANÒ, Pietro: *Utopies réalisables,* in Exibart on Paper, August/September 2004, p. 46.

MAAK, Niklas: *Architecture: Yona Friedman,* in 032c, no. 7 ("At War with the Obvious"), summer 2004, p. 113.

ROUILLARD, Dominique: *Superarchitecture. Le futur de l'architecture 1950–1970,* Paris, Editions de la Villette, 2004.

WILLEMIN, Véronique: *Maisons mobiles,* Paris, Editions Alternatives, 2004.

DE MUYNCK, Bert: *Various Prospects on the Principle of Over Population,* in Graz Architektur Magazin, no. 2, 2005, pp. 79–99.

VIDLER, Anthony: *Diagrams of Utopia,* in Lotus international, no. 123, 2005, pp. 28–41.

VAN SCHAIK, Martin and MÁCEL, Otar (eds.): *Exit Utopia. Architectural Provocations 1956–1976,* Munich, Prestel, 2005.

JAMESON, Frederic: *Archaeologies of the Future: The Desire Called Utopia and Other Science Fictions,* London, Verso, 2005.

SADLER, Simon: *Archigram. Architecture without Architecture,* Cambridge (MA)/London, MIT Press, 2005.

AURELI, Pier Vittorio and ORAZI, Manuel: *The Solitude of the Project,* in Log, no. 7, spring 2006, pp. 21–32.

LIPPOLIS, Leonardo: *La nuova Babilonia. Il progetto architettonico di una civiltà situazionista,* Milan, Costa & Nolan, 2007.

BUSBEA, Larry: *Topologies: The Urban Utopia in France, 1960–1970,* Cambridge (MA)/London, MIT Press, 2007.

ORAZI, Manuel: *Repêchages involontaires,* in AMC, no. 179, May 2008, p. 74.

id., *Utopia's Revival,* in Log, nos. 13 – 14, fall 2008, pp. 37 – 40.

CERIZZA, Luca, DANERI, Anna et al.: *Yona Friedman,* Milan/New York, Fondazione Antonio Ratti-Charta, 2008.

VAN DER LEY, Sabrina and RICHTER, Markus (eds.): *Megastructure Reloaded. Visionary Architecture and Urban Design of the Sixties Reflected by Contemporary Artists,* Ostfildern, Hatje Cantz, 2008.

LUCAN, Jacques: *Composition, non-composition: Architecture et théories, XIXe – XXe siècles,* Lausanne, Presses Polytechniques et Universitaires Romandes, 2009.

NEWSOME, W. Brian: *French Urban Planning, 1940 – 1968: The Construction and Deconstruction of an Authoritarian System,* New York, Peter Lang Publishers, 2009.

DE WIT, Wim: *The Papers of Yona Friedman,* in Getty Research Journal, no. 1, 2009, p. 191 – 96.

ORAZI, Manuel: *Gehry + Friedman: dialoghi di utopie,* in Abitare, no. 504, July 2010, p. 17 – 21.

RODRIGUEZ, María Inés (ed.): *Yona Friedman. Architecture with the People, by the People, for the People,* Barcelona, Actar Birkhäuser, 2011.

COHEN, Jean-Louis: *The Future of Architecture since 1889,* London, Phaidon, 2012.

ORAZI, Manuel: *Escatologia della città. Genesi e sviluppo della Ville-Spatiale di Yona Friedman,* in DE MICHELIS, Marco (ed.): *La città nuova. Oltre Sant'Elia. Cento anni di visioni urbane 1913 – 2013,* Milan, Silvana, 2013, pp. 105 – 13.

ORAZI, Manuel: *Budapest, Haifa, Dubrovnik: Yona Friedman e le origini della megastruttura,* in Territorio, no. 67, 2013, pp. 85 – 91.

SCHIBECI, Stefania: *Yona Friedman,* in TRIONE, Vincenzo (ed.): *Il cinema degli architetti,* Milan, Johan & Levi, 2014, pp. 106 – 11.

ACKNOWLEDGMENTS

This work was born from my PhD dissertation held in Venice in 2007. My severe but ironic tutor was Marco De Michelis. If it is true that every work is a collective work, then it is necessary for me to thank a number of people who have made a substantial contribution, through their criticism in particular, to this essay: Federica Ciavattini, Pier Vittorio Aureli, Guia Camerino, Gino Giometti, Maddalena Scimemi, Nader Seraj and Valter Tronchin†.

I am also grateful for the help I have received, in many forms, from Cristina Barbiani, Stefano Boeri, Pino Brugellis, Marco Bruni, Donatella Calabi, Jean-Louis Cohen, Pippo Ciorra, Giovanni Damiani, Cynthia Davidson, Wim de Wit, Jean-François Drevon, Peter Eisenman, Lodovico Folin Calabi, Shulim Vogelmann, Stefano Graziani, Benjamin Malkin, Sara Marini, Gabriele Mastrigli, Daniele Pisani, Marco Pogacnik, Marianne Polonsky, Giorgio Pressburger, Marco Rispoli, Sharon Rotbard, Nitza Szmuk-Metzger, Cristiano Toraldo di Francia, Bernard Tschumi, Michel Valensi, Stefano Verdicchio and Cyril Veillon.

Finally, without the kindness and accessibility of Yona Friedman – who on several occasions has made available his personal archives and his time with extreme generosity – this thesis would have been far poorer.

Manuel Orazi

We are very grateful to Yona Friedman and Manuel Orazi for placing their trust in us to publish their work.
Our warm thanks go to Marianne Homiridis and Jean-Baptiste Decavèle for giving us access to their active archives thereby ensuring the considerable enrichment of this book.
We would also like to acknowledge the following people for their efforts, support and advice throughout the editorial process:
José Abásolo, Fernando Botton, Tareq Daoud, David de Buck, Elise Gaud de Buck, Glenn Deulofeu, Ramón Durántez, Nicolas Dürr, Matias Echanove, Gilles Gabriel, Stefano Graziani, Paul Goodall, Emmanuele Lo Giudice, Jean-Robert Gros, Hernan Guerrero, Eduardo Gurian, Satchmo Jesop, Marc Kalinka, Thomas Kramer, Pascale Luck, Josephine Macintosh, Luca Ortelli, Thomas Paine, Andrea Patti, Giorgio Pesce, Glenn Phillips, Picto – espace d'art polyvalent, Marianne Polonsky, Cédric Roquier, Quentin Rosset, Seraj family, Christine Vaudois, Leonardo Vimos and Brice de Warlincourt.

The editors

PICTURE CREDITS

COPYRIGHT YONA FRIEDMAN

COURTESY OF MARIANNE HOMIRIDIS:
p. 48 (no. 002), pp. 52–55 (nos. 006–9), p. 60 (nos. 015–17), pp. 63–65 (nos. 027–28, 030–35, 037), pp. 68–69 (nos. 039–44), pp. 71–77 (nos. 046–70), p. 81 (nos. 074–77), p. 86 (no. 083), pp. 98–103 (nos. 114–28), pp. 108–13 (nos. 138–45), p. 116 (nos. 149–50), pp. 118–19 (no. 152), pp. 120–23 (nos. 154–60), pp. 125–27 (nos. 162–73), pp. 128–32 (nos. 175–81), p. 134 (nos. 183–84), pp. 138–10 (nos. 189–95), p. 142 (no. 203), pp. 146–11 (nos. 213–27), p. 178 (no. 251), pp. 180–81 (nos. 253–54), pp. 184–87 (nos. 257–66), p. 192 (nos. 277–79), p. 194 (nos. 281–82), pp. 196–10 (nos. 284–300), p. 202 (nos. 302–4), p. 206 (nos. 311–12), p. 208 (nos. 314–17), p. 212 (nos. 321–22), pp. 214–15 (nos. 324–6), p. 243 (no. 390), pp. 256–57 (nos. 398–400), pp. 397–98 (nos. 492–94), p. 425 (no. 528), pp. 435–36 (nos. 540–42), p. 448 (nos. 548–49), p. 451 (nos. 556–62), p. 481 (no. 578), p. 483 (nos. 581–84), p. 493 (nos. 586–89), p. 497 (no. 595), p. 531 (no. 612), p. 532 (no. 614–22), p. 533 (no. 624–25).

COURTESY OF MANUEL ORAZI:
p. 51 (no. 005), p. 80 (no. 073), p. 87–11 (nos. 084–101), p. 128 (no. 174), p. 141 (no. 196–201), pp. 144–45 (no. 212), p. 153 (no. 229), p. 216 (nos. 327–30), pp. 342–43 (nos. 441–42), pp. 382–83 (nos. 489–90), p. 397 (no. 491), p. 398 (no. 495), pp. 399–11 (nos. 498–500), p. 434 (no. 538), p. 467 (no. 564), p. 471 (no. 572), pp. 481–82 (nos. 579–80), p. 492 (no. 585), p. 494 (no. 590), p. 525 (no. 608), p. 533 (no. 623).

COURTESY OF JEAN-BAPTISTE DECAVÈLE:
pp. 92–93 (nos. 102–6), p. 143 (nos. 204–11), p. 156 (nos. 230–31), pp. 158–63 (nos. 233–44), p. 204 (nos. 306–9), pp. 218–22 (nos. 332–51), pp. 224–11 (nos. 353–73), pp. 238–42 (nos. 374–89), pp. 244–45 (nos. 391–6); *Strip Cartoons* (pp. 30–33, pp. 36–40, pp. 164–68, pp. 248–52, pp. 260–65).

ARCHIV FÜR ARCHITEKTUR UND INGENIEURBAUKUNST NRW / COURTESY OF MANUEL ORAZI:
p. 425 (no. 529), p. 448 (no. 550).

CENTRE POMPIDOU / © ADAGP (dist. RMN), GEORGES MEGUERDITCHIAN:
p. 57 (no. 011), p. 63 (no. 029), pp. 78–79 (no. 071);

CENTRE POMPIDOU / © PHILLIPE MIGEAT:
p. 80 (no. 072), pp. 406–7 (nos. 507–9), p. 437 (no. 543):

CENTRE POMPIDOU / © BERTRAND PRÉVOST:
p. 411 (nos. 513–16), p. 449 (no. 551–52), p. 471 (nos. 571, 573).

CNAP, MINISTÈRE DE LA CULTURE ET DE LA COMMUNICATION / COURTESY OF MARIANNE HOMIRIDIS:
p. 106–7 (nos. 135–37).

FRAC CENTRE, FRANCE / @ FRANÇOIS LAUGINIE:
p. 61 (nos. 018–025), p. 65 (no. 036);

FRAC CENTRE, FRANCE /© PHILIPPE MAGNON:
p. 398 (no. 496–97).

GETTY RESEARCH INSTITUTE (2008.M.51) / COURTESY OF MANUEL ORAZI:
p. 24 (no. 001), p. 50 (no. 004), pp. 58–59 (nos. 012–14), p. 62 (no. 026), pp. 66–67 (no. 038), p. 70 (no. 045), pp. 96–97 (no. 113), p. 117 (no. 151), p. 124 (no. 161), p. 133 (no. 182), p. 135 (no. 185), pp. 136–37 (nos. 186–8), p. 152 (no. 228), p. 169 (no. 245), p. 182 (no. 255), pp. 188–89 (nos. 267–73), pp. 344–45 (nos. 443–47), pp. 352–11 (nos. 460–73), pp. 379–11 (nos. 486–88), pp. 403–5 (nos. 502–4, 506), pp. 408–10 (nos. 510–12), p. 422 (no. 522), p. 446 (nos. 545–46), p. 450 (no. 555), p. 466 (no. 563), p. 531 (nos. 609–11, 613).

GETTY RESEARCH INSTITUTE / COURTESY OF MARIANNE HOMIRIDIS:
pp. 104–5 (nos. 129–34).

MOMA, MUSEUM OF MODERN ART, NEW YORK / COURTESY OF MANUEL ORAZI:
p. 56 (no. 010);

MOMA, MUSEUM OF MODERN ART, NEW YORK / COURTESY OF MARIANNE HOMIRIDIS:
pp. 114–15 (nos. 146–48), p. 120 (no. 153), p. 405 (no. 505).

MAM, MUSÉE D'ART MODERNE, PARIS / COURTESY OF MARIANNE HOMIRIDIS:
pp. 82–5 (nos. 078–82).

NOUVEAU MUSÉE NATIONAL DE MONACO / COURTESY OF MARIANNE HOMIRIDIS:
pp. 94–95 (nos. 107–12), p. 446 (no. 544).

OTHER SOURCES

© ARATA ISOZAKI:
p. 413 (nos. 520–21);

© ARCHIGRAM ARCHIVES (078-001-OC01) / COURTESY OF DENNIS CROMPTON:
p. 450 (no. 554).

© CENTRE POMPIDOU / MNAM / BIBLIOTHÈQUE KANDINSKY / FONDS JEAN PROUVÉ:
p. 346 (no. 448).

© CONSTANTINOS AND EMMA DOXIADIS FOUNDATION, ATHENS:
pp. 523–24 (nos. 604–6).

© DEUTSCHES LITERATURARCHIV, MARBACH:
p. 301 (no. 409).

© ECKHARD SCHULZE-FIELITZ / COLLECTION FRAC CENTRE, FRANCE:
p. 424 (no. 526).

© FONDATION LE CORBUSIER:
p. 402 (no. 501).

© FONDATION MOMA / GIFT OF THE HOWARD GILMAN:
p. 413 (no. 519).

© LAS VEGAS STUDIO / COURTESY OF DENISE SCOTT BROWN:
p. 480 (no. 575).

© LUIGI PELLEGRIN / COURTESY OF CHIARA PELLEGRIN:
p. 449 (no. 553).

© MÁRIÁSSY FÉLIX / COURTESY OF YAD VASHEM:
p. 282 (no. 401).

© STUDIO GIANCARLO DE CARLO / COURTESY OF ANNA DE CARLO:
p. 541 (no. 634).

© THE ESTATE OF NIGEL HENDERSON AND THE MAYOR GALLERY:
p. 480 (no. 574).

© THE SMITHSON'S FAMILLY COLLECTION:
p. 376 (nos. 474–77), p. 480 (no. 576).

© VICTOR GRUEN, PHOTOGRAPH BY NINA LEEN / TIME LIFE PICTURES / GETTY IMAGES:
p. 378 (no. 485).

@ ATELIER POISSON / ARCHIZOOM EXHIBITION POSTER:
p. 562

Every effort has been made to identify owners of copyrights. Errors and omissions will be corrected in subsequent reprints.

This book was published in conjunction with the exhibition "Yona Friedman – Genesis of a Vision", which was presented in 2012 at Archizoom, École Polytechnique Fédérale de Lausanne (EPFL), Switzerland. Both projects were conducted by Nader Seraj, architect and independent researcher.

The first part brings together a large number of projects and proposals by Yona Friedman into a classified anthology, which includes unpublished works. The second part presents an essay by Manuel Orazi that reconstructs the many facets of Friedman's work since his formative years and places it within the political and geographical context of its time.

Archizoom is the exhibition space and public programme of the ENAC Faculty at EPFL. Developed by Cyril Veillon, it produces and hosts exhibitions, lectures and publications, with the aim of fostering interactions between art and the various disciplines of knowledge composing urban sciences.

Authors
    Yona Friedman, Manuel Orazi
Editor
    Nader Seraj
Project Manager
    Cyril Veillon
Publishers
    Park Books, Editions Archizoom
Translations
    Huw Evans, Genevieve Hendricks
Proofreading
    Huw Evans, Lisa Schons
Graphic Design, Typography and Prepress
    Atelier Poisson / Giorgio Pesce, Cédric Roquier, Christine Vaudois
Printing and Photolithography
    DZA Druckerei zu Altenburg GmbH

ISBN 978-3-906027-68-5

Cover photograph © Yona Friedman, Paris Spatial, 1970

Copyright © 2015 Park Books, Archizoom-EPFL,
    Yona Friedman, Manuel Orazi, Nader Seraj

Park Books
Niederdorfstrasse 54
8001 Zurich
Switzerland
www.park-books.com